"Best single overview..."

"The best single overview—both conceptual and practical—of direct marketing as a key component in integrated marketing programs. I have selected it as the text for my next direct marketing class."
—KARL LENDENMANN, PH.D.
Director of Planning and Research
Bozell/SKS
Instructor
University of California, Irvine

"For neophytes and pros..."

"This book is a 'must read,' not only for the neophyte who needs to know where direct marketing is now but also for the pro who needs to know what's ahead as our industry embarks on the superhighway."
—LEE EPSTEIN
President
Mailmen Inc.

"Practical know-how..."

"Somehow Ed Nash has managed to stay in the forefront of Direct Marketing developments. Given the magnitude of recent changes, that's not easy! This worthwhile book is up-to-date and readable as well. It remains an excellent source of practical know-how."
—H. ROBERT WIENTZEN
President, CEO
Advanced Promotion Technologies

"Of great value in training..."

"I found Ed Nash's book to be of great value both for myself and in training members of my staff. I cannot imagine a better reference book for the seasoned veteran or neophyte."
—CHARLES WICKHAM
Senior Vice President
Disney Publications

"A must-read..."

"A must-read for anyone interested in improving the performance of direct marketing programs. Covering essentials of both strategy and implementation, it is a primary and advanced text on how to do direct marketing right!"
—KEVEN J. CLANCY, PH.D.
Chairman
Copernicus Marketing Strategy Group
Professor of Marketing
Boston University

DIRECT MARKETING

DIRECT MARKETING

STRATEGY, PLANNING, EXECUTION

EDWARD L. NASH

THIRD EDITION

McGRAW-HILL, INC.

NEW YORK   SAN FRANCISCO   WASHINGTON, D.C.   AUCKLAND   BOGOTÁ
CARACAS   LISBON   LONDON   MADRID   MEXICO CITY   MILAN
MONTREAL   NEW DELHI   SAN JUAN   SINGAPORE
SYDNEY   TOKYO   TORONTO

Library of Congress Cataloging-in-Publication Data

Nash, Edward L.
    Direct marketing : strategy, planning, execution / Edward L. Nash.
—3rd ed.
       p.   cm.
    Includes index.
    ISBN 0-07-046032-9
    1. Direct marketing.   I. Title.
HF5415.126.N37   1994
658.8'4—dc20   94-21282
                                            CIP

ISBN 0-07-046032-9

The sponsoring editor for this book was Jim Bessent, the editing supervisor was Jane Palmieri, and the production supervisor was Donald Schmidt. It was set in Garamond by McGraw-Hill's Professional Book Group composition unit.

Printed and bound by R. R. Donnelley & Sons Company.

This book is printed on recycled, acid-free paper containing a minimum of 50% recycled, de-inked fiber.

To Amy Nash, my daughter,
with respect
for her and her generation

CONTENTS

CHAPTER 3   THE MARKETING PLAN   38

CHAPTER 4   THE PROPOSITION   60

CHAPTER 19   MAIL-ORDER MATH   381

CHAPTER 20   DIRECT-RESPONSE TELEVISION   399

CHAPTER 21   INFOMERCIALS   417

Preface to the First Edition

Direct marketing is not only a technology, it is a process. It not only seeks to make a sale, it builds profitable customer relationships.

In doing this, any medium may be used—not only direct mail, but newspapers, magazines, radio, television, matchbook covers, and other media not yet dreamed of. The defining characteristic is not the method of reaching the prospect, or even the method by which the prospect responds to us. It makes no difference whether the inquiry or order comes to us by mail, phone, Mailgram, interactive cable, or a visit to a retail location.

What is essential is that the customer's name and address be "captured," to be recorded on a list which becomes the heart of the marketing process. The mailing list is the means by which we fulfill our obligations to the customer or prospect; provide satisfactory service; collect payments due us; and make subsequent offers of products, services, or information.

Those of us who make our living in direct marketing entered the field from widely divergent directions. Among us are mail-order entrepreneurs seeking profits from the amazing leverage of direct marketing; advertising executives fascinated by its measurability; academicians captivated by its logical and scientific foundations; writers and artists pursuing its virginal creative opportunities; and suppliers of paper, printing, and other services who have discovered its present immensity and its future potential.

Lately our ranks have been joined by skilled practitioners in financial, packaged goods, retail, and other marketing methods who have suddenly been called upon to apply the direct marketing process in one way or another to their own fields.

In the advertising agency business, I have worked with people who have approached this business from all these varied perspectives. There has always been the need to train new people who voluntarily chose or accidentally stumbled into this unique and immensely satisfying field.

I originally conceived this book as a means of sparing myself the trouble of explaining the basic principles of direct marketing over and over again. The book gradually expanded into a guide for anyone who must conceive, plan, or execute all or part of a direct marketing program.

My intention is to take the reader step by step along the road to eventual success in any direct marketing endeavor. For novices, it is the basic training needed to succeed in this fast-moving field. For specialists, I do not presume to teach about their own field, but to provide a sense of context—how their specialty interrelates with every other area of this business. For everyone, I offer some new insight and wide abstractions about my particular forte, direct marketing strategy. Though not every reader may agree with all my hypotheses on strategy, it is my expectation that this book will at least initiate starting points for the identification of each reader's own strategic conclusions.

In addition, I have tried to apply some of the writing principles of the field to the book itself. If the book is interesting and fast-moving, that is because the subject is interesting and fast-moving. If the book is long, that is only because there is a lot to say. If the book is lively and conversational, that is because I believe that the style of the written word should not differ significantly from that of the spoken word.

I welcome you, the reader, to *Direct Marketing*, the book. If you are new to the field, I welcome you to that, as well. May you find both as stimulating and satisfying as I do.

New York, 1982

Preface to the Second Edition

"The more things change, the more they remain the same," reads an old French proverb. In the last five years, since the publication of the first edition of *Direct Marketing*, our field has undergone vast changes—but, in many ways, it is still the same.

Many years ago, when copywriters were the sages of what was then called "mail order," successful advertising was built on instinct—a writer's instinct for a phrase, an entrepreneur's instinct for a product, a designer's instinct for an attractive mailing package or advertisement.

Later the field "progressed" from an art into a science; the computer became king. Lists could be processed. Results could be modeled and forecast. Profitability could be tracked for each individual key number. Catalogs could be designed by calculating profit potential per square inch.

Today, we've come full circle. Those who dare to break the rules achieve the greatest breakthroughs, while copycat catalogs and formula advertising fades into oblivion. Once again, creativity rules.

The new strength of creativity is that we know more about our own instincts and more about the consumers' instincts. And we know more ways to bring the two together.

In this second edition, you'll find frequent references to the use of psychology—in research, in understanding consumer needs, and in communicating with the consumer. Today we can plan products to meet unspoken and highly personal emotional needs; we can deal with fears and anxieties, with aspirations and fantasies, with sensual satisfactions and subtleties of self-imagery. We can touch on issues that cannot be expressed in words, only with pictures. And thus, we can cater to the needs not only of the body but also of the soul.

This recognition of psychology is present in many of the revisions and updates throughout the book. It has resulted in virtually a new chapter on research, whole new sections on creativity, and a complete revision of past theories about using television—the most emotional medium of them all.

Psychology has made it possible for us to replicate the magical instincts of the creative greats of yesteryear, to logically analyze illogical needs, and to precisely calculate the best way to fulfill a vague emotional desire.

To the tens of thousands of readers who bought the first edition and are coming back for more, I promise not to disappoint you. The changes will make reading the new book worth your while.

To new readers, who may be discovering this field or my writings for the first time, this book will give you a basic foundation in the principles—old and new—that make the difference between success and failure, between amateurism and professionalism.

New York, 1986

Preface to the Third Edition

As I write these words, the rest of this revision has long been completed and at the publisher. This preface was delayed because my father was hospitalized and, after five weeks, passed away. We buried him two days ago. I ask the reader's understanding if he is very much on my mind.

My dad and I were very different. He printed words. I write them. Our interests were different, as was our style. Yet I cannot ignore the fact that his ideas and spirit are part of me, and that I cannot seek different goals without at least understanding the ways we were the same.

I see this lesson applying to direct marketing, which I have seen grow and expand and become more sophisticated in the same way. Yet we who love this field do not do it justice if we fail to understand its roots. Those roots are in the mail-order business, and always will be.

There is no question that the field has grown up. The earlier prefaces record that progress: first, acceptance into the world of general advertising, then at least token integration. There are no longer challenges to our size. Every statistic shows that direct mail as a medium, and direct marketing in its many forms, are among the fastest-growing segments of the entire economy. And there is no question that our methods work. Where once we listed with pride the handful of Fortune 500 companies who had some involvement in our field, now it is difficult to find one that does not.

But what is still missing is respect. Respect for the ways in which we are different. Respect for the knowledge that may be based on tests of old-fashioned products but that are still valid. Respect for the judgment and instincts of those who have made it their life's profession.

Though experience has proven the value of direct marketing, too many of the entrenched practitioners of general advertising lack the respect for this less familiar (to them) discipline. Two of my present clients are the largest and best-known advertisers in their respective categories. One of them thinks nothing of spending a million dollars on a television spot, but sets direct mail budgets so tightly that they can rarely afford more than a letter and reply card. The other is a leader in using visual imagery to build brand equity, but allows only stock photos to be used for the mail medium. In both cases direct marketing has been relegated to the more junior executives who have more to lose if they go 5 percent over their budgets than they can gain if they should double expected sales goals.

Many companies wouldn't place an ad in a trade magazine without careful planning and professional help. But they don't hesitate to trim their budgets by using freelance writers to do conceptual planning, and art studios to write direct-response copy. This is somewhat like building a customized house without an architect. It's done all the time, but the house looks it, and the roof leaks.

No wonder I still meet people who dispute the experience of direct marketing by saying they tried something and it didn't work. Their mailpieces are often nothing more than an ad in an envelope and lack the unique relationship-building aspect of direct mail. And when they do write a letter, it sounds like an ad rather than a one-on-one communication. The lists are wrong. The offer adds no real motivation or immediacy. The copy platform is nothing more than "50¢ off." *Of course* their tests didn't work, any more than it would work to run a letter as a magazine ad or an ad as a television spot.

One problem is the proliferation of specialties. Today you'll find shingles hung out for financial specialists, customer loyalty specialists, database specialists, infomercial producers, and interactive technicians. There are anlysts, telemarketers, order entry firms, computer processors—all of them offering their services on a piecemeal basis to experienced and inexperienced direct marketing users alike.

While in the hospital my dad was a victim of this kind of specialization. Pulmonologists, cardiologists, urologists, neurologists, surgeons, and others each poked and prodded and performed their own procedures. To find out his status I had to speak to each of them separately, none of whom could give me the whole picture. They each did their own job as well as they could. They each pronounced their own treatment successful and the patient cured of that ailment. The hospital looked at all the charts and called me to say he had therefore improved and was ready to come home. Later that same day they called to say he was dead. How many direct marketing projects die the same way, for lack of an experienced, competent leader with a clear, strategic approach to the objective?

In every field, the analogy to a chain's weakest link holds true. A sound system, for instance, is no better than its weakest component, regardless of what the others cost. Yet companies continue to waste the power and precision of direct marketing in all its forms by not recognizing that it is more complex than it looks. Direct marketing requires the same standard of professionalism, the same top management interest and involvement, as any other marketing or communications activity.

There are many who say that direct marketing has arrived. Maybe so. But where have we arrived? And what is the next destination? Is size the standard? Or acceptance by famous advertisers? No, the standard is, always was, and always will be: will it work, will it be worthwhile, will it make a contribution? For direct marketing, and direct marketers, to make it work, we must know and respect our roots. That's what it's all about. That's what this book is all about.

Ed Nash
New York, 1994

Statements of Appreciation

FIRST EDITION, 1982

Where does one begin to thank those who have taught the lessons or provided the opportunities to enable one to write a book like this?

There are the people who trained me at various points in my own career: Tom Collins, Mel Fauer, Lee Friend, Ray Hagel, Alan Livingston, Stan Rapp, Dave Reider, Vic Schwab, Warren Smith, Sam Sugar, Aaron Sussman, and George Violante. They can be said to have been my teachers, and every client with whom I have ever worked, every specialist and staff member who has ever worked with me or for me, has also been my teacher. So have been the authors of the books which came before mine, the lecturers whose talks I attended, and the brilliant men and women who invented some of the theories I only report. These include Richard Benson, Mike Fabian, Jerry Hardy, Rose Harper, Si Levy, Ben Ordover, Maxwell Sackheim, Robin Smith, Robert Stone, Frank Vos, and Lester Wunderman.

I must extend my warmest appreciation to the staff of the Direct Marketing Association, whose manuals, materials, and advice proved invaluable. These include, among many others, Richard Brennan, Karen Burns, Bob DeLay, Bonnie DeLay, Richard Montesi, Ed Pfeiffer, Bonnie Rodriquez, Marilyn Ross, Laurie Spar, Donna Sweeney, Merrill Tomlinson, Ruth Troiani, Sue White, and Dante Zacovish. Pete Hoke, the publisher of *Direct Marketing* magazine, offered not only advice and information, but also encouragement when I needed it most.

More immediately, there are those who provided specific information or who helped me by reviewing specific sections of the manuscript: Renee Birnbaum, Sol Blumenfeld, Susan Bynum, Tom Collins, Joel Feldman, Tom Garbett, Hal Glantz, Lloyd Kieran, Ellen Kraus, Carol

Ladanyi, Marge Landrau, Jeramy Lanigan, Craig Mansfield, Walter Marshall, Fran McCown, Murray Miller, Charles Orlowski, Fred Rola, Murray Roman, Joe Shain, David Shepard, Iris Shokoff, and Mike Vigil.

My executive assistant, Caroline Cohen, supervised the endless hours of typing, proofing, and working with the editorial and production specialists at McGraw-Hill. I would never have met the final deadlines without her help. I would like to thank my editor, William Newton, who has been superb.

Having saved the most important for last, I now thank my patient and loving wife, Diana, who provided the inspiration and encouragement to start this project in the first place, and to keep it going night after night, week after week, as what started as a labor of love seemed to become a monstrous burden and an impossible chore. She made it all worthwhile, and still does.

A word of apology to my five-year-old daughter, Amy. When she's old enough to read this passage, perhaps then she'll understand why Daddy was spending so much time at "the typewriter" (sic) instead of with her.

To all of you, for all your contributions, thank you.

SECOND EDITION, 1986

For all the people who guided me and helped me write the first edition of this work, my appreciation has not diminished. However, the list has grown longer.

Today I must thank Brian Anderson, who pioneered the new method of broadcast buying reported here for the first time, and Lucille Guardala, who wrote the television commercials which demonstrated that direct-response broadcast standards should be no lower than those of general advertising.

I must thank Sheron Davis, Fran Kahn, and Jeff Kintgen of BBDO's research division, who helped to adapt some of the most sophisticated, psychological research techniques to the unique needs of direct marketing.

Many of the executives at BBDO Direct helped me review the facts and update examples from the first edition to this. Lois Seiden contributed much to the chapter on print media. Lloyd Kieran wrote the computer program to solve the need for a statistical validity table that could be used and understood easily. Cindy Benes-Trapp conceived the jacket. Sharon Ross provided the patience and care needed to work with McGraw-Hill's demanding editors and production specialists, and the planning to keep the whole project on schedule amid a hundred other priorities.

Many industry leaders reviewed chapters for me and submitted suggestions. I am particularly indebted to Dave Shepard, Jules Silbert, Stan Fenvessey, and Ed Burnett.

My dauther, Amy, will be ten when this is printed, and can already type out a good ad on her own. But my wife, Diana, has not grown older at all. She is as young and beautiful as when I first met her, and she remains the source of my strength and inspiration when I take on projects like this.

This new edition would never have been commissioned by the publisher if it had not been for the many readers of the first printing whose word-of-mouth advertising made possible the next printing, and the next, and eventually this new edition. I must, above all, thank those men and women—many of whom are just entering this wonderful field—for contributing their own new ideas, new energy, and new opportunities for us all.

THIRD EDITION, 1994

To thank everyone who has contributed in one way or the other to the writing of this book would require a book in itself. Every client has taught me something as I have worked with them. Every employee has given me something back, even in the questions they ask. Every other book and magazine article and lecture has added to the knowledge that I have assembled here.

Some names do come to mind though, in no particular order. Bill Harvey of Next Century Media and Tim Hawthorne of Hawthorne commercials, who provided much of the material for the chapters on Interactive and Infomercials respectively. Judy Black, Bozell's media futurologist, who helped with both. My friend Bob Wientzen, now president of Advanced Promotion Technologies, who hired me to do a project for P&G seven years ago and challenged me to cope with and contribute to the world of database marketing as applied to packaged-good companies. Tricia McGivney, formerly my assistant and now list manager at Bozell Direct, who fielded the foul balls so I could concentrate on serving clients and completing this edition.

And, last and best, my wife Diana, who has helped me and encouraged me and kept my spirits up through good times and bad.

In short, I extend my thanks to all those to whom the previous editions were dedicated: "To my teachers—everyone for whom I have ever worked, or who has ever worked with me or for me. Each has taught me something new about direct marketing or, more importantly, about life."

1

INTRODUCTION

"All the armies of the world are not as powerful as an idea whose time has come." This liberal translation of the famous Victor Hugo quote applies to direct marketing as it stands today—a dozen years after the first edition of this book was written.

Today direct marketing is an idea so timely that it almost has a life of its own, so popular that it has spread through every kind of business and every country of the world, so effective that despite a proliferation of well-meaning amateurs it chalks up so many victories and successes that a half-dozen trade publications can't cover them all.

One measure of its success is that it is now the basis for a half-dozen subdisciplines. "Database marketing" is now a basic tool of some of the largest packaged-goods companies. "Relationship marketing," "one-on-one marketing," "maximarketing," "integrated marketing," and others all offer interesting extensions and variations of its basic techniques.

Companies that once scoffed at "mail order" and "junk mail" have since opened their own direct-to-the-consumer sales operations. Who would ever have guessed that both Procter & Gamble and General Foods would have fully-staffed direct marketing divisions, that Bloomingdale's and Neiman-Marcus would be known to many consumers as the names of mail-order catalogs, that IBM, Apple, and Compaq—unable to ignore the growth of the mail-order computer company created by Michael Dell—would decide to join the fray and create their own catalogs? Who would have guessed that a field in which one "rule" was that you couldn't sell by mail anything over $10 would be used effectively by banks, stockbrokers, and automobile companies, by jewelers, tourism promoters, and real estate ventures?

Another measure of success is a paraphrase of a statement I once heard about a philosophical movement: "Direct marketing has finally come into its own; we have our own lunatic fringe." In our case it is the sensation-seeking lecturers who predict that "one day all advertising will be direct marketing," that "all retailing will be mail order," that "infomercials can sell anything," or that "everyone will shop through interactive video connections."

The truth is that even with enormous advances in analytical and computer capabilities, most direct marketing attempts fail to achieve their potential or, worse, fail to work at all. Companies with minor successes stop there and fail to exploit their breakthroughs with further testing. Financiers still fail to properly value two of the most powerful assets: a responsive marketing database and an established "brand equity."

To master direct marketing and take full advantage of its potential, marketers must understand that all of its current applications are rooted in the art and science of a once-scoffed-at field called mail order. One cannot pretend to be a direct mail or database practitioner without having a solid understanding of how magazine subscriptions, book clubs, office supplies, and credit cards are sold, without appreciating the thinking and testing behind a mailing for Publishers' Clearing House, a magazine ad for Columbia Video Club, a television spot for Ginsu knives, Marshall Islands coins, or Topsy Tail hair accessories. Only then should anyone attempt to plan or execute even the simplest database application.

The direct marketing discipline can be preserved and profited from only if its roots are respected and understood. Only by building upon the foundations of the past, can today's innovators succeed in using direct marketing as it should be used.

A BRIEF BACKGROUND

Only 20 years ago, direct marketing was considered a specialty to be employed by book publishers, record clubs, magazines seeking subscriptions, correspondence schools, and sellers of kitchen gadgets and low-priced fashions. No one then would have guessed that it was destined to become a marketing tool utilized by more than half the *Fortune* 500 companies.

Anyone looking through old magazines will find early examples of what was then called mail-order advertising. Many of the classic advertisements of all times were mail-order ads: "They laughed when I sat down to play"...or Charles Atlas's bully kicking sand in our hero's face, or "Do you make these mistakes in English?"

Advertisements were crowded with small-type copy, appealing to every human desire. The most mundane products were offered as keys to fame, success, popularity, riches, admiration, sex appeal, security, and eternal happiness. Mailing pieces began to utilize the simplest kinds of personalization, such as a prospect's handwritten name on an invitation to subscribe to *Business Week*. And mailing lists progressed, slowly and painfully, from typed labels to Scriptomatic cards to rooms filled with trays of ink-covered Elliott addressing stencils. Clerks pushed long metal rods through trays of hole-punched stencils to select prospects by elementary categories, then refiled them manually.

It all seems primitive today, and yet in those early efforts a solid foundation already was being laid for direct marketing as it is today. The earliest advertisements, as far back as I have been able to search, all include the one tiny element that has made it possible for a copywriter's art to become a marketer's science, that has enabled modern writers to declare what works and what doesn't with a sense of certainty unknown to most other kinds of advertising.

The Incredible Key Number

That tiny element is, simply, the key number. This is the common denominator of every type of direct marketing activity, in every medium, for every product, in the years that have passed as well as those that are yet to come.

The incredible key number, carried in coupons, reply cards, and, today, in television announcements, is what makes direct marketing unique. It is the foundation of our knowledge, the key to our science, the signpost to our future.

The early giants of our field—Maxwell Sackheim, Victor Schwab, John Caples—did not have to rely on a client's subjective opinion to gain acceptance and fame for their advertising. They *knew* it worked. The clients knew it when the responses, bearing the key numbers of advertisements that they or their agencies prepared, poured out of mail sacks. The advertising community knew those ads were "great" the same way we do today: by seeing them repeated, over and over again, in ever-expanding media schedules.

As the reservoir of knowledge grew, copy-oriented executives looked to other areas for response improvement: price testing, media testing, and premiums. Products began to be created just for mail-order advertising. Sherman & Sackheim created the Little Leather Library and then another innovative proposition, the Book-of-the-Month Club. An innovative retailer named Sears started to develop a catalog offering merchandise to railroad station agents, and another industry was born. In later years, Lester Wunderman helped Columbia Broadcasting System (CBS) create the now-famous concept called the Columbia Record Club. Jerry Hardy, creator of the original Time-Life Books concept, later became president of the Dreyfus Fund and revolutionized the financial industry by selling mutual funds by mail without using stockbrokers.

As the industry emerged, computers and optical scanning devices counted the same incredible key numbers and produced a wealth of data showing marketers not only how many coupons were returned from a particular advertisement but how many people bought how much and what they paid for it. Simple concepts such as cost per order gave way to precise forecasts of return on advertising investment. The key number led not only to new ads and new mailing lists, but to the creation of entire new businesses.

The Miracle of Statistical Projectability

One reason for the rapid evolution of the industry is its unique ability to test new ideas with minimal downside risk. The key to this ability is statistical projectability. Direct marketing is a statistician's paradise, for all the practices of this mathematical application are used daily as an intrinsic part of its marketing and its operations.

If a test mailing to a valid sample produces a 5 percent response, there is a reasonable probability that the rest of the list or similar lists will, within a predictable margin of error, produce the same result. It is therefore possible, by spending relatively small amounts, to accurately determine the best copy, offer, or list for a given proposition, or even to test one product against another. The same principle is present in magazine advertising, where regional editions and split runs can provide a very accurate reading of which ad "pulls" best or whether the publication itself is potentially profitable.

To make this miracle possible, thousands of prospective customers turn the pages of a magazine or look in their mailboxes in a frighteningly predictable manner. They elect to rush to the phone or put our coupon aside—each acting independently—until a precisely graphable "later." The total pattern makes it possible for direct marketing to be more of a science than any other field of advertising or marketing.

OTHER ADVANTAGES OF DIRECT MARKETING

The predictability of direct marketing, arising out of its measurability and the science of statistics, is only one of the unique elements of this field. Others are (1) concentration, (2) personalization, and (3) immediacy. Businesses built on direct marketing live with these advantages every day, for they are what makes the existence of such businesses possible. And any company planning to apply direct marketing techniques to its established business or to enter the direct marketing field must first understand how these advantages work and how to apply them to their objectives.

Concentration

Concentration is a media concept. It is the ability to take promotional dollars and direct them to the most likely prospects with great accuracy.

When general advertisers, seeking a larger share of a market, blanket entire communities with newspaper, magazine, and television messages, selectivity is necessarily very limited. Readership surveys and Simmons data make it possible to achieve relative efficiencies, but not anywhere near the precision targeting available to direct marketers.

The successful campaign for Starrett City, a major housing development in Brooklyn, New York, is an excellent example of this capability. Previously the conventional approach had been used—ads in the real estate section of the prestigious *New York Times*. The fixed budget produced low awareness, no perceptible attitude changes, and—most important—a lack of new leases from the target audience: middle-income families with children.

The new effort switched the same dollars into a different media pattern. Instead of the *Times,* with distribution throughout the metropolitan New York area and its affluent suburbs, the designers of the campaign switched to the mass-audience *New York Sunday News,* using preprints distributed only in those areas of Queens and Brooklyn where the client's development presented a distinct advantage. Instead of being just one ad among many, the preprint format offered a full-color, high-impact story and a response coupon asking for an appointment.

This concentration enabled the client—with the same media budget—to rent out the balance of the 25,000 apartments in Starrett City. Later, because of a change in objectives, direct-response television was used to target prospective tenants in a specific income range.

When General Electric wanted to promote its wide line of television sets and other video products, it turned to direct mail. Where general media would have spread a diluted message to a general audience, the direct mail campaign offered high-tech products with explanations of engineering excellence to lists of people who would understand and appreciate technological advantages, while featuring beautiful cabinetry and design in mailings to new home owners and people who subscribed to magazines like *Architectural Digest.*

Direct mail offers even greater concentration, by offering even greater selectivity. From tens of thousands of mailing lists an advertiser can select those people who have identified themselves as being interested in buying products of a certain type in a particular price range, and buying them through the mail. In addition, one can select—instead of or in addition to so-called buyers lists—an incredible range of community and individual characteristics compiled from census, Simmons, and telephone directory data.

The search for selectivity and segmentation reached new heights with the development of database marketing. Beginning with questions such as "Do you smoke?" this field quickly evolved into category usage and brand preference for virtually every product. Interests and personality indicators made it possible to apply the principles of direct marketing to other fields: automobiles, packaged goods, investments, travel, with hardly any limitation.

Personalization

Another cornerstone of direct marketing, particularly within the direct mail media, is the ability to personalize communications. Not only can we select very specific audiences for concentrated promotions, we can address them in a manner that dramatizes our conviction that the product or service we are offering is particularly right for each person who gets our message.

Addressing a person by name is one obvious example, which can range from a label showing through an envelope window to much more dramatic display: giant ink-jet letters, computer-addressed salutations, or handwritten fill-ins on envelopes or invitations.

Of much greater effectiveness is personalization incorporated in the concept of the mailing itself. A *Newsweek* mailing talks openly about the kinds of subscribers they are looking for, and the characteristics indicated by the address of the recipient. *Reader's Digest,* in a sweepstakes promotion, lists the names of winners in the same or nearby towns. Business mailings refer to the industry type or sales volume or employee count, as indicated by Dun & Bradstreet (D&B) mailing lists.

One mailing to promote weekend car rentals for Avis included one paragraph that showed through the envelope and dramatized the kinds of weekends the prospect might take. The examples changed depending on the location of the prospect. Different weekend suggestions were written for each zip-code group to make the appeal as real as possible.

A Lanier promotion for word-processing equipment used not only computer personalization but a half-dozen variations in the printed brochure to illustrate the specific applications of a new product to each of several industries. Only the cover and a couple of pages changed, but the mailing became more relevant when the recipient's industry type was boldly displayed. "How this new product can save time and money for advertising agencies (or engineering firms, or law offices)" is much more likely to be read than any general appeal.

Today, the novelty of seeing one's own name in an ad or mailing piece is often perceived as mere gimmickry. There have been two important advances in personalization.

The first is personalized imagery: a letter that is not from a company trying to sell something, but from an actual person who is sharing his or her sincere enthusiasm for a product or service. This approach has proven particularly effective in the new database applications.

The second is the recognition that relevance is the handmaiden of personalization. It is far more effective to select and segment lists in such a way as to enable reference to their community, their occupation, their interests. One application is to refer to known interests—identified from an NDL or similar list—in relation to the product being offered. For instance, "Next time you go bowling, you'll feel better and look better with..."

Immediacy

The third and most vital element of direct marketing is *immediacy.* Conventional advertising invests millions of dollars to establish product awareness and positive attitudes. It can establish a desire; but it can't fulfill it.

On the way to buy an advertised product, our prospects may be exposed to competing messages, conflicting desires, alternative uses of discretionary spending power. The store may not have our client's product, or the salesclerk may not know where it is, how to use it, or why the customer should buy it.

The decline of selling skills in retailing is one of the great forces propelling the growth of direct marketing. Advertisers who count on the wisdom of store buyers or the ability of store salespeople to move their products may find that even the finest products can become marketing casualties.

Direct marketing messages, in all media, ask for the order now, or at least for a response that enables us to ask for an order on the next communication. If general advertising's objective is *awareness* and *attitude,* direct marketing is the third A—*action.*

There is a wide spectrum of actions we can ask for. The ultimate is to ask for a sale: a mail order, a subscription, a membership, or a contribution. We can ask for it on a loose "send-no-money-now" trial basis or on a hard "check-with-order" basis.

We can establish a contact, by making an appointment or providing a less specific motivation to bring our prospect to a retail outlet or a showroom, or we can arrange to have our salesperson visit the prospect's home or office.

On the less committed end of the spectrum, we can offer a booklet or sample as a means of identifying prospects who are worth the expense of additional mailings, phone contacts, or personal visits.

Immediacy is a strength of direct marketing, but it is also a requirement. Our promotions are successful only to the extent that we facilitate immediate action. It is for this reason that our copy disciplines find ways to urge action now, rather than later; that our offer disciplines require simple, easy-to-use, sometimes prefilled-out reply forms; that our media planners place a premium on bound-in insert cards or other easy-to-use reply devices. A sacred rule of direct marketing is that response devices must be easy to use, for if they are not used immediately, they may never be used. In direct marketing, as we'll explain in Chapter 2, procrastination is as serious a challenge as a conscious decision to refuse your offer, and in some ways it is an even more serious challenge.

THE REVOLUTION IN DIRECT MARKETING

Earlier I pointed out that direct marketing is being accepted as a fundamental marketing tool in a growing variety of businesses—from giant multinational financial corporations to local retailers offering an interesting new product to their customer lists or a specialized item in the shopping sections of national magazines.

The greatest attention has been given to the companies starting or acquiring direct marketing businesses, or deciding to offer their existing product line by mail order. But the most important development, and one that has proven to have the greatest role in the widening importance of this field, is the fact that the techniques of direct marketers can be valuable even for businesses that do not utilize any type of mail-order distribution. The principles of direct marketing are already widely in use in financial institutions of every kind. The largest manufacturers of office equipment are rapidly discovering how lead selling can increase the efficiency of the most powerful sales organizations who never needed it before. Oil companies, telephone companies, and hotel chains are using it. Applications of direct marketing have been developed for automobile companies, appliance manufacturers, toy makers, and camera manufacturers. And packaged-goods companies of all sizes have embraced direct marketing's most advanced application, database marketing as an ongoing strategic marketing tool. The list is unlimited.

The Two-Way Discovery

Just as the world of general marketers is discovering the tools of direct marketers, we in direct marketing have made a discovery of our own. We, as an industry, have looked down our noses at the undefinable, unmeasurable, seemingly unscientific methods of general advertising. Suddenly we have all, in our own ways, woken up, rubbed our eyes, and looked around to make an incredible discovery: We didn't know all the answers!

As we educated the barbarian practitioners of communications techniques that lacked the almighty key number, our pontifications were interrupted by the startling realization that maybe, just maybe, all these giant marketing organizations with years of experience investing larger budgets than direct marketers even dream of might just have something to teach us after all.

Little by little, direct marketing specialists became exposed to the workings of general advertising. Executives with packaged-goods experience came to work for direct marketing agencies and clients. Realizing the growing importance of direct marketing as a tool for every kind of advertiser, major advertising agencies such as Young & Rubicam (Y&R) and Doyle Dane Bernbach (DDB) purchased the most famous specialized agencies in this field and worked with them to bring both general and direct marketing clients the combined expertise of both disciplines.

Today the field has changed completely. Yes, the basic principles are still intact—and still correct. The old books are still correct; they're just not complete. Today there are new tools and new sciences that enable us to reach levels of professionalism never before attainable. There are five such areas that I consider extremely important:

1. Computer technology
2. Strategic planning

3. Structured creativity
4. Predictive research
5. Nonverbal communication

The Coming of the Computer

The availability of computer systems has been to the direct marketing industry what airplanes have been to transportation. No development has had such a far-reaching, truly revolutionary impact on our way of doing business.

The computer's first applications in our field were similar to those in every other field of business. They saved us time. Mailing lists were transferred to punched cards, which could be sorted and filed easily. Customer records could be maintained on magnetic tape and, later, instantly recalled for billing, shipping, and promotional mailings. The cards gave way to tape, and the tape to floppy disks. Punched cards became high-speed printouts and ink-jet labelers that operated faster than the eye could see. Labels became heat-transfer fill-ins, and then became computer-typed and later laser-printed letters.

The ability to file and retrieve data changed the procedures, the personnel, and the profitability of direct marketing. But this was only the beginning. These first applications of the computer were, in effect, only simpler, faster ways to do everything we always used to do before. The real excitement was yet to come.

Responses, once laboriously broken down by ledger cards, are now not only tallied but compared to expectations, compared to test cells, forecast to infinity, factored for relative customer quality, analyzed for trends, and tracked for profitability through the life of the customer relationship. Regression analysis and other sophisticated mathematical methods predict with uncanny certainty which postal areas and which combinations of personal characteristics are most likely to produce an optimum profit.

Sophisticated firms now use computers for "modeling": printing out scenarios based on subtle changes in pricing or renewals. This is done most often in the magazine field, but in other direct marketing fields as well.

Both customer lists and prospect lists can now be subjected to infinite selectivity, merging, purging, matching, eliminating of present customers, and screening of individual names or census tracts for likely credit risks.

A merchandiser now, for instance, can go through the company's customer list and make an offer only to those who have purchased an item in a specific category, in a specific time frame, and within a chosen price range. The customer can be selected by neighborhood, credit experience, sex, or any other deducible factor. Once the customer has been selected, a computer letter can refer to past purchases or known interests.

Computerized list segmentation has made it possible for mailings to be directed to those most likely to respond, sparing others from unwanted offers and advertisers from unnecessary expense.

Credit can now be extended more easily, on the basis of more reliable data. Screening of bad credit risks can be based on past experiences in a half-dozen areas. And we can be more creative than ever in displaying our customer's name and other data with dramatic, computer-driven printing methods.

Thanks to the computer, our industry can be not only more accurate than ever but also more personal. The technology invented to process enormous volumes of data and keep track of millions of customers has made it possible for us to treat each one individually and to be more personal than ever in our offers, our appeals, and even the products we develop.

The Emergence of Strategic Planning

Another great evolution has been the growth of strategy as a recognized factor in direct marketing.

When the bulk of mail-order ads promoted a single product or self-help book, each advertisement stood on its own to a much greater extent than today. We concerned ourselves with building sales, not reputations, with very few exceptions. The occasional farsighted advertiser—such as the Book-of-the-Month Club—established an identity in copy style and layout. The legendary Oscar Ogg painstakingly drafted calligraphic-style layouts for the Book-of-the-Month Club that accurately portrayed the respectability and sincerity of this mail-order institution.

Most firms, however, searched for the elusive "hot product," wrote headlines and copy that promised the moon, and relied on research methods that can be fully described as "Let's run it somewhere and see if it works."

Things are very different today. The market is bigger. The options are more numerous, and the stakes are gigantic. There are at least dozens of direct marketers with sales volumes over $100 million, and many more aiming to join their ranks. The rewards are greater, and so are the risks. Fortunately, the tools to work with have improved also.

The success of a product today begins in its very design. You can't take a product off a retail shelf and expect it to succeed in a mail-order ad without some special advantage. That's why many products are designed especially for mail-order markets and are "Not available through stores."

The offer is more than just a good price. It involves calculations of market potential and advertising cost. It requires consideration of returns, credit, premiums, trade-ups, and additional items that can be sold.

Media are much more complex also. What's the size of the universe? Can multimedia support methods expand it? Is there a core market that can be segmented out for special attention? Should our strategy "skim off" the most likely prospects from a large audience, or concentrate on squeezing every sale out of a smaller target market with what we call a high-penetration strategy?

Creative copy is no longer the starting point. Brilliant headlines are no longer enough. Professionals in this field resolve questions of positioning, emotional appeal, benefit extension, and credibility before the first word of copy comes out of a word processor.

Today marketing strategy involves long-range objectives seldom considered in the past. Every advertisement not only brings in orders but creates impressions that will influence the result of future offers by your firm. Every customer relationship is a value in itself, to be treated as carefully as if you were running an exclusive retail shop. Furthermore, it is likely that you will face direct, effective competition within months after your success has become well known.

Structured Creativity

Another great change that is rapidly sweeping this industry, and many other industries as well, is the emergence of *structured creativity*.

When I was running the Capitol Record Club, I remember Capitol's president, Alan Livingston, telling our board, "You can't have a hundred-million-dollar corporation dependent on whether or not four dope addicts get their act together and give us a hit single."

The same advice applies to direct marketers. We can't build and maintain multimillion-dollar businesses on the occasional brainstorm of the rare and unpredictable genius who comes along from time to time. If you're running a Doubleday or a Time-Life or a CBS, you need new ideas and new products when you need them, not when an idea happens to be available.

The solution to this dilemma was found in the development of techniques to stimulate and evaluate new ideas on a dependable basis. Some of the early attempts at this included positive thinking and what we now call "brainstorming" in various forms. "Synectics," a method of problem solving based on creative thinking, offered an original approach to problem definition and formal creativity that in turn inspired many spin-offs and variations.

During the initial planning stages for a new client or introduction of a new product, I often recommend that some type of open-ended structured creativity session be part of the plan. These sessions always include both client and agency personnel, as well as some objective but talented people not steeped in the client's business. Sometimes they are run by a skilled staff member as an "idea-generation" lab. Sometimes we bring in outside facilitators.

Such sessions produce hundred of ideas. Many of them are unusable, a necessary by-product of any free-thinking creative process. But without exception, one or two brilliant approaches, which would not have been created in any other way, emerge. Some of these have, in turn, become spectacular direct marketing successes.

Seeing the Future: Predictive Research

The fourth major revolution has been the recognition of the potential of *predictive research.*

In a field where, for years, only "split-run testing" was respected, research has finally come into its own.

I'm not talking about fact-finding research—questionnaires and interviews to help define a market or determine a product's previous positioning. And I don't mean creative research—the use of focus panels and similar techniques to get reactions to a proposition and zero in on customer vocabulary. Neither of these techniques has been effective in determining which advertising approach will work best in the media marketplace.

The new development, predictive research, does tell us just this. Now that there is so much invested in a major campaign, where speed is so often part of the marketing strategy—to test a proposition and roll it out before a competitor can react—some type of advance research has become essential. In addition, the high cost of full-color plates and small-quantity direct mail executions made its use an economic necessity.

Chapter 9 will reveal some of the techniques used today, not necessarily to pick winners, but to eliminate the losers and give our split-run tests a better chance to come up with a winner.

Nonverbal Communication

Of all the "secrets" direct marketers have learned from their interaction with general advertisers, none has had as much impact as the recognition of the role of nonverbal communication in advertising.

In a field where the rule used to be that "copy is king," art directors, photographers, and researchers with training in psychology now make significant contributions to direct marketing communications in all media.

Progressive direct marketers now recognize that consumers get impressions from every aspect of a communication, not just from the headlines and the copy. A cluttered, messy, cheap-looking layout makes the company and the product seem cheap, and all the verbal assurances and guarantees in the world won't overcome the impression.

If every mailing piece yells "Bargain!" and "Clearance!" eventually the recipient gets the impression that bargain is the nature of the company, and expectations of a quality product steadily diminish and finally disappear. On the other hand, if a company has built a reputation over the years, by the overall impression it conveys and by its actions in providing good products with good service, then future communications are more likely to succeed. The appearance of an ad, the character and personality communicated by the photographs or graphics used, can do more to enhance or destroy credibility than any words.

Indeed, many messages can be communicated with images and photographs more dramatically than with words. If you said, "Use this product and find happiness," people would not take you seriously. If you said "Romance can be yours if you follow the advice in this magazine," you would lose all credibility. Yet advertisers can "say" such things, and prospects "read" exactly these messages when the message is conveyed pictorially. A happy couple using your product associates happiness, the couple, and the product in the eye and mind of the reader.

Like any new tool, nonverbal communication must be understood and practiced to gain the best results. As a result, the creative process today is more difficult than it used to be, but also infinitely more capable of solving any marketing problem.

Other Important Developments

The five developments discussed above are not the only major changes going on. They are, however, the ones responsible for the present scientific and professional level of direct marketing. Even as I write this, other changes have emerged that are having dramatic and far-reaching consequences in the direct marketing world.

The telephone is one change, as both an ordering opportunity and a selling tool. Credit cards are another, bringing advertisers the ability to offer "credit" terms while getting cash payments. Independent delivery systems are another, offering direct marketers at least the hope that we may someday have an alternative to the costly, inefficient, slow, wasteful, and bureaucratically frustrating postal system. Globalization is still another—the tendency for direct marketing businesses, like all business, to extend across the world's borders. Only rarely can a successful direct marketing proposition in one country not be transferable in some way to others around the globe.

INTEGRATED MARKETING

For years there was a wall between the disciplines of general advertising and direct marketing. Today those walls have come tumbling down, and advertisers can demand and expect direct marketing based on the combined experience of general advertising and direct marketing. In many agencies, direct marketing is a strategic element routinely considered when new campaigns are planned. Conversely, the resources of the general agency—sophisticated research methods, precisely measured media planning, and brilliant creative departments—are available to back up the direct marketing group. It is not, as has existed before, a coexistence or mutual toleration, but a total assimilation that retains the strengths of both. It is not a matter of hanging the name "direct marketing" on a general agency department, or vice versa. In the old days there was a wall between direct marketing and general advertising. The former used reason to generate action; the latter harnessed emotion to influence awareness and attitudes. Today each discipline has learned to respect the other, and the walls have come down.

Reason and Emotion

Direct marketers have always been the masters of reason. We excelled at lengthy advertisements that involved the reader, proclaimed benefits, made promises, overcame objections, and asked for the order. Our advertisements in all media argued with the prospect. Sometimes we yelled our story with bold-type newspaper headlines, and sometimes we used loud, strident broadcast announcers. The highest state of the art was "17 reasons why...," and a great breakthrough was "19 reasons why...."

At the same time, general advertisers had mastered the art of emotion. Photographs associated a smile with a product and good times with a company name. They brought tears to our eyes and smiles to our faces, creating emotional involvements far beyond those which are possible using written communication alone.

Modern direct marketers learned to use *both* reason and emotion. We tested our ideas explicitly, adding photographs that communicated emotional ideas which might lack credibility in verbal form. Significant lift factors were noted. The use of nonverbal, photographic communication in an emotional message is now tracked and tested just as precisely as any other kind of copy.

Action and Awareness

Direct marketers have always concentrated on the immediate goal of action: coupons (or phone calls) now! The old rule was "Every ad stands alone. There's no such thing as cumulative effect."

General advertisers, on the other hand, concerned themselves with changes in aided and unaided awareness, and measured the positive and negative associations consumers had with a brand name. They cared about frequency of impression and multimedia impact. They tracked the extra value people would pay for a trusted name, and knew the effect of building long-range reputation even while they urged people to buy a product at their supermarket or department store. General advertisers emphasized the long-range attitude of the consumer, while we direct marketers concentrated on making a fast buck.

Today, both kinds of advertising have to do both, Some stimulus to immediate action helps general advertising to pay off. Some concern with long-range awareness helps direct marketing propositions to remain viable for a longer period.

Every communication has an "awareness" by-product. It's free. But it can be positive or negative. You can build product image and company name, as well as the overall image of direct marketing, with every communication—or you can hurt all three. The difference is a little extra planning and a long-range view.

We know from third-party propositions and from support advertising that impressions are transferable. In third-party propositions, the endorsement of a company trusted by the consumer makes it possible to sell everything from luggage and diamond rings to insurance policies that might not be successful otherwise. In support advertising, we know that we can place TV spots or radio commercials calling attention to a newspaper ad or mailing, and have a response rate greater than advertisements in either media would produce independently. Why has it taken us so long to accept that every time we send out a mailing we create attitudes that will affect the response to every future mailing?

We have always concerned ourselves with the 5 out of 100 people who responded to a mailing. We have ignored the rest. But 30 or 40 others probably opened the envelope and read at least part of the contents. They may not have ordered *this time,* but they have formed some impression of the product and the company. If it's good, they're more likely to say yes next time. If it's bad, they may not even open the envelope on the next effort. Taking the long-run view will pay off in future campaigns.

STRATEGIC PLANNING

If you hand a mailing piece to a group of direct marketers, you will have a scene reminiscent of the Indian tale of several blind men describing an elephant. Somebody will comment on a brilliant letter, another on a clever headline, still another on an original format or an exciting layout. Someone else may overlook the communications vehicle altogether and note an attractive offer or appealing product.

Direct marketing is no one of these things. It is all of them together: a sum more powerful than its ingredients, a harnessing of the forces of art, science, psychology, and common sense to achieve a marketing objective.

WHAT'S DIFFERENT?

Many marketers encounter direct marketing after years of experience in general advertising and marketing, and sometimes they experience difficulties in attempting to reconcile the different approaches. Here are some highlights of what's different about direct marketing, all discussed in more detail later in the book.

Targeting. Direct marketers are concerned only with logical prospects, whether on a mailing list, among a magazine's readership, or a television station's audience. In approaching this we take into account that some customers are worth more than others (the 20-80 rule) and that new customers may not have exactly the same characteristics as past ones.

Concentration. We concentrate our advertising budget and our creative attention on the targeted readers or viewers, not on averages. For instance, while an audience average may best be reached with one simple idea, a genuine prospect often needs (and even wants) as much information as possible. This leads to longer copy, larger mailings or advertisements, and longer TV formats. How long? Long enough to make the sale. In direct marketing, our efforts usually are not measured by impressions and changes in attitude, but by actual sales—whether by phone, mail, or at the supermarket counter.

Involvement. In direct mail or in longer-format mass media, we enjoy a luxury unknown to general advertisers: sufficient space or time to tell the whole story. To hold the readers' interest we must involve them, whether in an interesting story, an intriguing illustration, fascinating information, or playful formats: stamps, cards, coupons, etc.

Personalization. In direct mail, the ability to personalize is infinite—not just by being able to simulate a letter or refer to the reader by name, but by making the message as relevant as possible to the reader's own interests. But this does not apply to direct mail alone. Newspaper ads often produce higher response rates by referring to the city; magazine ads to the publication or the special interests of its readers.

Response-ability. As we are going after a response, not just an impression, we want to make it as easy as possible for the prospect to respond. That's why coupons must be easy to fill out, phone numbers must be legible. If we can fill out the name and address, so much the better. Even when we are seeking a retail transaction, it pays to give the address of the dealer, or to provide a clip-out reminder of the purchase intention.

Accountability. No matter what we are selling or how it is to be purchased, it always requires a response, and that response must be measurable. That is the only way we can test one list or medium against another; the only way we can continue to say "I know" that this worked and that didn't. Direct marketing is the ultimate in accountable advertising, the attribute that has allowed this field to evolve and grow as it has.

Test-ability. Direct marketing uses research to help develop ideas or to understand why one ad worked and another did not. However, it is not usually accepted as a substitute for testing—the use of split runs, test markets, and relatively small samples to determine what the consumer will really respond to. That's why executives trained in direct marketing will often try several products or marketing approaches in relatively inexpensive test campaigns, holding back the bulk of the marketing budget until actual results can be measured and projected.

STRATEGY DEFINED

The one critical element that must be understood to master this field is strategy. But first we must agree about what strategy really is. Am I using *strategy* in the sense that military planners use it when planning or discussing wars won or lost? Yes. In the sense that Machiavelli wrote about it, in his advice on how to manipulate masses and topple princes? Yes. Will we deal with it in the dictionary sense of *harnessing combined resources to achieve a selected goal?* Yes. Further, we will see how and why strategic planning is the great essential difference between amateurism and professionalism in direct marketing particularly, and probably in most other fields as well.

FIVE ESSENTIAL ELEMENTS OF STRATEGIC PLANNING

The first step in any marketing endeavor is to determine a basic strategy. There are five elements of strategic planning in direct marketing:

1. Product
2. Offer
3. Medium
4. Distribution method
5. Creative strategy

No one of these is all-important. No one of these is unimportant. Each of these five elements demands careful study, perceptive problem definition, innovative solutions, and logical decision making.

The tendency in most organizations is to emphasize one or the other of these elements, depending on the strengths and interests of a corporation's management. That is how they eventually get into trouble, providing opportunities for new management to become heroes by coming up with new solutions in a neglected area.

These principles apply when planning a major launch of a giant new program or when preparing one mailing piece for a kitchen-table mail-order business. They are universal and, used with some imagination and lots of hard work, can increase the profitability of any size or type of direct marketing endeavor.

While many of these examples refer to direct marketing's roots in classic mail order, they are the foundation of direct marketing, and it is necessary to understand the keys to mail-order success in order to be successful in its newer applications.

PRODUCT STRATEGY

Originally, most businesses were based on the idea that a product is a fixed, inflexible entity that is developed by one area of business management, then handed to a sales or marketing department with the order: "Now you guys figure out how to sell it!"

Today the emphasis has been reversed, with product-development teams directed to find products or services to meet marketing opportunities. In place of the old dictum "We made it, you (the consumer) should buy it," we now have "You want it, we'll make it."

Direct marketing has been a pioneer in this approach. The ultimate application would be a product that is designed and priced "from scratch" exclusively for direct marketing.

Such products are designed to provide appealing offers that can be sent on a trial basis, with both product and packaging that looks good on a printed page. They are priced to permit credit sales, introductory offers, and repeat sales in subscription or club programs. They are exclusively direct marketing in that, at least in the version offered, they are "Not available in stores."

The giants of our industry have their best marketing teams developing and testing new products for sale to their house lists—products that benefit from the reputation of the originating company and the expertise of its management.

For most direct marketers, the options are more limited, A retail product can be adapted for mail-order sales. A group of printed publications can be repacked as a direct marketing program. A successful overseas proposition can be tailored for introduction in another country.

An even more challenging situation is the stale product that has to be revitalized—a process akin to reopening dry oil wells or mined-out gold veins. That is a more common objective. The principles remain the same.

Changing a Product without Changing It

The most economical way to revise a product is to change it without actually adding anything to it. There are several ways to make "changes" in direct marketing.

Positioning is a whole subscience, so important that Chapter 11 is devoted to it. Briefly, it involves "repositioning" the product or service by presenting it in a different placement vis-à-vis competition, by aiming it at a different market segment, or by selling it at a different point in the buyer's decision-making process—my own invention, which I have named *horizontal positioning*.

One example of conventional or *vertical* positioning is a campaign to sell Avis used cars as "The New Car Alternative," appealing to new-car buyers instead of the conventional used-car market. An example of horizontal positioning is Doubleday Book Club's "Fantasy" advertisements, selling prospects on the idea of reading itself rather than on book clubs in general or on their particular book club offer.

The "breakout" technique is another valuable tool of the trade. This involves taking a component of the basic package and isolating it to be featured as part of the offer. You'll spot the breakout technique in a mailing or an advertisement that takes a packaging element—such as the plastic case in card file offers, or a reference service's binder or index section—and sells it as "Included at no extra cost."

Many products have attachments, accessories, manuals, or even service contracts that can be broken out and featured as ways of giving new life to old offers.

Multiple-part products can be taken apart, or put back together, to make what appear to be entirely different offers. A catalog of socket wrenches and tools with individual prices would probably not be successful in general markets; yet "100-Piece Tool Sets" including assorted sockets, tapes, tools, and—as a bonus for fast action—1000 assorted nuts and bolts are offered in full-page ads in dozens of publications.

I remember a variation I once did for Walter Black's Classics Club, which basically offered three books for $1 with a subscription to others. I added a panel 6 square inches in size that dramatized the end product: "Build a fine collection of great classics like this," showing a shelf of the beautifully bound books. It worked so well that the panel eventually became the theme for an ad that was still running many years later.

On the other hand, a set of encyclopedias can be taken apart and sold volume by volume, or a Barbie doll can be sold on an offer which brings new doll outfits each month. A manufacturer of pots and pans, for example, can sell a deluxe set of pots, or a subscription to a pot-a-month club, or a basic set with other kitchen equipment added, or a set of pots along with "The coffee pot free just for trying this amazing...."

None of the products in these examples have changed. They have just been repositioned, redescribed, or recombined to make them seem fresh and different.

Turning Lemons into Lemonade

One of the most interesting approaches to revitalizing a stale proposition is the dramatization of a product feature that may have been either buried in body copy or left out of advertisements completely. You can build an ad around any aspect of a product or service. This includes not only the major features but the minor ones, not only the new improvements but the features that have been taken for granted.

Don't presume that the customer knows everything there is to know about your product. Reintroduce it, and look for every product benefit that can legitimately be dramatized.

Is the product small? Stress space saving and portability. Does it lack controls that its competitors offer? Talk about simplicity and ease of operation. Is it an older model? Write that they don't make products like this anymore, and that this model is in limited supply.

Is your company not the largest in its field? You may be able to stress personal service or family ownership, or the idea that the principals are intimately involved, read every letter, and personally stand behind their product.

Are your prices a bit high? Then make a plus out of it and feature the idea that not everyone appreciates extra quality and this offer is only for those who do, and are willing to pay for it.

Is your magazine thinner? Then perhaps it can be read quickly, and has more selective editorial matter. Is your charity the smallest in its field? Then its work is probably more personal. I have never seen a marketing product where there wasn't something that could be pulled out and dramatized.

All this presumes that the claims given in the examples above are legitimate. If your product doesn't offer real value of some sort—if being different doesn't provide the consumer with some advantage—then maybe you should start all over again with a new product. You can turn lemons into lemonade only if you include some sweetener in the mixture.

Enhancing Perceived Value

Your product strategy isn't limited to the extremes of developing whole new projects on one hand and repositioning or reassessing your product on the other. It often pays to invest in adding some genuine value to enhance the product's perception. Such additions are "paid for" by reduced order cost resulting from greater advertising response, and they can be tested easily and inexpensively.

Premiums are a simple addition. So is utilitarian packaging (such as a carrying case or storage container). If you're planning to send follow-up mailings anyway, why not include a newsletter that you can mention as an added benefit in your initial offer? A cosmetic firm's Personal Beauty Plan, for instance, can include an Insider's Fashion Forecast newsletter as an attractive feature of a customized beauty makeover. A plants-by-mail service can include a magazine that doubles as a catalog and adds value to the basic proposition.

Some other value add-ons include a really strong, long-term guarantee, which can become a powerful advertising appeal in itself. Or a food manufacturer or cookbook publisher can offer a follow-up telephone service, such as a call-for-assistance recipe preparation service offered toll-free.

The essence of strategic product planning requires basic decision making: a commitment about what your product or service is and how you want it perceived. You can't have it be all things to all people. It can be the best or the cheapest, traditional or innovative, entertaining or educational. To try to be everything at once is to be nothing.

Whether you reposition your product, change it, dramatize a new feature, or invent something entirely new, the product itself must respond to research and test results in the same manner as every other ingredient of the five-part marketing equation. Unfortunately, the product is often the last consideration of many advertisers, who prefer to place blame on the ad or the medium rather than look objectively at their own product.

OFFER STRATEGY

Though it is only one of the five critical elements, offer strategy is the element most easily revised for a fast-result improvement. Even the slightest change in the price, though buried in body copy or coupon, can have dramatic effects on front-end performance.

Expressing the Price

Not only the price itself but the way the price is expressed can drastically influence the cost per order. For example, let's say a monthly magazine has a newsstand value of $1 per copy, or $12 a year. The subscription offer is set at $6 per year. Here are some of the ways this offer can be expressed:

- One year for only $6; basic price statement
- 50 cents per copy; basic price expressed by unit
- Half price; price expressed in fractions
- Six issues free; savings dramatized by units
- Save $6; savings expressed numerically
- Save 50 percent; savings expressed in percentages

Note that all these offers represent exactly the same price. Only the means of expression varies. Of course, most of these statements must comply with Better Business Bureau (BBB) standards and Federal Trade Commission (FTC) regulations and, if used to sell magazines, will be subject to the additional standards of the Audit Bureau of Circulation (ABC) codes.

I have had occasion to test all of these price expressions, using bind-in cards in newsstand issues of the magazine. The best of these versions did three times as well as the worst; twice as well as the average.

Price Sensitivity

One test I conducted for a film-processing client shows how sensitive pricing and price expression can be. The numbers are altered for confidentiality, but the relationships are correct. The offer is an introductory film-processing order, with a sliding scale of prices ranging from $1.99 for a 12-exposure roll up to twice that for 36-picture 35-mm rolls. The objective was to attract film-processing customers who could then be sold additional processing at progressively higher prices. Table 2-1 shows what happened.

This test demonstrates several important lessons. In the first place, you can see how important offer expression can be. The same average price produced a cost per order ranging from $5 to $12 or $14. (The discounted film offer was simply another way of offering savings.) If the 1-cent

TABLE 2-1
TEST RESULTS OF A FILM-PROCESSING OFFER

Price statement	Twenty-print price	Average price (all sizes)	Cost per order	Margin	Units	Net	Contribution
Basic, $1.99 up	$1.99	$3.50	$19	$10.00	6,315	($9.00)	($56,835)
Film, only 39 cents	1.39	2.50	14	9.00	8,571	(5.00)	(42,855)
1-cent sale	1.00	2.50	12	9.00	10,000	(3.00)	(30,000)
$1 off	.99	2.50	9	9.00	13,333		
99-cent offer	.99	2.50	8	9.00	15,000	1.00	15,000
Half price	.99	1.75	5	8.25	24,000	3.25	78,000
39-cent limited offer	.39	2.20	2	8.70	60,000	6.70	402,000

sale was your control offer and produced 10,000 orders at a cost of $12 each, the half-price offer would have produced 24,000 orders at $5 each. If your allowable margin at $3.50 was $10 per order, the 1-cent sale offer would have produced a $30,000 loss; the half-price offer would have produced a $78,000 profit, even after reducing the margin by 75 cents per order.

The 99-cent offer, which had a higher average price but a $3 higher cost per order, would have resulted in a profit of $15,000. It is often the case that a client finds a satisfactory offer like this one and stops experimenting, therefore never finding a more profitable offer, such as the half-price one in this example.

The more daring 39-cent offer would produce far more orders—60,000 in this example—and a very dramatic $402,000 profit. This is true if the "back end" doesn't deteriorate and the margin holds up despite the poorer-quality orders. In most cases there would be some deterioration of quality, but not enough to offset the dramatically higher number of responses at a much lower order cost.

It is a mistake, however, to look solely at cost per order as the ultimate indicator of profit. As is further discussed in Chapter 19, Mail-Order Math, there are times when a higher cost per order may result in a lower net profit per order but many more orders and a better overall return on investment (ROI). Plans should aim at total profit measured against investments, not just profit per item sold.

Elasticity of Price

In setting a pricing strategy, price elasticity must be taken into account. There are customers who must have your product and will pay almost any price to get it. If there are enough of them, you may be able to set your price very high.

However, inelasticity is more often the rule. If you are selling a product or service that people can live without—a strictly discretionary purchase—then it is likely that you are asking your customer to make an impulse decision.

Just look at some of those executive toys in the airline gift catalogs. Let's face it. No one really *needs* a battery-operated travel alarm that plays your favorite tune and tells you what the time is in two time zones. However, for $5 or $10, few of us would have trouble justifying such a purchase in our own minds. We could probably talk ourselves into it at $29.95 as well. But what about $129.95? Suddenly it is a considered purchase for most of us, and while we wouldn't mind getting it as a gift, it's not something we'd rush out to buy. This is an example of an inelastic price. It can stretch only so far, and no further.

Price Break Points

In setting a price, the key break points are related to currency units. Prices should be just under currency break points. In the United States, 99 cents will do better than $1.20, $4.99 much better than $5.50, $10 better than $11, and $19.95 much better than $21.

On the other hand, often you can approach such a break point with no noticeable decline in results. If you're at $8.95 you can often move up to $9.95 with a negligible decline in response rate. But go to $10.95 and watch for a 20 to 30 percent drop-off.

You'll notice in this example that I use both rounded (i.e., $5) and broken (i.e, $4.95) prices. Frankly, I suspect that the consumer is smarter than most people think and that no one is fooled by the nickel change, or perceives $4.95 as a significantly lower price. However, I have no definitive recommendation. There have always been more important things to test, and none of my clients has ever had a test cell to spare for this question. Whether the client with the $10 subscription price should charge $9.95, or whether the $9.95 marketer has unnecessarily sacrificed a treasure in nickels, is a question I'll leave for others to decide. My feeling is that prestige-related offers should use the rounded figures, price-appeal offers the broken prices. My advice is to decide what's appropriate for your own business and stick to it.

Add-On Pricing

I'm often asked about shipping and handling costs, which are a frequent complaint raised in customer correspondence. Should you set your price at $10 plus $1.50 postage and handling, or should it be $11.50, or a flat $10? I have tested this, and it is a perfect example of how the consumer has a way of surprising us. The tests indicate that a price of $10 will do about the same as $10 plus shipping and handling, without statistical significance one way or the other. The only "bad" price would be $11.50, which would do about 20 percent worse than either alternative.

It appears that consumers don't mind paying for shipping costs as an add-on.

The Almighty "Free!"

No discussion of pricing would be complete without homage to the almighty "Free!" I call it almighty because, when I was a young copywriter at Schwab & Beatty, no use of the word ever escaped being capitalized by my copy chief, as if the word represented a deity deserving of respect.

In a way the treatment is deserved, because even in this day of FTC-specified qualifications and rampant consumer skepticism, "Free!" is still the single most powerful word in the vocabulary of direct marketing offers.

The film-processing price test I described earlier was an exercise necessitated because the most famous film offer of all time—the one developed for Film Corporation of America—was specifically barred by the FTC. That offer was "Free film—send $1.00 for postage and handling." The customer was sent film only to discover that it apparently had to be processed by the same company for additional costs.

The power of the word *free* is such that it often makes possible two-step offers in which a customer is offered a free booklet, free information, a free trial, or a free short-term subscription in order to build a mailing list for later solicitation.

The enormously successful Time-Life Books operation initially built its business on one offer: free examination of the first book in a series.

One variation is what magazines call the "comp-copy offer," which is shorthand for "complimentary initial copy sent on trial." Most comp-copy offers are free only to respondents who do *not* eventually subscribe. If they do, the first issue is made part of the subscription. In my view, this isn't really "free." As a result we have evolved the "true comp-copy offer," which makes the first issue free whether or not the respondent elects to cancel. The problem is that ABC rules will not count this first copy in the magazine's circulation figures.

A healthy approach to this dilemma is that used by *Geo* magazine when it was first introduced. They developed an initial "collector's issue," which was offered as the free incentive. These could be printed in quantity and sent out to new subscribers promptly, without waiting for the next issue date. The regular issues then all counted as circulation for advertising purposes.

Time magazine's development of exciting premiums such as almanacs or videotapes are offered in much the same way, and enable the magazine to make an honest free offer.

Other Considerations

There are many other considerations besides price to be considered when planning offer strategy. Many of them are discussed in Chapter 4, The Proposition.

One question is credit. Depending on the nature of the product and the audience, you may or may not want to establish a credit relationship with your customer. "Send no money now" is a powerful result-builder, especially when used with a full guarantee, but it involves sending out bills, setting up credit-evaluation procedures, and writing off some percentage of bad debt. Installment sales and credit cards have their own unique problems, as do cash-on-delivery (COD) shipments.

Contests and sweepstakes are another aspect of offer strategy, one that can have dynamic but dangerous consequences. The "lift" of a sweepstakes can be like a narcotic. It makes you feel good for the moment, but you can get hooked on it. While sweepstakes have been very important for many advertisers, they create a whole new set of problems in terms of poor quality, high costs, and the need to come up with bigger and better contests in order to maintain the hyped sales level. The effects show up in everything from bad debt to poor renewals to lower list-rental income. "Sweepstakes-sold" is, to a sophisticated advertiser, a warning that the magazine or list whose circulation is offered consists largely of people who like to enter contests, not necessarily of people truly involved in the type of magazine, product, or service sold.

Evaluating the Time Factor

The most overlooked factor in planning offer strategy is time. Usually an advertiser must make some type of advertising or premium investment (such as a loss-leader sale) to attract a customer. We often refer to "buying" a customer, as it is not uncommon to deliberately lose money by selling an item for $10 that cost us $5, at a cost per order of $20. In this case we have "bought" a customer for $15—the order cost less the net income from the initial sale.

How fast we get back that $15 depends on what type of proposition we set up, the popularity of our products, and the effectiveness of our creative material. In other words, the same factors that go into planning customer acquisition strategy go into back-end strategy.

Many advertisers aim for a first-year break-even. That is, they want to recover their initial investment within twelve months of the initial solicitation. They then start pulling ahead and developing a satisfactory return on investment in the second, third, and subsequent years. Renewals, repeat purchases, list-rental income, trade-ups, and cross-sell projects bring in profits over a period of years. Sometimes the break-even point does not occur during the first year, but only after two, three, or even four years.

This time factor accounts for the great profitability of magazines, mail-order catalogs, and club operations that have been in business for many years. They control the "mix" of old and new customers so as to produce a stable profit. Too many new customers in one year may bring the profit for that year down. To be a "hero," all one has to do is cut back on new-customer acquisition and let the profits from old customers overwhelm losses from new ones.

A similar trick of the trade is the enactment of an unwarranted price increase. New customers come in at a higher price. Long-term models look good. But the balloon often bursts when customers who came in at an old, lower price are asked to renew at the new, higher one. Buyer resistance from old customers can set back any gains for a period of two or three years, until the mix of new customers, brought in at the higher price, catches up.

Mathematical Models

All of these approaches can be evaluated with the aid of mathematical models. While mathematical modeling can be done manually, there are many fine companies that can do it by computer at very reasonable fees. With today's spreadsheet software, you may be able to set up a workable model on an in-house computer.

The basic data of your operation is programmed and entered, taking into account order cost, promotion expenses, conversion rates, renewal rates, cancellations, and bad debts. With magazines they add advertising space sales and newsstand circulation as well. At the touch of the right buttons, a model of the next few years can be printed out, showing profitability, cashflow, circulation or volume levels, and even production requirements. At any time, day or night, you can change an element of the model and see what happens.

For example, let's say you want to consider tightening an offer but you expect that cost per order will increase. You advise the model that you are changing conversion and payment expectations up 5 percent but you expect response rates to go down 10 percent. The entire business plan, utilizing these revised figures, is printed out in minutes. You can try out any scenario until you find the one that best suits your company's objectives and capabilities.

Whether you forecast the effects of offer changes manually or by computer, you will see that subtle changes will have the most profound—and sometimes most surprising—impact on your entire business. Any company that fails to think through offers and try new ones independently of what they do in the product, media, and creative areas is missing a bet. Any company that presumes that the best offer for one product line is automatically the best for every product line is going to be unnecessarily writing off some very good products. In the mysterious alchemy of direct marketing, the right offer is the indispensable catalyst that activates every other ingredient. It is the key ingredient in turning the paper we write our plans on into gold.

MEDIA STRATEGY

In direct marketing, the medium is the market. We generally do not use lists or publications to reach predetermined market segments; each list or publication or broadcast audience is a market in itself.

Conventional advertisers pick out cities or market segments and plan schedules to build awareness within these target groups in the most efficient manner possible. Readership studies, audience profiles, and

Simmons data are correlated with circulation figures in order to obtain a cost per page per target audience. This might be 200 or 300 percent higher than a publication's cost per page for general circulation, depending on the selectivity.

In direct marketing, we usually don't care whether a new customer comes to us from one city or another or even in one month or another (except for circulation guarantees or fiscal-year profitability goals). A customer is a customer is a customer. Since UPS, Federal Express, or the U.S. Postal Service is our distribution system, we do not have to worry about proximity to retail outlets or distributor routes. Therefore our strategies are concerned not with markets but with media as markets. Since every medium is subject to precise testing and result measurement, we can determine the most effective medium objectively instead of subjectively.

The Media Universe

Direct marketers often refer to a media "universe," meaning the maximum of known lists, publications, and other media that can be expected to be productive for a given product or service. The planning of strategy requires a full understanding and precise identification of the media universe for a given product.

At one time, the identification of a media universe was largely a product of instinct. Advertisers would go through magazines and look for those with a suitable editorial environment, or with large numbers of repeat mail-order advertisers. Today, instinct still has its place, but the tools are more sophisticated. Reference books available in every advertising agency list the competing advertisers and the publications or cable TV stations they have run in. Simmons and other services identify the demographics, interests, and media preferences of users of virtually every product or service.

No product has an unlimited universe, for no product appeals to everyone. A universe is limited in its width by the range of lists and publications available, in its depth by the intrinsic appeal of the product, the offer, and the creative strategy.

Consumer Reports presents a classic example. In 1977 and 1978 their universe consisted of about 10 million names on mailing lists and one national publication: *TV Guide*. A new creative approach enabled them to dramatically increase the number of publications that were profitable. At one point, over 30 magazines and dozens of newspapers were on their media list. Both radio and television became major media sources as well.

A media universe, like the planetary universe, contracts and expands. In fact, "expand the media universe" is the general strategic objective of many major new offer and creative tests.

For a large advertiser intent on maximizing its facilities and reputation, planning may begin with the availability of a media category that has not responded to otherwise successful propositions. Direct marketers will, for example, develop short-term offers for some media, special products for others, and different credit terms for still others. A magazine might try a short-term offer in an impulse medium such as package inserts. A book club might offer a preselected group of books instead of a choice in a television offer that requires phone response. A mail-order firm might require credit card payments or ask for additional information when advertising in a publication that has previously produced poor credit experience.

Support is another way of expanding a universe. Support will be fully discussed in Chapter 7, Broadcast Media. Broadcast is the most common support medium, but not the only one.

Core Lists and Publications

In direct marketing, media and list-buying strategies are not as concerned with numbers as they are with relevance. If you are selling fishing reels, a small list of known buyers of fishing equipment is worth more than ten times that circulation consisting of demographically selected prospects—i.e., males, 35 and over, nonurban. A list of people who have bought such products through the mails is worth more than a list of patrons of local sporting-goods shops.

Magazine audiences are selected in the same way. A publication directed at fishing enthusiasts is likely to do well for the fishing-reel proposition. If the bulk of its readers are "direct-mail-sold," they are more likely to respond than readers of a publication who bought it primarily through newsstand circulation.

Interestingly, this is the opposite criterion from that used by packaged-goods advertisers, who generally prefer newsstand readers. Such readers go out to buy their purchases in retail stores, and so are more likely to buy a retail-distributed product.

Lists of relevant buyers of related products, or other lists that compose the most logical or previously most productive lists, are called *core lists*. Similar publications are called *core publications*. These core media usually are the most productive for any product or service.

Pilot Testing

In a typical media schedule, lists and publications are assembled into categories related to the potential markets for a product or service. Such categories might include, for a female-oriented product, "Women's Homemaking," "Women's Career," "Women's Lifestyle" (such as *Cosmopolitan*), and "Women's Special Interests." In mailing lists it might include "Subscribers to Women's Magazines," "Cosmetics Plan Expires," and "Book Club Members."

These categories are assembled according to the logical relationships affecting the particular product being sold. If the product is particularly costly, price range might be more relevant than product type in assembling a list universe.

If you were selling a power saw, a media universe might include "Mail-Order Tool Buyers," "Mechanics-Type Magazine Subscribers," and "Home Repair Catalog Inquirers." Usually, advertisers of such things as power tools would devote the bulk of their media plan to repeat insertions in lists or proven publications. Test advertisements or mailings would be scheduled in new lists or publications within the same category. Other tests would be dedicated to probing related categories not previously tested.

The objective here is to limit downside risk. We want to test the new categories without committing so much of our budget that the new categories, if unsuccessful, would offset the profitability of the rollouts and test extensions.

Risk Limitation

It is important to limit the number of untested variables. What is being tested—the x factor—is the category of publication. This is, therefore, not the place to also test untried space units, new formats, or new creative strategy.

If your control ads have worked with a full page, small space is not the way to test a new category. In space the way to minimize risk is, usually, to use a publication in the proper category that has small circulation but has been proved for other direct marketers. If you must use a larger-circulation, more costly magazine, then look into regional editions. Provided you are not penalized with a "back-of-the-book" position, a regional insertion should be projectable (with some geographic adjustments if run in a particularly poor or effective part of the country) to indicate what the cost per order would be on a national basis. It is important to adjust your cost figures to reflect the difference between the higher regional rate and the national rate.

Mailing lists are much more flexible, as it is less costly to test each new list. However, the principles are the same. The lists tested should be proven within each category. The types of lists should be comparable. For instance, don't compare "hot-line" names if the bulk of the lists are year-old names. When analyzing results, adjust test printing costs for what the mailings would have cost on a large-quantity rollout basis.

Testing will be more fully explored in Chapter 10. For now, it is only necessary to understand how a media program is put together—a very different process than that used by general advertisers.

CPM, CPP, OPM, and CPR

When planning a media program for your proposition, don't fall into the trap of presuming that cheap is good. A low CPM (cost per thousand) circulation is no bargain if the list or publication doesn't pull in the quantity and quality of buyers you need.

Some publications have a low CPM, but low readership. If readers only skim the publication, there is less chance that your advertisement will be noticed. Others have a very small, "digest" page size. If you need space to show your merchandise or tell your story, such a small page is not worth as much as a page in a publication of conventional size.

If you have access to computerized Simmons or other readership data, you will be able to study the circulation analysis of a publication, or a broadcast buy, in terms of CPP (cost per thousand prospects). Such data offer more than a breakdown of readers by age or education; they can tell you whether the readers have bought an item in the product or service category recently, whether they intend to, and whether they have ever bought by mail. Information about other members of the family may also be available—whether any member has joined a book club, for instance, and the name of the club. With this kind of data, the CPP for a magazine campaign can be compared with what it would cost to reach prospects through other media. Surprisingly, CPP analysis often indicates that magazines or broadcast can be as cost-efficient as direct mail—a prediction often borne out by later result analysis.

Micromarketing

Increasingly, with certain luxury consumer products or business-to-business services, a marketing program must be directed to very few prospects.

When such prospects can be identified using specialized direct mail lists, the choices are obvious. Where they can be reached only by using broader lists or media, a different approach is required.

Media efficiency is, in such cases, no longer the ultimate standard, for there will always be a waste factor of irrelevant names. For instance, an insurance mailer seeking veterans has built an enormous business by using lists with a good proportion of veterans, but these lists also contain the names of many who are not veterans. The mail is addressed to "Dear Veteran," and simply ignores the nonveterans who may receive the piece. They are not a concern in this strategy. This attitude must often be adopted for print media and broadcast campaigns as well. The campaign concentrates on those who are prospects and ignores those who may not be. In some cases only a handful of readers will be legitimate prospects, but they are the only ones that count.

Ultimately, OPM (orders per thousand) becomes a planning factor. OPM is an index of how many orders (or inquiries or donations or subscriptions) are produced from promotion efforts in the various media. OPM is an index of responsiveness. It provides a standard of reasonableness. That is, if we double the cost of the mailing package, is it reasonable to presume that we can double the OPM? In some cases the answer will be yes, in others no.

CPM and OPM figures are both superseded by one universal index: CPR (cost per response). CPR (sometimes called CPO, for cost per order, or CPL, for cost per lead) is the indicator of "front-end" effectiveness: the relationship between responsiveness and cost. It is obtained simply by dividing the advertising cost by the number of responses.

The "quality" of respondents takes into account various kinds of conversion efforts: how many inquirers will buy, how many book club applicants will honor their commitment, how many business leads will see a salesperson and become customers. It also eventually takes into account the size of orders and the length of the relationship: renewal rates, frequency, etc. This eventually leads to projected ROI: return on advertising investment. A good strategic plan should consider these factors and forecast them for each and every media recommendation.

Other Media Considerations

A media strategy must consider all of the above factors and build a logical testing plan that reflects the acceptable degree of risk as compared with the need to exploit a productive campaign as quickly as possible. Time is a major aspect of strategy.

One must consider turnaround time: how long it will take to get the results from one effort, and whether you can then act fast enough to exploit the next peak season.

Response formats are an important factor in publication advertising. Does your proposition need a bind-in card to facilitate a quick, impulsive response? That limits your options somewhat. Does it need an envelope to facilitate payment? That knocks out more than three-fourths of your potential magazine circulation.

Secrecy often is important. If you are testing a new product, use direct mail outside your competitor's home base. It is less likely to be noted, and they have no way to determine how big your test is.

Competition is another factor. You don't want to be in the same issue with a direct competitor and, often, not even in the issue immediately following, unless you have a much more powerful offer. Mailing lists usually are rented on a protected basis, meaning that no competitor can use the same list in the same 30-day period.

You must consider what type of space unit is needed to present the creative story. If you are offering a choice of 50 books or magazines or records, you'll obviously need a larger unit than if you have a simple story.

The editorial content also is a factor. Does it create a climate beneficial to your offering? Does its own reputation enhance or diminish the credibility of its advertisers?

A media strategy usually must combine caution in testing with aggressive risk-taking to exploit a success before competition "rips it off." Your media strategy must be uniquely tailored to your own product, your market, and current availabilities.

DISTRIBUTION STRATEGY

One overlooked element of marketing strategy is the distribution method itself. Too often it is presumed that the method of getting the product to the customer will be the same as that used for all of the other company's products, or the same as that used by the company's competition.

In fact, some of the most exciting marketing breakthroughs have taken place because corporations have been willing to rethink this basic question for one or more of their product lines or services.

Distribution is an element of marketing, but in too many organizations distribution is not part of the marketing director's responsibility or authority, even though it must be taken into account. In such cases, though, it should still be one of the considerations in determining marketing strategy.

On the broadest scale, there is the question of whether or not to use direct marketing methods at all. Often this is the fundamental decision.

Take the example of a company selling an industrial product or service directly to businesses, using sales representatives. Over the years the better salespeople have left, and the company has had difficulty replacing them. Do they drop the product line? Or do they consider alternatives? They can sell the product in rural and marginal areas directly by mail. They can use telephone operators to solicit reorders from previously sold customers rather than use the valuable time of the remaining sales force. They can solicit leads, using their sales force for calls on prequalified interested prospects rather than waste their time on cold canvassing. With sales calls exceeding $200 each, this can be a profitable approach even if the sales force is strong and effective.

Let's consider products that traditionally have been sold in the conventional retail manner—to, say, drugstores. Shelf space is hard to get for new products from new companies. Store personnel are unable to explain product features or answer customer concerns. And discount chains are squeezing the price margins mercilessly.

Many companies have chosen to introduce such products through mail-order selling directly to the consumer. They can target their efforts to those customers most likely to be interested. They can concentrate their efforts on explaining how the product works, offering proof of performance, and overcoming objections. And they can give people incentives to try the product immediately.

Products dealing with sources of embarrassment lend themselves extremely well to direct mail. Sensitive problems such as incontinence, thinning hair, and teenage skin problems can be dealt with in great detail in the privacy of direct mail, whereas most customers would hesitate to discuss such problems with a retail sales clerk. If the product is a good one, word of mouth will start to work for the company and eventually retailers will *ask* for the product. The marketing effort then can change to a retail one, but behind a now-established product.

Products that traditionally have been sold through direct marketing can also benefit from a rethinking of the basic distribution method.

The American Management Association traditionally sold their courses as "one-shots." Circulars made the offer of individual courses and asked for cash with the order. They eventually found they could do better with some courses if they sold them by soliciting inquiries first and then converting the inquiries with a mail series and phone calls, as well as by issuing a catalog offering all the courses.

Some large organizations are geared for selling by continuity (periodic automatic shipment) systems, and resist changing to a club (negative option) system even when research shows that their customers would prefer it. Others built their business with clubs, but quickly recognized the potential of continuity publishing and single-package promotions and, by using these approaches, expanded their business dramatically.

Magazine publishers can consider putting their product in books. Book publishers can consider part-works (newsstand-sold segmented periodicals) or seminars. These concepts are explained further in Chapter 4, The Proposition.

Financial institutions have found that, once they have a customer relationship, it pays to offer as complete a package of services as possible. And then they can use any of these services as lures for new customers. Rethinking the basic proposition of what a bank or an insurance company or a stockbroker *is* has led to greater marketing flexibility and greater consumer choice.

Of course it is not necessary to use mail-order or lead-selling distribution systems to use direct marketing. In recent years, many advertisers have been using direct mail every effectively to support retail sales or to supplement direct-selling organizations.

Automobile manufacturers and packaged goods companies use the principles of direct marketing to encourage test drives or product trial, as well as the loyalty of their existing customers. Both Avon and Mary Kay have created major direct marketing programs to generate additional sales of products originally designed to be sold only through person-to-person selling.

It is these applications that have benefited most from database marketing, a direct offshoot of direct marketing. This method—the subject of an entire book I have written on the subject—*Database Marketing* (McGraw-Hill, 1993)—differs primarily by its ability to select and address prospects individually, based on individual interests and known brand or category usage.

CREATIVE STRATEGY

No aspect of direct marketing is more discussed than the creative side. This is the glamour part of the industry. This is what makes direct marketing an art as well as a science. However, for purposes of planning, creative strategy (the copy, layout, and either media unit or direct mail format) is the last consideration—not because it is the least important but because it is the most flexible.

The Need for Flexibility

The crafts of the writer and the artist demand versatility. It is no trick to produce every advertisement in one distinctive style, no matter how effective it might be. This kind of advertising strategy is like an actor who plays himself or herself no matter what the role calls for, or an artist who paints the same subject in the same style over and over again. True genius requires the ability, and more important, the willingness, to adapt one's skills to fulfill any objective.

A creative department must be able to solve the creative requirements of any product, any offer, any media. It must be able to adjust style and vocabulary to any market segment, to adjust length to any size advertisement or letter, and to write headlines and conceive illustrations that attract any desired audience.

The Need for Subtlety

In the old days, a copywriter's task was clear-cut. Benefits were offered, dramatized, guaranteed. Attributes were proclaimed, proved, glorified. Selling propositions were stated, restated, and stated again—in visual presentations crowded with copy and liberally sprinkled with exclamation points.

Today the creative process is infinitely more subtle. The old-fashioned "hard-sell" approaches can still work in the short run, but they are short-sighted. Hard-sell copy picks up core markets—the easy prospects—but fails to build credibility or positive attitudes for the future. Today we not only look at the 2 to 5 percent of people who respond to a mailing piece, or the much smaller percentage of a magazine's audience who respond to an advertisement. We must consider that our advertisement is being seen and noted by a much larger percentage of readers or viewers who, though not responding now, are prospects for future promotions by the same company. Today, just as general or "awareness" advertisers find situations where it is desirable for them to ask for a response with direct marketing techniques, we in direct marketing must consider the awareness- and attitude-building factors in our response-seeking advertising.

International Silver's American Archives division happened to run a half-page list-building advertisement offering a condiment set for $4.99 in the same issue as a full-page advertisement picturing an elegant silverware service available at retail outlets. Starch reports for the issue indicated that the half-page mail-order advertisement had higher "Noted" and "Read Most" scores than the full-page advertisement intended solely for those purposes. I had a similar experience with an ad for ITT's telephone services.

Ninety percent of communication is nonverbal, and "first impressions" are based not only on what you say but how you say it. An analogy I have used frequently is that copy style is like tone of voice whereas layout is like body language. Both communicate credibility or lack the of it, and say as much about your company and its product as anything in your basic copy platform.

When planning a creative strategy, you must consider not only those who respond today but those who may respond in the future.

Emotional Factors

The concepts expressed in the previous section of this chapter gradually evolved into a whole new approach to strategic planning. Some years ago I had access to packaged-goods methods and experience that had never been applied to the direct marketing field. Many such methods dealt with an understanding of human perceptions and needs and with the various avenues, many of them nonverbal, for communicating with the consumer.

I incorporated many of these general advertising methods into the basic procedures of the agency I headed, adapting them within the basic creative work plan used for every new assignment. The results were incredible. We found that, by using photography more precisely and utilizing certain emotional themes relating to the prospect's self-image, we were able to produce significant lift factors. These will be discussed in more detail in Chapter 9, Research, and Chapter 12, Creative Tactics. For now I will just say that the choice of strategy must consider not only the practical person's reasons for buying a product, but also the emotional needs the product can fulfill; not only the immediate action-inducing methods to be used, but the imagery of the product that will determine the long-range success of the marketing effort.

Good advertising today must answer not only the question, "What will this product do for me?" but also the equally important question, "What does this product *say about* me?"

CHOOSING A STRATEGY

This chapter has dealt with strategic alternatives in five areas: product, media, offer, creativity, and distribution method. In preparing a strategy, it is important to consider all five of the basic elements and to make definite, clear-cut decisions. Many of the choices will be difficult, but they must be made. I have found that the worst strategy, in any of these five areas, is the so-called safe strategy. If you are competing against General Motors it is folly to produce cars just like theirs at the same kinds of prices. Somewhere you have to take a chance and be different in as many respects as possible. Lee Iacocca did not achieve Chrysler's great marketing turnaround by doing the same as everyone else.

There are many ways to help make these decisions. A written plan is essential. Research can help. And when the alternatives are boiled down to a few significant fundamentals, you can always use split-run testing to let the consumer tell you the best way to go or which market is the best to aim for.

If you are introducing a new product, saving an old one, or looking for a major breakthrough or market expansion, then you must be willing to rethink all five main strategic areas.

Your strategy will, of course, be influenced by your corporate personality. In World War II, British Field Marshall Bernard Montgomery was known for his cautious, logical, carefully planned campaigns, based on the best intelligence available. American General George Patton had a radically different style. His armored divisions would plunge ahead as fast as his tanks could go, seizing bridges, bypassing pockets of resistance, exploiting opportunities as they occurred. I won't venture an opinion as to which approach was the best then, or which would be best for your company now. But I will urge you to consider not only the directions you want to go in, but how fast or how cautiously you want to proceed once you set your direction.

Strategy requires the selection of goals, the defining of objectives. Tactics are the methods of achieving those goals. Planning is the conscious decision-making process that must precede any act of creation.

THE
MARKETING
PLAN

Only a written plan makes it possible to obtain useful professional advice from coworkers and consultants. Without it, any expert is only reacting to the scanty information and predigested prejudice of his or her client.

Only a written plan brings everyone involved into the total strategy. The greatest media buyers or copywriters cannot do their best work in a vacuum.

Only a written marketing plan documents strategies and test objectives as originally conceived, so that results obtained months later can be properly evaluated.

Most important, only a written plan enables its preparer to fully think through every essential element that affects decision making—not only the big decisions, but countless day-to-day implementation choices vital to the final result.

HOW SHOULD A PLAN BE PREPARED?

In the following sections I'll describe the "what" of a marketing plan. But "who" should write it, and "how" should it be assembled?

Ideally the head planner should be a marketing strategist, no matter what the title, and regardless of whether the planner is the boss, a product manager, or an outside advertising executive or consultant. One person has to be responsible for assembling and coordinating the preparation of the plan, but seldom can one person write it. A team is needed.

Each component of the overall plan should be prepared by a specialist in the particular area being covered, after an overall briefing and with frequent consultation with other members of the marketing planning team.

Much of the detailed assembly of information can be delegated. The decision making cannot be delegated, nor should one person make the decisions unilaterally. Just as it is impossible for most writers to be objective about their own writing, so it is with marketers. Planning must be an open, honest dialogue among professionals whose integrity precludes pleasing a client or the boss with "lip service."

The head planner who is too directive will not get honest opinions. On the other hand if the planner is not directive enough, the plan will be aimless or contradictory. There must be an honest dialogue. As William Wrigley said, "When two people in a business always agree, one of them is unnecessary."

The format of the plan is not critical. It can be written in simple outline form, with elements listed, or in an exhaustive narrative format with charts, tables, and exhibits. I have seen and endorsed excellent plans written in only a few pages, as well as one for a major national corporation that required 300 pages to summarize a year of research and planning.

Once written, the plan is relatively simple to update from year to year. Segments should be in a loose-leaf binder to facilitate adding new competitive information, new marketing data, and the hard facts of research and testing.

The basic elements of a marketing plan are, in the broadest sense: product description, marketing environment, objective, strategies, and economic considerations.

I PRODUCT DESCRIPTION

The first section of a marketing plan is generally a statement describing the product or service. It sounds a great deal simpler than it is.

The obvious first level of product description is its basic attributes. What exactly are we offering? What is the size, the material, the function? How does it work? Although you might attach samples or photographs of the product, it helps to verbalize each and every attribute, including the color, the feel, the weight, even the sound it makes when it operates. (Ogilvy's famous Rolls-Royce ad about its loudest sound being the electric clock might never have been written if someone hadn't first verbalized the attributes of the product.)

Then there is the scientific level. How was the product made? How does it work electronically, chemically, or mechanically? Exactly what does happen inside, where the customer can't see but the writer can describe? Is the product made of a scarce material? Tell about it. Is there hand-craftmanship, or exacting precision tooling, or rigorous quality control? How long will it last? How long will it operate? How is it better than the competition?

The third level, and in some ways the most important, is the emotional. What real or imagined need does the product fill? What will it do for the buyer? How might it change the customer's self-image or image to others? What benefit might it add to the customer's life: comfort, convenience, spare time, confidence, prestige, wealth, romance, beauty?

There are intangibles to be considered also. Is there a guarantee or service contract? Is the company well known? Is there an endorser or other authority? How is it delivered? (Fast delivery is an asset, for instance.)

Some might say this doesn't apply to intangibles: telephone services, retail chains, banking services, insurance. The fact is that the less tangible the product or service and its advantages, the more important it is to work at describing just what it is we are trying to sell.

Perhaps the best way to dramatize the levels of product description is to share with you an exercise that is sometimes used to train copywriters. The assignment: Describe a pencil.

The Classic Product-Description Example

"It's yellow. There's black lead inside a wooden tube. There's a point on one end and an eraser on another." How many writers would stop right there?

Another might go on to describe how the pencil lead is made, what kind of wood it's encased in, or the country of origin of the rubber eraser. Still another writer might describe the manufacturing process, tell how long the manufacturer has been in business, or dramatize the many types of pencils offered by the company.

Better. But then along comes the scientific writer, who has painstakingly used up a pencil to find out how many times it can be sharpened, how long it will hold a fine point, and—after hours of work—exactly how many words can be written with a single pencil.

Much better. But we can still do more, by trying out competing pencils and determining whether ours "lasts 20 percent longer." That's a lot of work, surely, but nobody has ever said advertising is easy.

Even with all this we've only just begun, for advertising is an art as well as a science, and our prospective customer is emotional, as well as logical. Imagine for a moment the psychic satisfactions: the security of being able to erase errors easily, the peace of mind in knowing that the pencil will not leak or stain or smear.

Further, imagine what using a pencil says about our customers. They will impress their friends with practicality, conservatism, and frugality, and the courage to admit that they can make mistakes.

Let's carry the copywriting art one step further and, adding a sense of poetry, suggest that such a pencil as ours might enable its possessor to write a moving play, develop a brilliant business idea, or compose a touching love sonnet. Thus our buyer might achieve—by buying a pencil—fame, riches, and romance. Want to buy a pencil?

How Is the Product Perceived?

The product-description section is the place to include all relevant research on how your product or service is presently perceived by various components of your customer base. Both quantitative and evaluative research, such as focus panel sessions, should be summarized here. The purpose is to summarize not the research itself, but the conclusions the marketing plan preparer is drawing from this research.

What consumers think your product is can be just as important as what it really is. Perception is an aspect of reality. If the product is perceived as better than it really is, you may face returns and complaints unless you either change the product or reveal the shortcomings in your promotions. The well-known Joe Sugarman often includes a sentence in his long-copy advertisements pointing out features that a product is lacking, then adding a line making light of it, such as "Of course, at this price you can't expect everything."

If your product is perceived as worse than it really is, or if there are fears that have to be overcome, a good writer can make sure that every concern is overcome in the copy presentation. The knowledge that these perceptions exist, and the decision to deal with them, must be elements of the marketing plan.

Levels of Perception

The perception of a product or a service may be thought of as being organized into ascending levels. The first level is that of basic attributes; for example, a car is a means of transportation. The second level involves what might be called "detailed" attributes: the car can travel at a particular rate of speed. However, attributes can always be translated into benefits. The practical benefit of a car—the third level—is that it can get you from point A to point B faster than you could get there by walking or taking the bus. But is that really the motivation to buy? Increasingly we are finding that many benefits are psychological. We are dealing more and more with feelings: e.g., feelings of power (the car) or feelings of security (the pencil, which allows you to erase a mistake). We are also dealing with fantasy, as described above in the paragraph discussing the potential uses of a pencil. So far our ladder of perception looks like this:

Fantasy benefits

Emotional benefits

Practical benefits

Attributes—detailed

Attributes—basic

In recent years, theorists have proposed that there is a still higher level that marketers must deal with:

Self-image

In addition to all the reasons for buying a product having to do with attributes and benefits, there is a fundamental question that a prospect may never consciously ask but that represents a powerful motivating factor: *How will this product affect my image of myself?* This is very different from the "How will this impress my friends?" approach.

Research has shown that people have an idea of what sorts of people use different kinds of products. If the sort of people they are (or would like to be) use a certain product, they identify with the product. If not, they would be embarrassed to admit (even to themselves) that they wanted it. If people see themselves as "sophisticated" or "macho" or "chic," or as part of an "in" group, they will desire a product they perceive as sophisticated, or macho, or chic, or "in." If people perceive a product as silly, or only for old folks, or kids, or poor people (again, depending on self-image) they may shy away from the product regardless of how much they really would like to have it. This can apply to individual brand names or to entire categories of products or services.

We know from research that family heads invest in products from life insurance to encyclopedias not because of their practical benefits but because doing so reinforces their self-image of being good parents. Other products from sports cars to beverages have carefully cultivated brand images that help buyers to see themselves as young and vital.

Self-image buying can best be influenced nonverbally, by including in the advertising piece phrases and illustrations depicting the typical user in such a way that the prospect wants to identify with them. This is a highly sophisticated approach, one that has now been applied to direct marketing efforts and has produced astonishing results.

It is therefore important not only to note what is known about a product and to describe the product in terms of how it will be perceived at the various levels previously discussed, but also to identify the consumer's attitude about what kind of people buy it.

II MARKETING ENVIRONMENT

The marketing environment is the cumulative total of every factor that might influence the development of marketing strategy. As you'll see, it includes competition, media, distribution, government regulations, and economic trends.

Competition

The competitive situation is a constant and continuing factor in your own strategy development. Every legitimate information-gathering process should be used, and all information recorded.

The marketing plan should summarize the current knowledge about each competitor's activity and draw conclusions, in writing, about what appear to be trends, their strategies, their offers, and their copy platforms.

The first step is obvious. Start collecting every tear sheet and direct-mail sample that falls into your possession from any source. Ask media representatives for back issues known to contain competitive advertising. Ask your staff, your suppliers, and even your friends and relatives to send you anything they happen to get in the mail in the particular product category.

When you get the samples, "break them down." Spell out, in writing, what audience they seem to be aimed at and how they are positioned against your product. Reconstruct their copy platform, by listing each and every point used in the copy of each competitor. If there are many competitors, set up a chart and compare who is saying what.

Look for the evolution of the appeals, offers, and copy claims. This is often very revealing, especially if you don't make the common mistake of underestimating your competition. The safest course is to presume that if point A has been added or point B left out since last year, it may have been done because of research, testing, or results that would apply just as well to your product.

Today the sources of information are greater than they have ever been. However there is still a need to build your own files of competitive activity, as it is still difficult to get full data about direct mail used in most business categories.

Magazine Advertising. Using reference services such as Publishers' Information Bureau, magazine advertising can be tracked over a long term. This will tell you what magazines other advertisers are using, in what months, and in what size units.

However, it will not tell you what ads they are running, or how their copy has evolved. If you are concerned with a competitor who advertises in magazines, you will want to examine their most-used magazines on a regular basis.

It is particularly important to examine copies of these publications at newsstands, comparing several copies to see if there is a split-run test—different creative treatments or offers being tested. These should be carefully logged in to see which split is repeated. It is safe to presume that the ad repeated is the one that proved to be most successful.

Broadcast Advertising. Like magazine advertising, broadcast advertising has similar information posted in LNA/Arbitron, which lists the dayparts and major markets used for direct marketing advertisers as well as all others, by month. It does not, however, reveal which particular stations they use and which dates they ran on. Also, the books generally are issued too late to help with most direct-response advertisers who do not repeat their propositions from quarter to quarter.

To get current information, you generally have to put together your own network of spotters—friends and associates around the country who will tell you when they see or hear a certain commercial and the time and station it was on.

Copies of TV spots can be purchased from a service, Broadcast Advertising Reports, that can provide videotapes of most commercials. They are also available on paper, in storyboard form.

Direct Mail. Direct mail has become much more trackable in recent years, at least with direct mail packages. While it is valuable to see what the competition is doing, what kinds of offers and promotions they are using, it is still virtually impossible to learn what lists are being used and what quantities are being mailed.

One exception to this is a company called MIN (Marketing Information Network). MIN has more than 18,000 lists accessible by computer, with updated information every three months.

A service created by Denison Hatch, called "Who's Mailing What" (Philadelphia, PA), has filled an important void. It is a newsletter and archive service with the largest collection of direct mail in the United States. The publication is available by subscription, and the sample-copy service is charged for by the number of pages of copies.

Another recent improvement in data gathering is provided by a company called DBM/Scan (Armonk, NY), created by John Cummings. Originally a tracking service for database marketing activities by packaged-goods products, it has been expanding into automotive and other categories. They will provide a survey of activity in a particular product category, along with copies of samples, on a fee basis.

General Business Information. By all means order the product, subscribe to the service, or join the club or plan offered by your competitor. In fact, join it several times, through different people in your office, and see how they respond to different actions on your part, such as prompt payment, slow payment, and no payment. Keep track of every date you receive or send something. While you're at it, send in similar dummy memberships for your own product or service. You may be surprised, particularly if your fulfillment is being done at another location or by an outside service.

On top of this, use all the conventional research techniques for business information. Get annual reports. Look up articles that may have appeared in the business press or newspapers. Read books, articles, and interviews written by your competitors or their agencies.

Today there are several fine magazines and newsletters covering news and developments in the direct marketing field. I particularly recommend *DM News, Direct,* and *Direct Marketing*—each of which has a unique perspective. The field is now so widespread and fast-moving that one must read all of these just to keep up with what's happening.

Friday Report and *The DeLay Letter* are two excellent newsletters of particular value to senior executives, advertising agencies, consultants, and others in the service industry. The former provides excellent coverage of talks at meetings and conventions. The latter features exclusive interviews with industry executives and "inside" information not generally available elsewhere. There is surprisingly little duplication between the two.

It's amazing what people sometimes let drop in the course of seminars or business meetings. In the direct marketing field, a unique and valuable source of information is the enormous library of cassettes available from *Direct Marketing.* Order and listen to every cassette of talks by your competitors and by their advertising agencies.

The Direct Marketing Association (DMA, New York) is a gold mine of valuable information about the industry in general, and well worth the membership fee. One of their lesser-known services is a library of contest entries that can be visited in New York or purchased on microfiche. These entries are in bound books that include statements of objectives, mailing plans, samples, and results. If your competitor has submitted campaigns for awards, this can be a surprisingly beneficial reference source. Members can also obtain computerized summaries of news items, contest entries, and other data about types of direct marketing programs by industry, specific company, or marketing method—at a very reasonable processing fee.

Another valuable source is the list-rental cards issued by your competitors. Often they indicate the number of customers brought in within a given period of time, the size of their total list, the average sale, the source of the names, and a demographic breakdown. Some allowances are necessary because they are presenting the data in the most favorable light to rent their lists, but some valuable data still can be deduced.

The Media Universe

This marketing environment section is also the place to record the media universe—a speculative, highly optimistic compilation of the mailing lists and publications that might be relevant to your particular proposition.

Standard Rate and Data Service (SRDS) publishes various catalogs of publications and mailing lists. Go through these SRDS publications and begin to assemble, in categories, the various media that you might someday hope to use. Indicate the basic costs for print media, presuming a standard space unit. Also indicate what you might spend on mailing lists, figuring not just the list cost but an estimated package cost. You may find that certain media categories are so large that it's worthwhile to tailor your strategies to find ways of making those categories work.

Certainly the information on what media your competition has used, and repeated, should be taken into account here, as well as the media they tried and evidently discontinued. There's no dishonor in learning from someone else's experience. Don't make the mistake, however, of presuming that a medium has been "used up" by a competitor. International Masters Publishing has followed Betty Crocker into markets all over the world, and found that a quality product, the right offer, and a good creative strategy can make even the most saturated media pay off for their Mary Masters "My Great Recipes" cards. Don't let the competition scare you off. Go where the action is; just find ways to be better than they are.

Time is a factor in media selection, as well as cost. While you are formulating your marketing plan is the time to estimate how long it will take to get into the various media categories with your ad or mailing— and how long it will take to read the results. Turnaround time will be important, because you always will want to read the results of one mailing or ad in time to make decisions on the next.

To summarize, you should, for each medium listed, estimate cost for a standard unit, record apparent competitive experience, indicate the lead time in preparing an ad or mailing, and, finally, indicate how fast you should be able to read results.

Fulfillment

This term applies to the steps needed to convert the response to an advertising message into a form that results in a profit. Obviously, what those steps will be depends on the nature of the business.

Magazine subscription companies require not only the mailing of the publication but procedures for billing and, eventually, renewals. Fund-raisers must enter the donation and send appropriate thank-you letters. Companies that sell through agents or salespersons need a lead distribution system, complete with methods of tracking conversion rates. Packaged-goods companies count redemption of store coupons or use other research methods. And, of course, catalogers and other mail-order marketers must deal with packaging, shipping, returns, customer service, and similar issues.

All companies must provide for adequate handling of the responses themselves, whether by mail, phone, or at retail establishments. Many an otherwise successful promotion has failed because the phone lines were busy, or the operators improperly trained. And there are cases of major direct marketers who have gone out of business because of poor computer planning. Fortunately there are consultants who specialize in these issues, and suppliers who have gained substantial experience in handling any of these functions. With very few exceptions, I usually recommend handling fulfillment with such outside suppliers, at least during the first couple of years of a new direct marketing venture.

Where these decisions have been made, they should be part of the plan shared with all participants in the planning process. This information often will help to identify steps that might otherwise be overlooked.

Economic Trends

Are there economic trends that affect your business, or other trends? Here's the place to spell them out, in narrative, figures, and charts. If your product is sensitive to the economy as a whole, include pertinent economic indicators such as the Consumer Confidence Index, the Dow-Jones Index, and Housing Starts. These are the tables I most often find relevant to mail-order predictions.

Is your product related to a specific hobby, interest, or fashion? Then spell out available information, and speculate about the life-cycle of the interest. Usually, the best time to ride in on a new fad is near the beginning. Once it becomes so popular that general magazines and Sunday supplements deal with it, the fad is usually almost over.

CBS brought out *Popular Gardening Indoors* just in time for indoor gardening to be yesterday's enthusiasm. International Silver introduced a CB (citizens-band) necklace and a gorilla pendant just in time for CB radio to fade and for the remake of *King Kong* to have come and gone.

Unless your product can be issued on a timely basis, with fast turn-around media, save your money. You can make a fortune if you're one of the first to offer mood rings or collectibles, but you can lose your shirt if you're one of the last.

III THE MARKET

In direct marketing, we deal with "media universes," "target markets," or "audiences." We try to quantify these markets by age, education, and income; by zip code and census tract; by demographics and psychographics. But this is just the beginning of defining a market.

Your Customer Is Not a Statistic

All market data can tell us is who our audience has been, based on previously selected product, offer, and media choices. It shouldn't be a surprise, but often is, that years of positioning a product toward older people, for example, eventually result in a research study showing that older people have been buying the product. It doesn't show what could have been, or still could be, if the total market potential were considered and if different creative efforts were aimed at alternate lists or media. Anyone in direct marketing should read *The Marketing Revolution* by Clancy and Shulman (Harper Business, 1992) for an enlightening discussion as to how and why new customers may not look like present customers.

The first lesson to remember is this: Your customer is not a statistic. The buyer is not packaged in neat demographic profiles waiting for your message to arrive. There is only one common denominator that you can count on: interest in your product.

Interest can be developed, with the help of the right creative strategy, among people who compose virtually any statistical unit; but their interest is individual. What they do have in common is that they are *accessible at an economic cost through a common list or other medium.*

An average age or income is useless unless it is related to the accessibility of those characteristics through various media. Too narrow a definition, such as "people who like hummingbirds," also is useless, unless there are substantial numbers of publications or lists directed to such people. Inaccessible statistical profiles are academic exercises.

This is a fundamental difference between a typical packaged-goods marketing plan and a direct marketing plan. Although statistical data is a keystone of packaged-goods marketing, it is usually just an idle curiosity for direct marketers. Available data should be included, of course, if it is known, but it should be precisely identified. The typical market study included in such a plan should not be called "Market for Our Product" when, in literal truth, it should be titled "Statistical Survey of Questionnaire Respondents by People Who Bought Our Product as a Result of Previous Creative Efforts in Previous Media."

The Lifestyle Approach

Logical reasoning will take you further than statistics in a direct marketing plan, and should be the starting place for the market section of a plan.

Begin with the product: its function, its purpose, its benefits. Who needs it? Who might be persuaded to need it? What absolute limitations are there? What essential prerequisites exist with regard to where the prospective customer is in his or her life, career, or avocation?

One exercise used by some major agencies is the "ideal-prospect" scenario. Imagine an ideal buyer. Make up a story about where he lives, what he does, how his job is going, how he's getting along with his wife, what his ambitions are, what he does in his spare time. Does he have a beer after work at the local pub? Does he build craft projects in his workshop on Sunday afternoons? What are his political preferences? What's his favorite movie, TV show, or magazine?

Just letting your imagination go wild in this way will help you, and the copywriter, to zero in on what's really important and relevant about the market characteristics for your particular product. In case the point hasn't been made yet, what's the chance that the relevant characteristics of the ideal buyer are age, income, and education? Not very likely.

Often there are common demographic denominators, and they should be taken into account, but usually these common denominators are pure speculation until a full range of list and media and positioning tests has been run.

Common Media Characteristics

Reading media and list results is an art form in itself. While a media universe may be conceptualized arbitrarily at the beginning of a marketing program, it must be reshaped when the hard reality of result figures is available.

After adjustments have been made for media format, competition, regionalization, date, and position (in print media), a clear picture starts to come into focus. Usually some list or publication categories are clear winners, others are clear losers, and some are marginal.

The art is all about looking beneath the obvious and searching out what winners and losers have in common. Often it is not the obvious publication title or list name, but characteristics beneath the surface. Astute analysts and strategic planners insist on reviewing editorial content of magazines, media sources of mailing lists, and the entire competitive environment before drawing conclusions about what works and what doesn't.

Common sense goes a long way toward identifying abstractions about successful media. Direct marketing results are always subject to logical analysis and interpretation. But beware of the blaring exception to logic. Every time I have been stumped by a seeming contradiction to an otherwise clear pattern, the villain has been not logic but the reliability of available testing procedures. I've found that a magazine that was supposedly a split run sent most of ad A to newsstand dealers and ad B to subscribers. Though the print run was 50-50, a large percentage of the newsstand copies were returned unsold, thus depressing that side of the split.

In mailing lists, I've seen list suppliers—accidentally or intentionally—provide the most recent names rather than a typical cross-section, thus making a marginal list look better than it really is. If something looks odd, don't act on the test results until the contradiction can be explained or until a retest can be arranged under tight supervision.

All test results, and the abstractions drawn from them, should be summarized in the marketing plan. The market portion of the plan should include all relevant data and all speculation about who the ideal buyer seems to be and what possible buyer profiles might be added. It should include the history, the interpretation, and a statement of objectives for the future. And it should all be spelled out in writing.

IV THE STRATEGIES

Strategic planning is possible only when the product, the market, and the environment have been clearly identified. There is always more than one possible strategy. Alternatives should be developed and then reviewed according to preestablished criteria, and the best strategy should be selected. Often it is possible to test more than one fundamental strategy. The consumer's response will determine which is the most effective. The selection of strategies depends on several considerations: budget, timing, market conditions, and the inherent personality of the corporation making the decision.

One important determinant is a substatement of the objective: the goal. Both should have been listed in the preliminary material. Usually the objective is general, such as "Expand media universe," "Open youth market for product," or "Lower cost per order." The goal, however, is specific: "Expand media universe by $500,000" or "Reduce cost per order by 25 percent." The more ambitious the goal, the more daring the strategy that can be justified and the greater the downside risk merited. If the goal is modest, strategies should avoid daring new concepts or bold offers and stick to logical progressions from existing control ads and packages.

Comprehensive Testing

Let's say, for example, that we are dealing with an existing and reasonably successful proposition that is ready to break into the big time. Our survey of the product, the environment, and the possible markets has identified several areas for possible improvement. Maybe the proposition has worked well in women's magazines in full-page black-and-white ads. The goal is to double sales for the next year.

We would probably list a variety of possible strategies, including a price change, a premium addition, the use of credit cards, new creative strategy to widen the appeal of the product, and some new media and formats. The trick is to test all these approaches in a short period of time so as to permit a massive rollout in a later prime season.

The first step would be to list and evaluate all of the possible strategies for testing. The key factor would be the likelihood, in the judgment of the people who have to make the decision, that the change would result in the desired improvement. At this point, some possibilities would be ruled out in favor of others. Perhaps some form of predictive research would be used to help select those variations most likely to appeal to the potential customer.

Testing

It is likely that, no matter how tight the decision-making process has been, there will be a variety of possibilities to be tested. At this point, a testing strategy should be established.

The testing strategy generally isolates test ads or mailings into three categories: media or list tests, simple offer or format tests, and basic creative concepts.

One creative concept, generally the most logical and proven approach, is selected—by past results, or arbitrarily—to be the control ad or mailing piece. This control is the vehicle for testing one medium or list against another. Where possible, all offer and format variations also are tested within one or two media: a core list and an expansion probe list, for example. The basic control might run in 10 or 20 purely media test cells. The variations might take two of the media and test four or five variations against each, and then the basic creative format testing might be tried. The result would form a grid like the one shown in Table 3-1.

TABLE 3-1

	Mailing lists (10,000 names in each cell)							Publications		
	A	B	C	D	E	F	G	H	L	M	N
Basic control	*	*	*	*	*	*	*	*	*	*	*
New concept	*	*							*		
Offer variation			*	*						*	
Price test A			*	*						*	
Price test B			*	*						*	
Add lift letter			*	*							

In this case, lists A and B and publication L are pure split runs of the basic package against the new creative variation. Lists C and D and publication M are basically the same as the control except for the variation indicated. Lists E, F, G, and H and publication N are to give us readings of the new media.

One consideration in publication testing is the normal inability of publications to match split-run advertisements to bind-in cards. In this test, the L publication might be a split run of a full-page advertisement, while the M publication is the control ad with a bound-in card. All variation testing is confined to the card itself. In this way an infinite number of variations on the card can be accommodated simply by preprinting and premixing the cards before supplying them to the publication. This bind-in card method is often used to test the more cost-effective format of page and bound-in card, which is often difficult to test reliably. Industry experience indicates that the results are transferable. Testing is further discussed in Chapter 10.

With simple adjustments and interpolation, it is possible to calculate what any of the ads or mailings would have done in any of the lists or publications.

The Product Viability Test

One frequent situation is the need to prepare a test strategy for a brand-new product or concept. Under such circumstances, budgets generally are more limited and the need for more information is less demanding. What is needed here is not an estimate of the best copy or the ultimate media universe, but a quick answer to the query, "Does this product have any life at all?"

In such a case the test program is confined to larger samples of four or five very logical media, usually in direct mail. Only lists that represent categories large enough to sustain the business by themselves are tested. It will do the client no good to learn that a small core list is highly successful if there is no place to go from there—if the list category cannot supply the needed volume.

It is vital to determine at what price the product or service can sell. Usually the creative concepts are limited to very basic approaches, perhaps a general discount certificate package and a sweepstakes approach. Within each basic list, both approaches are tested, as well as some basic product or price concept.

One purpose of the test is to produce a large enough customer base to get a reading on back-end performance. If a 5 percent response is expected and a 10,000-customer base is considered minimal to get a valid reading, then this initial mailing would be 200,000 pieces. This might be spread over five lists of 40,000 names, each to be mailed four different mailing packages, thus giving us 20 test cells of 10,000 names each.

If the test is going to be a "one-shot," now-or-never decision on a new product, then it is also necessary to test any basic alternative medium. For instance, if competitors previously have used package inserts and broadcast to a larger extent than direct mail, then the control approach should be adapted for these media and the tests run simultaneously. While direct mail may be the best medium for testing variations, it is still necessary to include basic media categories that could produce a viable business in themselves. Both broadcast and package inserts are, independently of direct mail or publications, large enough media to support enormous businesses.

V ECONOMIC CONSIDERATIONS

A marketing plan should stand by itself as a source document and as a working plan. Therefore the plan should include, perhaps in an appendix, all pertinent economic considerations.

All information on costs, allowable margins, and past results should be recorded. I also find it helpful to do a simple chart showing the response needed to produce a break-even cost per order at different mailing package costs. See Table 3-2.

TABLE 3-2

Direct mail, cost per thousand	Response rate needed at various target CPOs, %		
	$10	$50	$100
$200	2	0.4	0.2
300	3	0.6	0.3
400	4	0.8	0.4
500	5	1.0	0.5
600	6	1.2	0.6

Such a chart is helpful to creative people, who occasionally have to be reminded that the more expensive the package, the larger the response must be just to break even. Sometimes, in a product with a limited market and a large unit sale, the same chart will justify spending the money on a high-penetration, multiple-part mailing program.

Another piece of information that should be included here is a statistical validity indicator. A simple table is called for, listing the minimum size sample that is needed to produce a 90 or 95 percent confidence level at various response rates and allowable error margins. This requirement will be covered in Chapter 10, Testing, in more detail.

All of the economic assumptions should be detailed here as well. What are the basic costs for product and premium? What return, trade-up, and collection assumptions are being made? What overall budgets are established and what profit and loss (P&L) is it expected to produce?

The availability of such economic considerations in the marketing plan makes it possible for everyone concerned in promotion to look at the overall picture. It might, for example, show that a modest back-end improvement in units sold per customer or in renewal rate might lead to more significant profit improvement than lowering the cost per order. This data would lead to appropriate strategies for back-end improvement.

VI LEGAL CONSIDERATIONS

Today, more than ever, an attorney should be consulted at the earliest stages of preparing a marketing plan. It is almost impossible for any layperson to be thoroughly familiar with every nuance of national and state government regulations and restrictions, and with various courts' interpretations of the law.

Different applications of postal regulations can make a significant difference in your total financial picture. For instance, companies operating with nonprofit status are entitled to dramatically reduced postal rates. Other companies might benefit from sending merchandise out under classifications that require much less postage than does parcel post.

The Federal Trade Commission (FTC) is very concerned about consumer protection. They require that commitments be spelled out clearly and completely, that product representations be honest and in no way misleading, and that words such as *free* or *guarantee* be handled in very precise ways. Even the size of type is often specified.

If you are dealing with a banking or investment service of any kind, you will have to be apprised not only of federal rules and regulations but of those of the states as well. Some states are more restrictive than others, and some have procedures that cause considerable delay in granting approvals.

Some specific areas of great importance include procedures for notifying customers in the event of shipping delays, rules regarding merchandise substitution, and the parameters of "dry testing"—announcing a product before it is actually produced.

A knowledge of the FTC "thirty-day rules," which apply to delayed shipments and require specific notices and actions, is extremely important. One prominent marketer spent years in lawsuits because, at a critical point, he elected to notify customers of a delay by phone instead of mail. While most marketers would consider a phone notice better service, it has only recently become acceptable, provided certain records are kept. Logic cannot be relied upon when dealing with government rulings.

"Unordered merchandise" is an area of particular sensitivity, as are the various practices involving unauthorized billing. If you sell on credit, Regulation Z of the Treasury Department may apply. If you are in the financial area, the Securities and Exchange Commission (SEC) will have much power over what you can and cannot say.

Be sure you consult "Do's and Don'ts," a pamphlet published by the Better Business Bureau, and the *Guidelines* issued by the DMA Committee on Ethical Standards. Robert Posch's chapter in the *Direct Marketing Handbook* (McGraw-Hill, 1992) is very helpful, as is his full-length treatise, *The Direct Marketing Legal Advisor* (McGraw-Hill, 1983).

The laws governing direct marketing change rapidly, and so I deliberately did not attempt to record specific advice in this book, whose use is intended to span a number of years. Keep in mind that whatever strategies you devise will have to be within the bounds of government regulations, industry ethical standards, and simple fairness to the customer. Define those standards now, before you've finalized your marketing plan, so you won't risk going over the line in the letter or spirit of your marketing proposition.

VII IMPLEMENTATION

Now, at last, it's time to get down to action. The background has been clarified and the strategies chosen. All that remains is to implement the plan. This section of the marketing plan includes all the basics that, in less professional approaches, are likely to compose the entire plan. This section is not so much a logical, step-by-step, decision-making process as it is a blueprint for action.

Basic Scheduling

This section should start off with a simple statement of the purpose of the plan. If the purpose is a viability test, a universe probe, a search for breakthrough creative concepts, or a rollout of a proven approach, this is the place to say it, in so many words. Then set up the plan to do it.

Media schedules, timetables, and budgets are basics that should be included here in appropriate detail. If testing grids or keying systems are called for, include them. If product changes or revisions in the fulfillment system are necessary, this is the place to lay them out.

Further, with each step, this is the place for detailing exactly who is responsible for what: who will do it, who will approve it, and by what date it must be approved.

Creative and Offer Concepts

Creative and offer concepts should be separately outlined. They should approximate the same form as an advertising agency work assignment, containing everything copywriters need to start their work. For each offer and creative concept, there should be a simple statement of the objective and goal for that one version, and an explanation of the strategy chosen for this specified ad or mailing piece.

Any revisions in the basic copy platform should also be mentioned next to each creative concept, as well as any special economic considerations, cost limitations, timing problems, etc. Sensitivities—legal matters, styling considerations, and subjective client preferences—also should be noted, so that all concerned can agree on what they are.

A positioning statement also should be included, with special emphasis on any ways advertisements are expected to differ from previously established positioning. This positioning statement should refer specifically to copy style, level, and tone, as well as to graphic style and image. Often this type of detail is not part of the basic marketing plan but is added later in the form of individual strategy statements for specific advertisements, mailings, and broadcast commercials.

The final step is a statement of result targets: how the program as a whole is expected to affect the profit and loss sheet. This is the place to temper the goals and make allowances for the probability that not every new format is going to beat the control.

Budgeting

The budget should be prepared on the "task method." This means that recommended cost estimates should be provided for achieving the objectives stated in the plan. Possible budget shortcuts and abridgments should be included if it is possible that the task-based budget is in excess of management's expectations. However, the task-based budget should be stated even if it is unlikely that the necessary monies will be appropriated.

Where there are alternatives, their effect should be clearly expressed. If a smaller test budget will require a second stage of extension testing and a season's delay in the rollout, it should be graphically depicted, as should the risks and economic effects of such a delay.

If it is not yet possible to forecast results from recommended mailings or media insertions, a range of possible CPOs should be shown, with the economic effect of each worked out and shown.

It's a mistake to end a marketing plan with the cost of implementing the plan, for many executives scan the last pages first. The final wrap-up should restate the sales and profit expectations. This keeps the final focus on what is to be gained, not on what investment is required.

Timetable

The wrap-up is the schedule. How long will everything take? What are the key decision points? What answers are needed, at what dates, in order to move everything along. Who is expected to do what?

More marketing plans are killed by inaction than by deliberate rejection. If you want your marketing plan to have the approval of your management, then make it very clear who is expected to approve what, by what date, so that at least the blame will be clear if someone sits on your proposal.

Perhaps a note about overtime factors is in order. Often as little as a one-week delay in the early stages of a program will result in adding 50 percent or more to production costs incurred for overtime and rush services. If you have the figures available, they make a dramatic footnote for the timetable section of a marketing plan.

Whether your plan is a complete statement of every element and alternative, as outlined here, or a simple design for the next mailing, put it in writing and add data as you go along. The simplest plan is better than none, providing it is a written document that everyone can agree upon in advance and look back upon later.

THE MARKETING PLAN FORMAT

In the previous pages of this chapter I have outlined what kind of information should go into a marketing plan and explained why the background data is as important as the strategy itself—both in creating the strategy and in reviewing it.

Now let me summarize the format of the plan in more conventional marketing language:

Title
Marketing Plan for PERIOD for XYZ COMPANY Product Line. Prepared by NAME, DATE

Introduction
How and why the plan was prepared, at whose request, and with whose endorsement. The qualifications or point of view of the preparers. The process, if relevant. The data and briefings that were or were not available for inclusion in the plan.

Product Description
Physical description
Scientific data
Emotional data
Benefits

Present positioning
Possible variations

Marketing Environment
Competitive situation summarized
Competitive media utilization
Competitive copy point breakdown
Miscellaneous competitive information
Media availabilities

Media Cost, Timing, and Testing Factors
Distribution—cost, timing, effectiveness
Government regulations—dos and don'ts
Economic trends: fads and fashions
Known problems and opportunities

Market Potential
The media universe
Profile of prospective customer
Product, offer, or positioning changes needed to appeal to other
  likely market segments
Results of previous list and media tests
Available demographic or psychographic data

Strategic Planning
Objectives of marketing program
Goals: quantified objectives, within time frame
Strategic alternatives
Criteria for selection
Recommended prioritized strategies

Implementation
Basic campaign outline
Test grid, if applicable
Media or list recommendation
Offer or creative concept
Budgets
Timetables
Result targets

The writing style for a marketing plan should be as simple as possible. The object is to impress the boss or client, not with the number of words but with the soundness of the thinking. An outline form, with bulleted points and telegraphic copy style, is very appropriate as long as it is clear.

Loose-leaf binders are recommended. They permit updating, revision, and addition during the course of a campaign. New data, new ideas, and result reports should all be added to the basic marketing plan during the course of the year, so that the plan is not just a historical record of an original intention but a living, working document of a campaign in progress.

EVALUATING A
MARKETING PLAN

For many executives, particularly in larger businesses, the preparation of a marketing plan is left to an advertising agency, a consultant, or staff members. The real problem for such executives—one that is just as important as writing the plan—is its evaluation.

If the plan has been prepared as outlined here, or in any similar format, it is a self-contained document that includes all relevant background material. The evaluator should be able to take one binder on an airplane or to a poolside lounge chair and read through the plan without reference to outside data.

The first thing evaluators should note is whether all pertinent considerations have been taken into account. If they have, the other pieces should logically fall into place. The evaluators should then ask whether the plan looks ahead. Does it provide marketing and creative direction for the future?

If the plan is for a presently successful campaign, are there provisions for testing ads and mailing pieces for future seasons when the present control will eventually wear out?

The budget will be important, of course, especially as it fits into overall corporate budgets. However, it should be considered only in terms of downside risk. Even the unsuccessful portions of a campaign produce some orders.

Is the plan legal? Does it follow the spirit as well as the letter of the law? Sending the copy platform to lawyers for review now, rather than waiting for finished copy, may be helpful.

Most important, is it unique? Does it present fresh, original, creative thinking? Or could it be your competitor's plan just by changing the product name? You should expect some new approaches and some challenging ideas, as well as obvious marketing logic.

After the plan has been completely reviewed, one final test remains. In some ways, this may be the most important. Call in the people who wrote the plan and approved it. Look them in the eye and ask them this one question: "Do you really think this plan will be successful?" The people who wrote the plan should really believe in it. You have a right to expect them to believe in it and to have enthusiasm about it. If they don't, start looking for new people and a new plan.

Plan or Process?

While this chapter deals with planning, it is now popular—particularly in the academic world—to recommend that direct marketing and database marketing be approached as a process, not a plan.

This concept suggests that marketing decisions cannot be fixed, but must respond to changing environments and the constantly shifting status of the groups and individuals who make up the pool of customers and prospects. I agree that this is an ultimate ideal, and it is a reality in many companies whose databases and resources are large enough to respond quickly to market changes. But even a process requires planning.

First a company must have sufficient information to understand which market groups or individuals are responding to which offerings, possibly even to which positionings or creative themes. These are considered individually, not as an "average." With this information it should be possible to forecast the long-range income and profitability from each sector, and to appropriate marketing budgets accordingly.

Given the rapid evolution of technology, someday this approach may be universally feasible and in common practice. If so, I will be delighted to describe it in detail in this book's fourth edition! For now, I suggest that most practitioners should regard process as a goal, to be implemented where and to the extent possible. It represents an ideal approach, and idealism has its place. But in the world of marketing, as in life itself, it must not distract us from dealing with the realities of today.

4

THE PROPOSITION

Except for changing the product itself, nothing can make as big a difference as a change in the basic proposition. There are exceptions, but this is still the rule. Changes in the price, the terms, the guarantee, the way the product is combined or segmented—all of these will show up faster in result tabulations than most changes in copy and layout. The rule: The substance of the offer outweighs the form of its presentation.

PRICE OFFERS

Does price make a difference? You bet it does. We'll start with the simplest category: the types of propositions available to a business selling a single product or service directly to the consumer in a "one-step" approach that asks for the order on the initial contact.

Hidden Price. If the product is new, has a new feature, or answers a real need, you may want to deemphasize price until after the benefits have been fully presented. In such a case the price may be buried in the last paragraphs of the main copy. LaSalle Extension University concealed its tuition under a flap on the enrollment form. *Geo* magazine used a sealed envelope to be sure the price was the last and not the first information communicated.

Featured Price. "Giant wall map, only $1" can be a powerhouse offer. If the price *is* the news, then scream it out at the beginning, right in the headline of an ad, the superscription of a letter, or superimposed on a television commercial. Most general advertising can't feature price because of legal restrictions, but direct marketers—like retailers—can and should.

Comparative Price. Did the product sell for more at an earlier time? Is it the equivalent of a retail product that sells for a higher price? Would your book club titles cost more in "publishers' original editions"? Then by all means let the consumer in on this fact. The more striking the comparison, the more prominent it should be. But make sure it's legitimate and make sure you can prove the claim. Government and industry self-regulators are frowning on stretched comparisons justified by a few token sales at a higher price.

Introductory Price. If you're offering a new product or service, the introductory offer is a great way to get attention and encourage immediate action.

Discount Offers. If the offer can be expressed in terms of a comparison with a previous price, a retail price, a newsstand price, etc., then consider expressing that price in percentages or fractions. "Half-price" will usually do better than "Originally $10, now $5.

Savings Feature. Consider featuring the savings in a price comparison, rather than the low price. "Save $11" can be a stronger lead than "Now only $19," if price is the feature.

CREDIT PROPOSITIONS

The availability of credit in its many forms can be as valuable a sales stimulus as a product enhancement or price reduction. Credit is costly, not only in "no-pay" sales but in interest costs if you carry your own receivables, or in financing discounts or credit card charges if you don't. Don't forget paperwork processing, billing, postage, and the cost of added returns.

Whether or not you offer credit is a fundamental decision that will be affected by the value of your product and the nature of your market. In some product-market combinations, it is not an option; the proposition will not work at all without it. With still others, it may be a marginal consideration requiring extensive testing of whether the front-end lift is worth the back-end cost and complications.

Free Trial Offer

Credit combined with a guarantee is the strongest credit proposition available. Its powerful benefit is the implication that you have such confidence in your product that you are willing to let the consumer use, read, examine, or try it before deciding whether to return or pay for it.

As returns will be significant, it is necessary to consider the cost of the product before trying this offer. If you do try it, then make the most of it by using "Free trial," "Send no money now," and "Use it for 10 days at our risk." If you plan to refurbish and reship returned merchandise, use the term "Free examination." There are legal problems in reshipping "tried" merchandise.

Conditional Free Trial

Essentially the same as the previous offer, the conditional free trial has one vital difference: The offer is subject to acceptance. A clause in the coupon can state this reservation. The marketer can then apply a variety of credit-screening techniques. Here are some examples.

- *Internal match.* Previous bad-pay customers, or those who have already taken advantage of a "one-time only" or "one-to-a-family" offer, can be eliminated by computer matching, usually by address.

- *External match.* Prospective customers can be checked against lists maintained by credit compilers such as TRW, Hooper-Holmes, and local credit bureaus.

- *Zip-code characteristics.* The credit history of previous respondents from the specific postal area or like postal areas, defined in clusters, can be checked. This data is sometimes tempered by media source data that justify accepting quality publication or list respondents despite the overall record of the zip code.

- *Individual indicators.* Substantial credit differences can result from the types of information provided in the coupon. Although a full credit application—inquiring about employment and banking histories— might be theoretically desirable, it would depress response rate severely. The bulk of bad-pay prospects often can be spotted simply by asking for additional information, such as a phone number or a signature.

A separate question is what to do with customers whose orders are rejected. The orders should be acknowledged in the interest of courtesy if not profitability. I prefer honest replies, advising the customers that previous history prevents shipping their orders on credit and asking for prepayment, credit card payment, or additional information.

Installment Sales

With a large enough unit sale, or where a credit relationship already exists, installment sales often can be profitable. The most common application of installment sales is a simple three- or four-part billing, usually used with a trial offer. Installment sales also can require that a deposit be paid or that the order be charged to a credit card, a charge card, or a new or existing charge account.

Care should be taken to comply with applicable Regulation Z requirements regarding full disclosure of interest terms. Even if there is no interest but you give a premium or discount for cash, there is a presumption that the installment payments include interest, and a disclosure statement is still required. I personally negotiated with the Treasury Department for a waiver for magazine offers, but other products may still be subject to this requirement.

Charge and Credit Cards

One of the greatest changes in the entire direct marketing industry was the ability to utilize charge and credit cards in direct marketing. While this may not represent a majority of the population, it probably represents the bulk of consumer spending power. The utilization of credit cards can be expanded still further for some purposes, by arranging for acceptance of oil company, telephone, hotel, airline, and other specific-purpose cards.

Obviously, cards will be most effective when used with offers that are appropriate in both market and price range, but there is another important consideration: the response element itself. A credit card offer requires space for number, expiration dates, and the name of the card used. The customer may get frustrated trying to squeeze the 15 digits into a tiny space. A solution for print-media advertisers is to offer a conventional coupon asking for check with order, and then to combine credit cards with phone ordering, as in, "Credit card holders may order by phone. Call 800...."

Broadcast offers an excellent opportunity to "trade up" a send-no-money proposition to a credit card order by having the incoming phone operator offer a premium for such an order.

COD Sales

Cash-on-delivery sales are a form of credit only in that the consumer is able to order without enclosing payment in advance. In this method, either the U.S. Postal Service or United Parcel delivers the package and collects payment. It is one alternative that some marketers use when selling impulse products to people who do not have an appropriate credit card, especially when orders are taken by telephone.

COD requires extensive and costly paperwork. More important, refusals tend to be excessive for several reasons. Sometimes the customer doesn't have the cash available when the order is delivered. At other times no one is at home, and it is too much trouble to arrange redelivery or to pick the package up at the post office. More often, the impulse to buy has simply cooled off, particularly as the COD collection process usually presents an anonymous package with no presell, a request for immediate payment, and unexpectedly high postal charges. Even when all COD costs are passed on to the customer, the refusal rate generally is so high that most advertisers in the United States avoid this technique.

Easy or Preapproved Credit

An age-old retail technique that is very effective for offers to demographic groups that traditionally have trouble getting credit at all is offering easy or preapproved credit. A typical application is the utilization of preapproved credit offers to those on lists that have been computer-prechecked by TRW and local credit bureaus. Such mailings have been overused by banks offering checkbook loans, with the cliché opening, "You have already been approved for $2000 in credit."

An application of this technique that still has not been fully exploited is the offer of preapproved credit to prospective mail-order buyers of jewelry, collectibles, or similar high-ticket items.

Low Down Payment

If you're offering credit or installment sales, a low down payment can be as important as a low price, particularly if it reflects an advantage to the consumer. One correspondence school, to add news value to its series of enrollment mailings, lowered down payments at three different points in their conversion series.

Low Interest

As an alternative to a price reduction, a dramatic low interest rate can get attention and stimulate sales. If you are competing with department stores that carry their accounts at 12 or 18 percent interest, an offer of an installment item at 6 percent, for instance, might have greater appeal than an equivalent price reduction.

GUARANTEES

In direct marketing, a guarantee of some sort is not an option. It is a necessity. We are asking consumers to trust us by placing orders and, sometimes, sending payment for items they have never actually handled. It is necessary to return that trust by standing behind the product and services we offer with the most liberal return or refund policies possible.

I believe it is not all coincidental that the companies with the most generous policies seem to be consistently among the most successful.

Norm Thompson, a very professional catalog house featuring classic casual wear, makes this guarantee:

"YOU BE THE JUDGE™"
When we say "You Be the Judge™", we mean just that! Every
product you purchase from Norm Thompson must live up to
your expectations, not ours. If at any time a product fails to satisfy
you, return it to us, postage prepaid, and we'll either replace the
item, or refund your money in full, whichever you wish.
This is definitely not a 2-week guarantee. It's good for the normal
life of the product. (You being the judge of what that normal life
should be.) We'll stand behind everything we sell to the fullest
extent...no ifs, ands, or buts.

Sears Roebuck & Company puts the same idea in more succinct language with this guarantee statement that they credit as a major contributor to Sears success:

SATISFACTION GUARANTEED OR YOUR MONEY BACK.

Unconditional Guarantee. The two statements quoted above are
examples of unconditional guarantees. While a small minority of customers may abuse such a guarantee by returning obviously used and
abused merchandise or by falsely claiming dissatisfaction, the guarantor
is usually more than compensated by the goodwill of and the added
sales from the majority of its customers.

Conditional Guarantee. If you must limit your guarantee, the law
requires that you label limitations precisely. Some types of guarantees are

- *Time limit.* The most common type of guarantee, the time limit is
  stated in a sentence such as, "If not satisfied, return within 10 days for
  full refund."

- *Repair or replacement only.* This form of guarantee includes an
  assurance that the item will work, rather than that the customer will be
  satisfied with it.

- *Liability limit.* Where a customer might claim secondary damages,
  the guarantee takes the form of a limit on liability—for example,
  "Liability limited to replacement of film," as used by a film processor.

- *Usage condition.* For some products, including fragile items, the
  guarantee may be written in a form such as "When used according to
  instructions" or "Providing it has not been dropped or abused."

Double Guarantee. While most financial officers will welcome this
idea like an attack of eczema, its "lift" power is so substantial as to merit
its consideration with most products offered to civilized audiences.
"Double your money back" will be abused, but by so few people that
you still come out ahead. Like any other offer, it must be tested first.

Competitive Guarantee. If you believe your product is as good as any competitor's, try this: Offer to send them your competitor's product as a replacement, or free, if they don't like yours. One variation of this was tried by *Newsweek:* "Try *Newsweek* for 3 weeks without cost. If you don't like it, we'll ask *Time* to send you their best offer."

Dramatized Guarantee. You may not want to offer to eat your hat or roll a peanut down the street with your nose if your customer isn't satisfied, but there are more appropriate ways to dramatize your guarantee. For example, "Bring this coupon to our store; if our prices are not the best in town, we'll even pay for the gas you used to drive here."

"Keeper" Offer. When you're offering a premium, you can dramatize your confidence in your product by telling buyers they can keep the premium, even if they elect to return the purchase.

Trial Subscription. If your product is sold serially, as are magazine subscriptions and continuity programs, you can give buyers the right to cancel either "at any time" or after examining the first shipment.

Value Protection Guarantee. Some organizations selling collectibles or investments have advertised a willingness to buy back the item at some future time if it has lost value or has not achieved a specific gain in value. Such offers should be made only by large, well-financed companies that can make good this claim. Anyone making this kind of guarantee recklessly may run into a personal charge of mail fraud. The "limited liability" protection of a corporation won't help anyone charged with fraud.

CONTINUITY PROGRAMS

The most successful mail-order proposition generally involves the establishment of a customer relationship that extends beyond the initial transaction. Continuity is one of the most critical, and unfortunately most neglected, aspects of the direct marketing profitability equation.

A retailer can establish good customer relationships by providing the service, quality, and environment to support the simple invitation, "Come again." A catalog marketer accomplishes repeat sales in the same manner, except that the marketer's image is created by the catalog and service.

In many direct marketing propositions, either a series of products such as books, videos, or skin-care items is offered, or a product is segmented or serialized to facilitate continuity programs. Anyone promoting via direct marketing should look for ways to combine, break apart, or add to existing products in order to make possible some type of continuity offer.

Subscription

The word *subscription* is most frequently associated with magazines. This form of publishing is not only the most common user of this proposition, it is also one of the most sophisticated. However, the technique can be applied to other products as well.

Basically, a magazine is an information or entertainment product sold in installments over a period of time. The most common time period is a year, but most publications are willing to discount rates for longer subscriptions—two, three, or more years.

Shorter subscriptions often are used as introductory offers, to make a trial inexpensive for a new customer. One innovation is the variable-term introductory subscription, which permits a new subscriber to choose any number of copies at a low price per copy.

Subscription selling is probably the longest customer relationship in direct marketing. As a general rule, 50 to 60 percent of first-year subscribers will renew for a second term; 70 to 90 percent of renewed subscribers will then renew again for subsequent terms—on to infinity. This renewal rate is influenced by the professionalism of the renewal series but, obviously, depends to a much greater extent on the reader's satisfaction with the magazine's editorial content.

Subscription propositions are sometimes offered to the consumer as "item-a-month" or "pay-as-you-go" plans, where the total price is committed but payable in monthly installments.

The defining characteristics of subscription sales are that the term is fixed and the service is billable at its inception. The same technique can be applied to a library of books, a set of collectibles, or even linens or tablewear.

Automatic Shipment Plans

Unlike subscription selling, the automatic shipment plan seeks not one sales transaction but a series of individual ones.

The customer is asked to participate in a sales plan that provides for the sale of individual units at a predetermined interval—a month, or six weeks, or even annually. The most famous examples are the various libraries or sets of books offered by Time-Life Books, Grolier, Meredith, Harlequin, and other major publishers.

In this type of continuity plan the customer agrees to buy a unit per interval. The units could be books in an encyclopedia set, cosmetic samples, components of a teaching plan for children, parts of a desk set or matched luggage,, annual diaries or yearbooks, or issues in a collectible series. A unit could even be a service such as furnace inspection or window cleaning. The possibilities are infinite.

Here's a typical automatic shipment offer, from a Grolier ad:

I am enclosing [check/money order] for one dollar. Please enroll
my child as a trial member and send me the four Bright and Early
Beginner Books shown here plus the free book, *In A People's
House,* and the free booklet. If not delighted, I may keep the free
book and booklet and return the four books within 14 days and my
one dollar will be fully refunded. Otherwise approximately every
4 weeks hereafter, please send two other Beginner Books at
only $2.75 each (instead of the retail price of $3.95) plus delivery.
I may cancel at any time.   `

Note that in this case the customer is offered the first volumes at a substantially reduced price, with return privileges, and may cancel at any time.
The free book and booklet is a *keeper:* a premium that may be retained
whether or not the customer decides to continue with the program.
Sometimes such coupons provide for accelerated shipments at a later date
or the right to "load up" subsequent books once credit is established.

The essential principle is that the customer authorizes automatic shipments and agrees to pay for them or return them. Usually the customer
does not have the right to return a single shipment without canceling the
program—a pressure to induce acceptance of the entire series.

The psychology of this principle is that inertia—one of the most powerful elements of human psychology—is converted from a negative buying force to a positive one. Customers no longer have to say yes to buy
the product; instead, they must say no to *not* buy it. This is the underlying psychological principle of all continuity plans.

Club Plans

Though some firms use the word *club* rather liberally to describe any
type of continuity plan and even noncontinuity membership plans, the
technical usage of the term should be reserved for the club concept as
originated by the Book-of-the-Month Club.

The defining characteristic of the club concept is its addition of choice
to the basic automatic shipment plan. In a conventional club, automatic
shipment is not limited to one preselected product each interval, but a
choice is provided—usually by means of a club bulletin or advance
announcement. The club "member" is free to accept a recommended
item (often called a "selection of the month"), choose no item that
month, or select an alternative.

When you consider that generally there is not only advertising
expense but also some type of inducement offered to persuade people to
join such a club, two serious concerns must come to mind:

1. How do you get the members to respond to each announcement bul-
    letin?

2. What is to keep members from always declining purchases?

These are very valid concerns, and they have led to some ingenious solutions that now apply to many types of direct marketing propositions:

1. The negative option
2. The positive option
3. The commitment
4. The membership plan

Negative Option

Basically, the negative option refers to the customer's need to say no in order to keep a preselected shipment from arriving in the mailbox. It applies to continuity programs in which the definition of *no* can be "Pass this shipment only," "Cancel entirely," or a choice between the two types of refusal. In clubs, the negative applies only to the selection. It provides the leverage to overcome inertia and force a reply. The consequence of not replying in a reasonable time period is that the selection will arrive and have to be paid for or returned. Some writers have successfully presented this feature as a positive benefit, stressing its convenience and its contribution to self-discipline.

The purpose of negative option is emphatically *not* to ship unwanted merchandise, for that is to no one's benefit—it would result only in returns, no-pays, and cancellations. The objective is simply to overcome inertia and force a conscious, considered decision. Usually about 25 percent of club members will take the selection (if it is a desirable one) and another 25 to 50 percent will take an alternate. The figures vary widely from business to business and interval to interval, depending on the attractiveness of the product offered and the soundness of the presentation. Negative option can force a decision; it can't force a sale.

Note that I used the word *interval* rather than *month* or *year*. The original Book-of-the-Month Club concept has evolved into plans in which many book or record clubs offer 15, 16, or even 18 different announcements per year.

Positive Option

To make this presentation complete, we must touch on the antithesis of negative option. Theoretically, a continuity plan might be constructed wherein the customer is sent preannouncements but need not reply. A commitment, discussed below, might apply and so the customer would have to buy something eventually. In principle, such a plan should have a higher initial response, because it would attract people who don't want to be bothered with making a decision or sending a notice every month. In principle, the commitment should offset the loss-of-inertia reversal.

It's a nice theory, except for one problem: I have never seen it work. The closest thing to its being used on a large scale is the membership plan, discussed on the following page.

Commitment

A commitment is simply an obligation for the customer to buy a minimum number of units or a minimum dollar volume within a limited time period: traditionally a year or two. There have been clubs that tried to eliminate the commitment, just as some have tried to operate without negative option. While it might be possible to dispense with one, there is no way to do without both.

Why would customers accept the obligation of a commitment? For the same reason that they accept the negative option: an attractive inducement. A back-end obligation such as "I agree to buy as few as four more tapes at regular club prices in the next three years" is the price the customer pays for a front-end reward such as "seven tapes for 1 cent."

Note that the customer is as sensitive to the commitment as to the inducement. Large advertisers continuously test "three books for 98 cents" versus "four books for 10 cents" and similar offers. They also test whether the commitment on a given offer should be one item more or less, and whether the obligation should be fulfilled within one year, two years, an unlimited time period, or once every three months.

Membership Plans

Most continuity plans offer the customer what Capitol Record Club called "Savings in Advance." Membership plans flip this concept around and, incredibly, offer the customer a pay-now, save-later option.

The way these usually work is that members are invited to join a plan, sometimes called a club, which will give them some immediate benefits or the right to future benefits in return for a fee paid at the onset. To the extent the fee is paid at the beginning, it is more like a subscription than any other type of continuity plan. There are several basic applications of this scheme, each of them with variations that may or may not be interchangeable.

Discount Buying Service.   The customer is asked to pay a fee in advance. Membership then entitles the customer to buy from a catalog at presumably bargain prices not available to the public. Usually the company counts on the membership fee to cover or at least defray advertising costs. The profit depends on the markup from subsequent sales.

Catalog Subscription.   If a catalog has intrinsic value in itself, it can be the heart of a membership plan. Typically, it is a *magalog*—a term coined by Maxwell Sroge Associates—that combines editorial content and product offers.

This catalog format often is quite effective, even when mailed conventionally. Not only are the editorial pages a reason to keep the catalog and read it more carefully, but they generate interest in the product or service category, educate the reader, and create desire. It is particularly effective in specialty catalogs dealing with outdoor apparel, hobbies, and technical subjects (such as computer software).

A typical variation is to put a price on such a catalog and make it available at that price to anyone, but to send it free to buyers. Some such catalogs have even been sold on newsstands.

Customized Service. Another membership approach is based on providing some type of personal service to the customer in return for the membership fee, leading into offers of related products. One dramatic example was the Sarah Coventry Personal Beauty Plan, which invited the customer to send $25, a photograph, and the answers to a questionnaire. The photograph was enlarged and sent back with a professional face makeover, using real cosmetics on an acetate sheet. The colors recommended were available only in their own line of cosmetics. Modern computer technology makes it possible to produce personalized horoscopes, career plans, investment analyses, life expectancy predictions, and diet plans—all as part of related mail-order programs.

An interesting recent variation of customization, though not part of a continuity program, was advertised by a weight-reduction product called Ultra Slim-Fast. Readers were invited to send in a photograph of themselves and answer some questions about weight-reduction goals. In return they received a computer-generated Polaroid picture showing their own picture at their desired weight. New technology such as this provides a constant challenge and opportunity to direct marketers developing the propositions of the future.

Most current membership plans have everything built in except some type of automatic shipment element. The real challenge for such companies is to find a way to combine the up-front appeal of their present propositions with the back-end profitability of some of the other continuity plans outlined here.

DATABASE BUILDING

What was once called *two-step marketing* is now generally referred to as *database building*. While database marketing has opened up many new applications of direct marketing—particularly in packaged goods, automotive, appliance and other marketing areas not previously using direct marketing—basically it is the first step of any form of a "two-step proposition." The only difference is that a traditional direct marketer usually has a specific second step in mind, while the database marketer often is building a list as a marketing tool without having tested specific applications.

In my book *Database Marketing: The Ultimate Selling Tool* (McGraw-Hill, 1993), I cover this subject in much more detail. But I also point out the truth that database marketing is rooted in classic mail order, and suggest that to master the newest forms of this marketing art one should understand its history and have some experience with it.

The previous sections of this chapter have dealt with offers that "ask for the order" for a product or service at the initial contact. Certainly the most qualified name on a mailing list is that of someone who has already made a purchase. But even catalog marketers will run advertisements in nondirect-mail media, simply offering the catalog. This type of ad is a two-step list-builder or, to use the modern expression, an example of database building.

The general objective is to locate new prospects—leads, inquiries, sample requesters—to be followed up later with a more intensive sales effort than would be affordable on a large-scale basis to marginal or unqualified prospects. The later follow-up might be through a personal visit by a salesperson, an invitation to a showroom or sales event, a telephone call, or more direct mail—elaborate conversion packages, a videotape, or a series of selling letters.

This two-step technique is used by many of the largest corporations in the direct marketing business. Encyclopedia publishers offer a free booklet, which is delivered by a salesperson. Insurance companies offer a book of maps or a gardening guide, which also is brought by a sales representative.

Financial institutions offer free information or a prospectus, which is followed by an intensive series of mailings and telephone calls. Real estate developers invite prospects to make an appointment to see model homes; the sales effort begins at the site. Or a pipe tobacco may be offered in a 25-cent trial size, just to introduce the product, with the hope that the flavor will sell itself.

Free Information.   The simplest and most logical two-step plan is the offer of free information. It can be strengthened by further definition, such as, "Send for free information about the amazing new XYZ device, including pictures, diagrams, detailed operating instructions, and our pay-as-you-go installment purchase plan."

Free Booklet.   When your advertising is aimed at an earlier horizontal positioning stage, it is often effective to offer a booklet about the generic subject rather than the specific topic. North American Coin & Currency, for instance, offers the "Gold Guide" rather than asking for an investment right off the bat. The guide, of course, sells not only the generic advantages of precious metal investments, but also the particular services offered by its publisher.

Free Planning Kit.   A further way to build on preceding offers is to make up a more complex "kit" of everything the client may need to plan a vacation or diagnose a lawn problem, for example. For Marriott Hotels, I developed a series of meeting and convention planning kits for particular cities where Marriott has hotels. The idea was to produce very hard leads, instead of the usual contest entries or booklet requests. Offers of these guides would appeal only to sales managers or other executives who were seriously planning a major meeting in a particular city.

Free Videotape. With the proliferation of VCRs, videotapes have become one of the most effective ways to respond to a lead (or to get one in the first place). Duplication Factory in Chaska, MN, has dozens of case histories in a wide variety of fields. Now that videotapes cost little more than a good color brochure, it is an option that should not be overlooked.

Free Book on Related Subject. Lanier, for instance, offered a copy of a book called *Time Management* along with information about their dictating equipment. The subject set the stage for saving time by dictating, and the book had a perceived value of $2.50 or so, comparable to what the public then expected to pay for paperback books.

Free Gift. Here's the classic insurance offer again. "Just send us your birthdate and we'll send you a free book of maps"—or a tool kit, gardening guide, or some other popular item. The thinking here is that supposedly everyone is a prospect for insurance, it is not capable of being presold, and all you want is to get the salesperson in any door.

Free Survey. "Let us survey your telephone costs." "Let us check your roof for leaks." "Let us inspect your car's tires." All of these offer a genuine service that should appeal only to people who have a suspicion that they have something to gain from such a survey. Hence the leads should be good ones, and the service profitable to offer. .

Free Sample. If your product lends itself to sampling, and if it is really good, so good that it sells itself, then consider giving it away in small units. Tobacco companies have handed out samples of new cigarette brands. Soap companies have placed samples on doorknob hangers. Why not offer a free sample and send it along with an effective selling message by mail or salesperson?

Free Catalog. Some companies just send their catalogs to every logical mailing list. Where the catalog is costly or the lists are marginal, a two-step offer is sometimes preferable. Space advertising is an excellent way to get fresh names for a catalog business, just by offering the catalog. These catalog inquiry names often are better than buyer names from other catalog companies.

Choice of Booklets. A choice of booklets (or catalogs or samples) is an accurate way of identifying which of several products or services someone is most interested in. This is a device that I have frequently recommended for database building.

Nominal Cost. All the above propositions can not only be made on a "free" basis, but they can also be offered for a quarter, a dollar, or more. Even the slightest charge qualifies the inquiry and makes it worth following up.

List-Building Offer. Some merchandisers, instead of offering a catalog or other information in their promotions, go right ahead and sell some product that is an example of their line and that represents an unusual value. You'll find clothing catalog merchandisers advertising in *The Wall Street Journal,* for instance. Often, these ads don't produce a profit over the cost of goods and advertising, but they do produce a list of qualified buyers for the company's full line of products at a lower cost per name than a straight "free catalog" offer.

LEAD SELLING

In a lead selling system, two-step initial transactions are completed by a dealer, agent, or salesperson rather than by the company's own direct mail.

Lead Flow Considerations

In supporting a sales organization, it is often necessary to maintain a steady supply of leads for all members of the sales force, in all seasons. This introduces a new consideration into media planning, as it is often necessary to mail or advertise in seasons that might be comparatively unresponsive. It is more important to keep the conversion rate high in most cases than to maximize the cost-per-lead figures.

Often leads come in geographically in a manner that brings in more leads in some parts of the country—perhaps the West or rural areas. Other areas need supplemental programs, sometimes using regional publications or local compiled lists in order to keep the sales force content. At LaSalle Extension University we called this a "local support program."

Too many leads sent to one salesperson will be "burnt off." The salesperson will prejudge them, and pick and choose the ones his or her hunches (almost always wrong) say are the easiest to sell. Too few leads sent to other salespeople will cause them to quit their jobs because they are not making enough money.

There is a chicken-and-egg dilemma in terms of planning for lead selling. Do you plan your lead supply to satisfy your sales force? Or do you allocate your sales territories and dealerships to reflect the lead flow? Usually this is a matter to be resolved between the sales force manager and the direct marketing manager, preferably without bloodshed.

Lead Freshness

One question that everyone agrees on is that leads must be followed up promptly. Every day that passes before a prospect is contacted by a salesperson will noticeably reduce the conversion rate. In some cases I have advised companies to set up systems for computer transmitting or faxing leads to dealers or sales offices, to avoid the delay of postal transmission.

If a company's computer system takes too much time to get leads processed, it is often advisable to bypass the computer initially and send a manual lead to the sales force. A copy can be sent to the computer department for data entry on a more convenient schedule.

Lead Distribution

Usually a lead is supplied on some type of computer form. The forms should obtain as much information as possible to help the salesperson relate to the prospect. Not only name, address, title (if a business lead), and phone number should be included, but the date of lead, the company's Standard Industrial Classifications (SIC) code or business classification, and the exact nature of the inquiry. The salesperson should know what ad or mailing piece the prospect responded to and in what publication the ad appeared.

The lead recipient should have one copy for filing and another to be transmitted back to the computer center for tabulation. The report form should indicate the date of contact and initial disposition, to be tabulated into sales reports.

A lead should be supplied, in my opinion, with some type of expiration date. Perhaps the lead can be exclusive for a given period and then become nonexclusive, with other dealers or the company's own mail conversion effort cutting in after a deadline. My experience has proved that salespeople will convert more if they have only a limited time to call on the prospect.

The computer should be programmed so that lead distribution is not automatic. Whether you are dealing with salespeople or dealers, the transmission of additional leads should be contingent on the prompt reporting and effective handling of leads previously sent. The computer should automatically cut off lead flow if the open lead ratio is too high or if subsequent confirmation questionnaires indicate that reporting wasn't accurate. Cutting off lead flow should not be left to the discretion of the sales manager, who should concentrate on getting the lead recipient to shape up or ship out. Unassignable leads should be sent to a dealer or salesperson in an adjoining area or converted by mail order rather than sent to an uncooperative or ineffective destination.

Appointment Assignments

Some organizations that sell directly to the public, such as vinyl siding contractors, carpet companies, or security system installers, use a more controlled method. Rather than providing their salespersons with leads, they have their own telemarketing department call each prospect, requalify them, and schedule appointments. Large national phone services such as National Marketshare can do this on a national basis, keeping track of sales performance, days off, routes and schedules. Typically sales representatives are given three or four such appointments; when there are more leads than sales representatives in a given area, more salespeople are recruited as quickly as possible. Where the reverse occurs, leads are given only to those with the best conversion records.

Lead Reports

Reports should indicate, both to local and headquarters sales managers, exactly how many leads have been distributed, how many are "open" or uncontacted, and how many have been sold. If possible, the dollar volume of the sales should be related to the dollar cost of the leads. Such reports should be cross-tabulated by type of product, type of prospect, salesperson, or dealer, and by the initial promotion codes: mailing lists, media, etc.

The frequency of these reports—weekly, monthly, or quarterly—depends on the ability of management to find time to read and study the results. I prefer to reduce the frequency of reports and really work with them rather than have them come out frequently only to be stacked on a windowsill.

These reports are not historical curiosities. They are blueprints for action, and it is essential that management respond by changing advertisements, schedules, products, or salespeople as necessary.

QUALITY OF LEADS AND INQUIRIES

The quality of leads can be fine-tuned like a stereo set. As the volume of leads goes up, the quality goes down, and vice versa. The slightest change in the advertisement or mailing piece can produce significant changes in lead quality, and so can changes in the type of publication, station, or mailing list used.

We refer to the relative "hardness" and "softness" of leads. A hard lead is super-qualified, ready to buy. A soft lead may be someone sending for a free gift. Usually we are operating between the two extremes and adjusting the lead flow and quality to meet immediate needs in the marketplace and to satisfy the concerns of the sales organization.

It is very useful to know how to harden leads or soften them as required.

Lead Hardeners

If dealers or salespeople complain about the quality of leads, here's how to "harden" them:

- *Mention price.* Indicate what the product will cost.
- *Mention sales call.* Say someone will call.
- *Tell more.* Reveal more information about the product, including any potential negatives.
- *Ask for more information.* Get the telephone number and the best hours to call. Find out how many employees the company has.
- *Charge something.* Even a token amount for a booklet or sample will smoke out the real deadbeats.
- *Require a stamp.* Don't use a business reply card or envelope. Let the prospects buy the stamps—maybe even supply their own envelopes.
- *Narrow the offer.* Make it very relevant to the product or service you are selling.

Lead Softeners

If more leads are needed, here's how you can loosen up the lead quality and permit more leads to come in from the same promotion expenditures:

- *Tell less.* Leave something to curiosity.
- *Computerize the response coupon.* Fill in the names and addresses of the prospects. Give them less to do.
- *Add convenience.* Supply the stamp, the envelope, and maybe even a pencil.
- *Give more.* Add a gift or premium—maybe one that is valuable independently of the product offered.
- *Charge less.* Make it free, free, free.
- *Ask less.* The fewer questions, the better.
- *Add a prize.* A sweepstakes is the ultimate quality-softener.

Don't forget that the medium also will have a material effect on lead quality. The low-cost-per-lead publication or list may be composed of teenagers or others who send for everything. Study the source data and change mailing and media schedules to improve quality. Fine-tuning the media is just as important as fine-tuning the coupon copy.

CONTESTS AND SWEEPSTAKES

One sure way to boost the number of responses is a contest or sweepstakes. A prize of as little as $10,000 has been known to lift response rates between 30 and 50 percent. Larger prizes, selected creatively, have done even better.

If you use a contest, consult a contest management company such as Ventura Associates or D. L. Blair to help you select prizes, set up rules, and administer the contest. The legal restrictions are very exacting, and an independent management and judging organization will be well worth the small cost.

The cost of the prizes has to be taken into account when planning the costs of mailing. The larger the mailing, the less significant the sweepstakes cost. A mailing of 10 million pieces with a $100,000 contest costs only an additional $10 per thousand pieces, and therefore needs only a slight lift over a nonsweepstakes package to be profitable.

The problem is not in initial cost but in quality. The added lift of a sweepstakes package represents a large number of people who are forced into a yes-or-no decision on the product offered with the sweepstakes, or who mistakenly believe that saying yes will help their chances of winning.

Sweepstakes produce a noticeable deterioration in the quality of business produced, not just in the initial acceptance, conversion or payment, but all the way along the line. In magazines, the payment rate, the initial conversion rate, and subsequent renewal rates all are reduced. The only remedy is to keep offering more sweepstakes, on the back end as well as with future new offers. To managers faced with maintaining sales levels originally set with sweepstakes offers, sweepstakes seem like an addiction.

Lately sweepstakes have been losing their novelty, and have needed larger and more interesting prizes in order to remain effective. Some variations have artificially hyped response by concealing the "yes" alternative in deliberately confusing formats. This is another form of self-deception that will cost its user a great deal in back-end performance.

The purpose of a sweepstakes is to get readership and generate a yes-or-no decision on the product offer, usually a trial subscription. It is a strategic anomaly of sweepstakes that adding more product sell, which might be expected to increase response, usually depresses it. That's why you see so many sweepstakes offers that seem to feature the contest to the exclusion of the product.

REFERRAL OFFERS

Get-a-friend (GAF) or member-get-member (MGM) propositions are useful for almost any type of product or service. Their effectiveness depends heavily on the genuine satisfaction the customer derives from the product or service. There is no way to "bribe" a customer into recommending a proposition that has not been pleasing. However, if an offer is genuinely good, GAFs are a way of accelerating the word-of-mouth publicity that would ordinarily take place anyway. Whatever they are called, these offers come in the several different forms discussed next.

Name Requests.   Simple requests for names and addresses of people who would be interested in the proposition can be very fruitful in building a mailing list, particularly if you also request permission to mention the referrer's name in your initial letter. Such a request can be a simple printed notice on the back of a statement or an inexpensive buckslip. Most advertisers do not offer an incentive for such names in order to avoid lessening their quality.

Pass-Alongs.   In the pass-along technique, a simple brochure describing the basic proposition is included in a product shipment, along with a request to either mail it or give it to a friend. The order form might include space for the present customer number or name and address, so that a thank-you gift can be sent if the pass-along generates an order.

Sales Brochures.   In this case, customers are asked to function practically as sales agents, showing the product they have received to a friend or neighbor and soliciting orders in return for a commission, prize, or merchandise credits. Some companies have used this technique very effectively, creating an unofficial army of part-time salespeople.

This approach is most effective when the original customers have reason to feel smart about the purchase (maybe because it is well priced) and can feel they are doing friends a favor. The feeling of passing along a good thing is an essential ingredient—even more critical than the value of the incentive.

I don't know of anyone who has successfully sent out mailings devoted only to MGM offers. In most cases they are successful only to the extent that they enjoy a "free ride" as a catalog page or package insert.

Front-End Referrals.   Recent tests have shown surprisingly strong response to requests for names as part of the front-end prospect mailing. In continuity promotion for a packaged-goods company, we generated two referral names on one-half of the new customers—one referral per order. These names, when sent a mailing mentioning the referrer's name, produced a 20 percent response. This experience was repeated for another client.

I would not suggest this for video clubs and other propositions with generous up-front offers and high credit risk. Experience in these circumstances indicates a need to send them only to customers who have proved that they honor their agreements and pay their bills. The theory is that good credit customers produce good credit referrals, and vice versa.

The proposition is the heart of any direct marketing effort, and it requires concentrated creativity independent of the more glamorous tasks of designing interesting new headlines or colorful mail pieces. Unfortunately, many companies seem to restrict their outside creative sources to implementing existing offers. Why bring in agencies or consultants to write fresh headlines, when their talent may have a much greater impact creating fresh offers?

Offers can be any combination of the offers outlined here, or any others. There is no limit. It is precisely the new offer that will have been created while this book is on press or after it is published that will be the most exciting news in the industry. Its very freshness will help it to be effective.

The search for offers requires constant monitoring not only of your competitor's propositions, but also of what's going on in the whole field of direct marketing—in the United States and all over the world. It requires your best talent, your most courageous thinking, and your most daring testing.

MAILING
LISTS

Direct mail is the world's largest advertising medium, and mailing lists are the key to its success. It is an industry axiom that a poor mailing to a good list can be profitable, but that no mailing—no matter how well conceived—will work if sent to the wrong list.

Those who know how to use this medium—how to select from over a billion names on 50,000 different mailing lists—have in their hands the most powerful and profitable tool in the world of marketing.

THE WIDE WORLD OF
MAILING LISTS

There are four broad categories of lists: response lists, compiled lists, business lists, and house lists. (Database marketing, which relates to each, will be covered in Chapter 23.) We'll review them one at a time.

Response Lists

Other than a company's own house lists, response lists are the workhorse of consumer direct mail. Sometimes called *buyers' lists,* or *mail-order lists,* they include every classification related to a consumer's previous response to a direct marketing offer.

The names can be those of buyers, subscribers, inquirers, donors, members, or depositors. They can be new customers, active ones, or former ones. They can and do represent every conceivable area of human interest.

All have two things in common: one, they have identified themselves, by their own choice, as people with a specific interest, and two, they have demonstrated that they are willing, when properly motivated, to respond to a direct marketing offer.

While many companies and agencies maintain their own list specialists, the definitive way to select and order mailing lists is to use established list brokers. These businesses are staffed with professionals, assisted by custom computer systems, and enriched with a wealth of experience. Not only is their information up-to-date, but they are in a position to make recommendations based on their knowledge of which lists have been selected for other clients and which have been tried but not repeated. The advertiser gets irreplaceable advice and service, yet pays no more than if ordering directly. In *Mailing List Strategies* (McGraw-Hill, 1986), Rose Harper, chairperson emerita of The Kleid Company, makes very clear that there is much more than meets the eye to this critical phase of creating a successful mailing.

Many list compilers publish directories of lists they have available, but the definitive reference guide is published by SRDS (Standard Rate and Data Service, Wilmette, IL). Their *Direct Marketing List Sources* contains over 1700 pages of detailed information about every list available. While this directory is an indispensable tool in the planning stage of a mailing program, it is wise to work through an established list broker for the latest costs, quantities, and other data.

The directory is divided into three broad categories: *business, consumer,* and *farm*. Both compiled lists and response lists are included.

Consumer lists include broad interest categories with every type of demographic, geographic, and psychographic breakdown, including responders to every type of solicitation imaginable. Anyone who has ever joined, subscribed, inquired, donated or answered a questionnaire is on one or more of these lists.

Business lists include over 150 categories with not only available names of businesses but also buyers of products, subscribers to publications, professionals in various business specialties.

When using DMLS, it helps to be aware of the broad classifications it contains. Each one includes dozens of mailing lists offered by a wide variety of end users and compilers. Their full list of classifications is reprinted here as Fig. 5-1.

Consumer Lists

Though thousands of mailing lists are offered, it is astounding to note that each one generally is available in a multiplicity of segments, and can be further selected and segmented.

The following is an example of a consumer listing, the Columbia House Compact Disc Club. Note that this is just one of the lists offered by this major direct marketer, which also has lists of video buyers and

BUSINESS LISTS

3—Advertising & Marketing
5—Air Conditioning, Plumbing & Heating, Sheet Metal & Ventilating
7—Amusements
9—Appliances
11—Architecture
13—Arts
15—Automatic Data Processing— Computers
17—Automotive, Automobiles, Tires, Batteries, Accessories, Service Stations, Garages
19—Aviation & Aerospace
21—Baking
23—Banking & Financial
25—Barbers
27—Beauty & Hairdressing
29—Boating
31—Books & Book Trade
33—Bottling
35—Brewing, Distilling & Beverages
37—Brick, Tile, Building Materials
39—Brushes
41—Building
43—Building Management & Real Estate
45—Business Executives
46—Business Firms
47—Camps & Camping
49—Cemetery, Monuments & Funeral Suppliers
51—Ceramics
52—Certified Public Accountants and Accountants
53—Chain Stores
55—Chemical & Chemical Process Industries
57—China & Glassware
61—Clothing & Furnishing Goods (Men's)
63—Clothing & Furnishing Goods (Women's)
65—Coal Merchandising
67—Coin-Operated and Vending Machines
69—Confectionery
71—Control & Instrumentation Systems
73—Corsets, Brassieres & Undergarments
75—Cosmetics
77—Dairy Products
79—Dental
81—Department, General Merchandise and Specialty Stores
83—Discount Marketing
85—Display
87—Draperies & Curtains
89—Drugs, Pharmaceutics
91—Educational
93—Electrical
95—Electronic Engineering
97—Engineering & Construction
99—Engineers
101—Farm Implements & Supplies
107—Feed, Grain and Milling
109—Fertilizer and Agricultural Chemicals
113—Fire Protection
115—Fishing Commercial
117—Floor Coverings
119—Florists & Floriculture
121—Food — Processing and Distribution
123—Funeral Directors
125—Fur Trade, Fur Farming, Trapping, Etc.
127—Furniture & Upholstery
129—Gas
133—Giftware, Antiques, Art Goods, Decorative Accessories, Greeting Cards, Etc.
135—Glass
137—Golf
139—Government Administrative Services & Public Works — Municipal, Township, County, State, Federal
141—Grocery
143—Hardware & Housewares
145—Home Economics
147—Home Furnishings

149—Hospitals & Hospital Administration
151—Hotels, Motels, Clubs & Resorts
161—Industrial Distribution
163—Industrial Purchasing
165—Infants', Children's & Teen Age Goods
167—Institutions
169—Insurance
171—Interior Design/Space Planning
173—International Trade
175—Jewelry & Watchmaking
177—Journalism
179—Landscape, Garden Supplies, Seed and Nursery Trade
181—Laundry and Dry Cleaning
183—Leather, Boots & Shoes
185—Legal
187—Lighting & Lighting Fixtures
191—Luggage & Leather Goods
193—Lumber & Forest Industries
195—Maintenance
197—Maritime, Marine, Shipbuilding, Repair & Operating
201—Materials Handling & Distribution
203—Meats & Provisions
205—Medical & Surgical
207—Metal, Metalworking & Machinery
213—Mining (Coal, Metal & Non-metallic)
215—Motion, Talk, Sound, Commercial Pictures, Etc.
217—Motor Trucks & Accessories
219—Motorcycle & Bicycle
221—Moving & Storage
223—Music & Music Trades
225—Notions & Fancy Goods
229—Nursing & Health
233—Ocean Science and Engineering
235—Office Equipment & Stationery
236—Office Equipment Mail Order Buyers
237—Office Methods & Management
241—Optical & Optometric
245—Packaging (Mfrs.) Paperboard
247—Packaging (Users)
249—Paint, Painting & Decorating
251—Paper
253—Parks, Public
255—Petroleum & Oil
257—Pets & Pet Supplies
259—Photographic
261—Plant & Manufacturing Executives
263—Plastics & Composition Products
265—Plumbing
267—Police, Detective & Security
269—Pollution Control, Environment, Ecology, Energy
271—Poultry & Poultry Products
273—Power & Power Plants
275—Printing & Printing Processes
277—Produce (Fruits & Vegetables)
279—Product Design Engineering
281—Public Transportation
283—Radio & Television
285—Railroad
289—Religious
291—Rental and Leasing Equipment
293—Reproduction — Inplant & Commercial
295—Restaurants and Food Service
297—Roads, Streets, Etc.
299—Roofing
301—Rubber
303—Safety, Accident Prevention
305—Sales Management
309—Schools & School Administration
311—Science, Research and Development
315—Selling & Salesmanship
317—Sporting Goods
319—Stone Products, Etc.
323—Swimming Pools
327—Telephone & Communications
329—Textiles and Knit Goods
331—Tobacco
333—Toys, Hobbies and Novelties
335—Trailers & Accessories
337—Transportation, Traffic, Shipping & Shipping Room Supplies
339—Travel
341—Venetian Blinds/Storm Windows

343—Veterinary
345—Water Supply & Sewage Disposal
347—Welding
349—Wire & Wire Products
351—Woodworking

CONSUMER LISTS

502—Almanacs & Directories
506—Art & Antiques
508—Automotive
510—Aviation
512—Babies
514—Boating & Yachting
516—Brides
518—Business Leaders
520—Children's
520A—Collectibles
521—College & Alumni
522—Contributors (Philanthropic)
524—Crafts, Hobbies & Models
525—Credit Card Holders
528—Dogs & Pets
530—Dressmaking & Needlework
532—Education & Self Improvement
534—Entertainment
536—Epicurean & Specialty Foods
538—Ethnic
544—Fashions — Clothing
546—Fishing & Hunting
548—Fraternal, Professional Groups, Service Clubs & Associations
549—Game Buyers, Contest and Puzzle Participants
550—Gardening (Home)
551—Gay & Lesbian
552—General
553—General Merchandise Mail Order Buyers
554—Gifts — Gift Buyers
556—Health
558—Home & Family Service
559—Horses, Riding & Breeding
560—Insurance Buyers
561—Investors
562—Labor — Trade Unions
563—Land Investors
564—Literature & Book Buyers
566—Mechanics & Science
568—Men's
572—Military, Naval & Veterans
578—Music & Record Buyers
584—Occult, Astrological & Metaphysical
586—Occupant & Resident
588—Opportunity Seekers
590—Photography
592—Political & Social Topics
593—Premium & Catalog Buyers
594—Professional
596—Religious & Denominational
598—Senior Citizens
600—Society
602—Sports
604—Teenagers
606—Travel
608—Video & Home Computers
612—Women's

FARM LISTS

700—Dairy & Dairy Breeds
702—Diversified Farming & Farm Home
704—Farm Education & Vocations
710—Field Crops & Soil Management
714—Land Use & Conservation
716—Livestock & Breed
718—Poultry

Figure 5-1. Classifications numbers and titles. [REPRINTED FROM DIRECT MARKETING LIST SOURCE, BY PERMISSION OF SRDS.]

record and tape buyers. The latter list, like the one shown, has about two million names.

Note that the list shown is useful in several ways. People on this list not only are likely to be interested in music but also to be "new triers" or "early adopters" because they own the latest tool for music reproduction. Accordingly they are more likely to try other new products. In addition the music preferences tell you something about the personality of the member, to the extent that music preferences are consistent. For example, classical music members are more likely to respond to an art offer, and country music members are likely to honor their obligations more than members in some other categories.

COLUMBIA HOUSE COMPACT DISC CLUB
Member: D.M.A.
Columbia House
1221 Ave. of the Americas, New York, NY 10020.

1. PERSONNEL
   Mgr/Inserts & Lists—Jeannie Wheaton Shaw, 212-596-2427.
   Fax: 212-596-2475.
   Dir/List Mktg—Evelyn Deitz, 212-596-2421.
   Acct Serv Mgr—Sabrina Anthony 212-596-2428.

2. DESCRIPTION
   Members of negative option compact disc club.

3. LIST SOURCE
   Direct mail and space ads.

4. QUANTITY AND RENTAL RATES
   Rec'd Oct. 27, 1993

	Total Number	Price per/M
CD club members	4,918,324	90.00
Easy listening	239,056	90.00
Popular	1,040,754	"
Jazz	223,593	"
Country	637,321	"
Rock	2,817,321	"

   Selections: state, SCF, sex, hotline, 4.00/M extra; ZIP Code, 5.00/M extra; key coding, 1.00/M extra; exact age, 8.00/M extra; incidence of children, 12.00/M extra. Minimum order 10,000.

5. COMMISSION, CREDIT POLICY
   20% commission to recognized brokers.

6. METHOD OF ADDRESSING
   4/5-up Cheshire labels. Pressure-sensitive labels, 6.00/M extra. Magnetic tape, 15.00 fee

8. RESTRICTIONS
   Sample mailing piece required for approval.

11. MAINTENANCE
   Updated triyearly

This list, as most consumer lists, is available in whole or in part. The rental cost is $90 per thousand names, and the minimum order is 10,000 names. You can select segments such as sex, age, state or postal Sectional Center (SCF) for $4 per thousand extra for each characteristic selected. You can even select individual zip codes—either because you have learned which are most likely to be productive, or because you are promoting a regional service or product—for $5 extra per thousand names. Exact age can be added for $8 per thousand, or incidence of children at $12 per thousand. These are probably "enhanced" by outside sources. It is possible to rent such a list yourself and do the same type of enhancement, with these or other characteristics. The costs might be higher, however.

As you can see, this listing includes the owner of the list and the name of the list manager: a company that has been retained to manage and promote the list on a commission basis. The list manager is the source of specialized information and the clearinghouse for rental availabilities. However, the customer need not contact the owner or manager. Instead, you should work with a list broker: a company specializing in recommending and coordinating list rentals for customers. Such companies usually have all the data you need in their own files, plus experience on how the list has worked for their other clients. They will contact the manager when and if it is necessary to do so.

These listings include the rental price per thousand names for each of several subcategories, plus surcharges for additional segmentation. Usually there are also notations on minimum test quantities and on requirements for advance approval.

Many advertisers find it convenient to assemble their own file of list cards, usually 8 × 5½-inch horizontal cards with this same basic data. List brokers usually provide such cards as backup for their recommendations.

Compiled Consumer Lists

People not familiar with direct marketing often think of compiled lists first. These might be names and addresses drawn from the telephone book, automobile registrations, association memberships, directories, warranty card registrations, or any similar source. The defining characteristic—what dramatically differentiates compiled lists from response lists—is that there is no indication of previous willingness to subscribe, buy, donate, or otherwise respond by mail.

Such lists provide expanded coverage of market areas, including certain psychographic and demographic characteristics as well as large quantities of names in precise definitions not available in response lists.

There is a theory in direct marketing that people who have recently made one key decision in their lives, or a basic change of any type, are more likely than most to make other changes. Consequently, very successful lists have been established identifying new parents (BIRTHS—FAMILIES WITH CHILDREN: 275,000 new names per month), newlyweds (COUPLES—NEWLY MARRIED: 50,000 names per month), and recently moved families

(NEW MOVERS: 800,000 names per month). This type of psychographic characteristic can be successful for a wide range of products and services. Obviously, children's products do well with new-parents lists; but so do cameras, correspondence schools, and self-help publications. Evidently, the new addition to the family adds a new sense of ambition and responsibility as well.

Automobile-owner lists, in those states where compiling them is still permitted, are an extremely valuable means of selecting prospects by lifestyles. Number of cars, type of car, model (minivan or sports car, for instance), and age of car can all be significant.

Business Lists

The area of business-to-business selling is very different from consumer selling. As with consumer marketing, prospects on a list of people who have already responded to something related are much more likely to accept your offer than prospects on any compiled list. Unfortunately for most business propositions, there simply are not enough such lists.

Financial propositions can sell to the substantial subscriber lists of *Money, The Wall Street Journal,* and *Boardroom Reports* readers, as well as to smaller but very responsive lists of subscribers to newsletters and advisory services. There are lists of buyers of business equipment, inquirers about business services, subscribers to trade publications, and attendees at trade conferences. Lists of this type are handled in exactly the same way as consumer response lists.

THE DIRECT MARKETING DATABASE
Cowles Business Media
Box 4949, Stamford, CT 06907-0949. Phone 203-358-9900. ext. 326.
Fax: 203-348-5792.

1. PERSONNEL
   List Mgr—Jill Bacchiocchi

2. DESCRIPTION
   Subscribers to Direct and Catalog Age; names of direct marketers and catalog executives.

4. QUANTITY AND RENTAL RATES
   Rec'd Nov. 23, 1993.

	Total Number	Price per/M
Total list	48,000	95.00
Business classification:		
Agencies/sales/promo/dm agency/consult	12,720	+10.00
Manufacturers	5,626	"
Retailers/catalogers	13,443	"
Wholesalers	1,572	"
Publishers	4,089	"
List broker/compiler/manager	1,183	"

	Total Number	Price per/M
Data/processing/fulfillment/tel mktg..................	1,515	"
Associations/fundraisers	1,007	"
Health care/social svcs/pub adm govt	607	"
Education/seminars/trade shows.........................	730	"
Communication/transpr/utilities..........................	902	"
Banks/insurance/real estate/finc svcs.................	2,185	"
Job function:		
Corporate/general management	18,000	"
Sales/marketing management	16,000	"
Advertising/promotion management...................	5,800	"
Circulation/list media management....................	3,000	"
Fulfillment/mail order..	1,400	"
Production/creative management.......................	3,000	"

Selections: key code, 2.50/M extra. Minimum order 5,000

5. COMMISSION, CREDIT POLICY
Frequency and broker discounts to recognized brokers.

6. METHOD OF ADDRESSING
Cheshire labels. Pressure sensitive labels, 9.00/M extra. Magnetic tape, 25.00 flat.

7. DELIVERY SCHEDULE
Ten working days.

8. RESTRICTIONS
Sample mailing piece and agreement required on all orders. One-time use only. Not available to competitive offers.

Note that this list is segmentable by business classification or by job function, and the quantities duplicate. Note that this list rents for $85 per thousand names, with a minimum order of 5000 names. Segmentation costs an additional $10 per thousand, and they will charge $2.50 extra if you want separate key codes imprinted for each segment.

Whereas such response lists are the keystone of consumer direct mail efforts, usually they are a secondary consideration in business selling. Here the primary list sources are so-called compiled lists—those prepared by Dun & Bradstreet, Database America, and others. The basic selectors of such lists are size and type of business.

Also called *vertical lists,* they reach all types of executives in all sizes of businesses within a specific industry. The narrower the category, the more precise you can make the message, the offer, and the product offering.

Originally, such lists were compiled from the Yellow Pages issued by telephone companies, with all the obvious limitations and inaccuracies such a list would include. A look at Yellow Pages directories will show you that many categories are inconsistent, repetitive, and hard to define.

SIC codes were added to such lists as an attempt to narrow these business definitions even further. These four-digit classifications arc published under the supervision of the U.S. Government Office of Statistical Standards, and called Standard Industrial Classifications.

The first digit of the four-digit code defines a broad business category:

01-09   Agriculture

10-14   Mining

15-17   Construction

20-39   Manufacturing

40-49   Transportation, Communication, Utilities

50-51   Wholesaling

52-59   Retailing

60-67   Finance, Insurance, Real Estate

70-89   Services

Within these broad areas, hundreds of different business types have been identified and coded with very fine differentiation. When the first edition of this book was published, one list compiler made news by creating five-digit subclassifications. Today, six-digit business classifications are routinely available from several compilers.

In Dun & Bradstreet's classifications, SIC Code 73 includes four-digit codes for Advertising Agencies (7311), Outdoor Advertising Services (7312), Radio, Television, Publisher Representatives (7313), Advertising NEC (Not Elsewhere Categorized) (7319), Adjustment and Collection Services (7322), Direct Mail Advertising Services (7331), and other business services—25 in all.

If you want to reach advertising agencies, you can select from any of the subsegments of codes 7311, 7312, 7313, and 7319, listed below. But it pays to examine the list closely, because you might stop at 7322 and 7323, which deal with credit and collection, and miss what might be the best prospects of all in category 7331, Direct Mail Advertising Services. This segment of D&B's list catalog follows as an extract. Note that the four-digit codes are totals of the six-digit segments that follow them, and that "nec" means "not elsewhere categorized."

SIC	Description	Primary	Total
73	*Business Svcs*	509206	627060
7311	Advertising Agencies	28816	32973
731100	Advertising Agencies	26049	29595
731199	Ad Agencies, nec	2767	3378
7312	Outdoor Advertising Svcs	2067	2399
731200	Outdoor Advertising Svcs	1383	1616
731299	Outdoor Advert Svcs, nec	684	783
7313	Radio, Television, Publisher Representatives	2233	2560
731300	Radio, Television, Publisher Representatives	775	933
731301	Electronic Media Advertising Representatives	629	705
731302	Printed Media Advertising Representatives	829	922
7319	Advertising, nec	2157	2509

SIC	Description	Primary	Total
731900	Advertising, nec	68	81
731901	Transit Advertising Svcs	139	156
731902	Distribution of Advertising Materials	701	798
731903	Aerial Advertising Svcs	117	156
731999	Advertising, nec	1132	1318
7322	Adjustment & Collection Svcs	6203	6891
732200	Adjustment & Collection Svcs	1859	2014
732299	Adjustment & Collection Svcs, nec	4344	4877
7323	Credit Reporting Svcs	2482	3170
732300	Credit Reporting Svcs	1097	1177
732399	Credit Reporting Svcs, nec	1365	1993
7331	Direct Mail Advertising Svcs	6512	8234
733100	Direct Mail Advertising Svcs	3435	4138
733199	Direct Mail Advertising Svcs, nec	3077	4096

It is important to note that not all compilers use exactly the same coding, or have the same standards for data storage, pricing, and segmentation. A particular question is the depth of coverage. Some compilers offer mostly presidents and financial officers, while others can provide a wide range of executives in depth. As of this writing, I know of no business list that provides complete in-depth penetration of an industry or occupation, but some compilers are getting there. Recently the Cahner's publishing group announced the availability of over 5 million business names "at hundreds of managerial levels." While most of these would be addressed by title only, an impressive 1.8 million of them have both names and titles "at 270,000 locations of the 15,000 largest companies." This is discussed in more detail in my book *Database Marketing* (McGraw-Hill, 1993).

Primary and Secondary SIC Codes

As many firms are in more than one business, another variable exists in the designation of companies, usually by credit services, of the business they consider their primary one and others they may consider secondary.

An advertising agency, for instance, might be classified as 7311. If they consider themselves to be in the public relations and direct mail business as well, they may carry secondary codes of 7392 and 7331.

Usually a business firm is looking to sell to everyone in a particular business, whether it be their primary or secondary business. Ordering a particular SIC code would get both. However, there are times when you may want only those firms that consider a business their primary one, or vice versa.

There are many refinements in working with SIC-categorized lists. Not the least important are the varying techniques for seeking out individuals you need within each corporate address. These are discussed later in this chapter.

House Lists

No discussion of direct marketing would be complete without including the most obvious but most neglected list of all: a company's own house list.

Direct Marketing magazine points out, "Every transaction in the direct marketing field, whether it begins with direct mail, print, broadcast or telephone selling, always ends up on a list—of inquiries, of orders, of sales leads, of contest entrants, or whatever."

While building a list may not be the primary purpose of entrepreneurs running their first mail-order ad, it is the beginning of the process that makes the difference between a one-shot mail-order sale and a long-term direct marketing business. Even the smallest, newest company should begin, at the outset, to make the most of its mailing list. The same applies to *any* business asking for direct responses.

First of all, a house list is the most profitable source of future resales. Second, list-rental income or the ability to exchange names can be very important. For these and other reasons, a house list can be a company's single greatest asset. Ways of protecting and utilizing this asset are discussed later in this chapter.

HOW TO SELECT RESPONSE LISTS

The economic facts of life in using direct mail are that an advertiser will be spending 10 to 20 times what it would cost to reach a prospect compared to using print media, and even more when compared to broadcast.

This concentration of marketing effort on individual prospects is justified only by the concept of *selectivity:* the ability to pick out prospects much more efficiently than in mass media. Sometimes print and broadcast are called "the big guns" of marketing. Direct mail, then, is the medium of the sharpshooter. At the high cost of direct mail, you can't send your messages wildly into the night as in broadcast. You have to decide who your best target is and where to find that target, and you have to take careful aim.

In all direct marketing, the medium is the market. In direct mail this applies doubly. The mailing list is not a way to reach a market; it *is* the market.

The Principle of Affinity

In selecting mailing lists, the most important principle is the need for *affinity,* a logical connection between your offer and the prospects on a mailing list.

Some are easy. If you are selling gourmet cookware, you might try buyers of sophisticated cookbooks. If you are soliciting money for a charity, lists of donors to similar causes (health and religious organizations, the arts, etc.) are the first place to look.

If you are soliciting leads for an expensive, high-performance automobile such as a Porsche, you might mail to owners of yachts and airplanes (who are affluent and love fine possessions); engineers (who would appreciate performance); readers of *Road & Track* and *Playboy* (whose self-image might include a Porsche); and top executives in advertising, entertainment, and other dynamic fields (who could afford such a car and not be criticized for owning one).

Fortunately, direct mail methods permit the testing of a wide variety of lists with some possibility for success. A list does not have to be a "sure thing" to be worth testing. It only has to have some logical affinity.

It's helpful to remind yourself, when picking lists to test, that not every person on a list has to be right for the offer. If you're looking for a 5 percent response, you can probably get it if 25 or 30 percent of the list consists of reasonable prospects. You can afford to build in a "waste factor" of people who definitely are not prospects, as long as there are enough people who are. The total quantity of prospects in the list counts for less than the quality of the prospects. Better 20 very good prospects out of 100 than 40 so-so prospects.

Recency, Frequency, and Unit Sale

When looking at DMLS or a list information card provided by a broker, some of the most valuable data is the buying history of the list being offered. The three factors of buying history, other than the type of product purchased, are *recency, frequency,* and *unit sale*. These should be compatible with the offer being made, independently of any other selection factor.

Recency is the time element between the date the list is rented and the date the people on the list sent in their order, inquiry, donation, or subscription. The more recent, the better.

Frequency is the number of times a prospect has purchased from the company renting the name, or the length of the subscription, membership, or other association. The longer or more frequent, the better.

Unit sale is the amount of the highest transaction the customer has made through the mail. If your offer involves a substantial commitment, it is more likely to be accepted by people who have made other substantial purchases than by people who have not.

Sources

It's also important to look at the source of the mailing list. Lists of people who bought by direct mail will be most likely to work for other direct mail offers. People who responded to telephone or television solicitations may not necessarily be accustomed to responding to mail offers. If the list has been built with sweepstakes offers, they are likely not to be responsive except to other sweepstakes offers.

TESTING NEW LISTS

After consultation with a list broker and independent examination of list cards, DMLS, and directories issued by list brokers, every possible list worth testing should be sorted out into logical groups based on their common denominators. These categories can correspond to DMLS categories, or they can be arbitrary.

Lists should be grouped by the common denominator that makes them of interest to you, whether or not it is their basic identity. For instance, some groups could be purely affinity-based, grouping readers of magazines in related fields, buyers of similar products, buyers of books on the subject, buyers of items in a related price category, or any other segment.

Pilot Lists

Once the lists have been sorted into categories, the next step in preparing a test mailing is to select one or more "pilot lists" in each category: the lists most likely to succeed. These pilot lists should be representative not only of the potential of the whole list but also of the entire group.

Quantities should be considered, of course. If you are using 10,000-name test cells, don't test a list of only 20,000 names, for there will be no place to roll out to if the list does succeed. The pilot lists should be larger lists or, at least, representative lists from a group of smaller lists with a substantial total.

LIST SEGMENTATION

Once a mailing list has been chosen, there are still other alternatives available to the media manager. Mailing lists can be segmented in any way the list owner chooses and the computer can execute.

Some of the largest companies will make their lists available according to the type of merchandise purchased by their customers. Fingerhut offers these categories:

Paid buyers—current year:	4,420,000
Paid buyers—previous year:	1,678,000
Hispanic—current year:	400,000
Hispanic—previous year:	135,000
Hotlines:	1,406,000
New residents:	413,000
Customer referrals:	264,000
Sweepstakes, no respondents:	1,100,000
Other individuals in households:	6,516,000
Children (0–18), last 2 years:	1,916,803

In addition, each of these lists can be further segmented not only to the fairly common sex, age, state, or zip code, but also to their unique characteristics, such as these:

Credit card buyers

Cash or credit buyers

Single or multi-buyers

Nielsen market

Sweepstakes yes responses

Type of product

The last item means you can select buyers of apparel, home furnishings, appliances, automobile accessories, stereos, cameras, power and hand tools, and many more categories. With this list, as with many others, if the selection you want isn't listed, ask for it.

Doubleday Book Clubs, with millions of members, offer a wide variety of similar subsections, but also another exceptional aspect: the type of book that members of their various book clubs have selected. So if you're interested in any of the following, they can give you names of people who have purchased a book in exactly that subject area:

Art

History and biography

Gardening

Cooking and crafts

Nature, exploration, outdoor sports

Personal finance, current affairs

Romance

Self-help

Military

Mystery

Plays (Fireside Theater)

Science fiction

Some owners sort their lists by size of purchase and whether or not the buyer has made more than one purchase. Almost all of them have a time frame built in, so you can start with the most recent names and work back to the older ones if results justify.

Lists can be selected by sex, by state, and by zip codes chosen for geographic or demographic criteria. Large mailers can identify clusters of zip codes where response rates and quality are exceptionally rewarding, and concentrate on those when sending out their mailings. Conversely, clubs or other credit propositions can screen out zip codes with historical bad-debt problems. Magazine publishers sometimes preselect zip codes in mail subscription solicitations in order to influence the demographic mix of their magazine's circulation.

Hot-line names are eagerly sought after. These are people who have recently bought, subscribed to, ordered, or inquired about the product of the company renting the list—usually within the last 90 days. The hottest of the hot-line names are those that are less than 30 days old. Such lists have been proved to do very well, and some advertisers contract for such names on a year-round basis.

One caution about hot-line names. Some list owners have included customers who eventually failed to pay for or returned their purchase, and thus are much poorer quality than names that stayed on the list long enough to become regular customers. One magazine rented out hot-line names that included complimentary-copy customers who had not yet paid their bills and converted to regular subscribers. Such names should not be on hot-line lists, and it is worth asking about them specifically if you do use this category.

Virtually every selection factor costs a bit more—maybe 10 to 15 percent—than the basic list, and many list owners charge a premium for sex or geographic selection. Considering that these charges are an even smaller percentage of the total mailing cost, and that selectivity is the essential ingredient of making the campaign work, such extra charges are a small price to pay.

There are different approaches to selecting segments for list testing. One school says that hot-line names and particularly favorable geographic areas or buyer classifications should be avoided, in order to make the test as "fair" as possible. This is true if research is the objective. My approach is to put the best foot forward and give the list every chance of working by selecting the most favorable segments. If those are not successful, the list can be dropped anyway. If they are, testing can proceed with caution through balancing the better names with older names and less affinitive segments.

The exception would be a campaign where, for competitive or other reasons, a major rollout must be conducted in the next season, with no time for extension testing. In that case I would go with a list segment representative of the quantity that would be needed in the rollout.

The factor here is the total anticipated rollout quantity. If it's moderate, then the list program can be built gradually, beginning with the best segments, which should supply enough names without reaching into the bulk of the list. If the plan requires an ambitious rollout, then by all means test only large lists in typical segments.

THE MAILING PLAN

The previous remarks dealt with selecting lists for a test schedule. Actually, this process continues in one form or another throughout the life of a product.

An initial test probably would test 50,000 or so names for various pieces of copy. These names might be taken from one or two lists that appear to be very logical choices. Another 50,000 names might be divided among 5 or 10 pilot tests representing substantial list categories.

An ongoing campaign would have three major groupings. The most important would be the rollout of lists that have been successful in previous testing. Then there would be list extensions: retests in larger quantities of lists that have proven successful in previous testing but where it is not yet considered safe to roll out the full quantity. Then there is additional list testing, which is divided into two areas. One area of list testing for an ongoing campaign would be the exploration of additional lists in categories where the pilot list was successful. The other is in searching for new list categories.

Let's say that 10 lists (which we'll call A to J) were tested in an initial campaign, and 5 were successful. Those 5 would be rolled out or retested as extensions, depending on the quantities involved. Then additional lists in the successful categories would be tested, plus some new categories. The original unsuccessful test lists would be dropped, as would any other lists in the same categories.

Such a hypothetical schedule might look like this:

List A	Rollout	125,000; full list, less previous tests
List C	Rollout	87,000; full list, less previous tests
List E	Extension	50,000 of possible 1,250,000
List G	Extension	50,000 of possible 650,000
List I	Extension	50,000 of possible 325,000
List K	List test	10,000; same category as A
List L	List test	10,000; same category as A
List M	List test	10,000; same category as A
List N	List test	10,000; same category as C
List O	List test	10,000; same category as E
List P	List test	10,000; same category as G
List Q	Category test	10,000; new category pilot list
List S	Category test	10,000; new category pilot list

In this schedule, the original 100,000 mailing is now built up to 442,000, of which over 80 percent is rollout or extension. The percentage of testing is kept to less than 20 percent, so that even if all the tests did only half as well as the rollouts and extensions, total results would be depressed only 10 percent. Even this is unlikely, as most of those tests are in categories that have already been proved successful.

This type of evolution, from highly subjective initial test to logical combination of tests, extensions, and rollouts, quickly converts the direct marketing manager from a chance-taking gambler into a statistician and scientist.

USING COMPILED LISTS

The two major considerations in selecting direct-response lists are mail responsiveness and affinity. Neither of these is presumed when working with most mass-compiled lists. Why, then, is this such a large industry, and how do these lists fit into the world of direct marketing?

Compiled lists offer two attributes ordinarily not available in the direct-response list field: *saturation,* and *precision segmentation.* These attributes are interdependent. It is only the large quantity of compiled lists that makes precision segmentation economical, and it is only segmentation that makes it profitable for advertisers to use compiled lists.

There are two major types of segmentation: *area selectivity,* and *individual household selectivity.* The former is based primarily on information about individual postal areas, sometimes organized into clusters with like information. The theory here is that people in similar neighborhoods tend to have similar tastes and attitudes, independently of their income.

The latter is based on individual or household information, a source that has become increasingly more sophisticated since the previous edition of this book was published. Where we once had only demographic data or lifestyle changes such as "new parents," we now have all the results of the database marketing phenomena—individual interests, hobbies, health problems, product usage and brand preferences, etc.—and all in significant quantities.

For more information about using or building marketing databases, I refer the reader to my book devoted to this subspecialty of direct marketing, *Database Marketing* (McGraw-Hill, 1993).

Metromail

Local advertisers—retailers, banks, political candidates, charities—often need the geographic concentration of compiled lists. A compiled list such as Metromail's contains much smaller and sharper delineations than the usual zip-code selection.

The United States Census Bureau has divided 323 Metropolitan Areas, and other highly populated counties, into neighborhood units called *census tracts.* Each census tract contains on the average about 4000 persons. *Block numbering areas* cover all counties that do not have census tracts, and the Census Bureau publishes the same types of data for block numbering areas as it does for census tracts. Census tracts and block numbering areas are subdivided by clusters of census blocks into over 250,000 subunits called *block groups,* which average about 400 housing units each.

Metromail calls these units *audience cells* and *subcells.* For each audience cell and, where available, subcell, an incredible array of demographic information is available for analysis or selection. As people of like interests tend to live in like neighborhoods, this demographic data delivers an enormous degree of selectivity. Audience cells and subcells are available throughout the United States; however, rural post offices usually are too small to be effectively subdivided into audience cells and subcells. Nevertheless, the same type of demographic information is available by zip code.

Virtually any census tract data can be used to select which cells, subcells, and untracted zip codes you wish to be mailed, in combination with geographic preference and individual characteristics. Metromail has created over 400 area demographics, using counts from the 1990 Census. The following is a list of some commonly used area variables that can be easily selected from Metromail's Audience Cell File.

Audience Cell and Subcell Demographics
1. Median income
2. Median value of owner-occupied units
3. Percent owner-occupied units with value of $500,000 or more
4. Percent owner-occupied units with value of $200,000 or more
5. Percent owner-occupied units with value of $100,000 or more
6. Home value index
7. Home value percentile
8. Median years of school completed (for population 25 years old and over)
9. Percent of population age 25 years and older with a bachelor's degree or higher
10. Persons per household
11. Percent of households with 3 or more persons
12. Percent of households with 1 or more persons under 18 years of age
13. Index of social position for small areas (ISPSA)
14. ISPSA docile
15. Median age of householder
16. Percent of households with householder age 34 years and under
17. Percent of households with householder age 35–44 years
18. Percent households with householder age 45–54 years
19. Percent of households with householder age 55–64 years
20. Percent of households with householder age 65 years and over
21. Percent of households with householder age 55 years and over
22. Percent of households that are families
23. Percent of households with householder of hispanic origin
24. Percent of households with householder of black race
25. Percent of households with householder of white race
26. Percent owner-occupied households

27. Percent of Metromail households that are 1-unit structures

28. Percent of Metromail households that are 3-or-more-unit structures

29. Percent of Metromail households that are 10-or-more-unit structures

The 1990 Census has added extensively to the range of data that will be available by cell and subcell. Metromail and other suppliers will undoubtedly be adding to the sophistication and the diversity of their list segmentation.

In addition to area demographics, households can be selected by individual characteristics, or by dwelling unit characteristics, or any combination of the three types of data. Individual characteristics include data such as age and mail responsiveness. Dwelling unit characteristics include homeowners and other information obtained from realty sources. Also, characteristics such as length of residence and size of dwelling unit can be inferred from telephone directory listings over a period of years. Metromail's data goes back to 1954.

Each of these individual characteristics can be of value in itself, or can be looked upon as a significant aid in increasing the probability of locating age, income, and family-size target groups:

- *Length of residence.* How long this family has lived (or at least had a telephone listing) at the present address. Long residence generally indicates an older head of household. A ten-year resident is likely to be 20 years older than a new resident.

- *Sex of household head.* Deduced from the first name of the person in whose name the phone is listed.

- *Type of dwelling unit.* Either single or multiple.

- *Surname ethnicity.* An imperfect but sometimes valuable selector, used often in fund-raising and political campaigns. Classifies last names according to their likelihood of being Catholic, Italian, Jewish, Hispanic, or of a particular national origin.

- *Research-based preselections.* Based on correlations of research with individual and area characteristics, aimed at reaching a high proportion of older people (over 55 or over 65), affluent families (likely to have incomes over $25,000), and "influentials," based on educational and occupational characteristics and correlations.

Specialized Consumer Lists

These very important and effective lists are based on psychographic characteristics rather than geographic or demographic factors, and there are many of them. While geographic and census tract data can be used as additional refinements, the appeal of the specialized lists is that they give some indication of the lifestyle of the prospective customer, and offer points of departure for specialized product, offer, or copy appeals. These are some of the most used compiled lists:

- *New parents.* Names of people who have had a child or who are expecting a child, selectable by number of months since birth and by number of other children (based on previous inclusion in the list).
- *Newlyweds.* Couples who have just been married or who have indicated that they are about to be.
- *New residents.* Changes of address, indicating a strong possibility that the residents have bought a house or are fixing up a rented home or apartment. These are good prospects for decorating offers.
- *Families with children.* Children's Census, prepared by Demographic Systems, Inc., offers a list of more than 7 million families with 10 million children. The selection factors are the age of the mother, the age and number of the children, and correlations with any census or individual telephone directory data.
- *Automobile owners.* An interesting lifestyle indicator, based on common denominators of station wagon buyers, sports car buyers, new-car versus used-car buyers, luxury car versus economy car owners, etc. Offered by Polk for most of the United States.

R. L. Polk

Area Selectivity. Polk maintains a number of files with geographic characteristics compiled by the U.S. Census Bureau. These characteristics are available through Polk's Small Area Characteristics, or SMACS file. Information is maintained for block groups, census tracts, and zip codes. Categories of information include

- Population statistics
- Race/origin
- Age
- Household size
- Marital status
- Housing/structure
- Household composition
- Home value
- Income
- Mobility
- Occupation
- Education

- Military
- Ancestry
- Birthplace
- Language
- Vehicles

Polk also maintains another file containing postal carrier route characteristics. Called Carrier Route Marketing Information, or CRMI, this file contains the following types of information:

- Census variables from the 1990 U.S. Census
- Polk variables from exclusive commercial files compiled by R. L. Polk & Co.
- Automotive variables from official state registration records, compiled exclusively by R. L. Polk & Co.
- Other variables from USPS sources and various marketing resources

Categories of data include

- General population
- Family composition
- Education and income
- Ethnicity
- Housing
- Automotive spending
- Automotive size/style

Individual Household Selectivity. Polk's TotaList contains over 80 million U.S. households. It is built from over 20 sources and contains various selectivity options. Sources contributing to TotaList are

1. Current automobile registrations
2. Current truck registrations
3. Current recreational vehicles
4. Current motorcycle owners
5. Current monthly new car buyers*
6. Current monthly new truck buyers*
7. Household census list*
8. Telephone list
9. Last available automobile registrations
10. Last available truck registrations
11. Last available recreational vehicles

12. Last available motorcycle owners
13. New car buyers (back to 1964)*
14. New truck buyers (back to 1968)*
15. New birth, high school, college information
16. Mail response coding
17. Adult birthdate information
18. Questionnaire data
19. Credit card holders
20. Homeowner Information
21. Product registration data
22. Mail-order buyer data
23. U.S. Census Bureau statistics
24. U.S. Postal Service information
25. Children's age data
26. County assessor information

*Exclusive to R. L. Polk & Co.

BUSINESS LISTS

The beginning of this chapter indicated that, while there are some business response and subscriber lists, the great bulk of business mailing activity involves compiled lists, usually sorted by SIC codes. The need for this selectivity is obvious for products that are usable by only one or two industries. However, if you are selling a general business product, such as imprinted business forms, small computers, typewriters, copiers, office furniture, or consulting services, then you have a different problem.

Often an advertiser will send out a sampling "across the board" to a typical cross-section of SIC codes, company characteristics, and geographic areas, and then set up a response analysis (Dun's offers this service to their list customers) analyzing the number of responses and the response rate percentage by every relevant factor. In this way, subsequent mailings can exclude SIC codes or other determinants that were not responsive. There can be a 400 to 500 percent difference, for example, depending on the company size and the SIC code.

Several segmentation factors can have a bearing on your list, and all of them are available:

- *Age of business.* When it was founded
- *Size of indicators.* Sales volume or number of employees
- *Type of business.* The primary or secondary SIC codes

- *Ownership.* Private or public
- *Headquarters or branch office.* Or the fact that this might be a single-location business
- *Credit.* The D&B credit rating, and the general trend of the particular business

One particular advantage, especially where personalized letters are appropriate, is the large number of individual officer names and titles available through this supplier. They have already offered the names of presidents and chief financial officers, and have now added over 6 million additional names of various titles including vice president, secretary, manufacturing director, and purchasing agent, bringing the total to over 8½ million.

Unfortunately, no one supplier can give you the name of every Vice President, Manufacturing, in every type of company, and it will probably be necessary to deal with several list suppliers. Publishers of trade publications in specific fields often have very complete lists of the industries reached by their publications. Chilton, for instance, produces a very complete list of executives in the automotive field—one that is often used by companies offering credit or banking services.

HOUSE LISTS

The single most valuable list used by the majority of advertisers is their own house list. Sadly, it often is the most neglected. For most direct marketing companies, it is their single most precious asset—the one whose loss could put them out of business. Usually it is the list most responsive to a company's additional offers.

There are several important ways in which this investment can be protected and maximized. The first is to set the list up right in the first place. Too many companies, when first starting out, simply copy a customer's name and address off a coupon the way it comes in and preserve this name on labels, address systems, or at a computer service.

Even the best computer service can be a mistake if they do not have specific experience in direct marketing list management. Companies such as Polk, Metromail, MBS, and other specialists in list management should be considered. If you are publishing a periodical, by all means talk to Neodata in Boulder, Colorado, and similar magazine fulfillment specialists. Reinventing the wheel is not a good idea; there is just too much that can go wrong.

Your lists should be carefully edited to conform exactly with the *Direct Marketing Manual* (DMA, Manual Release No. 200.2), which details exactly how to handle first names, titles, addresses, cities, and other information according to accepted industry standards.

Abbreviations, codes, and tape formats should be worked out so that they are compatible with other tapes used in this field, in order to enable you to use matching, updating, and suppressing techniques as discussed later in this chapter. Also, if you're going to rent the list, you don't want a reputation for having a "dirty" list (one that is not updated or not in a consistent format). Such a reputation would lower your rental income substantially.

Sales History

Another important factor to consider, right from the beginning, is the sales history or other activity that will help you to fine-tune your own marketing efforts.

Your list should be identified with key information such as

- *Recency.* When did the customer make the first purchase—and the latest one?
- *Frequency.* How often has this customer ordered from you during the relationship, or in the latest year?
- *Unit sale.* What is the average order size? The last order size? The highest order ever?
- *Source.* Where did this customer originate—from what ad, media, or copy appeal?
- *Credit.* If you are selling on credit, what is this customer's history? What is the largest credit limit you will permit?
- *Product line preference.* What does this customer buy from you?

This last item enables you to send offers only to those customers who are known buyers of a given type of product, making many mailings profitable that would not otherwise be. It is common to send out mailings to segmented lists such as this, appealing to known interests, before offering the same product to your own full list or to outside lists. If these buyers won't buy it, the chances are no one will.

Some companies use a Recency-Frequency-Unit Sale formula to evaluate the probability of individual names responding. Such formulas weight these three factors according to their own priorities, usually with frequency as the highest value. A company may thus decide that some names are worth mailing to ten times a year, while others merit a mailing only once or twice.

Protecting Your List

Anyone in the field will tell you at least one horror story about attempted list fraud. The value is just too great for some people to avoid temptation. I personally received a phone call, at one company, from the president of a competitor who had been offered my list for sale. It took a detective less than two days to track down the dishonest employee, with the help of the competitor, and turn him over to the police—but don't let it come to this.

The first protections are obvious ones. The tape processing must be protected from theft as well as from fire or vandalism. Tapes should be stored in a locked room with tightly enforced access restrictions and a sign-in–sign-out system. Alarms should be built into the room, as well as fire extinguishers. Most important, a "grandfather system" should be instituted, in which original tapes and the latest update tape are sent to a remote location for storage. Once a working tape has been updated, it replaces the previous tape in storage. The idea is that there should always be, in another location, the basic data for reconstructing the current working tape.

"Seeding" names is another important step. Place some names and addresses on the list—your own, and those of several key employees and friends—with deliberate misspellings as codes. Whenever the list is used, you'll be able to spot the source of the list by the coded name. If an unauthorized mailing comes in with a misspelling, then you'll know something is wrong.

Postal Sorting

You'll probably want to maintain the list in zip-code sequence, with postal carrier coding as it becomes available. Mail rates offer valuable incentives for presorting mail in zip sequence and by carrier route.

List Cleaning

Every "nixie" should be removed from the file immediately. Nixies are mailings returned by the Postal Service with notations such as "No longer at this address." When new addresses are known, the listing can be updated and put back in the active file.

Address changes also should be entered promptly. This is vital, as bulk mail is never forwarded, and even first-class mail seems to have a mixed record for forwarding reliability.

There also should be a "match code" to enable you to spot new inquiries or orders from people who are already on the list, possibly under the name of another family member. The new order should supersede the previous file, but must be matched in order to avoid the expense of sending two mailings to the same household. The customer name should supersede the similar prospect name.

List Rental

The list-rental business can be very profitable. There is no reason to worry about "protecting" your customers from other mail offers. They will be getting them anyway. The only question is, who will be getting the list-rental income? You won't have to worry about directly competitive offers, because you can refuse to rent to any offer you feel is competitive with you or offensive to your customers.

The first step is to set up your segmentation and pricing structure so as to make it appealing to other list-rental customers. The second step is to get a list management company to handle the promotion and administration of your list-rental business. A good list manager will have a good administrative operation and, more important, a strong sales organization to promote your list to likely users.

Some companies find the list-rental business to be so important that it contributes more profit than the sale of products. This can have a profound effect on marketing decisions.

Using Your List

In addition to using your list for your own products or renting it out to others, you may find that your list will be so important that you will be looking for new ways to "mine" it.

One way is to use syndicated mailings—offers of products prepared and packaged by others for mailing to your list. It could be an insurance plan, a language course, or any other product. The letter goes out under your name to your customers, but all the expense and handling are the responsibility of the syndicator. All you do is handle the list and the orders. The syndicator will pay for the mailing, handle the product, and ship it out to your customers. You get your commission on each sale, and it can amount to a substantial sum if the product is the right one for your list.

The ultimate use of your list is to develop products that fit the reputation your company has built and the interests of the people on your list. As you are working toward a known customer base, it is relatively simple to work with researchers to arrange focus panels, questionnaires, or other forms of pretesting to help you develop an offer that will sell. The chances are that, if the offer appeals to your current list, it will also appeal to the readers or viewers of the media that you used to build your list.

ORDERING AND PROCESSING MAILING LISTS

Selecting the right mailing lists may be a fine art, but ordering and processing them correctly is an exact science. As in every direct marketing activity, excellence requires the best of both worlds.

Ordinarily, lists are rented through a list broker. A good list broker should be a willing and enthusiastic part of your marketing team. Select the best, regardless of location.

Then you will need a list processor. This is sometimes subcontracted by your direct mail letter shop or advertising agency. Many suppliers are tempted to increase their own profit margins by trying to do this type of work themselves, but often they don't have the computer capabilities or the depth of experience of the companies that specialize in list processing: companies such as Magi, Wiland, Printronics, Marketing Electronics, and Creative Automation.

Placing the List Order

List orders should be worked out with the list broker. There are many details to be worked out, and often they vary from list to list. Treat your list broker like a partner, not just a supplier.

List Description. For each list, you have to define exactly what you want. Include the name of the list and an exact specification of the segment you are ordering, such as "1995 Buyers" or "1994 Expires" or "Latest Hot Line."

Quantity. Usually, you want to test a fixed quantity or to utilize a previously ordered quantity of direct mail packages. Often, though, you may want all available names in a geographic area, or hot-line names as available, or as many names as are available within recency parameters. In such a case, specify that instruction and be sure the list owner is told to provide an actual list count.

If you must estimate the amount of a mailing designated for a geographic area before the list is run, one handy way is to use state or SMSA counts published by the Census Bureau. Your list broker can supply this information.

This data includes the percentages of population, manufacturing, and retail sales for each state. Use the population figure for consumer lists, the manufacturing figure for business lists, and the retail sales figure for retail or professional lists. Just take the appropriate percentage and apply it to the total national list size.

Manufacturing and retail sales figures may not be available by individual SMSA market. To get these, take the state figure you need and then apply the "percentage-of-state" population figure to the manufacturing or retail figure. It's far from perfect but usually it's close, with an error margin of 5 or 10 percent.

Selectivity. If you want a typical cross-section for test purposes, the usual practice is to ask for an "Nth-name sample, to be taken from all reels." This means you want the total list size divided by your test quantity: a 300,000-name list used for a 10,000-name test would require that $N = 30$, or every thirtieth name.

I would avoid testing with what is called a *fifth-digit zip select*. Arbitrarily taking a last number of a zip code and running those names does not give you 10 percent of the entire list. I have had this checked, and there is a dramatic difference in response by fifth-digit zip number.

The reason is that lower numbers, such as 0, 1, and 2, often are the downtown areas of major cities, while the higher numbers are more likely to be suburbs away from the city center. Also, many areas do not have the higher zips at all, and so a smaller postal area may have only the first few last digits.

On a test extension or rollout, you may want to specify certain geographic areas that you believe to be the most responsive to your offer, or you may designate a list of zip codes to be selected from or suppressed, as the case may be. You can also select by city size, seeking either urban or nonurban buyers.

You can designate sex by asking for "males only" or "females only." If your letter refers to the recipient by gender, you may want to avoid offending the opposite sex by adding this phrase: "Omit unidentified gender names." This will drop out those with only initials for first names and also those names that could be male or female.

Compiled and business lists can, of course, be selected by all the criteria indicated in the previous parts of this chapter, and such specifications should be clearly stated. Where names are not available individually, you may instruct the supplier to add a specific title, such as "purchasing agent" or "stationery buyer."

Key Coding. Your key numbers, by list, should be assigned at the very beginning, so that lists will be supplied to match your key numbers. You may request that the key number be printed on the label in a location you specify.

Dates. You must indicate the planned drop date and advise the list house if there are any substantial delays. Usually you will receive protection against competing use of a particular list one week before and one week after your scheduled mailing date. During this time another company should not be able to mail this list. This should be indicated on the order. If a longer protection period is necessary, it will have to be negotiated in advance.

Your order should indicate both the scheduled drop date and the date you want the lists in order to begin processing.

Telephone Numbers. Some compiled lists can be supplied with telephone numbers, if so requested. This is a great convenience if you are using a list for telephone instead of, or in addition to, direct mail.

Multiple Use. If you are planning a second or third use of the same list, order them all at the same time. Most list owners will agree to a reduced rental rate (usually 50 percent) for repeat uses of the same tape as part of a series mailing.

If you are preparing a master prospect list, some list compilers will lease their list, at a higher price, for unlimited use during the contract period.

For instance, if your lists are going to be used for generating sales leads, you may want to order one set on labels for your mailing; another on 3 × 5–inch cards with telephone numbers for salespeople to use in making follow-up calls; and a third set in register form, by sales territory, for local managers to use in following up on sales efforts.

Seed Names. A list of seed names—names and addresses to be inter-mixed for checking mail delivery—should be included from the beginning and attached to each list order. These will be valuable in checking on the accuracy of the mailing house and the delivery time of the post office.

Deliverability Guarantee. Your printed list order form should include a standard line requesting a guarantee of deliverability by the list owner. A figure such as 95 percent should be acceptable, and the list owner should be willing to pay the minimum third-class or nonprofit postage rate on all returned mail over the 5 percent figure.

Such a guarantee should provide an incentive for the list owner to keep the list cleaned regularly, and to drop the names on returned mail from the list for future mailings.

Mailing Identification. The mailing order should clearly identify the product being offered and should be accompanied by a sample mailing piece. All orders are subject to the list owner's acceptance. Scrupulous honesty in regard to identifying mailings and barring reuse is expected not only by the list owner but by the entire direct marketing establishment.

LIST FORMATS

Cheshire Labels. The original addressing vehicle was the Cheshire label, a continuous form containing four labels to a line, side by side (or "east to west"). These labels are 1 inch by slightly less than $3\frac{1}{2}$ inches wide. Ungummed and unperforated, they can be affixed only by machine.

Peel-off Labels. At slightly higher cost, list owners can supply adhesive labels on a waxed-paper backing, each label being slightly smaller than a Cheshire label. These can be machine-affixed in the same manner, in situations where you want the customer to peel off the label and place it on an order form. They also can be hand-affixed very easily when labels are supplied to retailers or salespeople for local mailings.

Sheet Listings. A printout of data in listing form, sheet listings usually consist of 50 lines to a page. It is usable only for reference or checking, or for telephone selling operations.

Card Files. Each individual record can be printed on a 3 × 5–inch card, or on a form having one or more parts, for distribution to salespeople or for similar uses. Such formats often include additional information. Dun's sales prospecting cards include sales volume, number of employees, lines of business, telephone numbers, and the chief executive's name in a format intended for convenient use by field sales personnel.

Magnetic Tape. Larger mailers often prefer to order lists on magnetic tape, in a format specified by their list processor. These tapes can then be sent to a list processor for any of the services outlined in the following paragraphs, or they can be sent to mailing houses for the preparation of personalized computer letters using high-speed chain printers, laser printers, or Mead Digit ink-jet printing.

Delivery Instructions. The list broker should be told exactly where the lists are to be shipped and how they are to be marked. Usually you will have the lists or tapes not shipped to your office but sent directly to the mailing house or computer service that is to process them. The tapes should be clearly marked with key numbers, purchase order numbers, drop dates, and your company name, so that the lists will be properly routed when they arrive at the destination.

Other items. Your list broker also will want to clarify such questions as how the lists are shipped, what the cost is with tax and all surcharges, and what payment terms are mutually acceptable. You may also be required to sign an agreement not to reuse the names except as specifically agreed upon.

LIST PROCESSING

Most large mailers eventually will need the services of a list processor. These firms offer even the smallest advertisers the type of sophisticated computer equipment and advanced programming that otherwise only a handful of direct marketers would be able to afford.

The advantages of these processes are directly related to volume. Duplication may not be an important factor if you are mailing only 100,000 names nationally. But it can add up to a lot if you are sending out 10 or 20 million names a year.

Duplicate Elimination

Duplicate elimination, or de-duplicating, is the most common list-processing service. Sometimes called *merge-purge,* it basically consists of matching names and addresses from several lists against each other, searching for similarities (including family members at the same address), and consolidating duplications.

Magi's Mailsave II system uses different logic patterns for urban, suburban, and rural addresses to maximize overall de-duplication accuracy to better than 99 percent. Their system uses phonetic logic, which spots similar names although spellings are slightly different; transposition logic (which detects transposed characters); data entry error logic (for address keying errors); and zip-code logic (to correct incorrect zip codes). This system, as well as others like it, works with magnetic tape input in any format supplied by list owners and sent directly to their facility.

The duplicate names are combined and merged into a separate multi-buyer tape that can be mailed and tracked separately. Such names, because they appear on more than one logical list, usually have a higher response rate than the bulk of the lists that consist of de-duplicated names.

A duplication allocation system produces a report showing the duplication by list. This can be done on a priority basis, matching new names against a house list or other master list, or by the system Magi calls *stratification allocation,* which distributes duplication evenly.

Other by-products of the system are suppressions, if desired, of noncontinental United States, APO/FPO, military bases, prisons, and other unique zip-code categories. Postal bag tags are computer-generated and printed to meet Postal Service requirements for various zip sorts. A report of "net counts by key" also is prepared, based on the final de-duplicating mailing.

Merge-Purge Rate Adjustment

When ordering names from many lists to be "merged" into one file and "purged" of duplicates, how do you pay the list owner? And what about when you are eliminating names that are already your customers?

In such cases you must ask your list broker to secure an "85 percent agreement" beforehand. This means that you agree to pay the list owner for no fewer than 85 percent of the names on the list mailed. Some also charge $3 per thousand deleted names, to cover computer costs. If the actual percentage after the merge-purge has been completed is higher, then you will have to pay the higher rate.

Such agreements customarily are granted only on orders of 50,000 or more names of a large list, or the full run of smaller lists. Without such an advance agreement, you will be expected to pay the full rate regardless of the number of unused names.

The computer house must submit proof of the number of names purged from the list. If 93 percent of the list is mailable, the renter has to pay for 93 percent of the names. But if only 65 percent of the names are mailable, the renter is still obliged to pay 85 percent, as per the agreement. This system protects the list owner and broker and also provides some discount for the list user.

Large-scale mailers sometimes can negotiate a 75 percent agreement. On the other hand, some list owners permit no discount at all. The Metropolitan Opera House, for example, requires 100 percent payment for its subscriber list, regardless of the net number of names used.

List Cleaning.   Any mailer or list owner must keep its list "clean" to eliminate wasted duplication of "nixies" in its own use of it, and to give renters fair value. While there are other, privately maintained techniques, the most popular one today is the postal system's NCOA (National Change of

Address) Service. Large computer-processing firms are licensed by the post office to match lists against post office files of active recipient addresses and move notices. While even this process isn't perfect, it is almost always worth the small cost. According to MBS Multimode, this list-cleaning process can eliminate 10 to 20 percent of otherwise wasted mail that would be better sent to "live" prospects.

Two valuable types of information can be added to a mailing list as a by-product of the matching process. One add-on is carrier route codes, which can result in faster mail handling in the short term and probably postage savings later on. Another is demographic data by census tract or individual family characteristics, to be used in list-suppression or data-overlay processes.

The savings resulting from a "clean" list will pay for the address-correction process from the first large mailing, and it is certainly cheaper than current Postal Service charges for individual address correction.

The significance of this type of service lies in the fact that one out of five Americans moves each year, so that if your list is not updated, 20 percent of it becomes obsolete each year. Statistically, a one-year list is 80 percent accurate, a two-year list 64 percent, a three-year list 51 percent, and so on.

List Suppression

Another process that has become standard for many large mailers is the suppression of selected names, performed by computer matching techniques. The names that might be suppressed from a mailing include

- The DMA "Name Removal List"—people who have asked that they not be sent mail of any kind.

- Customer lists, to avoid sending introductory offers to persons who are already on your house list.

- Any other characteristic, individually or by zip code, selected because of credit history, poor response records, or simple inappropriateness for the particular offer.

- People who have indicated that, while they wish to receive mail from a company they do business with, they prefer not to have their names rented to or exchanged with other companies. More and more companies are offering this option to their customers.

Customer History Files

When list processors are used for maintenance of a company's own list of active customers, they can perform many valuable services in addition to list maintenance and the preparation of labels for mailing.

Business mailers can add to their customer lists any Dun & Bradstreet information, as discussed earlier, plus information on specific sales, sales commissions, purchases, and relative rankings.

Consumer catalog mailers can add a product-preference code, average and latest purchase amount, credit history, sex, birth date, ages of children, census tract data, and a profitability index taking into account the number of catalogs mailed.

Fund raisers can compile similar information for contributors, including interest groups, initial and subsequent contributions, date of last gift, and individual and census information.

Circulation promotion mailers can add subscription term, renewal information, income, advertising cost, additional purchases, and anything else that might be of value.

Reports can be compiled by source, by customer type, by product category, by month, by state, or SMSA. Virtually any type of data can be produced, provided it is in the system in some form in the first place.

Special Systems

Some list processors and compilers have prepared total systems for list management, lead procurement, or direct marketing.

There are too many suppliers to try to mention all their services. At least one company supplies a business lead system integrated with mailings, reports, sales follow-up, and lead distribution. Another has a special program for the insurance industry, where local agents may select demographic specifications within their own areas and order mailings sent to their immediate neighborhood, with related lead follow-up systems.

Some companies have stock systems for continuity programs or card file mailings. Others have software ready to go for catalog operations, with or without credit sales. Your best bet is to talk to many potential suppliers and to find those who have learned how to handle your problem the hard way—by making their mistakes at some earlier client's expense. It is much easier to adapt an existing computer program to meet your needs than to teach a company the basics of list processing.

SOME ADVANCED MAILING-LIST TECHNIQUES

Here are some of the list-buying and list-processing techniques used by some large advertisers. Most of these will be necessary only for companies that have exhausted conventional sources and who require very substantial mailing lists. In some cases, however, they may help a marginal company get bigger, if it has the time and patience to work out some of these sophisticated methods.

Multibuyer Match

One way to pretest a mailing list is to match it against either your customer list or known profitable lists. The higher the match factor, the more likely it is that the total list will be successful. This is used to predict the likelihood that a list will work.

Data Overlay

It is possible to match response lists against either the census tract or the individual characteristics of compiled lists, producing a list that combines both known response history and demographic factors. For instance, for a home repair book, you might overlay the factor of "individual residence" against known mail-order buyers, to produce a list of mail-order buyers who live in single-family homes. Or you might match a list of people who have responded to any book offer against other lists of families with children, to send out a mailing offering a set of children's books.

Title Conformance

If you are looking for female mail-order buyers and have exhausted all known female names on your best lists, you can try arbitrarily adding a "Mrs." before the male names on the lists. The chances are that "Mrs. John Jones" will reach the woman of the household, even though a certain amount of such mail will be wasted on bachelors.

In neighborhoods with children, you can correct a title to read "To the children of Mrs. Smith" with a reasonable chance of successfully reaching your prospect. When you have the names of children, there's no problem in having the computer print out "To Amy Nash's Daddy" or something similar.

Cluster Analysis

Companies such as Claritas and Database America have perfected systems that enable you to analyze your customer data and determine which zip codes have the greatest chance of success for your mailings. Gross response, credit performance, buying patterns, and other factors are used to pick out which areas are worth mailing to and which are not.

Waste Factor Calculation

Some advertisers back off from using lists because their message is too narrow. An example might be a special credit offer to college graduates. Such lists are difficult to obtain in quantity, yet in some neighborhoods more than half the household heads are college graduates.

The waste calculation strategy deliberately ignores the off-target addresses and concentrates on the doughnut instead of the hole. Sure, some people will get mail with an offer that they will not be qualified for; but if the mailing produces an overall 2 percent response, and if that 2 percent is acceptable, then it is no longer important that a pure college graduate list might have produced twice the response. A half-efficient list is better than none.

Skimming versus High-Penetration Strategies

"High penetration" is needed when you have few prospects and a high unit sale. Companies such as Avis Rent-A-Car and International Gold Corporation do well with a series of letters at a CPM over $1000. On the other hand, many charities send inexpensive mailings to large lists, a technique called *skimming*.

Other Techniques

The more advanced techniques in this field are often carefully guarded secrets. Even some of the examples used here have been changed to respect confidences. We urge you to look at the techniques discussed here more as a way of thinking—of stretching your mind to the potential of what can be done with mailing lists—than as specific ideas for your company. I strongly recommend that you read some of the articles by list specialists in *The Direct Marketing Handbook* (McGraw-Hill, 1992).

PACKAGE INSERTS AND COOPERATIVE MAILINGS

Two mediums that are often lumped with mailing lists are *cooperative mailings* and *package inserts*. Like mailing lists, both are listed in SRDS Direct Mail, and like mailing lists, they are ordered through list brokers.

Package Inserts

Several companies sell the right to insert an offer in their package mailings, or their statement suffers. Because they get a free ride with postage that would have had to be paid anyway, such stuffing opportunities can be made available very inexpensively.

Here are two typical package inserts listed by SRDS, along with quantities and prices:

	Annual quantity	Price per thousand inserts
Gurney Seed & Nursery Co.	1,230,900	$35
Sessions Records	1,100,000	25

These inserts have stringent weight and size limitations and so are most useful where a skimming strategy has proven effective. A disadvantage of these inserts is that it is difficult to coordinate them with other media or seasonal plans.

Cooperative Mailings

Probably the best-known cooperative mailings are Donnelly's Carol Wright, which sends out some six mailings a year to over 20 million people, and those by Larry Tucker Associates. There are also many specialized cooperative mailings to teenagers, seniors, and specific occupations or business types. The Tucker organization has been particularly helpful in providing flexibility to help test solutions for special marketing situations.

Costs range from $25 to $50 per thousand inserts, depending on the degree of selectivity, the amount of clutter (discussed next), and the number of inserts. Rates vary with the size and weight of the pieces inserted. Printing is extra. Some advertisers, especially those offering mass general magazines, recipe cards, or film processing, consider this medium very important and reserve choice dates and geographic areas years in advance.

Clutter is the result of too many other pieces inserted with yours in a cooperative mailing. Too many pieces will dilute attention and therefore response. More important is the professionalism of the other inserts and the perceived quality of the products offered. Both will rub off on yours.

Cooperative mailings are inexpensive to test. Direct marketers whose offers can be expressed in a small space should consider them.

This is easily the longest chapter in the book. No other medium is as important, varied, or complex. Working with mailing lists will never be as dramatic as designing a new mailing package, but it is more challenging. Suppressing or segmenting out the unproductive half of a mailing list is as valuable as doubling a response rate. It is just as profitable, just as feasible, and just as worthy of our time, attention, and talent.

PRINT MEDIA PLANNING

In the fast-changing world of direct marketing, newspapers and magazines are the Cinderellas of media. While these communication tools have lacked the instant stardom of broadcast, or the high-tech mathematical and personalization tools of direct mail, they are still productive and—when used correctly—can be profitable for every kind of direct marketer.

True, little has changed when it comes to the classic uses of print media. Small-space ads in shopping sections. Inquiry-pullers in financial, travel, real estate, and other newspaper sections. Special-interest business and consumer magazines. Multipage record club sections, and other free-standing inserts in the Sunday papers.

The change here is that direct marketing methods have become the key to the survival of these media. Advertising lineage has declined in many once-prosperous publications, as marketing funds have been diverted to direct mail and other accountable media. Yet direct marketers know that well-done advertisements in these mass media have the power to reach and identify prospects who can't be identified on existing mailing lists.

Business advertisers need print media to reach the elusive "initiators" and "approvers" who play a key role in purchasing and supplier decisions. Consumer advertisers need it to reach the fresh, highly responsive prospects who have not already been worked over by their competitors: the newly prosperous, the newly married, the new adopters of an interest or activity who are often the most enthusiastic.

Don't despair if tacking on a phone number to your clever image ads hasn't generated the response you expected. Instead, have direct marketers design an advertisement where response-generation is a prime objective rather than an afterthought, and see the difference. It is no more accurate to say "Print media don't work" than to apply that to any other media category. All that means is that you haven't figured out how to make them work. Newspapers and magazines will always be with us, and will always be an effective if not glamorous communication tool; they cannot be ignored.

WHEN TO USE PUBLICATION MEDIA

The principles of planning newspaper and magazine schedules are not unlike those that apply to selecting direct mail lists. The medium is the market, not just a way of reaching a market. There must be a logical affinity between product and audience. The quality of audience is more critical than the quantity. Divisibility permits segmentation and, therefore, both fine-tuning of profitability and limitation of downside risk in test situations. The principles are the same, but the practice is significantly different.

Most businesses are launched in direct mail, and some giant firms use direct mail as their single most important way of reaching potential audiences. However, in every marketing situation some important role is played by other media. Some examples follow.

Extending Direct Mail

A frequent problem with successful direct mail users is that they reach a point where the list universe is exhausted. Despite tailored appeals, segmentation refinement, and the testing of alternative direct mail strategies, there simply are no more names to be tested.

At this point many advertisers, particularly magazine subscription managers, try to increase the frequency of mailing, but they find that lists that did well on an annual or biannual frequency roll over and die when mailed twice a year. The highest-affinity core list simply has only so many fresh names, and so many old names becoming ready to accept a product offer—and no more.

In such a situation, print media extends direct mail. If subscribers to a magazine are an effective list, for instance, then an advertisement in that magazine enables you to reach not only the subscribers but also the newsstand buyers of the magazine. You'll also reach the publication's pass-along readership. According to some studies, this can be two or three times the circulation and up to six times the number of subscribers.

If a list such as Lillian Vernon is highly effective, then it is often possible to do well by going into the same magazines that Lillian Vernon did to build their list in the first place. This is another approach to extending mail.

Advertisers usually discover that, after house lists and a limited group of core lists, print media—and in some cases broadcast—are the most effective media sources. Noncore lists take up the next position in effectiveness and provide an opportunity to push sales volume ahead every year or two when the economic situation and the existence of a particularly effective direct mail package permit.

Alternatives to Direct Mail

There are some propositions that simply work much better in print media than in direct mail. The four occasions for this are (1) economics, (2) credibility, (3) buckshotting, and (4) creating new markets.

Economics. Print media reach a much larger number of people, at much lower cost, than direct mail, but possess much lower identified affinity levels with a given product. Chapter 3 discusses skimming as a strategic alternative to high penetration in direct mail. The skimming approach is carried to a greater extreme in print media, where a message can be presented to larger numbers of less motivated people at less expense.

Skimming is particularly appropriate for offers involving a low unit cost or for two-step propositions with initial free offers. There is simply not enough margin to support a 40-cents-per-unit ($400-per-thousand) mail contact on an offer that has no more likelihood of getting a response from any one prospect than a 4-cents per-contact ($40 per thousand) print-media message. In other words, unless there is 10 times the likelihood that a list addressee will respond—because of either list affinity or the added impact of a longer, more involving direct mail message—it will be more profitable to reach that prospect and others in a less involving, less expensive print-media message.

Credibility. Other direct marketing offers require the implied endorsement of a publication's pages to be successful, just as some direct mail programs need the *imprimatur* of a well-known company. Readers presume, and rightly so, that a magazine or newspaper will stand behind the products advertised in its pages. Some publications, such as *Good Housekeeping* and *The New York Times,* are very strict about this, and so have greater credibility than publications that may not be as stringent in their requirements.

If your company is unknown, and especially if your product raises health or safety concerns on the part of the consumer, it may do much better in established magazines than in any direct mail other than that endorsed by a well-respected third party.

Buckshotting. Some companies have a product or service that can afford a highly targeted, high-penetration direct mail effort, but simply do not have enough good lists. This is frequently the case in the business equipment and financial fields. The opposite of targeting is buckshotting.

Mailing lists that identify key executives by name will do well for a maker of dictating or copying equipment, or a solicitor of investments in gold, gems, or money market funds. But there are just not enough of those names. Dun's Decision Makers, for instance, can provide the names of half-a-dozen top executives in a corporation, but hundreds more may have the authority to buy a dictating machine, reserve a car, or plan a plane trip. While direct mail may be much more effective on a cost-per-order basis, such products still require extensive print-media campaigns to reach all of their potential prospects.

Creating New Markets.   Starting something new often requires going into the widest possible marketplace and letting the product seek its own level or find its own market.

In some cases—such as prepaid health services, a magazine for tennis buffs, or a club for indoor gardeners—there are not enough mailing lists to build a business, no matter what the strategy is. That's where print media can be extremely useful. In fact, I sometimes recommend using general publications for an initial round of ads, followed by a regression analysis of respondents to find unexpected list-affinity areas.

A valuable by-product of this approach is the building of a unique mailing list of buyers of your own product. This should have high value in the list-rental marketplace or as a foundation for additional product introductions.

Again, direct mail is a sharpshooter's medium, while print media and broadcast are shotguns. If your targets are few, worthwhile, and identified, nothing beats direct mail; but if they are hard to find, small in number, or hard to identify, then there's nothing like a shotgun. It will be sure to hit something.

SOURCES OF INFORMATION

Before we go into selecting newspapers and magazines, the first step is to know where and how to get the information you need.

Standard Rate and Data Service

As with direct mail, the basic tools are the directories published by Standard Rate and Data Service for consumer publications and other advertising media.

The consumer magazine directory alone contains data on about 1500 magazines sorted into 63 classifications. The main classifications are worth noting:

1.   Airline Inflight/Train Enroute

1A.   Almanacs & Directories

2.   Art & Antiques

Page 120

---

3. Automotive
4. Aviation
5. Babies
5A. Black/African-American
6. Boating & Yachting
7. Bridal
8. Business & Finance
8A. Campers, Recreational Vehicles, Motor Homes & Trailers
8B. Camping & Outdoor Recreation
9. Children's
9A. Civic
9B. College & Alumni
10. Comics & Comic Technique
10A. Computers
11. Crafts, Games, Hobbies & Models
12. Dancing
13. Dogs & Pets
14. Dressmaking & Needlework
15. Editorialized & Classified Advertising
16. Education & Teacher
17. Entertainment Guides & Programs
17A. Entertainment & Performing Arts
18. Epicurean
19. Fishing & Hunting
19A. Fitness
20. Fraternal, Professional Groups, Service Clubs, Veteran's Organizations & Associations
20A. Gaming
21. Gardening (Home)
21A. Gay Publications
22. General Editorial
22A. Group Buying Opportunities
23. Health
23A. History
24. Home Service & Home
25. Horses, Riding & Breeding
25A. Hotel Inroom
27. Labor, Trade Union
28. Literary, Book Reviews & Writing Techniques
28A. Mature Market
29. Mechanics & Science

29A. Media/Personalities
30.   Men's
30A. Metropolitan/Regional/State
30B. Metropolitan/Entertainment, Radio & TV
31.   Military & Naval (Air Force, Army, Navy & Marines)
31A. Motorcycle
33.   Music
34.   Mystery, Adventure & Science Fiction
35.   Nature & Ecology
36A. News—Weeklies
36B. News—Biweeklies, Dailies, Semimonthlies
36C. Newsweeklies (Alternatives)
37.   Newsletters
38.   Newspaper Distributed Magazines
38A. Parenthood
39.   Photography
41.   Political & Social Topics
41A. Popular Culture
42.   Religious & Denominational
43.   Science/Technology
43B. Sex
44.   Society
45.   Sports
45A. Teen
46.   Travel
47.   TV & Radio/Communications & Electronics
49.   Women's
50.   Women's/Men's Fashions, Beauty & Grooming
51.   Youth

Most people are surprised at the wide range of little-known and high-ly specialized magazines. The classification "General Editorial," for instance, is one that most advertisers might guess they would already be familiar with; but I doubt that anyone would be able to recall all the fol-lowing audited publications classified in the 1994 *Consumer Magazine SRDS* as "General Editorial."

Air & Space/Smithsonian   Atlantic, The
American Heritage   Audubon
American Legion Magazine, The   Bon Apetit
Archaeology   Changes
Architectural Digest   Condé Nast Select

Consumers Digest

Country America

Ebony

Emerge

Globe

Grit

Harper's Magazine

Harrowsmith Country Life

Hispanic

Historic Preservation

Journal of Accountancy

Kiplinger's Personal Finance Magazine

Life

Modern Maturity

Money

Mother Jones

National Enquirer

National Examiner

National Geographic Magazine

Natural History

New Age Journal

New Choices

New Yorker, The

Parade

Private Clubs

Reader's Digest

Robb Report, The

Saturday Evening Post, The

Sierra

Smithsonian

Spy

Star

Town & Country

Utne Reader

Vanity Fair

Washington Post Magazine, The

Wildlife Conservation

World Press Review

When we deal with less general publications, or with the 8000 or so magazines in the classifications in *Business SRDS*, the challenge is even greater. Media buying cannot be done "off the top of your head." It is a rigorous and demanding science that demands the best tools of the trade.

Each listing of a single magazine incorporates, in a standardized format, all the objective data needed to analyze potential media. Unlike rate cards supplied by the magazines themselves, SRDS listings are always comparable, point by point. Each listing includes all of the following information.

Introductory material
- Title of publication
- Media identification code
- Frequency of issue
- Name of publisher
- Address of publisher
- Telephone number
- Fax number
- Publisher's editorial profile

1. *Personnel*
   - Names and titles of those executives who have responsibility and authority relative to national advertising accounts

2. *Representatives and/or branch offices*
   - Representative's name only
   - Branch office
   - Name
   - Address
   - Telephone number
3. *Commission and cash discount*
   - Amount of commission allowed to agencies
   - Cash discount
4. *General rate policy*
   - Contract cancellation clause
   - Policy on rate protection and rate revision
   - Conditions and/or regulations related to all advertising space contracts not given in Contract and Copy Regulations
5. *Black/white rates*
   - B/w discount structures
5a. *Combination rates*
   - Rates when sold in combination
5b. *Discounts (gross expenditures)*
   - Discounts applicable to total dollars invested
6. *Color rates*
   - Color availability
   - Rates for standard colors
   - Rates for selected colors
   - Color discount structures
7. *Covers*
   - Availability
   - Rates
8. *Inserts*
   - Base rates
   - Special charges
   - Tip-ons
9. *Bleed*
   - Space and color charge
   - Gutter bleed
10. *Special position*
    - Availability
    - Rates
    - Spreads
11. *Classified/mail order*
    - Classified rates
    - Display classifications
    - Mail-order rates
12. *Split-run*
    - Rates
    - Requirements
    - Circulation data and source

13. *Special issue rates and data*
  - Rates and data pertaining to special or thirteenth issue (exclusive of regular issues)
  - Issuance dates for special issues
  - Circulation data and source

13a. *Geographic and/or demographic editions*
  - Rates
  - Requirements
  - Issue and closing dates
  - Circulation data and source

14. *Contract and copy regulations*
  - Numbers shown here refer to standard regulations used by many publishers and summarized on a special page of the directory. Such terms refer to volume contracts, copy acceptability, payment terms, and various legal matters.

15. *General requirements*
  - Trim size, number of columns to page
  - Binding method
  - Color available
  - Mechanical requirements for geographic and/or demographic editions, where different from basic publication
  - Dimensions—ad page (width and depth)
  - Minimum depth R.O.P. (run of paper) for newspaper formats

16. *Issue and closing dates*
  - Frequency of publication
  - Closing dates for: black-and-white, color, inserts, set copy, and special feature issues

17. *Special service*
  - MCC Business Publication Data Form
  - A.B.C. Supplemental Data Report
  - Ad readership studies
  - Advertising preparation services
  - Direct mail services
  - Direct-response services
  - Merchandising services
  - Reprints
  - Reader service card
  - Special stock printing

18. *Circulation*
  - Year established
  - Single-copy and annual prices
  - Circulation data and source
  - Territorial distribution
  - Publisher guarantee or "rates based on"
    This discloses whether a publication is subscription or single-copy. Direct marketers, looking for evidence that readers will respond to mail offers, usually prefer the subscription-sold publications to newsstand ones.

19. *Distribution*
    - Year established
    - Distribution data and source
      (Applicable to periodicals placing copies in distribution to specific places.)
20. *Print order*
    - Copies printed and offered for sale
      (Applicable to annuals, semiannuals, and magazines with less than quarterly frequency that are printed and offered for sale with definite "on sale" dates, and with established single-copy or issue prices.)

There are several other various specialized features that are lesser known but can also be very helpful.

Magazine and farm publication representative
Shows name, address, telephone number of home and branch offices of firms representing consumer magazines and farm publications. In alpha sequence.

Promotional dates
Shows special days and weeks, such as National Baby Week, Law Day, etc. Listed chronologically and updated monthly.

Census divisions map
Shows the states comprising each Geographical Division. Breakdown under "Territorial Distribution."

Magazine group-buying opportunities
An alphabetical index of all group titles appearing in *Consumer* magazine and *Farm Publication Rates and Data,* with reference to editorial classifications in which listings have been assigned.

Magazines with geographic and/or demographic editions of split-run advertising
A two-section index, listed in alphabetical order.

Magazines with shopping advertising pages

International consumer magazines

Shopping Pages lists magazines that accept small-space mail-order advertisements in special sections. Presumably, such sections are very effective because the rates are lower and the ads are grouped together near compatible editorial matter. This type of shopping-section ad has been the lifeblood of many small mail-order businesses.

Demographic and Geographic Editions lists magazines that can be segmented by type of reader or by area of the country—a valuable way to target expenditures to a specific market or to minimize downside risk on a test.

Split-run availability shows magazines that will accept split-run advertising, facilitating copy testing with or without combination with geographic or demographic editions.

Some Other Tools of the Trade

While SRDS is the indispensable tool of the media planner, other tools can sometimes be very useful.

Audit Statements. Audit statements began as a way of verifying circulation claims and providing an independent verification of publishers' sworn statements. The best-known individual magazine statements are those published by the Audit Bureau of Circulation. Today their most valuable function is their breakdown of circulation by source. An ABC statement will disclose whether a magazine is subscription-sold or newsstand-sold; whether it has been sold at cut rate, with premiums, or with a sweepstakes; and whether it has been sold by direct mail or through agents such as Publishers' Clearing House. All this data can he analyzed to indicate the quality of a publication's circulation. Direct mail–sold readers who have come in through full-price subscriptions can be the most meaningful circulation if your own product is sold the same way. However, if you have a reduced-price introductory offer or are selling with a sweepstakes, it may be important to know that similar offers were successful in attracting the magazine's readers in the first place.

Usually, the data is helpful the other way around—in tailoring the offer. If a magazine ad has been marginal in response despite a logical affinity of editorial matter, it may be helpful to look at how it was sold in the first place. If the magazine was sold by sweepstakes, it might be worth trying your own sweepstakes offer there.

Another factor revealed by audit statements is the status of the circulation, as opposed to the source. If most readers are new, introductory readers, they may not be reading the magazine intensely if it is not what they expected. However, a large percentage of renewed renewals (RRs) indicates that the publication is being read thoroughly, giving your advertisement a better chance of being read as well. From a direct marketer's point of view, the quality of a magazine might be represented by the formula MS% × RR% = QF, or percentage of direct mail–sold times percentage of renewed renewals equals quality factor.

The quality factor can be applied to total percentages or to cost per thousand readers to produce a quality-adjusted circulation or cost per thousand. There should be a correlation between quality-adjusted cost figures and resulting cost-per-order data from actual insertions.

PIB Reports. Another tool is *PIB Reports*, issued by Publishers' Information Bureau. As discussed in Chapter 3, The Marketing Plan, the primary reason for reading *PIB Reports* is to check on the competition by seeing what publications they are using repeatedly.

Simmons Reports. Simmons reports, available in voluminous binders at great expense, are the most sophisticated application of research to publication-media buying. Simmons conducts extensive surveys, asking readers what magazines they read and what their hobbies and interests are, and draws valuable conclusions about magazine readership and reader interests.

Many agencies have this data on computer, and can quickly run through categories to produce media efficiency studies. For instance, if you wanted to run an ad selling golf clubs by mail, they would correlate readers who play golf and readers who buy by mail. They could then combine the results with income, education, age, family size, or any other factors to produce a media list based on cost per thousand targeted readers. This "CPMT" factor is discussed in more detail later in this chapter.

THE MATHEMATICS OF MEDIA

For companies new to this field, a review of some of the basics will be helpful before going on to selection of magazine and newspaper media.

CPM versus CPR

The basic tool of media buying is cost per thousand, meaning that advertising cost divided by one-thousandth of the circulation gives you the cost per thousand in circulation. This is a traditional index, and at one time SRDS used to quote CPM for a typical black-and-white page at the end of each listing. However, it is not the only index and certainly not the most important one.

The figure that counts, in the long run, is one that correlates results— or at least expected results—as cost per response (or order, or lead, or subscription). The CPR, the ultimate index for direct marketers, is simply advertising cost divided by number of responses.

Some advertisers and agencies also use a figure called *orders per thousand* to provide a constant figure for responsiveness of a given media space unit against all propositions and all advertisers whose data they can compare. OPM eliminates distortions due to volume discounts, remnant rates, or exchange space deals, and indexes the potential "life" of the magazine's audience without cost distortion. The value of the OPM factor becomes very clear if you presume that each publisher is reasonable and negotiable, as most are, and that—given the facts—they will bring their costs into line with other publications to make their magazine attractive to advertisers.

The OPM factor is also important when conducting tests in split-run or regional editions. Such smaller segments are always more expensive on a CPM basis. The use of the OPM factor evens out the premium cost and provides a consistent standard for comparing results.

Mail-Order Rates

Many magazines and newspapers offer special reduced rates for classifications of advertising that they consider particularly desirable, or where competition with other publications is particularly severe. Philanthropic rates, cultural rates, publishers' rates, and retail rates are all common, and can make a big difference in projected CPR.

I know of one mail-order book advertiser whose most important medium was *The New York Times.* The advertiser opened a retail store just to get that paper's retail rate. The retail store prospered unexpectedly and became the forerunner of half-a-dozen such stores.

Volume and Frequency Discounts

Many publications offer lower rates, called *frequency discounts,* for multiple insertions, either in a single issue of a publication or over a period of time. Publications also offer volume discounts, based on the total lines or dollar amount of space used during a fiscal or calendar year. Such discounts often allow large advertisers to support marginal propositions where other advertisers would not be able to make them work. In some cases, however, such discounts are not available if a mail-order discount is also being taken. Check with the publications.

At the end of a contract period, it sometimes pays to run some additional advertising that will help the entire schedule to reach a lower rate breakpoint. CBS, for instance, is able to run advertising for its magazines and for specialty mail-order clubs in the same *TV Guide* issues as its Columbia House ads, making a much lower rate available to the smaller proposition than it would enjoy if it were independent.

One unfortunate by-product of such volume and frequency discounts is their tendency to accelerate the decline of small individual direct marketers. Such rates make it possible for a giant advertiser to buy a smaller competitor or overwhelm their advertising. Volume discounts are attractive to big advertisers but, in my opinion, grossly unfair to smaller ones.

Printing Costs

In direct marketing media, advertisers often buy units with bound-in or tipped-on insert cards, multipage sections, or newspaper inserts. In such cases the printing cost should be considered part of the overall cost in all schedules, even though it is not billed by the magazine. A media schedule and subsequent analyses of results should always include printing costs as if they were part of the media cost.

Rates

Premium Rates. Almost all publications charge a higher CPM for regional or demographic editions than for full-run advertising. This is only fair, as a publication is segmented at great cost and difficulty, and only for the convenience of advertisers. However, the resulting CPR will be higher than if a full-run insertion had been used. This should be kept in mind, and appropriate adjustments made, when determining whether regional or split-run advertisements can be rolled out on a full-run basis.

Remnant Rates. Many publications offer various kinds of remnant deals, particularly in the Sunday supplement field. The offer applies to units that remain unsold after premium regional edition buyers have made their pick. In some cases, publications will offer unsold space on a remnant deal, subject to preemption if a full-price advertiser comes along. Even the prestigious *New York Times* has a half-price offer contingent on permitting the *Times* to select the date within a certain time frame. *Time* magazine offers flexible-date advertising at 35 percent less than the full rate.

Surcharges. Another rate consideration is the cost of surcharges. Most publications will charge extra for a premium position, such as a back cover, although few will charge for (or guarantee) positions such as the front of the magazine. Some newspapers charge different rates, or surcharges, for ads in a specific Sunday section, such as a magazine section.

One of the most common surcharges is for "bleed" pages: the right to run your advertisement over the entire page, right to the edge, rather than just to the margin. Many progressive publishers, recognizing that four-color bleed ads make their magazine more interesting and colorful for readers, are discontinuing this charge.

Agency Commissions and Cash Discounts

Most magazines and newspapers grant recognized advertising agencies a 15 percent agency commission. This is a practice that dates back to the days when agencies literally bought space in blocks and resold it to advertisers. Today agencies earn this commission by providing the creative services that used to be supplied by individual publications.

There was a time when any recognized member of the American Association of Advertising Agencies would be expected to work strictly on the commission system. Today that applies mostly to very large advertising accounts that require a full range of agency services. Some large clients who demand less than full service—perhaps excluding the agency from marketing planning or media buying—negotiate arrangements where the agency is paid only a partial commission. Or agencies may be paid on a fee or hourly basis, rebating all or part of the commission to the advertiser.

With smaller accounts this agency commission may be only part of the compensation paid by the advertiser to the agency for marketing, creative, media buying, and executional services. A minimum income guarantee or supplementary fee often is required in addition to earned commissions. Sometimes the commissions are credited against a guaranteed monthly income.

It is possible for an advertiser to set up a "house agency" to keep the commission, thus lowering advertising expense by 15 percent. Generally this is a false economy, due to the cost of the staff required and the loss of the professionalism and objectivity provided by an outside agency. Any client who thinks a house agency is a good investment has probably never worked with a first-class advertising agency. In the direct marketing field particularly, any agency that can't lift its clients' results by much more than the 15 percent commission isn't doing its job. The best solution in such cases is not a house agency but a different outside agency.

Production Costs

The costs of preparing artwork—type, photography, paste-up, etc.—can be substantial. Should these costs be figured into the media budget and the result analysis? My recommendation, and the general industry practice, is a negative answer.

If an ad runs only once, production costs will be substantial in relation to the overall budget. If it runs many times, in many publications, production costs may be insignificant. I have never seen a formula that anticipates this problem. The general practice is to treat production costs as a separate "below-the-line" budget against the total advertising appropriation—not against individual advertisements. The costs should be controlled, and economies should be related to the extent of intended use as a control on the production budget, not as a burden to individual media expenditures.

Whatever rates your company can earn, and whatever fees, surcharges, commissions, or discounts are involved, the bottom line remains the same: cost per response.

SELECTING THE RIGHT PUBLICATIONS

How do you pick the best magazines or newspapers in which to place your first advertisements? If you have already proved that print media works for you, where do you run your next ads?

No matter what stage you're in, the selection process is the same, and the principles are very similar to those we explained for selecting direct mail lists. If the media is the market, you want to know which media will pay off for you. The "affinity" approach is a logical place to start—with some exceptions.

Cost per Thousand Target Audience (CPMT)

Magazines included in Simmons will have circulation breakdowns, based on their research data, indicating estimated circulation in terms of various breakdowns, such as "Has More than $100M of Life Insurance." Two percentage figures are shown: *vertical,* or percent of such households reached by the publication, and *horizontal,* or percent of the publication's circulation with the sought characteristic, i.e. the "target" audience. In addition an index is provided, giving the user a quick indicator of the circulation efficiency for that characteristic as compared with other listed publications.

In addition to the percentage figures, there are also estimates of the readers of each characteristic in actual numbers. The planning process used by the account executives I train is to compare these actual numbers with the applicable rates, usually discounted or at the rates they can be purchased through a direct marketing media service such as The Stephen Geller Company. The rates are divided by the target circulation figures on a spreadsheet to produce "Cost Per Thousand Target Audience."

This CPMT ranking is a valuable directory of media efficiency, in terms of cost. But it doesn't become a media schedule in itself. We must still take into consideration such experience-based questions as editorial affinity, audience responsiveness, and the availability of economical and reliable testing options. These are all discussed later in this chapter.

Mail Responsiveness

You might think that an art publication would be the right place to advertise art supplies or prints. It seems logical because of the affinity between audience and product. Most likely, however, you'd be wrong.

When you're selecting from lists of mail-order buyers, the factor of mail responsiveness is already built in. That's where the list came from. But that's not necessarily the case with magazines.

Certainly look first at those publications where there is a clear relationship between their editorial subject and your product or service, but within that group of magazines, look for the factor of mail responsiveness. That's where you'll need either the ABC statement or a space salesperson who's willing to do more than take you to lunch.

Is the magazine sold by subscription or on the newsstand? Subscription buyers have at least responded to the subscription offer. Is the magazine sold by mail? That's good. Is it sold through association memberships or sweepstakes-based agents? That's bad. Whether you observe them empirically or go to the trouble of calculating the quality factor discussed earlier, these factors have to be taken into account.

A simpler approach is to play follow-the-leader. Look at several issues of the magazine and see if it carries a great deal of other direct marketing advertising. Then look up some of the advertisers in PIB and see if the ads are first-time insertions or repeats. If the latter, you can presume the earlier ad was successful. You might even talk to some advertisers that are not directly competitive with you and ask how the magazine pulled.

Ask whether the advertising is paid space. Don't be misled into going into a publication at full rate when the bulk of previous direct-response space has been there on an exchange or remnant basis.

If plenty of other advertisers have been repeating coupon advertising or if the publication has a high quality factor by observation or calculation, then it's worth a try—provided the audience is the right one.

Editorial Affinity

How do you determine whether a magazine's audience is right for you? The key is *editorial affinity*, or an observation of the editorial environment—an observation that relies entirely on the subjective judgment of the person responsible for making the media recommendation or decision.

A vertical publication dealing directly with the field at which your product is aimed may not be right because the readership is too advanced or too amateurish for your particular product. A general magazine with a strong mail-order advertising representation may be too downscale or upscale, or may exclude the audience or market segment you need. This is where judgment comes in, and is one of the ways direct marketing is still an art as well as a science.

It is just as much of a mistake to go by audience demographics alone and ignore the editorial environment. Just as business direct mail does better when sent to business addresses, and vice versa for personal offers, so too it is dangerous to ignore the context of the advertisement.

When I read *Cruising World* or *Popular Photography* or *Condé Nast Traveler,* I am thinking about an interest that is a source of pleasure. While I might be interested in investments or insurance or a new long-distance service, it is an intrusion at that particular time. To a large extent, I would probably not even be interested in a travel ad when I was reading a sailing magazine. The few attempts at defying this theory that I have seen were not successful.

There is no substitute for examining the actual magazines and getting a feel for the editorial content and the level of other direct marketing advertisements. The environment has to be right for your particular advertisement; or maybe you will have to prepare a special offer and advertising approach that will make this particular medium work for you.

The Elusive Audience

The people you are trying to reach read many magazines and newspapers. They get direct mail. They listen to radio and watch television. There is no one way to reach them, but usually there is a best way.

It is essential to remember that usually we are trying to get a response from less than one-half of 1 percent of a publication's readership. That means we are concerned with only 10 or 20 percent of the publication's circulation, at best. Our target market segment does not have to be the majority of a magazine's readers; it just has to be there somewhere.

That "somewhere" doesn't have to be in the mainstream of the publication's circulation. They could be at the lower edge of an upscale publication or the upper edge of a downscale one. A mass-market mutual fund, for instance, can do equally well in *Barron's,* which is primarily directed at sophisticated investors, or in *Money,* which deals largely with budget planning and shopping guidance rather than investments per se. Both may have attracted enough prospects to be successful for you. The only way to find out is to examine the magazine, use your own judgment, and—if you're not sure—take a chance and see what happens.

Media Constellations

If the total potential media for a proposition is called a *media universe,* then the logical subcategories of that whole might be termed *constellations.* Just as astrologers arbitrarily group stars into constellations, so advertisers arbitrarily group publications into categories.

Once you've examined SRDS, considered the wide scope of possible magazines, and examined the data and the magazines themselves, you can sort the publications by any common attributes you desire. Your categories are as good as anyone else's.

Perhaps you'll have vertical publications, downscale ones, prestige magazines, city or regional publications, newspaper Sunday supplements, foreign language papers, women's magazines. If your market is narrower, you might break down a category such as women's magazines into even finer subconstellations, such as women's homemaking magazines, women's career magazines, women's cooking publications, and women's escapism magazines. With newspapers you might use categories such as size of market, area of country, level of editorial, and political slant. Any category can be refined down to the ultimate subcategory: an individual publication.

The categories in SRDS are a handy place to start, but they are as subjective as the categories you would invent. That's why many magazines list themselves in more than one SRDS category, and that's why categories must be broken down into those that are relevant for you and your business.

Pilot Publications

Once you've established the categories, you're ready for the next step: picking one representative magazine within each constellation to be your pilot publication. This is the magazine or newspaper that you will advertise in, the one that will enable you to make a decision about the entire grouping that it represents. As such, it must be typical of the constellation.

A pilot publication should not be the place to experiment on a single magazine that might be new or untried by others. You want to give this pilot every chance of succeeding and representing its group, and so it should be the publication in the group that appears to be most used by other direct marketers and most representative, editorially, of the group as a whole.

To minimize downside risk, a pilot publication does not have to be a full run of a given magazine or newspaper. It can be a region or a split run, provided that the publication will not double-handicap you—not only charge you a premium rate but also place your ad in a marginal back-of-the-book position.

Don't be concerned about picking a publication that is likely to do a bit better than most other publications in the constellation. If your group is news magazines, for instance, and you are looking for older, more serious readers, then by all means start with *U.S. News & World Report.* A *Time* regional buy might be more representative, but if your offer doesn't work in *U.S. News* it won't work in *Time* or *Newsweek.* So give yourself the edge by going with the better magazine and then rolling out cautiously after you see the results.

TV Guide. This single magazine is a media constellation in itself, and no discussion of media would be complete unless its unique attributes were reviewed. It is the key medium for some of the nation's largest direct marketers, and it has been an important test medium for many others.

Because *TV Guide* reaches an audience whose common denominator is simply ownership of television sets, it covers an almost universal audience. At the beginning of 1994 its total circulation exceeded 14 million households.

The magazine has over 100 editions, distributed according to TV markets, and offers a perfect A-B split in each of those markets. It is a weekly, which means you can get fast turnaround for testing. You can test a wide variety of copy appeals very quickly, sometimes in advance of a general national campaign.

This publication's readers have many interests: the outdoors, decorating, shopping, entertainment. It is a unique place to use the skimming strategy and let a proposition seek its own audience.

Part of the success of the magazine is due to its low cost per page, a product of its small page size. Actually, on the basis of cost per square inch per thousand circulation, it is quite expensive, but an offer that doesn't need much space to fully explain and sell it can do very nicely.

Inserts and foldout units are eagerly sought after, but they are very sensitive to position, timing, and competitive factors, With printing costs, a typical book club or encyclopedia insertion can cost over $300,000 an insertion—yet there's usually a waiting list for the most responsive issues.

Letting the Consumer Make the Decisions

In general advertising, expert opinion and statistical data lead to a high budget for scheduling each magazine for several insertions, to build frequency. In direct marketing, on the other hand, where each ad has to stand alone, a small budget is appropriated for pilot publication testing, with one insertion per publication. Then the direct marketer waits to read the results. The balance of the appropriation is held in reserve for a campaign to run during a good season after getting the results of the pilot test. In an ongoing campaign these tests might alternate with rollouts. Summer tests, for instance, sometimes are intended to influence the following summer schedules, not the winter campaign. Turnaround time becomes very important in integrating tests and rollouts.

Fast closing dates might influence the selection of a pilot publication. Weekly rather than monthly publications offer a plus in testing. Weekly magazines are readable a full month sooner, after the sale date, than monthlies, and usually have faster closing dates as well.

General advertisers often have difficulty in accepting the constant change and step-by-step decision making of direct marketing media plans. They are accustomed to taking $1 million and scheduling it all at once. A direct marketing schedule might commit a fourth of that to testing, put the other three-fourths in reserve, and then ask for an additional one or two million dollars if results justify it.

MAGAZINE CONSIDERATIONS

Circulation numbers and characteristics are only one consideration in planning a magazine schedule. You also have to know what kind of space unit to use, what position to ask for, and whether or not to use some type of segmentation.

Space Units

Let's look at the space unit first. Should it be large or small? One page or two? What about those spectacular units like multiple-page inserts or heavy-stock preprinted bind-ins, perhaps with a reply-card flap?

The traditional rule is to use as little space as possible to get your message across, and to avoid wasting money on white space and irrelevant illustrations. That's a good starting place, but it's not a rule without exceptions.

On one end of the spectrum, a small 3- or 4-inch one-column advertisement in a shopping section can be the safest and most profitable insertion you can make, on a return-on-investment basis. After this unit is placed in every applicable publication, as often as results hold up, what's the next step?

Running larger ads seems to be the obvious solution, but often the larger ad produces little more response than the original ad. That's because space alone is not an attention-getter. As I'll explain in Chapter 14, Art Direction, the perceived size of an ad is not the size of the space unit but the size of the largest single element in the advertisement. Just blowing up an ad to a larger size gives you a larger element, but not necessarily more selling power or more impact.

A larger ad should be redesigned and conceptually thought through from the beginning. If the ad is to have proportionately greater result-getting appeal than the original ad, it must use the space better. Perhaps the larger version can add testimonials, or dramatize a guarantee or product feature that there wasn't room for before. Or perhaps the main attention-getting element—a headline or illustration—can be made even more dramatic so as to multiply the stopping power of the ad even more than the increase in the size of the space.

For some types of products or services, a standard fractional unit like a half-page or page can be important because of the credibility it adds, by itself, to the advertisement. This is the only case where sheer size can add results. An "exciting announcement" is much more exciting in a full-page ad, as a message from a company that purports to be large and important. This theory is more important with companies that are not well known. A major institution that already has a widely established name can get away with smaller space units than a newcomer to the field.

Once a space unit reaches its optimum level of responsiveness, increasing the space unit to a larger size can still be worthwhile. For example, a philanthropic advertiser soliciting contributions used double-page spreads in the best-pulling magazines, rather than single pages. The cost per donor was slightly higher, but the incremental return for the second page was still greater than if the same money had been spent on a marginal medium or greater frequency.

Spectacular Units

So-called *spectacular units* are very substantial investments that produce equally substantial improvements in results. The old rule of thumb is that a page with an insert card costs two and a half times the cost of a page alone but produces four times the results.

There are several kinds of spectacular units. The simplest is the bound-in reply card. The greatest importance of this unit is the ease of reply that it offers the reader interested in your proposition, but it also "indexes" the magazine, causing it to open at that page while being thumbed through.

Full-page inserts, with your ad printed on both sides, also offer the same advantages, plus even more impact due to the sheer weight of the inserted page.

When it is necessary to offer a large choice or a long presentation of copy points, four-, six-, or eight-page inserts, or even longer ones, can also be bound in. Such units are often on coated stock, card stock, or standard magazine coated paper. They may or may not include a reply card, but some advertisers deliberately omit the business reply card as a way of trading response rate for quality improvement.

Such units often are hard to schedule, as publications have relatively few such positions available in each issue. Advertisers who have used them before generally have an option to continue to use the same unit on the same date in subsequent years.

Color or Black-and-White?

There's no hard-and-fast rule to this question either. Color is particularly valuable if used well—especially to illustrate a colorful product. The only test I know of color versus black-and-white showed that color paid for itself, although it did not lower the cost per order. The rule is to use color only if it adds to the visual appeal of the product or the impact of the advertisement—both highly subjective evaluations.

One alternative that is always wrong is two or three colors. If your message isn't appealing in black-and-white, a color headline or background isn't going to make a difference. And certainly it's not worth the money just to put your company trademark in a second color. Either go with black-and-white, or go all the way to four-color with lifelike illustrations.

Magazine Positions

Virtually all advertisers agree on the relative ranks of various positions in most magazines, although they disagree on the exact percentage difference between them. However, everyone agrees that position is an important influence on results.

In magazines, insert card positions are the most effective, with the first better than the second and so on. Pulling power declines until just before the back of the magazine, where the last insert card does only 10 percent less than the first. This is a general rule, and results vary depending on the type of magazine. Fashion publications, handicraft magazines, and financial publications seem to hold up better throughout the magazine than other types of publications.

In general space, right-hand pages pull better than left-hand, with the first right-hand page the very best and others declining at 5 or 10 percent for each subsequent right-hand page.

Back covers are particularly desirable, and will do as well as a first right-hand page, if the publication does not impose a punitive surcharge for the position. The inside back cover will do as well as a first right-hand page, with the page facing it producing as well as a second right-hand page. These unique back-of-book positions are more likely to be available than first right-hand pages, and should always be considered when negotiating with a space representative.

One of the errors direct marketing beginners make is presuming that the magazine will give them the best possible position, or that nothing can be done to influence the choice of position. It may be easy to mail out an insertion order reading, "Far forward right-hand position requested," but this is not doing everything you can. Talk to the ad sales representative for the publication and stress the importance of position, particularly in terms of potential repeat insertions. Specific pages should be negotiated for and an understanding reached, even if they cannot be guaranteed. One insertion order clause that is sometimes accepted by magazines is "Page xx or better right-hand position urgently requested, or notify agency prior to cancellation date."

Segmented Editions

As previously discussed, it is not necessary to buy a full national circulation of a magazine, and there are many times when it will be desirable to pay a higher rate per thousand circulation in order to target a specific area or demographic group, or to limit downside risk.

A wide variety of options is offered by magazines. Here are some examples of the alternatives available.

Better Homes and Gardens is a good example. With 8 million circulation, it offers the following choices:

- 55 regional marketing editions, generally states, with circulations ranging from as little as 15,000 to almost half a million, with any combination available.

- 64 top markets, generally metropolitan areas, with circulations as little as 30,000 (Providence, Rhode Island) or as much as 437,000 (New York).

- Metro Suburban. A single edition covering the metro marketing area surrounding and including every A county in the U.S.—25 top marketing areas sold in one four-million-copy edition.

- Travel sections. State circulations grouped for the convenience of the travel industry, each comprising more than one million people in travel origination areas such as East, Great Lakes, West, South, Central.

- Alternate copy. One half of the circulation, sold on an every-other-copy basis evenly distributed throughout the publication's circulation.

Time has been particularly innovative in segmentation, and offers over 150 different markets in editions of as little as 25,000 copies. They also offer some unique demographic editions:

- *Time* Campus — 391,388 — College students
- *Time* B — 1,661,726 — Business executives
- *Time* T — 617,512 — Subscribers in top management
- *Time* Z — 1,448,605 — Subscribers living in 1414 top income quintile zip-code areas
- *Time* 33 Major Metros — 2,962,168 — 50 top cities

Not to be outdone, *Newsweek* has several similar editions, plus one unique one:

- *Newsweek* Woman — 700,000 — Female subscribers

These examples give an idea of the opportunities available in special editions. Over 250 magazines offer segmentation opportunities for advertisers.

NEWSPAPERS—ROP, SUPPLEMENTS, AND PREPRINTS

In general advertising, the most important attributes of the newspaper medium are its ability to achieve a very high penetration of each market, its high credibility, and its immediacy.

These same attributes are of interest to direct marketers, but overall they are offset by the medium's lack of "mail responsiveness." Very few newspapers are sold by mail, and few carry significant amounts of direct marketing advertising in relation to other advertising. This trend is changing, as home-delivered papers use direct mail and telephone calls to solicit subscriptions, but generally it still prevails.

ROP Newspaper Advertising

There are very few national direct marketers who advertise ROP ("run of paper") in daily or Sunday newspapers in preference to national magazines or other forms of newspaper advertising. When such ads are not specified for a specific section, such as the financial section, they are ROP.

Gerber's life insurance division has been running full- and double-page ads offering term policies for many years, and other insurance companies seem to be following suit.

It is more common for continuity and collectible advertisers to use Sunday rotogravure sections, or photo-finishing and magazine circulation offers to appear as free-standing inserts. However, these uses seem to be the exception.

In addition, newspapers are used when the product or service is local, or when a specific newspaper editorial section targets a needed audience.

In direct marketing, schools and seminars advertise in newspapers to build enrollments for their classes. In such advertising, location and starting date should be prominently featured, as in "Fayetteville Classes Start October 1." This makes the ad a news item in itself, with its own elements of localness, immediacy, and newsiness. In effect, this adapts the ad style to the media environment.

Many advertisers use newspapers to tie in with local dealers, particularly where the product must be sold through a dealer. This is not strictly a direct marketing application but more of a sales promotion scheme, although direct marketing agencies work with such projects frequently.

The most effective use of local newspapers by national direct marketers appears to involve "reader notice" advertising, where 50- or 100-line ads are designed to resemble newspaper items. (There are 14 agate lines to an inch; this is a standard way of expressing newspaper sizes. A 100-line ad can be 100×1 or 50×2, the second figure indicating the number of columns.)

Successful newspaper "reader notice" ads include many self-improvement subjects, in areas such as memory, vocabulary, and conversation.

An interesting application was Bradford Exchange's schedule of advertisements, with testimonial headlines like "Claremont woman buys dish in garage sale for $1—worth $1100."

Newspaper advertising rates are covered in a *Newspaper SRDS* that is very similar to the one previously described for magazines. Newspapers are listed by market area, with rates generally expressed in agate lines. Most newspaper advertising is sold ROP. Your ad can be placed anywhere. Specific classifications or sections of the paper, such as "Food Editorial," "Main News Section," "Sports Section," "Financial Pages," and "Business News" usually have a separate higher rate or require a position surcharge. There are also surcharges for specific positions such as "top of column."

Newspaper positions can and should be negotiated in the same manner as magazine positions. A prominent, far-forward or top-of-page position is often worth any extra surcharge. In buying newspaper ads, caution should be taken before automatically placing advertisements in "appropriate" classifications. The education section often is not the best place for a school ad, just as the stamp and coin page would not be the best place for an ad selling coins to investors—especially if you were seeking to bring new people into the market.

Both placement (location in the newspaper) and position (location on the page) should always be tested.

Sunday Supplements

The two principal newspaper supplements, *Parade* and *USA Weekend,* together deliver over 317 million households in 497 newspapers. This is a big medium, and one that is often used by direct marketers.

Sunday supplements are published on a large scale, usually in a magazine format, sometimes as comics. They are distributed in newspapers around the country. The larger ones can be broken down into regions or "target groups." Because Sunday supplements usually are printed on calendered stock, the four-color reproduction rivals that offered by magazines.

Back covers are particularly effective, but hard to get. National advertisers such as Doubleday and CBS have tied up many of them, and they arc also sought eagerly by cigarette and other general advertisers. Some of the national supplements are shown in Table 6-1.

In addition there are excellent individual magazines published by newspapers in many large cities. The magazine sections of the *New York*

TABLE 6-1

Supplement	No. of Papers	Circulation
USA Weekend	397	17,882,430
Metro-Puck Comics	247	46,080,572
Parade	351	35,115,831
Sunday	28	16,260,352

Times, New York News, Chicago Tribune, and *Los Angeles Times* are excellent editorial vehicles and have been successful for a wide variety of direct marketing advertising. Some specialized publications, such as the *Los Angeles Times Home Section* and the *New York Times Book Review,* are recognized as important media in their own right.

Sunday supplements have a very different readership pattern from newspapers in general. The supplement is likely to be treated as a magazine and kept around the house for several days until it can be read leisurely.

Consequently, many ads work in supplements that do not work in newspapers. Small-space shopping-section ads often do well, as do major units. Many advertisers place half- and full-page ads on a standby or remnant basis. In return for a substantially reduced rate, they accept date flexibility or editions left over from other advertisers' regional buys.

Newspaper Preprints

Sometimes called *free-falls* or *freestanding inserts,* newspaper preprints are the big guns of modern direct marketing. They offer all the impact of the most spectacular magazine or direct mail unit, complete with envelopes, reply cards, or pop-up membership cards, with the saturation effect of Sunday newspaper circulation.

Preprints are exactly what the name implies. The advertising unit is printed by the advertiser, generally in large quantities, and shipped to individual newspapers for insertion with the Sunday paper. It is like a separate "section" of the Sunday paper and most likely tumbles out when the paper is opened, just as a blow-in card falls out of a magazine. The reader has to handle the preprint even if only to throw it away—and if it is handled, it is likely to be looked at.

The range of propositions that work in preprints is truly amazing, from the most general of book club, insurance, or magazine propositions to highly selective invitations for ballet subscriptions or mutual funds.

The cost of preprints is high. Including space costs, printing, and freight, a preprint campaign can cost $50 to $100 per thousand circulation, depending on the format. However, the results are higher still.

Preprints offer the opportunity to use a reply device and to have enough space to tell the entire story and ask for the order. There are booklet formats, gatefold formats, and envelope formats. The choice is so versatile that the medium is sometimes considered closer to direct mail than to print advertising. The main difference is that the newspaper, rather than the post office, delivers the message to the customer.

There is another advantage as well. Many newspapers can permit preprints to be distributed to specific geographic areas within the newspaper market. You can often specify the kind of neighborhoods you need. An investment product might go into higher-income areas only. A home repair or gardening product might be advertised only in suburbs rather than in apartment building areas. A bank or real estate proposition might select only their own trading area rather than have to buy the entire city's circulation.

The Starrett City apartment complex in New York utilized newspaper preprints by concentrating on the most likely target areas. The same budget that had been spread over the whole metropolitan area in routine ads was reallocated to preprints to be disseminated in select neighborhoods. There was no increase in budget, only a redistribution of it. The improvement in cost per response was over 500 percent.

Preprints also are an ideal medium for television support, which is discussed in Chapter 7, Broadcast Media.

BUSINESS MEDIA

The same principles apply to business magazines and business newspapers as to general publications. General business magazines such as *BusinessWeek* and *The Wall Street Journal* can be very responsive; others are not.

There are two basic kinds of business publications. "Horizontal" ones cut across industry lines and address themselves to job titles or management levels, financial officers, engineers, purchasing agents, and marketing specialists. "Vertical" publications such as *Hardware Age* and *Modern Plastics* talk to everyone within a specific industry.

Most specialized magazines do not do well for direct marketing offers, at least not as compared to renting the lists of the same publications and addressing the readers by mail.

However, specialized business publications often are a key to reaching important executives whose opinions influence others. They can also be valuable aids in building a custom prospect list. Consequently, an overall communications campaign should cover this media category even if the campaign cannot be totally justified on the basis of cost per response.

The Wall Street Journal and *BusinessWeek* straddle the fence between being general business publications and business-oriented consumer magazines. They are listed in both editions of *SRDS*. Segmentation is offered for both, and they can be tested by using a regional edition first and projecting what the results would have been on a national basis.

If you do use specialized business publications, I suggest that you ask the publication not to list your product in their "bingo" card—the reply card that the magazine provides to readers so they can easily request information about products. The ease of reply is so great, and the temptation to circle a few more numbers while filling it out so inviting, that such bingo leads have a reputation for very poor quality. This doesn't mean that all the responses are bad; only that the good ones are lost among the curiosity-seekers. This applies to any type of publication, but the cards are much more common in business publications.

Increasingly, business decisions can be made at any level of a corporate structure, and it is important to reach every potential buyer. This requires covering a wide range of media. In the last few years, air express and telephone service marketers have been using television to reach the wide number of people who make day-to-day business purchases in those areas. Such campaigns are fully rounded out, with advertising in both horizontal and vertical business media and with extensive use of direct mail. Today, virtually any medium can be used for business campaigns.

WHAT'S THE BEST SEASON FOR ADVERTISING?

After you pick the right magazines for your direct marketing program, you still have to decide what time of the year would be the best for your advertising campaign. Seasonal influences can cause substantial differences in results.

Many advertisers have tested direct mail seasons and have been able to precisely plot the best times of the year for mailings. However, testing is not as easily done in print advertising. If the same ad runs month after month, a fatigue factor sets in, automatically making the first months look better than the later ones.

However, here's the "state of the art" agreed to by most major advertisers:

1. The best month is January, meaning January magazines with on-sale dates just after Christmas, or January weeklies or newspapers.

2. February and October tie for the number 2 position, about 10 percent behind January.

3. July and September also are acceptable, with only another 10 percent decline behind February and October.

4. March and November are possibilities, especially if you can't find an open date anywhere else. Another 10 percent drop.

5. The second quarter—April, May, and June—is the worst part of the year, along with December and August. Another 10 percent drop, so avoid these months if you can.

To translate these comments into a scale would produce an index like this:

January	100
February	90
March	70
April	60
May	60
June	60
July	80
August	60
September	80
October	90
November	70
December	60

Theories about why certain months do better than others are plentiful. Prevalent is the "change-of-season" theory, which says the second quarter is when people are looking forward to summer, and October is when they are finally "back to work" in the new fall season. Everyone agrees on the reason for January—another "back-to-work" feeling after the hectic Christmas season, plus a sense of affluence from Christmas bonuses and the feeling that the New Year is the time to start new projects or fulfill newly adopted self-improvement resolutions.

There are many other factors as well. Weather can play a big role in results, particularly in newspaper schedules. Bad weather is good, as people will stay in and read the paper—provided the weather is not so bad that they can't get the paper at all. Good weather is bad, for people may go out on a Sunday drive instead of staying home to read your advertisement. Broadcast is even more sensitive to weather factors. Newspapers are sometimes saved to be read another day, and magazines always are, but usually a missed radio or television announcement is missed forever.

Elections can have an influence. Just after a hotly contested presidential election, about half the country will feel a letdown because their candidate lost, and this can show up in ad results. Before an election, there may be too many interesting items to read in a newspaper. In fact, anything worth reading can depress ad results. A major news event of any kind that's worth reading leaves your prospect less time to look at ads. The Gulf War, California brush fires, and the Missouri River flooding all produced marked reductions in response rates in all media, but particularly in newspapers, television, and news magazines. Fortunately, these are not frequent occurrences.

Now that we've covered the *science* of media planning, let's conclude with a word about the *art*. There's no way to plug in a computer and produce an ideal media schedule. There's still a great need for subjective judgment in evaluating editorial environment, selecting audience targets, and picking the best publication and the best season—particularly when the ones you really want have already been reserved by some other advertiser.

There's still a place for instinct in media buying. The hunch, based on years of experience, is usually too complex to recall and explain, but more often than not, it's right. That's why there is no substitute for professional direct marketing media specialists. Just as a good list broker should be part of any company's team, so should an agency with a top-notch media staff.

7

BROADCAST MEDIA

When the first edition of this book was released, it made news as the first book on direct marketing to recognize that there are other ways to generate responses than direct mail.

Today, I can no longer describe broadcast as a new development in this field. Indeed, today it is fully recognized, widely used, and the subject of entire books devoted to this specialty.

Not only are radio and television advertising logical expansions for successful mail-order or database-building programs, but there are many propositions that work in broadcast that do not work at all in direct mail.

Every medium is unique, with it own strengths and weaknesses, and broadcast is no exception. Nothing else reaches mass audiences so cost-effectively to identify new prospects. Nothing else permits the advertiser to demonstrate, prove, dramatize. And nothing else provides the ability to portray emotion and self-image—the powerful selling tools direct marketing has borrowed from the toolbox of national general advertising.

BROADCAST IS UNIQUE

Radio and television require a very different approach from direct mail or print. On the one hand, they lack a "hard-order" device; there's no card to fill out, and not even a coupon. On the other, they offer incredible impact, coverage, and credibility.

Broadcast is perishable. It can't be torn out and read carefully at a more convenient time. It's now or never.

Broadcast is impatient. You have seconds to tell your whole story—to attract attention, offer a benefit, demonstrate your product, and motivate a desired action. Then you still must communicate an address or telephone number in a way that will make it memorable. In broadcast, you have to say it quickly, say it simply, say it effectively—or save your money.

However, the opportunities are fantastic. Broadcast goes into the home and talks to your prospect. It finds a viewer. It doesn't wait for a page to be turned or an envelope opened.

Because it offers sight, sound, and motion, broadcast communicates 100 percent, not 10 percent. The body language and tone of voice that must be simulated in copy style and graphics in other media are available to support your message with appropriate degrees of sincerity, enthusiasm, conviction, or urgency.

Broadcast has credibility. In focus panel research, the most often repeated objection to buying by mail order is the wish to see the product. On television it can be seen from every angle. Consumers can see it working. They can see what it does, what makes it tick, and how to operate it. Television is the ultimate illustration, and it does its work at the lowest cost per thousand of any medium.

TWO KINDS OF BROADCAST

Basically, there are two different kinds of broadcast direct marketing—and I don't mean radio and television. There is another, more fundamental dichotomy: the one between *direct response* and *direct support*. They are as different as night and day. They require different formats, different copy treatments, different media strategies. And they have entirely different purposes.

Direct response applies to advertising designed to produce an immediate inquiry, order, or donation. By definition, it must offer an address and/or a telephone number. By necessity, it must be lengthy enough to accomplish several creative objectives—usually 60 or 120 seconds in length, compared to the 30-second ads most used by conventional advertisers.

Direct support, on the other hand, is exactly the opposite. It needs no address or telephone number. It can be effective in very short units, even 10 or 30 seconds. It is bought in the same way, and usually at the same rates, as conventional advertising commercials.

The purpose of direct support is not to get inquiries or orders but to increase the effectiveness of other media. I've called direct support a *media extender,* the "Hamburger Helper" of direct marketing. It is always used in conjunction with direct mail or print campaigns that would still be effective without broadcast. It makes a good medium larger, not necessarily better.

DIRECT-RESPONSE BROADCAST

Direct-response broadcast is not for every product. It requires products or services that either appeal to very general audiences or to audiences segmentable by program adjacencies. A kitchen knife or a set of pots may work because everyone who cooks is a prospect for it.

A set of books on World War II may work best when it is adjacent to a war movie, a violent sports program, or another form of violence—in some cities, the local news. Although detailed programming usually is not available in quantity, special-interest propositions can still be very successful on general programming, provided the allowable margin is adequate.

The "old" rules of direct-response television dictated formats and placements that made this medium successful only for mass-market products. In recent years, new media buyers have been able to use sophisticated general-agency analysis methods to make direct-response broadcast effective for investments, fine arts publications, intellectual magazines, business products and services, insurance, and the entire range of upscale direct marketing propositions.

Television stations use "dayparts" as newspapers use different editorial sections. Daytime shows often are soap operas and game shows appealing to homemakers, who are responsive to offers of household products. News and sports shows deliver predominantly male viewers. Tennis and golf deliver smaller but more upscale audiences than baseball or boxing. Children's shows and family-appeal movies attract their own unique audiences. Usually selectivity in direct response is limited mostly by the daypart that is available.

Radio stations have adopted single-format programming. Each station generally has a reputation for a type of news or music, rather than the original concept of balanced programming with a little of everything. Rock stations reach teenagers, easy-listening stations find older adults, country and western selects blue-collar workers, and news programs reach more general audiences. In radio you reach specific audiences by selecting the station that aims at your audience.

It is sometimes possible to reach specific audiences on radio by sponsoring a specific show, such as farm or stock news, if the programming is relevant to your product.

As in all other direct-response media, the medium is the market, and your offer will be successful in broadcast only if the market is the right one for your product.

Direct-Response Offers

Just as different propositions do well on broadcast rather than in print or direct mail, so do different offers. If your conventional offer requires a great deal of explanation or legal copy, it won't fit on a radio or television spot. If it requires a signed agreement, you won't have a form to give out. If you usually give people a choice of 50 records or 15 sizes and colors, it will be too complicated.

Credit quality is another problem. If your offer involves a free magazine or other premium, the percentage of people taking the gift and electing not to buy or pay for the rest of the offer will usually be greater than with any other medium. Broadcast, as the name itself indicates, casts a broad net over a wide variety of people and personalities. It will pull in the deadbeats along with the good customers, unless your offer is designed to be selective. Fortunately, there are many ways to do so.

More often than not, successful offers in print or direct mail have to be changed in order to be successful in radio or television. Choices have to be eliminated or reduced. Credit has to be simplified. Offers have to be attractive and easy to understand. Here are some examples:

- A magazine that generally sells a full-year subscription in print media offers a short-term introductory offer on television.

- A book club that usually offers a wide choice of gift books for new members offers a preselected library.

- An appliance usually sold "off the page" is featured in a two-step offer, offering a free information kit.

- Another special-interest club offers a single book at a nominal price— a straight deal that does not require explanation or legal copy. The buyers then are converted with a letter that suggests they "tear up the bill" and take the book free as part of a standard club offer, which is explained in full in the letter.

- A major catalog merchandiser, who usually sells only on a prepaid basis, makes an exception and accepts credit card orders on television in order to get qualified prospects.

- An insurance company offers low-cost term life policies, qualified during the phone call, and achieves greater profitability and volume than direct mail. For another type of policy, this same insurer offers information and price quotes to be given to their agents as highly qualified leads.

- A collectible manufacturer sells coins related to a current event, and generates hundreds of thousands of new customers.

Integrated Advertising Offers

Today's growing trend to integrating all forms of advertising to achieve marketing goals has fostered some dramatically effective uses of direct-response broadcast.

While most advertising budgets have traditionally allocated funds between different marketing disciplines—advertising, public relations, sales promotion, direct marketing—the modern approach is to define objectives and allocate funds to achieve them according to which tools turn out to be the most effective. That's one of the reasons why some advertising agencies, including the one I'm working for now, include all disciplines in their planning and services without favoring one over another.

The result has been the evolution of techniques that use media to achieve short- and long-range goals simultaneously. Applied to broadcast, this often results in advertising that gets leads for immediate sales and builds brand equity at the same time. Or that offers further information or free samples as a by-product of budgets originally devoted exclusively to image building.

One sees offers like this now for a wide variety of products—phone services, computers, travel destinations, automobiles, and packaged goods. And it works. In effect, they use broadcast to build awareness and at the same time identify prospects meriting further communication or sales contact. As this aspect of database marketing increases as part of direct marketing, the use of broadcast also becomes more important.

Preemptible Time-Buying

In its early days, direct-response media-buying required a kind of guerrilla media operation. While general agencies massaged audience figures and paid card rates, direct-response agencies wheeled and dealed for good buys. "Who you know" was a more important credential than "what you know."

The best buys went to advertisers and agencies that could pay cash, had good credit, and had "clout," or whose buyer had a personal relationship with a station time-buyer. In those good old days, station representatives seldom got involved in direct response, and most buying was conducted by phone directly with executives at the station.

Today, all that has changed. While some entrepreneurs still do business the old way, more sophisticated practitioners have made direct-response buying much more of a science. For one thing, getting the lowest rate is often not as important as achieving clearance goals. Run-of-station frequency has been replaced by pressure to reach those dayparts that deliver the specific audience type most likely to be profitable.

Even cable stations, once dominated by direct-response advertisers, have been fully discovered by all types of general advertisers. The result has been both an increase in rates and a decrease in availability. While the number of cable stations keeps increasing, those that have proven to be the most profitable are in great demand.

In addition, numbers influence decisions today more than "connections" or personal experience. Ogilvy Direct has perfected its STAR system, which correlates past results from a wide variety of advertisers so as to forecast probable results for new advertisers. Bozell Direct has input rates and demographics for 2400 dayparts on 300 stations, to generate its "Audience Affinity Analysis"—a ranking by cost per thousand for any demographic characteristic. These are just a few of the systems now in use, each custom-developed for advertisers and agencies that recognize the need for a scientific basis for direct-response media selection.

While the approaches have changed, the basic theories and goals have not. For one thing, most direct-response propositions cannot afford the same rate cards paid by general advertisers, or even the discounts often negotiated for them. Typically, our clients can afford only 25 to 33 percent of the general rates. Most stations are willing to accommodate this need by offering preemptible availabilities.

The trade-off in preemptible availabilities is that the station will give you a very low rate providing they can use your spot as a standby for unsold time. Time is a perishable commodity for stations. Magazines can cut back on the number of pages, but not on commercial broadcast seconds, which will never exist again.

Advertising agencies often cultivate personal relationships with station managers. Media buyers are assigned to groups of stations and keep in touch with them every week, putting together mutually advantageous deals. Buyers visit the stations and attend conventions of station managers to reinforce these contacts.

Officially, the deals often are for run-of-the-station spots, with dayparts requested but seldom guaranteed. Unofficially not only dayparts but even particular adjacencies are often verbally agreed upon.

The catch is that they are always preemptible. If a general advertiser comes along and offers full rate, the direct-response spot is moved to another time slot or bumped altogether. During busy seasons it is necessary to order 20 or 50 percent more time than is really needed in order to buy the desired coverage.

The personal contact between media buyer and station manager continues after the spots are run. Each week, and sometimes on a daily basis, the buyer checks the results and calculates the cost per order. The commercials are continued as long as the order cost is satisfactory. If the response is inadequate, the buyer "pulls" the schedule. Sometimes an effective buyer can get a marginal station to throw in "bonus spots," in order to bring the station to a profitable level so the campaign can continue. These are de facto result guarantees when arranged in advance.

The bottom line is the only consideration. The media buyer must have the responsibility and authority to spend a given budget as effectively as possible, in any stations in that buyer's area of responsibility. Neither the client nor the account group can be consulted on every decision. The buyers must make decisions on the spot, while talking on the phone, to revise schedules or pull them.

Contemporary Media-Buying Techniques

The object of the time-buying activity described in the previous section used to be getting the most gross rating points (GRPs) for your money. Gross rating points are the sum of the percentage of homes viewing the group, or "flight," of commercials in a given market. Ten spots with a 7 percent AA (average audience) have 70 GRPs. This is sometimes expressed as

$$GRP = R \times F$$

where R is reach (the average audience coverage, expressed as a percentage) and F is frequency (the number of times the commercial is aired).

GRPs are the currency, so to speak, of the broadcast industry. Just as circulation is what magazines have to sell, GRPs are what stations have to sell. (The equivalent magazine formula to the one for GRPs is circulation times frequency is equal to impressions.)

Until recently, getting the most GRPs was the simple goal of some of the best-known agencies and media-buying organizations, and the results of using this method led to the conclusion that only downscale, low-priced mass market products could be sold by direct-response television. But the science of direct-response television has advanced significantly in the last few years. Newer approaches treat direct-response broadcast in much the same manner as the direct marketing discipline treats other media: with emphasis on targeting the prospects.

In all fairness, I should point out that state-of-the-art time buying is not the only key to making direct-response campaigns work for such a broad array of products.

Another has to do with creativity—and with the station owner. The station owner, an often forgotten factor in the media equation, is sensitive to the opinions of viewers and, understandably, to the opinions of other advertisers. Direct-response commercials with music, entertainment value, believable announcers, credible situations—all the tools of general advertising—get placed on better time spots and program adjacencies than the old-fashioned direct-response commercials that come on to the audience with phony enthusiasm.

Working people who watch the news, and families watching better-quality programs, are, not surprisingly, better customers for more products and services than the insomniacs and soap opera buffs who comprised the old direct-response audience.

I do not mean to say that there was, or is, anything wrong with the original system. It still works for sets of records and offers of pots and pans, as it always has. But those who have defended it as the *only* way to go have been proved wrong. It is right for some kinds of products, not for others. Modern time-buying methods, combined with creative techniques that result in commercials that don't insult the viewer's intelligence, are a viable, proven alternative—one that has opened television up to a wider range of advertisers than ever before.

Commercial Length

How long should a direct-response commercial be? The industry started with sponsored 15-minute programs, which were whittled down to 5 minutes, then 2 minutes. When I wrote the previous edition of this book, the unchallenged consensus of the field was that the direct-response commercial should be 120 seconds.

Today, the answer to the question of length, like everything else in the business world, is more complex. It depends—on a number of factors. It has been demonstrated that 60-second commercials outpull 120's on a cost-per-response basis, and on a quality basis, for some products, not for all products. There are now indications that 30's may be workable for some propositions. In the case of infomercials, many have achieved enormous success by going full circle to 30-minute and even one-hour sponsored advertising programs. There are several considerations:

- *What do you need to get the story across?* Some propositions can be expressed only in a 120. On the other hand, successful continuity offers have been done, complete with all required legal copy, in a 60. And they worked.

- *How narrow are the placement opportunities?* If the proposition is a general one that can work on almost any kind of station, in any day-part, length may not matter. But if the audience is a narrow, highly specialized one, the 60-second format will give you more flexibility and access to better program adjacencies.

- *Can you hold the viewer's interest?* Some messages actually come out better in a shorter format, and there is less risk of boring or antagonizing the viewer. This is especially true if the commercial is part of a high-frequency market-saturation effort. For clients such as Mutual of Omaha, I have placed as many as 20 spots a week in some markets to meet lead acquisition goals. This high a level of activity could never be sustained with long, drawn-out 120 formats. Musical themes, or a variety of interesting situations in rotation, lend themselves better to a 60-second format.

- *How complex is the proposition?* Sometimes the nature of the offer is such that 60 seconds is not enough. Repeated phone numbers, a special trial offer, credit card availability, a premium for fast action—all together, these can require up to 20 or 30 seconds in addition to the time needed for the basic message. Then you may have no choice but to use a 120.

- *What works best?* The ultimate question is always, "Which length produces the lowest cost per response?" This applies to broadcast media, as it does to any medium. Where possible, my preference is to produce both a 60 and a 120, try both, and see which works best. In many cases the two can be produced during the same "shoot" at little additional cost.

Setting Up a Broadcast Schedule

As little as $100,000 can get an initial reading on the possibility of broadcast direct response for a direct marketing proposition. This includes not only the cost of the time purchased but also the production of the commercial and a fee for professional marketing and creative counsel.

The choice of cities and stations should be made on the same basis. A new-offer viability test is not the place to experiment or succumb to "deals" offered by untried stations. It should be placed with tried and proven stations that have worked well for other direct marketing propositions. Dayparts and adjacencies are a different matter. There can be very dramatic differences in response by daypart, including weekday versus weekend, and testing several dayparts within the selected stations will be necessary.

Awareness of television builds, and a two- or three-week flight is necessary in order to read the potential of the station. Unlike direct mail and print, there is no statistical curve by which you can forecast early results. The building of response rates is erratic, but once it reaches the full response level it usually holds at that level as the flight is extended for several more weeks. After a while a noticeable downward curve develops, and the spots are continued only as long as they are still profitable.

Three-week flights generally are scheduled, with the third week pulled on stations where initial results are disappointing. The buyers then transfer that money to other stations so as to reach fresh audiences. Usually the client agrees to keep providing additional advertising funds as long as the CPR is holding up.

A typical campaign in a medium-size market might build like this:

Week	1	2	3	4	5	6	7	8	9
Responses	110	190	270	390	410	380	400	270	130

If 250 orders per week were needed to make the station pay, it would have been a mistake to pull the campaign after only two weeks. This is the most common error made by companies using broadcast media for the first time. They pull out too soon and draw the sweeping conclusion, "Broadcast doesn't work."

In the example above, the campaign should have been pulled at the end of week 8, demonstrating the need for prompt result reporting and continuous decision making. Once pulled, the proposition can be taken to other markets or "rested" for a year or so.

As test results come in, daypart selection should be adjusted and adjacencies revised. Weak cities are dropped. Trends are identified for the successful stations, dayparts, and adjacencies. A pattern soon emerges for the best size of city, type of programming, and relationships to other direct marketing results. An index is established, based on cost-per-thousand target audience, to guide future negotiations. When the first results come in, the schedule can build rapidly as fast as cashflow permits, and a modest test schedule can become a $1-million-a-month campaign in a matter of weeks.

In direct-response broadcast, one typical error seems to come up frequently: imposing personal taste on scheduling. It happens that the top-rated or most intellectual shows often are not the best place for direct-response broadcast. We cannot sneer at schedules that include reruns and old movies, because such schedules often are exactly what works best.

Response Options

Every direct marketing message ends with a request for some type of action. But what kind of action do we ask for on radio and television? There are currently only two choices: mail and telephone.

Eventually, there will also be a significant number of viewers who will be able to respond by simply pressing a button on a remote control.

Mail is desirable when you're trying to screen out unqualified respondents or asking for a token payment to ensure quality. Also, older people are more likely to respond by mail. If you use mail, you may have to prepare a slide for each station, including the product name, the address, the price, and a key number. The station will add this at the end of your commercial. If the address or U.S. Postal Service box number is complicated, the chance of errors is increased. Usually you'll also have to reveal the actual name of the sponsoring company and state some type of guarantee, in order to satisfy station requirements. Slides with key codes are necessary, because mail responses come in slowly and would otherwise be difficult to track against particular stations or dayparts.

Many such companies use Postal Service box numbers, but I feel that they should be avoided unless the sponsoring company is well known. Boxes have a suggestion of impermanence and don't inspire consumer confidence. I'd rather include a real address, where people can walk in if they have a mind to, even if that address is a bit more complicated.

Telephone response has become the prevalent reply device of mass direct marketers. Despite some problems, telephone numbers now are used with the great majority of direct marketing commercials.

The greatest problem is the busy signal customers get when hundreds call the same number immediately after a commercial has run. The impulse factor vanishes quickly, especially if the program gets exciting and lures your customers back to the television set. Jammed telephone lines are a major problem, and the most important consideration in setting up a means to handle telephone orders or inquiries.

A more detailed discussion of inbound telemarketing appears at the end of Chapter 8, Telemarketing.

INFOMERCIALS

In recent years the infomercial, or "long-form" commercial, has become one of the most exciting developments in broadcast media, not only for direct-response advertisers but for many general advertisers who have become fascinated with its unique ability to explain and convince.

Over the last few years, well-done infomercials have built multimillion-dollar businesses for products such as Victoria Jackson's cosmetics, or for purveyors of get-rich-quick training in real estate, sales, used cars, or even mail order itself. Organizations such as Synchronal and TMI created omnibus formats such as *Amazing Discoveries,* which enabled them to sell enormous volumes of different products in a program format.

Whereas it took 20 years for general advertisers to recognize and respect the applications of direct marketing in general, it took no time at all for all kinds of general advertisers to rush into infomercials. Automobile manufacturers, investment counselors, record producers, and many others have rushed into the category. Companies like Braun, Singer, and Nordic Track have sold tens of thousands of appliances directly to the public, while at the same time increasing demand at retail. The result has accelerated both the opportunities and the problems in this field.

Opportunities

The chief opportunity is the upgrading of the quality of infomercials. Just as with short-form spots, advertisers have found that quality counts. Infomercials with talented actors, unique story concepts, and genuinely interesting formats have proliferated, building the public's confidence in the format itself. This has also opened up previously unavailable dayparts on important cable stations and major-market local stations.

I have been told that infomercial respondents are very different from respondents to other direct-response media. For one thing, they don't respond to direct mail, as they are products of the television generation and have little patience for, or responsiveness to, the written word. Supposedly, only telemarketing has been effective for follow-up offers. As a result, names of infomercial buyers seldom are effective for direct mail use by others, and they do not command a premium price in the list rental market.

Problems

The problem is that all this has limited the inventory of effective dayparts. Sure, it's possible to buy half-hour segments if you're Ross Perot and price is no object. But experience shows that, as in all direct marketing, the final determination of success depends on cost per response, and that in turn is very dependent on cost per thousand audience. In the rush to use this media tool, it is too often overlooked that most infomercials haven't worked, and that most individual long-form media options haven't worked. Certain cable stations, and certain dayparts on spot stations, have been priced at a point where they can be successful. Most others are not.

To complicate the process, the best buys often have been sewn up by those advertisers who have a variety of infomercials for different products, and who can book blocks of time on a seasonal or year-round basis. Some companies even are considering running their own channels, using new cable and satellite options, in order to find more time to place their messages on the air.

In the long run, the infomercial phenomenon presages a possible return to the beginnings of broadcast, where advertisers produced and sponsored their own shows. Avon, for instance, introduces products such as their perfume collection in this format, without soliciting orders or inquiries. As opposed to sponsoring network or station-produced shows, the sponsor creates an editorial environment that reflects positively on the advertiser. Who hasn't heard of *The Hallmark Hall of Fame,* the Texaco orchestral presentations, *The Chrysler Showcase?*

This option is open to companies large and small, national and local. Imagine how effectively a restaurant might put together a cooking show highlighting its unique dishes, or a boutique conduct its own televised fashion show, or even the local hardware store put on a home-improvement show. The opportunities are limitless.

Creative Considerations

Today, infomercials are a true subdivision of direct response, and despite everything, are still subject to all of its methods and mystiques. In fact, most failures are due to the same problems confronted by those general advertisers who use direct mail without understanding it. Some "put an ad in an envelope" without appropriate involvement and immediacy elements. Others hype their message with gimmicks and trickery that get a good initial response from the least sophisticated members of the audience but fail to build brand equity for the long run.

I predict that Victoria Jackson's infomercials, in which Cher and other celebrities calmly discuss makeup and beauty, will be around much longer than the screaming, butch-haircut spokeswoman on *Stop the Insanity,* selling her approach to weight control. The television format mirrors life itself. Weirdness will get attention, and there's a sucker born every minute for the aptly-named "incredible buys," but in the long run it is civility and common sense that will endure.

They say that most strengths also are weaknesses. The great strength of the infomercial format is its length. Like direct mail, when it is used properly you have the time to tell the whole message: to explain, to demonstrate, to dramatize, to provide endorsements from users and authorities. But length is also the problem. As of now, no one looks up infomercials in their program guide because they want information on a product or service, although eventually I believe they will. In the meantime we have to appeal to what I call "accidental audiences": viewers who fell asleep during one program and woke up to find our spokesperson on the screen, or channel-surfers skipping around during commercials and looking for something interesting to watch.

"Interesting" is the key to the creative process for infomercials. There is some tendency, as in badly done direct mail, to rely on gimmicks or formats. In infomercials I have worked on, I have found it to be no problem to simulate an interview show, or a game format, or other audience participation show. It also is not a big problem to find an appropriate celebrity to endorse a product and act as a spokesperson. However, these are no guarantee that a sufficient audience can be stopped and held long enough to make the sale. As with all advertising, we must respect the AIDA rule: attention, interest, desire, action. To turn interest into a buying decision, the product or service itself has to provide the fascination for the viewer. In my experience, a skilled direct marketing copywriter—accustomed to the long-copy requirements of direct mail—has a better chance of accomplishing this than a slick television scriptwriter.

In the end, direct-response infomercials are not a different kind of commercial message, simply a longer one. The terms *short-form* and *long-form* ultimately refer only to the amount of time being bought.

BROADCAST SUPPORT

Support commercials are closer to general advertising than any other area of direct marketing. As in general advertising, shorter commercial—30- or even 10-second—spots are bought to achieve the most economical combinations of reach and frequency. As in general advertising, the creative theme must be single-purpose, chosen to be easily dramatized and remembered. There is only one action request: Look for this offer in your newspaper or mailbox.

Broadcast support is not a medium in itself, only an adjunct to other media. As such, it always must be planned in terms of its effect on the media it supports.

Probably the best example of this type of advertising is its use by Publishers' Clearing House and its competitors, running during the week their heavy mailings are due to arrive in homes around the country.

In recent years this device has not been used as often as it once was, largely because direct mail has become more effective. Also, it has been found that there is an improvement in response rate simply by coordinating the timing of broadcast commercials, whether image-building or direct response, with the arrival of direct mail. Nevertheless it is a valuable tool, and can be used whether the support is of mail, newspaper inserts, or even door-to-door distribution of samples.

No matter what the use, the principles are the same, and such campaigns always must be planned in terms of their effect on the medium being supported.

When to Use
Broadcast Support

With few exceptions, support does not lower cost per order. What it does do is increase the number of orders that can be obtained from other media.

If a $100,000 preprint insertion ordinarily would produce 20,000 responses at $5 each, the addition of support cannot be counted on to lower the cost to $4. What it can do is increase the number of $5 orders from that insertion, in proportion to its own added cost. If the preprint in this example is supported by a $50,000 television support campaign, the objective should be to garner 30,000 responses from the combined insertion.

In order for such an investment to be effective, the coverage of the supported media within the television market must be substantial. Unless you are deliberately spending out of proportion for testing purposes, a proposed support program must be measured in terms of broadcast support cost per thousand prospects (BSC/M). But what is a prospect in this case? Not every television viewer reached by the station is a prospect, for the commercial is relevant only to people who receive your ad, preprint, or direct mail piece.

If your newspaper preprint reached 250,000 households in a city of 500,000, you would have 50 percent market coverage in that medium. If you supported this with broadcast that produced an average rating of 25 percent, you would be reaching 25 percent of homes using television (HUT).

If the HUT is 80 percent, for example, then 80 percent, ∟r 400,000 homes, are watching TV, and 25 percent of them see your commercial. That's 100,000 homes. Expressed another way, this means a "reach" of 20 percent. This 20 percent reach applied to the 50 percent preprint coverage gives you a "support penetration" of 10 percent. Fifty thousand homes in this market will see both the preprint and the TV commercials supporting it.

Let's say the preprint costs $12,500 and the purchase of 300 GRPs in this market, to give you 20 percent reach, costs $5000. The $5000 is effectively reaching only the 50,000 homes that are getting both. The BSC/M is $100. If the supported preprints cost $50 per thousand, the combined cost is $150 per thousand—200 percent more than the preprints alone. Therefore a 200 percent lift is required—usually an impractical objective for support advertising.

Putting it another way, if the support cost is applied to the total preprint cost, the investment is 250,000 × $50/M or $12,500 for the preprints, plus $5000 for the support. Divide 5000 by 12,500, move the decimal point two places to the right, and you get 40 percent—the overall lift required to make the support investment pay.

This is the way the total campaign will be measured, but the BSC/M method is the best way to test the reasonableness of expecting a particular support investment to achieve a desired lift. A 200 percent lift on the BSC/M method is unreasonable, a conclusion you would not get from the 40 percent overall lift requirement.

We have an entirely different picture if we use direct mail instead of preprints in the same hypothetical market. If direct mail costs $400 per thousand, reaching the same 250,000 households would require $100,000. The same 300 GRPs still cost $5000, and the broadcast reach is still 20 percent, producing a support penetration of 10 percent.

The BSC/M is still $100 for the 50,000 households, but this is now only 25 percent more than the cost of the mailing alone to the supported households, and only a 25 percent lift factor is required. Compare the 200 percent lift required in the previous example. On an overall basis, the $5000 support investment is just 5 percent of the $100,000 mail cost, so only a 5 percent overall lift is required to justify the expenditure. The likelihood of success is much greater here.

One major advertiser buys as many as 3000 GRPs in prime seasons—ten times this example. This advertiser aims for a 50 percent overall lift and usually gets it. Increasing the GRPs, the reach, and subsequently the penetration level is effective, provided there is a sensible relationship to the media being supported.

One rule of thumb is that the mailing or other supported medium must reach one of three homes in a television area for support TV to be cost-effective. Often a combination of media is used to accomplish this. I'm told *Reader's Digest* mails to as much as 50 percent of some markets, combining several product offerings under the same support umbrella.

Theoretically that means that, if we can invest 25 or 50 percent in support dollars instead of 10 percent, we should be able to get 25 or 50 percent more orders. This presumes that the additional support dollars are spent effectively to get increased reach and penetration. But how do we know if we are spending it effectively?

Support Media Buying

As indicated in the previous section, all support schedules must be in relation to the media being supported. The more media that can be concentrated under one support umbrella, the more effective the support program will be.

One advertiser uses a common sweepstakes to send out various product offerings to different people in the same market and thus widen the coverage. This enables the support program to cover all the products by referring to the sweepstakes instead of the product. I have proposed similar tactics for multiple-product book club groups, using a copy theme or response device as a common supportable theme.

The examples given here had a penetration factor (supported media coverage times support media reach) of no more than 10 percent. A good media buyer should be able to achieve between a 30 percent and a 50 percent penetration factor by making a comparable investment in the support media. Some advertisers believe this is a minimum range for support to be worthwhile.

The budget for support is developed by working backward from the media coverage and expenditure, and calculating how much penetration is available in various TV markets for a given level of expenditure.

Let's say a market has $75,000 in all supported media, and a decision has been made to aim for a 33 percent lift for a comparable expenditure. The media buyer then determines what can be bought for 33 percent of the $75,000, or $25,000.

The budgeted sum then is spread over a variety of targeted dayparts in a very precise pattern over a period of three days adjoining the expected on-sale date of the publication or the date a mailing is expected to be delivered. The objective is to see how many GRPs (gross rating points, obtained by multiplying reach times frequency) can be purchased in the particular market.

Advertisers with access to audience composition forecasts can go a step further, and work with GRPs or TGRPs (target audience gross rating points) to reach a target audience (see the earlier discussion, under Contemporary Media-Buying Techniques). Estimates are prepared indicating the type and number of individual households reached by the number of GRPs obtained, and calculations quickly indicate whether the penetration of target households receiving the supported media is sufficient to justify the expenditure.

In some markets this may not be feasible. In others, it may be relatively simple. No matter which comes first—GRP level, penetration level, or support budget as a percentage cost of media supported—all the factors must interact before final recommendations can be assembled.

In direct response, a campaign can be run a few weeks later or in a different market. But support schedules must be precisely timed. To be effective, the campaign must run as scheduled. This means that at least the foundation of the schedule usually has to be placed at negotiated but nonpreemptible rates. This is closer to 80 percent of the rate card rather than the 20 percent paid for direct-response campaigns.

Direct-response campaigns flourish on marginal programming and midnight movies, but support must produce raw audience counts in the same manner as general advertisers. Thus prime-time dayparts and top-rated shows must be part of the schedule.

One method used increasingly is to set up a minimum schedule, say at the 30 percent budget level, with orders placed at negotiated card rates, and then arrange a campaign in direct-response programming, at 120-second or 60-second length, to supplement the minimum schedule. The full-rate minimum schedule guarantees the required penetration, while the preemptible direct-response schedule adds additional exposure at bargain rates if time is available.

Major advertisers have found that direct-response commercials, while not referring at all to "look in your mailbox" or other support references, do as well as pure support commercials on a dollar-for-dollar basis. Planning this simply requires concentrating a heavy schedule of direct-response commercials just before the mail is expected to arrive.

Another problem involves direct mail support. When a campaign is being supported, it is critical that the mailing arrive on time. This requires close coordination and special arrangements with Postal Service customer representatives. If the mailing is delayed, the support campaign will be delayed too. One of the very largest users of TV support had a major snafu in timing, with their multimillion-dollar support campaign appearing just when a competitor's mailing was arriving instead of theirs. A major management shakeup took place soon afterward.

Does this all sound complicated? It is. It's very time-consuming as well, which is why agencies and time-buying services seldom will handle broadcast campaigns of any kind, support or direct-response, without getting a full commission and sometimes even supplementary fees or incentive arrangements.

RADIO ADVERTISING

In most of the previous sections, television has been the representative example of the various broadcast media. I do not want to overlook radio, which has similar tools, methods, and objectives.

The differences in radio lie in the nature of the medium itself. Radio is not visual, but this is not a handicap for business services or products that the consumer is already familiar with. Radio often is heard outside the home, when it is not convenient to write down a phone number, but this is no problem when the radio message is being used for support purposes or for a service listed in the phone book. An exception is California and other areas where mobile phones are widely used.

One great advantage of radio is the nature of its programming. Whole stations often are devoted to a specific kind of music or to news, bringing the advertiser a very predictable type of listener. And special-interest programs—business news, farm news, ski reports, even advertising news—give us access to specific interests and occupations.

Radio can be particularly effective for business products or services, lending audio impact and immediacy to offers appearing only in business publications and business sections of newspapers. With radio, as with any other medium, creative copy must be tailor-made for radio, taking into account its strengths and limitations. Because radio often is a "background" sound, you must attract listeners' attention and sustain their interest. And because many people don't focus on radio as they do on television, it is often necessary to repeat messages more frequently.

Creative Approaches

Often, radio is an afterthought of a successful television effort—added to a broadcast schedule in an effort to find more outlets for an effective spot. In such a case it is tempting to take the successful television spot and adapt it for radio. However, without visual impact, such messages sometimes are effective, sometimes not. There is no problem with the reasoning to try such a creative approach. The only problem is concluding, if it is not successful, that "radio doesn't work."

As is true of all media, radio has its particular strengths and weaknesses. Its strength is based on its programming consistency. On some stations the listener expects entertainment, and a musical spot or comedy script is often more likely to maintain attention. On others, the listener expects news and commentary. To the extent that the product or offer has news value, such a style is more likely to succeed on such stations.

One minor but important piece of advice: Don't write your spot so tightly that the message must begin at the first fraction of a second. Give listeners a break so that they can differentiate your spot from the previous one. Then get their attention with a "stopper statement" or sound effect. And another suggestion: A whisper is often louder then a shout, as a way of getting attention. As with direct-response broadcast, don't feel you have to shout your message. The sound of sincerity is always more winning than that of forced enthusiasm.

OTHER BROADCAST FACTORS

When testing both direct support and direct response, we often use matched markets—pairs of like markets selected according to station and media characteristics, population demographics, and the client's own experience in the markets. Perhaps six markets are selected, half of them supported and the other half not. Two different commercial treatments or offers also can be tested in this way.

The techniques of support advertising are equally applicable to coupon programs. More general advertisers will probably begin supporting product coupons with television spots saying, "Look for this coupon in your paper." This technique will be a natural application of direct marketing techniques to general advertising.

Sometimes direct marketing broadcast applications are applied to retail marketing. The Eicoff agency, a pioneer in this field, uses the same general theories outlined here to force distribution of mail-order products through retail drug chains and discount houses rather than through mail order. They reportedly have achieved some incredible sales successes for products distributed in this manner.

In the first edition of this book I wrote: "Direct-response television is a multimillion-dollar medium, but it is still in its infancy technologically. It is somewhat like a baby elephant: big, strong, but not yet housebroken."

Part of the problem was that the initial users of this medium were often those with the least regard for the public. In some cases product quality left something to be desired. In others, there was simply contempt for the taste level of the viewing audience.

I went on to say that "'in New Jersey call…' should not be the public's only impression of direct marketing on television. There is room for creativity and imagination, for adding entertainment values that not only attract and hold an audience but also make selling points subtly, memorably, and effectively."

Today, I am delighted to report that as direct-response advertisers have begun to apportion a larger share of their advertising budgets for broadcast, and as their expectations of success have risen, production budgets also have risen to the point where creativity, imagination, and high entertainment value are the rule rather than the exception. Direct-response advertisers are producing both radio and television spots that are as good as anything coming out of the finest general agencies.

Today's direct-response broadcast doesn't just bring in the orders. It adds measurably to the image and reputation of the advertiser and all its products, building credibility and desire that will make all its future advertising more effective, no matter what medium is being used.

TELEMARKETING

There is nothing new about using the telephone as an advertising medium. The "boiler room" filled with telephones has been a sales institution as far back as anyone can remember. Insurance agents have called newlyweds, compiling their lists from the wedding announcements in the local newspaper. Stockbrokers have called newly promoted executives, scanning trade papers for names of prospects. The most aggressive users of all have been politicians, whose paid and volunteer workers canvass voters, raise funds, and get supporters to the polls on election day.

Today telemarketing is big business in itself. Its techniques have become more efficient. In many cases it is a substitute for other direct marketing efforts, in others it is a supplement. Many companies, large and small, build their own telemarketing capabilities; others use one or more of the telemarketing firms that, like co-op mail, serve the needs of many companies more cost-effectively than they could individually.

ATTRIBUTES OF TELEPHONE SELLING

Like direct mail, telephone selling is highly selective. Like direct mail, it is expensive, even with WATS lines and independent long-distance networks, and its high cost is only justified by utilizing maximum selectivity. Like broadcast, it reaches out to its customer with ultimate immediacy and ultimate ease of responding.

All the customer has to do to get the entire message is not hang up. A muttered "Okay" will replace filling out a coupon, finding a stamp, and going out to the mailbox. A recited charge-card number will prepay the order.

However, unlike all other media, the telephone call is involuntary for the prospective customer, who cannot simply turn the page, look away from the TV set, or toss a letter into a wastepaper basket. Prospects are contacted—one-on-one with another human being—in their own home, at a time when they might have been enjoying a nap or eating dinner. The prospect gets out of a chair or bed and walks over to the telephone, where a commercial message is the last thing expected. Once in conversation, most people feel an obligation to be courteous. Few people just hang up.

The power to capture and hold the attention of the prospect is the strength of telephoning—and its weakness as well. Nothing will irritate a consumer quite as much as a poorly timed, poorly conceived, or poorly executed telephone call. Nothing will terminate a long-term customer or donor relationship quite as quickly, or generate as angry a letter to a congressional representative.

For this reason, the telephone must be used with caution and with good taste. Late calls should be avoided, as well as Sunday calls, with particular attention to local custom. Farmers should not be called after nine o'clock in the evening, as they retire early so they can attend to farm chores in the morning. Jews and Seventh Day Adventists, if their religious affiliations are known, should not be called on Saturday. Business people should not be called early in the morning when they are scrambling to leave for work, nor should they be bothered at the office about personal matters. Maintaining the goodwill of the consumer is the responsibility of everyone in direct marketing who uses the telephone.

USES OF THE TELEPHONE

The best uses of this medium involve preexisting relationships. A phone call from a company to its customers may be positioned and perceived as a service. The same call to a stranger may be an intrusion. Though there have been very successful mass telephone campaigns (Ford Motor Company once made 20 million phone calls to produce leads for automobile salesmen), I recommend utilizing this medium with caution except where there is some prior relationship. Also, because of its cost, it generally should be used only after less expensive media, such as direct mail, have been utilized. In fact, the combination of direct mail followed by telephone may be the most profitable way to use this medium.

Service Calls

"To approve your credit application." "Your order has been delayed." "The color you wanted isn't available, may we substitute another?" (Note that delayed orders must still be confirmed in writing as well, according to FTC procedures which, for some reason unknown to anyone in business, do not recognize this superior form of customer communication.)

Trading Up and Cross Selling

"We have your order, but wanted to let you know it's now available in a deluxe format." "There's a new accessory for your...we thought you'd like to know about." "We're having a special sale, three for...and thought you might like to increase your order." "The item you bought once is now on sale, and we thought you might like to purchase another at this low price." "We're having a private sale for our credit card customers. We wanted to give our present customers first chance to..." "If you're happy with the present service you buy from us, we invite you to try another...."

Direct Mail Follow-Up

"We haven't received your reservation yet for our hummingbird collector's plate, and before we close out the edition..." "We have been saving a place in the next excursion bus to our resort development for you, and before we release it...." "There is still time to take advantage of the introductory offer we wrote you about..."

Business Contacts

Personal sales calls are costing over $500 each, according to a McGraw-Hill survey. Telephone contacts may cost about $5, and produce fast and substantial results. Purposes can range from sales calls positioned as restocking to old-fashioned collection calls. Help is available in the form of "phone power" training courses and brochures from most telephone companies, or there are companies that will train your staff for you.

"Summer is coming, and you might want to check your stock on our..." "We've had reports that our...is selling out, and we wanted to see if you need more." "Our ad campaign is about to break, and we thought you might need some of our..." "We know you like to be among the first to stock new items, and so I wanted to tell you about..." Calls to dealers, sales agents, and franchises are the most effective way of exchanging information—getting it out fast and getting a fast reply. Sometimes a simple, "I'm not calling to sell you anything, just to thank you for last year's business" can be one of the best long-range investments a company can make.

Renewals and Reactivation

Telephone selling is uniformly recommended as part of a magazine's renewal series. After a series of letters has gone out, another label is generated and sent to a telephone center rather than a mailing house. "Your subscription is expiring, and we wanted to give you a last chance to..." Reactivation of inactive customers is another use: "We've enjoyed having you as a customer, and wonder why you haven't bought from our catalog lately."

"Immediacy" Situations

The telephone offers a very believable sense of immediacy, and fits well with efforts such as these: "Have you read about the plight of the children in Thailand? Well, we're raising a special fund to help, and we thought you, as one of our past donors..." "The election looks very close, and if we can just raise another $100 from each contributor for a last-minute TV campaign..." "We only have a limited supply of this product, and wanted to give you a chance to place your order..." "The price is about to go up, but if you get your order in now..."

Prospecting

In both consumer and business selling, telephone lead solicitation is a widespread application that has proved very effective. In some cases the telephone is used to ask for the order, usually for a low-unit sale—newspaper or milk delivery, a magazine subscription, or a trial examination of the first volume in a set of books.

Another common telephone use is *bird-dogging*. The term refers to hound dogs trained to "point" at birds or game. Cold-canvass field salespeople used to have trainees set up their appointments for visits later in the evening, and the trainees were called "bird dogs." Today the term applies to telephone lead prospecting.

The end product of a bird-dogging call is not a sale but an appointment. The mailing list uses every appropriate type of list selection, as described in Chapter 5, Mailing Lists. The offer can be any of the lead-generating approaches described in Chapter 4, Propositions. The caller can offer information, a free booklet, a valuable gift, a discount—anything that proves to be effective.

Insurance salesmen now offer financial planning. Encyclopedia salesmen offer booklets. Real estate agents call owners of desirable homes and offer free appraisals or tell of a buyer who has expressed interest in their home. Coincidentally, the same offers that work on broadcast are likely to work over the telephone.

ECONOMICS OF THE TELEPHONE

The telephone is a direct marketing medium in that its cost can be measured in relation to its results. The concepts of CPR (cost per response), conversion rates, and allowable margin, as well as every aspect of mail-order math, apply in exactly the same way.

If you deal with one of the established suppliers of telephone contact services, you will know your costs exactly. They can give you an all-inclusive estimate based on your own particular needs and taking advantage of their own established systems, telephone automation, and trained personnel.

If you plan your own telephone campaign, you will have to anticipate a variety of costs, including

- Renting and processing of mailing lists
- Phone number acquisition, from a list supplier or by looking up numbers in the telephone book
- Telephone operator costs, including time, overhead, supervision, and any incentive bonuses
- Phone company equipment and toll charges
- Management, creative preparation, forms, scripts, operator training, meetings, and results analysis

In determining costs, a great deal will depend on the selectivity of the list, the percentage of valid telephone numbers that can be obtained, and the efficiency of the telephone operators. The operators must be trained to dial quickly, terminate unproductive conversations, and stick to a proven script.

Telephone number look-up costs are an important consideration. Few mailing lists are available with the numbers already provided, and those that are charge extra. For most mailing lists you'll have to rent your list from one source and then have the numbers provided by another. Metromail and Army Times have a service that computer-matches phone numbers to lists with an average 60 percent match-up rate. Additional names then can be obtained from other look-up services at a cost between 7 and 10 cents a name.

Wide Area Telephone Service (WATS) is most efficient when calls are made in rapid sequence, with little downtime. Some large telephone services maintain computer switchboards that automatically select the most economical calling route, depending on time of day, utilization of phone lines, and other factors. Electronic dialing systems dial prospect lists automatically, connecting operators only to numbers where the party is at home and answers. A skilled operator need not waste time dialing or waiting for an answer.

As a general rule of thumb, telephone responsiveness can average ten times that of direct mail—as high as 25 or 35 percent of all calls made. This, of course, is for a successful campaign. At the same time the cost of making calls (depending on the length of the call, the distance, and the cost of lists, among other things) can average between $2 and $5 a call. Considering the cost of small-quantity direct mail, this is usually less than ten times direct-mail cost, and the cost efficiencies become obvious. However, as always, there is no such thing as an "average" proposition. Yours will do better or worse depending on its applicability to telephone selling. This medium, like any medium, requires its own evaluation.

THE TELEPHONE SCRIPT

The presentation of a telephone message has become a unique and highly creative art form. The script must never be clever, tricky, or gimmicky, for it must sound sincere and courteous. This is no place for dramatics.

A phone message generally begins with a simple introduction, including the name of the caller and the company being represented, followed by a request for or confirmation of the identity of the person called. The next statement is a qualifier or screener—giving enough information to get a reaction as to whether this call is worth continuing.

There has to be room for the person to respond if the call is not going to sound like a one-sided lecture. Once the qualification response has been obtained, the basic message is delivered.

The script is not simple. Depending on answers at various points in the conversation, the script must provide for various alternate messages. In some cases, it moves to "Thanks anyway. Good-bye." In other situations, it asks other questions or provides more information. Questions have to be answered and objections overcome. The operator cannot improvise; everything has to be provided for in the script. The late Murray Roman, recognized as the pioneer of large-scale outbound telemarketing, had great success with one technique that still has merit. Operators would tell the party being called that they had a brief message from a celebrity—perhaps a TV star or political office-holder. Once they had the permission of the party called, they would play a recorded message, perhaps an appeal to vote or contribute to a cause. The operator would then return to make the appeal or present an offer.

The following is an example of a classic type of telephone script—a style that was in use 10 years ago and that was very effective at the time. The purpose of the script was to ask Consumers Union subscribers for contributions. The call format included the fund-raising appeal in a concise, logical, warm, person-to-person interaction, and detailed truthful responses to questions and objections. Several fund-raising strategies were tested, and the one finally chosen included a $35 donation request, with an appropriate drop to $25 and then a further step-down to $10.

CONSUMERS UNION FOUNDATION FUNDRAISING COMMUNICATOR SCRIPT ©CCI 1983

1. INTRODUCTION TO HOUSEHOLD

Hello. May I speak with (NAME ON CARD)?

IF ASKS WHO'S CALLING: This is (YOUR NAME) calling for Consumer Reports Magazine. Is Mr(s)_____in?

IF ASKS WHAT ABOUT: We're calling our subscribers about some help we need. Is he/she there?

IF NOT AVAILABLE: Fine. We'll call again. Can you tell me when is a good time to reach him/her? (NOTE) Thank you.

2. INTRODUCTION TO SUBSCRIBER/MEMBER

Hello, Mr(s)_____. This is (YOUR NAME) calling for Consumer Reports. How are you (today/this evening?) (LISTEN AND RESPOND). I'm calling because you're one of our subscribers. I'd like to thank you for your subscription and take a minute to talk to you about a difficult situation we're in right now. May I do that?

IF NO/TOO BUSY: May I call you back at a more convenient time? (LISTEN AND RECORD)

IF NO/IS VERY IRRITATED: I'm very sorry to have disturbed you Mr(s)_____. I hope you have a pleasant (day/evening).

IF YES: We're asking our subscribers for help Mr(s)_____, because regrettably Consumer Reports is in a financial crisis. As you know, we're a nonprofit organization, and unlike any other consumer magazine we refuse to accept any advertising. This guarantees that we remain impartial in our testing and stay independent from any companies or retailers we evaluate in the magazine.

3. FIRST REQUEST

As you may have read in the January issue, all nonprofit organizations were hit with a huge and unexpected postal rate increase. Because of this increase, we're now faced with a $2 million deficit.

That's why we must appeal to our friends, Mr(s)_____, and ask them for their help. We need your contribution to help us surmount this present crisis. A tax-deductible contribution of $35 will go a long way in helping us through these difficult financial times. If you're able to help us with a pledge, don't send us any money yet. We'll send you a pledge acknowledgment in the mail and we'll enclose a reply envelope for you to send your pledge back to us. So, can you help us with your support by making a tax-deductible contribution of $35 or more, Mr(s)_____?

IF YES: Thank you. GO TO CARD 8

IF NO: I see. GO TO CARD 4

IF RETIRED & MENTIONS LACK OF FUNDS: GO TO CARD 5A

4. SECOND REQUEST

Of course, a contribution of *any* amount would be greatly appreciated. Our ability to maintain the high cost of quality testing requires that we turn to you and ask you for help. Even $25 will go a long way in helping us continue to provide the best in product testing and reporting. As we mentioned in our January issue, we've been calling our subscribers all around the country and so many of them have been responding to this appeal. Can we also count on you for a $25 tax-deductible contribution, Mr(s)_____?

IF NO: GO TO CARD 5

IF NO (VERY ADAMANT/IRRITATED): GO TO CARD 10

IF YES: Thank you. GO TO CARD 8

5. THIRD REQUEST

I can certainly understand the way you feel, Mr(s)_____. If we could count on you for just $10 at this time we'd be that much closer to overcoming our present deficit. Can you support us with a $10 pledge?

IF YES: Thank you. GO TO CARD 8

IF NO: GO TO CARD 10

5A. REQUEST/RETIRED

Mr(s)_____, many of our subscribers are retired and I certainly understand your position. We hope that Consumer Reports has helped you to be able to get the best buys for your money. Our ability to continue to provide all consumers with the very best in product testing requires that we do ask for your help.

If we could count on you for just $10 at this time we'd be that much closer to overcoming our present deficit. Can you support us with a $10 pledge Mr(s)_____?

IF YES: Thank you. GO TO CARD 8

IF NO: GO TO CARD 10

6. WILL CONTRIBUTE— AMOUNT NOT SPECIFIED

Mr(s)_____, I understand. I'll send you a donation form and a pledge reply envelope so that you may make your decision at a more convenient time. Let me make sure I have your correct name and address. Is it (NAME & ADDRESS ON CARD)? (RECORD ANY CHANGES)

Thank you, and have a good evening.

6A. HESITANT ABOUT SPECIFIC DOLLAR AMOUNT

The *only* reason we're asking for a specific dollar amount, Mr(s)_____, is because it is so critical for us to know how close we are to meeting our $2 million dollar deficit.(PAUSE SLIGHTLY FOR RESPONSE)

IF GIVES AMOUNT: GO TO CARD 8

IF STILL REFUSES TO GIVE $ AMOUNT: GO TO CARD 6

7. MAY CONTRIBUTE

Mr(s)_____, I realize this telephone call may be bringing your attention to a situation you'll want to know more about. So I'll send you some information about what we're trying to accomplish. Let me make sure I have your correct name and address. Is it (NAME & ADDRESS ON CARD)? (RECORD ANY CHANGES) Thank you. I hope that after you've had a chance to give it some thought, you'll decide to make a contribution. Thank you for your time.

8. CLOSE/PLEDGE

(RECORD AMOUNT OF PLEDGE) That's very generous of you, Mr(s)_____.

We'll send you a pledge acknowledgment in the mail—along with a reply envelope for your contribution of $_____. Okay? Let me make sure I have your correct name and address. Is it (NAME & ADDRESS ON CARD)? (RECORD ANY CHANGES)

Thank you again for your pledge, Mr(s)_____. Before you hang up, I'd like to make sure you have my name in case there are any questions when you receive your pledge acknowledgment in the mail. (GIVE YOUR NAME, AND WAIT IF NEEDED FOR SUPPORTER TO RECORD) Thanks, and have a good (day/evening).

(IF ASKS WHEN THEY WILL GET THE PLEDGE ACKNOWLEDGMENT, SAY:) Mr(s)_____, we'll be sending that out in the next day or two.

9. NOT NOW— UNEMPLOYED/SICK

I understand, Mr(s)_____. We want to thank you for supporting us by subscribing to Consumer Reports—and we hope we've been able to help you with important buying decisions. (LISTEN AND RESPOND)

Thank you for your time. Have a good (day/evening).

10. CLOSE/WILL NOT CONTRIBUTE

I understand. There is, however, something you can do for us, Mr(s)_____.
(PAUSE) When you get your renewal notice, would you let us know right away
that you'll be renewing your subscription to Consumers Union? That will save
us the expense of mailing more notices. Thank you. I hope we can continue to
count on your support.

The script went on to include 25 or more "cards" with additional dialogue, responding to specific questions or situations. However, this type of scripting is now used only by company-owned telemarketing departments, where operators can be intensely trained in a single company's policies and products.

Commercial telemarketing organizations, particularly inbound ones, today serve dozens of clients. The general practice today is to simplify the script and let a supervisor handle objections or problems. It is also possible to use "on-line transfer," in which a specific prospect can be connected to the client's own customer service staff, or to a local agent or dealer, to make an appointment, close the order, or resolve problems.

One classic use of outbound telemarketing was planned by National Marketshare, which made over one million calls on behalf of Pizza Hut, mostly to reactivate customers who had not ordered recently. The script asked about prior service and quality, and then made an offer to deliver pizza that evening at a special price. Other mail and telephone offers followed up these calls, varied according to the information received and the policies of the local Pizza Hut outlet. A custom computer program planned the calling so as to correspond to slow days and hours at each outlet, when the special-price offer could easily be implemented.

INBOUND TELEMARKETING

Telephone marketing has become a highly specialized subcategory of direct marketing, and I have presented only highlights here. For further information about this aspect of direct marketing, I recommend that you consult the book, *Telephone Marketing,* by Murray Roman (McGraw-Hill, 1976). This book, with a foreword by Prof. Theodore Levitt of the Harvard Business School, is still the definitive work on using the telephone as a marketing tool.

Inbound telemarketing is a marketing discipline in itself, with its own suppliers, its own standards, and its own techniques.

While some companies offer both inbound and outbound telemarketing, most have particular strength in one or the other.

Though outbound telemarketing is a medium to be evaluated as part of the overall media mix, inbound telemarketing is a service, the costs of which are added to cost per lead as another fulfillment expense.

However, inbound phone services do much more than act as order-takers. With proper planning and careful testing, they can be used to "qualify" a lead, prescreen credit, and—most commonly—trade up the customer to a deluxe option, a longer term, or a larger quantity.

Selecting Inbound Telephone Services

Many organizations, including NDC in Atlanta and Matrix in Ogden, Utah, are in the business of providing this type of incoming telephone service. Avis Rent-a-Car's Telecommunications division is able to use their huge reservation facility in Tulsa for handling direct marketing calls, because direct marketing calls peak at times when automobile reservations are slow. Other companies with large reservation phone systems might consider this business as well.

For the buyer of telephone service, the key considerations are the number of phones available, how many of them are staffed, and what their load factors are. Before selecting a telephone service, get a list of the company's clients and check references. Also, call in on a broadcast offer for one of their clients to see how long it takes to get through and how courteously and efficiently the telephone is answered. If you have a bad experience, go elsewhere. Don't let anyone argue that you reached the one exception. There shouldn't be any exceptions if the staff has been properly selected and trained before being placed on line.

Because jammed telephone lines can cost you an estimated one-half to two-thirds of your potential response, selection of a telephone service is serious business. Take the time to pick the right telephone supplier for your needs and to check out every detail in person. The available numbers should be easy to remember and unique to the particular advertiser if at all possible.

Phone answering companies should have efficient systems—manual or computerized—for indicating all necessary information about the offer and the order. The best systems are those in which the operator has a cathode-ray-tube (CRT) computer terminal and can display information on the product and a list of questions on the screen. The operator says exactly what is on the screen, giving information or asking for it as necessary. Questions to be asked appear on the screen. If there is information to be checked, such as available inventory for a particular item being ordered or the validity of a credit card number, the checking is done automatically and simultaneously while the customer is still on the phone. The customer's answers are punched right into the computer, displayed on the screen, and stored in memory.

Really professional telephone suppliers can do more than just answer the telephone and capture name, address, and item ordered. They can train their telephone answerers to be salespeople as well. They are also the company's goodwill ambassadors, and for this reason also, care in the selection and training of operators is essential. One insurance firm, Prudential, gives its operators who deal with AARP members special sensitivity training in dealing with senior citizens.

Telephone trade-ups are a growing trend, but they require trained salespeople. Some magazines offer short-term subscriptions on the air and then offer "added savings" on the telephone to try to convert the respondent to a longer subscription. Some companies invite COD or to-be-billed orders on television and then have the telephone operator offer a premium if the customer pays by giving a credit card number on the telephone. Some advertisers invite viewers to mail cash to a certain address but suggest that only credit card holders may call and order by phone.

Whatever system or supplier you select, I strongly urge that you have a backup or a second supplier lined up before you start to shoot your commercial. Otherwise, if your telephone service goes broke or gives you bad service, you'll have to go to the expense of reshooting the phone-number portion of the commercial unless you have designed it so that the number can be changed easily. Also, if the commercial is a big success, it's a good idea to use more than one supplier when running on several stations at one time, to reduce the busy-signal ratio.

Inbound Telephone Scripts

Here is an example of an inbound telephone script for a one-shot mail-order proposition being sold by COD or credit card. Note that in this script no questions are asked to determine the source of the call, as the called number activates the computer program automatically to tell the answering service operator the nature of the product and the proposition.

PRODUCT:	$19.95 widget
PAYMENT:	Credit Card—Mastercard, Visa, Amex, Discover
	COD—$5
SCRIPT:	1. HI, THIS IS_____. MAY I HELP YOU?
	2. MAY I HAVE YOUR POSTAL ZIP, PLEASE?
	3. YOUR LAST NAME? FIRST? MISS OR MRS.? (if female)
	4. YOU LIVE IN_____, _____ (city, state)
	5. MAY I HAVE YOUR STREET ADDRESS?
	6. WHICH CREDIT CARD WILL YOU BE USING? (MC, VISA, AMEX)
	7. (If Customer says "no") DID YOU KNOW THAT YOU CAN SAVE $5 COD POSTAGE AND HANDLING BY USING YOUR CREDIT CARD?
	8. MAY I HAVE YOUR CREDIT CARD NUMBER, PLEASE? (Credit card payments, skip to line 10.)
	9. YOUR AREA CODE IS _____. MAY I HAVE THE REST OF YOUR HOME PHONE, PLEASE?

10. YOU CAN HAVE TWO WIDGETS FOR $35.00—AN
    ADDITIONAL SAVINGS OF ALMOST $5.

11. THANK YOU FOR CALLING. YOUR WIDGET WILL
    BE DELIVERED IN 4 TO 6 WEEKS.

The zip code is punched into the computer, and the city and state are revealed so that the operator can confirm the zip code. The same information also gives the telephone area code to facilitate getting the home phone number, which is mandatory for this company before either credit card or COD shipment will be accepted. The credit card question is presented as a presumption: "Which credit card will you be using?" rather than "Will you be using a credit card?"

Note the trade-up suggestion, line 10: an additional savings for multiple purchases. I have had exceptional results trading up $5 coin collectibles to multiple orders or a $25 silver version.

Similar suggestions can be made to turn credit orders into cash, one-year subscriptions into two-year ones, and information leads into qualified appointments for salespersons. The creative opportunities for telephone scripts are much greater than most people realize.

900 Numbers

Billing charged automatically to a phone bill was, when introduced, supposed to be the ultimate convenience to the direct marketing customer, and therefore the key to new response breakthroughs. It is a convenience, but the phone companies and the media poisoned its usefulness by letting its first users include propositions such as sex phone services, paid information on credit cards (good only for one company's merchandise), and similar embarrassments.

Another problem is that phone companies do not have the conflict-resolution systems offered by credit card companies. If buyers dispute a charge on an American Express Card, they are given automatic credit until the question is resolved. With a phone charge, they must pay the bill or have their phone service cut off, and there is no help at all from the phone company.

As a result, the mere use of a 900 number raises a credibility question about an offer. While this method has proved useful for applications in which the sponsor is well known, such as memberships in public service television, I generally do not recommend it.

Electronic Answering

Several in-bound phone services now offer automated data-entry services, which are generally less expensive than systems that use live operators. These systems generally prompt replies by asking the caller to press a touch-tone button on the phone. This facilitates multiple questions, as for database surveys, and has even made possible complex games such as rotisserie sports contests and stock market selection games.

While the household name and address can be determined by capturing the in-bound phone number, the weakness usually has been the difficulty of getting the caller's first name. Some systems deal with this by asking customers to state or spell their names, which then are transcribed by operators. While some buyers would object to the impersonal treatment of such a system, others are fascinated by the technology.

Checks-by-Mail

Many consumers, particularly older ones, prefer not to give anyone their credit card numbers over the telephones, severely restricting the total sales resulting from television offers. Others simply do not have credit cards. One answer to this has been the development of services that can accept the customer's check number and arrange to debit the account.

While it is too early to determine the impact this will have on the direct marketing industry, I find it difficult to imagine that consumers who do not want to give their credit card number will be willing to give their check number. There should be some incremental convenience for those consumers who simply do not have credit cards, but I'm skeptical about how large or valuable that segment would be.

TELEMARKETING'S PROBLEMS

The problem with telemarketing is that, while it is an industry in itself, it largely uses the same type of mailing lists used by direct mailers. To the extent that their offers are illegitimate or their use of such lists intrusive or irritating, they have exacerbated negative attitudes toward both mail and telemarketing, leading to serious threats to the collection and use of both business and consumer prospect lists.

Eventually, telemarketers will have to band together to clean their own house, or direct marketers will have to distance themselves from the whole telemarketing industry and join the calls for restrictions. We are not in the same business. Mailers put their offers in writing, and are willing to leave both addresses and phone numbers. Our messages arrive in a mailbox or a magazine or on the air; a prospect has the right to toss the envelope, turn the page, change the channel. We do not incur a prospect's anger at having to leave the dinner table to answer the telephone, or at having been interrupted during a busy business day by the need to deal with a supposedly "personal" call. What I personally find so amazing is the way substantial organizations such as Citibank allow their lists of customer names to be used for such irritating promotions.

Like it or not, telemarketing is here, and it has its legitimate uses, particularly where a prior relationship exists or where there has been a request for information. We don't have to use it; we do have to understand it.

RESEARCH

One of the most significant results of the influence of general advertising disciplines on the traditional processes of direct marketing has been the increasing role of research.

Long utilized by conventional advertisers, it is now recognized by most direct marketers as being the powerful tool that it is. While it is used routinely by a few of the largest and most sophisticated direct marketers, the great majority of firms in our field still mistakenly believe research to be either irrelevant or uneconomic. Only in the last few years has research been included in books on this subject or incorporated into agendas of direct marketing training programs and industry conferences.

On the other hand, general advertisers who now are beginning to use database marketing have long ago recognized the importance of research in their marketing process. While these general advertisers have benefited by adding direct marketing methods to their promotional options, so too has the direct marketing industry gained by learning how to use the research methods they have perfected.

Those using research wisely will find that it often can make the difference between the success or failure of a new campaign; that it can provide the edge needed to revive a failing proposition or to ensure the success of a new product.

RESEARCH VERSUS TESTING

It is important to differentiate between research and testing, as the two terms are often used interchangeably, and thereby misused. This book deals with each in a separate chapter.

For the most part, direct marketers rely on testing—an art and a science that has always been a unique strength of the industry. *Testing,* as we use the term, refers to producing an advertisement, mailing piece, or commercial, putting it in the media, and seeing what happens. It produces some responses, and so at least partially pays for itself.

Testing may tell us *what* works, but never *why.* Like a good accountant, it can tell us what we did wrong, but not what we should do instead. It can tell us who is buying a product, but not why certain people are buying it. It can tell us that our proposition appealed to some people on one mailing list or in one type of community, or among subscribers to one publication, but not the reasons for the difference in response.

Research, on the other hand, involves a learning process. It does not produce orders or leads, and so it is usually treated as an expense. Companies who would not hesitate to try out a new direct mail package or invest in the production expense of a new advertisement often freeze up when it comes to approving several thousand dollars for a research project.

Research as an Investment

Research should be as fundamental a part of an advertiser's annual budget as production costs or creative fees. It should be looked on not as an expense, but as an investment.

The question is not "Do we need research?" but "How much research do we need?" Think about this example: If you were considering adding a sweepstakes, you wouldn't look at $15,000 in prizes and expenses as a cost, but as an investment. If you were mailing out a million pieces, the cost of the contest would be $15 per thousand pieces. The question then is not whether you can afford $15,000, but whether you can afford $15 per thousand. If the mailing package cost $300 per thousand, the $15,000 would represent a 5 percent increase in mailing cost. The question then is whether you can reasonably expect a 5 percent lift in response, say from 1 percent to 1.05 percent. In that case the expectation is reasonable, and you might try the sweepstakes.

On the other hand, a million-dollar prize would cost $1000 per thousand at the quantity in this example, and would require a 333 percent lift—a 4.3 percent response instead of 1 percent. That is unlikely, although not impossible.

Why all this talk about sweepstakes economics in a chapter on research? Because the arithmetic is exactly the same. And so are the examples. Substitute a research investment of $15,000 and ask yourself the same question: "Is there a reasonable probability that this investment will pay for itself in added response?" Depending on the size of your total budget, and on the previously available data, decide whether a particular research proposal will help you to develop a product improvement or a new creative theme; then determine whether it can give you a response increase sufficient to pay for the cost of the research. If the cost is out of line with the response needed to justify the expense, or vice versa, pass it up. Otherwise, you have as good a chance of finding a new breakthrough from a research investment as you do in trying a new test cell.

PURPOSES OF RESEARCH

There are many different research techniques, going far beyond the simple "focus panel" most advertisers are familiar with. Most full-service direct marketing agencies and many advertisers have consultants on staff to advise them about which research method is most appropriate for a specific objective. First, however, we have to identify the objectives that are most appropriate for research.

Some broad areas are

- *Market research,* which seeks to understand the marketing environment, including its various geographic, demographic, and psychographic segments
- *Creative research,* which seeks to identify new creative themes and prioritize copy points
- *Predictive research,* which seeks to narrow the number of approaches that are brought to the testing stage
- *Post-test analysis,* which analyzes test results or compares respondents and nonrespondents to identify marketing and creative steps for the future

Let's look at each of these objectives separately.

Market Research

Market research attempts to both identify and understand the prospects for the product or service being offered. While testing will eventually tell us which lists or publications or broadcast programming will produce the most responsive audience with the least cost, market research tells us who the likely prospects are, independently of how we can reach them.

Researchers can tell us not only the *who*—in terms of age, income, education, and geographic location—but also the *why:* Why do some people crave our product while others couldn't care less? Why do some people see it one way while others see it very differently? We can learn about lifestyles: the psychographic indicators of how our prospects live; what kind of work they do; their hobbies, sports, interests; their tastes and preferences. Data like this make mailing list selection less subjective and more scientific than direct marketers of the old school ever thought possible.

Research also can answer such questions as: What do our prospects know, or think they know, about our product or service? How do they react to it? Do they understand it? Does it need more explanation? Are there undesirable features that should be eliminated, or other features that can be added? Do customers really need what we have to offer? And—an entirely different question—do they know they need it?

And what about the offer? Pricing is a suitable subject for research, but so far the results have not been satisfactory. People will tell you whether they would or would not buy a product at a certain price, but the information from such offer testing has not proved reliable, and new methods are needed. Research will, however, help to identify premiums, or uncover a need for a guarantee, or determine reactions to elements of the proposition other than pure pricing.

Finally, researchers can answer a vitally important new question about our prospects: What is their self-image, and the image they have of people who use products like ours? This "user imagery" question, discussed in more detail later in this book, can be very significant in determining product positioning and the use of visual communication in all forms of advertising.

Segmentation

Great strides have been made in developing research tools that help us to segment the market for products according to geographic, demographic, or psychographic information.

These tools are generic ones, not always linked to specific brands or products, but nevertheless able to provide clues to the interests and lifestyles of prospects. In turn, this aids in the selection of media and even mailing lists.

Simmons is probably the leading continuing analysis report. Long used as a tool by general advertising media departments, it provides a continuous survey of people around the country and relates their interests, hobbies, purchasing histories, and intentions to those of the readership of particular publications.

Agencies and companies who have this service on computer can customize the data by comparing various statistics to find correlations between two purchasing styles. For instance, if women who frequently buy hosiery also are working women, and also are likely to travel or read, this tells us something about what kind of lists are likely to work and what kinds of situations to show in our illustrations. It also gives us the information it was originally designed for: an index to measure the likely effectiveness of print media schedules.

Simmons studies always have included characteristics such as whether a prospect purchased anything by mail or joined a book club. Recently they also have begun to develop a purchase log that enables them to relate their data in terms of actual mail-order purchasing history rather than just recalled purchases. Interestingly, many more participants logged in mail-order purchases than stated they had bought by mail.

SRI, formerly Stanford Research Institute, has introduced a study called VALS (Values and Lifestyles Program), which has had important applications to direct marketing. This method divides consumers into three broad categories and eight subcategories.

The *outer-directed* categories are

Belongers—preservers of the status quo

Emulators—conspicuous consumers

Achievers—comfort-loving people

The *inner-directed* categories are

"I am me"—impulse buyers

Experiential—consumers who ask, "What does the product do for me?"

Societally conscious—people who ask, "Is this product environmentally sound?"

The *need-driven* categories are

Survivors—people concerned with price

Sustainers—people concerned with price

Reading habits, purchasing intentions, and relevant copy appeals differ for each group. Often a product clearly appeals to one group rather than another, and the data can affect the entire advertising plan: the media, the creative concept, the offer, and even the style of execution. Though not every product may be subject to VALS segmentation, in many cases companies can benefit from knowledge of this system.

Geodemographics, a research tool developed specifically for the direct marketing industry, is now very much in use by the more sophisticated advertisers in the industry. This method involves studying available census data about different geographic units—zip codes, census tracts, or even smaller units such as postal carrier routes—and relating them to demographic or lifestyle indicators. Such data has long been available on a demographic basis, enabling direct mailers to select high-income areas, homeowning areas, or areas with large families. The newer applications relate to lifestyle data, and were obtained by reducing over 1000 available variables into fewer than 100 significant indicators. Some of the companies in this field add their own proprietary data as well.

Some of these segmentation methods include Claritas's Prizm, CACI's Acorn, and Donnelly's Cluster Plus. These, and others, enable an advertiser to analyze an existing house list and locate the significant variables that indicate the probability of success. Some of these are lifestyle indicators that define geographic areas with names such as the following, from Claritas's Prizm study:

Blue Blood Estates	New Beginnings
Money & Brains	God's Country
Furs & Station Wagons	Towns & Gowns
Pools & Patios	Levittown, U.S.A.

Two More Rungs	Gray Power
Young Influentials	Rank & File
Young Suburbia	Blue-Collar Nursery
Blue-Chip Blues	Middle America
Urban Gold Coast	Coalburg & Corntown
Bohemian Mix	New Melting Pot
Black Enterprise	Old Yankee Rows
Emergent Minorities	Back-Country Folks
Single City Blues	Share Croppers
Shotguns & Pickups	Tobacco Roads
Agri-Business	Hard Scrabble
Grain Belt	Heavy Industry
Golden Ponds	Downtown Dixie-Style
Mines & Mills	Hispanic Mix
Norma Rae-Ville	Public Assistance
Old Brick Factories	

Such information not only helps us to use otherwise marginal mailing lists, but provides us with a feeling for the type of people who are buying our product. This naturally can lead to changes in the substance and style of the advertising communications prepared for these markets. Often, such data reminds us to be less clever, less subtle, and more in touch with basic needs and desires.

Creative Research

Focus panels, field interviews, and questionnaires can give advertisers a chance to get a current reading on the thinking of the marketplace. Advertisers can check on whether their messages are understood, determine the jargon used by readers and viewers, and uncover objections that otherwise would go unanswered. Most important, research can identify opportunities that might otherwise be missed.

Today's creative directors must be objective enough to realize that they are not omniscient and should make full use of modern research. But research directors must recognize that their methods are a source of creative inspiration, not a substitute for it.

Creative research, as the name suggests, is concerned with the creation of advertising messages rather than with overall marketing questions. Of course, the areas of major interest do overlap, and the same research project often may have objectives relating to both areas.

The definition of creative objectives is best done in relation to a creative philosophy that seeks answers to test the applicability of a specific strategy.

Awareness.   If there is little awareness of the product, we need to "Create a need" with educational copy addressed to those entering the market. Virtually every product needed such an approach at some time, and even established products can be sold to some market segments in this way. Research can tell us where and when this approach is needed.

Is the consumer aware of the category but not of our brand? This requires a different approach. Are consumers aware of the product, but not of its advantages? Has the public received misinformation that should be corrected? Or is the product one that is both needed and wanted? In this case our problem is to stress offers that can motivate immediate action. Research can answer these questions.

Attitudes.   What are people's preexisting attitudes toward, and associations with, the product or service? Often we find a basic problem of credibility. People know our claims but don't believe them. In one such case, an entire advertising program was built around dramatization of the guarantee. In another, scientific explanation was used. And in still another, credibility was achieved with the help of a respected spokesperson.

Once you know what the problem is, creative directions emerge from a logical thought process. Otherwise, there is a tendency for some creative people to pursue cleverness for the sake of cleverness. Sound solutions to identified problems always produce better results.

Needs.   We can also learn what the consumer's real needs are, and how our product or service can fulfill these needs. Such needs usually deal not only with real, tangible concerns, but with emotional and imagery needs as well.

A mobile telephone, for example, enables one to keep in touch when traveling. But is that the real need? Research shows us that it may be only an executive toy, a symbol of success, a gadget to fulfill curiosity and enhance self-esteem. In such a case, the needs of the office are a way of justifying the purchase, but are not the primary motivator. This would lead to ads using illustrations to enhance self-image and dramatize the play value of this product.

In fund-raising, most creative appeals are based on the nature of the good work of the philanthropy. But some research seems to indicate that reward and recognition are equally important. Philanthropists want to achieve something more than a sense of doing right. They want others to know they have done right. Some research even indicates that a philanthropist may be buying "immortality" and "disalienation." This may explain why appeals for children often do better than those for adults, why building funds for "monuments" do well, and why people seem to respond to being part of a "crusade," joining hands with others.

There are just a few examples of research that expose emotional needs which might otherwise be overlooked in the creative process.

Intentions.   The potential buyer's intentions are another area of interest. Do we have to create a need? Or fulfill it? Do we have to persuade our prospect to buy our particular brand rather than a competitor's? Or is our problem simply to overcome inertia with a sale or special offer, to get them to act now rather than later?

Very often I find that the subjective judgment of client and agency is correct, but only for one segment of a market. Research sometimes reveals enormous market segments that represent unanticipated problems or opportunities that require different approaches.

Behavior. When we've identified the families—or companies, in the case of business products—who are our prospects, it is valuable to know how they previously handled the problem solved by our product or service.

If we are selling long-distance telephone services, for example, we discover different behavior among different market segments. Some families may, as alternatives to long-distance calls, send cards or write letters. Others simply make such calls very brief or very infrequently.

In another example, if you're selling a lawn product, it's helpful to know whether the present prospect is a do-it-yourselfer who spends countless back-breaking hours pulling up crabgrass, or someone who just suffers with a poor-looking lawn, or a consumer who uses an expensive service that is more costly than yours. With such information, your choice of creative strategy becomes very clear: you know whether to base it on "Save time and trouble" or "Get a better lawn" or "Save money." Though a good direct-response ad or mailing will include all these copy points, a choice must be made as to which to lead off with to attract the prime prospect in the first place.

Execution. Some research methods also can be helpful in perfecting the execution of the creative theme or concept finally selected.

Simple interviews or focus panels may not be helpful in telling you whether an ad is "liked" or whether the panel members would "respond." But these techniques can tell you whether your message comes across as you meant it to, or whether your illustration conveys what you think it does, or whether people will stop to read your ad at all.

Where there is a great deal at stake in a successful ad or mailing, such creative research can be a good investment. This is especially true when there are differences of opinion within a client's or an agency's organization. Some quick research can quickly break a deadlock or resolve a disagreement.

User Imagery. Probably the most significant development in the world of creative research is the application of "user imagery" to the field of direct response. This method seeks to influence the image prospects have of who buys a product or service. "Do people like me use this? Do I want to be associated with others who use this product?"

Such imagery is readily apparent in ads for products such as perfume or fashion, which suggest a lifestyle that many consumers would like to adopt as their own. What is less clear is that people and companies have images in connection with virtually every kind of product, and that some products are perceived to be "right" for a particular self-image, whereas others are "not right."

We have conducted imagery studies for direct marketing clients in fields such as banking, air express, investments, credit cards, book clubs, and magazines, and we have never failed to find a creative opportunity. Sometimes an imagery study influences the entire basic thrust of the campaign; at other times it provides an "awareness by-product" direction, facilitating a gradual improvement of the advertiser's image through presentation of users in different situations and illustrations.

There was a time when research was perceived as a hindrance by old-fashioned copywriters. Today, writers and artists welcome both the stimulation of research and the sound creative strategies that it leads to. Research has made the creative task more professional, though not easier. It enables the creative team to put more energy into creative expression than into speculation. Most important, a solid creative plan based on research takes the guesswork out of the creative process.

Predictive Research

One of the most common reasons that research has not been used adequately in direct marketing is the relative weakness of predictive research, or pretesting methods. While pretesting has been used extensively in the general advertising world, where multimillion-dollar test market campaigns have been the only logical interim step to a rollout, no research method has approached the effectiveness of the split-run and sampling methods that are an integral part of direct marketing methodology.

However, even the largest advertisers cannot afford unlimited split-run testing. Sample sizes and the number of cells in a direct mail campaign should have some relationship to a total budget. Print advertising is limited by the flexibility of the print media being tested. Where color ads or brochures are involved, production costs can quickly become prohibitive if several four-color executions are being tested against each other.

Predictive research techniques range from simple screening methods to complex physiological methods involving voice pitch, eye movement, and even brain waves. More than 50 different approaches to copy testing are used by general agencies.

Pretest techniques, in my experience, cannot pick a winner; they are no substitute for split-run testing. What they do is identify the losers. If there are a dozen possible concepts for a campaign and only four can be tested, pretesting can eliminate the half-dozen least likely to succeed. Then, with only six left to choose from, the odds that the combined subjective judgments of client and agency will pick the best four are greatly improved.

Pretesting often is desirable for a new product under development, when both secrecy and flexibility are mandatory. On the other hand, if pretesting is used to reduce the number of alternate creative approaches, usually it is because no single direction was agreed upon previously. In such cases, the various directions often can be tested using conventional research methods.

I have seen pretesting methods used in naming a proposition, in selecting a spokesperson, in establishing priorities among the elements of a copy platform, and in identifying a visual presentation. Where four-color plates are involved, or quality television production, or complex mailing formats, testing every possible element is often too expensive.

The methodologies of pretesting research will be discussed later in this chapter. However, it is important to note the limitations of predictive or pretesting research. The results of such endeavors usually provide only an index of relative appeal, never an absolute figure. In other words, you may learn which ad will pull best, but not whether any of them will work. Unless you have established some previous standard or model with which to compare future results (as some very large advertisers have), you will still have to conduct a conventional sampling or split-run test.

Post-testing

An axiom of direct marketers is that we always know what went wrong, or right, after the results of a split-run test are in. Theories abound to account for breakthrough results or to explain away the concepts at the bottom of the response rankings. It appears that hindsight is a gift possessed by all practitioners in this field.

Too many advertisers are willing to settle for knowing which ad did best without knowing *why* it did best. Although research can't determine who will really order a product, it can find out why people responded to an offer. And once we know who responded to an offer and who didn't, telephone surveys, in-depth interviews, and mail questionnaires can uncover the differences in their attitudes and feelings, motivations and perceptions. Usually some of the differences relate to the nature and needs of the prospect, and may or may not point to the possibility of segmented appeals in the future.

In other cases, we can learn what appeal most influenced the buying decision of the responders. Sometimes it is not the one we featured, and future efforts can thus be strengthened. Or we may find that a point was overlooked by the nonresponders, possibly because of the layout or because it was expressed too subtly by the copywriter.

We can try hypothetical questions with nonresponders, to guide us in future efforts. What if we lowered the price? What if we offered a guarantee? What if you didn't have to send money now and could just try it? What if we included a free training course? What if you knew that many other customers had already bought it? What if you knew that this offer was being made by such and such a well-known corporation? If the nonresponder might have acted differently when given different information, a key element that might affect future efforts can be identified. The only other way to uncover this element would be by repeated trial and error.

Such questions should, of course, be asked of people who remember getting the offer, who have some conceivable use for the product or service, and who are qualified as prime prospects. The opinions of others are irrelevant. Especially unimportant are those who say, even swear, that they didn't get the mailing. They are as reliable as the large percentage of consumers who swear they never order by mail, even though their names are on multibuyer lists.

RESEARCH METHODS

Up to now we have been discussing what can be done with research, and why we direct marketers should use it with much greater regularity and effectiveness than we have in the past.

The next part of this chapter touches on available research tools—in two broad categories, *qualitative* and *quantitative*—not to provide a catalog of methods to choose from but to give you some understanding of the large variety of methods. This will be followed by an introduction to some of the newer nonverbal research methods.

Too many advertisers just ask their advertising agency or research firm for "a couple of focus panels" or a "questionnaire." This is like asking for a self-mailer without first determining the offer or even the right medium.

Research is a great industry today, with countless companies in the field. Many have unique or proprietary methods, and several have successfully applied their methods to the problems of direct marketers. The first place to start is with professional research counsel: the specialist at your ad agency, a consultant, or your own experienced staff member. The choice of research methods should be determined after the objectives are established, which is why this chapter is written in exactly the same sequence. Good research can be very helpful, but bad research can be more than a waste of money: it can lead you to wrong decisions and consequent losses.

QUALITATIVE METHODS

There are two broad categories of qualitative research: group discussions, sometimes called *focus panels,* and individual interviews, which may take place at home or in an office, on the street, or even on the telephone.

Focus Panels

Focus panels are the antithesis of direct marketing's scientific testing methods. They are not subject to measurement at all. Individual panel members may be atypical of the market as a whole, and there is almost never a definitive resolution of any question. Yet their value is immense.

Basically, a focus panel is like a group therapy session. Its basic structure involves between 6 and 12 people, who engage in an open discussion. A moderator, who must be more of a psychologist than a researcher, guides the group into areas of interest to the advertiser. The whole proceeding is watched, through a two-way mirror or on closed-circuit television, by clients who are in a position to influence the direction of the meeting and direct further exploration into topics of special interest.

Planning. The first step in using focus panels is to consult with a research specialist and prepare a plan. This plan must include several vital subjects: objectives, geography, composition, screening criteria, and a discussion guide.

The objectives may be open-ended, and must recognize the limitations of the focus panel. A focus panel objective cannot be quantifiable, as in "Determine percentage of market familiar with client's trademark." A realistic objective would be, "Obtain consumer reactions to client trademark." It cannot be selective, as in, "Select which advertisement to run." It can be subjective, as in, "Determine understanding of advertising concepts as expressed in various treatments."

Some of the most productive panels have the most open-ended objectives. One asked how people opened a direct mail package—and how they felt about it. Others sought attitudes toward new book clubs or other direct marketing ventures.

Geography is another consideration. Most focus panel researchers are affiliated with testing services around the country and are in a position to obtain screeners, panels, and focus group rooms in any city.

Usually it is possible to assemble panels representing different lifestyles and demographics within almost any city. Sometimes a researcher will recommend a suburban location, if that is where the market is. More often it is necessary to sample groups in a variety of areas—in the United States, perhaps the east, midwest, south, and west—to get a good cross-section of opinion.

One group of six panels was held in New York, Charlotte, and Kansas City, with younger and older age groups in each city. Geography produced little variation in attitudes, but age or prior product usage produced very different reactions.

Composition refers to the makeup of the groups. Groups can be selected within any age, income, education, or lifestyle parameters. Often there are very significant reactions depending upon age, sex, or education. Career women and housewives may have different reactions to a product.

The standard I recommend for all research is usability. Education or income standards may do very little good, because usually it is impractical to select lists or media by education or income, but other categories are very useful. For one financial product I separated *Wall Street Journal* readers, our core group, into separate panels from the general audience of savings account depositors. The different insights could be addressed differently in the two media categories—financial and general.

Sometimes attitudes toward products can be important. A magazine may want to explore the attitudes of groups who logically should read the magazine but never have, of newsstand buyers who have never subscribed, and of former subscribers who failed to renew. Obviously each of these groups should reveal very different attitudes.

How many groups should one have, then? Some arbitrary choices have to be made, especially as a professionally done focus group can cost between $2500 and $5000, not including the travel expenses of the moderator and marketing personnel. Holding two different panels in each of three cities can cost between $20,000 and $30,000. It is preferable to limit the number of panels and reserve some money for quantitative research. Additional panels can always be scheduled after the first reports have been studied. The additional panels then can concentrate on target groups or focus topics that require further exploration.

Screening Criteria.   Once location and composition have been established, it is necessary to establish screening criteria, the key determinant of a panel's usefulness. A necessary requirement for direct marketing focus groups is that they be composed of people who have bought by mail. People who are hostile to mail order will be useless, and their opinions and attitudes will color the comments of the rest of the panel. Only people who have bought by mail in the past have opinions that are relevant for our purposes.

Other criteria include employment, media readership, and history of purchasing similar products, as chosen by the researcher and the client. The criteria also should include a question designed to eliminate competitors, people in related fields, or people in the news media who might compromise the trade information exposed to the focus panel.

"Screeners" employed by the research firm telephone lists of people supplied by the client or assembled from local directories. They telephone hundreds of people until they can get the handful needed for each product—people who are qualified according to the criteria established and who are willing to participate in a panel in return for a nominal payment. The more restrictive the screening criteria, the more people must be called in order to assemble the panel.

Discussion Guide.   The discussion guide is the step that requires the most work, and researchers usually will not prepare the guide until they have been awarded the contract.

The discussion guide is basically an agenda—a step-by-step guide to the various discussion topics as they are to be exposed to the audience, including a list of the samples or promotional materials to be shown to the groups.

There is no one right way to prepare a guide. Moderators develop styles that fit their own personalities. No two are alike. Some are analytical. Some are flamboyant. Yet most of them have some elements in common. The following composite of many panels I have observed is basically an attempt to abstract common denominators.

Opening Remarks.   The first objective is to relax the participants and to set the ground rules for the next couple of hours. Most moderators encourage the members of the group to say whatever is on their minds—to be honest in their opinions and feelings. A casual environment is established, with refreshments and light conversation. A joking comment or two doesn't hurt.

Introductions are made for two reasons. One is to help the participants to feel comfortable with one another. The other is to make it easier to relate individuals' backgrounds to their comments when audio-video tapes later are reviewed.

Some moderators disclose the presence of observers on the other side of the mirror; most do not. Almost all of them advise participants that the discussions that are to take place are not being judged nor rated, and that there will not be any resolution of the topics. Panel members are told that one person's opinion is as good as any other's, and that there is no pressure to obtain agreement.

Attitudinal Exploration. The next step is to inquire about general attitudes toward the product category, buying by mail order, or other relevant topics. Questions are open-ended, and designed to elicit background for the more specific comments that will come later.

During this stage, psychoanalytic methods are used to encourage amplification. "Mmm-hmm, I see. Why do you feel this way?" "Can you tell us more about that?" "Who else feels this way?" All these are appropriate comments that serve to draw out the group's feelings and attitudes.

Development Stages. The subject at hand is brought up in a variety of ways. If the subject is a magazine, the panel may be asked where they get information about a certain topic or how they have learned certain things. They will be led into mentioning magazines in general, and the specific magazine being studied, in a way that conceals that the magazine is the central interest of the moderator. These indirect methods are used in order to forestall any bias, and to elicit comments that might be withheld out of courtesy if the sponsor were known right away.

Often competing advertisements or products are shown, sometimes with the advertiser's name blacked out. This is done to obtain comments about the product or advertisement uncolored by positive or negative attitudes that have developed toward the brand name.

One excellent focus panel explored attitudes toward conventional mail-order propositions and identified positive and negative reactions. The sponsor's proposition, which overcame many of the objections of conventional propositions, was then introduced. The features of the new proposition would have been less evident if they had not been contrasted with the previous ones.

Subject Exploration. Finally, about halfway through the session, the subject of the panel is unveiled, with the same casual manner in which the previous queries were presented. By now the group should be warmed up, and comments should come freely.

One technique is to show a commercial or read the headlines of an ad or mailing piece and then, at a signal, ask the participants to quickly jot down the points they recall that were important to them. Comments are solicited later as to what these points were and why they were important. It is important for participants to write down their points; otherwise the panel members would tend to echo the first comments they heard rather than expose their own honest reactions.

Where several ads are shown, the panelists may be asked to rate the likelihood that they would buy the product on a zero-to-ten scale in the same manner. They are then asked for their scores and their reasons for the scores.

The Redirect. Up to this point, the moderator has been in complete charge, pursuing a line of questioning previously worked out with the client. Then, 30 minutes or so from the end, the moderator makes an excuse to leave the room, invites the group to have some refreshments, and proceeds to the room where the clients have been watching. In hurried conference, the moderator and the clients exchange ideas on how the next segment should be handled.

Clients may ask that a particular person's viewpoints be explored further, that a point be stressed, or that a major change be introduced. "Stress the guarantee and see if that changes anyone's mind." "Tell them who is behind this new product and see if it adds credibility." "Would they join this club if they didn't have to pay anything up front?"

The moderator rejoins the group and finishes the session, using the requested approaches. After each panel, the client, agency, and research people discuss their observations on the spot. Often they revise the discussion guide before the next session. Sometimes new layouts or package designs are created between one session and the next, in response to comments.

The Write-Up. When everyone is back home, the researcher's work begins anew with a comprehensive written summary of the various focus panels, objectives, and conclusions. Correlations are made with the backgrounds of the focus panel members, and patterns and differences are observed from one group to the next. These written reports are extremely valuable, and usually are circulated to all interested parties. Such reports are notoriously unable to predict the success of a direct marketing idea, but they do provide valuable insight into idea comprehension and often lead to modified plans, products, and promotions.

Individual Interviews

For some situations, group interviewing may be impractical. Sometimes it is impossible to identify enough prospects in a given geographical area to form a group. At other times the subject may be too technical, too diverse in its applications to different individuals, or too personal to discuss in group sessions.

In these situations, the most common approach is the in-depth individual interview, based on the same kind of comprehensive discussion guide as that just outlined for focus groups.

As with focus panels, a critical element is the determination of whom to interview. Another is the training and skill of the interviewer.

Individual interviews can take several forms, ranging from the simple runthrough of a questionnaire to open-ended discussions. These discussions can be highly complex. Some companies interview doctors on medical subjects or engineers on their areas of interest, and even pay them for their time. Others need only go door-to-door or stop people on a street corner or in a shopping center.

At least one organization has been successful at using the telephone for in-depth interviewing, although this method has some limitations where visual communication or the presentation of a product sample is involved. Joseph Castelli, writing in *The Direct Marketing Handbook* (McGraw-Hill, 1984), suggests one solution: advance mailing of materials in a locked metal box, which can be opened only after the combination has been revealed during the phone interview.

Individual interviewing can cover all the areas and all the steps used in focus panels. Its weakness is that it does not provide the cross-stimulation that occurs when respondents spark each other's reactions. This may make it harder to get to respondents' real feelings. On the other hand, the individual interviewer can probe into personal issues—emotional reactions, selfish desires, sexual associations—that some respondents might hesitate to discuss in front of a group.

Individual interviews also lend themselves to physiological and psychological methods that would not be practical in groups. Some of these are discussed later in this chapter.

QUANTITATIVE METHODS

Quantitative research, as the name implies, endeavors to measure the various components of the marketing equation.

For general advertisers, such measurements often are the only index, other than sales figures, of the effectiveness of an advertising investment. For direct marketers, the needs for quantitative research are more limited, as new directions or concepts often can be tested more economically through exploratory split-run advertising and mailing than through research. However, there are some notable exceptions.

One company uses telephone interviewing of people on new mailing lists to gauge the probability that the list will succeed. Another uses Simmons data on magazine readers to determine the best combination of print media for specialized products and services. Some agencies also use audience composition data to buy broadcast time, as discussed more fully in Chapter 7.

For a quantitative study to be meaningful, it must be statistically reliable. Therefore the sample size must be large enough to be meaningful within the guidelines of statistical validity. Such studies can be conducted by telephone, as indicated above, which provides speed and the ability to conduct a truly national sample. Or they can be made in person at home, at the office, or in any public place. The common denominator of such studies is that they always end up with numerical rankings rather than simply lists of observations and conclusions.

In some research efforts, quantitative studies are used to set priorities among observations produced in earlier qualitative studies. For instance, one method invites consumers to complain about a product or category rather than simply state their preferences. Lists of perceived problems arise from the qualitative step, which are then arranged in order of priorities in a quantitative step. The resulting study informs clients of the frequency with which a problem occurs, the importance or seriousness of it, and, most interestingly, its preemptibility—the likelihood that an advertiser can position the product as the answer to the problem. We have applied such methods to the problems of direct marketers with amazing results, identifying advertising themes that were later proved successful in split-run tests and subsequent rollouts.

In-Person Interviews

The first question to consider, as with all research, is whom you want to talk to. The second is where. At home? At the office? At a factory gate? A supermarket? An elegant shopping area? The choice of place will, to some extent, determine your success at finding the mix of respondents needed for the particular survey.

Door-to-door interviews gives you a mix in a specific geographic area, but the diversity may not be wide enough. Also such interviews are time-consuming, and, particularly in urban areas, many people do not like to open their doors to strangers.

Fixed-site interviews, sometimes called "intercepts," provide a good mix of people with some common denominator. If they are held at a shopping center, you know you are talking with someone who shops at a center with a particular style attributed to it (fashion, bargain, etc.). If you are in front of an office building or a factory, you have a different set of demographic probabilities.

You are also able to talk with people at the time when a certain type of purchase or activity is on their minds. For example, an amusement park is a good place to talk about attitudes toward recreational activities, and a bank is a good place to discuss financial questions.

Telephone Interviews

Some packaged-goods organizations have established the correlation between telephone responses, response rates, and actual marketplace experience so finely that they can make decisions about major direct mail programs from a few hundred phone calls. While I am still uncomfortable with this approach, especially when it is accompanied by a dearth of copy and offer cells, I am impressed by its reliability.

It is now relatively simple to make several hundred phone calls from one central location to selected prospects throughout the country. Lists of customers, or names selected from mailing lists, or respondents to a mailing or advertisement can be used. The calls can be made quickly; often important information can be compiled in less than 24 hours by using a telephone survey.

One purpose of telephone interviews is to measure the probability of converting respondents to paying customers. You can ask people who have replied to different offers or different media sources, "Now that you've seen the free sample, do you intend to continue?" A relative index like this would take months to determine by any other method.

Another purpose of telephone interviews is to obtain information about a sample advertisement mailed to a specific list. The mailing can be sent "cold" and followed up with a telephone call asking whether the recipient recalls it. Or it can be sent in a sealed envelope, with the request that it not be opened until the call is received.

Though telephone surveys have limitations in the areas of cost and depth capabilities, no other method can give you answers so quickly.

Mailed Questionnaires

To many, the word *research* brings to mind *questionnaire.* Yet mailed surveys are one of the least reliable research methods.

There are two dangers in such surveys. One is that they seem simple to prepare, and therefore too many advertisers fail to retain professional researchers to handle them. The other is that they are too difficult to answer, resulting in skewed responses—a disproportionate ratio of responses from people with nothing better to do, who may not be typical prospects.

The solution to the first problem is obvious: Work with a professional. The second problem is more difficult to solve. I recommend validating that the questionnaire respondents are typical of the prospect list as a whole before acting upon questionnaire results. This can be done by following up a mail questionnaire with a telephone survey to nonrespondents, attempting to determine—even if just on a spot basis—whether nonrespondents are substantially similar to respondents. Once this has been established, mail questionnaires can be used freely.

Mailed questionnaires are unlike in-person interviews in that you cannot control the questions. If you ask about unaided recall in one question, there is nothing to stop the reader from scanning a list later in the questionnaire. Also, you don't know whether the questionnaire has been filled out by the prospect or by the prospect's spouse, secretary, or janitor.

If you do use questionnaires, here are five suggestions to help make them more effective:

1. *Make it easy.* The ease of filling out the form is a critical factor. Except for unaided recall questions, where you should ask for a one-word reply, everything else should be answerable by making a sim-

ple check mark or circling a number. Don't ask for complicated rankings. Put touchy queries, such as those about age, into groups rather than asking for specific data.

2. *Make it interesting.* Begin with the "meat" of the survey, and use any illustrations, trademarks, headlines, or product packages in the earlier questions. Ask the dry (and sometimes too personal) questions about age, education, and so on at the very end. Also, include some questions that the respondent will enjoy even if they are not very important to you.

3. *Make it personal.* Wherever possible, include a letter addressed to the individual, and make it clear that only a small number of people are being sent this form and that every answer represents tens of thousands of consumers.

4. *Make it important.* Explain, if it is true, that a major corporation is holding up a multimillion-dollar new-product launch until the person's opinions have been received, or that it is the practice of the company to act on this type of information in the name of good consumerism. The questionnaire also should look important. This is not the place to skimp on paper quality or typesetting.

5. *Make it profitable.* Most researchers use some type of premium: a small gift either promised in return for the questionnaire or enclosed with the quiz. The future gift is difficult because it requires disclosure of the name and address of the respondent. I prefer a small cash gift—perhaps a $2 bill, which is an interesting oddity in itself, or a check for $5 or $10. When sending questionnaires to business prospects, you can suggest that they may want to donate the gift to their favorite charity if there is a policy prohibiting the acceptance of such incentives.

One company uses questionnaires to pretest new products, even before they have been fully developed. Descriptions, not promotional copy, of half-a-dozen product concepts are given in three or four paragraphs each, and all shipping and billing terms are spelled out. Customers are asked to register their reactions this way:

( ) Would order

( ) Might order

( ) Some interest

( ) No interest

The questionnaires are sent to people on the company's own mailing list. Once the responses have been ranked, the company knows which product idea most interests their customers and which interests them the least. They can screen out the dogs before spending any money on developing or promoting the product.

Mathematical Analysis

These segmentation methods involve geographic clusters. Based on the idea that "birds of a feather flock together," they surmise group dynamics from the common denominators of postal zones, census tracts, and various subsegments of each. Today, with the evolution of database marketing, similar information and applications can be based on individual households to a degree never before possible.

Over 100 million individual households in the U.S. have provided some kind of lifestyle and product usage information. For millions more, we can add specific ages and marital status, as well as all the census and other information compiled by residence location.

While no one supplier owns all of the data, an extensive system of cross-licensing and data sharing has evolved so that virtually any existing data—from a half-dozen sources—can be overlaid onto your own list or onto an especially relevant outside list. Some of the suppliers who specialize in this are Donnelly Marketing, Database America, DirectTech, MBS/Multimode, Axciom, Metromail, InfoBase, and Polk/NDL. Your direct mail list broker can help you to determine which of these companies can best help you to meet your own needs.

Your own buyers can be pinpointed with all of these characteristics by first enhancing your list with this type of data and then subjecting it to mathematical analysis. Sometimes called *regression analysis,* this method matches characteristics and then uses one of several mathematical formulae to develop a profile of the list segments. This can be further analyzed in terms of market share, profitability, potential, and other goals. This analytical method is interesting and informative in itself, but it also helps to provide segments that can be subjected to conventional research methods, keeping in mind that different segments may respond to entirely different tactics.

RESEARCH ON NONVERBAL COMMUNICATION

Perhaps the most exciting frontier of research and its applications to direct marketing is nonverbal communication. It is only fitting that new applications in the art of communicating visually, without words, should be accompanied by new research methods.

The applications of psychology to all forms of advertising have led to some powerful breakthroughs that are only beginning to be applied to direct marketing. Foremost is the recognition that people cannot, or will not, always express themselves in words. Many people are not capable of expressing their feelings. In addition, some feelings cause guilt or embarrassment, such as "I'm sick and tired of reading to my child every night," or "I'm not sure I'm smart enough to invest in stocks," or "I like this car because it makes me feel powerful and sexy."

Such feelings can be the key to whole new advertising strategies, but they are difficult to ferret out in conventional interviewing. For this reason, a great many methods have been developed that enable advertisers to identify reactions which may be too difficult or personal for prospects to express verbally.

Physiological Methods

Measurement of involuntary reactions to stimuli, such as the sight of an advertisement, a commercial, an illustration, or even a simple benefit statement, can be done by several methods in common use today.

Brain Wave Measurement. An electroencephalograph records spontaneous electrical activity in the brain when the subject is shown different items. The results not only show attention and arousal but also indicate whether the response is favorable or unfavorable.

Eye-Movement Tracking. An optical device records exactly what the eye is looking at, how long the focus is maintained, and the sequence in which the message is perceived. This method presumes that greater attention to an element of an ad or mailing piece denotes greater interest.

Galvanic Skin Response. This method utilizes a psychogalvanometer which, when in contact with the subject's fingertips, records the rate of sweating every $2\frac{1}{2}$ seconds. Degrees of arousal indicate the frequency and intensity of the subject's feelings about the subject matter. I have seen demonstrations of this method that later correlated very closely to split-run test results, closely enough to eliminate sure losers. The theory here is that arousal may indicate good or bad feelings, but no arousal is always a sign that the ad won't work.

Pictorial Methods

To the extent that self-imagery is a factor in a buying decision, in general marketing or direct marketing, it is essential to measure the perceptions that people have of a company, a category, a product, and equally important, themselves.

Customers have clear impressions of who shops at a particular store, who wears a certain kind of fashion, who travels on a certain kind of transportation. If they think your product is not for "my kind of people," all the logical convincing in the world will not get them to send in the coupon or make a purchase. But a change in their impressions can!

One approach is to inquire what kind of automobile (or bird, or animal) a product connotes, and then compare it with one that the prospect identifies with personally. If you're in the investment business, symbols of strength and wisdom are desirable. If you're selling an upscale product, you don't want downscale images, and vice versa. I have seen a bank associated with foreign cars (a negative association in this case, as the bank was considered an outsider in the community). I have seen another bank associated with winos and bums. While shocking at first, these images indicate the presence of a problem that is solvable, and that would not have been solved if the problem had not been identified.

Photoimages are an incredibly precise measurement. One agency uses a method called Photosort. In this method, photographs of people are shown to individual prospects, who are asked to sort them into piles. The piles can represent different brands, different ways of cleaning a house, different ways of buying. The photographs, each of which represents previously identified personality and character attributes, also are rated according to the prospect's personal preferences. The result is a detailed score of the personality traits linked with a brand or a company.

No matter which technique one uses, the more sophisticated and psychological the research method, the more important it is to have professionals administer the program and interpret the results.

New Approaches

Some new research approaches, advocated in such books as *The Marketing Revolution* by Clancy and Shulman, are particularly applicable to direct marketing's selectivity and versioning capabilities. For instance, they point out that all customers are not alike, and averages of likes and dislikes are not as valuable as understanding specific market segments that would respond to product advantages or creative positionings. What counts is not what *most* people think, but what the thoughts are of those people who can be motivated to respond.

In another area, they point out that your present customer base is not necessarily the one most profitable to market to. Often it is more productive to open up a whole new segment than to squeeze the last few buyers from an overworked demographic group. This has been confirmed frequently in direct mail testing, which has demonstrated that supposedly marginal mailing lists often will respond well if sent different creative messages than so-called core lists.

10

TESTING

The measurability of direct marketing is such an integral part of this business that the word *testing* is used very lightly. Direct marketers talk of testing media, testing copy, and testing an offer. We run test campaigns, dry tests, split-run tests, element tests, and concept tests.

In its simplest form the word can be used as a synonym for *try*, as in running an advertisement in a publication or using a mailing list for the first time and then seeing if the results are satisfactory. In its most complex form, two- and three-dimensional grid tests can be constructed to simultaneously read media, offer, and copy variables on a new business proposition.

If a mailing list has one million names and you mail to the entire list the first time you try it, you aren't testing, you're gambling. The pragmatic defining characteristic of "testing" in direct mail is the desire to minimize downside financial risk.

How many pieces of mail do you have to send out in order to rely on the test results? Because direct mail is believed to be subject to the rules of statistical projectability, you should be able to mail as few as 3000 or 5000 pieces and determine a range of response rates that might be expected from the entire list. Most books on direct marketing, including the first edition of this work, included statistical validity tables to help determine the answer to this question. These tables are all based on formulas derived from game theory, the laws of chance, algebraic interpretations of sampling practice, and established formulas of statistical probability. Unfortunately, most of them have been difficult to put to practical use and have required many pages of explanation.

While the principles of testing are unchanged, I have tried to make the application as easy as possible. I have asked Lloyd Kieran, a respected direct marketing consultant now living in Laguna Niguel, California, to prepare an easy-to-use set of probability tables. Unlike tables in other books that list response rates and tell you how many samples you should have mailed, these tell you what the variations will be at selected practical sampling quantities and projected rates.

These tables, up to a 12 percent response rate, first appeared in my recent book, *Database Marketing* (McGraw-Hill, 1993). In that book, the tables range as high as 30 percent, reflecting current experience in this expanding application of database marketing.

PROBABILITY TABLES

One of the great advantages of the direct mail medium is its predictability. If one has information about past direct mail efforts, then it is not only possible but highly desirable to forecast the results of planned mailings. This is possible if some simple rules are followed.

When projecting the results of a planned mailing, one must keep in mind the basic rule of comparing "apples to apples." For example, it is essential to roll out a new mailing with the same package as used in the test. If you were to change the offer, the rollout really would be a new package, and the results would not be projectable based on the previous effort.

The laws of statistical probability will apply only if you minimize the variables and measure like to like. However, there are some variables that cannot be controlled. Time is a good example of such a condition. Even though you may mail exactly the same package a second time to exactly the same lists, you cannot overcome the time differential. You can minimize the variable to be sure—by mailing at the same time of year—but it is impossible to change the fact that you will have mailed in two different years. So there is always some difference, however small. (And if market conditions have changed dramatically, then time is a major differential.)

Probability Table Description

The probability tables (Tables 10-1 to 10-3) are based on a standard statistical formula for predicting a future outcome based on sample results. In all, there are three tables: one each for a 95 percent confidence level, a 99 percent confidence level, and a 90 percent confidence level. Each table shows the following:

- Sample sizes, ranging from 1000 to 100,000 pieces, expressed in thousands

- Response rates, expressed as percentages, ranging from 0.5 percent to 12 percent, in 0.5 percent increments

- Percent variation; that is, margin of error expressed as a percentage of the response rate
- Low projection; that is, the test response rate less the margin of error
- High projection; that is, the response rate plus the margin of error

How Probability Tables Work

For example, if you mailed 5000 pieces and achieved a 2 percent response rate, you can predict a future response rate if you replicate the test *exactly*. Now refer to Table 10-1, page 1, which has a 95 percent confidence level. In the column for the 2 percent response rate on the line for a 5000 sample, you will see a percentage variation of 19.4 percent in the "% Var." column. That means if you replicate the test exactly, you can expect to achieve a 2 percent response rate, plus or minus 19.4 percent, 95 times out of 100 replications. (There is the statistical probability that 5 times out of 100 replications you will *not* achieve that response rate, plus or minus 19.4 percent. However, 95 times out of 100 is pretty good odds.) Then, looking in the "Low" column, you will see 1.61 percent. That projection is the low end of the range, or 2 percent less 19.4 percent. Looking in the "High" column, you will see 2.39 percent, which represents 2 percent plus 19.4 percent, the high end of the range. In other words, if your test mailing was one of 5000 pieces and it achieved a 2 percent response, you can expect to achieve a rollout response as low as 1.61 percent and as high as 2.39 percent, or somewhere in between. Your confidence (or odds) of attaining that result is 95 times out of 100.

Now, for the moment assume that a 95 percent confidence level isn't good enough. Refer to Table 102, page 1, which has a 99 percent confidence level, and you will see that the margin of error has changed to 22.1 percent. The response rate now can be projected in a range from 1.56 percent to 2.44 percent, 99 times out of 100, if the test is replicated exactly. While the differences in the two response rate ranges may seem small at first glance, it is important to note the difference between the margins of error for a 95 percent confidence level and a 99 percent confidence level. Note that the former is 19.4 percent, the latter 22.1 percent. There is a 14 percent differential between the two that can be significant in some cases.

Let's complete our example now with a look at the 90 percent confidence level, using the same example of a 5000 piece mailing and a 2 percent response rate (Table 10-3, page 1). In this case the margin of error is 16.3 percent, and the range of the response rate will fall between 1.67 and 2.33 percent. While the projected response rate range is tighter, the confidence is not as great, for that response rate range can be expected only 90 times out of 100—not quite as good as a 95 percent confidence level, and certainly not as good as a 99 percent confidence level.

TABLE 10-1
DIRECT MAIL PROJECTION TABLE

95% Confidence Level—Standard Deviation: 1.960 (Page 1)

ANTICIPATED PERCENT RESPONSE

Sample Size (000)	.5% ±%	Variance Low	High	1.0% ±%	Variance Low	High	1.5% ±%	Variance Low	High	2.0% ±%	Variance Low	High	2.5% ±%	Variance Low	High	3.0% ±%	Variance Low	High
1.0	87.4%	.06%	.94%	61.7%	.38%	1.62%	50.2%	.75%	2.25%	43.4%	1.13%	2.87%	38.7%	1.53%	3.47%	35.2%	1.94%	4.06%
2.5	55.3%	.22%	.78%	39.0%	.61%	1.39%	31.8%	1.02%	1.98%	27.4%	1.45%	2.55%	24.5%	1.89%	3.11%	22.3%	2.33%	3.67%
5.0	39.1%	.30%	.70%	27.6%	.72%	1.28%	22.5%	1.16%	1.84%	19.4%	1.61%	2.39%	17.3%	2.07%	2.93%	15.8%	2.53%	3.47%
7.5	31.9%	.34%	.66%	22.5%	.77%	1.23%	18.3%	1.22%	1.78%	15.8%	1.68%	2.32%	14.1%	2.15%	2.85%	12.9%	2.61%	3.39%
10.0	27.6%	.36%	.64%	19.5%	.80%	1.20%	15.9%	1.26%	1.74%	13.7%	1.73%	2.27%	12.2%	2.19%	2.81%	11.1%	2.67%	3.33%
12.5	24.7%	.38%	.62%	17.4%	.83%	1.17%	14.2%	1.29%	1.71%	12.3%	1.75%	2.25%	10.9%	2.23%	2.77%	10.0%	2.70%	3.30%
15.0	22.6%	.39%	.61%	15.9%	.84%	1.16%	13.0%	1.31%	1.69%	11.2%	1.78%	2.22%	10.0%	2.25%	2.75%	9.1%	2.73%	3.27%
17.5	20.9%	.40%	.60%	14.7%	.85%	1.15%	12.0%	1.32%	1.68%	10.4%	1.79%	2.21%	9.3%	2.27%	2.73%	8.4%	2.75%	3.25%
20.0	19.6%	.40%	.60%	13.8%	.86%	1.14%	11.2%	1.33%	1.67%	9.7%	1.81%	2.19%	8.7%	2.28%	2.72%	7.9%	2.76%	3.24%
25.0	17.5%	.41%	.59%	12.3%	.88%	1.12%	10.0%	1.35%	1.65%	8.7%	1.83%	2.17%	7.7%	2.31%	2.69%	7.0%	2.79%	3.21%
30.0	16.0%	.42%	.58%	11.3%	.89%	1.11%	9.2%	1.36%	1.64%	7.9%	1.84%	2.16%	7.1%	2.32%	2.68%	6.4%	2.81%	3.19%
35.0	14.8%	.43%	.57%	10.4%	.90%	1.10%	8.5%	1.37%	1.63%	7.3%	1.85%	2.15%	6.5%	2.34%	2.66%	6.0%	2.82%	3.18%
40.0	13.8%	.43%	.57%	9.8%	.90%	1.10%	7.9%	1.38%	1.62%	6.9%	1.86%	2.14%	6.1%	2.35%	2.65%	5.6%	2.83%	3.17%
45.0	13.0%	.43%	.57%	9.2%	.91%	1.09%	7.5%	1.39%	1.61%	6.5%	1.87%	2.13%	5.8%	2.36%	2.64%	5.3%	2.84%	3.16%
50.0	12.4%	.44%	.56%	8.7%	.91%	1.09%	7.1%	1.39%	1.61%	6.1%	1.88%	2.12%	5.5%	2.36%	2.64%	5.0%	2.85%	3.15%
60.0	11.3%	.44%	.56%	8.0%	.92%	1.08%	6.5%	1.40%	1.60%	5.6%	1.89%	2.11%	5.0%	2.38%	2.62%	4.5%	2.86%	3.14%
70.0	10.5%	.45%	.55%	7.4%	.93%	1.07%	6.0%	1.41%	1.59%	5.2%	1.90%	2.10%	4.6%	2.38%	2.62%	4.2%	2.87%	3.13%
80.0	9.8%	.45%	.55%	6.9%	.93%	1.07%	5.6%	1.42%	1.58%	4.9%	1.90%	2.10%	4.3%	2.39%	2.61%	3.9%	2.88%	3.12%
90.0	9.2%	.45%	.55%	6.5%	.93%	1.07%	5.3%	1.42%	1.58%	4.6%	1.91%	2.09%	4.1%	2.40%	2.60%	3.7%	2.89%	3.11%
100.0	8.7%	.46%	.54%	6.2%	.94%	1.06%	5.0%	1.42%	1.58%	4.3%	1.91%	2.09%	3.9%	2.40%	2.60%	3.5%	2.89%	3.11%

TABLE 10-1
DIRECT MAIL PROJECTION TABLE (Continued)

95% Confidence Level—Standard Deviation: 1.960 (Page 2)

ANTICIPATED PERCENT RESPONSE

Sample Size (000)	3.5% ±%	Variance Low	High	4.0% ±%	Variance Low	High	4.5% ±%	Variance Low	High	5.0% ±%	Variance Low	High	5.5% ±%	Variance Low	High	6.0% ±%	Variance Low	High
1.0	32.5%	2.36%	4.64%	30.4%	2.79%	5.21%	28.6%	3.22%	5.78%	27.0%	3.65%	6.35%	25.7%	4.09%	6.91%	24.5%	4.53%	7.47%
2.5	20.6%	2.78%	4.22%	19.2%	3.23%	4.77%	18.1%	3.69%	5.31%	17.1%	4.15%	5.85%	16.2%	4.61%	6.39%	15.5%	5.07%	6.93%
5.0	14.6%	2.99%	4.01%	13.6%	3.46%	4.54%	12.8%	3.93%	5.07%	12.1%	4.40%	5.60%	11.5%	4.87%	6.13%	11.0%	5.34%	6.66%
7.5	11.9%	3.08%	3.92%	11.1%	3.56%	4.44%	10.4%	4.03%	4.97%	9.9%	4.51%	5.49%	9.4%	4.98%	6.02%	9.0%	5.46%	6.54%
10.0	10.3%	3.14%	3.86%	9.6%	3.62%	4.38%	9.0%	4.09%	4.91%	8.5%	4.57%	5.43%	8.1%	5.05%	5.95%	7.8%	5.53%	6.47%
12.5	9.2%	3.18%	3.82%	8.6%	3.66%	4.34%	8.1%	4.14%	4.86%	7.6%	4.62%	5.38%	7.3%	5.10%	5.90%	6.9%	5.58%	6.42%
15.0	8.4%	3.21%	3.79%	7.8%	3.69%	4.31%	7.4%	4.17%	4.83%	7.0%	4.65%	5.35%	6.6%	5.14%	5.86%	6.3%	5.62%	6.38%
17.5	7.8%	3.23%	3.77%	7.3%	3.71%	4.29%	6.8%	4.19%	4.81%	6.5%	4.68%	5.32%	6.1%	5.16%	5.84%	5.9%	5.65%	6.35%
20.0	7.3%	3.25%	3.75%	6.8%	3.73%	4.27%	6.4%	4.21%	4.79%	6.0%	4.70%	5.30%	5.7%	5.18%	5.82%	5.5%	5.67%	6.33%
25.0	6.5%	3.27%	3.73%	6.1%	3.76%	4.24%	5.7%	4.24%	4.76%	5.4%	4.73%	5.27%	5.1%	5.22%	5.78%	4.9%	5.71%	6.29%
30.0	5.9%	3.29%	3.71%	5.5%	3.78%	4.22%	5.2%	4.27%	4.73%	4.9%	4.75%	5.25%	4.7%	5.24%	5.76%	4.5%	5.73%	6.27%
35.0	5.5%	3.31%	3.69%	5.1%	3.79%	4.21%	4.8%	4.28%	4.72%	4.6%	4.77%	5.23%	4.3%	5.26%	5.74%	4.1%	5.75%	6.25%
40.0	5.1%	3.32%	3.68%	4.8%	3.81%	4.19%	4.5%	4.30%	4.70%	4.3%	4.79%	5.21%	4.1%	5.28%	5.72%	3.9%	5.77%	6.23%
45.0	4.9%	3.33%	3.67%	4.5%	3.82%	4.18%	4.3%	4.31%	4.69%	4.0%	4.80%	5.20%	3.8%	5.29%	5.71%	3.7%	5.78%	6.22%
50.0	4.6%	3.34%	3.66%	4.3%	3.83%	4.17%	4.0%	4.32%	4.68%	3.8%	4.81%	5.19%	3.6%	5.30%	5.70%	3.5%	5.79%	6.21%
60.0	4.2%	3.35%	3.65%	3.9%	3.84%	4.16%	3.7%	4.33%	4.67%	3.5%	4.83%	5.17%	3.3%	5.32%	5.68%	3.2%	5.81%	6.19%
70.0	3.9%	3.36%	3.64%	3.6%	3.85%	4.15%	3.4%	4.35%	4.65%	3.2%	4.84%	5.16%	3.1%	5.33%	5.67%	2.9%	5.82%	6.18%
80.0	3.6%	3.37%	3.63%	3.4%	3.86%	4.14%	3.2%	4.36%	4.64%	3.0%	4.85%	5.15%	2.9%	5.34%	5.66%	2.7%	5.84%	6.16%
90.0	3.4%	3.38%	3.62%	3.2%	3.87%	4.13%	3.0%	4.36%	4.64%	2.8%	4.86%	5.14%	2.7%	5.35%	5.65%	2.6%	5.84%	6.16%
100.0	3.3%	3.39%	3.61%	3.0%	3.88%	4.12%	2.9%	4.37%	4.63%	2.7%	4.86%	5.14%	2.6%	5.36%	5.64%	2.5%	5.85%	6.15%

TABLE 10-1
DIRECT MAIL PROJECTION TABLE (Continued)

95% Confidence Level—Standard Deviation: 1.960 (Page 3)

	ANTICIPATED PERCENT RESPONSE																	
	6.5%			7.0%			7.5%			8.0%			8.5%			9.0%		
		Variance			Variance			Variance			Variance			Variance			Variance	
Sample Size (000)	±%	Low	High	±%	Low	High	±%	Low	High	±%	Low	High	±%	Low	High	±%	Low	High
1.0	23.5%	4.97%	8.03%	22.6%	5.42%	8.58%	21.8%	5.87%	9.13%	21.0%	6.32%	9.68%	20.3%	6.77%	10.23%	19.7%	7.23%	10.77%
2.5	14.9%	5.53%	7.47%	14.3%	6.00%	8.00%	13.8%	6.47%	8.53%	13.3%	6.94%	9.06%	12.9%	7.41%	9.59%	12.5%	7.88%	10.12%
5.0	10.5%	5.82%	7.18%	10.1%	6.29%	7.71%	9.7%	6.77%	8.23%	9.4%	7.25%	8.75%	9.1%	7.73%	9.27%	8.8%	8.21%	9.79%
7.5	8.6%	5.94%	7.06%	8.2%	6.42%	7.58%	7.9%	6.90%	8.10%	7.7%	7.39%	8.61%	7.4%	7.87%	9.13%	7.2%	8.35%	9.65%
10.0	7.4%	6.02%	6.98%	7.1%	6.50%	7.50%	6.9%	6.98%	8.02%	6.6%	7.47%	8.53%	6.4%	7.95%	9.05%	6.2%	8.44%	9.56%
12.5	6.6%	6.07%	6.93%	6.4%	6.55%	7.45%	6.2%	7.04%	7.96%	5.9%	7.52%	8.48%	5.8%	8.01%	8.99%	5.6%	8.50%	9.50%
15.0	6.1%	6.11%	6.89%	5.8%	6.59%	7.41%	5.6%	7.08%	7.92%	5.4%	7.57%	8.43%	5.3%	8.05%	8.95%	5.1%	8.54%	9.46%
17.5	5.6%	6.13%	6.87%	5.4%	6.62%	7.38%	5.2%	7.11%	7.89%	5.0%	7.60%	8.40%	4.9%	8.09%	8.91%	4.7%	8.58%	9.42%
20.0	5.3%	6.16%	6.84%	5.1%	6.65%	7.35%	4.9%	7.13%	7.87%	4.7%	7.62%	8.38%	4.5%	8.11%	8.89%	4.4%	8.60%	9.40%
25.0	4.7%	6.19%	6.81%	4.5%	6.68%	7.32%	4.4%	7.17%	7.83%	4.2%	7.66%	8.34%	4.1%	8.15%	8.85%	3.9%	8.65%	9.35%
30.0	4.3%	6.22%	6.78%	4.1%	6.71%	7.29%	4.0%	7.20%	7.80%	3.8%	7.69%	8.31%	3.7%	8.18%	8.82%	3.6%	8.68%	9.32%
35.0	4.0%	6.24%	6.76%	3.8%	6.73%	7.27%	3.7%	7.22%	7.78%	3.6%	7.72%	8.28%	3.4%	8.21%	8.79%	3.3%	8.70%	9.30%
40.0	3.7%	6.26%	6.74%	3.6%	6.75%	7.25%	3.4%	7.24%	7.76%	3.3%	7.73%	8.27%	3.2%	8.23%	8.77%	3.1%	8.72%	9.28%
45.0	3.5%	6.27%	6.73%	3.4%	6.76%	7.24%	3.2%	7.26%	7.74%	3.1%	7.75%	8.25%	3.0%	8.24%	8.76%	2.9%	8.74%	9.26%
50.0	3.3%	6.28%	6.72%	3.2%	6.78%	7.22%	3.1%	7.27%	7.73%	3.0%	7.76%	8.24%	2.9%	8.26%	8.74%	2.8%	8.75%	9.25%
60.0	3.0%	6.30%	6.70%	2.9%	6.80%	7.20%	2.8%	7.29%	7.71%	2.7%	7.78%	8.22%	2.6%	8.28%	8.72%	2.5%	8.77%	9.23%
70.0	2.8%	6.32%	6.68%	2.7%	6.81%	7.19%	2.6%	7.30%	7.70%	2.5%	7.80%	8.20%	2.4%	8.29%	8.71%	2.4%	8.79%	9.21%
80.0	2.6%	6.33%	6.67%	2.5%	6.82%	7.18%	2.4%	7.32%	7.68%	2.3%	7.81%	8.19%	2.3%	8.31%	8.69%	2.2%	8.80%	9.20%
90.0	2.5%	6.34%	6.66%	2.4%	6.83%	7.17%	2.3%	7.33%	7.67%	2.2%	7.82%	8.18%	2.1%	8.32%	8.68%	2.1%	8.81%	9.19%
100.0	2.4%	6.35%	6.65%	2.3%	6.84%	7.16%	2.2%	7.34%	7.66%	2.1%	7.83%	8.17%	2.0%	8.33%	8.67%	2.0%	8.82%	9.18%

TABLE 10-1
DIRECT MAIL PROJECTION TABLE (Continued)

95% Confidence Level—Standard Deviation: 1.960 (Page 4)

ANTICIPATED PERCENT RESPONSE

Sample Size (000)	9.5%			10.0%			10.5%			11.0%			11.5%			12.0%		
	±%	Variance Low	High	±%	Variance Low	High	±%	Variance Low	High	±%	Variance Low	High	±%	Variance Low	High	±%	Variance Low	High
1.0	19.1%	7.68%	11.32%	18.6%	8.14%	11.86%	18.1%	8.60%	12.40%	17.6%	9.06%	12.94%	17.2%	9.52%	13.48%	16.8%	9.99%	14.01%
2.5	12.1%	8.35%	10.65%	11.8%	8.82%	11.18%	11.4%	9.30%	11.70%	11.2%	9.77%	12.23%	10.9%	10.25%	12.75%	10.6%	10.73%	13.27%
5.0	8.6%	8.69%	10.31%	8.3%	9.17%	10.83%	8.1%	9.65%	11.35%	7.9%	10.13%	11.87%	7.7%	10.62%	12.38%	7.5%	11.10%	12.90%
7.5	7.0%	8.84%	10.16%	6.8%	9.32%	10.68%	6.6%	9.81%	11.19%	6.4%	10.29%	11.71%	6.3%	10.78%	12.22%	6.1%	11.26%	12.74%
10.0	6.0%	8.93%	10.07%	5.9%	9.41%	10.59%	5.7%	9.90%	11.10%	5.6%	10.39%	11.61%	5.4%	10.87%	12.13%	5.3%	11.36%	12.64%
12.5	5.4%	8.99%	10.01%	5.3%	9.47%	10.53%	5.1%	9.96%	11.04%	5.0%	10.45%	11.55%	4.9%	10.94%	12.06%	4.7%	11.43%	12.57%
15.0	4.9%	9.03%	9.97%	4.8%	9.52%	10.48%	4.7%	10.01%	10.99%	4.6%	10.50%	11.50%	4.4%	10.99%	12.01%	4.3%	11.48%	12.52%
17.5	4.6%	9.07%	9.93%	4.4%	9.56%	10.44%	4.3%	10.05%	10.95%	4.2%	10.54%	11.46%	4.1%	11.03%	11.97%	4.0%	11.52%	12.48%
20.0	4.3%	9.09%	9.91%	4.2%	9.58%	10.42%	4.0%	10.08%	10.92%	3.9%	10.57%	11.43%	3.8%	11.06%	11.94%	3.8%	11.55%	12.45%
25.0	3.8%	9.14%	9.86%	3.7%	9.63%	10.37%	3.6%	10.12%	10.88%	3.5%	10.61%	11.39%	3.4%	11.10%	11.90%	3.4%	11.60%	12.40%
30.0	3.5%	9.17%	9.83%	3.4%	9.66%	10.34%	3.3%	10.15%	10.85%	3.2%	10.65%	11.35%	3.1%	11.14%	11.86%	3.1%	11.63%	12.37%
35.0	3.2%	9.19%	9.81%	3.1%	9.69%	10.31%	3.1%	10.18%	10.82%	3.0%	10.67%	11.33%	2.9%	11.17%	11.83%	2.8%	11.66%	12.34%
40.0	3.0%	9.21%	9.79%	2.9%	9.71%	10.29%	2.9%	10.20%	10.80%	2.8%	10.69%	11.31%	2.7%	11.19%	11.81%	2.7%	11.68%	12.32%
45.0	2.9%	9.23%	9.77%	2.8%	9.72%	10.28%	2.7%	10.22%	10.78%	2.6%	10.71%	11.29%	2.6%	11.21%	11.79%	2.5%	11.70%	12.30%
50.0	2.7%	9.24%	9.76%	2.6%	9.74%	10.26%	2.6%	10.23%	10.77%	2.5%	10.73%	11.27%	2.4%	11.22%	11.78%	2.4%	11.72%	12.28%
60.0	2.5%	9.27%	9.73%	2.4%	9.76%	10.24%	2.3%	10.25%	10.75%	2.3%	10.75%	11.25%	2.2%	11.24%	11.76%	2.2%	11.74%	12.26%
70.0	2.3%	9.28%	9.72%	2.2%	9.78%	10.22%	2.2%	10.27%	10.73%	2.1%	10.77%	11.23%	2.1%	11.26%	11.74%	2.0%	11.76%	12.24%
80.0	2.1%	9.30%	9.70%	2.1%	9.79%	10.21%	2.0%	10.29%	10.71%	2.0%	10.78%	11.22%	1.9%	11.28%	11.72%	1.9%	11.77%	12.23%
90.0	2.0%	9.31%	9.69%	2.0%	9.80%	10.20%	1.9%	10.30%	10.70%	1.9%	10.80%	11.20%	1.8%	11.29%	11.71%	1.8%	11.79%	12.21%
100.0	1.9%	9.32%	9.68%	1.9%	9.81%	10.19%	1.8%	10.31%	10.69%	1.8%	10.81%	11.19%	1.7%	11.30%	11.70%	1.7%	11.80%	12.20%

TABLE 10-2
DIRECT MAIL PROJECTION TABLE

99% Confidence Level—Standard Deviation: 2.236 (Page 1)

ANTICIPATED PERCENT RESPONSE

Sample Size (000)	.5% ±%	.5% Variance Low	.5% High	1.0% ±%	1.0% Variance Low	1.0% High	1.5% ±%	1.5% Variance Low	1.5% High	2.0% ±%	2.0% Variance Low	2.0% High	2.5% ±%	2.5% Variance Low	2.5% High	3.0% ±%	3.0% Variance Low	3.0% High
1.0	99.7%	.00%	1.00%	70.4%	.30%	1.70%	57.3%	.64%	2.36%	49.5%	1.01%	2.99%	44.2%	1.40%	3.60%	40.2%	1.79%	4.21%
2.5	63.1%	.18%	.82%	44.5%	.56%	1.44%	36.2%	.96%	2.04%	31.3%	1.37%	2.63%	27.9%	1.80%	3.20%	25.4%	2.24%	3.76%
5.0	44.6%	.28%	.72%	31.5%	.69%	1.31%	25.6%	1.12%	1.88%	22.1%	1.56%	2.44%	19.7%	2.01%	2.99%	18.0%	2.46%	3.54%
7.5	36.4%	.32%	.68%	25.7%	.74%	1.26%	20.9%	1.19%	1.81%	18.1%	1.64%	2.36%	16.1%	2.10%	2.90%	14.7%	2.56%	3.44%
10.0	31.5%	.34%	.66%	22.2%	.78%	1.22%	18.1%	1.23%	1.77%	15.7%	1.69%	2.31%	14.0%	2.15%	2.85%	12.7%	2.62%	3.38%
12.5	28.2%	.36%	.64%	19.9%	.80%	1.20%	16.2%	1.26%	1.74%	14.0%	1.72%	2.28%	12.5%	2.19%	2.81%	11.4%	2.66%	3.34%
15.0	25.8%	.37%	.63%	18.2%	.82%	1.18%	14.8%	1.28%	1.72%	12.8%	1.74%	2.26%	11.4%	2.21%	2.79%	10.4%	2.69%	3.31%
17.5	23.8%	.38%	.62%	16.8%	.83%	1.17%	13.7%	1.29%	1.71%	11.8%	1.76%	2.24%	10.6%	2.24%	2.76%	9.6%	2.71%	3.29%
20.0	22.3%	.39%	.61%	15.7%	.84%	1.16%	12.8%	1.31%	1.69%	11.1%	1.78%	2.22%	9.9%	2.25%	2.75%	9.0%	2.73%	3.27%
25.0	19.9%	.40%	.60%	14.1%	.86%	1.14%	11.5%	1.33%	1.67%	9.9%	1.80%	2.20%	8.8%	2.28%	2.72%	8.0%	2.76%	3.24%
30.0	18.2%	.41%	.59%	12.8%	.87%	1.13%	10.5%	1.34%	1.66%	9.0%	1.82%	2.18%	8.1%	2.30%	2.70%	7.3%	2.78%	3.22%
35.0	16.9%	.42%	.58%	11.9%	.88%	1.12%	9.7%	1.35%	1.65%	8.4%	1.83%	2.17%	7.5%	2.31%	2.69%	6.8%	2.80%	3.20%
40.0	15.8%	.42%	.58%	11.1%	.89%	1.11%	9.1%	1.36%	1.64%	7.8%	1.84%	2.16%	7.0%	2.33%	2.67%	6.4%	2.81%	3.19%
45.0	14.9%	.43%	.57%	10.5%	.90%	1.10%	8.5%	1.37%	1.63%	7.4%	1.85%	2.15%	6.6%	2.34%	2.66%	6.0%	2.82%	3.18%
50.0	14.1%	.43%	.57%	9.9%	.90%	1.10%	8.1%	1.38%	1.62%	7.0%	1.86%	2.14%	6.2%	2.34%	2.66%	5.7%	2.83%	3.17%
60.0	12.9%	.44%	.56%	9.1%	.91%	1.09%	7.4%	1.39%	1.61%	6.4%	1.87%	2.13%	5.7%	2.36%	2.64%	5.2%	2.84%	3.16%
70.0	11.9%	.44%	.56%	8.4%	.92%	1.08%	6.8%	1.40%	1.60%	5.9%	1.88%	2.12%	5.3%	2.37%	2.63%	4.8%	2.86%	3.14%
80.0	11.2%	.44%	.56%	7.9%	.92%	1.08%	6.4%	1.40%	1.60%	5.5%	1.89%	2.11%	4.9%	2.38%	2.62%	4.5%	2.87%	3.13%
90.0	10.5%	.45%	.55%	7.4%	.93%	1.07%	6.0%	1.41%	1.59%	5.2%	1.90%	2.10%	4.7%	2.38%	2.62%	4.2%	2.87%	3.13%
100.0	10.0%	.45%	.55%	7.0%	.93%	1.07%	5.7%	1.41%	1.59%	4.9%	1.90%	2.10%	4.4%	2.39%	2.61%	4.0%	2.88%	3.12%

TABLE 10-2
DIRECT MAIL PROJECTION TABLE (Continued)

99% Confidence Level—Standard Deviation: 2.236 (Page 2)

ANTICIPATED PERCENT RESPONSE

Sample Size (000)	3.5% ±%	3.5% Variance Low	3.5% High	4.0% ±%	4.0% Variance Low	4.0% High	4.5% ±%	4.5% Variance Low	4.5% High	5.0% ±%	5.0% Variance Low	5.0% High	5.5% ±%	5.5% Variance Low	5.5% High	6.0% ±%	6.0% Variance Low	6.0% High
1.0	37.1%	2.20%	4.80%	34.6%	2.61%	5.39%	32.6%	3.03%	5.97%	30.8%	3.46%	6.54%	29.3%	3.89%	7.11%	28.0%	4.32%	7.68%
2.5	23.5%	2.68%	4.32%	21.9%	3.12%	4.88%	20.6%	3.57%	5.43%	19.5%	4.03%	5.97%	18.5%	4.48%	6.52%	17.7%	4.94%	7.06%
5.0	16.6%	2.92%	4.08%	15.5%	3.38%	4.62%	14.6%	3.84%	5.16%	13.8%	4.31%	5.69%	13.1%	4.78%	6.22%	12.5%	5.25%	6.75%
7.5	13.6%	3.03%	3.97%	12.6%	3.49%	4.51%	11.9%	3.96%	5.04%	11.3%	4.44%	5.56%	10.7%	4.91%	6.09%	10.2%	5.39%	6.61%
10.0	11.7%	3.09%	3.91%	11.0%	3.56%	4.44%	10.3%	4.04%	4.96%	9.7%	4.51%	5.49%	9.3%	4.99%	6.01%	8.9%	5.47%	6.53%
12.5	10.5%	3.13%	3.87%	9.8%	3.61%	4.39%	9.2%	4.09%	4.91%	8.7%	4.56%	5.44%	8.3%	5.04%	5.96%	7.9%	5.53%	6.47%
15.0	9.6%	3.16%	3.84%	8.9%	3.64%	4.36%	8.4%	4.12%	4.88%	8.0%	4.60%	5.40%	7.6%	5.08%	5.92%	7.2%	5.57%	6.43%
17.5	8.9%	3.19%	3.81%	8.3%	3.67%	4.33%	7.8%	4.15%	4.85%	7.4%	4.63%	5.37%	7.0%	5.11%	5.89%	6.7%	5.60%	6.40%
20.0	8.3%	3.21%	3.79%	7.7%	3.69%	4.31%	7.3%	4.17%	4.83%	6.9%	4.66%	5.34%	6.6%	5.14%	5.86%	6.3%	5.62%	6.38%
25.0	7.4%	3.24%	3.76%	6.9%	3.72%	4.28%	6.5%	4.21%	4.79%	6.2%	4.69%	5.31%	5.9%	5.18%	5.82%	5.6%	5.66%	6.34%
30.0	6.8%	3.26%	3.74%	6.3%	3.75%	4.25%	5.9%	4.23%	4.77%	5.6%	4.72%	5.28%	5.4%	5.21%	5.79%	5.1%	5.69%	6.31%
35.0	6.3%	3.28%	3.72%	5.9%	3.77%	4.23%	5.5%	4.25%	4.75%	5.2%	4.74%	5.26%	5.0%	5.23%	5.77%	4.7%	5.72%	6.28%
40.0	5.9%	3.29%	3.71%	5.5%	3.78%	4.22%	5.2%	4.27%	4.73%	4.9%	4.76%	5.24%	4.6%	5.25%	5.75%	4.4%	5.73%	6.27%
45.0	5.5%	3.31%	3.69%	5.2%	3.79%	4.21%	4.9%	4.28%	4.72%	4.6%	4.77%	5.23%	4.4%	5.26%	5.74%	4.2%	5.75%	6.25%
50.0	5.3%	3.32%	3.68%	4.9%	3.80%	4.20%	4.6%	4.29%	4.71%	4.4%	4.78%	5.22%	4.1%	5.27%	5.73%	4.0%	5.76%	6.24%
60.0	4.8%	3.33%	3.67%	4.5%	3.82%	4.18%	4.2%	4.31%	4.69%	4.0%	4.80%	5.20%	3.8%	5.29%	5.71%	3.6%	5.78%	6.22%
70.0	4.4%	3.34%	3.66%	4.1%	3.83%	4.17%	3.9%	4.32%	4.68%	3.7%	4.82%	5.18%	3.5%	5.31%	5.69%	3.3%	5.80%	6.20%
80.0	4.2%	3.35%	3.65%	3.9%	3.85%	4.15%	3.6%	4.34%	4.66%	3.4%	4.83%	5.17%	3.3%	5.32%	5.68%	3.1%	5.81%	6.19%
90.0	3.9%	3.36%	3.64%	3.7%	3.85%	4.15%	3.4%	4.35%	4.65%	3.2%	4.84%	5.16%	3.1%	5.33%	5.67%	3.0%	5.82%	6.18%
100.0	3.7%	3.37%	3.63%	3.5%	3.86%	4.14%	3.3%	4.35%	4.65%	3.1%	4.85%	5.15%	2.9%	5.34%	5.66%	2.8%	5.83%	6.17%

TABLE 10-2
DIRECT MAIL PROJECTION TABLE (Continued)

99% Confidence Level—Standard Deviation: 2.236 (Page 3)

| | ANTICIPATED PERCENT RESPONSE | | | | | | | | | | | | | | | | | |
| | 6.5% | | | 7.0% | | | 7.5% | | | 8.0% | | | 8.5% | | | 9.0% | | |
Sample Size (000)	±%	Variance Low	High	±%	Variance Low	High	±%	Variance Low	High	±%	Variance Low	High	±%	Variance Low	High	±%	Variance Low	High
1.0	26.8%	4.76%	8.24%	25.8%	5.20%	8.80%	24.8%	5.64%	9.36%	24.0%	6.08%	9.92%	23.2%	6.53%	10.47%	22.5%	6.98%	11.02%
2.5	17.0%	5.40%	7.60%	16.3%	5.86%	8.14%	15.7%	6.32%	8.68%	15.2%	6.79%	9.21%	14.7%	7.25%	9.75%	14.2%	7.72%	10.28%
5.0	12.0%	5.72%	7.28%	11.5%	6.19%	7.81%	11.1%	6.67%	8.33%	10.7%	7.14%	8.86%	10.4%	7.62%	9.38%	10.1%	8.10%	9.90%
7.5	9.8%	5.86%	7.14%	9.4%	6.34%	7.66%	9.1%	6.82%	8.18%	8.8%	7.30%	8.70%	8.5%	7.78%	9.22%	8.2%	8.26%	9.74%
10.0	8.5%	5.95%	7.05%	8.2%	6.43%	7.57%	7.9%	6.91%	8.09%	7.6%	7.39%	8.61%	7.3%	7.88%	9.12%	7.1%	8.36%	9.64%
12.5	7.6%	6.01%	6.99%	7.3%	6.49%	7.51%	7.0%	6.97%	8.03%	6.8%	7.46%	8.54%	6.6%	7.94%	9.06%	6.4%	8.43%	9.57%
15.0	6.9%	6.05%	6.95%	6.7%	6.53%	7.47%	6.4%	7.02%	7.98%	6.2%	7.50%	8.50%	6.0%	7.99%	9.01%	5.8%	8.48%	9.52%
17.5	6.4%	6.08%	6.92%	6.2%	6.57%	7.43%	5.9%	7.05%	7.95%	5.7%	7.54%	8.46%	5.5%	8.03%	8.97%	5.4%	8.52%	9.48%
20.0	6.0%	6.11%	6.89%	5.8%	6.60%	7.40%	5.6%	7.08%	7.92%	5.4%	7.57%	8.43%	5.2%	8.06%	8.94%	5.0%	8.55%	9.45%
25.0	5.4%	6.15%	6.85%	5.2%	6.64%	7.36%	5.0%	7.13%	7.87%	4.8%	7.62%	8.38%	4.6%	8.11%	8.89%	4.5%	8.60%	9.40%
30.0	4.9%	6.18%	6.82%	4.7%	6.67%	7.33%	4.5%	7.16%	7.84%	4.4%	7.65%	8.35%	4.2%	8.14%	8.86%	4.1%	8.63%	9.37%
35.0	4.5%	6.21%	6.79%	4.4%	6.70%	7.30%	4.2%	7.19%	7.81%	4.1%	7.68%	8.32%	3.9%	8.17%	8.83%	3.8%	8.66%	9.34%
40.0	4.2%	6.22%	6.78%	4.1%	6.71%	7.29%	3.9%	7.21%	7.79%	3.8%	7.70%	8.30%	3.7%	8.19%	8.81%	3.6%	8.68%	9.32%
45.0	4.0%	6.24%	6.76%	3.8%	6.73%	7.27%	3.7%	7.22%	7.78%	3.6%	7.71%	8.29%	3.5%	8.21%	8.79%	3.4%	8.70%	9.30%
50.0	3.8%	6.25%	6.75%	3.6%	6.74%	7.26%	3.5%	7.24%	7.76%	3.4%	7.73%	8.27%	3.3%	8.22%	8.78%	3.2%	8.71%	9.29%
60.0	3.5%	6.27%	6.73%	3.3%	6.77%	7.23%	3.2%	7.26%	7.74%	3.1%	7.75%	8.25%	3.0%	8.25%	8.75%	2.9%	8.74%	9.26%
70.0	3.2%	6.29%	6.71%	3.1%	6.78%	7.22%	3.0%	7.28%	7.72%	2.9%	7.77%	8.23%	2.8%	8.26%	8.74%	2.7%	8.76%	9.24%
80.0	3.0%	6.31%	6.69%	2.9%	6.80%	7.20%	2.8%	7.29%	7.71%	2.7%	7.79%	8.21%	2.6%	8.28%	8.72%	2.5%	8.77%	9.23%
90.0	2.8%	6.32%	6.68%	2.7%	6.81%	7.19%	2.6%	7.30%	7.70%	2.5%	7.80%	8.20%	2.4%	8.29%	8.71%	2.4%	8.79%	9.21%
100.0	2.7%	6.33%	6.67%	2.6%	6.82%	7.18%	2.5%	7.31%	7.69%	2.4%	7.81%	8.19%	2.3%	8.30%	8.70%	2.2%	8.80%	9.20%

TABLE 10-2
DIRECT MAIL PROJECTION TABLE (Continued)

99% Confidence Level—Standard Deviation: 2.236 (Page 4)

ANTICIPATED PERCENT RESPONSE

Sample Size (000)	9.5% ±%	Variance Low	High	10.0% ±%	Variance Low	High	10.5% ±%	Variance Low	High	11.0% ±%	Variance Low	High	11.5% ±%	Variance Low	High	12.0% ±%	Variance Low	High
1.0	21.8%	7.43%	11.57%	21.2%	7.88%	12.12%	20.6%	8.33%	12.67%	20.1%	8.79%	13.21%	19.6%	9.24%	13.76%	19.1%	9.70%	14.30%
2.5	13.8%	8.19%	10.81%	13.4%	8.66%	11.34%	13.1%	9.13%	11.87%	12.7%	9.60%	12.40%	12.4%	10.07%	12.93%	12.1%	10.55%	13.45%
5.0	9.8%	8.57%	10.43%	9.5%	9.05%	10.95%	9.2%	9.53%	11.47%	9.0%	10.01%	11.99%	8.8%	10.49%	12.51%	8.6%	10.97%	13.03%
7.5	8.0%	8.74%	10.26%	7.7%	9.23%	10.77%	7.5%	9.71%	11.29%	7.3%	10.19%	11.81%	7.2%	10.68%	12.32%	7.0%	11.16%	12.84%
10.0	6.9%	8.84%	10.16%	6.7%	9.33%	10.67%	6.5%	9.81%	11.19%	6.4%	10.30%	11.70%	6.2%	10.79%	12.21%	6.1%	11.27%	12.73%
12.5	6.2%	8.91%	10.09%	6.0%	9.40%	10.60%	5.8%	9.89%	11.11%	5.7%	10.37%	11.63%	5.5%	10.86%	12.14%	5.4%	11.35%	12.65%
15.0	5.6%	8.96%	10.04%	5.5%	9.45%	10.55%	5.3%	9.94%	11.06%	5.2%	10.43%	11.57%	5.1%	10.92%	12.08%	4.9%	11.41%	12.59%
17.5	5.2%	9.00%	10.00%	5.1%	9.49%	10.51%	4.9%	9.98%	11.02%	4.8%	10.47%	11.53%	4.7%	10.96%	12.04%	4.6%	11.45%	12.55%
20.0	4.9%	9.04%	9.96%	4.7%	9.53%	10.47%	4.6%	10.02%	10.98%	4.5%	10.51%	11.49%	4.4%	11.00%	12.00%	4.3%	11.49%	12.51%
25.0	4.4%	9.09%	9.91%	4.2%	9.58%	10.42%	4.1%	10.07%	10.93%	4.0%	10.56%	11.44%	3.9%	11.05%	11.95%	3.8%	11.54%	12.46%
30.0	4.0%	9.12%	9.88%	3.9%	9.61%	10.39%	3.8%	10.10%	10.90%	3.7%	10.60%	11.40%	3.6%	11.09%	11.91%	3.5%	11.58%	12.42%
35.0	3.7%	9.15%	9.85%	3.6%	9.64%	10.36%	3.5%	10.13%	10.87%	3.4%	10.63%	11.37%	3.3%	11.12%	11.88%	3.2%	11.61%	12.39%
40.0	3.5%	9.17%	9.83%	3.4%	9.66%	10.34%	3.3%	10.16%	10.84%	3.2%	10.65%	11.35%	3.1%	11.14%	11.86%	3.0%	11.64%	12.36%
45.0	3.3%	9.19%	9.81%	3.2%	9.68%	10.32%	3.1%	10.18%	10.82%	3.0%	10.67%	11.33%	2.9%	11.16%	11.84%	2.9%	11.66%	12.34%
50.0	3.1%	9.21%	9.79%	3.0%	9.70%	10.30%	2.9%	10.19%	10.81%	2.8%	10.69%	11.31%	2.8%	11.18%	11.82%	2.7%	11.68%	12.32%
60.0	2.8%	9.23%	9.77%	2.7%	9.73%	10.27%	2.7%	10.22%	10.78%	2.6%	10.71%	11.29%	2.5%	11.21%	11.79%	2.5%	11.70%	12.30%
70.0	2.6%	9.25%	9.75%	2.5%	9.75%	10.25%	2.5%	10.24%	10.76%	2.4%	10.74%	11.26%	2.3%	11.23%	11.77%	2.3%	11.73%	12.27%
80.0	2.4%	9.27%	9.73%	2.4%	9.76%	10.24%	2.3%	10.26%	10.74%	2.2%	10.75%	11.25%	2.2%	11.25%	11.75%	2.1%	11.74%	12.26%
90.0	2.3%	9.28%	9.72%	2.3%	9.78%	10.22%	2.2%	10.27%	10.73%	2.1%	10.77%	11.23%	2.1%	11.26%	11.74%	2.0%	11.76%	12.24%
100.0	2.2%	9.29%	9.71%	2.1%	9.79%	10.21%	2.1%	10.28%	10.72%	2.0%	10.78%	11.22%	2.0%	11.27%	11.73%	1.9%	11.77%	12.23%

TABLE 10-3
DIRECT MAIL PROJECTION TABLE

90% Confidence Level—Standard Deviation: 1.645 (Page 1)

ANTICIPATED PERCENT RESPONSE

Sample Size (000)	.5% ±%	Variance Low	High	1.0% ±%	Variance Low	High	1.5% ±%	Variance Low	High	2.0% ±%	Variance Low	High	2.5% ±%	Variance Low	High	3.0% ±%	Variance Low	High
1.0	73.4%	.13%	.87%	51.8%	.48%	1.52%	42.2%	.87%	2.13%	36.4%	1.27%	2.73%	32.5%	1.69%	3.31%	29.6%	2.11%	3.89%
2.5	46.4%	.27%	.73%	32.7%	.67%	1.33%	26.7%	1.10%	1.90%	23.0%	1.54%	2.46%	20.5%	1.99%	3.01%	18.7%	2.44%	3.56%
5.0	32.8%	.34%	.66%	23.1%	.77%	1.23%	18.9%	1.22%	1.78%	16.3%	1.67%	2.33%	14.5%	2.14%	2.86%	13.2%	2.60%	3.40%
7.5	26.8%	.37%	.63%	18.9%	.81%	1.19%	15.4%	1.27%	1.73%	13.3%	1.73%	2.27%	11.9%	2.20%	2.80%	10.8%	2.68%	3.32%
10.0	23.2%	.38%	.62%	16.4%	.84%	1.16%	13.3%	1.30%	1.70%	11.5%	1.77%	2.23%	10.3%	2.24%	2.76%	9.4%	2.72%	3.28%
12.5	20.8%	.40%	.60%	14.6%	.85%	1.15%	11.9%	1.32%	1.68%	10.3%	1.79%	2.21%	9.2%	2.27%	2.73%	8.4%	2.75%	3.25%
15.0	18.9%	.41%	.59%	13.4%	.87%	1.13%	10.9%	1.34%	1.66%	9.4%	1.81%	2.19%	8.4%	2.29%	2.71%	7.6%	2.77%	3.23%
17.5	17.5%	.41%	.59%	12.4%	.88%	1.12%	10.1%	1.35%	1.65%	8.7%	1.83%	2.17%	7.8%	2.31%	2.69%	7.1%	2.79%	3.21%
20.0	16.4%	.42%	.58%	11.6%	.88%	1.12%	9.4%	1.36%	1.64%	8.1%	1.84%	2.16%	7.3%	2.32%	2.68%	6.6%	2.80%	3.20%
25.0	14.7%	.43%	.57%	10.4%	.90%	1.10%	8.4%	1.37%	1.63%	7.3%	1.85%	2.15%	6.5%	2.34%	2.66%	5.9%	2.82%	3.18%
30.0	13.4%	.43%	.57%	9.4%	.91%	1.09%	7.7%	1.38%	1.62%	6.6%	1.87%	2.13%	5.9%	2.35%	2.65%	5.4%	2.84%	3.16%
35.0	12.4%	.44%	.56%	8.7%	.91%	1.09%	7.1%	1.39%	1.61%	6.2%	1.88%	2.12%	5.5%	2.36%	2.64%	5.0%	2.85%	3.15%
40.0	11.6%	.44%	.56%	8.2%	.92%	1.08%	6.7%	1.40%	1.60%	5.8%	1.88%	2.12%	5.1%	2.37%	2.63%	4.7%	2.86%	3.14%
45.0	10.9%	.45%	.55%	7.7%	.92%	1.08%	6.3%	1.41%	1.59%	5.4%	1.89%	2.11%	4.8%	2.38%	2.62%	4.4%	2.87%	3.13%
50.0	10.4%	.45%	.55%	7.3%	.93%	1.07%	6.0%	1.41%	1.59%	5.1%	1.90%	2.10%	4.6%	2.39%	2.61%	4.2%	2.87%	3.13%
60.0	9.5%	.45%	.55%	6.7%	.93%	1.07%	5.4%	1.42%	1.58%	4.7%	1.91%	2.09%	4.2%	2.40%	2.60%	3.8%	2.89%	3.11%
70.0	8.8%	.46%	.54%	6.2%	.94%	1.06%	5.0%	1.42%	1.58%	4.4%	1.91%	2.09%	3.9%	2.40%	2.60%	3.5%	2.89%	3.11%
80.0	8.2%	.46%	.54%	5.8%	.94%	1.06%	4.7%	1.43%	1.57%	4.1%	1.92%	2.08%	3.6%	2.41%	2.59%	3.3%	2.90%	3.10%
90.0	7.7%	.46%	.54%	5.5%	.95%	1.05%	4.4%	1.43%	1.57%	3.8%	1.92%	2.08%	3.4%	2.41%	2.59%	3.1%	2.91%	3.09%
100.0	7.3%	.46%	.54%	5.2%	.95%	1.05%	4.2%	1.44%	1.56%	3.6%	1.93%	2.07%	3.2%	2.42%	2.58%	3.0%	2.91%	3.09%

TABLE 10-3
DIRECT MAIL PROJECTION TABLE (Continued)

90% Confidence Level—Standard Deviation: 1.645 (Page 2)

Sample Size (000)	3.5% ±%	Variance Low	High	4.0% ±%	Variance Low	High	4.5% ±%	Variance Low	High	5.0% ±%	Variance Low	High	5.5% ±%	Variance Low	High	6.0% ±%	Variance Low	High
1.0	27.3%	2.54%	4.46%	25.5%	2.98%	5.02%	24.0%	3.42%	5.58%	22.7%	3.87%	6.13%	21.6%	4.31%	6.69%	20.6%	4.76%	7.24%
2.5	17.3%	2.90%	4.10%	16.1%	3.36%	4.64%	15.2%	3.82%	5.18%	14.3%	4.28%	5.72%	13.6%	4.75%	6.25%	13.0%	5.22%	6.78%
5.0	12.2%	3.07%	3.93%	11.4%	3.54%	4.46%	10.7%	4.02%	4.98%	10.1%	4.49%	5.51%	9.6%	4.97%	6.03%	9.2%	5.45%	6.55%
7.5	10.0%	3.15%	3.85%	9.3%	3.63%	4.37%	8.8%	4.11%	4.89%	8.3%	4.59%	5.41%	7.9%	5.07%	5.93%	7.5%	5.55%	6.45%
10.0	8.6%	3.20%	3.80%	8.1%	3.68%	4.32%	7.6%	4.16%	4.84%	7.2%	4.64%	5.36%	6.8%	5.12%	5.88%	6.5%	5.61%	6.39%
12.5	7.7%	3.23%	3.77%	7.2%	3.71%	4.29%	6.8%	4.19%	4.81%	6.4%	4.68%	5.32%	6.1%	5.16%	5.84%	5.8%	5.65%	6.35%
15.0	7.1%	3.25%	3.75%	6.6%	3.74%	4.26%	6.2%	4.22%	4.78%	5.9%	4.71%	5.29%	5.6%	5.19%	5.81%	5.3%	5.68%	6.32%
17.5	6.5%	3.27%	3.73%	6.1%	3.76%	4.24%	5.7%	4.24%	4.76%	5.4%	4.73%	5.27%	5.2%	5.22%	5.78%	4.9%	5.70%	6.30%
20.0	6.1%	3.29%	3.71%	5.7%	3.77%	4.23%	5.4%	4.26%	4.74%	5.1%	4.75%	5.25%	4.8%	5.23%	5.77%	4.6%	5.72%	6.28%
25.0	5.5%	3.31%	3.69%	5.1%	3.80%	4.20%	4.8%	4.28%	4.72%	4.5%	4.77%	5.23%	4.3%	5.26%	5.74%	4.1%	5.75%	6.25%
30.0	5.0%	3.33%	3.67%	4.7%	3.81%	4.19%	4.4%	4.30%	4.70%	4.1%	4.79%	5.21%	3.9%	5.28%	5.72%	3.8%	5.77%	6.23%
35.0	4.6%	3.34%	3.66%	4.3%	3.83%	4.17%	4.1%	4.32%	4.68%	3.8%	4.81%	5.19%	3.6%	5.30%	5.70%	3.5%	5.79%	6.21%
40.0	4.3%	3.35%	3.65%	4.0%	3.84%	4.16%	3.8%	4.33%	4.67%	3.6%	4.82%	5.18%	3.4%	5.31%	5.69%	3.3%	5.80%	6.20%
45.0	4.1%	3.36%	3.64%	3.8%	3.85%	4.15%	3.6%	4.34%	4.66%	3.4%	4.83%	5.17%	3.2%	5.32%	5.68%	3.1%	5.82%	6.18%
50.0	3.9%	3.36%	3.64%	3.6%	3.86%	4.14%	3.4%	4.35%	4.65%	3.2%	4.84%	5.16%	3.0%	5.33%	5.67%	2.9%	5.83%	6.17%
60.0	3.5%	3.38%	3.62%	3.3%	3.87%	4.13%	3.1%	4.36%	4.64%	2.9%	4.85%	5.15%	2.8%	5.35%	5.65%	2.7%	5.84%	6.16%
70.0	3.3%	3.39%	3.61%	3.0%	3.88%	4.12%	2.9%	4.37%	4.63%	2.7%	4.86%	5.14%	2.6%	5.36%	5.64%	2.5%	5.85%	6.15%
80.0	3.1%	3.39%	3.61%	2.8%	3.89%	4.11%	2.7%	4.38%	4.62%	2.5%	4.87%	5.13%	2.4%	5.37%	5.63%	2.3%	5.86%	6.14%
90.0	2.9%	3.40%	3.60%	2.7%	3.89%	4.11%	2.5%	4.39%	4.61%	2.4%	4.88%	5.12%	2.3%	5.37%	5.63%	2.2%	5.87%	6.13%
100.0	2.7%	3.40%	3.60%	2.5%	3.90%	4.10%	2.4%	4.39%	4.61%	2.3%	4.89%	5.11%	2.2%	5.38%	5.62%	2.1%	5.88%	6.12%

TABLE 10-3
DIRECT MAIL PROJECTION TABLE (Continued)

90% Confidence Level—Standard Deviation: 1.645 (Page 3)

ANTICIPATED PERCENT RESPONSE

Sample Size (000)	6.5% ±%	Variance Low	High	7.0% ±%	Variance Low	High	7.5% ±%	Variance Low	High	8.0% ±%	Variance Low	High	8.5% ±%	Variance Low	High	9.0% ±%	Variance Low	High
1.0	19.7%	5.22%	7.78%	19.0%	5.67%	8.33%	18.3%	6.13%	8.87%	17.6%	6.59%	9.41%	17.1%	7.05%	9.95%	16.5%	7.51%	10.49%
2.5	12.5%	5.69%	7.31%	12.0%	6.16%	7.84%	11.6%	6.63%	8.37%	11.2%	7.11%	8.89%	10.8%	7.58%	9.42%	10.5%	8.06%	9.94%
5.0	8.8%	5.93%	7.07%	8.5%	6.41%	7.59%	8.2%	6.89%	8.11%	7.9%	7.37%	8.63%	7.6%	7.85%	9.15%	7.4%	8.33%	9.67%
7.5	7.2%	6.03%	6.97%	6.9%	6.52%	7.48%	6.7%	7.00%	8.00%	6.4%	7.48%	8.52%	6.2%	7.97%	9.03%	6.0%	8.46%	9.54%
10.0	6.2%	6.09%	6.91%	6.0%	6.58%	7.42%	5.8%	7.07%	7.93%	5.6%	7.55%	8.45%	5.4%	8.04%	8.96%	5.2%	8.53%	9.47%
12.5	5.6%	6.14%	6.86%	5.4%	6.62%	7.38%	5.2%	7.11%	7.89%	5.0%	7.60%	8.40%	4.8%	8.09%	8.91%	4.7%	8.58%	9.42%
15.0	5.1%	6.17%	6.83%	4.9%	6.66%	7.34%	4.7%	7.15%	7.85%	4.6%	7.64%	8.36%	4.4%	8.13%	8.87%	4.3%	8.62%	9.38%
17.5	4.7%	6.19%	6.81%	4.5%	6.68%	7.32%	4.4%	7.17%	7.83%	4.2%	7.66%	8.34%	4.1%	8.15%	8.85%	4.0%	8.64%	9.36%
20.0	4.4%	6.21%	6.79%	4.2%	6.70%	7.30%	4.1%	7.19%	7.81%	3.9%	7.68%	8.32%	3.8%	8.18%	8.82%	3.7%	8.67%	9.33%
25.0	3.9%	6.24%	6.76%	3.8%	6.73%	7.27%	3.7%	7.23%	7.77%	3.5%	7.72%	8.28%	3.4%	8.21%	8.79%	3.3%	8.70%	9.30%
30.0	3.6%	6.27%	6.73%	3.5%	6.76%	7.24%	3.3%	7.25%	7.75%	3.2%	7.74%	8.26%	3.1%	8.24%	8.76%	3.0%	8.73%	9.27%
35.0	3.3%	6.28%	6.72%	3.2%	6.78%	7.22%	3.1%	7.27%	7.73%	3.0%	7.76%	8.24%	2.9%	8.25%	8.75%	2.8%	8.75%	9.25%
40.0	3.1%	6.30%	6.70%	3.0%	6.79%	7.21%	2.9%	7.28%	7.72%	2.8%	7.78%	8.22%	2.7%	8.27%	8.73%	2.6%	8.76%	9.24%
45.0	2.9%	6.31%	6.69%	2.8%	6.80%	7.20%	2.7%	7.30%	7.70%	2.6%	7.79%	8.21%	2.5%	8.28%	8.72%	2.5%	8.78%	9.22%
50.0	2.8%	6.32%	6.68%	2.7%	6.81%	7.19%	2.6%	7.31%	7.69%	2.5%	7.80%	8.20%	2.4%	8.29%	8.71%	2.3%	8.79%	9.21%
60.0	2.5%	6.33%	6.67%	2.4%	6.83%	7.17%	2.4%	7.32%	7.68%	2.3%	7.82%	8.18%	2.2%	8.31%	8.69%	2.1%	8.81%	9.19%
70.0	2.4%	6.35%	6.65%	2.3%	6.84%	7.16%	2.2%	7.34%	7.66%	2.1%	7.83%	8.17%	2.0%	8.33%	8.67%	2.0%	8.82%	9.18%
80.0	2.2%	6.36%	6.64%	2.1%	6.85%	7.15%	2.0%	7.35%	7.65%	2.0%	7.84%	8.16%	1.9%	8.34%	8.66%	1.8%	8.83%	9.17%
90.0	2.1%	6.36%	6.64%	2.0%	6.86%	7.14%	1.9%	7.36%	7.64%	1.9%	7.85%	8.15%	1.8%	8.35%	8.65%	1.7%	8.84%	9.16%
100.0	2.0%	6.37%	6.63%	1.9%	6.87%	7.13%	1.8%	7.36%	7.64%	1.8%	7.86%	8.14%	1.7%	8.35%	8.65%	1.7%	8.85%	9.15%

TABLE 10-3
DIRECT MAIL PROJECTION TABLE (Continued)

90% Confidence Level—Standard Deviation: 1.645 (Page 4)

ANTICIPATED PERCENT RESPONSE

Sample Size (000)	9.5% ±%	Variance Low	High	10.0% ±%	Variance Low	High	10.5% ±%	Variance Low	High	11.0% ±%	Variance Low	High	11.5% ±%	Variance Low	High	12.0% ±%	Variance Low	High
1.0	16.1%	7.97%	11.03%	15.6%	8.44%	11.56%	15.2%	8.91%	12.09%	14.8%	9.37%	12.63%	14.4%	9.84%	13.16%	14.1%	10.31%	13.69%
2.5	10.2%	8.54%	10.46%	9.9%	9.01%	10.99%	9.6%	9.49%	11.51%	9.4%	9.97%	12.03%	9.1%	10.45%	12.55%	8.9%	10.93%	13.07%
5.0	7.2%	8.82%	10.18%	7.0%	9.30%	10.70%	6.8%	9.79%	11.21%	6.6%	10.27%	11.73%	6.5%	10.76%	12.24%	6.3%	11.24%	12.76%
7.5	5.9%	8.94%	10.06%	5.7%	9.43%	10.57%	5.5%	9.92%	11.08%	5.4%	10.41%	11.59%	5.3%	10.89%	12.11%	5.1%	11.38%	12.62%
10.0	5.1%	9.02%	9.98%	4.9%	9.51%	10.49%	4.8%	10.00%	11.00%	4.7%	10.49%	11.51%	4.6%	10.98%	12.02%	4.5%	11.47%	12.53%
12.5	4.5%	9.07%	9.93%	4.4%	9.56%	10.44%	4.3%	10.05%	10.95%	4.2%	10.54%	11.46%	4.1%	11.03%	11.97%	4.0%	11.52%	12.48%
15.0	4.1%	9.11%	9.89%	4.0%	9.60%	10.40%	3.9%	10.09%	10.91%	3.8%	10.58%	11.42%	3.7%	11.07%	11.93%	3.6%	11.56%	12.44%
17.5	3.8%	9.14%	9.86%	3.7%	9.63%	10.37%	3.6%	10.12%	10.88%	3.5%	10.61%	11.39%	3.4%	11.10%	11.90%	3.4%	11.60%	12.40%
20.0	3.6%	9.16%	9.84%	3.5%	9.65%	10.35%	3.4%	10.14%	10.86%	3.3%	10.64%	11.36%	3.2%	11.13%	11.87%	3.1%	11.62%	12.38%
25.0	3.2%	9.19%	9.81%	3.1%	9.69%	10.31%	3.0%	10.18%	10.82%	3.0%	10.67%	11.33%	2.9%	11.17%	11.83%	2.8%	11.66%	12.34%
30.0	2.9%	9.22%	9.78%	2.8%	9.72%	10.28%	2.8%	10.21%	10.79%	2.7%	10.70%	11.30%	2.6%	11.20%	11.80%	2.6%	11.69%	12.31%
35.0	2.7%	9.24%	9.76%	2.6%	9.74%	10.26%	2.6%	10.23%	10.77%	2.5%	10.72%	11.28%	2.4%	11.22%	11.78%	2.4%	11.71%	12.29%
40.0	2.5%	9.26%	9.74%	2.5%	9.75%	10.25%	2.4%	10.25%	10.75%	2.3%	10.74%	11.26%	2.3%	11.24%	11.76%	2.2%	11.73%	12.27%
45.0	2.4%	9.27%	9.73%	2.3%	9.77%	10.23%	2.3%	10.26%	10.74%	2.2%	10.76%	11.24%	2.2%	11.25%	11.75%	2.1%	11.75%	12.25%
50.0	2.3%	9.28%	9.72%	2.2%	9.78%	10.22%	2.1%	10.27%	10.73%	2.1%	10.77%	11.23%	2.0%	11.27%	11.73%	2.0%	11.76%	12.24%
60.0	2.1%	9.30%	9.70%	2.0%	9.80%	10.20%	2.0%	10.29%	10.71%	1.9%	10.79%	11.21%	1.9%	11.29%	11.71%	1.8%	11.78%	12.22%
70.0	1.9%	9.32%	9.68%	1.9%	9.81%	10.19%	1.8%	10.31%	10.69%	1.8%	10.81%	11.19%	1.7%	11.30%	11.70%	1.7%	11.80%	12.20%
80.0	1.8%	9.33%	9.67%	1.7%	9.83%	10.17%	1.7%	10.32%	10.68%	1.7%	10.82%	11.18%	1.6%	11.31%	11.69%	1.6%	11.81%	12.19%
90.0	1.7%	9.34%	9.66%	1.6%	9.84%	10.16%	1.6%	10.33%	10.67%	1.6%	10.83%	11.17%	1.5%	11.33%	11.67%	1.5%	11.82%	12.18%
100.0	1.6%	9.35%	9.65%	1.6%	9.84%	10.16%	1.5%	10.34%	10.66%	1.5%	10.84%	11.16%	1.4%	11.33%	11.67%	1.4%	11.83%	12.17%

When you examine the tables in some detail, you will see a pattern emerge that helps to clarify the concepts of margin of error and confidence in the projections. Simply stated, the pattern is that confidence decreases as sample sizes and response rates decrease. Conversely, confidence will increase as response rates increase and as sample sizes increase. Putting it another way, if you expect a relatively low response rate, be sure to use a sample large enough to enable you to have confidence in the results. Otherwise you may have a test that cannot be projected to a satisfactory degree of acceptance.

Using Probability Tables in Planning a Mailing

Let's assume you are planning a test mailing that will ultimately lead to a large-scale rollout. You wish to have results that will give you a response rate plus or minus 10 percent, and you decide that you wish to have a confidence level of 95 percent. Finally, you anticipate a response of 3 percent. (Either your product P&L [profit and loss] requires a 3 percent response rate, or you may have some prior experience that leads you to that conclusion.) Now refer to the 3 percent column in Table 10-1, page 1. By scanning down the column, you see that a 10 percent margin error is possible with a mailing of 12,500 pieces, and a replication of that test projects a yield of between 2.7 and 3.3 percent. So, a 12,500 mailing will be a "safe" test within the parameters you have set. A "safer" test would be 15,000 pieces, which has a 9.1 percent margin of error.

After reviewing the 95 percent tables further, you see that you can use a smaller test sample if your anticipated response rate is higher—for example, a 4 percent response rate would require a mailing of only 10,000 pieces to fall within the ± 10 percent margin of error parameter (Table 10-1, page 2). However, a lower anticipated response rate—for example, 1 percent—would require a much higher test mailing quantity (40,000 pieces for a 1 percent response rate) to have validity within your parameters (Table 10-1, page 1).

The decisions you make before your test mailing are quite important, because all of your rollout efforts can be predicated on a test. Therefore it's a good idea to err on the conservative side when constructing a test. Once you have conducted a test, it's impossible to go back and change vital factors.

Using Probability Tables in Evaluating a Mailing

Having accomplished a test mailing, you can then evaluate the results in terms of a projection. Let's assume in this case that you mailed 10,000 pieces and achieved a response rate of 2.5 percent. Table 10-4 shows what you can read out of Tables 10-3, p. 1; 10-1, p. 1; and 10-2, p. 1, in that order.

TABLE 10-4

	Confidence level, %	Margin of error, %	Projected low response, %	Projected high response, %
Table 10-3, p. 1	90	10.3	2.24	2.76
Table 10-1, p. 1	95	12.2	2.19	2.81
Table 10-2, p. 1	99	14.0	2.15	2.85

As discussed previously, the margin of error is less for a lower confidence level and greater for a higher confidence level. In this example, if you are satisfied with a confidence level of 90% (that is, 9 times out of 10), then you can plan on a rollout response of between 2.24 and 2.76 percent. However, if you want to be more certain, look at the 99 percent confidence level (99 times out of 100), and note that you can then expect a wider range in your rollout response. How do these different possibilities work with other factors in your plans? If your product P&L is very tightly constructed, it may be advisable to try the more conservative projected response rate. If you have some latitude, however, then a less conservative approach may be appropriate.

Construction of Probability Tables

For those who are interested, the probability tables use a standard statistical formula for large samples. Using certain factors, we can determine the margin of error as follows:

Let E = margin of error (expressed as a decimal variable—plus or minus—to be added or subtracted from the response rate)
r = response rate (expressed as a decimal)
n = sample size
S = standard deviation

The formula for margin of error is as follows:

$$E = \sqrt{\frac{(r)(1-r)}{n}}\,(S)$$

To determine the sample size for a given margin of error, the formula just given is converted to the following:

$$n = \frac{(r)(1-r)(S)^2}{E^2}$$

The tables were constructed on a personal computer, using Lotus 1-2-3. The Lotus formula for determining the margin of error, expressed as a percentage, is as follows:

$$\{@SQRT[E\$66*(1 - E\$66)/(\$B7*1000)]\}*196/E\$66$$

(E\$66 and \$B7 are cell addresses with constants.)

TESTING CAUTIONS

Theoretically, statistical probability tables are absolutely reliable and, after testing the proper sample and getting acceptable results, a company should be able to roll out any number of pieces it wishes. In practice, a favorable test result usually is followed by a test extension—a cautious remailing to a larger quantity—before a company's entire program is committed to a new mailing package, offer, or audience. There are several theories about this.

I received a letter from a California marketer who suggested that the reason for this lack of confidence is that we, as an industry, "lack faith in the competence or honesty of the list broker or list source...that everyone has at least one horror story of salted lists or computer foul-ups." The same writer suggests that mailers should make it a practice to always physically inspect a mailing list in its Cheshire or other printed format. "That way, when they think they are mailing 10,000 needlepoint catalogs to sewing hobbyists, they will learn before, not after, the mail is dropped that what they really had was 10,000 car dealers." This writer may or may not be correct. More likely, the root of the dilemma may lie in the fact that we are dealing in a fluid environment. A mailing sent out even a few months after a test might encounter changed attitudes, economic circumstances, or competitive activity, not to mention weather, news events, and other influences on direct marketing results.

Grid Testing

The quantity used for each test being conducted, whether of copy or lists, is called a "test cell," and each test cell is assigned its own key number. If five new lists were being tested, you would have five test cells. If other mail were being sent to previously tested groups of names, each separately keyed group would be called a "rollout cell" or an "extension cell."

Often a variety of tests are being conducted simultaneously—perhaps new concepts, offer variations, and new lists. If the combination of anticipated response rate and required error limit produces large mailing samples, and if there are many variables to be tested, the test quantities can be enormous. In the interest of minimizing downside risk, an alternative method is needed, and that alternative is grid testing.

Under the grid method, each test cell is still the minimum quantity indicated in the discussion of sample size earlier in this chapter. The difference is that each cell may represent more than one variable, as long as the total number of cells for each variable meets the minimum sample-size test.

TABLE 10-5

| Copy | Lists | | | Total |
	A	B	C	
X	20,000	20,000	20,000	60,000
Y	20,000	20,000	20,000	60,000
Z	20,000	20,000	20,000	60,000
Total	60.000	60,000	60,000	180,000

Let's say we have three copy tests and three list tests, and that a sample size of 60,000 was indicated. Ordinarily that would require a mailing quantity of 540,000 pieces—nine cells of 60,000 names each. However, if you structure the test as shown in Table 10-5, you can cut the total mailing quantity, and therefore the total test investment, by two-thirds.

Note that the total mailing required is only 180,000, yet there is a 60,000 quantity against each variable being tested. The results are read against the totals for each variable, not against each cell. Any observation of results against each individual cell would be futile, because of the wide error limit for the smaller quantity; only the totals can be read.

For more substantial testing programs, greater economies can be achieved by not testing every variable in every list. If every variable is tested on one list and every variable is tested against a control somewhere in the grid, results can be interpolated. This is illustrated and further discussed in Chapter 3 of this book.

Economies in Direct Mail Testing

The grid test is one way to lower the investment in testing. There are others that depend on what is being tested.

List tests require only changes in the key number. Offer tests should require changes only in those areas where the offer appears. Substantial production economies can be effected by omitting the offer, if it isn't absolutely necessary, from the four-color brochure or other printed elements. A premium versus no-premium test can be accomplished by keeping the entire package the same and only adding a buck slip (a slip of paper stating the offer), changing the reply device, and adding a paragraph to the letter. It isn't necessary to do an entirely new package for every variation.

When CBS Publishing introduced a new gardening magazine, there were several fundamental approaches that had to be tried: a conventional announcement package, a how-to positioning for beginners, and an "exotic plants" positioning for advanced gardeners. This was accomplished very inexpensively by designing an envelope with a full-back cellophane window and a circular in which each appeal was centered on a different section. The brochure was designed so that it could be folded with a different appeal facing out, visible through the window. Only one press run of the brochure was required, effecting substantial economies; only the folding had to be varied.

For Weight Watchers, I developed a package that varied only in the response card, part of which showed through a window of the outer envelope face, and in one insert. Everything else remained the same, except for the opening paragraph of the letter. A minimal production budget permitted two very different appeals to be tested: one dramatizing the social aspect of weight-reduction groups, the other the eating pleasure of the varied menus.

List Sampling

In testing a mailing list, it is essential that the names tested be representative of the entire list. In Chapter 5, Mailing Lists, there is a discussion of why Nth-name samples are the most accurate way of doing this. This system will provide a true cross-section of the entire list, if it is supplied correctly by the list owner. Any shortcuts, such as taking a single geographic area or a fifth zip-code digit, add a considerable measure of risk.

Also read the discussion in Chapter 5 of the relative merits of hot-line names, active customers versus expires, and other factors, all of which must be taken into account when testing lists.

PRINT MEDIA TESTING

Whereas direct mail testing opportunities are limited only by imagination and economics, newspaper and magazine testing is limited by the production capabilities of the publications themselves.

There are two principal objectives of testing in magazine space. One is to test a magazine as a medium; the other is to test alternate copy, offers, or products.

Testing a New Magazine

In Chapter 6, Print Media Planning, there is a lengthy discussion of the pilot testing theory applied to magazines. It deals with grouping magazines in constellations and testing the most representative magazine in each group.

Often, downside risk can be minimized further by using only one portion of a magazine rather than the entire publication. Some magazines permit you to buy one-half of the circulation, across the board on a national basis. Many magazines will permit you to buy one or more sections of the country. Either plan will enable you to run an advertisement and discover a magazine's response rate without having to buy the entire circulation. Adjustments must be made, in such tests, for seasonal or position variations. Often regional insertions are placed in the back of a magazine, where response would be materially less than the same ad placed nationally.

As little as $5000 can test full-page ads in the largest magazines, such as *Time* and *TV Guide,* in small regional or city editions. As little as a few hundred dollars can test small-space advertisements in any of hundreds of magazines.

The small-budget advertiser can start with a fractional unit and work up, little by little, to larger sizes and even spectacular units. Some of the largest firms in the direct marketing business started in just this way. The only difference between them and advertisers with more substantial budgets and wider-reaching test programs is the element of time. The larger firms compress the testing experience and step-by-step building of smaller advertisers into one season, enabling them to quickly establish a multimillion-dollar business rather than to build it slowly.

A-B Split-Run Testing

There is no more accurate way to determine which magazine advertisement is the best than split-run testing. Whether you are testing an offer, a copy approach, or one product or business against another, this testing approach will always give you a clear and meaningful basis for decision making.

SRDS defines *split run* this way: "A technique to measure the relative strength of different copy approaches...for example, by means of coupon returns from equally divided portions of a specific edition or issue of a publication's circulation, each identical except for the varying copy approaches." There are more than 50 magazines that offer split-run testing. Some require that a full page be purchased for the test; others offer A-B split runs on fractional units. The SRDS listing follows.

Consumer Magazines with Split-Run Advertising

American Legion Magazine, The	Discover
Athion Sports Communications, Inc.	Discovery
Atlantic, The	Down East
Baby Talk	Elks Magazine, The
Bicycling	Esquire
Bon Appetit	Essence
Bride's and Your New Home	Expecting
Business Women Leadership Media	Family
Capper's	Family Circle
Car Craft	Family Handyman, The
City Pages	A First Baby
Collegiate Sports/Alumni Network	Fishing World
Condé Nast Traveler	Fortune

4-Wheel & Off-Road

Four Wheeler

Gentlemen's Quarterly

Glamour

Good Housekeeping

Granta

Grit

Guide Package, The

Guns & Ammo

Healthy Kids: Birth–3

Healthy Kids: 4–10

Hemispheres

Hot Rod

Ladies Home Journal

Longevity

Maclean's—Canada's Weekly
  Newsmagazine

McCall's

Men's Health

Metropolitan Home

Modern Maturity

Money

Mother Earth News

Motor Trend

National Enquirer

National Lampoon

National Speed Sport News

New Woman

New York Times Company
  Magazine Group, The

New Yorker, The

Newsweek

Omni

Organic Gardening

Our Sunday Visitor

Parents

Penthouse

People Weekly

Petersen Magazine
  Network

Petersen's Photographic
  Magazine

Playboy

Prevention

Reader's Digest

Redbook Magazine

Rodale's Scuba Diving

Scene

Self

Ski

Sport

Sporting News

Sports Illustrated

Superman Batman Group

Teen

TV Guide

TWA Ambassador

U.S. News & World
  Report

USAir Magazine

Vermont Magazine

Vista

Weight Watchers
  Magazine

Women's Day

Yankee

YM

Your Prom

To run a test, you simply prepare two different versions of your advertisement, each with a different key number, and place both of them in

the publication as a split insertion on the same date. Usually some small extra fee is charged.

The publication probably is printed "two-up" on one or more enormous web or rotogravure presses. The magazines either are bound separately and the streams of finished magazines merged, or a double magazine comes off the press and is sheared in half after binding.

In either case, every second magazine has a different advertisement. Usually, looking through a pile of magazines on a newsstand, you can see ad A in one magazine, B in the next, A in the next, and so forth. As these magazines are distributed throughout the country to magazine distributors or mailed out to subscribers in this same fashion, there is an absolutely perfect sampling of the whole: 50 percent for one, 50 percent for the other. The validity of this type of test is virtually unchallenged, provided that the difference between test results is large enough.

What result size is "large enough" to be meaningful is a controversial question. One commonly used guide for determining statistical significance in split-run print advertising involves "significance factors"—the percentage difference between two alternatives at a varying total number of responses. Although at least one very well-known company relies on this type of table, many statisticians appear to be at a loss to identify the underlying mathematical formula.

The chart in Table 10-6 is widely used and simple to understand. Just combine the total response to the two versions of your ad, usually the

TABLE 10-6
SIGNIFICANT FACTOR IN SPLIT-RUN ADVERTISING
(95 PERCENT CONFIDENCE LEVEL)

Total responses (both sides)	Factor
50	64.24
100	60.00
200	57.07
300	55.77
400	55.00
500	54.47
1,000	53.16
1,500	52.56
2,000	52.23
3,000	51.83
4,000	51.58
5,000	51.41
10,000	51.00
20,000	50.71
30,000	50.58
40,000	50.50
50,000	50.45
100,000	50.31

control and the variation, and you'll have the total response figure. Then divide the numbers for each split to produce the percentage of the total response (not the response rate). Look up the total response figure in the left-hand column, and refer to the significance figure in the right column. If your test result, expressed as a percentage of total response, is greater than the figure listed, then you have a significant improvement. The test ad should become your control ad in the future. If the test result is less, and if the control figure also is not greater than the significance figure, then you have a "tie," and you can use the new advertisement, or not, based on nonstatistical considerations, such as its effect on the long-term image of your product and company. Some companies with extensive schedules will elect to use such "tie" ads to alternate with other ads and thus avoid the "fatigue" factor.

Multiple Split-Run Testing

The A-B split provides a reliable comparison of one advertisement against another in a given publication. But what happens when there are a half-dozen valid concepts to be tested in magazines?

Multiple split-run testing, sometimes called *telescopic testing,* is designed to solve this problem. It combines the A-B split, just described, with the availability of regional editions of magazines. If a magazine has four regional editions, you can test four different ads against your control ad. For example, see Table 10-7.

The results of such a test might be as shown in Table 10-8. The helter-skelter of result figures can quickly be made meaningful by either (1) calculating the "lift factor" for each insertion, independently of the results of the control ad A; or (2) by adjusting the ad A results to a national aver-

TABLE 10-7
MAGAZINE GEOGRAPHIC EDITIONS

West	Ad A versus ad B
South	Ad A versus ad C
Northeast	Ad A versus ad D
Midwest	Ad A versus ad E

TABLE 10-8
MAGAZINE TEST RESULTS

Edition	Control	Response	Variation	Response
West	Ad A	351	Ad B	416
South	Ad A	297	Ad C	376
Northeast	Ad A	328	Ad D	302
Midwest	Ad A	345	Ad E	420

TABLE 10-9
MAGAZINE SPLIT-RUN TEST

Edition	Adjusted cost	Control	Number	CPR	Test	Number	CPR	Lift %
West	$ 1,836	A	351	$2.62	B	416	$2.21	18
South	2,856	A	297	4.81	C	376	3.80	26
Northeast	3,060	A	328	4.66	D	302	5.07	(7)
Midwest	2,448	A	345	3.55	E	420	2.91	21
Total	$10,228		1,321	$3.86		1,514	$3.37	

age, calculating the adjustment against all of the other numbers and restating the figures accordingly.

Either of these techniques compensates for geographic or distribution variations and enables you to read the results correctly. Similarly, the various advertisements can be indexed, with the control ad designated 100. Table 10-9 shows an example of an adjusted result report, including all the preceding factors and with the figures adjusted against the control. Note that the greatest lift resulted from ad C, although ads B and E had lower CPR figures because of regional variation.

Referring to the significance chart in Table 10-6, we see that at this level of total response we need only a 54 percent factor for the new ad to be declared a valid winner. Ads B, C, and E all are valid winners. Statistically, ad D also is equivalent to ad A, though it did not beat it.

Some magazines have so many editions—*TV Guide* with 107 local editions, or *Time,* with 51 state editions and 50 spot market editions, for instance—that it is possible for the sample sizes to get too small to be meaningful. In such cases the practice has been to cluster the editions by regional demographics, with each cluster containing a mix of urban, rural, eastern, and western areas of the country.

Flip-Flop Testing

Unfortunately, many magazines don't have split-run testing facilities, particularly those whose circulations are not large enough to enable them to be printed two-up. Very few newspapers offer this service, although most magazine sections of Sunday papers do.

The best available technique is *flip-flop testing,* and even this requires geographic editions. *The Wall Street Journal* is sold in four editions but is printed in seventeen different plants, and each plant can carry separate copy. A local newspaper might have a city and a suburban edition.

In this kind of testing you run ad A in one edition and ad B in the other, on the same day. Then, a week or two later, you reverse the ads, running B where A ran and vice versa. By running two ads and reading the combined total response rates rather than individual ones, you cause the distortion factors to offset each other. One edition or region might be stronger than another. The ad that runs the first time will probably do better than the second ad in each section, because it has "creamed" the market somewhat. However, this qualification applies to both ads and both editions. The total response rate of ad A compared with ad B should be valid.

Full-Page Bind-Ins

There are times when the best testing medium may be full-page bind-in cards, although they are too costly for most advertisers. These are preprinted by the advertiser and supplied to the publication for insertion in the magazine. Usually they are "perfect-bound" rather than saddle-stitched. The unit can include a perforated reply card, gummed areas for tokens or stamps, numbers for sweepstakes, pop-ups, or a variety of other techniques not possible with a conventional soft-space unit.

As the cards are preprinted and premixed by your own printer, virtually any number of variations can be tested simultaneously. This is an excellent technique for major advertisers whose potential investments are so large that 6, 8, or 12 concepts must be tested before a major campaign is launched.

The unit is atypical, in that the ad must be designed to utilize both sides of the bound-in card. Some advertisers have gotten around this requirement by placing a separate advertisement for a different product on the reverse side of the page. When this is done, one side of the reply card for one ad appears on the other side. This could be confusing, but my experience indicates that the format is successful.

If you are selecting a publication for this type of testing, you'll want to pick one that is sold mostly by subscription rather than newsstand. Though your space rates are based on actual circulation, you still have to print enough card units for the magazine's total press run, including unsold newsstand copies. Newsstand-sold magazines have a much greater waste factor than those sold mostly by subscription.

Bound-In Reply Cards

A more common format for major advertisers is the combination of a single- or double-page advertisement with a bound-in reply card, usually called an *insert card*. While this is a very successful unit, producing four times the result of a page alone at an average cost increase only two or three times higher, it does have limitations as a test vehicle.

With few exceptions, there is no way to match cards to an alternative A-B split. If the card is to match the page, it is impossible to be sure that the cards are inserted in synchronization with the page. One error, and the entire test can be ruined.

One solution is to confine the test to the card alone, without changing the advertisement for the page. This is really only suitable for testing offers or minor proposition variations. If it does not appear on the page, several different offers can be featured on the card itself. For instance it is easy to test one card with a premium featured and another with no premium at all, to determine the lift factor of the premium. Or you can try modifying the coupon wording, simplified commitment copy, postage and handling costs included in the price, the availability of a trade-up option, or quality-improvement tests such as requiring respondents to an inquiry ad to provide their own stamp as opposed to a business reply card paid by the advertiser.

Another way to do split testing when insert cards are involved is to use a transfer code. This is a useful device when several basic concepts are being tested for a proposition, which usually is successful only when an insert card is used. In this case, the insert card is constant and the ads change, with as many variations as A-B splitting and regional editions permit.

One version of the transfer code is to offer a choice of book bindings or other options, asking respondents to use a designated letter for one color and a different letter for the other. The letters change not only for the color but also for the different advertisement. In one ad, the customer is asked to select A for a black binding and B for a brown one. In the other, C represents black while D represents brown. The customer is asked to place the letter in a designated space on the insert card so as to indicate the choice. Better still, if you have product order numbers, put an A after each number on ad A, a B after those in ad B, and so on. These letters are later translated into key numbers, and the results are analyzed as with any other split run.

Where a choice is not available, a premium can be used instead. The respondent can be asked to place a designated letter on the card for a free poster, for example.

The most direct and straightforward approach of all seems to work as well as the others, but it may depend on the type of product being offered. This is a simple statement on the printed page that says "To help us evaluate our advertising, please put this letter in the space indicated on the reply card."

Deliberate Underspacing

If a proposition usually works in a page but as a half-page doesn't do well, we say it is *underspaced*. The same consideration applies to format as well as space size. If a proposition works best with an insert card or a bound-in multipage unit, and we run a simple black-and-white page instead, we have also "underspaced" the ad.

Deliberate underspacing is one way that an advertiser with a modest budget can enjoy the benefits of multiple testing. All that is needed is to use regional editions and A-B splits for a smaller unit than would otherwise be profitable, knowing in advance that the overall results will be disappointing. If the primary objective is to test various copy appeals, for instance, and the basic proposition has already been proved, it may be less expensive to use soft-space black-and-white pages than to make the space, printing, and production investment of card testing. The reduced responses may be less of a price to pay than the multiple testing costs, but the relative pulling power of the different appeals will still be meaningful. One caution, though: Don't expect black-and-white ads to demonstrate the relative effectiveness of those advertising appeals for which the visual element is critical and must be in color. This approach will work only when the concept is not dependent on color.

One example of this technique is to use Sunday newspaper supplements or the listing pages of *TV Guide* in clusters of local editions to reduce regional distortion. This approach is far less costly than testing in preprinted full-page units.

Another technique is the use of half-page black-and-white ads in Sunday supplements of newspapers in a few regions before investing in a full-page, full-run, full-color advertisement. The trick with all of these underspacing approaches is to keep your focus on the original objective and the original expectations.

NEWSPAPER PREPRINTS

The possibilities for copy testing in preprints are infinite. You can arrange with your own printer to produce as many different versions of your advertisement as cost and statistical validity permit, and to deliver them, premixed, to newspapers for insertion in their Sunday editions. The only limitation would involve trying to mix formats, as the insertion equipment can only be set to handle one size and thickness of your preprint and they can't be interspersed.

The problems with preprint copy testing don't come at the publication; they come at your printer. It is essential that someone visually check the shipment of inserts after they have been mixed and before they are sent out to the newspapers.

Some printers don't have the presses to automatically "stream" the different versions together on press, and they rely on something they call *hand spanning.* This means that they pack the inserts from different stacks or skids, one handful from this stack, another from that stack, and so on. This is adequate for a test, if it's really done. Unfortunately, there are too many temptations for the individual supervisor to take shortcuts and invalidate your test. For instance, in a four-way split, if the press is doing only two versions at a time, the printer has to store the entire run of the first two versions before packing anything to wait for the beginning of the production of the second two versions. Unless the printer has adequate floor space, this may not happen—and no one is going to tell you. There are many scrupulous and careful printers who would never permit this to happen, but caution still requires that your own inspector check the skids before they are shipped.

Another caution might be to include a pure key test if possible, with no changes other than the code number itself. The results should be identical, within statistical error limits. If they're not, you'll know that something is wrong. However, it will be too late to do anything about it other than change printers in the future. The on-site inspection is still the preferred choice.

Statistical validity is always a consideration, as with any other test factor. Use the same statistical validity chart as with direct mail, except that the response rates may be too low for the chart. It is reasonably accurate, as a rule of thumb, to adjust decimal points; that is, if you expect a 0.05 percent response, use the quantity indicated for 0.5 percent and multiply it by 10. For instance, at a 0.1 percent error limit you would need a circulation of 191,000 for each split.

Picking Test Markets

With the exception of a few large cities with more than one newspaper, print media provide a very broad range of demographics—rich and poor, educated and not, mail-order buyer and retail buyer—representing the entire scope of the area covered by the newspaper.

Geographic characteristics, such as median income and buying power, are the key variables, and so they are the prime consideration in selecting which newspapers to use in conducting a preprint test. Size of market is generally the most influential characteristic. For a test, pick a variety of papers in different-sized markets: one or two large cities, several medium ones, and a handful of smaller towns.

In all cases the newspapers should be those whose sales representatives can demonstrate a large number of repeat insertions by other mail-order advertisers, with rate structures that are not punitive.

Within these broad parameters, availability will be the prime consideration. On key dates you may find that your competition has already reserved space, or there may be too many other advertisers scheduling preprints on the dates you want. You will have to check availabilities and weigh the tradeoffs of preferred dates versus preferred markets in making your selections.

FORMAT TESTS

One of the old maxims of testing was that it was possible to split only within a given format—one preprint versus another, one full page versus another. Few magazines would permit tests of small-space units.

However, just as rate cards are not always indicative of the rates available to direct-response advertisers, so they are not always the best guide to what kind of splits are available.

If your own budget or your agency has enough buying power and influence, and if your media specialist is respected by the media and a good negotiator as well, virtually anything is possible. For example:

- Black-and-white versus color
- Large space versus small
- Card versus no card
- "Square" third page versus vertical column

- Multiple splits in publications that supposedly offered none
- One position versus another in the same publication
- Custom-tailored geographic segmentation

While such tests are not generally available, and if available, usually only on a limited and confidential basis, they can provide definitive answers very quickly to media strategy questions that might otherwise take years of trial-and-error approaches to resolve.

BROADCAST

As discussed in Chapter 7, there are two very different kinds of broadcast: *support* and *direct-response*. They are very different in their purposes and methodologies, and just as different with regard to the ways of testing their usefulness or refining scheduling.

Direct-Response Testing

This is the place to use the "best-foot-forward" approach. The place to test is not the stations expected to be most typical of the broadcast media at large. Testing should begin on those stations most likely to succeed, where experience shows that your own propositions or those of other direct marketers have been successful.

There can be substantial differences in response by type of market, and so a variety of stations should be included in a test schedule: urban, rural, East, West, South, Midwest, independent stations, network affiliates, and cable stations. Often there are patterns showing that one type of station works better than others. More often the key variable is the willingness of stations, regardless of type of market or programming, to establish a rate structure and make available time slots that will be cost-efficient.

Dayparts. The time of day is usually the most constant and controllable variable other than the station itself. The time of day is the most effective selector of audience segments. Weekend mornings reach parents whose children are watching children's shows. Afternoons reach women at home, enjoying the never-ending stream of soap operas and talk shows. News programs and adventure shows reach a higher number of men. Late-night programming seems to find older people, or at least restless ones. Programming adjacencies, to the extent that they are available for direct response, offer even finer selection, for certain shows seem to attract audiences of predictable affinities.

Other Testing. Other than the stations or type and time of programming, there are often times when it is necessary to test other factors, such as frequency, length of commercial, or the content of the commercial itself.

The technique most used is a variation of flip-flop testing discussed earlier in this chapter in the section on print media. A different phone number is assigned to the new campaign, and it is run in alternate weeks on several stations, beginning with the new campaign on half the stations and the old one on the other half. Half the stations are running A-B-A-B-A, while the others are playing B-A-B-A-B. This tends to offset differences by station and by whether a commercial is played earlier or later in a flight.

This test method generally is used to test entirely new commercials, and sometimes frequency. It would not be possible to test prices or other offer variations this way. Such testing requires a "paired-market" test.

Audience Valuation

The newest testing technique, discussed in more detail in Chapter 7, attempts to evaluate specific audience segments in order to predict the success of possible television schedules. The result is a specific allowable media cost for audiences targeted by different stations.

To initiate such testing, spots are arranged for various times during a particular week, and then the actual audiences reached by the spots must be subjected to computerized analysis. This type of analysis requires access to all the audience evaluation tools used by general advertising. The analysis is difficult and complex, but produces an analytical tool that reaches far beyond the old standard of pure cost per response. By being able to target future buys, it has been possible to make upscale, narrow-audience, regional, business-to-business, and cultural propositions work that might not have worked with past test methods.

Support Broadcast

The choice of markets in support broadcast is dictated by the media to be supported. Within each market, however, there are usually several stations to choose from, and within each station, there is a choice of day-parts and frequency.

Often it is necessary to use every station in a market in order to reach the 300 or so gross rating points most direct marketers feel is a minimum for effective media support. As support spots must be aired in a precise pattern during three or four days adjoining the appearance of the ad or mailing being supported, it may be difficult to line up enough good availabilities.

Usually the first objective is to test the effectiveness of support broadcast itself. The standard technique is to select between six and ten similar markets, supporting some of them at one frequency level, others at a higher level, and some without any support at all.

The costs of the broadcast are added to the costs of the preprints or direct mail being supported. The total advertising cost is divided by the number of responses received and—voilà!—we have cost-per-response figures for each market, and a conclusion as to whether support costs are justified and at which GRP level.

Similarly, an ongoing campaign can test various daypart concentrations, commercial lengths, or even different creative appeals.

I would advise readers considering any type of broadcast testing to reread Chapter 7, and to keep in mind the objective of a broadcast support test. Support advertising cannot be expected to lower CPR, although sometimes it does. A more reasonable expectation is to extend the media being supported—a higher level of orders at the same CPR, or a CPR that is higher than unsupported preprints or direct mail but still less costly than other media alternatives.

TESTING STRATEGY

Now that we've covered how to test in each medium, let's look at the basic philosophy that applies to any and all kinds of testing. The first consideration is planning the test: how many tests to run, what kinds are the most important, and how to use the information you get from testing. And the approach to this depends on the personality of your company.

Continuing with the military analogy we made use of in Chapter 2, we can say that General Patton and Field Marshall Montgomery became archetypal examples of two different military strategies. Patton was aggressive: a man who seized every opportunity, took risks, bent the rules of warfare, and swept across miles of enemy terrain without bothering to mop up pockets of resistance. Montgomery was cautious. He planned carefully, regrouped slowly, and moved his forces ahead step by step, with due care to logistics and supply lines.

While I regard myself as a Patton fan, I will not say that the Montgomery approach isn't right for some companies. One of my banking clients is a Patton-type company. They will test one or two fundamental approaches and, if successful, roll out a major national campaign so fast that the competition is unable to copy the concept. Another corporation is a Montgomery-type company, with each direct mail program studied and planned and poked at for such a long time that, by the time the smallest test gets in the mail, the competition already may have tested, rolled out, and reaped the profits from similar programs.

What to Test

What you can test depends on your budget, mailing size, objectives, and willingness to assume risk. It is easy to test a wide variety of mailing lists, or a simple direct mail variation. Each split costs very little to execute. It is more costly to test different TV commercials, color magazine ads, and total mailing concepts. The cost of testing should be in relation to the size of the expected benefits.

The greatest difference in results can be expected from changes that affect the product being offered or the way the product is positioned.

Offer changes run a close second, with very dramatic changes resulting from changes in price, premium, commitment, term, etc.

Creative changes are next, with very broad differences sometimes created by a change in headline or illustration, or in print and direct mail formats. Layout revisions or different copy treatments of the same theme usually show very little difference, presuming they were professionally executed in the first place.

The big differences—200 and 300 percent lift factors—almost always come from product positioning, offer changes, or the selection of different lists or publications.

As you can't afford to test everything, the selection of what to test has to be done methodically. First, list test opportunities within your basic mailing or media schedule—publications you are using anyway that make testing feasible. Then list the things you would like to test, in the order of expected result improvement.

In a recent mail-order product introduction, I still had 12 possible ad variations even after focus panel reviews and predictive research. There were 8 testing opportunities, between direct mail and a Sunday supplement regional–A-B split. When the opportunities were reviewed, all the copy alternatives were set aside in favor of testing product and offer variations.

Evolutionists versus Fundamentalists

Another issue is how boldly to test. One school, which I'll call the evolutionists, advocates strictly "readable" testing, with all elements in an ad or mailing piece identical except the single factor being tested. If you are testing a headline, they will tell you, don't change the layout anywhere, and leave every element of type size and color exactly the same. The question to ask of this approach is, "When the results come in, what conclusions will I be able to reach?" If more than one element changes, the ability to make a final pronouncement on what works or doesn't work is muddied.

The fundamentalists, on the other hand, are looking for the big breakthrough, the dramatic result, regardless of whether or not they ever know why one approach works and another one doesn't. Publishing consultant Dick Benson has long advocated testing one creative resource against another. His advice is not to try to work out an overall testing plan that leads to definitive knowledge, but to pit one supplier against another and see which approach does the best.

I personally lean to the evolution approach, as I find that even the best creative directors are pressured by the fundamentalist system into looking for creative gimmicks and major departures, sometimes overlooking the less exciting but more profitable breakthroughs that often occur with a simple coupon revision or offer change.

I think the best approach depends on what you have to lose. If you are running a successful business, then changes should be evolutionary, building upon existing success in a manner that identifies principles that can be

used in other mailings and for other products. On the other hand, if you're
in trouble, go for broke with completely fresh, way-out approaches.

Which Medium to Test In

Each medium has its unique advantages. Direct mail offers great flexibility if you are testing a wide variety of offers, and great economy if the
basic color circular can remain the same with only the letter and reply
card changing. It also offers a very low profile, if you don't want your
testing activity to be spotted by your competition.

Print media, on the other hand, let you test broad creative concepts
very dramatically and inexpensively in black-and-white magazine or supplement splits. Such basic design differences cost less to execute in art,
type, and platemaking for print media than for direct mail.

Broadcast is expensive to test, with each commercial variation costing
thousands of dollars. If you are working under Screen Actors Guild
(SAG) and American Federation of Television and Radio Artists (AFTRA)
regulations, then even the slightest variation requires payment of added
session fees and residuals.

It is possible to do broad testing in media units other than those that will
eventually be the most profitable. Larger units such as bind-in cards, or
smaller ones such as black-and-white fractional units, may give a reading
that will project accurately to color pages with bind-ins or other units that
will be the mainstay of the basic campaign. The added CPR, because of the
less efficient unit, is a cost to be charged against your testing budget.

In direct mail, for instance, tests sometimes are sent out as first-class
mail, with a small panel of bulk mail sent at the same time. The faster-
arriving first-class mail gets responses to you fast, and gives a quick reading of which mailing approach does best. The bulk-mail panel determines which class of postage to pay in the subsequent rollout—a
decision that can be made after everything has been printed. This permits a much faster turnaround than would be possible if testing were
done by bulk mail.

An interesting advantage of print advertising is its virtually certain trans-
ferability into other media, including direct mail. A print-tested concept
almost always proves out in direct mail and broadcast. A direct mail concept, on the other hand, hardly ever translates into a successful print ad.

When to Break Out the Champagne

In the introduction of a new product, or the challenge of bettering an established control, there is necessarily an element of impatience in awaiting the
results. Part of the impatience is due to the desire to make use of the
knowledge as soon as possible; more is due to just plain curiosity.

"Doubling" is a convenient way to read results, as earlier returns usually are not reliable indicators of eventual results. The doubling date

sometimes is called the "half-life" point, a concept borrowed from the world of nuclear physics.

Direct mail results start dribbling in immediately. Even the machine operator at the mailing house can send in an order or inquiry before the official mailing date. Nothing is significant, however, until the first Monday after a first-class mailing or the third Monday after a bulk-rate mailing. With first class, half the results usually are in two weeks after the first large Monday mail. With third class, this point comes three weeks later. Usually first-class mail will have a doubling point three weeks after mailing, bulk mail in the sixth week. After that, results dribble in for years.

Now that I've set forth the rule, let me warn you against counting on it. Mail delivery is nothing less than erratic. It varies at different times of the year and in different post offices. Carrier presorted mail travels fast. Mail with business reply envelopes may linger a few days at your local post office on the way back to you. And so on.

Print Results

Just as direct mail uses a doubling date, and just as responses will arrive in a pattern suggestive of the way the mail is delivered and read, magazines and newspapers also have predictable patterns. Daily papers are read immediately or never, and so the half-life point is less than a week away. In a local Sunday paper, you can usually double the results that are in as of the following Thursday. (If the ad is part of a national schedule, you have to allow more time for the mail to arrive from across the country.)

Most monthly magazines have a doubling point three weeks after the first heavy Monday, or about four weeks after the magazine's on-sale date. An earlier, less reliable, 20 to 25 percent point may be reached after two weeks, for those who insist on making early forecasts.

Weekly magazines such as *TV Guide* have a similar pattern. Once the returns start arriving, the halfway point is reached about 12 days later, or about two weeks after the publication first went on sale.

"Hard space" such as business reply insert cards will come in faster than soft space, which requires the respondent to hunt for an envelope and stamp. Inquiries or responses to free offers will come in faster than those that require the writing of a check or the filling in of a credit card number.

Magazines with mostly subscription readers are usually received throughout the country at about the same time. The responses will come in as much as a week faster than responses from a newsstand-sold magazine that is picked up by readers over a month's time.

Magazine response curves also vary by the editorial content. A magazine with a long, particularly interesting article may be saved for weeks, keeping the responses coming in for a longer time. A shelter book may be kept and referred to, while a news magazine usually is read the day it arrives. All these factors affect response curves.

To develop experience in the publications you use, I recommend tracking the results of your ads in each magazine on a daily basis, logging in the results, and drawing curves on graph paper until you discover what seems to be right for your ads with coupons sent to your geographic area.

Broadcast and Telephone

There is no curve in broadcast media or in telephone selling. Most responses come in within hours or they don't come in at all. On telephone orders received in response to a radio or television offer, at least 90 percent will arrive in the first three or four hours. When a mail-in offer is used on broadcast, the response curve is the same as with a daily newspaper.

In telephone selling the responses are, of course, instantaneous. Each day's tallies can be obtained by phone to give you an immediate indication of the success of the techniques used that day.

Rollout Strategies

Once the results are in, there is usually little time to analyze the results and make decisions. New publication closing dates demand decisions as to whether to place orders and run more ads or print more mail. Competitors already are speculating about the effect of your test program on their campaigns. Good mail-order seasons must be exploited or passed up.

Some cautions should be observed. A new approach may work because it is fresh and new, not because it is better. It may work the first time it is run or mailed, but not again. Some ads tire more quickly than others. An approach may not work because of some unusual coincidence. Whenever results seem illogical, always check the medium in which the ad ran. Perhaps a competitive ad ran in the same issue, diluting your responses. Maybe a major news event kept readers from getting into the ads, or a weather aberration kept them from reading the paper or watching television at all.

Whether to act on half-life figures or wait until final results are in and back-end experience is gained is another decision that will depend on corporate personality.

Usually the best approach is somewhere in between. Unrepeatable opportunities—a key season, a difficult-to-get insert card or back-cover position—should be reserved at an early date, because the opportunity is perishable. Lists can be reused with increased quantities, but not yet with the whole list. With broadcast, you can drop the weak stations and add a larger number of new stations in order to gradually build up the schedule.

My own observations are that the risk-takers do better in the long run, and that a winning proposition should complete its rollout within a year. Taking longer to complete the rollout means that marketing circumstances may change, mitigating the success of the early results. Remember, timing is a factor in the original test results as well, and next year may not be as good as this year. The old maxim about making hay while the sun shines is very applicable to the field of direct marketing.

11

POSITIONING

The single most important creative decision in the making of a successful ad or mailing piece is positioning. This concept can apply to basic marketing strategy or to the writing of a single mailing piece. It can be constant—the same for all products created by a company and for all media and offers—or it can vary from campaign to campaign and from mailing to mailing.

First developed as an aspect of packaged-goods marketing and popularized by Rosser Reeves, positioning has become a basic part of advertising jargon. It has become like the weather: Everyone talks about it, but few people do anything to change it.

In direct marketing, we have the ability to refine our positioning very precisely, to measure the results, and to make dramatic changes from one advertisement to another. We can, in effect, be all things to all people, just not at the same time.

The difference is that we are not living off a history of awareness and associations built up over years. Each ad stands alone, adopts its own position, and seeks out and sells the portion of the market segment attracted to that position.

VERTICAL POSITIONING

The classic approach to positioning is based on the dictionary definition of the term: *the portrayal of a product in its proper status vis-à-vis other products*. A hierarchy is presumed: the most obvious categories are price and quality. The products are classified as good, better, best or cheap, cheaper, cheapest.

Value is, of course, only one possible spectrum of positioning. A camera can be easy-to-use as opposed to one with more controls, or a portable computer can be lightweight as opposed to more powerful. A soap can be gentler or stronger. A business service can be a ready-to-use no-brainer, where all the thinking has been done for you, or a highly customized one. Automobile brands can be positioned as safer or faster, sportier or more comfortable. Indeed, such companies go beyond tailoring their advertising to different appeals and actually design models to appeal to different consumer preferences. Someone once said that the essence of the creative process is choice. Certainly, it is the fundamental decision that must be considered in positioning.

All the conventional uses of this discipline involve some type of relative placement over or under others. Thus I call this kind of positioning "vertical positioning" to differentiate it from horizontal positioning (to be described after this).

Perception as the Standard

Before going into the various kinds of positioning, I first want to point out that positioning is not necessarily related to reality. It is, instead, a function of perception.

From a pure marketing standpoint, it is not important whether your product is the best of its kind. What is important is whether people *think* it is the best. Positioning in the marketplace means positioning in the mind. Though it is easier and more ethical to place a product where it should be placed on the basis of merits, its position in the marketplace is not necessarily dictated by considerations of merit. The ratings in *Consumer Reports* magazine often shoot down our previous conceptions of which products were the best, while pointing out little-known products that really are.

Product Placement

Within the sphere of vertical positioning, product placement is a more common consideration than its companions: offer placement, audience placement, and media placement.

Product placement is a function of how the product is presented in relation to competing products. It involves choice: choice about what real attributes are selected for prominent attention, or choice about the images, associations, and conventions that are to be attached to the product's public perception.

A product can be "New!" or it can be "A Tradition since 1829." It can be "Solid," built to last, or it can be "Lightweight and Portable." It can be "Bigger" or "Compact."

A camera can be super-simple—"Just point it and shoot"—or it can offer the ultimate in dials, knobs, gadgets, and other controls for maximum flexibility.

None of these positions is necessarily right or wrong, but all of them are different, and all of them give you something to say about your product that differentiates it from competition. The position that is almost always wrong is "right in the middle," with a committee-designed concept that tries to be all things to all people at the same time.

Offer Placement

Book clubs constantly maneuver against each other with offers such as six for $1 or three for 49 cents, and magazines present their introductory subscription prices in countless variations. (See Chapter 4, The Proposition.)

The offer is a positioning consideration as well. The examples above are attempts to offer the lowest price—or at least to appear to. This is the most common direction, but it is not the only one and certainly not always the best one.

A full-price offer sets your product apart. So does, "A little more expensive, but worth it." There is a subtle difference, with not so subtle results, between "Regular price 50 cents" and "$1, but for you, half-price." The first is just cheap: the second is a bargain. It may not be logical, but neither is human psychology.

The offer is another way of placing your product. A high price is presumed to represent conservative quality. Too low a price is presumed to be cheap. A price slightly higher or lower than the competition can be fine, provided the placement is justified. A price dramatically higher is a way of appealing to snobbery. A price dramatically lower often is not believable. This applies not only to pricing but to introductory or trial offers that result in de facto new prices.

Personally, I prefer to go after the "slightly higher" position in most cases, with a good-quality story to justify the added cost and some premium or discount for immediate action. It is usually easier to point out the better features in a high-priced product than to explain why the cheaper product is low-priced.

Audience Placement

The classic audience positioning is related to age, income, education, occupation, and other demographic or geographic characteristics.

A product may be salable to many audiences, but a given advertisement in a given medium usually has to choose one audience segment as its primary objective. Within any given medium—magazine or newspaper, direct mail or television—there are a wide variety of audiences. How else can you explain the success, within one publication, of many widely varied promotions? Which audience you reach is a function of both copy and art, and both of these crafts can be adapted to attract whichever audience segment is desired.

Some headline styles and typefaces connote elegance; others imply news or bargain images. Some appeal to most women, others to most men.

Older people are more willing than younger to read long copy messages, provided the type is legible. Color makes a difference, and so does the choice of illustrations. The age and apparent personality of a model, for instance, will attract similar readers and repel dissimilar ones.

Psychographic considerations are, in my opinion, a more important aspect of audience placement than demographic ones. The lifestyle and life stage of the prospect is a more sensitive positioning selector for direct marketers than any categories related to age and income only.

For example, more dramatic result differences occur from aiming a message at newlyweds, new parents, homeowners, and retirees than from any demographic selectors. On a finer level, positioning a product as one for people who value independence, macho sex appeal, culture, or other psychological delineators is the most dramatic difference of all.

Such emotional placement is the ultimate audience selector. Conventional market segmentation would never lead you to write an ad with this headline: "Lonely?" Yet lonely people who are precisely targeted by such a lead may be just the right audience for self-confidence courses, dating services, dance lessons, or even bowling shoes.

Media selection is another way of implementing overall market planning. What we do within the media is a matter of positioning. Usually we are positioning not just against other products, but against every other direct-response advertisement in the magazine or mailbox.

Size

Size is the exposition of media positioning. You say a lot about what you are selling by the space unit you select and by the location in the publication.

A double-page spread or a full-page newspaper ad tells the reader, before a word is read, that this message is big! It's important! It also says that the advertiser is substantial (or else they couldn't afford such a large-space unit).

A philanthropy, on the other hand, might prefer a smaller, half-page unit, to convey a humbler, more appropriately frugal image.

In direct mail, this effect is infinitely more flexible, as described in Chapter 15, Direct Mail Formats. Relative placement against other mailing pieces can be accomplished with infinite creative combinations, but the choice of positioning is relatively simple.

A personal message is conveyed in one group of techniques, an ethical or financial message in another. A bargain catalog is presented one way, an expensive collectible another. A sweepstakes offer aimed at young mothers calls for styling in copy, art, and format selection very different from a proposition addressed to presidents of corporations.

The size aspect of positioning is the choice of how you want the communications vehicle, as a medium, to be perceived by your prospect.

HORIZONTAL POSITIONING

Horizontal positioning is the new dimension in positioning—one that I identified while preparing marketing recommendations for a variety of clients and of which I have become the principal exponent. Horizontal positioning adds a new perspective: time.

Horizontal positioning refers to the point in the consumer's decision-making process chosen as a starting point for an advertising message. It can deal with any of the four basic parameters: product, media, offer, and audience. It is a supplement to conventional positioning, not a substitute for it. This leads to a positioning grid, such as that illustrated in Fig. 11-1, offering a matrix of placement opportunities rather than one dimension or another.

The spectrum of horizontal positioning begins, at the left side of Fig. 11-1 with "create a need." At the right is "overcome inertia." In between are "fulfill a need," "sell competitively," and "motivate by value." All of these are primary appeals that should be chosen as creative starting points as carefully as other positioning factors are chosen. Let's review them one at a time, in the order of their evolution in the mind of the consumer.

Create a Need

Does anyone remember carbon paper? Not too many years ago, that was how we made duplicate copies of letters. Today xerography is the standard, and most manufacturers sell competitively against other copiers. When copiers first came out, however, specific product features, pricing, and other approaches would not have been as relevant as the merits of the product generically.

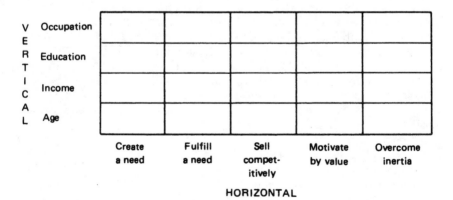

Figure 11-1. The positioning grid.

But what if you now can offer a new, lightweight copying machine with an unusually low price? The expected strategy would be to dramatize the price or the features and compete with the established copiers, but there is another strategy that may do much, much better and is certainly worth testing: creating the need, meaning selling the category before you sell the individual product.

Take the same copier, and instead of featuring product benefits or pricing, aim your message at the "new-user" market. Imagine an ad headlined, "Why every home should have a copier," and describing general uses: keeping tax records, preparing shopping lists, making copies of valuable papers. Imagine a targeted version in a school newspaper: "How a copier can help your grades."

Such an ad doesn't begin with the product at all, except as a general product category. It stops the reader who hasn't been considering such a purchase and says, in effect, "Hey, you! You need one of these."

Once that point has been established, the role of this particular copier and its suitability for home use becomes very relevant. It then becomes a simple matter to be the particular product that just happens to be in the right place at the right time. A lead procurement version might, in fact, simply offer a booklet about the use of copiers in the home. The sales call and follow-up literature would, of course, promote the particular product.

At any given time, and in any given marketplace, there are always some market segments in each stage of the decision-making process. Which one should be selected will depend on just how many are at each stage.

For instance, home computers are still a new product for most homes, and most advertising for such products should be (but amazingly isn't) selling by creating desire. Obviously, at this point, the bulk of the marketing possibilities lie in the creation of desire.

However, there are some people who have already decided that they must own a home computer and are looking for one with the right features, comparing different brands, or waiting for the price to come down—or simply have to be pushed into buying now. All these segments represent stages of horizontal positioning, and all exist side by side.

For an investment product, I wrote a headline, "Just what *are* money market accounts, anyway? And why should I keep my savings in one?" This is the create-a-need position, and according to research with beginning investors, was the headline that was most appealing and would most generate interest and readership.

To create a need, a smoking deterrent should sell readers on quitting smoking, rather than addressing itself "To people who want to stop smoking." A pocket calculator ad should sell parents on the merits of giving one to their child, rather than announcing the latest price reduction or the addition of an exotic mathematical function. A typewriter or computer manufacturer should sell high school students on "How typed papers get better grades" rather than pointing up a new feature or a reduced price.

In each of these examples, the choice is not either/or. It is "Which comes first?" The choice of positioning, properly executed, will demand very different copy, art, and even media choices, even if every possible copy point appears in every possible version.

Fulfill a Need

In the previous position, a need had to be created. In this position, the need already exists, the consumer is aware of it, and advertising only has to announce that there is now a way to satisfy that need.

Using the copier example, this position leads to advertising that says, "Looking for a lightweight home photocopier? Here it is."

Fulfilling a need is probably the most common position for most advertising, and it appears to be the starting place for those advertisers who do not employ strategic planning generally or positioning in particular. The presumption, and it is one, is that the world knows it needs what you have to sell.

"Motor's Auto Manual Helps You Fix Any Car Fast" is such a presumption, even though it also states a benefit. This classic ad runs in publications where large audience segments want to fix their own or others' cars and believe they can do it. For that segment, the ad offers help.

For a more general, less handy portion of the population, the need might have to be created in the first place, with something like, "Make Money, Have Fun—Now Anyone Can Fix Cars." Here the theme is the generic one, and the desire is being created rather than fulfilled.

One difference in fulfillment ads is that the customer knows there is a need prior to reading the ad. Time-Life begins an ad for its American Wilderness library with a glorious mountain scene and the word "Escape!"—fulfilling a psychological need. *Bon Appetit* tempts you with a close-up photo of a scrumptious chocolate cake, appealing to a sensual need to enjoy the food one eats. The Dreyfus Tax Exempt Bond Fund appeals to a universal need with its headline "Zero Tax." All these examples are proven winners, having been the subjects of split-run testing.

Sell Competitively

This middle position is probably the second most used direct marketing position but the single most common general advertising position.

Most advertising presumes that a portion of the media audience already knows it has a need (say transportation), wants to fulfill that need (by buying a car), and has only to choose (which car to buy). For automobiles, that is probably correct. But it would be interesting to see someone do a direct mail campaign to non-car owners on why they should own a car, or to one-car families on why they need a second. The very successful direct mail and phone campaigns used by Ford, Mercedes, and Chrysler, aimed at motivating owners of two-, three-, four-, and five-year-old cars, are creating a desire to own a new car rather than an old one.

Most advertisers generally presume that a product is needed and wanted, and that the only consideration is which brand to buy. Using the copier example, such ads might have the theme, "Why the XYZ copier is the one you need for home use because of this unique feature." Competitive selling can be very competitive and may, in fact, be most powerful when it takes on competitors by name. You've seen car ads do this, but very few direct marketers seem willing to meet the competition head-on. Those who do are often very successful.

Equitable's Money Market Account was introduced as "the new alternative" to certificates of deposit, while savings banks were countering with ads attacking mutual funds. Discount stockbrokers compare their rates openly, not only with the full-service brokers such as Merrill Lynch but with other discounters, by publishing charts listing examples of actual commissions for each firm.

Motivate by Value

Price emphasis is another distinctly separate aspect of horizontal positioning—the aspect most common to advertising by retail establishments. It is the easiest, least imaginative, and usually least profitable form of advertising, saying in effect, "Buy now, because we're cheap."

In direct marketing, pricing motivation is usually manifested by announcements that you can now get thirteen records for 1 cent from the Columbia Record Club, six books for 99 cents from The Literary Guild, or a Sharper Image closeout on a travel alarm for only $14.99.

The limitations of price emphasis are obvious. For one thing, it is only effective if the pricing is genuinely attractive. For another, attractive pricing may cut into allowable margin so severely as to make the offer unprofitable.

It is far preferable, and a much greater challenge, to find motivations, positions, and appeals that will sell a product without resorting to price emphasis. Good marketing and advertising are capable of doing this. Price emphasis should be a last resort after all conventional price options have been fully explored.

Notwithstanding this admittedly utopian goal, pricing and offers will produce a dramatic variation in response rate and CPR, virtually without exception. This is why major advertisers always give price testing a high priority in the selection of ads or mailing pieces to be tested.

Capitol Record Club, in an early split run in a *TV Guide* centerspread position, tested 30 offers, including "Take 8 Free," "Take 9 Free," "Take 10 Free," "Take 12 Free," and "7 for $1.00."

Fotomat, in its testing of the mail-order film processing market, began with an eight-way offer split in newspaper-inserted envelopes. These offer tests included: "This certificate good for ONE DOLLAR off our already low prices." "1¢ Sale. Pay for processing your first roll at our regular low price. Pay only 1¢ for processing your second roll." "HALF PRICE. Yes—take 50% off our already low regular prices for film processing."

The position based on price, discount, premium, or introductory offer may be the least imaginative from the creative viewpoint and the most obvious from the strategic planning standpoint, but it is still the easiest and fastest way to produce a dramatic change in advertising response.

Overcome Inertia

The middle positions—fulfilling need, competitive selling, and price competition—are already used extensively, if not scientifically. I advocate testing all five positions in split-run testing when research indicates they may be appropriate.

The middle three positions already are used often and effectively. The forgotten positions are at the two extremes. The create-a-need position is discussed above. The other extreme is overcoming inertia, or to put it another way, basing the fundamental theme of the advertisement on immediacy. This is not the same as adding an immediacy element to an ad based on another position, which is one of the fundamental tactics discussed in Chapter 12.

In retail advertising, the immediacy concept is based most frequently on a sale, a closeout, a discount, or a cents-off coupon good for a limited time only.

In direct marketing, when immediacy is the position, the offer, the copy, and the layout must all be developed with the dramatization of immediacy as a primary objective.

This position is driven by the inertia theory. In brief, it presumes that at any given time in the life cycle of an established product, there are people who have never heard of the product, others who have tried and rejected it, and still others who have bought or are about to buy it. In addition, another large, very significant market segment has heard of it, likes it, intends to buy it someday, and just hasn't gotten around to it yet. This last segment is the prime target of this position. Its intent, in very simple language, is to flag these people down, grab them by the shoulders, and yell, "Do it now! Don't put it off a minute longer!"

Save the Children advertising is a clear example of this. After years of exposure to their advertisements and that of other child-sponsorship philanthropies, a large audience was ready and waiting, according to a Yankelovich survey. All that had to be done was to overcome inertia.

The ads presumed prior knowledge and went right for the order—now—with headlines like "Fill out this coupon now and save a child." This simple position change, first tested in split runs, turned Save the Children around completely, and helped to produce one of the lowest-percentage fund-raising expenditures of any philanthropic advertiser.

Telegram approaches, with their abbreviated sentence structure and implied urgency, communicate immediacy in style, but so do handwritten messages and other devices described in Chapter 12, Creative Tactics. The difference is that they are dominant rather than supportive themes.

Deadlines are, of course, one of the most effective methods of all, whether real, as with a limited quantity or special offer, or implied, as in, "Please reply by date indicated."

Many magazines, for example, promote their subscriptions once or twice a year, when their replacement or growth needs require it. Often these offers promise savings of between one-third and one-half off the newsstand price.

Imagine how much more effective such offers might be if, instead of relying solely on price, they moved the position to that of immediacy by making the reduced-rate offers true special offers, good only for the 60 days or so of the promotion, with a meaningful and legitimate deadline for responding at that price.

POSITION SEGMENTATION

Research can be very helpful in determining the most effective positioning for a given product or proposition. One method is to use mailed questionnaires or telephone interviews to buyers or customers, to determine which feature or appeal motivated them to buy.

In some cases the conclusions are obvious, as when one approach is clearly and consistently the most appealing. However, one must be careful to avoid what I call "the average trap," where results are pooled together to indicate a one-size-fits-all solution that, like some apparel with the same description, actually fits no one.

For example, a very inexpensive car might be the choice of young people who can't afford anything else, and also of more affluent, older people who use it as a second car. If you were to look only at the average, you would mistakenly conclude that your market was somewhere in the middle.

General advertisers relying on mass media often mistake such difficult choices, watering down their appeals so as to try to cover (and not exclude) the extremes of their market. In direct mail, particularly, we are freed of the need to play the averages, and can direct different messages to different geographic segments.

Research Matrix

A useful tool is a *research matrix,* such as the hypothetical example in Fig. 11-2. This would be for a product such as a camera, and compares two ranges of responses: modernist self-image, and desired complexity.

Each dot represents one of 25 interviews with people who bought the product. It is clear here that buyers who consider themselves modern (Pepsi drinkers?), or triers of new products, bought the new item because of its ease of use. However, buyers who consider themselves traditional (Coke drinkers?) also bought the product, but in their case they were attracted to some of the new controls and options that it concluded.

Here again, an averaging of the interviews might lead to an incorrect middle position. The same kind of grid can be prepared to visualize other research responses—say, the correlation between age and feature desired, or price preference and intended product use.

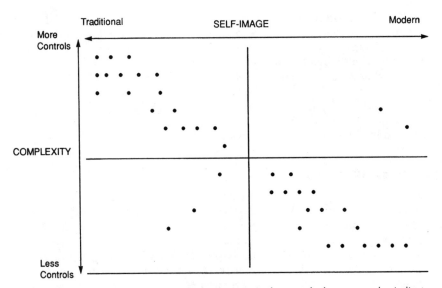

Figure 11-2. Hypothetical research matrix. Forty respondents ranked on two scales indicate pattern of preferences.

In this case it clearly demonstrates that, to the extent media and list planners can identify cost-efficient ways of reaching people with the specified self-images, different positioning is needed.

ESTABLISHING A POSITION

How do you determine which position is right for your advertising campaign? How do you revise a position that has been firmly established in the consumer's mind?

Locating the Correct Positioning

First, when do you do it? Some advertisers go through the positioning exercise only at the inception of a new product launch. Others consider positioning only when a basic ad program starts to fail. Of course, positioning is one of the considerations that should be raised at such times, even though most advertisers will, instead, concentrate on revising lists and media. It is incorrect to presume that an entire publication or list no longer works when, in fact, what is really happening is that the relatively small portion of each medium that has been responding is no longer doing so to the same extent as before.

A different position may "talk to" a different segment of the same media universe. It may hit an emotional "hot button" with a larger percentage of the original audience segment than before. More likely, the number of prospects who were reached by the original horizontal position has declined. Advertising must then address itself to those who have moved to a later point or to those just entering the market who must be addressed at an earlier position placement.

Relocating either the horizontal or the vertical positioning can radically alter your entire marketing picture, significantly increasing response rates and substantially increasing the size of the total media universe, which is in some ways more important.

Vertical Alteration

Advertising can be adjusted vertically in very subtle ways not immediately discernible to previous users or to competitors. An important requirement is that present audiences not be lost in the search for a slightly higher or lower demographic profile.

As discussed in more detail in Chapter 13, The Art of Copywriting, and Chapter 14, Art Direction, vertical positioning can be altered simply by revising copy style and graphic appearance.

You can move a product upscale or downscale by changing typefaces, copy vocabulary, graphic image, and the selection of models or actors used in the advertising. For multiproduct companies, of course, the selection of which product is featured will make a material difference in the type of customers produced for later promotions.

Beer and cigarette advertising have adopted the concept of vertical positioning in dramatic ways. There is the "Marlboro man," attaching a masculine image to a previously "sissy-image" cigarette. On the other hand, Virginia Slims appealed to an emerging feminist market with "You've come a long way, baby."

Some brands of beer—Heineken and Beck's, currently—position themselves for the white-collar suburbanite entertaining in the home. Others aim for the larger blue-collar beer market, with scenes set at ball games, bowling alleys, and bars, showing macho spokesmen implying that viewers could be as tough as truckdrivers or construction workers if they would just drink more of this particular brand of fermented hops.

Direct marketing still has not taken full advantage of the science of vertical positioning, and it has taken even less advantage of horizontal positioning. The influence on direct marketing agencies of giant general agencies has accelerated this consciousness. Direct-response ads and direct mail now routinely reflect carefully thought-out audience positioning.

Using research methods, we can determine whether both business and consumer prospects believe a product or service is "for people like me." Knowing that people want to associate with brands and products that reflect their self-image, we can position our products visually by carefully selecting the kind of people we show in our ads, mailings, or other communications. Split-run tests have proven that the addition of the right photograph can produce dramatic improvements in the results of direct-response advertising.

Horizontal Alteration

Almost always, changing horizontal positions requires a fundamental change in advertising concept. At times it is possible to broaden an existing advertisement by adding appeals to another horizontal placement, but usually an entirely new ad, mailing piece, or commercial is required.

An early ad for Black's Classics Club offered works by Aristotle and Bacon as a premium for joining the Classics Club, presuming there was already a desire to know the classics—fulfilling a need.

Later ads changed the picture considerably. At one time I added a theme creating a desire for such books as "furniture," showing a shelf of classics with the line, "Start now to build this fine home library." Later ads by the brilliant Len Reiss created a different image, and sold readers on the educational and cultural satisfaction of reading such great classics. I don't know the relative results, but these approaches are both examples of moving the proposition back to an earlier position so as to appeal to new audience segments.

Franklin Mint's Franklin Library division at one time relied, for a couple of years, on television commercials in which several reviewers guessed at the value of these finely bound books, while an announcer intoned "Wrong!" This was a dramatic and well-done exposition of the value position. Challenged to find a commercial to replace this tiring spot, I moved to the first position, creating the need. The bindings and value story were relegated to a secondary position behind a dramatization of a young man reading, and getting pleasure out of, one of the classics: *Moby Dick*. This spot proved successful at opening a whole new market segment for Franklin Library by dramatizing what should be obvious: that great books are also great to *read!*

Let's look at another example, the simple calculator. When calculators first came out they could be sold by creating a desire for them among non-calculator users or by fulfilling the need of office calculator users for a small portable model. One ad would sell their usefulness, the other would presume knowledge of what a calculator does and stress size, weight, and portability.

Eventually, many calculators came into the market, and smart advertisers abandoned their earlier ad themes and moved into competitive selling (if they had a superior product) or into the pricing position (if price was a viable appeal). Even while new, sophisticated calculators at unbelievably low prices were flooding the retail market, direct marketers still reaped huge sales. Older, higher-priced models took the route of overcoming inertia, placing attractive reasons to "act now" in prospects' hands via space ads and direct mail.

At any given time, even today, each and every horizontal position can be used by some manufacturer. The desire to utilize such marketing appeals impels research and development departments to find ways to make their products better or cheaper in some way, to some market. Examples are children's educational calculators, game calculators, race handicapping calculators, programmable calculators, and miniature calculators the size of a business card.

Let me make clear that, in direct marketing, you are not limited to a single position for all of your marketing efforts. A position can be adopted for a specific medium or list, as the best position for the particular target audience. For instance, Consumers Union has used a food-oriented product position for women's lists and magazines, an automobile-related position for male lists and publications, and a home-repair emphasis for lists of homeowners. A direct mail campaign I created for General Electric positioned television sets as technologically superior for one kind of list but as attractive furniture for another, and stressed the convenience of having additional sets (creating a need for still another mailing). The choice of which of their wide product line to feature varied as appropriate for the particular mailing.

As new products are developed, marketers are called on to find new ways to appeal to new audiences. In return, manufacturers are called on to innovate, improve, and economize in order to please the consumer. This free, competitive interplay of marketer and manufacturer is the strength of America's capitalist economy, and the search for better advertising is its catalyst.

12

CREATIVE TACTICS

The artist Willem de Kooning, in a *New York Times* interview, said "I see the canvas and I begin!" His results are bold, spontaneous brushstrokes with no comprehensible theme or subject—a result that would be absurd in advertising.

The late Victor Schwab, cofounder of Schwab & Beatty, used to quote Corey Ford's story about the rider who jumped on his horse and rode off in all directions—an allusion to copywriters who sit down at their typewriters and write subjective copy without adequate planning.

One of the great copywriters, Tom Collins, took the pro-planning position a step further, with fewer words. His credo: "Advertising is hard!"

Brilliant ideas and sudden inspirations come to people who have done their homework, who have done the basic conceptual thinking that is essential before trying to write copy or design layouts.

The largest ad agencies require their account staffs and writers to prepare "creative strategy statements" or "creative workups" as one of the first steps in the ad-making process—*after* the marketing plans have been written, *after* the product and its positioning have been selected, *after* the offers have been finalized, and *after* the media or list schedule has been determined. Preparing the creative workup is the step that comes before the fun starts: the exciting, challenging, stimulating, fulfilling process of creating the advertisement or mailing piece to meet prescribed positioning and tactics.

A large advertiser may want a formal copy platform to be reviewed in meetings with several supervisors. A smaller advertiser may write a list of copy points on a pad, talk it over with a coworker, and sleep on it before selecting creative priorities. The process in the two cases is identical: (1) develop alternative concepts, and (2) select and prioritize.

Chapter 11 discussed positioning, the single most critical aspect of the creative process. In later chapters we will go into the actual processes of copywriting and graphic design. Here we will limit ourselves to the principles that precede the conceptualizing of headlines and the writing of copy. In essence this chapter deals with the creative planning, other than positioning, that any writer needs to do in order to deliver an on-target assignment.

THE IMAGERY TRIANGLE

One theory I have devised in the days since I wrote earlier editions of this book is the need for what has been called the Imagery Triangle in creative planning. I have used this as a practical tool for clients, in staff training, and in creative workshops for direct marketers such as American Express and IBM. While it is only a theory, it has been included in some research projects and been the basis for some split-run testing. While I cannot claim it as an absolute law of nature, it has worked for me and—unless the reader has found or developed a better approach—it can be of value to any direct marketer planning a creative project.

In brief, it is an exposition of the belief that the prospect must have three clear images in mind before he or she can feel confident about responding to a direct marketing offer. These are product image, self-image, and company image, as expressed in Fig. 12-1.

Product Image

The lower-left corner of Fig. 12-1 represents the product story, or "What does this do for me?" This is the basic product presentation that most

Figure 12-1. The Imagery Triangle.

companies and copywriters handle superbly, and is the foundation of the simplest trade announcement or catalog blurb as well as major packaged-goods database campaigns.

When the product is new, or has an attractive new feature, by all means it should have the major emphasis, with 60 or 70 percent in that direction. When it is established, you would not spend time explaining the basics, such as how it works or what it's used for, and would stress product only if there was some new feature or benefit. Certainly this changes as the product goes through different stages of its life-cycle.

However, no matter how prominent the feature, some space must be devoted to company image or self-image, if only as insurance for the future. With today's fast-changing product evolution, virtually any product feature is bound to be imitated or surpassed within the space of a season or two. Your protection is to establish a self-image position, or clear trust in the company, that can serve as an advantage even after other edges have been lost.

For example, imagine a bank issuing a credit card with a new feature—perhaps private club privileges at airports, or credits towards stays at resort hotels. Either of these would be very attractive to super-frequent flyers such as myself, as I can't possibly join all the airline clubs and I already have enough "miles" for all the trips I want. I would definitely drop one of my credit cards to sign up with the bank that offers these new features. But eventually my original card-issuer might offer the same advantage. In that case I might just switch back, unless I also have a sense that this new company is one I'd rather do business with, or that somehow fits in with my image of myself. Over the long term, product features by themselves are not enough. I must have clear images of all three elements.

Self-Image

The lower-right corner designates the percentage of attention for self-image, or "What does it say about me?" Putting it another way, "How does this buying decision enhance my self-esteem, my own image of who I am?"

For years, direct marketers thought that impressing others was a consumer motivation. The idea of the "coffee-table book" came into vogue. The pictorial element of an advertisement was designed to show "others" admiring your good taste.

We sold Bibles and encyclopedias in the same way, assuming that they would never be opened by most customers, concerned only with impressing others with their devoutness or scholarship. We knew it wasn't to help the children in the family pursue these goals, because in most cases the buyer's children were too young to read.

Later research revealed that neither neighbors nor family were the real underlying motivation, although the latter might be offered as an excuse. The real reason was the buyer's need to reinforce his/her *own* self-image as a devout person or as a good parent, as the case might be.

That's why brands all have clear positioning images, which usually correspond to the buyer's own self-image. They are more youthful, more traditional, more elite, more popular, more technical, or more carefree. And so they appeal to consumers who see themselves in the same way.

Today, many products and services are basically parity offerings. Their advantages over past or competitive versions may be too tiny to make much of a fuss about. In these cases, only the ability to appeal to self-image distinguishes one from the other.

Company Image

If product image is "What does it do for me?" and self-image is "What does it say about me?" then company image is "Can I believe the advertiser's answers to the first two questions?" Company image establishes the credibility needed, to some extent, for any marketing proposition.

To the extent that the offer is a costly one, or involves personal safety, this is a major issue. To the extent that the product is intangible, or in an area where the customer has learned to be skeptical, it may well need to occupy 40 to 50 percent of the message.

One client offered precious-metals investments in an environment where some less reputable firms had poisoned trust in this proven inflation hedge. Their solution was to arrange with a well-known bank to store the gold bullion, which could not be delivered because usually it was sold on margin. The ad: "Monex offers something new in gold investments—the gold!"

Similarly, magazine agents encountered skepticism among some consumers about their huge sweepstakes mailings. Publishers' Clearing House ran heavy schedules on television showing real winners. American Family used a well-known celebrity, Ed McMahon, to add credibility, using him both in television advertising and in direct mail.

Even the largest companies must sometimes devote space to establishing their credibility, especially when appealing to a new market segment or entering a new field. For example, when Sears bought Coldwell Banker and Dean Witter, they insisted on adding the Sears name but did nothing at all to justify the new brand. Instead, their catalog image diminished credibility for these high-end brands. They ignored the new relationship, whereas I believe they should have dedicated a percentage of every direct marketing communication to changing their own image.

Imagery Balance

When used as one element of a creative plan, so-called *imagery balance* dictates the relative emphasis copy and art should give to each of the three elements. Where an element already is strong, such as the reputation of the company in the mind of the prospect, little emphasis is needed. Where the company is unknown, at least to those being marketed to, then it is necessary to give some emphasis to making the image clear.

In practice I have my planners agree on a percentage to be placed in each of the three image corners, adding up to 100 percent in all. While some propositions may seem to require a great deal of attention to all three segments, in practice choices must be made. The point is that the most attention should be given to those areas that are the least clear.

For instance, an established company such as IBM or Time-Life would have an entry of only 5 percent in the company image corner, not because it is unimportant but because it can be presumed. Even this percentage is a reminder to prominently display the logo and company name. For an unknown company, particularly one asking for investments or dealing with a personal health product, this figure might be 25 or 35 percent.

Where a product is brand-new and has distinct and obvious advantages, the product should be the hero, with a large percentage of attention there. The same applies where a product has new and exciting features. Where there is no product story, then self-image often is the key and, at any rate, one factor that always must be present to some degree.

In using this method, I have occasionally had the opportunity to test different percentage allotments in split runs, and have found significant differences. Sometimes different list segments require different combinations. A magazine's expired subscribers may want to know what's new. New prospects may need to have it related to their self-image or may require some knowledge of the credentials of the publisher.

EIGHT TACTICAL ELEMENTS OF CREATIVE SUCCESS

In addition to the Imagery Triangle, there are eight additional areas that should be thought through, talked over, and carefully chosen. These are

1. Audience targeting

2. Product presentation

3. Involvement devices

4. Convenience factors

5. Immediacy incentives

6. Speed of delivery

7. Credibility

8. Style

Once the basic marketing plan has been completed, including the positioning decisions, it is necessary that these eight factors be considered for each individual mailing or advertisement that is to be tested or rolled out at each stage of a program. Not only the front-end solicitation of orders or inquiries is involved, but also the back-end follow-through to obtain payment, renewals, and reorders.

These steps do not have to change with each separate test or each letter in a sequence. Within a fixed combination of the eight factors there is room for dozens of different copy and layout executions. In my experience, however, fundamental conceptual differences will produce a greater difference in results than will different creative executions of the same concept.

In some organizations the selection of these concepts is left to the copywriter or copy-art creative team. In others it is selected by the account person or product manager, and included as part of the specifications for a creative execution. In either case it should be a separate and distinct process, participated in or at least reviewed by both marketing and creative personnel. Agreement should be reached before anyone jumps on a typewriter and rides off in all directions.

AUDIENCE TARGETING

Once you have selected your audience, you have to figure out how to get to them. Presuming you have picked your lists and media correctly, you know you are reaching them, but you don't know whether they are seeing your message.

The classic AIDA—attention, interest, desire, action—formula begins with the concepts of *attention* and *interest.* Another way of saying this is, "How do you get the right people to stop and read your advertisement or open your letter, in the midst of dozens of competing advertisements or mailing pieces?"

Attention Appeals

The obvious way to target an audience is simply to announce whom your message is for. A money market fund begins its ad, "A new alternative for people who have $2500 in a savings account or certificate of deposit." You can't get much more specific than that.

A book club directed at new market entrants begins, "If you've never joined a book club before, maybe its because you never knew about..."

Here are some other, less wordy applications of this type of headline: "Hard of hearing?" "Good news for denture wearers!" "For women with narrow feet."

Appeals to Needs

If your product or service appeals to too broad an audience, you won't have much luck applying this principle. "Readers!", or "To people who like to dress well," may be too general. In most cases you'll do better getting the attention of your audience by addressing their needs, physical and psychological alike.

Such needs include the entire range of human desires and emotions: independence; importance; self-image; the respect of others; energy and health; wealth and security; pride and satisfaction; adventure and excitement, or tranquility and escape; eating well; dressing well; having a good job, a nice home, a healthy family; finding love and affection, sex and romance; being amused, excited, and entertained; being smarter, or at least appearing smarter; being happy, or at least happier; doing good, feeling good, looking good, and maybe even being good.

Select any of these needs and see how they fit the product or service you have to sell. A book club can appeal to any of these needs through one book or another. Even a specialized product can appeal to many of them.

Take, for example, a product or plan that helps readers to stop smoking. The broad "attention" approach would be simply, "For people who want to stop smoking." But let's say you want to talk to smokers who have not yet made that decision. You could write a headline about health or long life, or you could state that food tastes better to nonsmokers. You could say that the reader will look better without nicotine stains or smell better without smoky hair and clothing, and point out how this improvement could lead to new friends, a better job, or a new romance.

Try this exercise with any product, and you'll be amazed at how many needs your product can fulfill. Then make a deliberate choice before you start to write a headline.

The Floating Audience Appeal

Sometimes, with an unusual product, it's important to let a product find its own audience by appealing to curiosity, snobbery, or independence. Some examples: "Why is *Rolling Stone* the most misunderstood magazine in America?" "What is *Ms.* magazine, and why is it saying all those terrible things?" Any ad that says "X—it's not for everyone."

PRODUCT PRESENTATION

Chapter 3, The Marketing Plan, suggested that you describe your product or service from every possible viewpoint, and gave the example of how as simple a product as a pencil can be described from physical, historical, scientific, emotional, and psychological perspectives. The time to make that exercise pay off for you is when you are ready to present your product.

Once the product has been described, you can then select certain attributes or appeals around which to build your advertising. The choices may depend on the positioning decision made for a specific ad or mailing piece, as discussed in Chapter 11. They may depend on your understanding of the nature and needs of the target audience. They may vary depending on the available media and the format you have to work with. (Decorator colors, for example, would not be as demonstrable in a black-and-white ad as in a color one; an impressive action or motion would come over better on television than in print.)

Feature Dramatization

One creative tactic is to find a way to dramatize one or more attributes of the product or service. This can be done as a logical presentation, as in, "Seventeen reasons why you should read *U.S. News & World Report,*" or a dramatic one, such as, "See how this wonder knife cuts through solid steel."

Dramatization often involves exaggeration—giving an example or case history that is accurate but atypical. Demonstrating that your glue can lift a suspended elephant or pull a freight train has nothing to do with your prospect's intended use, but serves to dramatize the attribute of strength. The case history of a homeowner who built a whole new wing with the help of a do-it-yourself book may not echo the prospect's intention, but it will serve to dramatize the attribute of usefulness.

While working on the introduction of a money market fund, I discovered the importance of dramatizing liquidity in the form of the check-writing feature of such funds. This appeal proved to be indispensable, even though operating data indicated that very few such investors ever took advantage of the feature. They just wanted to know it was there in case of a sudden emergency or opportunity.

Unique Selling Proposition

The concept of the unique selling proposition (USP) is most important in general advertising where a single association is needed to aid recall and association, but it is also useful to direct marketers. It is most relevant at two levels of horizontal positioning (discussed in Chapter 11): (1) creating a need, and (2) competitive selling.

In creating a need, the USP is often a generic concept for an entire category of products. In such instances the ad must point out the desirability of your product as compared with the product in prevailing use.

When television was first introduced, its USP, a visual image, was sufficient to sell a great many sets by companies that are no longer factors in the business. Today, in order to sell competitively, electronic manufacturers constantly search for new USPs, such as color-correction signals, room light-adjustment devices, remote control units, and built-in accommodation for cables, recorders, game controls, computer attachments, and phone hookups. The computer industry is now undergoing a similar change.

Selling Benefits

Most important, every product attribute must be interpreted in terms of benefits, whether it is generically unique, competitively unique, or not unique at all.

Never assume that a customer knows why a certain feature is important. No matter what you're selling, look for interpretations of product attributes as potential planks for your copy platform. For example, a Krugerrand contains exactly 1 ounce of pure gold—an attribute. Because the price of an ounce of gold can be found in the daily paper, it is easy to determine the value of a Krugerrand—a benefit. An appliance may have a plastic body for lightness, a metal body for sturdiness, or a glass body so that you can see how it works or keep it clean easily. No matter what the attribute, thinking in terms of benefits can lead to important and effective selling points.

Building an Edge

In direct marketing, we presume that the market and its needs are the given, and any product can be adapted to fit. Therefore, where there isn't a unique selling proposition or a feature whose benefits can be drama-tized, we can always invent one.

Even with a going business, there is always some way to give it an edge and thereby help sales. Add a guarantee, a service, an updating method. Invent an accessory, an attractive display case, or some element that will make the product a bit easier or more effective to use. Or give it an intangible edge: peace of mind, confidence, pride, certainty.

The power of marketing can and should be used as a two-way street—not only to sell consumers on using new products but also to motivate manufacturers to improve products to meet consumer needs and desires.

Getting to the Point

The specifics of a copy platform are governed by the attitudes of the consumer. These attitudes have changed over the years and will contin-ue to change.

If you look at the typical buyer scenario suggested in your marketing plan, it probably will be evident that this prospect is very different from the prospect who was enticed into reading such long copy messages of yesteryear as "They laughed when I sat down to play the piano...." Today's consumer is distinguished, in the eyes of direct marketing copy-writers, by laziness, impatience, and procrastination.

Many consumers are reluctant to seek out information on different brands and to analyze which is best. You must bring the facts to them. They don't want to wade through long copy messages to find reasons why your product is the one they should buy. You must make your mes-sage interesting and rewarding to read. Furthermore, when presented with the facts, consumers don't want to interpret them. You must make an interpretation for them.

Most consumers not only don't want to read long copy messages in advertising and direct mail, they don't want to read your ad or direct mail at all—no matter how short the message. Ads such as "Forty-nine reasons why you should buy..." usually are not as successful today as they once were, precisely because your prospect won't keep reading until he/she finds the one reason that would really be convincing. If you've got some-thing to say, you'd better say it up front, simply and clearly.

A classic philanthropic ad read, "For $16 a month, you can help Rosario Torres. Or you can turn the page." The motivations were buried in the body copy. Most readers just turned the page. It was later discovered, in split-run testing, that this ad did only one-third as well as a new advertisement built on the concept of involvement. To quote from Victor Schwab's poetic rendering of a consumer's advice to writers, "Tell me quick, and tell me true, or else my love, to hell with you."

INVOLVEMENT DEVICES

Assuming that your prospect has been stopped and has enough interest in your product to hesitate on the way to turning the page or tossing the letter in the wastepaper basket, how do you hold that interest long enough to get your whole message across? The key need here is some way to "involve" your prospect. Here are some ideas.

Quizzes

"Do you make these mistakes in English?" is an old classic that ran for years. Another is, "Should you invest in a tax-exempt bond fund?" Both ads ask a question and offer information that stimulate the reader's desire to learn the answer.

Checklists are a variation: "Which of these important stories have you missed because you haven't been subscribing to...?" Another variation is a headline with a simple yes-or-no request.

Fascination

Every once in a while a copywriter has an opportunity to hold the reader's interest through the sheer eloquence of the story being presented. Often such a message is an entertaining narrative, an intriguing case history, or step-by-step instructions on building a craft project or cooking a sumptuous recipe. A message that is rewarding in itself, because it entertains or informs, can be one of the best ways to hold a prospect. Alas, writers who can turn out this kind of copy are rare today.

Value

A coupon that, graphically, appears to have value in itself, will involve the reader of an ad or mailing piece. While "checks" must be used carefully in a way that will not deceive the reader, any item that in fact can save the reader money does have value and should look valuable. No one wants to throw away an envelope that contains a valuable certificate. Fewer still will toss out one that has a coin showing through a window, contains a bona fide check (even for a token amount like 10 cents), or has a real postage stamp on the reply envelope.

I have received mailings containing a $2 bill (from *Money* magazine), commemorative stamps, packets of seeds, and good-luck charms—all attempts to get me to pay attention to a message by offering me obvious and immediate value.

Personalization

Nothing is as fascinating to a person as his/her own name, and evidently the more frequently and prominently it appears, the better many mailings will do.

Even more effective is evidence that the advertiser is addressing not just a name but a person made "special" by an address, past purchase, political affiliation, or other data. Good personalization involves not only using the name often but using it well, with as much customization as computer technology and available data permit.

Play

Tom Collins quotes the saying, "Within every person there is a child, and that child likes to play." This is the underlying reason why stamps, stickers, and tokens of all kinds more often than not lift response. *U.S. News & World Report* achieved a major breakthrough by using a Westvaco-patented reply card that told the addressee, "Press here to subscribe." A trick fold popped out a picture of a handshake, indicating that the prospect was accepting the offer.

Other mailings ask readers to scrape off a coating, lift a flap, scratch a surface that will release a scent, pull a strip that will reveal a message in a window, look for a lucky number, examine a photograph through a colored filter, or moisten a surface to reveal an invisible-ink message. Corny? Sure. But like everything else in direct marketing, these kinds of play devices are used because they work.

Completion

The brilliant direct mail innovator Sol Blumenfeld identified the concept of "completion" as a factor in direct mail response devices.

This is the true magic of stamps, peel-off labels, and tokens, used particularly in direct mail. The "yes" or "no" stamp is not just a toy; it is a tool that fulfills the prospect's compulsive need to finish an apparently incomplete design.

Imagine a response card that shows a picture of a man looking into empty space with his arm outstretched and—yipes!—a hand missing! How can you resist pasting in the stamp that (1) adds the hand, (2) places the magazine being held by the hand in a position where the man appears to be reading it, and (3) coincidentally, indicates your acceptance of the publisher's proposition?

Try this experiment to see for yourself the power of completion. Draw a circle or a square on a blackboard, with one segment omitted. Leave a piece of chalk nearby and watch how visitors to your office feel a need to finish the shape.

Here's a simpler method. Start to tell a story on an envelope, and leave it in midthought. The completion urge will get your reader inside faster than any plea to "see inside." For the same reason, I always insist that direct mail letters be typed with the last paragraph on each page interrupted in midthought, as a powerful way to get people to turn the page and keep reading.

Choice

Perhaps one of the most successful involvement devices is the simplest: choice. "Which records do you want for only...?" "How many weeks of this magazine shall we send you for...?" "Do you want the red or green display case for your recipe card file?" "Do you want your contribution to help a needy boy or a needy girl?" Or simply, "Yes or no?"

CONVENIENCE FACTORS

"Make it easy to respond" has always been a fundamental requirement for direct marketing advertising. In fact, convenience is one of the cardinal reasons for the growth of direct marketing as an industry.

After all, shopping by mail means you don't have to use your precious time and even more precious gasoline to drive downtown. You don't have to look for a parking space, push through crowds, fumble through shelves and racks, and reason with a salesperson who knows nothing about sales and sometimes less about courtesy.

You see what you want in an ad or a catalog. You fill out a coupon or make a phone call. In a matter of days, someone from the Postal Service, UPS, Fedex, etc., brings it to your door. If you don't like it, you just pop it back in the mail.

The concept of convenience must be extended into every type of response advertising, and there are several ways that responding to such advertising can be made even easier.

Coupon Readability

Not only copy but especially coupons and commitment or guarantee information should be crystal-clear in style, meaning, and typography.

Some art directors seem to think that a coupon is a necessary evil, to be kept to a minimum size regardless of how much copy is to be included. Not so. As explained in Chapter 13, The Art of Copywriting, the coupon is the place to start writing, and the place to summarize your selling theme. It deserves as much space as it needs to be clear and easily readable. Some very successful ads I've been involved with have used an entire page as one giant coupon.

Just as important, the coupon should be easy to fill out. Lines should be long enough, and spaces high enough, so the consumer can write his/her name, address, city, state, and zip code comfortably, without abbreviating or printing in tiny letters. If someone writes illegibly, you're out an order. If another prospect gets frustrated trying to write in a cramped space, you're out another order. And if a third consumer has to look for a pair of eyeglasses in order to read the small type in the coupon, you're out a third order.

What a shame! Why put the right offer in the right medium, present it so you stop the right people and hold their attention through the copy and into the coupon, and then lose them because of simple readability?

Ease of Response

Most sales are impulse sales to some extent, and every second of delay minimizes your chance of getting a reply.

Format has a lot to do with ease of response. Soft-space ad coupons should be easy to tear out—not buried in the gutter of a magazine or the middle of a page.

Where budgets permit, bind-in cards, flaps, and tip-ons all are worth more than their added expense in increased response, not because they attract attention but because they make it easy to respond.

In direct mail you can make response even easier by providing an envelope or a reply card, ready to mail back. Computerization will let you fill out a reply form so that your prospect doesn't even have to write in a name and address, and business reply mail will even save a trip to the post office or the stamp box.

Some successful mailings have included a small pen or pencil. Where a choice is involved, stamps, tokens, labels, and other devices can be used to make selection and ordering simple.

Avoiding Calculations

It is safe to assume that most of your prospects don't really like to do math. I'll grant that veteran mail-order buyers can tackle a major catalog and calculate a maze of shipping costs and sales tax rates depending on the items ordered, shipping weights, and varying routes. However, I can't help wondering how much more business companies might do if the costs were all calculated in advance and included in parentheses next to each item.

If you're expecting multiple orders, don't confront your reader with a need for multiplication and postage calculations. Instead, make it simple with predetermined totals as much as possible.

Consider this example: "Send me_____widgets at $1.49 each, plus 50¢ postage and handling (additional widgets, add 35¢ postage and handling); Ohio residents add 5% sales tax." Instead, try this:

SEND ONE WIDGET for $1.49, plus 50¢ shipping. Total $1.99

SEND THREE WIDGETS for $3.99 (a 10% saving!) plus $1.20 shipping. Total $5.19

SEND FIVE WIDGETS for $5.99 (a 20% saving!) plus $1.90 shipping. Total $7.89.

Ohio residents please add 5% sales tax—7¢ for one, 20¢ for three, 30¢ for five.

Note that this example limits choice of quantity but encourages larger unit sales through both simplification and the discount. We have calculated shipping costs, multiple-order prices, and totals except for the Ohio residents, and for them the percentage sales tax has been calculated.

Ease of Payment

The easier it is to order, the greater the likelihood of impulse purchases. In many cases, selling on credit and including in the coupon the option "Bill me later" is worth the risk. On high-cost goods, of course, the risk can be excessive.

Credit cards are a godsend to the direct marketing business. They make it not only easy to pay but also easy to order. For most people, credit cards are more convenient to use than checkbooks. They can pull out the cards, copy in the numbers, and send their orders on the way.

Even more significant, credit cards have enabled the majority of mail-order buyers to pay by telephone, opening up the airwaves to direct-response radio and TV offers that previously could ask only for COD or prepaid orders.

The Magnificent Telephone

Permitting a customer to inquire or order by telephone is the ultimate convenience. A phone is always handy, and dialing ten or eleven digits of a toll-free number takes far less effort than mailing most reply cards.

Phone services can be open twenty-four hours, seven days a week, just as mailboxes are. Your phone operator also can answer simple questions, do calculations, advise whether an item is in stock, and take credit card payments over the phone.

Ironically, the anonymous telephone operator, trained to be courteous, knowledgeable, and quick, is rapidly replacing the personal service that most retail salespeople used to provide on a face-to-face basis.

The Need for Convenience

Our audiences have become less literate and less legible than they used to be. Most people coming out of public school systems either have not been taught to write or, just as deadly, don't like to write. If they can put sentences together, the chances are that any attempt at legible penmanship was abandoned in the third grade.

We have come a long way from the days when neat, handwritten letters were exchanged between sellers and buyers who treated each other with respect for literacy as they transacted their business. Today, in the age of the computer, we are well advised to make our messages easy to read, easy to understand, and easy to respond to.

IMMEDIACY INCENTIVES

One evangelical fund raiser sent its past supporters an imitation telegram with this short message: "Urgent. Please send $20 by return mail. Will explain later."

This may be the purest and shortest known implementation of the immediacy criterion in direct mail. It contains all the basic elements: urgency, copy, command terminology, graphic expression, and deadline. All these conceptual elements should be included in direct marketing copy whenever there is any justification for them.

Urgency Copy

Ideally, the immediacy concept should be an intrinsic part of the basic proposition, as discussed in Chapter 4. Even if immediacy is not intrinsic, however, there are many ways to convey a sense of urgency. The telegraph style in the example above is a style approach. News headlines, or words such as *now, new,* and *introducing* do the same.

The need for prompt action can be related to the proposition, if justified with reminders about limited quantity or possible price increases. In such cases it pays to dramatize the result of inaction, as in, "Why pay more later?"

Try dramatizing the imminent savings, comfort, or other advantages of the product or service offered, as well as the costs, discomfort, and disadvantages of putting off a decision. Some examples: "Winter is coming sooner than you think. Order this coat now so you'll be ready for the first frosty day." "Send your contribution today. A child's hunger has no patience."

The emotions can be tapped as well. "Imagine how much fun it will be when you receive this wonderful novelty in the mail...taking it out of the carton and watching it perform its amusing movements...sharing the excitement with your friends. Why put off this moment a day longer than you have to?"

Command Terminology

One copy approach that seems to be consistently effective is what I call "command terminology." This is the simple second-person declarative sentence: "Do it today," "Send it now," or simply "Mail this coupon." Somewhere, before a copy message has been completed, it is important to answer the reader's unspoken question: "So what do you want from me?" The answer should be a command: a statement of exactly what you want the person to do. In the AIDA formula, "action" is the payoff. The request for action should be as much like a command as good taste permits.

When I was marketing director of LaSalle Extension University, we had the opportunity to run a great variety of headlines dramatizing the tangible and intangible advantages of the school's educational courses. The most effective approach for this market, consistently, was the use of command headlines such as "Be an Accountant" or "Learn Auto Repair."

Graphic Expression

How do you make a layout look like it has news value? The key is *recency*. An old message doesn't demand immediate attention or action. A message that is hot off the presses conveys the impression that it is worth reading and acting on immediately.

Imagine that you are driving your car, looking for a parking space, and suddenly you see one near what appears to be a little-used driveway. Stenciled in faded letters is the warning DO NOT PARK HERE. It looks as if it has been there for a long time. Many people would ignore it. However, as you pull into the space, someone appears and hands you a note with the same message. Suddenly it's immediate. You are likely to pay immediate attention to it.

Some media have immediacy built in. Radio and television are prime examples, particularly because of the possibility of positioning commercials near news programs. Newspapers are more immediate than magazines, weekly magazines more immediate than monthly ones.

In direct mail, a telegram format is the ultimate immediacy. "Air mail" seems more urgent than other classes of mail. Even though all first-class mail now goes for the same rate, a simple red-and-blue diagonal border around an envelope or reply card still conveys the idea of speed, promptness, and importance.

Handwritten notes appear more recent, and thus more immediate, than printed letters. Rubber stamps or facsimile stickers also convey urgency. An interesting direct mail technique is to put part of the text, the postscript, and some marginal annotations in facsimile handwriting, to suggest that they are afterthoughts.

In print advertising, immediacy can be conveyed by setting the ad in a typewriter face, or the headlines in crayoned hand lettering. One retailer ran sales ads in such type with hand-printed or typed copy and photos with visible cut marks—a concept called *calculated crudity*.

The more finished the ad, the more permanent it looks—and therefore the less immediate. The trick is to strike a balance between the graphic respectability you want to convey and the need for immediacy. It isn't easy, but it is possible.

Deadline

The most important of all immediacy elements is the deadline. If the proposition permits, you can say "Offer expires on November 8." This is the strongest deadline of all.

"Offer expires in 10 days" is good, but not quite as strong as a specific date. I often recommend an undated deadline when there is risk that the mailing may not get out on time. Otherwise a dated mailing that is delayed could be a costly loss.

Where there is no genuine offer deadline, there are ways to suggest it. For instance, in a market where prices are rapidly increasing, you might say, "This price not guaranteed unless reply received before _____" or more simply, "Please reply by _____."

Other deadlines can be related to supply rather than date; for example, "Only 5000 plants available at this price." Sweepstakes often include a bonus for early entry—a proven stimulus to the total response. Some propositions offer a premium or discount only to the first few thousand people who reply.

The common denominator is the same in all these examples. Set a deadline or give a reason for action *now*. In direct marketing, it is now or never.

SPEED OF DELIVERY

A cardinal rule of direct marketing is to add immediacy, to encourage the prospect to act now rather than later. It is only fair, and good business, to pay off this sense of immediacy by turning on the service, shipping the merchandise, sending the information, or whatever, as soon as possible.

Don't wait to send letters back and forth to fulfill the customer's expectations. Use on-line transfer to turn a phone inquiry into an in-home appointment or installation. Use UPS, Federal Express, etc., to get your merchandise shipped in a day or two rather than take weeks with parcel post.

CREDIBILITY

The consumer today has probably never been more distrustful. Automobiles are recalled. Favorite foods turn out to have dangerous ingredients. Why should consumers trust a product they have never seen but have only read about in an ad or mailing piece that is transient by its very nature?

With newspaper or magazine advertising, some credibility is provided by the implied endorsement of the publication the ad appears in. But this is less relevant in newspapers and, because of the lack of acceptance standards in many stations, almost nonexistent in broadcast. It is hard to convey believability when your TV spot is adjacent to one for a telephone dating service.

The element of credibility is a must item on any copy checklist. Fortunately, there are many ways to provide it.

Advertiser Reputation

Nothing is quite as effective as sponsorship by a company that has built a good reputation over the years. If your company is well known, then make it clear that you stand behind the product being offered, and put your name in a prominent place. If your company is owned by or affiliated with a well-known substantial company, be sure to feature that company name. Split-run testing indicated a 25 percent lift for a new magazine introduction that featured the name of the broadcast network that owned the magazine over an identical ad that did not. When Condé Nast introduced *Self,* they felt their other magazines were better known than the publishing name, and so the opening campaign showed covers of *Vogue, Glamour,* and *Mademoiselle.*

If your company isn't well known but is large or reputable, has won awards, or is licensed by the government, then by all means say so. If you are just starting out, then make something of that; say that your president reads every letter, or that the item is your only product.

The Bandwagon

People flock to see why a store or restaurant is crowded. If your product is selling well, then say so. Tell them that your direct marketing business is prospering, that so many thousands of people have used your product, that certain big companies or such famous personalities as so-and-so have bought it. Everyone loves a winner.

Endorsers

If your company isn't well known, or even if it is, then consider finding an endorser, a well-known spokesperson who offers instant identity and therefore believability for your message, Where would National Liberty have been without Art Linkletter's endorsements during their peak growth period?

Corporate Personalization

Your spokesperson doesn't have to be a movie star or a national celebrity. It can be your own chief executive officer. A CEO who looks and sounds sincere might provide an ideal image in your advertising. Look at Ben & Jerry, or Gloria Steinem's *Ms.* ads. A personal message from the founder or the publisher can have a very nice ring—in copy style, and at the cash register.

Testimonials

Testimonials once were the mainstay of mail-order advertising, and it is surprising how few advertisers make good use of them today. They are still very effective. There is nothing quite like an honest face and the signature of someone in a nearby part of the country to add believability.

The problem is that testimonials are difficult to come by. In our lazy, nonliterate age, unsolicited testimonials are few and far between. When you do get one, you may not be able to get a release to use it in advertising.

For one packaged-goods client this element has proven to be critical to achieving the necessary response rate. Eventually we used laser printing to feature testimonials from each prospect's own state, changing from state to state. And we even included testimonials and photographs of real people, with similar lifestyles, using the product.

Today, you have to ask for testimonials. Send out a questionnaire soliciting opinions and comments, including a section with prewritten statements and the introduction "Which of the following statements would you subscribe to?" Respondents who check appropriate statements or add desirable statements in their own words can then be contacted by telephone and asked for a release. If the respondent agrees, a local photographer may be commissioned to take a photograph and secure the signed release.

Outside Guarantors

A guarantee is always helpful, and is more helpful if the guarantor is well known. If your company isn't well known, consider getting an outside source to back up the guarantee and ensure that money will be refunded if the customer is not satisfied. Perhaps an insurance company, such as Lloyds of London, or a local bank can endorse the guarantee. Perhaps an independent testing laboratory can vouch for the product claims. A newspaper clipping might be quoted, citing the effectiveness of your product's principal ingredient. An industry association may grant you its "seal of approval."

"Why Are You Being So Good to Me?"

To the extent that your offer sounds "too good," it may be perceived as unbelievable. Don't blame today's consumer for asking "What's the catch?" when the word *free* shows up.

Offer qualifications should be clearly stated up front, not just where required by law but as a matter of good business. Split-run ads have confirmed that the various rules requiring that club commitment and return policies be spelled out actually help response rather than hurt it.

CREATIVE WORK PLANS

In most agency and advertiser organizations, the pressure of daily work and the need to meet deadlines inevitably lead to shortcuts in the creative process. The worst shortcut is to start turning out mailing pieces and advertisements even when creative tactics have not been thought through.

The only way to keep creative work on target is to use a creative work plan for each and every project. Here are some elements that might be included:

General Information

- Client or product
- Project number
- Media, or list type
- Size or format
- Schedule and deadlines
- Assignments and required approvals
- Personalization or versioning options
- Image triangle—suggested emphasis (See Fig. 13-1)

Product Information

- Attributes and benefits
- Positioning
- Objective or offer
- Dramatization or demonstration possibilities
- Support of claims; guarantees; endorsers
- "What will this do for me?"

Market Information

- Demographics—age, education, etc.
- Psychographics—personality, interests, if known
- Prospect dramatization (Describe typical prospect.)
- Self-image considerations
- "What does it say about me?"

Company Information
- Required logos and tag lines
- Credibility supports, if needed

Response Stimulators
- Immediacy factors; reason for acting now
- Order or inquiry details
- Response device; card; envelope needed; etc....

Your approach should reflect the values and unique style of the organization or the creative director. But it must be in writing, and it must be prepared in advance and agreed to by the account supervisor or product manager.

13

THE ART OF COPYWRITING

Up to now we have dealt mostly with the science of advertising—the planning, the research, and the strategic and tactical considerations that precede writing the first word of copy.

It is as if the navigators have now set the course, and the pilot is ready to take over the highly skilled responsibility of getting the plane into the air. Or the architect and engineers have completed the plans for a new office building, and the artisans of many crafts now are ready to break ground.

Copywriting is the original "art" of advertising, and especially of mail-order writing. All the historic greats of the field started as copywriters, and all the early classics are essentially expressions of the copywriter's art.

An old-timer in the field once told me, "Copy is king." This is an exaggeration today, but copy is still the fountainhead of great innovations in direct marketing. The experience of copywriting is extremely valuable, perhaps indispensable, to those whose creativity would extend to the whole process of direct marketing management.

"ADVERTISING IS HARD" AND OTHER APPROACHES

Vic Schwab emphasized the importance of relating product benefits to human needs. In his classic *How to Write a Good Advertisement* (Harper & Row, 1962), he listed several basic needs: better health, more money, greater popularity, improved appearance, more comfort, more leisure, pride of accomplishment, business advancement, social advancement, and increased employment, among others.

David Ogilvy added story value, with text and illustration, subheads, and captions, all telling a story that bridges the common interests between the producer of a product and its potential consumer. The Ogilvy style, with booklike typefaces, sentence or title headlines, highly readable layouts, and dramatic illustrations, has become instantly recognizable. Above all, Ogilvy ads have been literate, showing proper respect for the English language, its structure and punctuation. I believe these ads are unusually effective because they treat the consumer with respect and invite the reader to respond in kind to the message and product.

Bill Bernbach was the first to adapt advertising style to its media context. Recognizing that advertising almost always appears in an entertainment medium, whether in the pages of a magazine or adjoining a television show, he added the dimension of entertainment to advertising itself. As a result, followers of his approach often include touches of humor, suspense, pathos, conflict, or contradiction to make them at least as appealing as the editorial or programming content they adjoin. It's a lot easier to get your point across if people *want* to read or watch your message.

Tom Collins summed it up with an aphorism reminiscent of Will Rogers: "Advertising is hard!" This classic understatement says it all. There's no easy route to successful advertising. The stroke of creative inspiration is a rare phenomenon that comes only to those who have been immersed in research, planning, strategy, and tactics.

The hard work of marketing scientist and creative artist pays off in successful advertising. The quickie tossed off by a free-lance or inexperienced in-house ad department may be an ad technically, but it will never realize the true potential of direct marketing done the hard way, the slow way, the sure way.

A SIMPLE FORMULA

Every writer has heard of the AIDA formula. As a reminder, the words stand for *a*ttention, *i*nterest, *d*esire, and *a*ction. This is the basic set of rules that guided me when I first wrote copy.

I was once asked by Murray Raphel, the well-known specialist in retail marketing, for my own formula, and with all homage to AIDA, I offered the "five S's" formula, an amplification of the one I grew up with. The letters stand for "Stop 'em! Show 'em! Seduce 'em! Satisfy 'em! Sell 'em!"

Stop 'em.   Write a headline that flags down the likely prospects from all of the readers or viewers out there.

Show 'em.   Communicate nonverbally as well as verbally. Use pictures, people, visual images to reinforce the headline.

Seduce 'em. Appeal to the highest psychological level, not just material benefit. Try emotional needs, fantasy, self-image.

Satisfy 'em. Deal with real needs and problems, and show how the product or service fulfills those on every level.

Sell 'em. Ask for the order, in a way that is simple to follow, reinforces the basic message, and assures satisfaction.

In this book we deal with creative plans, tactics, directions—all of which have to be done first. But the fine art of copywriting is probably best known for its tricks of the trade—how to get ideas, how to write a headline, how to make sure copy is read. Once upon a time, before we all got involved in strategies and psychology and research, when people read more and better, these skills were the foundation of direct marketing creativity. They may not dominate the substance of our communications today, but they still provide the style. And without readable, colorful, interesting writing, none of our strategies will ever be communicated at all.

THE DIRECT DIFFERENCE

Writers trained in general advertising often have a difficult time working in direct marketing. Even when the objective has nothing to do with generating an immediate response, their general advertising training often gets in the way. That's why real direct marketing writers and creative executives are in such demand, and command higher salaries than general agency equivalents. And it's why a young beginner, directed by a skilled direct marketer, will often turn out advertising that will outpull that done by a supposed heavyweight convert from general.

It is rare that I do not have, or at least know of, an opening for a good direct marketing creative. I probably see a hundred portfolios a year for writers and artists. Today, since so many good general advertising creatives are available, these portfolios often contain outstanding and well-known advertising for major general advertisers. But when I finally find the handful of direct mail pieces, they are virtually always disappointments.

The creative unfamiliar with direct marketing often produces parodies of what he or she thinks a direct mailing or direct response ad or TV spot should be. Often they are 6 × 9 formats, the least imaginative. The personalization is minimal, or used in a trite fashion. The letter is almost an afterthought, written more like an advertisement than a letter. (Adding "Dear Mr. Jones" doesn't make it a letter.)

The biggest difference is in the use of the space itself. General copywriters are trained to get across one idea, clearly and cleverly, in a manner that will be recalled and will influence attitudes. In a ten- or thirty-second commercial, or a page that will quickly be turned in a magazine, they have one shot to make an impression and get an idea across in a form that will stick. And so they should, in mass advertising.

But direct response, regardless of the medium, and direct marketing, regardless of the objective, is a different animal. Our purpose is not to leave an impression but to generate a positive decision to buy and a motivation to act—not later, but right now. Our job is not to make an impression, but to make a sale. Direct marketing is not just advertising, and it is not just sales. It is the bridge between the two, and must incorporate elements of both.

For one thing we either have more space, as in direct mail, or we are willing to use the space we have, as in long-copy magazine advertisements. We are not limited to one idea, but have the space to work in appeals to all segments of our audiences. We do not stop at making an impression, but go on to amplify, demonstrate, justify, motivate, and ask for an action. The writer must work harder, covering the entire sales message rather than just one point. And the art director must work with the writer, neither one dominating, because art and layout must be the vehicles for the selling message, not ends in themselves.

Although there are many award programs in the direct marketing industry—I myself have been chairman of the DMA's Echo Awards—the only award that counts is the end result. Leave out a selling point, and it shows on the bottom line. Put the body copy in reverse or against a distracting background, and the phones don't ring as often. Write a headline that's so subtle you're counting on the prospect to figure it out, and you may as well start looking for another job, because your client will be looking for another agency. In direct marketing, the only reality is results. And like it or not, your career, like mine, is governed only by the answer to the boss's or client's question: *What have you done for me lately?*

GET READY, GET SET...

Regardless of what other role you might play in your client or agency organization, for the purposes of this chapter you are now a copywriter. Even those company presidents who occasionally exercise their right to toss off an ad of their own are, at the time and place of writing, copywriters and only copywriters.

Whether your starting point is your own inspiration, an informal discussion, or a carefully prepared "project assignment" with marketing plans, briefings, and spelled-out creative specifications, the copywriter's first two steps are the same: *define the assignment* and *abstract all information.*

Define the Assignment. Are you doing concepts for discussion, or finished copy for a concept that has already been agreed upon? What are the medium and the space unit? Is there a formal marketing plan for the entire product line? Have creative tactics and positioning been worked out for this particular project, or are you expected to propose them? (If the latter, get agreement on them before you submit headlines or copy; you'll save yourself a lot of false starts and wasted time.) Also, what's the history of this project? Why is a new ad needed? How do the audience, medium, positioning, and strategy differ from previous ads? What is the result history of those ads?

The more you can learn, the more you can contribute. If it helps, quote me as recommending that no data should be held back from the copywriter. If there is a need for secrecy about actual CPRs and margins, then ask for some type of target or index figures that can be shared with everyone on the creative team.

Abstract All Information. Restate everything yourself, in your own words, in your own notes, and for your eyes only. Ignore the repetitious instructions and information you already know about, but spell out the key points you must add to your knowledge and the key criteria expected of you for this assignment.

It is important that the elements of strategy and tactics, as well as all relevant product and market information, be digested and restated in your own words. This is necessary to integrate this data into your own mental processes, and to be sure you understand and can explain it.

Beat the Winner

Often a writer has a broad assignment: to find a way to improve results— either up-front or through better-quality responses—as compared to either a previous winning effort or a competitor's ad.

You know that your ad or mailing will be put up against a control package that may have beaten dozens of tests before. The medium is fixed. The offer is fixed. You must overcome the winner with pure creative superiority.

The first step is to take the other package apart creatively. This too must be done in writing, as a way of helping you to fully identify what is important about it. The best approach is what I call a *reverse outline*—a list of copy points used in the piece being studied. Paragraph by paragraph, read the competing copy and draw conclusions such as these: What is the writer trying to say? What need is being appealed to? What position is being taken? What makes it work?

You know the winning ad works, so you can't dismiss it just because you wouldn't have written it that way. When a point is repeated, check it against your original list. Give the headline appeal 10 checks, appeals in subheads 3, and the main points in the coupon 2 or 3. Add up the checks to see where the emphasis is.

Then take the list and regroup it. What are the constants that you would have in your package anyway? Isolate the main themes. What does this package have that other tested packages did not have? Identify the variables—the optional appeals that you can retain or drop as you see fit.

Once you've done this you will be in a position to take the plunge: to gamble on what you think the strong points are and where you think the copy can be improved. Rather than trying an alternate approach or trying to please the client by being clever, begin with the basics and write out your own copy platform for the new effort.

The copy platform is your choice, as a writer, of which appeals you want to place your chips on. Take the ones you think are strong, and see how you can make them stronger. Take the weak ones and drop them or turn them around into positives. Then, as your edge, find the new copy points that you think will strengthen the previous effort and make yours the winner.

Check your benefits list, and see what you can add. Look at your positioning options, if they haven't been spelled out in advance. Even if they have been spelled out, feel free to contest the client's or marketing planner's selection. Just don't ignore it.

Three Secrets of Great Ad Writing

In real estate, the three most important considerations in selecting a property are location, location, and location. Similarly, the three great secrets of copywriting are research, research, and research.

Sure, any writer can fill up a page. The Blarney stone blesses all Irish and all ad writers with equal fervor. Consequently, it's no trick for any of us to spontaneously sound off for as many pages as we'd like on any subject we want. Politicians and debaters have been doing it for years, on whatever side of a subject is required. Making something out of nothing is a clever trick, not an art.

One common denominator of really fine copy is that it is "meaty"— filled with details, choice examples, and clever anecdotes, all of which make points with examples rather than with broad and empty claims.

I have had to write copy on electronic capacitors, automotive additives, books on bridge (which I had never played), and religious rituals that were unfamiliar to me. I knew nothing about these subjects before I wrote about them, and nothing soon afterward. While I was writing, however, I was steeped in each subject and knew enough to talk intelligently with experts.

Let's face it. If you can't talk about a subject in your own words, how can you write about it? If you haven't found out enough about it to interest you, how can you make it sound interesting to others? If you can't explain it to your spouse or best friend, how can you explain it to the person whom you want to read your mailing piece?

Someone asked me how I wrote this book. I answered, "One word at a time." Actors in commercials sometimes look at the cameras and freeze at the thought of the millions of people who may soon be watching them. They have to be reminded to think about and talk to just one person at a time. Copywriters too should heed this advice. If you can't talk to one person, you'll never talk to tens of thousands successfully. This means you must master each new subject with research, research, and more research.

First, get answers to every question that occurred to you when you read the briefing material or sat in on an orientation session. Don't be proud and stupid; be humble and smart. Let someone know what you didn't understand so you can get explanations of every point that isn't clear. No one is judging you in any way except by counting the coupons that will come in as a result of your efforts.

Study the product. If it is a magazine, go back two years or more to find articles with a wide range of appeals, and write out a catchy summary of each one. If it is a book, even an encyclopedia, go ahead and read it—or at least try to. As you read, make notes in copywriting form, as if you were writing a list of contents to be included in a mailing piece. (Maybe you'll use it this way, maybe not; but it's a great way to get examples for points you intend to make in your main copy message.)

Boardroom Reports became one of the most successful newsletters in the world by using this lesson consistently. Their writers are instructed to abstract selling points, in copy form, from current newsletters. Example: "What not to eat on an airplane." The points are called *fascinations,* meaning ideas that fascinate a potential reader. These lines are ranked, tested, and become the foundations for circulation-building ads and direct mail that are tough to beat.

One hint: Do note the page number and source of each such item you write out. Sooner or later a client or a lawyer is going to ask you for your sources, and it's a lot easier to make marginal notes as you go along. Some mailing pieces even add the page number to the copy, as a way of making the promise more specific.

After you have studied the product, head for the reference books. Go to the library, and look in the card files and in the *Reader's Guide to Periodical Literature* to get all the information you need on the subject. Call associations or technical groups and see what they can offer you. One such inquiry led me to spend three days at the library of the Society of Automotive Engineering just to support one key point for an advertisement for an automotive product.

Don't just talk to the product manager or ad director. Ask to speak with—in fact, insist on speaking with—the engineers, editors, technicians, or other specialists who really know what's happening. When I was asked to write a fund-raising mailing for The Free Store, Cincinnati's uniquely successful food distribution system for the needy, I visited the center personally. No briefing could have prepared me for the profoundly emotional experience of talking with the volunteers and those who needed help. As a result, the letter is one of my proudest and most successful efforts.

The more you know, the more you can write. Ideally, all the facts should be in the marketing plan, but it's more likely that the writer will be helping to write this section of the plan. In a small company without formal planning, you may be going through the processes on your own without benefit of a formal strategic plan.

The Creative Workup

You've defined the assignment. You've done your homework. Now you're ready to write—almost. Just one more thing: Make a list.

This list is a simple one. Put down all the copy points you want to make, based on your selection of positioning. Include the creative tactics you've selected and how you'll dramatize the offer and product attributes, interpreting everything in benefits. Perhaps you'll have 20 or 30 basic points. Even if you know them all, write them down, so that you can use the list later to help you sell the ad to whoever has to approve it.

Then put numbers or letters next to each point, indicating the relative importance of each. Which are major points, which minor? Which is the single most vital point to be worked into the headline? Which points should be clear even if the prospect reads only captions and subheads? Which ones are optional—to be left out if space limitations demand it?

Recently one of my creative teams submitted concept layouts to a new client. These were primarily headlines and subheads, with some callouts and captions as well. As might be expected, the client preferred some of them to others; the ones we liked most were not necessarily in the concepts selected for testing. We asked the client to look at them separately, putting an X next to those disliked, and one, two or three checkmarks next to the others. With this in hand, it was a cinch to put together final advertising that pleased the client.

Harnessing Your Subconscious

Now put away your research. Put away your notes. Tape your list to a wall, and get away from it all. Take a nap. Take a walk. Take a drink. Take whatever you need to let your mind digest all the research, strategy, and creative specifications. Sleeping on it works for some people. A walk around the block is my technique. The point is to let your subconscious mind digest all the information you have acquired.

Your brain will, in effect, switch to "automatic" and integrate all this knowledge with everything else you've ever heard, seen, read, or been taught—making connections with the whole of your life experience much as a "method" actor interprets a role.

If your thinking has been logical and scientific; if you've been a sensitive observer of the human process; if you've allowed yourself to think, feel, and communicate on both an emotional and an intellectual level; if you have managed not to block out your experiences as an adult or as a child—then you will be able to draw upon the sum total of your entire life to help you understand, create, and express the ideas you need to do your job.

Your job is infinitely challenging: to make the complicated simple, the dull fascinating, and the mundane marvelous; to bridge the communication gap between a lifeless product and a living consumer. The power to meet this challenge is already within you.

...AND GO!

Now you face the legendary blank sheet: the drawing pad or typing paper whose stark whiteness has, at one time or another, intimidated not only ad writers but novelists, poets, and playwrights as well.

Presumably you have done your homework. You know the subject. You understand the assignment. You have a picture in your mind of whom you are talking to. You know what you want to say. Now, where do you start?

The Mental "Dump" Process

Computer technicians use the word *dump* to mean emptying the data stored in memory. It's a process I recommend for copywriters as well.

The first attempt at writing should be not to write at all but to pour out everything that is on your mind about the subject at hand. It's a freeing process, if it is done right and honestly. You type, write, or doodle whatever comes to mind, including "What am I trying to say here?" or "I hate this job" or "I'd better wax my skis before I leave this weekend."

By getting random, irrelevant, and sometimes irreverent thoughts out on paper, you are freeing your mind to get to the task at hand. This dump process is for your eyes only, and it's simply a way of getting warmed up.

After a page or two of nonsense, resentment, or corn, the juices start to flow, and random ideas show up on the page. The first few are often terrible. They are the clichés, the slogans that someone else has done before, or obscene plays on words making fun of your task.

Some "pump-priming" phrases that have worked for other writers might be helpful. "The point I am trying to make is..." "Imagine yourself..." "Please buy my product because..." "Here's how I'm going to change your life...."

I find that this process not only gets rid of the blocks; it gets rid of the obvious. After a few pages of stream-of-consciousness writing, the ideas start to concentrate on the selling job you have to do. The checklists start coming to life, played back by your subconscious mind, and sooner or later some really choice ideas start showing up. The good ideas generate other good ideas, and soon the writer is on a creative "high," with usable phrases filling the pages. A genuine enthusiasm wells up. There is an anticipation, a sense of excitement. "Hey," you tell yourself, "this is going to be one of the best things I've ever written!"

Now you're ready. The hours or days of research, study, and planning at last pay off in a few hours of frenzied, productive writing.

If you build logically from the facts and begin to write, you will lack enthusiasm and that will show in your writing. If you jump in excitedly without having done your homework, the style will be there but not the substance. The process I recommend is certainly not the only approach, but it does offer one way for the direct marketing copywriter to set the mood for advertising copy that will be more than just satisfactory and may be great. One thing is certain: Your copy will be no better than the standards you set for yourself.

Begin at the End

This advice may seem strange, but it is sincere. The first thing to write is the coupon. Most writers save it for last and treat it as a necessary nuisance along with copyright notices. They are missing a bet.

Most people, when reading an ad, don't act on it immediately. Some do tear out the ad and act on it at once. Most, however, tear out just the coupon and put it in a pile of bills to be paid or in a notebook, or just pin it to a calendar or bulletin board.

Later, when the time comes to write out the envelope and perhaps a check, the coupon itself is the only reminder of the reasons behind why they tore it out in the first place. The headline is gone. The pictures are gone. All that remains is the reply card or coupon.

At that point, which do you think will get a greater response? "Send me _____ widgets at $4.95 each," or "Yes, I want to double my car's gasoline mileage without sacrificing speed or power, with your new Widget Wonderplugs (only $4.95 each), developed by the U.S. government for the space shuttle program. I understand that if I'm not completely satisfied I will get my money back by just..."

Writing the coupon first not only assures that it will get the important attention it deserves but also will help you to crystallize the main point of your advertising copy. Both ways, you win.

The First Draft

Some writers prefer to visualize the entire ad, jotting down a headline and subheads in a sort of skeleton concept. This is a fast shortcut to presenting a finished idea, and comes in handy when several different conceptual treatments must be visualized for presentation. Unfortunately, many advertisements that begin in this manner don't hold up in the finished version; the copy execution simply lacks the spark of the original idea.

My recommendation is to write the first draft of the advertisement before working out a detailed visualization and, in some cases, even before perfecting a headline or subheadlines. More often than not, good copy will suggest its own subheads, and any of them should be adaptable to main headlines.

There are as many approaches to the craft of copywriting as there are products to write about. My suggestion is to write the coupon first and the copy next, and then to extract the subcaptions and headlines from the body of the copy. If the copy is good, they'll be there. If they're not there, write new copy.

The first draft of a selling message should

- Begin where the reader is
- Bridge the gap between attention and interest

- Create desire

- Fulfill need

- Provide positive benefits linked to product attributes

- Dramatize the offer

- Provide proof, assurance, guarantee, and a reason to act now

In short, it should include all the selling motivations that have been determined to be appropriate for the particular proposition, even though only one of them is emphasized as the basic positioning for the advertisement or mailing piece.

The first draft is for content, and should be worked on until every selling point has been included in the most logical sequence and in the most persuasive manner. Then some basic decisions have to be made.

Style. Ninety percent of all communication is said to be nonverbal. How you say something has far greater impact than what you are saying. The same is true in advertising.

Copy style is like tone of voice. Layout is like body language. The tone of voice of your message has to be chosen as carefully as the elements of the copy platform. Style can support your message or contradict it. The choice of style, and its appropriate use, is one of the finer points of the copywriting art.

Flow. Once you've gotten readers into your message with the right headline and illustration, how can you keep them reading? If it's a mail piece, the prospect has other letters to glance at. With a magazine or newspaper ad, a hand is poised to turn the page at the slightest loss of interest. With a TV or radio commercial, there are refrigerators to raid, washrooms to visit, channels to change, the moment your message ceases to be appealing.

Tricks of the trade can help to create interest. Using numbers is one trick. Subheads breaking up blocks of copy into readable eyefuls is another. Still a third is a narrative style in which the message unfolds in sequence, as if you were describing the product to a friend.

These tricks are helpful, but they are no substitute for copy that is genuinely interesting, smoothly written, and easy to understand.

Level. The level of copy should also be chosen deliberately. Related to vertical positioning, copy level should reflect the self-image of potential purchasers by not being too simplistic, but recognizing that their self-image is probably well above their actual reading comprehension. The writer has to walk a tightrope in order to appear literate on the one hand and to assume a minimal vocabulary on the other. The safe bet is to keep the vocabulary simple and the style colorful, to presume nothing and explain everything.

Nonverbal Messages

Today, more than ever, the copywriter must think visually as well as verbally. This involves much more than the choice of drawings to illustrate a product feature, or photographs to stop the right prospect. It recognizes that some copy points—particularly appeals to sensitive emotions or fantasies or self-image—are better expressed with visual images than with the written word. This will be amplified in the next chapter on layout, but visual communication should be a tool considered by all members of the creative team, not just the art director.

Making It Sing

The first draft is done. The content is complete, readable, right on target. Well done. But you're still not finished.

Of course, many writers polish up the first draft and call it an ad, and many such ads are successful. Yet what makes the difference between a good writer and a great one is professionalism.

The pursuit of professionalism calls for another important step. Put the first draft aside until the next day, and forget about it. Go to a movie. Read a potboiler. Have fun. Then come back the next morning and look over the first draft as if you've never seen it before.

This time, look at it solely from the standpoint of style. Sit down and rewrite it completely, keeping the content but adding story value, entertainment, and fascination. Take the words you wrote yesterday, set them to music, and make them sing.

In the musical *My Fair Lady,* Liza Doolittle sings, "Don't talk of love, show me!" Copywriters should heed this advice, especially in the final draft.

Don't say that a book is entertaining. Give a sample of the humor, or some other satisfying element. Don't say a product will save you time in the kitchen. Describe exactly what you can make, in how many minutes. Don't talk of something being informative. Start informing! Support your copy claims with specific examples, interesting examples, pertinent examples, and more examples. Examples are what's interesting to your prospective buyer, and *that's* why you did all that research when you started.

Personalization

Once upon a time the word *personalization* meant mentioning the prospect's name as often as possible, or simply addressing the letter by name, as if that alone would equal the impact of a genuinely personal letter.

Today we know that it is more important to make the letter or other message as relevant as possible to the prospect's known interests. And to express that message in a sincere, conversational style, much as you might do if you were actually writing to a friend.

But that's only the beginning. Personal communication is a two-way street. In person, you would not tell someone about yourself without asking about their interests, nor would you do the opposite. In direct marketing copy as well, you must do both. This applies particularly to letters, which by definition should have a personal style. To be "real," they should reveal something about the writer. "Greasy dishes. Greasy pots. Greasy silverware. I used to hate dealing with them all, until I tried..." "If you have dry hair like I do..." "'Who needs another pair of sunglasses' I thought, until I tried..."

One of my "trademarks" is that my letters often are signed by a real person—a product manager genuinely proud of a new product, a quality engineer amazed at the great results. My daughter is the signer of a letter to teenagers about beauty products. And I even signed a letter about why I read *Yachting* magazine. Such letters practically ooze with sincerity, and the results prove that it's a worthwhile approach.

Stopping Power

Once the selling message has been worked out for both content and style, it's time to concern yourself with *stopping power:* the appeals you'll use to get the envelope opened, the ad noted, the TV viewer riveted to your commercial.

This final step in producing a really effective advertisement is the moment of truth in the craft of writing copy. The selling message may be superb, but if no one stops to read it, you've wasted your time and your client's money.

The headline must instantly flag down prospective buyers and intrigue them with an offer, a broad benefit or need fulfillment, or a curiosity-provoking specific selected from the body of the advertisement. The range of headline opportunities will have widened considerably once the copy has been written.

My suggestion is to put off writing the headline. Instead, go paragraph by paragraph and write pithy subheadlines with story value, curiosity, powerful benefits, and gripping emotional involvement. Then write captions for every illustration and try to come up with additional illustration ideas that will dramatize every major point. Each caption should translate the interest value of an illustration into a powerful selling point. All the subheads and captions, taken together, should add up to a convincing communication that will bring in the order even if the prospect doesn't read a word of the precious copy that spawned all these ideas.

If the research and planning are done right, the copy will be excellent. If the copy is excellent, the subheads and captions will be superb. The problem now should not be "coming up with a headline." It should be deciding which of several very fine, very persuasive subheads or captions to use as the main headline.

Of course, you can always write a headline as the first step, putting down on that blank sheet of paper the first thing that pops into your head after you're through studying the assignment. However, more often than not, such headlines either are clichés or concept statements, with-out benefit of the subjective integration, content assembly, style rewrite, and stopping-power processes recommended here. As always, the hard way is the sure way. That's why advertising is hard, and why it's right that it should be.

SOME GENERAL CONSIDERATIONS

No discussion of the craft of copywriting could be complete without pro-viding the answers to some of the standard questions that have been raised over the last decade and that will continue to be raised in the future. To those of us in the field, some of these questions have become downright boring. I address them here only in the hope of minimizing the number of times I will have to address them in the future.

How Long Should a Letter Be? An Ad? A Brochure?

The answer: long enough to do the job. There is a story of a boy who asked the unusually tall Abe Lincoln how long he thought a man's legs should be. Lincoln's now-legendary answer was, "Long enough to reach the ground."

If you are giving away something free, with no strings attached, you don't need a long letter to make your offer. If you are selling something that a prospect has never seen before, you have to show it, explain it, tell how it works, and dramatize the benefits. If your readers know you, just give your name and a tag line. If they don't, you may have to put in your whole corporate history and financial statement.

Don't be afraid of long letters—or short ones.

The thing to remember is that it is not length in itself that gives effec-tiveness, it is content. If you can cut a four-page letter down to two with-out losing a major selling point, the chances are that the two-page letter will pull just as well with a slight reduction in CPR because of the print-ing costs saved. The same applies to a speech, a book, or a presentation. Length is not significant; content is.

Which Comes First, Format or Copy?

In the previous section, I advocated writing the copy before the head-line, an admittedly "backward" approach that also involves doing the rough draft before sketching out a copywriter's "rough" of how the ad might look in the magazine, on the air, or in the mailbox.

In print ads or television, the format is usually fixed. Writers are told that they have a page or 120 seconds to work with—and that's that. The format usually is dictated by media economics, and there is little ability to accommodate copy innovations.

Direct mail, however, is another matter. I am constantly amazed by clients or account people who specify to the writer that a mailing piece should consist of "Four-page letter, 11- by 17-inch brochure, outer envelope, reply card, lift memo." There is nothing intrinsically wrong with such a format, but there is no reason to tie the writer's hands by dictating *any* format.

The format should grow out of the copy concept. The choice of brochure or booklet depends on copy flow and illustration requirement. Whether a mailing should be "all-in-one" or a group of small pieces—an invitation, a guarantee slip, a choice dramatization folder, a die-cut product representation—is a creative consideration that should await the writer's thinking process. Chapter 15, Direct Mail Formats, details the infinite variety of possibilities. For now, accept the idea that, in direct mail at least, the choice of formats should be a product of the creative process, not a specification.

Handling Rush Jobs

"All this is very nice," a writer may ask, "but where do I find the time to do this 'step-by-step process' when half the jobs I get are on 'rush' schedules?" The question is fair, and the problem is typical.

The first approach to rush jobs is to avoid them. Any account executive or product manager can appease a client or boss by saying yes to every request. The real professional will know when to say no, and will insist on giving creative sources adequate time to do their job properly.

The chances that something will go wrong in the execution increase dramatically with rush projects, and it is safer to risk offending a boss or client by saying no to an unreasonable request once, than to risk ending up with a job that no one is happy with. If the ad doesn't work, no one will remember the time allotted, and the failure will be your fault.

Accept a rush project only when you really want to, and when you are already so interested in the project and enthusiastic about the prospect of its working out well that you really want to do it. If that is the case, you'll find the time to go through each and every step listed above, taking less time for each.

Don't cut out research. Instead, have an apprentice do the research while you do your other planning. Don't eliminate the sleep-on-it phase. Just condense it into a quick nap or a fast walk around the block. If you have a rush job, don't take shortcuts. That way lies trouble. Travel the tried-and-true route, but walk a lot faster.

The Curse of Cleverness

Just as all of us fall in love with our own corny jokes, copywriters are especially prone to falling in love with their own pet phrases. That's why we can't begin with headline ideas and try to justify them with postnatal copy platforms. The planning must come first, the creativity later. That's also why copywriters cannot judge their own writing. Some element of objectivity is essential, from supervisor, account person, or client ad manager.

The greatest temptation to be clever rather than craftsmanlike comes from peer-group pressure. Every art has its critics, and artisans tend to try to impress their critics instead of their customers. You've seen it in novels or poetry with eccentric but unreadable styles, in plays with obscure plots, in paintings whose themes were conceived in marijuana and interpretable only under opium.

In art and literature, people sometimes gain national attention and critical acclaim just by being different, and this approach can also work in some fields of general advertising. In direct marketing, however, such acclaim—if it comes at all—will last only until the coupons come in. In this field the only real critics are the thousands of potential customers west of the Hudson River who won't give 2 cents if your concept is cute or your execution different, but will give $20 or more if you can convince them that your client's product is one that they need and want.

Sure, a clever ad or mailing may look good in your "book" when you apply for your next job, but consider that you might be better off with fewer clever samples and a reputation for results that makes it unnecessary for you to keep a book at all, or to apply for another job—ever!

Repetition: Right or Wrong?

Another area where battle lines frequently are drawn is repetition.

I don't mean the kind of repetition used by general advertisers, who find it desirable to repeat ad themes and brand names to reinforce awareness. I do mean the key point that's flagged in the headline, mentioned in the subhead, illustrated and described in a photo caption, referred to in a brochure and lift letter, and then summarized in the body copy and on the response card.

Reiteration is a better word than *repetition* for what I am advocating, for there *is* no need to say the same thing again in the same way. There *is* a need to put your best copy claim forward in every part of your message, in any medium that might be seen by your prospect.

You have no way of knowing what part of your message is going to be read first. Some research shows that a postscript is the most-read and often the first-read part of a sales letter. In some cases, depending on format and graphics, the brochure may be read before the letter, or a supplementary flyer may be the first thing out of the envelope.

In an ad, people attracted by the illustration may read the caption before they read the headline. Others may read the coupon before the body copy. If you have a principal selling point, get it out front in every part of your message that might conceivably turn out to be the first part read.

Newspaper preprints offer a clear illustration. Writers often put a great headline on page 1 of a four-page insert and use the back page for miscellaneous points. When the insert falls out of the newspaper, however, the back is just as likely to be seen first as the front. Thus the principal selling theme must be evident on page 4, perhaps worded differently.

Though repetition is desirable, there is no reason to present a selling point the same way over and over again. To avoid boring the reader who comes across the point a second or third time, reword it. Give a different example or a different analogy, and at the very least, use a fresh choice of words.

Presume that your first expression of the main theme is what stopped the prospects and got them to read your message in the first place. You know the message has appeal, or they wouldn't be reading, so keep it in front of the readers' minds by reinserting it in each and every main segment of the ad, mailing, or TV, commercial. Be sure to make the message fresh at the moment of truth when you are asking your reader to fill out the coupon.

EVALUATING ADVERTISING COPY

In evaluating your own or someone else's advertising copy, here are some simple tests that will separate the kids from the grown-ups.

The Tightness Test. Try to cut the copy. Sit down with a blue pencil and see how much shorter you can make it without deleting a material selling point. If it's easy, the copy is soft, mushy, fatty, or whatever pejorative fits your style. If the copy is hard to cut without breaking up the flow or omitting an important point, then you've got tight, meaty, hard copy—the real thing.

Interchangeability. Take out the name of your product and see if you can use the same copy for a competitor or another product. Your ad should be uniquely appropriate to your proposition. If it fits others just as easily, the creative approach lacks a unique selling proposition.

The Glance Test. Give yourself 5 seconds to look quickly at the headlines, subheads, and captions. Is there enough meat to convince you that you want to read the rest of the ad? If not, then move your project back to GO, and do *not* collect $200.

Then give yourself 10 to 15 seconds to read all the heads and subheads that call out to you in large, boldface type. Do they do a selling job in their own right? For instance, is a contents listing headlined "Table of Contents" or "The Secret of Eternal Life, and 88 other things you must know"? Every head, subhead, and caption should be a selling message in itself, and the whole should make the sale even if the reader does not read one single word of body copy.

Intelligibility. Ask your secretary, the receptionist, and the elevator operator to read the ad. They don't have to be prospects and the ad doesn't have to interest them, but they should be able to understand what in the world you are talking about.

I have been amazed to discover that points I thought were obvious and clear were completely misunderstood by exactly the people who should have followed them without difficulty. So let people who have had nothing to do with the creation of the ad or mailing piece read it, and have them play back what they think you said. If the playback is way off-base, you may want to do a more professional job of seeing whether the copy is clear by running it through a focus panel or two.

I have heard writers defend their work by elaborating on copy points. My answer is, "If you promise to accompany each and every copy of this ad or mailing and offer the same explanation, I'll approve it. Otherwise, make the ad stand on its own."

Actionability.   Now ask people to respond to the ad. Do they know exactly what to do, or do they start asking unnecessary questions? Is the coupon easy to fill out? Are the prices and any extra charges clearly understood? Is the phone number clear and legible, and is the fact that it's toll-free easily discernible?

You should be able to hand the ad to anyone in your office and say "Order this for me" with no further explanation. If an explanation is necessary, check through the response devices all over again.

A TRIBUTE TO COPYWRITERS

Maybe because I started as a copywriter, I expect writers to be the miracle workers of the advertising business. All the marketing planning, all the steps developing strategy and inventing tactics, have one basic presumption: that copywriters can do anything.

Like the debating society member who can argue any side of the question, the copywriter must be prepared to sell any product to any audience with any positioning. For anyone who thinks writing copy is easy, let me offer a challenge:

First, take a product, any product—preferably one that you see being handled poorly—or take fund-raising for a worthy charity.

Describe the product on every level—practical, scientific, and emotional—as discussed in the pencil example in Chapter 3. Imagine that you are the audience. Prepare a copy platform and write some ad concepts.

Then adjust the style upscale or down. Vary the horizontal positioning, and rewrite the ad for an earlier position.

Then change the size unit. What would you do differently in a small-space ad? In a double-page spread?

Then change the medium. Rewrite the ad for television or radio. Or change the style so that it is appropriate for direct mail.

Then dramatize a benefit, feature the offer, do an audience-selection ad, or lead with a premium.

The copywriter doesn't have to do all these things with every assignment, of course. Writers do have to have the inner conviction that their skills are ready and waiting and that they can produce winning direct marketing communications for any product in any medium at any positioning. Versatility is the mark of a truly professional writer. To paraphrase *Star Wars*: "May the skill be with you!"

14

ART
DIRECTION

Once, the art director was considered to be a mere implementer of creative strategies developed by marketers and writers. Today it is generally recognized that art directors can and should make a major contribution to the overall creative process. Exceptional art directors should be part of the creative team from the very inception of a project. They should be expected to contribute to strategic plans as well as make important contributions to the finished ad or mailing piece.

Visual Communications

While most artists have had their training in the techniques of graphics, and while the bulk of this chapter addresses the problems of advertising layout, the recognition of nonverbal communication as a major creative tool has increased the importance of the art function dramatically.

The art director can help to identify pictorial ways to communicate themes related to emotions, fantasy, or self-image. The mood of a photograph and the casting and direction of the models can be critical in suggesting intangible satisfactions to the user. Subtleties such as props and settings can create highly effective messages in themselves, all of which can be validated with research.

When a "user imagery" strategy is being employed, the people and expressions associated with the product are the key factors in the long-range awareness message, and their selection is the major responsibility of an art director. If fantasy ideas are to be communicated, the imagination of the art director is the only limit. Subtle changes in typeface, size, location, and format can convey different images and stress different aspects of the final message.

Copy style is tone of voice in nonverbal communication, and layout is the equivalent of body language. The art director should be capable of taking the same copy and adapting it to any positioning, any image, any emphasis, any medium, any audience.

The same message can be laid out to stress the headline, the illustration, the copy, the coupon, the offer, the lead item, the end product, the endorser, the guarantee. It is up to the art director to make the selections necessary to convey entirely different moods—elegance, bargain price, stability, excitement—all with identical copy.

Communicating Imagery

The role of the art director has become all the more critical with the increasing use of direct mail to create brand images, either as a primary or secondary goal. And the elements of emotion and self-imagery often are better communicated visually than verbally.

Emotional Messages.   One conclusion that appears obvious to me is that the closer the advertiser comes to an emotional "hot button," the more difficult it is to communicate in words. Perhaps a product really does make the user imagine his or her self as younger, bolder, sexier. Fine. But make those promises explicitly in a headline and, as research has repeatedly shown us, you will be greeted with incredulity. In our society you can dream anything. Do many things. But you can't talk about it, at least not in public, and certainly not with strangers.

So, you can show models being popular and having fun, but you can't say "Have more fun!" You can have the owner of your new car exchange suggestive glances with a passenger of the opposite sex and create an easily-read suggestion, but put the same idea in words and the same people will be offended.

Self-Image.   If you are appealing to people who see themselves as "thoroughly modern," then show the product in use with the latest styles and settings. If your prospect wants to "think younger," then pick your models and scenes accordingly.

Apparel catalogers understand the critical impact that the choice of models can have on the garments they display. At least one cosmetic ad manager has been known to say, "It's all casting. Everything else is detail." In any field, the personality conveyed by the model or spokesperson becomes the personality of the brand, store, or company.

A frequent direct marketing project involves popularizing a product or service that was originally marketed to a select core market. It is very difficult to find a message that says, "Now this is available to little guys like you." Whether the new prospect is a small business, a less affluent investor, a less sophisticated prospect for technical equipment, the issue is the same. Most verbal expressions will be in poor taste, and will produce poor response rates. The solution is to show it, not say it, by showing "people like you" in your illustrations.

Copy-Art Teams

In recent years, direct marketing agencies have started to establish copy-art teams as a part of the standard organizational structure. Long used by general agencies, this team approach keeps a balance between verbal and visual elements of the creative product. Writer and artist are able to work together over a long period of time and on many different projects, with the result that their thinking processes become thoroughly synchronized. Eventually the roles become less distinct, and either party may come up with a headline or the critical visual idea.

FIVE LAYOUT PRINCIPLES

Not withstanding the opportunities for art directors to contribute to overall creative direction, it is still just as necessary for an art director to know how to do a layout as it is for a copywriter to know how to write. The balance of this chapter will deal with basic executional questions. My work with art directors has led to the identification of five basic principles that all well-executed layouts have in common. These five Cs of advertising layout are *concentration, cohesion, convention, contrast,* and *convection.*

Concentration

Attention-getting ability is proportional to the size of the largest single element, not to the total size of the ad. A small-space unit with a single large element—a word, a headline, an illustration—will get more attention than a unit the same size or even larger, with smaller elements.

To understand this, look at newspapers. The article perceived to be the most important is not the longest one but the one with the biggest, boldest headline.

In any advertising layout, or in any art form for that matter, balance is dull. Everything can't be equal. An artist or the creator of an ad must make a deliberate choice as to which visual element should be the most important.

I have seen full-page ads so cluttered with so many conflicting subheads competing for attention that the reader has to be confused and bewildered. At the other extreme, I have done a successful ad that was only 2 inches on one column, with a 1-inch-high, black, bold headline: *Opium!* This small advertisement for Evergreen's reprint of the Jean Cocteau classic achieved very acceptable order costs.

Some ads are built around a dominant illustration, perhaps a square half-tone photograph taking up 60 percent of the page. Others have a clean, dominant headline that is obviously the place to start reading, and that does not have to compete for attention with other elements of the same ad.

Imagine, for a moment, two billboards along a highway. One is 50 feet high and has a 5-foot-high message. The other is 25 feet high and has a 10-foot-high message. It is obvious that the size of the message, not the size of the billboard, will determine from how far away motorists see it and how many it will attract.

Whether your unit is large or small, and whether your medium is print or broadcast or direct mail, it must attract attention by the inherent strength of the lead element, not by the total size of the page or printed piece or by the total length of the message.

Cohesion

The space in any direction between elements of a graphic presentation should not exceed the space between the message and the border of the layout. This rule sounds simple and obvious, but it is constantly ignored in direct-response advertising. The violations usually take place in the art studio, where a fine layout is turned over to unmotivated production artists for type specification and mechanical paste-up.

Cohesion is most frequently absent where it is most needed: in newspaper advertising. An ad "breaks up" if the space between the headline and the body copy is greater than that between the headline and the adjoining advertisement, or if the headline or closing copy is isolated by white space from the main selling paragraphs. Some advertisements might have been more effective if the agency had simply purchased less space, instead of a standard unit, and closed up all the elements.

Does this mean that "white space" doesn't belong in direct-response advertising? No. But white space, like any other styling, selling, or attention-getting element, has to be used in conjunction with all the other elements and not as an end in itself. For instance, I prefer to distribute leading throughout the body copy rather than have extra space between paragraphs.

What should the art director do when divisive space appears on the mechanical paste-up? Here are some idea-starters:

1. Enlarge the most important element, probably the headline or key illustration, and tighten up the remaining elements.
2. Reset the body copy in a larger or more leaded type.
3. Move all the elements toward the center of the advertisement or mailing piece, and let the white space add to the margin around the message.

The principle of cohesion is vital in fractional-unit advertising. Layouts for such ads should always be pasted in the newspaper or magazine to see how the ad will look on a busy page. Don't cheat! Pick the busiest page, not the one you would most like the ad to appear on. There should never be more space between elements of your layout than there is between your layout and the next ad.

Convention

There is a principle in fine art called *convention,* which refers to the perceiver's past experience and associations as an influence on how new perceptions are evaluated.

For instance, imagine for a moment that an artist has taken a canvas and painted the bottom half green and the top half blue. Most viewers, when asked to guess what is being portrayed, would call it a landscape, with the green bottom representing grass and the blue top the sky. Add some white blobs in the top area and, depending on their size and the color of blue used, they will be perceived as clouds or stars. A yellow blob might be seen as a sun or moon, depending on the total coloring. What you think the abstractions represent is influenced by what such colors or shapes *conventionally* represent.

Typeface studies have shown that the eye reads reflected light, not darkness, and that theoretically white type on a green or dark blue background should be the most readable. Yet because people are not used to reading books or newspapers in this way, reverse type is difficult to read.

Quality Perceptions.   Perceptions of quality, cheapness, bargain price, and elegance are all influenced by past experiences. If you look at department store windows, for instance, you'll see that a cluttered window is used to convey the feeling of a sale. A stark, relatively empty window, with only one or two mannikins displaying the new season's fashions, is used when the garments are exclusive and expensive.

Type Associations.   Typography also is associated with past experiences, and conveys its own form of nonverbal communication as the "body language" of an advertising message.

A sans serif typeface such as Univers or Helvetica is associated with modernity. A traditional book face such as Garamond, Caslon, or Times Roman is the classic kind of face associated with books, magazines, and newspapers, and so suggests reliability, authority, and credibility.

Type at an angle, or noncursive italic, gives the impression of speed or imminence. Bold faces convey importance or loudness, thin faces quiet or restraint. Gothics and other historic faces are associated with tradition, the old, perhaps the tried-and-true.

A bold Franklin Gothic face implies "Headline!" in most parts of the country, and the presumption is that its message is an important announcement. Century Schoolbook, a standard textbook face, seems right for an educational message. Bauer Bodoni is a modernized serif face, with a good combination of readability and a contemporary look.

Various pseudoengraving faces are reminiscent of invitations and wedding announcements, and suggest elegance and exclusivity.

Pictorial Associations.   Both the choice of illustrations and their style constitute another form of body language. Luxury settings imply a luxury product, which is why expert photographers spend at least as much time finding the right props as worrying about lighting. A picture of a spokesperson suggests sincerity and straightforwardness but also hard selling. A diagram or blueprint suggests that the product is well made.

All these illustration and typography associations, as you can see, do convey images and messages independently of the words and subjects involved. It is important that these layout considerations be planned in accordance with the basic strategy and tactics, so that the visual communication supports the copy theme rather than conflicts with it.

Contrast

The chameleon, which survives by blending into its environment, should be the mascot of any art department, not as an inspiration but as a reminder of the deadliest sin of advertising art.

The first law of layout is to be noticed. In any medium, to be noticed your message must look different from its environment.

If a newspaper ad blends into the newspaper's editorial content or looks like just another advertisement, if a magazine ad looks like every other ad in the publication, if a radio or television commercial blends into the program or into preceding commercials, you are throwing your money away.

Your advertisement must stand out. Your mailing must look fresh and different from the others in the day's mail. Your commercial must make people stop and take notice.

Boutique layouts that give a particular art studio or agency's work a distinctive look is good business for the supplier but not for the client whose money is being spent. The last thing in the world you want the prospect to say is, "Oh, isn't that clever. It's just like the ads for..."

The artistic expression should not call attention to itself at the expense of the message. The object is not to cause people to say "What a clever (or pretty) ad!" or (even worse) "What a clever artist (or agency)!" The object is to catch the reader's eye, to present the sales message clearly, and to use graphics to visually support that message, all leading to an immediate positive action in response to the proposition.

A corporate style is just as damaging. A corporate quality image or trade logotype may be desirable, to establish identity and authority once a message is being read, but it should not stand in the way of getting attention in the first place.

If people think they know what your ad is going to say, they won't read it. If a bank, for example, sends out all its promotions in envelopes that look identical (perhaps to falsely economize on printing costs), prospects will presume that the mailing is making the same offer as previous ones. The envelope will go unopened, the letter unread, and the proposition unconsidered.

Copycatting is self-defeating in a dozen ways, not the least of which is that the advertiser being copied is probably moving on to another format just as you are copying the old one. *Newsweek* started looking for new ideas at a time when almost everyone in the field was planning to imitate their Mead-Digit subscription package, which featured the prospect's name, for the first time, in large bold type. Every week brought an announcement from another supplier who was putting in that equipment or a request from a client who wanted to try the *Newsweek* approach. What *Newsweek* knew was that the technique was already losing effectiveness.

Cycles seem to exist in advertising layout. Sam Sugar of Sussman & Sugar, Inc., a leading book-promotion agency, once observed that the first step for an art director is to review the publication an ad is going to run in and to determine what the current fad is so you can go the opposite way. Sure enough, for two years I saw other book advertisers follow each other back and forth like sheep, with borders, white space, dark backgrounds.

The same thing happens in typography. Every typeface has had its fad. I have seen our industry overdose on Optima, Helvetica, Caledonia with descenders, and Century Schoolbook. It's as if some secret newsletters, like the ones in the fashion world, are forecasting the type of the month and so making the prediction come true. The smart move is to watch what everyone else is doing and find a way to make your own ads look distinctively different.

Convection

Once you've managed, through concept, copy, and layout treatment, to attract the right readers and get them into your message, the job that remains is to keep them there long enough to get enough copy read to make the sale.

This is a matter of *flow* or *convection,* the art of designing the message in a manner that carries the reader along in a logical fashion from one element to the other, right to the coupon.

In an ad you want to stop readers with a headline or illustration, then pay off the promise or curiosity in a subhead or in the first paragraph of copy. You then want the main copy to read in a manner that takes the reader to the point of action, the coupon or phone.

Support elements, the reading of which is optional, should be placed in a way that doesn't disrupt the primary copy flow. Items such as feature listings, testimonial panels, credentials, or detailed specifications should be there for those who want them but should be out of the mainstream.

If you are pulling for inquiries for an automobile, for example, the inclusion of technical specifications is necessary for some readers but for others it would be a distraction—a turnoff that would get them to stop reading altogether. Therefore optional elements must be handled in such a way that they are optional reading as well.

Draw a line down the main copy story to indicate how you think the reader will follow the message. Then ask someone else, an uninvolved writer or artist, to look at another copy of the same ad and draw a similar flow line. If the two lines are different, then perhaps the flow is not as obvious as you think it is.

In a mailing piece the flow should be just as well defined. The first thing prospects look at is their own names on the outer envelope, then they look again wherever their names appear. Nothing is as fascinating as our own image, signature, photograph, or other personalization.

The back of the envelope is less critical than the copy and image portrayed on the front. You cannot count on the reader to turn to the back, so there should be enough incentive to get the envelope opened even if the back is never seen.

The rest of the elements should then be collated in a logical manner. If you don't want the price to be the first thing seen, cover it with a fold or flap.

If you want the letter to be the first thing read, address the letter and let *that* be the envelope show-through, and let it be the first thing seen when the envelope is opened. The element seen through the window of an envelope will be the first thing seen inside, and everything else will be viewed after that.

If you want a color broadside to be the next thing read, then be sure it is the next thing viewed. Supplementary inserts should be smaller, or less colorful, so that they don't cover up or distract from the main pieces. If everything is equally important, or equally interesting, then you have no control over the flow of the message.

One trick of the trade that applies to both letters and long copy advertisements is to recognize that curiosity is a more powerful drive than a plea such as "see next column" or "see other side." Paragraphs should never be completed at the bottom of a column or a page, even though every secretarial school trains typists to strive for this. Instead, interrupt the last line in midsentence and, better yet, in midthought. Use the natural human desire to complete things as a force to encourage the reading of your sales message.

Don't build barriers within your ads. Subheads that are in a larger type size than the body copy will actually interrupt the reading of the copy rather than encourage it.

Bold borders that break up copy elements into panels will force the reader to "jump" from one to the other and leave half of them unread. It is better to use borders to separate optional reading elements or to separate your ad from others.

A photo can be a barrier also. Don't expect readers to continue reading a column of type if, in the middle, you distract them with a photo and caption. Such photos can break up the look of an ad to make it appear more attractive to read, but place them alongside the main theme rather than in its path. Illustrations should be supportive—pleasant additions to a copy point made on the way to the coupon payoff—rather than competitive.

The five principles of concentration, cohesion, convention, contrast, and convection apply to all advertising, but their violation shows up faster and more directly in the measurable world of direct marketing than in general advertising.

SOME SPECIFICS

Illustrations

The first question, almost always, is whether to use a photograph or a painting or drawing. There is no doubt about the answer; it has been the subject of split-run testing. Photography, with all its realism, is clearly the winner, particularly with product illustrations.

That is not to say that there won't be occasions when drawings or diagrams will be the better way to make a point or to illustrate something that doesn't lend itself to photographs. Good artwork often can contribute to a unique style, set a mood, or dramatize a benefit better than a photo.

When taking a photograph, you should strive for action, motion, and dimension. Even a straight product shot can be given a sense of action by surrounding it with props that make it appear to be in use or about to be used.

Motion is difficult to capture, but showing it makes the difference between "posed-looking" shots and candid news photographs. A good model doesn't look like a model.

Dimension, a matter of lighting and camera angles, is essential if a photograph is going to "come alive" and do more than lie flat on the page. The standard is realism.

Working with a photographer, the art director should be involved with every basic decision. Most important is the choice of models. This should never be left up to the photographer. Instead, go through the submissions of the model agencies yourself. The model should be able not only to look right, but to act right. Intangibles such as enthusiasm, contentment, tranquillity, and pride are all emotional states that are part of the message. Some models can be directed to convey an emotion; others just sit there and look pretty. I prefer to consider only models who list membership in one of the acting unions, as this is an indication of some acting experience and ambition.

The standard for selecting models is not whether you find them attractive but whether your prospects will relate to them. The ages and styles of models determine whether they are people the prospect can identify with or people who can be perceived as authority figures. The choice depends on the theme of the advertisement. One mistake to be avoided, however, is to select models who are faithful reflections of the target audiences. Research tells us that people want to relate to people who represent their ambitions, not their realities. They want to see themselves as a little younger, healthier, wealthier, wiser, happier, or thinner than they really are. I call this ambition "aspirational imagery."

Once the model has been hired, talk with him or her in person so that you can explain the nature of the shot and the kind of clothing and hairstyle that will be needed. It is amazing how little information is given to models by agents and photographers unless you take the time to do it yourself.

Then, be at the session. In a still photograph, the setting must be staged and the actor must be directed with the same care as in a television commercial. See the shot through the camera as the photographer does (even though it may be upside down). You may see something that other people overlook—subtleties like scratches on your product or too suggestive a pose. Also, of course, you and the art director should see the contact prints and select which shot should be blown up for final retouching.

Working with an illustrator is very similar, except that you see sketches rather than a photography session. The illustrator most likely will work with a "swipe file" of photos and other ads. Get agreement on the subject, the style, and the dress. I once had to reject an illustration because an artist dressed a character in a tuxedo in an ad for a mass-market book club. In another rejected illustration, retirees who were supposed to be pleased that they had invested in gold coins were drawn with insipid grins.

Cost control is always a problem. Negotiating art costs should never be left solely up to the art director, who is likely to be too sympathetic to the needs of peers in the art world. The art budget should always be approved by a product manager or account executive who has the total project budget in mind.

Costs have to be kept in perspective, and related to the value of the medium the illustrations are being used in and the total promotion budget. While I am usually the first to raise an eyebrow over the photography session that "must" be shot in the Caribbean or the commercial that can "only" be filmed in California, I will admit that there are times when such expenditures are justified.

Typography

Typography is the unheralded fine art of commercial layout. Of the tens of thousands of graduates of art schools, all are taught type as well as design and illustration, but only a handful—often relatives of printers or book designers—emerge with a genuine love for type.

Every creative organization should have at least one person who not only knows how to use typography but loves to work with it, for only that person will appreciate the infinite subtleties that go far beyond specifying type.

Sure, type must be selected and must fit the message to the available space, and anyone can be trained to count characters, use a Haberule, or otherwise "spec" type. But that has nothing to do with *designing* with type.

Type Has Style.   Each and every typeface has been designed to convey a feeling that is somewhat different from all other types that have ever been designed before it. The simplicity of Futura has given way to the subtler shading of Univers, Helvetica, and Optima. The classic readability of Caslon has been joined by varieties of Baskerville, Bodoni, and Roman. There is an infinite variety of stylistic faces: the heaviness of Cooper Black, the playfulness of Kaleidoscope, the starkness of Stymie, and the stylistic games of playful Mediterranean faces like Memphis, Karnak, Cairo, and Delta.

For an advertisement or mailing piece, a typeface must be selected that, overall, conveys the positioning selected for the project. It must have the flexibility to provide the shadings necessary for subheads, captions, emphasis, or parenthetical comments. Of course, it must also be easy to read.

You can choose more than one face if you really know what you are doing, but mixing and matching typefaces is as dangerous as trying to match slacks and jacket rather than buy a suit. Sometimes separates come out fine and sometimes they look awful; but you can't go wrong wearing a suit.

Within each typeface there are usually light and bold styles, regular and italic (cursive and/or noncursive versions), and an infinite range of sizes. There was a time when typography was ordered only by point sizes, and you were limited by those precise sizes. Now, with computer type, you can ask for any line width you want, and can even condense or expand a typeface to your needs. Hand lettering can also create a variety of very worthwhile special effects.

Leading.   Just as important as the selection of the type is the spacing between lines, called "leading" because of the rows of lead between lines in linotype printing. If you order an 8-point type and have no space between lines, it is set "solid" or "8 on 8."

This is usually somewhat difficult to read (except in the case of some typefaces that are "small-bodied," with oversize ascenders and descenders). As mentioned above, the eye supposedly reads reflected light, the white space around type, not the type itself. Therefore the spacing between lines may contribute more to readability than the size of the type. As a result, I usually prefer 8 on 9 to 8 solid or even 9 solid.

The size of type to choose for text copy is relative to the surroundings. In a publication like *TV Guide,* which uses fairly small faces, you can safely use 6 on 7 for body copy. In newspapers or a large brochure, a larger face usually is more appropriate.

Age is an important determinant. Children like large type, and older people, whether they admit it to themselves or not, may have difficulty reading conventional type sizes and would prefer not to have to put on their reading glasses. Many advertisers whose propositions are aimed at older people go out of their way to keep typefaces large.

Another key factor is motivation. If the headline and initial subhead are so interesting that the prospect wants to read the rest of the copy, size will be irrelevant. In fact, in earlier direct marketing ads, it used to be customary to drop type sizes down every few paragraphs.

Condensing a typeface can often save space more effectively than going down to a smaller type size or cutting out leading.

Simplicity is the byword of good type design. A safe way to design an ad is to pick a readable book face and use the boldface for the headline and all subheads. Using italic may work for captions, or you could use a smaller size. The body copy, subheads, and coupon copy could be the same size, with any insert panels a size smaller. You can't go wrong with this kind of design.

To be readable, lines of type can't be too long or too short. One rule says that for each line 30 characters is the minimum, 50 the maximum. The question is too complex for any one rule to answer, however, and really requires good judgment about what is readable and important and what is inviting to read.

Designing Coupons

In Chapter 13, I suggested that writers work on the coupon first, as a way of crystallizing the basic purpose of the advertisement. Although I do not give the same advice to art directors, the design of the coupon should nevertheless be assigned a great deal of importance.

I have seen too many art directors work out the placement of head-lines, copy blocks, and illustrations and then just leave a blank area for the coupon. As the coupon is likely to be torn out for later use, and at that time become a self-contained selling piece and response form, it must contain the basic elements and positioning of the overall message.

Within the borders of the coupon or reply card, there should be a simple restatement of the basic offer, possibly combined with a spur to action. "Mail this card today to get your free copy" is the right kind of headline, as opposed to just "Mail this card."

The ordering copy and the address should be simple, legible, and to the point, without crowding. Small type inspires distrust, and this is not the place to use a "typesqueezer" or "shoehorn."

The "name, address, city" part of the coupon should be easy to fill out, leaving enough space for long surnames and addresses.

Options or credit card information also should be designed with great care. The placement and positioning of these elements in the layout will materially affect the response.

For instance, if a credit option is built into the ordering paragraph and a cash-enclosed option is separate, you might have a 3:1 or 4:1 ratio for the credit responses. If the options are treated equally, after the order paragraph, the response will switch to 2:1 for credit, or perhaps come in evenly. Presenting the options "( ) Check enclosed" and "( ) Bill me later" forces a decision. Otherwise inertia pushes people to the option that does not have to be selected. The same principles apply to presenting options such as "large size" and "small size" or other trade-ups.

Telephone ordering options can be highlighted with a small drawing of a telephone or with a large telephone number, if telephone ordering is desirable for the particular proposition.

In a mailing piece, long commitments or credit terms can be contained in a stub or flap. This makes the ordering portion as simple as possible, yet still makes all sales and legal data visible at the time the coupon is filled out.

This doesn't just apply to mail-order coupons, though that's where it's most critical. If you're looking for a simple inquiry, or a complex database questionnaire, the principle is the same: The response device must be thought out carefully, and fussed over until it's just right.

Phone numbers also must be clear and easy to read. They must not only be legible, but as easy to tear out as a coupon, not buried in the body copy. The most consistent error of general art directors trying to handle a direct-response project is to bury the phone response in the body copy.

Don't be afraid of complicated coupons. The trick is to take the elements, experiment, and find a way to simplify them. At one point Columbia Record Club invited readers to: accept a long commitment; select a music division and write in the six-digit numbers of thirteen records; fill in their telephone numbers; choose cartridges, cassettes, tapes, or records; pick the first selection at a special discount; and use a "gold box" if they saw the offer on television—all within a standard-size coupon.

Starch ratings show that ads with coupons or phone numbers usually have higher ratings than those that do not. It might be compared to the difference between window-shopping at a closed store and an open one. The ad with a clearly visible device is always "open for business." So why turn out the lights by hiding the coupon or phone number?

FIRST-AID KIT FOR ART DIRECTORS

How to Spot a Bad Layout

If you are an art director who is on the firing line, or one of those who have to judge the art director's work, here are some telltale signs of a bad layout:

- The message doesn't stand out from other ads.
- The image is contradictory to the theme of the copy.
- The mood is completely inappropriate for the medium.
- The ad blends in perfectly with the publication.
- It reminds you of another mailing piece you liked or didn't like.
- It's another expression of the latest fad.
- It's static. People look at one phrase or illustration and never "get off the dime."

- It's too busy. Readers jump from point to point, contrary to the flow of the message.
- The ad calls attention to itself; it's designed to win awards rather than sell.
- Everything is important, or nothing is important.
- The ad is hard to read; the type is too small or crowded.

Improving a Bad Layout

If a layout has been finished and still doesn't look right, here are some ways to improve the ad or mailing piece:

- *Exaggerate or emphasize something.* Emphasize the headline, the illustration, the coupon, even the body copy. Take it "out of proportion" and deliberately throw the design "off-balance." Balance is static; we need motion, action, and dynamism. Taking one element, and filling 40 or 60 percent of the printed area with it, will give you a whole new look.

- *Add people.* A spokesperson, a delighted customer opening a box and seeing your product, or a picture of a satisfied user can help a bad layout. People are interested in people.

- *Put the product in use.* Take it out of the package and show it being used. Add diagrams, sequence photos, or anything that will make the product come alive.

- *Change the typography.* Start all over and get an entirely different mood by working with different typefaces. Simplify the type and work within one family exclusively, or add one contrasting face for emphasis. Warm the ad up with a serif face and a cursive italic, or modernize it with a sans serif face and a noncursive italic.

- *Pull the ad or mailing together.* Use white space at the exterior, use borders or background tints with consistent line spacing, or try to get a clearer flow of ideas from one point to the next.

- *Break the ad up.* Isolate the important elements with internal space and internal rules, or make the copy more inviting to read with bolder subheads and minor illustrations, with indents and handwritten annotations.

- *Follow Thoreau's advice: "Simplify, simplify, simplify."* Take a complicated headline and isolate one pertinent phrase. Take a headline with lead-ins and subheads and combine them into one long simplified statement. Take optional elements and isolate them with different faces, panels, or tints. Talk to the writer and share your problem, and see if copy can be cut to give you the space you need to simplify, simplify, simplify.

DIRECT MAIL
FORMATS

Format is the critical design element in direct mail, requiring the economical integration of creative and production processes to produce maximum communications impact.

In Chapter 14 we discussed design and layout principles that apply to any form of communication: a simple newspaper ad, a full-color magazine spread, a computer letter, a full-color brochure, a simple buck-slip insert, or the supers on a television commercial.

In direct mail, the art director's job increases a hundredfold, for the creative possibilities are multidimensional. The direct mail art director not only has to know all the disciplines and technology of the general advertising art director but also has to understand what can be done with paper, printing, computer forms, imaging techniques, and the flexibilities and limitations of envelope fabricators, label affixers, and processes for collating and inserting mail.

In direct mail you have the space you need to use every trick in the book of direct marketing psychology. You can dramatize and personalize, and you can provide incentives for immediate action. You can include samples or scent strips. You can take advantage of the play instinct with scores of involvement devices. You have all the space you need to ask for the order of the most complex or expensive purchase, to explain commitments, to ask for credit information. Direct mail is unlike space advertising or broadcast, in that you do not have to fit your message into the format; you can fit the format to your message.

CONSIDERATIONS IN DIRECT MAIL FORMATS

The essential considerations in every direct mail design project include *response stimulation, personalization, involvement,* and *economy.*

Response Stimulation

No matter how you stop the reader—with curiosity, self-interest, a powerful offer, a dramatic benefit—the payoff is asking the reader to come to an immediate decision: to make a call, visit a store, or mail in a reply card. No matter what action is required, the writer must have it clearly thought out, so that the copy message leads up to it clearly and conclusively.

If a phone call is requested, then the phone number and what it entails should be stated in a separate insert or even a Rolodex® card, which can be affixed to the letter. If a store visit is the objective, then provide a coupon or reminder piece. It can be a simple inquiry, or a multi-question database builder. It can be a one-shot mail-order form ("Send me *x;* I enclose *y* dollars") or it can be a complex continuity membership. In any case, for the purposes of planning and of this chapter, it is a response device.

Certainly, traditional mail order is the most complex and critical form of response device. For mail-order coupons, I recommend working it out first, even before you begin the creative planning or copywriting.

Ease of response is the first consideration. You want to make it as easy as possible for the prospect to fill out your coupon and mail it. Preaddressing the name and address with a computer or label not only facilitates response but ensures that you will retrieve key codes, account numbers, or other data.

Incentives for fast response should be visible right on the response card, including any premiums for fast action, or offer expiration dates. You should work on the assumptions that your prospect may not mail this card for a few days and that the rest of the mailing will have been discarded by that time.

Like all other pieces in a direct mail package, the response device should be capable of standing alone and should provide sufficient incentive even if nothing else is read.

Even if a card can be a self-mailer, it usually is worth the extra cost to also provide an envelope. If confidential, financial, or personal questions are asked, an envelope is essential.

Often the response card is the lead insert: the first piece visible through the envelope window, and the piece personalized with the prospect's own name. This piece will be seen first. Therefore it is necessary to emphasize the positives about the offer, and to obscure any negatives (such as price) until the prospect has had a chance to read the other pieces in the envelope.

In other cases, the reply card may be nested inside letters and brochures and may not be the first thing seen at all. It is then necessary to help the prospect find the card. To accomplish this, you have to refer to the card, and therefore it should have both a name and a color. For instance, "Send the reply card now" gives no help in finding the card in a complicated mailing. Consider, instead, "Send the red super-value certificate...."

Many of the involvement devices that will be discussed in a moment are intended to facilitate response, as are some personalization devices.

Personalization

Only direct mail, with the help of computer data and related high-speed printing technology, can facilitate the infinite range of personalization available today. It is one of this medium's most unique capabilities.

Sorting. Sorting is the simplest segmentation that can take place when lists are processed, permitting a message to be selected on the basis of demographic, geographic, or psychographic data. This personalization consists simply of inserting a different preprinted or lasered letter with each different list, or adding a special buck slip to address a type of prospect. For example, a magazine might include a special insert for people who once subscribed, or a slip announcing that a forthcoming issue will have an important article on a subject that, according to the list the prospect is on, should be of particular interest.

Name Reference. Another type of personalized direct mail design is the computer fill-in of the customer's name in the body of a letter, on the reply card that shows through the window envelope, or in other inserts.

It is also common to use a closed-face envelope, repeating the name and address on the outer envelope as well as on the contents of the envelope—usually the letter and reply form. However, caution is suggested. Many printers and lettershops claim to do this, but use laser on the inside envelope and a crude ink-jet address on the envelope, defeating the purpose of making it appear to be an individual letter.

Better quality currently is achieved with techniques that laser-print the envelope. This can be done on continuous forms, separately or at the same time as the letter, fabricating the envelope only after it has been addressed. The inserting is done either at the same time as fabrication, in a single manufacturing step, or later by optically matching the address or number codes. Some commercial lettershops now have equipment to laser-print prefabricated envelopes. There is another addressing method now available called *daisy wheel,* which is not as clean-looking as laser printing but is much better-looking than ink jet.

Multiple Personalization. It is possible to design a form that permits a letter or an invitation to be produced on the same form as the response device. Most computer letter formats permit a maximum length of 22 inches and a width of up to $18\frac{1}{2}$ inches. With various side-by-side or front-to-back folding, bursting, and slitting processes available, it is possible to easily and inexpensively assemble a wide variety of personalized combinations. One of the most practical is an $8\frac{1}{2} \times 11$ letter with a certificate, response device, or invitation on the top or bottom. This can be attached, or slit off during processing. And either the letter or the stub can be used for addressing, to show through a window envelope. Another common format is to print full-size letters, side by side or top and bottom. This is useful when there is a complex form, such as a credit application that must be filled out.

For economy, even smaller sizes can be designed, printed one-up or two-up. Or several personalized pieces can be included in the same mailing. For instance, you can design a 6×8–inch personalized letter with a 3×6–inch response form. Such a simple format enables the printing of six sets on each form sheet. More complex formats are cut out of this same size. They cost more, because the larger size per unit results in slower output.

One outstanding multiple format developed for International Masters used a $5\frac{1}{2} \times 7\frac{1}{2}$–inch four-page letter, a $3\frac{3}{4} \times 5\frac{1}{2}$–inch response slip, a $3\frac{1}{8} \times 5\frac{1}{2}$–inch guarantee, and a $3\frac{1}{8} \times 5\frac{1}{2}$–inch lift letter—each personalized with the prospect's name, and all printed out of a single $10\frac{5}{8} \times 16\frac{1}{2}$–inch form and machine-collated with five other inserts.

Electronic Letter Writing. In the mid-1970s, a variety of exciting new techniques were developed that took the art of personalization to new heights.

First Mead Digit, then Response Graphics, IBM, Itel, Xerox, and others developed various types of nonimpact printing. Some worked by ink jet, spraying very tiny dots on a page at high speed so as to form letters, lines, or images. Newer methods used laser technology to achieve clearer, bolder type images.

The first applications were in the use of new and larger typefaces. Suddenly it was possible to put the prospect's name on the letter in inchhigh capital letters, facsimile handwriting, or colored type. Suddenly you could print sideways or upside down, and thus open up new kinds of trick folds and seams to achieve special effects and new formats.

There was an explosion of creativity in personalization. Even more significant were the economic factors. Some of the new techniques could be attached to a printing press, permitting personalization, printing, folding, and assembly to take place in one high-speed motion. The ink jet, laser, and electrographic processes now permit great economy as well as unlimited creative flexibility. Every week brings new innovations across my desk or into my mailbox. Personalized messages within the pages of a magazine. Customized handwriting fonts that match the actual handwriting of the sender. High-definition photographs and simulated letterheads. Color laser messages. Laser printing anywhere on a 17×22 sheet, making it possible to have versioned messages as well as addressing anywhere within a catalog, or to create totally versioned newsletters.

The best way to utilize these new techniques is to work very closely with graphic designers, printers, and computer houses who have the equipment available. They can show you the work others have done with their processes, and help you to work out your own format problems. Good suppliers are an important part of your direct marketing team.

Noncomputer Personalization.   While the computer offers an infinite variety of sorting possibilities and letterlike or posterlike personalization, it is possible to get these effects in a simpler, more old-fashioned manner.

For years, *Business Week*'s control package was an invitation format, with the prospect's name handwritten. Avis scored a major direct mail breakthrough using an outer envelope with the prospect's name written in by hand. One unique format for business mail uses a facsimile rubber-stamped routing form, and the prospect's initials penciled in along with others.

And don't forget simple versioning: different letters or inserts for different lists or list segments. Elsewhere I describe the Polaroid success with different photos for different SIC codes, showing through a windowed outer envelope. Or "smart inserting," in which inserts can be varied at the inserting machine, depending on optically-read codes on the envelopes.

Involvement Techniques

Why do direct marketers make their mailings so complicated? Because they work!

With the exception of high-level business-to-business mailings, the devices of direct mail are repeated because they are successful. In some cases they are so successful that they are soon overused. A direct mail user can outflank the marketplace by going back to once-successful ideas as easily as by coming up with new ones.

Transfer Effect.   The purpose of involvement techniques is more than to keep the reader interested. They are also used most effectively to transfer reader attention from one component of a mailing to another. If the prospect will first see the response card, it is a good idea to point out that there is a label or stamp that must be found on the letter in order to get a premium or activate the offer. This will prompt more prospects to read the letter. Or the other way around, having a seal on a letter that is to be transferred to the order form is a way of directing the prospect to the order device.

One application is the inclusion of "bonus stamps" in Publishers' Clearing House contest mailings. The stamps, which are found on the same sheets as the magazine selections, are a way of encouraging entrants to handle and look at the offered magazines before responding.

Creative Devices.   Virtually anything can be included in an envelope or made visible through it. Virtually anything can be affixed to a mailing element for prospects to peel off, punch out, or otherwise get involved with. Any of these devices can be personalized by the computer. Here are some ideas:

- *Business cards.* For personal services, questions, warranties. Try them with a handwritten note printed on the front or back.
- *Carbon copies.* Of a previous letter. "Why haven't you answered?"
- *Checks.* A legitimately redeemable check or money order is a sure attention-getter, but see your lawyer first.
- *Coins.* A penny for your thoughts, or "Ten records for a dime, and we'll even give you the dime...."
- *Collectibles.* An Indian penny. Facsimile Confederate money. A foreign postage stamp.
- *Facsimile photographs.* A child to help. A baby seal to be saved. A beach hammock waiting for you. Very effective if the photo is emotional.
- *Gifts.* A packet of seeds or spices. A pencil. A bookmark. A key chain. Preprinted address labels.
- *Information.* Local police and fire numbers. A veterans' benefits guide. A map. A calorie counter. An after-tax investment-yield slide rule. You name it.
- *Numbers.* Serially numbered application forms, perhaps to indicate exclusivity. Often used in contests.
- *Peel-offs.* Reusable "piggy back" labels to transfer the address of any tokenlike symbol from one location to another.
- *Perforated stamps.* Easter seals for fund-raising. Record covers for a club selection.
- *Postage stamps.* To pay for the reply postage.
- *Punched holes.* To look through, giving the impression of a computer card, bingo card, or what have you.
- *Samples.* Recipe file cards. Fabric swatches. The product itself.
- *Seals.* Notary seals, certificates, etc., to indicate reliability.
- *Tokens.* To be punched out and placed in or on the order card, to accept an offer.
- *Yes or No or Maybe symbols.* A way of asking for an immediate decision.

Economic Considerations

Check with production specialists before proceeding to finished layouts. Production advice at this critical point can save the embarrassment of producing a mailing that has to be inserted by hand because there isn't clearance for automatic inserting equipment, or that wastes money by using an inefficient paper size.

Everyone in this business has made the mistake at least once of not providing enough clearance for machine labeling or inserting. An even more painful experience is watching a high-speed press print a brochure, with literally tons of unused wastepaper, paid for by you or your client, being trimmed off and baled to be sold as scrap.

Paper comes in standard sizes, depending on the type of paper and the press it will be printed on. Some standard sizes are book paper, 25 × 38 inches; bond paper, 17 × 22 inches; cover stock, 20 × 26 inches; newsprint, 24 × 36 inches; coated paper, 25 × 38 inches; and offset paper, 25 × 38 inches.

Flyers, brochures, and letters are usually cut out of standard sizes, and can be figured by folding or cutting such a sheet accordingly. Sometimes an extra insert can be printed without added cost by using paper that might otherwise be trimmed off and thrown away. One project I saw would have permitted four additional pages in a brochure without extra cost, just by using the full paper size.

On large-quantity press runs, paper companies often can prepare a special "mill run" of exactly the size and weight of paper you need, provided the quantity is large enough and you have the time to wait for it.

Art directors should familiarize themselves with paper for another reason as well. Interesting effects can often be added just by changing paper. Kraft paper portrays one feeling, bond paper another. Newsprint is good for sale brochures. Coated stock is essential where color is important. Specialty papers such as check safety papers can be very useful when conveying value concepts.

Envelopes also come in standard sizes. With rush jobs, weeks can be saved by using a stock envelope and printing a message on the face of it in simple type. Designing windows in unusual places or odd sizes requires special press runs. Usually the printing of the copy and art you provide is one job, and the subsequent conversion of the paper into envelopes through die cutting and fabricating is another. This is like two printing jobs in a row, and is usually the critical-path item in a direct mail job. Any envelope house, such as Transo or U.S. Envelope, will be happy to provide you with a complete directory of their envelope styles and sizes.

Mailing Weight. Postage is always one of the highest costs in a mailing. The total weight of a package is critical, particularly in first-class mail, where tipping the scale over the 1-ounce mark practically doubles the cost of the postage.

It is imperative that actual paper samples be cut to size and carefully weighed to determine mailing weight before the job goes too far. Often a slight change in paper weight or trimming will make an enormous difference in total cost.

In bulk third-class mail or not-for-profit mail, the weight is not as serious, because costs go up in intervals for each fraction of an ounce. Check with your postmaster or letter shop for the latest postage rates.

Working with Suppliers. Many pieces have to work together. The mechanical artwork. The computer specifications. The mailing lists. Paper and printing. Computer processing. Binding and collating. Subcontracting such as envelope fabrication. Sorting. Mailing. Getting the mailing to the post office. If there's any field where Murphy's Law applies, it is in the execution of direct mail: "Anything that can go wrong, will go wrong."

Probably the best economy is to work with reliable suppliers. Unless you have printing specialists on staff or as consultants, let one firm—an agency or printer—coordinate the entire job from providing you with mechanical specifications to getting it in the mail. That way it's their responsibility, not yours, if the pieces don't fit or everything doesn't arrive on time. As many agencies now buy printing at so-called trade prices, their total costs even with a mark-up are usually no more than those of buying directly from printers and mailing houses.

In short, to save money on direct mail,

1. Make sure it works mechanically.

2. Design it economically.

3. Let professionals coordinate the printing, computer, and lettershop processes.

4. Get postal approvals and permits before printing.

ELEMENTS OF THE MAILING PACKAGE

The Response Device

Everything in your direct mail package—every thought, word, and picture—is there for one purpose: to get the reply card returned to you with an affirmative acceptance of your proposition.

The format can be anything from a complex order form to a simple inquiry card. Usually a response card is about the size of the envelope, in order to permit it to be preaddressed with the address showing through a window in the envelope. It should be large enough so that it doesn't shift around and obscure the address. It should be small enough so that it easily fits the reply envelope without having to be folded.

Often a tear-off stub or flap at the side or bottom of the form will help to solve the size problem. A flap can be useful to cover information that you don't want to be seen right away, such as complicated ordering information or a credit application, or it can contain essential sales points or immediacy incentives.

Involvement devices can be placed on the stub—a gummed stamp, sticker, punched-out token, or any of the various devices listed above. The reader usually is invited to attach the device in a specific location on the response card. The purpose is to call attention to the reply card, or to transfer interest from one piece in the mailing to another.

Implied Value.   When the offer is the primary sales device, it is helpful to give the order form (or the token or stamp to be affixed to it) implied value. This can be achieved in several ways:

- Gift certificates or check-paper formats
- Borders such as those found on money orders or stock certificates
- Official-looking layouts, with punched holes, authorizations, or rubber stamps
- Engraved moneylike images, indicated by choice of typefaces and decoration elements
- Notary seals, ribbons, gold embossing, signatures
- Money orders, traveler's checks, bank checks, and passbooks, all of which by convention have implied value

Other Images.   Try to make the response card look like something other than what it is. If a sweepstakes is involved, dramatize the entry concept. If the product is in limited quantity, make the response card look like a reservation certificate.

Business-to-business correspondence should be on a restrained level. A simple white response card and a stamped envelope are very classy, or you can include a carbon of your letter and ask the recipient to initial it and return it.

Label Transfer.   A simple, dignified device that adds to ease of response and offers a measure of involvement is the address label transfer. If you order lists supplied on "piggyback" labels—pressure-sensitive labels with a wax-finish backing so they can be easily peeled off—the prospect can take the peel-off label off the letter or catalog cover and place it on the response card. For years, *Consumer Reports* used a unique double-response card with a one-year offer on one side, a three-year offer on the other. The prospect was involved by being asked to place the label on one side or the other.

Location in the envelope also has a bearing on results. The response card can be the first thing seen or the last. Some very successful mailings have had reply devices attached to the top or bottom of a computer-printed letter, to help generate readership for both. In other cases, where the letter really is trying to "pass" as a personal letter, the reply device should not, of course, be attached to it.

The Outer Envelope

The outer envelope is the headline of direct mail. Half the battle is to get the envelope opened—and much direct mail never *is* opened.

Imagine an envelope that would be difficult to open, offered the prospect no reason to open it, and aroused no curiosity or interest of any kind. Such envelopes do exist—the products of dull design, poor thinking, and sloppy execution. They offer every turnoff short of saying "Junk mail—don't bother to open this."

Fortunately, most people do open most of their mail. The problem is not just to get it opened but to arouse enough interest or curiosity to read the contents. You want your mailing to be the one that's "saved for last," the one that a prospect wants to read because of the promise it holds forth to satisfy basic needs or interests. Here are some of the ways to accomplish your ends:

Setting the Mood. My latest approach to this subject is to use the outer envelope solely to set the mood, to indicate the general field the offer deals with. My theory here is that people are complex and are not interested in all their interests all the time.

For the same reason that a landscaping offer would not do well in travel magazines, we want to trigger the appropriate self-image before the envelope is opened. Sometimes I want to read about advertising, other times about investments or sailing or travel, or how to understand teenagers. A simple graphic or pictorial clue can set the mood so that I open the letter when I am in the mood for it and thus am more likely to respond. Tricking someone may get more envelopes opened, but in the long run it is not the most profitable way to build a business.

Preselling. The obvious approach is preselling. It consists of putting the offer—or what would be the headline in an ad—right on the front of the envelope.

"Save 50% on *Time*" is a surefire headline, if the prospect already wants *Time*. If a simple offer statement is so effective, a simple turnaround document or double-postcard format will do the trick. In some cases, with presold products to core lists, it's all you need, and you can dispense with practically everything else.

"Stop Smoking Fast" is another example of preselling that either reaches prospects or turns them off instantly. With a really good appeal, getting to the point right from the beginning can work. More often, subtler appeals are necessary in addition to or instead of direct sell on the envelope.

Curiosity. The most curiosity-arousing envelope of all is the one that looks like a real business letter or a note from a friend. If you use a first-class stamp and a seemingly typewritten address, there is an excellent chance you'll get the letter opened.

You can also use headlines to build curiosity. Any provocative headline, ranging from "Do you make these mistakes in English?" to "Fifty stocks to avoid this year" will get people to read further to get the answer.

An incomplete statement will also get readership. Start telling a provocative story right on the outer envelope, and then just when it gets most interesting, you can...(Continued inside).

See what I mean? Curiosity pressures you to want to know the balance of the sentence.

A quiz also will do it, such as "Which should you buy?"—a *Consumer Reports* package that was mailed to over 20 million homes.

Audience Selection.   This approach can lend itself to interesting formats as well. One package for *Self* included a plastic mirror showing through the envelope, dramatizing the kind of person being looked for as a prospective subscriber.

The type of mailing list the prospect is found on can lead to interesting concepts. For instance, a mailing to engineers for a pocket calculator presented unique diagrams and formulas that would be of interest to that audience. Another to architects dealt with blueprints and diagrams.

For Polaroid, we designed a series of mailings geared to specific types of industries. Only a few pages and the envelope show-through changed from mailing to mailing, but to each reader the message appeared to be designed for the one particular industry.

Personalization.   The address label itself is a form of personalization, and showing the address through an envelope window can add an element of curiosity.

A larger window can disclose a larger, bolder name with the help of the new computer printing techniques. It can also disclose a longer message that also mentions an address, a personal fact, or even the name of a neighbor.

You can show an initial through a window, recreate a signature, or let a personal message show through. A mailing for the American Management Association featured the dates and location of courses near the prospect's own home, as selected by computer zip codes.

In a recent mailing for a soap sample, I arranged to have the address label repeat the prospect's name three times, as in "Diana, Diana, and Diana Nash." This created a curiosity factor in itself, which was repeated in the letter that repeated the three names in the salutation and went on to talk about "All the women you are—sometimes traditional, sometimes romantic, sometimes adventurous." This set the stage for the introduction of a well-known bar soap in three different scented varieties.

Any aspect of personalization mentioned anywhere in this book can be adapted for use on an envelope or to show through it.

Involvement Devices.   You can use any type of token, stamp, number, or device, as listed earlier, to show through a window in an envelope, and any type of gift or enclosure can be referred to on the envelope. The simple addition of "Valuable Savings Stamps Enclosed" can increase the rate of opening, and therefore the rate of response, very substantially. Another interesting device is a zip strip on the envelope, with instructions to pull a tab and reveal a copy message or illustration.

Implied Value. There are many ways to indicate that the contents of an envelope are of value. One obvious way is to say so. Another is to use very fine paper, an interesting colored stock, or a very professional (perhaps engraved or embossed) envelope. However, don't expect to combine such images with bulk mail, unless the indicia are handled very well.

Kraft paper can imply that the contents are of value. So can a seal. European direct marketers have reported fantastic results with facsimile wax-sealed envelopes.

Value can be added in other ways also: rubber stamps referring to valuable contents, or stickers with added messages. One idea is to die-cut a portion of the flap to look like a seal. If part of it is left ungummed, it flaps up and looks like a real label sealing the envelope.

A show-through of something that looks like it might have value—a certificate, coin, or stamp—is of course another way of suggesting value. Value can also be just stated, as in "Free Recipe Cards Enclosed."

The Official Look. You can use the power of convention to make your mailing look like an official communication, providing the overall effect isn't misleading. If your client is a bank, you can be sure that the kind of envelopes in which statements usually are mailed will get attention. Another effective technique is to use officialese language: "Notice of Price Increase," or "Nontransferable."

Adding Urgency. An expiration date is the ultimate urgency appeal. It can even be computer-printed on one side of an oversized address label. Let it show through to boost results. Another way to add urgency is to make the format look like a teletype or wire. Or you can use headline typefaces and copy styles, as in "NEW PRODUCT SLASHES COPIER COSTS!"

Bulky Contents. Fold the inserts down, and use a smaller envelope than is customary. The added thickness will imply that something of value is included. And don't presume that all the pieces must lie flat. An uneven fold can raise curiosity as to the contents as well as provide interesting visual effects once the mailing has been opened. However, keep in mind that to meet postal requirements, the package should not exceed $\frac{1}{4}$ inch in thickness.

Transparent Envelopes. Polyethylene envelopes are the closest thing to the disappearing envelope. They hide nothing, except those areas you may want concealed under a printed area of the polyethylene covering.

Materials are not inserted into these envelopes in the usual sense. Instead, the printed polyethylene is wrapped around the collated materials and fabricated into envelopes at very high speeds.

For a four-color circular, use a clear polyethylene envelope to let it show through. It will cost less than printing similar color art on the outer envelope.

Use of transparent envelopes for certificates or other enclosures of obvious value makes them visible immediately, adding to the pulling power more effectively than merely describing the enclosure.

Envelope Sizes

Envelopes come in many sizes. Twelve sizes of so-called official envelopes are usually available in stock from most suppliers, including monarch ($3\frac{7}{8} \times 7\frac{1}{2}$ inches), check ($3\frac{5}{8} \times 8\frac{5}{8}$ inches), the popular No. 10 ($4\frac{1}{8} \times 9\frac{1}{2}$ inches), and the more interesting No. 14 ($5 \times 11\frac{1}{2}$ inches), which accommodates a letter folded in half down the center.

Booklet envelopes come in an even wider variety of 32 standard sizes, including the popular 6×9–inch size. Many suppliers even have standard sizes or dies with various window configurations that can be imprinted quickly and inexpensively.

These standard sizes are very handy for test runs or small printing jobs. In larger quantities and with proper schedules, it is possible to design anything you want without any real cost disadvantage.

Convention is a vital consideration in envelope size selection. People are accustomed to certain sizes of envelopes being associated with bills, checks, invitations, personal correspondence, and business correspondence. They also expect matters of importance to arrive in No. 10, or 9×12–inch envelopes.

Oddly enough, the most-used direct mail size is one that has no associations except with direct mail promotions, the 6×9–inch envelope. It is an efficient size, and the largest that most Phillipsburg inserters can accommodate, but I prefer to use almost anything else. In fact, I have never come up against a 6×9–inch package that I wasn't able to beat, given the opportunity. I think it is a size that says "advertising" and puts the reader on guard. A squarer size has some interest. A $5 \times 7\frac{1}{2}$–inch envelope is unusual. A $3\frac{3}{4} \times 6\frac{3}{4}$–inch envelope can contain items folded to form a very thick and apparently valuable package. Almost anything is better than a 6×9–inch envelope, in my opinion, and yet, because it is the easiest to work with, design for, and produce, it probably will always be the most commonly used size.

The Letter

How Long Should a Letter Be?   Long enough to do the job. How many pages should it have? As many as are needed to tell the story.

There have been successful letters on one side of a monarch-size page, and other successes—like Tom Collins' classic fund-raising appeal for George McGovern—that ran for a dozen pages.

True, the usual sizes are two and four pages, but this may be the result of a failure to try alternatives rather than of careful testing. As the letter is one of the least costly segments of a direct mail package, you should not skimp on it.

What Size Should a Letter Be?   Convention determines size in most cases. Business letters should be standard business sizes and should be printed on one side only with each page separate, as if it came out of the typewriter. Consumer mail can be odd-sized just to be more interesting. It can be monarch-size to resemble a personal letter, or it can be $5\frac{1}{2} \times 8\frac{1}{2}$ inches with an apparently handwritten message to make it resemble an informal note. It can be in the form and size of memo paper, a telegram, or anything that fits the tactics chosen for the promotion.

What Should a Letter Look Like? First of all, it should be readable. Readability requires either that it look personal, with the prospect's name appearing on it, or that it look interesting. To get readership, use a headline in handwriting or giant typewriter type, or add a drawing or photograph.

Most of all, readability means that it cannot look like a dull letter with flush paragraphs. Some sentences should be indented, some should be underlined, and others should be annotated with handwritten marginal notes.

Formal paragraph rules can be thrown out the window. Instead, present your story in neat eyefuls of smaller readable paragraphs.

Why Imitate Typing? A question that comes up frequently is whether imitation typing really fools anybody, and if it doesn't, why bother?

The real issue is not whether typewriter faces deceive the reader but whether they suggest a letter by convention. The spirit of the letter format is that it is a one-on-one communication between two business executives or between a merchant and a consumer.

I have seen letters typed on IBM Executive typewriters that looked so perfect that they no longer seemed personal. Letters set in book or sans serif typefaces look even less like letters. The suggestion, dictated by convention, is what is important. Deception is not the issue at all.

Once upon a time, when most typewriters used reusable ink ribbons, letters had to be printed in halftone or a fine-line process in order to simulate the irregular appearance of letters typed with a ribbon. Today, with laser printers becoming more prevalent, simple offset reproduction adequately suggests typing.

Of course, computer letters or typed fill-in letters have to be carefully matched. The only way to do this is to type the body of the letter with the same computer printer or typewriter that will be used for the fill-in.

The illusion of personalization is sometimes broken by advertisers who illustrate a letter as if it were an ad, or who use clever devices like rebuses. While I doubt that such devices are desirable, I don't know of any that has been split-tested against convention-based letters.

The Brochure

The first question to ask is whether you need a brochure at all. I know of many successful mailings that omitted a brochure, and there have been some split-run tests of "brochure" versus "no brochure," where "no brochure" was the winner. (However, I have never seen a winning mailing that left out the letter.)

Whether or not a brochure is helpful really depends on the nature of the proposition and how well the brochure is done. If the proposition is an intangible, like a newsletter on financial privacy or an appeal for a contribution, the brochure may have little to add. For a philanthropy, a brochure might actually appear "slick" or "wasteful" and be a clear negative factor.

The brochure is usually one of the most expensive parts of a mailing, costing between 10 and 30 cents, depending on size, quantity, and complexity. The brochure also is the most expensive part of the mechanical production cost. Often, if a brochure costs 15 percent of the cost of the mailing, that mailing without the brochure can do 10 percent worse and still break even, with a better return on investment.

When Is a Brochure Needed?   A brochure is needed most often when the sales message requires illustration, amplification, or accreditation. A brochure is the television of direct mail. Like television it offers immense credibility, because words can lie but the eye cannot be fooled. It offers the prospect a chance to "see for yourself" the beauty of the product offered and how it will look at home, in the garden, or at the office. It provides space to diagram the most complex of working parts or the most elaborate of details. Unlimited except by the imagination of the artist and the skill of the photographer, it can make its presentations in full size, in color, and with dimension—from broad perspective to the finest close-up detail. In short, it provides an opportunity to use all the methods of visual, nonverbal communication discussed in earlier chapters.

What Goes in a Brochure?   Once you've decided you need a brochure, you should include, in one way or the other, every selling point that you listed in your general copy platform. Don't worry about duplicating points in the letter. In fact, use the letter as a checklist to be sure that every major point has been mentioned again. In direct mail, each piece must stand alone. Let it do the whole selling job as if the prospect will read no other piece, which may be true.

Use the largest broadside area or brochure spread for the most impressive illustration—usually the finished product, whether it is a set of encyclopedias, a nature garden, or a completed project that your house plans or craft kit will build. The illustration can show a choice: the wide range of books, records, toys, or doll clothes you can choose from with this initial offer. Or it can show the "exploded" contents: pages from a magazine or book, materials in a correspondence course, the pieces in a set of mechanic's tools or a build-your-own-computer kit.

The opening pages or folds should be used to make the basic appeal. If the tactic chosen is to stress the offer, then this is the place to dramatize the savings, the discount, or the premium. Even the simplest free trial offer can be dramatized, with an impressive certificate warranting the return privilege.

If the mailing is benefit-oriented, then show the benefit. In a book club, dramatize the relaxation of reading through pictures of people sitting with books on the beach or before a fireplace. Beyond that, bring to life the romance, adventure, excitement, or practical help that the books it offers contain. For as intangible a product as insurance, you can dramatize the comforts of worry-free retirement, the security of knowing that the family home is secure, or the reassurance that junior will, indeed, graduate from college "no matter what."

The Information Strategy. Whenever possible, structure the message in an educational tone, and select a format that suggests valuable information. For instance, a "Retirement Planning Guide," a booklet on "The Clear Skin Look" for an acne product, a "Fashion Fun Magazine" rather than just a catalog of Barbie premiums.

What about Format? *Brochure* is a term that usually describes a four- or six-page printed and folded sales message. A *booklet* is eight or more pages glued or stapled together. A *broadside* is larger than a brochure in that it is designed to unfold into a flat sheet, usually both vertically and horizontally. *Flyers, pamphlets, circulars, inserts,* and *stuffers* are all smaller items that usually unfold to a piece no larger than the letter.

Each has its own advantages. The smaller pieces are economical. The booklets and brochures are reserved, businesslike, and highly credible. The broadside is the heavy artillery of direct mail. It achieves a sense of dramatic impact that is not possible with any other format.

The principle involved in broadsides is the same as that involved in wide-screen motion pictures. If the visual image is wider or higher than the viewers' focal range, so that they have to move their heads in order to see the whole picture, it is perceived as more realistic than if they see the edges, margins, or other reminders that it is only a picture.

Consider the possibility of making the booklet or brochure an element of apparent value in itself: something that would merit your saying something like "Helpful Booklet Enclosed" on the outer envelope.

For instance, a computer kit brochure can be labeled "Instruction Booklet: Step One." Such information has further value in that it dramatizes the simplicity of building the product.

A cookbook's brochure can include some sample recipes. A fashion catalog can include a color coordination guide. A vitamin brochure can include an article on nutrition. A grouping of several items can be presented as if it were a catalog.

For Erno Lazslo, we presented a simple dealer list as a "Directory" for travelers. Avis prepared a "confidential proposal," and Marriott Hotels did a "meeting planner's kit." Both were basically sales booklets with their own apparent value. In the case of Marriott, we eventually were able to offer the "kit" as the premium in a two-step promotion.

Other Inserts

Other than the letter, a brochure, the reply card, and the outer envelope, what else do you need to make a mailing effective? Nothing, actually. These pieces give three or four repetitions of the main selling points, and should be capable of making the sale all by themselves.

However, for many mailers, the more inserts the better. The only requirement is that each insert have a raison d'être, a reason for being. An insert should not be just another piece of paper, but should have an obvious message or function.

The Lowly Buck Slip. I don't know how the buck slip got its name—maybe because it is often the size of a "buck"—but I do know it can make a big difference in results. Sometimes it's used to stress a point that may have been buried in the copy, like "Remember, you'll get a free tote bag...." Or it can offer a special premium that may have been an after-thought: "Reply by X date and we'll also send you a mystery gift worth at least $10 in catalog value...."

A buck slip may also contain news. "This widget has just been granted the seal of approval of the...." or "...selected for use in the space shut-tle." It can give a correction: "We regret that we are out of the beige cases described in the enclosed brochure; however, we will send the case to you in your choice of...." It might be a trade-up or referral offer: "Buy three and you'll also get...." "Give us the names of three friends and we'll send you a...."

No doubt buck slips began as a way of adding information or sales appeal at the last minute, after a mailing had already been printed. But the occasional addition of such slips proved so effective that they are now deliberately planned in many mailings, as a way of stressing major points. Like the postscript of a letter, they are often read first. If you use buck slips, be sure that they are self-explanatory and do not presume that the letter or other parts of the mailing have been read.

The Second Letter. The "second" letter has also been called the *lift letter* or *publisher's letter*. It has become an effective though now overused sup-plement to many mailings, particularly in the magazine subscription field.

As originally used, the second letter was a simple note from the publisher with a headline such as "Please read this only if you have decided to say 'No' to our offer." It went on to dramatize the no-risk aspect with copy like, "For the life of me, I can't understand why anyone would not send for...."

With sweepstakes mailings, second letters often reiterate the message "No purchase necessary." With insurance mailings, they stress an inex-pensive introductory offer.

Today scores of variations have sprung up. Some publishers put the sec-ond letter in a sealed envelope. Others have it sticking out of the reply enve-lope. National Liberty Insurance uses an interesting variation: a single folder printed as if it were an envelope, and held together with a spot of glue.

A new variation is the *double lift letter,* or basically two separate lift letters that may or may not be joined together. One is for people who have decided to say yes, the other for people who have decided to say no. Naturally, curiosity will lead both groups to read both letters.

Versioned Inserts. Often it is too costly to prepare different versions of a mailing piece for different mailing lists. One way to take advantage of customized appeals without losing the benefits of large-quantity printing is to add customized inserts, with variations depending on list segmentation. These can be geographic in nature, referring to local conditions, local service availability, or local dealers. They can also be demographic, with special notes relating the product or service to people likely to be young or old, wealthy, or homeowning.

These inserts can be related to the mailing lists and the known interests of prospects, indicated by what they have bought or subscribed to in the past. For a magazine, the insert can relate to a specific article coming up in a future issue. For a craft tool or book, it can zero in on the person's field of interest: making planes, trains, dolls, etchings, or what have you.

Selection Aids. The purpose of a selection aid is to make it easy to express a choice of one or more items offered in the mailing. It also has the effect of becoming an involvement device, and it gives you a second chance to list the products available.

In its simplest form, the selection aid can be an itemized order blank. All the customer has to do is check off the items desired, or indicate quantity.

Marboro Books used to list the number of each book offered, so that customers only had to circle a number to order a book. I remember this device well, because one of my first jobs included assembling and proofreading those lists of numbers.

Book clubs, record clubs, and magazine subscription firms routinely use sheets of gummed stamps, illustrating the selections and including the order numbers and a value comparison. Merchandisers could develop such a device for catalog sales. A department store mailer could present each item on its own sheet with a gummed, perforated order stamp that only needs to be affixed to a preaddressed order form.

Testimonial Flyers. Customer testimonials, a celebrity endorsement, a report of a testing laboratory, or other proof that your offer is sincere and valuable is often worth a separate insert.

Testimonials can be selected geographically, as in "What other Texans say about this offer." Endorsements can be in the form of a second letter.

The Reply Envelope

It does pay to have a reply envelope, even when the offer can be mailed back on a card, but this is the only simple aspect of dealing with reply envelopes.

First of all, even with restrictive postal design requirements on business reply mail, there is room to make the envelope interesting. Typefaces, reverses, patterned paper, colors, and borders all are tools that can provide a sense of design and value even with strict adherence to postal requirements. The company name and the way the envelope is addressed can help the sale as well. There seems to be no objection to adding a line like "Special-Offer Department" or "Rush Service, Please."

The only additional requirement is that you must fit the reply envelope into the outer envelope, and make it large enough to get your order form into it without difficulty.

The reply envelope can be "red-hot" to stimulate action with color, or yellow to imply telegraphic urgency. It can have a stamp affixed, or no stamp at all.

An interesting and effective development is the *double reply envelope,* used particularly with sweepstakes offers. One envelope is boldly marked NO and addressed to the contest judging company. The other is similarly marked YES and addressed to the mailer's fulfillment center.

Another way to accomplish the same end is to provide a window in the reply envelope so that the selection of yes or no shows through, allowing for easy sorting in the mailroom.

Some reply envelopes build in an action-now buck slip, designing it as a perforated tear-off slip at the flap or inner edge of the envelope. Even a business reply envelope can be designed in this way, as the stub will have been removed before the envelope gets to the post office.

Of course, a reply envelope doesn't have to be only an envelope. This general term might be used to refer to a Mailgram or telegram blank, the ultimate in immediacy.

Another possibility is to try to generate telephone response. Use a separate slip of paper to prominently display the phone number and the hours to call.

One trick is to provide the number on a gummed label, to be placed near the phone or in an address book or, for business mail, on a Rolodex card.

Postage

The largest expense of most mailings is postage, and the choice of bulk, first-class, or not-for-profit mail is worth consideration. The difference in rates is substantial, and more important, so is the difference in weight requirements.

First-Class Mail. This class offers the ultimate in the appearance of importance, and often is often worth the added expense for business mailings or where fast results are needed. The basic rate is applicable only to 1 ounce, and the slightest additional fraction requires almost as much. It is not difficult to take an elaborate mailing with a booklet over the 2-ounce line, and even up to the 3-ounce rate. For example, $2\frac{1}{16}$ ounce will require the same postage as 3 ounces.

First-class mail does move faster. It has priority in the post office, and usually it travels by air. If the piece is not deliverable, it will be forwarded or returned without added cost but often without the new address that would allow you to clean your list.

Even first-class mail now varies in rates, and substantial discounts are available for companies that can presort to various specifications. But even with the added delivery of the forwarding service, and the added importance conveyed by first-class mail, most large-scale consumer mailings will not justify the cost differential. The added cost often is worthwhile, though, in business and professional mailings.

One caution: If you are going to use first-class mail, make it look like first-class mail. Use stamps (for consumer mail) or postage-meter indicia rather than printed indicia (for business mail). Keep the envelope simple, except perhaps for a pseudo-stamped "First-Class Mail." There are some indications that postal employees may not always notice first-class indicia, especially if the envelope looks like advertising mail. You can't be too cautious about committing to spending on first-class postage.

Green diamond first-class borders, or red-and-blue airmail borders, can be added to the envelope, even though they no longer have any postal significance.

Third-Class (Bulk) Mail. This class is the key delivery system in the direct mail industry. Despite rates that are disproportionately high so as to enable the Postal Service to subsidize newspapers, franked mail, and individually hand-addressed mail, it is still the most effective communication system available to American business.

There are many reasons that third-class rates are lower than first-class ones. First, third-class mail is standardized, and must be the same size and weight for convenient machine sorting. Second, it is a basic presort by zip code, and can be handled in bulk, with entire trays or bags already tagged by the mailer for delivery to sectional centers. Third, it is paid for in bulk by the pound, and needs less handling and bookkeeping. Fourth, and most important, it is deferred, low-priority mail, which is permitted to sit around until the time is available to handle it, after the individual mail and newspapers have been delivered.

Postal rates and regulations change so frequently that it would be useless to include them in a book that takes a year to produce. Today there are discounts for five-digit and nine-digit sorting, for bar codes, for carrier delivery sequence, and with different rates depending on the envelope size. Some rates vary depending on how much of your mailing sorts into carrier-route quantities. A mailing concentrated in certain markets may be less costly than one spread throughout the country. Only your mailing house or the postmaster should estimate postage rates.

The most common (read *unimaginative*) way to use bulk mail is to put a little square in the upper right-hand corner and include the required wording ("Bulk Mail/U.S. Postage Paid Permit #___") and the name of the company or the city or zip code of origin. However, there are many alternatives. The same information can be designed into a facsimile postage-meter imprint, complete with circles simulating a postmark and a red eagle simulating the meter imprint.

There is no reason to limit yourself to printed indicia. Postal meters and precanceled bulk-rate postage stamps can be used instead. Most mailers can accommodate these requests, and can affix stamps by machine for a nominal added charge.

Not-for-Profit Rates. Legitimate not-for-profit organizations such as charities, religious groups, and foundations used to enjoy significantly lower postage rates. Even these have been under attack, and the gap between for-profit and not-for-profit rates is closing fast.

The catch is that the organization has to be authorized, and the penalties are stiff for any misuse or misrepresentation of this privilege. However, many organizations—Consumers Union, the Smithsonian, and others—support major magazines with the help of this not-for-profit rate. They can successfully mail millions of pieces at response levels that would bankrupt a company paying the regular bulk-mail rate.

The effect of this lower rate is so important that organizations have been known to restructure their activities in order to qualify. For example, *Ms.* magazine, which started out as a profit-making institution, completely revised its ownership and now operates as the Ms. Foundation for Education and Communication.

Not-for-profit mail also can be mailed with meter imprints, and pre-canceled not-for-profit-rate postage stamps.

Self-Mailer Formats

The bulk of this chapter has been devoted to typical direct mail formats with letter, envelope, and various inserts. However, enormous advances have been made in the science of self-mailers.

There have been many notable successes in self-mailers in recent years, and while they must still include the basic components outlined previously, often they can do so in formats that are both clever and economical. A dozen or so major "web" printers have made these formats so economical for larger-quantity mailings that the end cost per response rivals anything a more traditional format can achieve.

For one thing, the letter, envelope, brochure, and reply card can be combined and printed in one press run, at rates far less expensive than those for printing each piece separately. And these pieces can separate when opened into several highly involving components. "On-line fabrication" can even produce a standard envelope.

For another, these suppliers have perfected the art of in-line addressing and personalization. Catalogs come off the press in presorted ready-to-mail sequence, addressed not only on the cover but on an inserted order form. Mailing pieces, complete with simulated closed-face or open-face envelopes, include letters, reply devices, booklets, buck slips, or what have you—in a wide variety of sizes and configurations.

One of the major innovators in these formats is Webcraft Technologies of Princeton, New Jersey. They have provided sketches of several of the hundreds of such forms they have produced for me and other clients, and these appear in Fig. 15-1. and Fig. 15-2.

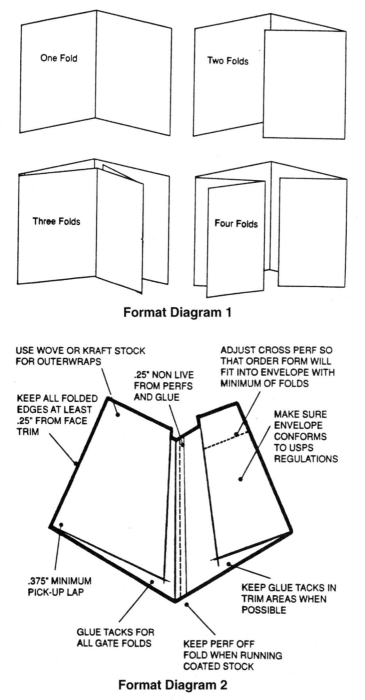

Format Diagram 1

USE WOVE OR KRAFT STOCK
FOR OUTERWRAPS

.25" NON LIVE
FROM PERFS
AND GLUE

KEEP ALL FOLDED
EDGES AT LEAST
.25" FROM FACE
TRIM

ADJUST CROSS PERF SO
THAT ORDER FORM WILL
FIT INTO ENVELOPE WITH
MINIMUM OF FOLDS

MAKE SURE
ENVELOPE
CONFORMS
TO USPS
REGULATIONS

.375" MINIMUM
PICK-UP LAP

KEEP GLUE TACKS IN
TRIM AREAS WHEN
POSSIBLE

GLUE TACKS FOR
ALL GATE FOLDS

KEEP PERF OFF
FOLD WHEN RUNNING
COATED STOCK

Format Diagram 2

Figure 15-1. Format diagram 1: Folding. Formats may be folded in many configurations to accommodate and fulfill a specific purpose or function. An enhanced in-line press offers the creative user a multitude of sizes, shapes, and format options. Format diagram 2: Bind-in order form/envelopes and outerwraps for use in perfect-bound and saddle-stitched publications. [WEBCRAFT TECHNOLOGIES, INC.]

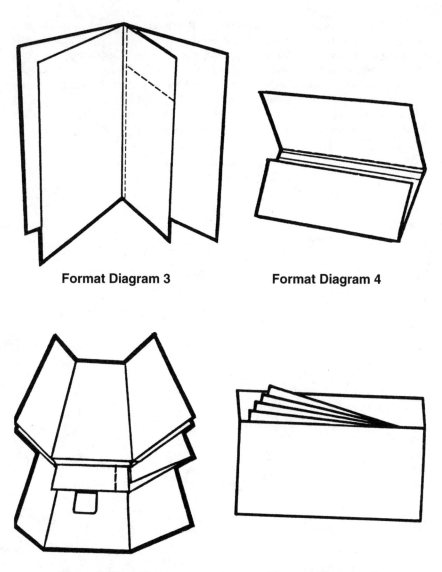

Format Diagram 3   **Format Diagram 4**

Format Diagram 5   **Format Diagram 6**

Figure 15-2. Format diagram 3: Mini-catalogs. Versatile, multipage formats with or without a built-in reply envelope. Available with 6, 8, 10, 12, or more pages in either digest or maxi size. Suitable for distribution by mail, as a take-one, a package-stuffer, or a magazine/newspaper insert. Format diagram 4: Round-trip mailer, the dual-purpose envelope. Format diagrams 5 (open-end mailer) and 6 (closed-end mailer): Both are economical, personalized web formats with closed-face or open-window envelopes. Match mailings are easily accomplished using the in-line process. Process colors, various grades of stock within a package, product samples, pop-ups, and fragrance applications are some of the capabilities. Format configurations are designed for the specific user. [WEBCRAFT TECHNOLOGIES, INC.]

This chapter has dealt with the physical aspects of taking a marketer's themes and a writer's words and getting them to the prospect. This physical process of format selection, design, printing, and lettershop work is often lumped together as *execution*. Creatively, it is a direct marketer's version of origami. We cut a sheet of paper, fold it, and print it to create a fascinating variety of envelopes, letters, flyers, inserts, tokens, stamps, ad infinitum. This chapter has described what has been done and is being done. The real excitement lies ahead, in your hands: what *can* be done!

16

PRODUCTION PLANNING

It is not necessary for every direct marketer to master the arts of production. The fine craft of planning, buying, and supervising the graphic arts aspects of print advertising and direct mail is the subject of dozens of books in itself. What every direct marketer should have, however, is an appreciation of the problems faced by production managers and their graphic arts suppliers, and a knowledge of how to work with them to achieve the optimum combination of time, cost, and quality.

The principles in this chapter apply to any type of production process—from a simple black-and-white ad for a newspaper to a full-color magazine ad with a bound-in insert card to the most complex direct mail campaign. I therefore encourage the reader to read the examples as principles, not as specifics which apply only to the media mentioned at the moment.

THE TIME-COST-QUALITY TRIANGLE

Imagine a triangle with the words *time, cost,* and *quality* each written on an edge. If you press one side, another bulges. If you press two sides, the third may stretch to the bursting point.

The same principle applies to the graphic arts, and probably to most other production endeavors as well. If all three dimensions are reasonable, then there is an equilibrium. If unreasonable demands are placed on one or the other, something has to give.

Want your ad super-cheap? No problem, if you give the production supervisor the time to send it off to a printer in Taiwan, or to get bids from new, untried suppliers. There's always someone who will lose money on an initial job in hopes of getting your later business.

Want top quality? Then be prepared to use the best suppliers and the slower processes, and allow enough time to check proofs carefully at every stage.

Want it yesterday? Anything is possible, if you are willing to pay for it in one of the other "currencies." If time is the only criterion, a multilith machine at a local duplicating shop can do it while you wait.

If you need both speed and quality, financial printing houses have the staff and equipment standing by on three shifts to handle rush jobs. They'll get out your color brochure in 48 hours or less, but be prepared to pay far more than what the same job would cost at a commercial printing house.

Your production manager, printers, and lettershops can do anything you want, but understand that the time-cost-quality interrelationship is a law of nature. All the haggling, screaming, bargaining, or cajoling in the world isn't going to change reality.

CONTROLLING COSTS

Each side of the cost-time-quality triangle has its own problems and opportunities. There is no trick to getting "the lowest costs." There *are* tricks to getting reasonable costs without sacrificing the other two considerations. These tricks involve

1. Planning the job
2. Defining it
3. Getting estimates
4. Avoiding errors
5. Avoiding rush work

Planning the Job

Whether you are working on a simple black-and-white ad for a newspaper, a multipage magazine ad with bind-in card, or a multimillion-piece printing run, the problems are the same, and so is the first step: planning.

It is too late to begin production planning after the layout is complete. The time to begin is after the writer and artist have worked out rough layouts, and before either finished copy has been written or final layouts completed. *That* is the time to bring in the production specialist or supplier.

In the simplest advertisement, the production specialist should have the responsibility for determining exact sizes and the kind of halftone that is acceptable for the publication. (Halftones vary from 60 to 120 screen; the lower the number, the coarser the illustration.) For a complex mailing piece the production specialist is responsible for knowing paper sizes, envelope formats, inserting requirements, and what you can and cannot do with computer personalization.

In general planning, you should do the following:

Plan for Changes. If you have different versions for testing or for different markets, plan them in advance. Usually it is not necessary to start from scratch with each version. If you confine changing areas to the black plate, different versions can be prepared on press at lower cost than making and setting up a whole new set of plates. If only an address or other element changes, then an overlay on the mechanical will be less costly than new mechanicals and will save on platemaking as well. Production considerations should be taken into account in the creative stage as well. For example, costly changes can be avoided if different mailing packages share a common window envelope, with copy changes positioned in the window, rather than require separate envelopes for each.

Check Paper Specifications. Review paper specifications with publications and printers, to be sure halftones are prepared correctly, ink won't show through, and your job will be cut out of the available paper with minimal waste. Even the paper's grain direction is important, especially for neat folding.

Plan for the Future. If you expect that color separations will be reused for other versions, do what publishers do when preparing books that will be printed in different languages. Order a "floating fifth" film from the color separation house. This is a second black film containing all text matter, while the original black film contains the black part of halftone illustrations. When printing, the two sets of film are combined into a single black plate, but the text can be changed without reshooting the expensive halftone areas.

Avoid Inflexible Dating. More than one disaster has been averted by keeping dates off the printed area of an insert card or mailing piece. If an expiration date is mentioned in print in several places, you're up a tree if the lists come in wrong, the season turns bad, or one of the other elements is delayed. It's much better to imprint the date as part of the laser printing.

Make Dummies. Take the time to cut out blank paper representing each piece of a mailing. Fold and insert it the way you want it. Errors, such as folders that open up and jam the inserter, or reply coupons that don't fit in the reply envelope, will be readily obvious and can be corrected before mechanical pasteups are begun.

Check with the U.S. Postal Service. Always check for postal acceptability and new regulations. Don't presume tolerance, understanding, or common sense. An extra fraction of an inch on a reply card can increase your business-reply postage costs. An error in postal indicia can lead to the refusal of an entire mailing. Go by the book, or they'll throw it at you.

Defining the Job

Once you've worked out everything, write down detailed specifications; don't count on a layout's being enough.

Bob Jurick, chairman of Fala Direct Marketing, prepared the following lists of questions that should be asked by sales representatives when writing up orders for printing, computer, or mailing services.

GENERAL PRINTING SPECIFICATIONS

1. *Name or subject matter of the job.*
2. *What is the quantity?*
3. *What is the size?* If a book or booklet, number of pages and the trim size of the page? Does it bleed?
4. *What is the paper stock?* *a.* Brand name if required. *b.* If brand name, can an equivalent sheet be used? *c.* What weight sheet? *d.* What finish is required: gloss, vellum, smooth, etc.? *e.* If a book or booklet, is there a separate cover? If a separate cover, what stock, weight and finish? *f.* Color of stock?
5. *How many colors—how many sides?* *a.* If two colors, are they two colors, not black or black and one color? *b.* If two colors on two sides, are they the same two colors? *c.* If four colors, is it four flat colors or four-color process?
6. *What type of art?* *a.* All line, ready for camera? *b.* Bendays: how many and what size? *c.* Halftones: how many, what size, square or silhouette?
7. *If process color.* *a.* Size of process area or areas? *b.* What art will be supplied for process areas: chromes, wash drawings, continuous negatives? *c.* If chromes, what size, and are they all in the same focus? Are they separate units or assemblies? *d.* Do the process areas print on one or two sides?
8. *What is the approximate ink coverage, in percent: 50%, 80%, 100%?*
9. *What kind of proofs are required?* *a.* Blueprints? *b.* Color keys (or chromalins)? *c.* Press proofs?
10. *What type of binding?* *a.* Saddle stitch? How many wires? *b.* Type and number of folds? *c.* Perfect bind? *d.* Stitched or pasted? *e.* Die cut? *f.* Embossing?
11. *What type of packing?* Skid, cartons, pallet, banded? Moisture-resistant? How should cartons be labeled?
12. *Delivery.* Where? Is delivery additional? Date of delivery? Receiving department hours?

13. *Are over-runs acceptable?* If so, is there a percentage or quantity limit?

GENERAL COMPUTER SPECIFICATIONS

1. *What type of job?* What is the quantity? Computer letter, list maintenance, labels?
2. *How is it to be run?* Impact, ink jet, laser? On continuous form or cut sheets?
3. *If computer letter. a.* Match fill-in—how many lines? *b.* Full computer letter—how many lines? *c.* Should everything be spelled out, abbreviated or exactly as on tape if tape is supplied (i.e., Ave., St., State, etc)? *d.* If prefix is not on tape, what are the rules for Mr., Miss, Mrs., Ms.? Should we look up female names on table? *e.* Type style: standard courier, wide courier? *f.* Proof and artwork information?
4. *Computer forms information. a.* One-up or two-up? *b.* Trim size of letter, excluding pin holes? *c.* Weight of stock, color? *d.* One- or two-sided printing? *e.* Bindery: perforations, die-cuts, or tip-ons?
5. *If labels. a.* One-up, three-up, four-up, or five-up? *b.* Type of stock: regular Cheshire, gummed, pressure-sensitive? *c.* Should match code, source code, or other information be printed on label?
6. *Admark ink-jet imaging.* Coated or uncoated stock. Tapes properly formatted?
7. *If list maintenance. a.* How will client submit changes? *b.* How often is list to be updated? *c.* Will list be used for rental? If so, should test tapes of various quantities be kept "hanging"?
8. *Tape information. a.* How many bits per inch (1600, 800, 556, etc)? *b.* What track, nine or seven? *c.* What is the blocking factor? *d.* What is the record size? Is the field fixed or variable? *e.* Are tape layout sheet, explanation of codes, sample printout, or "dump" available?
9. *Tape information—if conversion required. a.* How much information will go onto tape: codes, dollar amounts, references, dates, etc.? *b.* What purpose will the tape be used for: letters, labels, etc.? *c.* Will the client be doing "dupe" elimination? *d.* Will the list be used for rental?

GENERAL MAILING SPECIFICATIONS

1. *What is the quantity?*
2. *When will material be received, and what is mail date?*
3. *Envelopes. a.* Size? Booklet or open-end? Preprinted indicia? *b.* Window or closed? (If window, open or cellophane?) *c.* Paper or polybag?

4. *Number of inserts. a.* Sizes of each? *b.* Prefolded for machine inserting (i.e., no accordion gate or open end folds)? *c.* Order of inserts—from flap to front?

5. *Addressing. a.* If labels, what kind: Cheshire, pressure-sensitive, gummed? *b.* If labels, what is labeled: envelope, BRC, etc.? *c.* If computer forms, to be burst and trimmed? Size of forms: number up, trim size? *d.* If typed address, what font? On what piece? What is the source: directory, cards, galleys, handwritten?

6. *Mailing. a.* Is list provided in strict zip-code sequence? *b.* How many lists? Sizes from smallest to largest? *c.* Class of mail: first, third, bulk? *d.* Is indicia preprinted? *e.* To be metered? *f.* If stamps, what kind: regular, commemorative, bulk-rate, not-for-profit?

7. *Bursting and folding. a.* Size of full finished sheet? *b.* Number up: one or two? *c.* Number of folds and type of fold?

8. *Shipping. a.* Where? *b.* How—what carrier? *c.* Packed in cartons? Who supplies? *d.* Is shipping included in price?

9. *Incidentals. a.* Tipping, stapling, clipping? *b.* Keying? Separately or while labeling? How many different keys? Size and position of each key?

Getting Estimates

Once the specification sheet has been prepared, getting estimates is simple. Specification sheets are simply attached to a "request-for-bid" memo and given to various suppliers.

Ideally, three suppliers should be asked to bid on each part of each job. One should be a tried-and-true supplier who helped you plan the job. Another should be an alternate supplier who is sometimes used by your firm. The third should be a new supplier who has been soliciting your work.

Unless the savings are substantial, the supplier who has been working with you and helping you should get the job. It's only fair. The alternate supplier should get occasional jobs or parts of the overall job, because you don't want all your eggs in one basket. New suppliers should be tried occasionally to keep prices where they should be. If the job is exceptionally important or difficult, you won't want to work with a new supplier, but if they brought in a low bid, add them to the list for future bidding and break them in on simpler jobs.

It isn't cricket to play one supplier against the other, telling what another's bid is. You'll drive the prices down in the short run, as a hungry printer will meet your bid; but you'll pay for it in quality shortcuts or last-minute additional charges, or by putting the supplier out of business. Most likely, you'll also suffer by not getting the job out on time.

If you get a printer to do a job for less than cost, just to keep the presses busy, your job is the one that will get bumped if a normal-profit job comes along while yours is in progress.

Other Bidding Methods.   There are other ways to go, if you have a trained production person on your staff or acting as a consultant.

Some advertisers place their printing on a cost-plus basis—a fixed-percentage profit margin over the actual costs of the job. To do this, however, requires that you know estimating and be able to calculate press time, setup time, ink coverage, bindery, and letter-shop functions in the same way that the supplier's own estimator does.

Other advertisers act as their own printing brokers, buying the paper directly, dealing with the separators and platemakers, and buying press time (including labor) from printers around the country. Some firms regularly canvass printers or letter shops for idle machine time, to make deals that will save significantly. Here again, you have to have trained personnel who can manage the entire job through each individual graphic process, and you have to be willing to take the full responsibility for the finished job.

It usually costs no more to work with a printing broker or to let your ad agency handle everything. Not only do they supervise and take responsibility for the entire job, but often they get trade prices that enable them to charge the same as if you had bid on the job directly.

Another alternative that has arisen in recent years is the professional production consultant, who manages production programs on a fee basis without mark-up. One of the better known consultants in New York, Hal Glantz, reports that he is usually able to save his clients at least ten times the fees he charges.

Purchase Orders.   Award the job in writing, with the specification sheet appended and all details of price, overruns, delivery, etc., worked out in detail. The suppliers should be asked to sign an acceptance of the detailed order.

Photography.   Production managers should be particularly careful about dealing with photographic suppliers. In recent years these crafts have attempted to demand royalties, even on photographs where they are simply executing a layout designed by your art director. This can result in unpleasant disputes and unexpected costs when a test ad or mailing is ready to be rolled out.

Contrary to photographers' ambitions, this practice is not universal, and there is no reason to agree to it unless you want to. Even world-famous photographers and well-known models will often agree to a "buyout" price with no restrictions, or to specifically defined terms for reuse. These are your suppliers; insist that they agree to your terms, or get another supplier.

One common scheme is to send a bill with unagreed royalty terms on the back, or for a model to hand an art director a form that appears to be a simple confirmation of hours worked, but in small type limits the use of the photographs. Whatever you do, issue your purchase order and have it countersigned before the photo shoot; it is too late to negotiate when the talent is at the studio and your deadlines are approaching.

Avoiding Errors

There are two ways to avoid errors. One is to check everything yourself The other is to be sure that the client, or the senior executive in your own organization, sees and approves every detail at every stage. Use both.

Proofreading. Proofreaders check the various stages against the original copy. If the copy is wrong, the finished job will be wrong too. But don't count on proofreaders.

A proofreader once "corrected" Barbra Streisand's name to "Barbara" at the last minute, causing understandable consternation at her record company. To avoid problems like this, a proofreader must be given a detailed list of "dos and don'ts," including spelling of proper names; styles for numbers, grammar, and punctuation; and preferred usage.

Whenever anything is corrected, don't just check the one area that contains the correction. I once saw a piece of copy prepared on a word processor that retyped a revised paragraph and plugged it into an entirely different piece of body copy. On the revised copy the changed paragraph was perfect, but everything else described an entirely different product.

Getting Approvals. The most critical obstacle to cost control is revisions, whether made by agency, designer, or client. The way to avoid excessive revisions is to be sure to obtain all approvals at each and every step of the creative and production process.

A copy change on a press proof can cost thousands of dollars; on a blueprint, hundreds; on a mechanical or type proof, about $50; on typed copy, nothing. Obviously, the earlier changes are made, the less they will cost.

Be sure that everything is checked. Don't count on a client or a senior executive to know what to look for. If a layout isn't clear, or a mechanical paste-up is confusing, be sure to point out exactly what illustration goes where, what color the backgrounds will be, and any concerns you may have about the quality of the finished product.

I once saw a $30,000 printing job rerun because a client company president didn't realize that computer letters are not as neat as a secretary's hand-typed letters. I saw another job rejected because an executive didn't like the very subtle perforations on a Letterlope format. That no one else was bothered by these characteristics is irrelevant. The clients were not made aware of these details and had not been asked to sign off on samples as well as mechanicals. If they had, the projects would not have become victims of what has been called "the expectation-realization gap."

Figures 16-1 and 16-2 show some typical estimate forms. The column marked "Revisions" is a must.

Avoiding Rush Work

Overtime costs money, and overtime for unionized typesetters, engravers, and printers costs more than overtime for writers and artists. If you must rush a job, put the pressure on the early stages and the approval process, not on the very costly graphic arts stages.

Art and Mechanical Authorization

Client: Beneficial National Bank   Code:

Product: GEN   Code:

Project: DM #10 Window Package: Brochure, Outer Envelope, Reply Device, Letter   Code:

WORK CODE	WORK CATEGORY	ORIGINAL	REVISION	FINAL
J1	Comprehensives			
K2	Photography (3) cover, 2 cards & 2 cards	1150		
K6	Illustration	600		
L2	Models	210		
L3	Props Expenses			
L8	Travel Expenses			
M3	Chrm Dye C Print			
M7	Retouching (3 chromes)	700		
N5	Mechanicals	1320		
N8	Photostats	325		
N9	Copy Prints			
O2	Typo Photoltrng	1600		
O7	Engrvng-Rotgrv			
O8	Engrvng-Offset			
P3	Dup Materials			
P5	Printing			
R9	Miscellaneous (Comm)			
	COMMISSIONABLE SUBTOTAL	5,905		
	AGENCY COMMISSION			
S2	BBDO Trvl & Exp			
T6	Shipping			
T7	Messenger	100		
T8	Telephn Telegrm			
T9	Misc. (Non-Comm)			
V1	Sales Tax (4%)			
V5	Sales Tax (8½%)	487		
	N/C SUBTOTAL	587		
	TOTAL CHARGES	1,042		
	CONTINGENCY	649		
	GROSS TOTAL	$8,183		

Prepared By:	Approvals		Agency Use Only	
	Art	Date	Date received	Date
NOTE: This estimate is based on normal schedules and on reasonable revisions not exceeding 10% of time expended. Overtime, excessive alterations, or changes in direction will result in charges exceeding this estimate	Acct Exec	Date	Job No.	Date Input
				To Input Group
	Client	Date	Authorization Code	Input by

Figure 16-1. Typical production estimate form for mechanical preparation costs.

Schedule your job carefully, as described next, and then stick to the schedule. "Walk through" approvals and corrections rather than use mail or messengers, and be sure that everyone concerned knows the effect on timetables. It's amazing how often the people who insist that a job be finished on a certain date are precisely the same people who keep making changes or delaying approvals.

Production Authorization

Client: Beneficial National Bank	Job Description: Control Direct Mail
	1st Quarter - per attached
Product: Visa/Mastercard Credit	Code: specs
Date: November 9, 1984	Job No: C 91814

WORK CODE	WORK CATEGORY	ORIGINAL	REVISION	FINAL
PRINTING		1,130M + 3%		
DA	Outer Envelope	15,739.15		
DB	Business Reply Card Envelope	10,217.05		
DC	Letter S			
DD	Brochure 1	19,117.65		
DE	Brochure 2			
DG	Continuous Form	13,875.15		
DH	Response Device			
	SUB-TOTAL	58,949.00		
COMPUTER				
DL	List Rental			
DM	List Processing	16,525.00		
DN	Computer Printing	5,883.25		
DO	Reports and Analysis			
		1,180.00		
	SUB-TOTAL	23,588.25		
LETTERSHOP				
DP	Addressing			
DQ	Inserting			
DR	Meter Stamp			
DS	Sort Tie Bag Mail	16,018.75		
	SUB-TOTAL	16,018.75		
AGENCY COMMISSION		17,395.10		
T6	Shipping Air Freight			
T9	Miscellaneous (Inc. Travel, Telephone & Messenger)	500.00		
V4	Sales Tax			
DV	Postage	124,300.00		
	NON--COMMISSIONABLE SUB-TOTAL	124,800.00		
CONTINGENCY		24,075.10		
GROSS TOTAL		264,826.20		

Prepared By:	Approvals		Agency Use Only	
The above estimate is based on normal working schedules and routine corrections Overtime author s alternatives or changes of specifications will result in increased costs This will be reflected in the final billing Where major changes are requested a revised estimate will be submitted According to standard printing trade practices the total quantity delivered may be subject to a shortage or overage of up to 10% Such changes in quantity are not reflected in this estimate	Project Manager	Date	Date Received	Date
				Date Input
	Production Manager	Date	Job Number	
				To Input Group
	Client s Signature	Date	Authorization Code	Input by

Figure 16-2. Typical production estimate form for preparation of printing and mailing costs.

Each approval process should have a deadline, just as any other step does. The approver should be notified that delays past a due date will result in extension of the final deadline or perhaps even missing a deadline.

If the basic schedule is adhered to, most rush work will involve last-minute changes or correcting omissions that fell through the cracks.

Planning, specifying, and avoiding changes will be the best way to avoid rush jobs.

CONTROLLING TIME

When submitting a project for approval, I always make it a practice to submit a timetable as well as an estimate of costs. In some ways, the timetable is more difficult to control than the costs.

Time Requirements

Table 16-1 shows some timing allocations, a composite of schedules used by various graphic arts suppliers and ad agencies. It is important to note that no two are the same.

TABLE 16-1
OPTIMUM PRODUCTION TIMING

	Black-and-white ads	Color ads	Ads with cards	Labeled mailings	Computer mailings
Orientation and planning	2–4 weeks	2–4 weeks	2–4 weeks	2–4 weeks	2–4 weeks
Copy and rough layout	2–4 weeks	3–5 weeks	3–6 weeks	3–6 weeks	4–6 weeks
Comprehensive layouts	3 days	5 days	5 days	7 days	10 days
Approval and revisions	5 days	7 days	7 days	7 days	7 days
Typesetting and mechanicals	7 days	10 days	14 days	14 days	16 days
Mechanical approval and revisions	3 days	4 days	4 days	4 days	7 days
Color preparation, engraving, and proofing	5 days	10 days	10 days	15 days	15 days
List order and delivery				4–5 weeks	4–5 weeks
List preparation, including merge				3 weeks	4 weeks
Printing, including computer forms			3 weeks	4 weeks	5 weeks
Envelope conversion				1–4 weeks	1–4 weeks
Labeling or computer printing				5 days	10 days
Inserting and mailing				10 days	10 days

Note: These optimum schedules include scheduling and waiting time. On tightly scheduled projects, most of these steps can be cut in half if suppliers with available time are prescheduled. Very complex projects or mail quantities over 1 million pieces may take more time during the last two or three stages. Of course, very simple projects can take much less time. It is possible to get a simple ad or letter produced in a day or two if that is the objective.

Though any of these steps can take less time under rush conditions, these are reasonable guidelines for careful cost and quality control. They add up to six to eight weeks for preparing a color ad for a magazine, half that for a black-and-white ad, and between five and six months for direct mail, depending on whether or not it is computerized.

These are optimum schedules, within which costs and quality can be carefully budgeted and controlled. Unfortunately, such schedules seem to be the exception rather than the rule. The need to get a new product on the market before competition does, or to wait for results of a previous mailing before sending out the next, often requires that time allocations be reduced substantially. My experience is that they can be cut in half with great difficulty but without too serious an effect on cost and time. A bigger cut than that can require severe quality risks or "crash" costs necessitated by night and weekend work.

Critical Path Scheduling

Critical path method is a business planning technique originally developed as part of a process called Program Evaluation and Review Technique (PERT). It has been used to plan complex research and development projects such as the space program and major construction projects. In its most advanced usage, every step is programmed into a computer, progress is reviewed, and "critical dates" are called to the attention of appropriate managers.

Basically, the critical path method involves placing a time factor on each phase in a process, figuring what are the necessary preliminary steps for each, and laying the phases out in the indicated sequence.

This is sort of a "backward timetable," beginning with the finished project and working back step by step, perhaps plotting the time factors with lines on a sheet of graph paper.

Figure 16-3 is an example of this process applied to a complex direct mailing on a 16-week schedule. Note that this project was completed in four months only because several steps were conducted at the same time, so that lists and mechanicals would both be ready on the same date.

Different companies will have entirely different schedules, and so there is no way to prepare one standard schedule for every company. For instance, large corporations may require a week for legal approval. Regulated companies may need four weeks to get the NASD or other officials to pass on a simple letter. Companies with in-house computer facilities may be able to cut time on list processing. If only house lists are being used, the four or five weeks of waiting time for delivery of rented lists can be cut to a week or so.

Ways to Save Time

There are many ways to shorten a schedule or, at the very least, to prevent a job from getting behind schedule. Here are some that may be helpful.

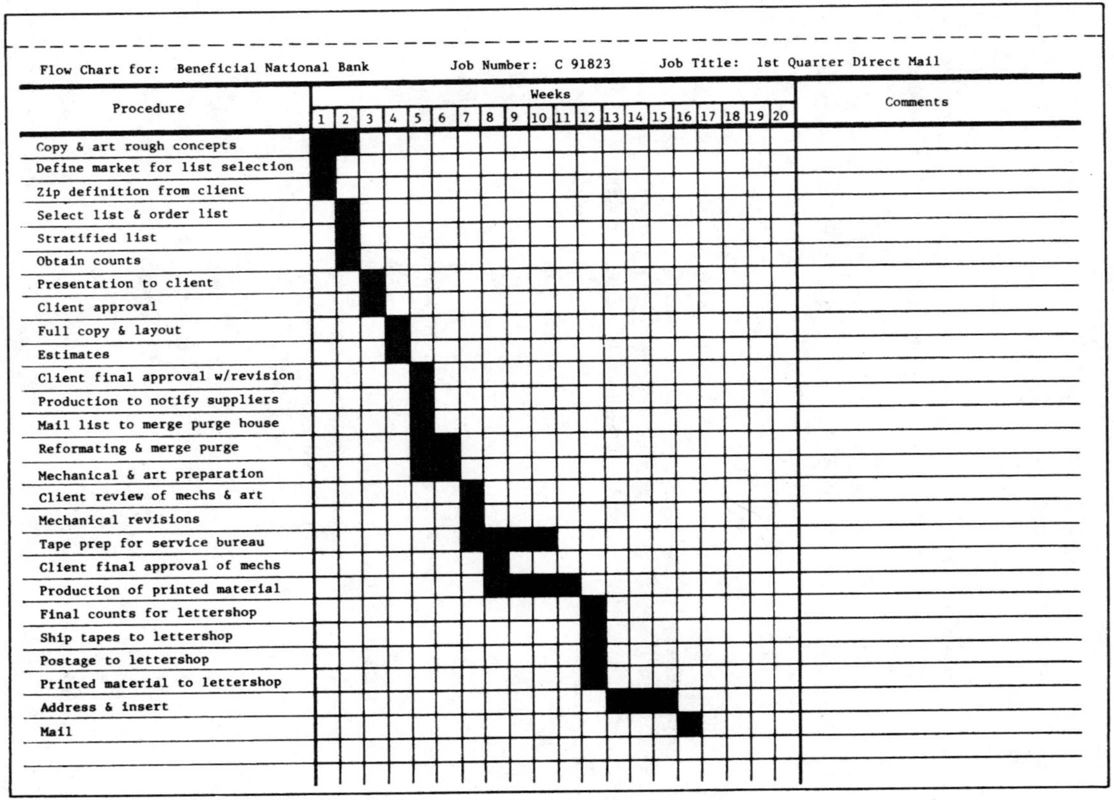
Flow Chart for: Beneficial National Bank
Job Number: C 91823
Job Title: 1st Quarter Direct Mail
Procedure
Weeks
1 2 3 4 5 6 7 8 9 10 11 12 13 14 15 16 17 18 19 20
Comments
Copy & art rough concepts
Define market for list selection
Zip definition from client
Select list & order list
Stratified list
Obtain counts
Presentation to client
Client approval
Full copy & layout
Estimates
Client final approval w/revision
Production to notify suppliers
Mail list to merge purge house
Reformating & merge purge
Mechanical & art preparation
Client review of mechs & art
Mechanical revisions
Tape prep for service bureau
Client final approval of mechs
Production of printed material
Final counts for lettershop
Ship tapes to lettershop
Postage to lettershop
Printed material to lettershop
Address & insert
Mail

Figure 16-3. This flowchart provides a convenient way to plan any promotional project.

Use Good Suppliers.   A rush job is no place to use untested or out-of-town suppliers. Use people you can count on.

Count Everyone In.   Let everyone—client, staff, and supplier—know what the deadline is and why it's important. If possible, bring all these people together in a "starter" meeting so that all of them will know what is expected of them and how their part of the job affects everyone else. You'll be amazed at what shortcuts they can work out if you let them talk to each other directly.

Order Lists Immediately.   Ordering lists is often the critical path on any job. As soon as you know the format and the lists you want, place your order with your list broker.

Get Interim Approvals.   Don't hold everything up for minor copy revisions. Ask for an OK to proceed with preparing color artwork, for instance, or envelopes. These can be done while other parts of a mailing are still being revised.

Order Paper Early.   Place the paper order as soon as the format has been approved, even if some copy and art elements are still being worked out. Paper is the most costly and least flexible part of the production process.

Get It Right the First Time.   This may seem contradictory, but rush jobs are precisely the ones on which you should slow down and be extra careful. There's no time to redo anything, or to fold or insert by hand; everything has to be planned carefully. Make dummies. Check with the mailing and computer firms. Be sure everything is right from the beginning.

Consolidate Corrections.   Don't take time correcting type errors or mechanical adjustments before showing them to your client. Just mark the changes you want to make on a tissue overlay and ask the client to add corrections. You'll save time and money by doing them all at once.

Be Mobile.   You can pick up days just by eliminating the need to send proofs back and forth for approval. Go to the printer or other supplier, and take your client or boss with you. If everyone knows the timing of the job, you should get full cooperation.

Arrange Batch Deliveries.   On large jobs that have to go to a binder, envelope fabricator, or computer printer, don't wait to ship all copies at once. Send the first million as soon as it's ready, to let the next processor get started. Send the rest in agreed-upon increments.

Pin Down All Interim Dates.   Be sure that delivery dates—and sometimes even the time of day—are indicated in writing and pointed out to each supplier. "As soon as possible" and even "rush" are meaningless. If suppliers have a specific time to aim for, they are more likely to make it, and will be less likely to bump your job for some larger customer's rush job.

CONTROLLING QUALITY

Presuming that the layout of the ad or mailing represents what you really are looking for, the problem of quality control in the production process is one of fidelity: being faithful to the original design.

Typesetting

Fidelity begins with the type-specification process, a task sometimes delegated to a member of a production department or an outside art studio. However, it must be done under the direction and with the approval of the art director who designed the original layout. The wrong choice of typefaces, sizes, or spacing can completely alter the feeling of a layout.

A frequent problem is that copy turns out to be too long, especially when lawyers or others have added long phrases that were not in the original copy. The wrong solution to this problem is to "make it fit," with illustrations reduced, spacing omitted, and type set small and crowded. This mistake can impair the entire body language of the ad or mailing. A better solution is to sit down with all parties concerned, including the copywriter, and make deliberate choices as to what can be cut or omitted.

Desktop Publishing

While some type is still set by linotype and other "metal" processes, it is much more common today to use computer typesetting, sometimes called *desktop publishing*. Virtually every kind of typeface or lettering is available, with infinite variations, using the excellent typefaces created by Adobe and other software producers.

Computer typesetting has become popular largely because of its substantial savings as compared with traditional methods. But there are many other advantages as well. Even companies who can't afford the highest-quality printing and proofing equipment can have access to these services, sending data by modem one day and getting finished proofs back by air express or messenger the next morning. And with printer quality improving constantly, all but the smallest typefaces can now be set on a simple home or office printer.

Obviously there are substantial savings in time and money. Type can be in galley form, ready to be pasted into position on mechanical forms as in the old days. Or, with properly trained operators, the entire mechanical and even the film can be generated directly by the computer. Approvals can be solicited by modem or network directly from a client or other departments. Type-fitting can be tried out right on the computer screen, with line spacing and letter spacing adjusted and widows cut to make it all fit perfectly.

Illustrations

If you're using photography, go to the photography session and look at all the details that the photographer might miss. Chances are, the photographer will be concentrating on lighting and composition. You should look at how the model is dressed and posed, whether your product is displayed at the best possible angle, whether the background is distracting, and whether the props create the right image. The photo will be no better than the scene at the moment the picture is taken.

Cropping and retouching usually can't add quality that's not in the photo. You can remove some defects or mask out an error, but the best bet is to get the picture right at the beginning.

If you're using artwork, then have it drawn oversized and insist that it be right. Revise it as many times as you have to, until you know it's what you want. This is no time to spare the artist's feelings.

Be sure to get a photostat and look at any artwork in the size that it will actually appear. Embarrassing details can suddenly show up when a 35-mm chrome or contact print is blown up to a larger size. On the other hand, an oversized painting that looks exciting can lose all its detail and blur together when printed in a smaller size.

Mechanical Paste-Ups

The mechanical stage is very important. This is where all the pieces fit together into camera-ready art. It's the last practical opportunity to make simple revisions or catch typographic errors.

As stated in previous chapters, spacing is very important. Usually it can easily be adjusted in the mechanical stage, but more can go wrong than right. Strictly speaking, the mechanical stage is an executional one, and although preparing mechanicals is a skilled and professional craft, it is usually not an additive process. Fidelity is the objective. The art is avoiding loss of fidelity. For instance, if photostats of type are ordered, those stats can lose a degree of sharpness from the original type proof. They can never make it sharper.

The mechanical should be prepared and checked with fidelity in mind. Any approval authorities should be cautioned that this is the last stage at which changes can be made without stopping the entire job.

Photographic Processes

Color separators and processors of reprographic film have the common objective of converting the mechanical paste-up into a form that can be turned into press plates and printed at a newspaper, magazine, or printing plant. The processes vary according to the end use and the artwork provided, but the objective is the same: fidelity.

The way to get what you want is to be sure that everyone knows what that is before starting. You have to supply good examples and clear instructions. For instance, if you are shooting gold coins and want a specific tone of gold, then be sure to show the photo processors a sample. They are not mind-readers. If two photos of the same coin start with different colors, the finished printing job will look the same way. High-quality photo processors can work miracles, but only on request. New computer-imaging processes can perform virtual miracles with illustrations, combining scenes from different photographs, changing colors, creating any illustration fantasy one can envision.

Usually the only adjustments that are necessary are color specifications, within very narrow ranges. Some minor adjustments can be made by lightening or darkening one of the color-separated positive films, or by expensive dot etching; but the color of the proof and the ensuing printing job can be no better than the artwork you provide.

One helpful hint: Be sure the engraver knows what kind of paper the job ultimately will be printed on. Insist that press proofs be pulled on the stock specified. Degrees of finish and absorbency can dramatically affect the fineness of the screen and the mix of the colors selected.

Printing

It would take years for an advertiser to learn everything a printer knows about achieving quality. All you have to understand is that by the time the job gets on the press, the printer's options are very limited.

Quality begins with the typesetting, the artwork, the mechanical, and the photo processing. By the time the piece gets on press, all that can be adjusted is the impression, the speed, and the color. Yet it is always the printer who gets blamed if the job doesn't look right.

Impression is a function of the make-ready process, in which the pressure between the printing cylinder (whether letterpress or offset) and the base cylinder behind the paper being printed is adjusted slightly.

Speed can affect the ink application and how fast the printed sheet passes through a drying station.

Color can be lightened or darkened on press, but it will turn out better if it starts out right in the proof stage.

Other Processes. If quality is the supreme requirement, then consider— when first planning the job—using letterpress or gravure printing rather than the more common offset lithography. These processes sometimes are used when printing illustrated books, photography magazines, and fine-art reproductions. The differences are dramatic, and the costs are not excessive. The problem is that most printers have converted to the higher-speed offset process and so will discourage letterpress and gravure printing, which cannot be produced in their own shop.

Mailing Lists. The simplest process should be placing orders for the mailing lists you previously selected. Unfortunately, because there are so many sources and subsuppliers involved, such orders frequently are mishandled. I once ordered ten lists for a test of a new product that included both sex-select and sectional center zip-select. Over 40 percent of the names did not meet specifications and had to be reordered.

Lists should be "dumped" as soon as they arrive, so that you can spot-check to see if they fit specifications. To wait until they are ready to be merged for labeling or computer printing is a mistake, as it can then be too late to have incorrect lists rerun.

Shipment. Here's another apparently simple process—but what disasters can take place! Be sure to specify whether a job is to be banded, in cartons, or stacked on skids, and choose how you want it shipped. I've shared many anxious moments with production managers, waiting for news that a magazine insert, last seen on a loading dock in St. Louis, had finally arrived at the publication only hours before final closing.

Shipping and freight are not to be taken for granted and should be considered, planned, and executed correctly. Any shipping instructions to suppliers should be sure to include not only when something should be shipped, but how.

Lettershop. What can go wrong in a lettershop? Plenty. For one thing, there have been plenty of horror stories about mailing the wrong insert to the wrong list. For another, it's easy to completely omit one of the pieces of a mailing.

Careful written instructions and clear insert coding must be provided. Each and every piece should have a code number clearly visible without unfolding the piece. And your inserting instructions should clearly list the sequence, the facing, and the nesting of the various pieces. A sample package, stapled together so that the sequence will not become confused, should be provided as soon as printed samples are ready.

A Phillipsburg inserter stacks one piece on top of another. A Pitney-Bowes inserter nests one inside another. Inserting equipment can have 6, 8, 10, or even 14 "stations," each inserting a single component. The more stations you need, the more costly the inserting will be and the more difficult it will be to find a supplier with the right equipment.

Also, if you don't want your mailing date delayed, be sure to send the letter shop a certified check to cover postage. They can't mail until the Postal Service has been paid. If postage is affixed on-line, the entire process will be held up.

Mailing Checks. How do you know the mailing went out on time and the way you wanted it? The final test is to see how and when it arrives in the mail.

Always "seed" a list with names of some of your key executives, and be sure they are merged into the list at the computer house, not at the letter shop. Or let the firm U.S. Monitor handle it for you.

It's also a good idea to include in your seeding of the list some people in other parts of the country, so that you can get an idea of the Postal Service's delivery at the time of the mailing. It will make a difference when you're trying to read results if you discover, for example, that your mail still has not been delivered on the other coast.

SUPPLIERS ARE PEOPLE TOO

Choosing graphic arts suppliers is more than a matter of getting three bids and picking the lowest one. You might save 5 or 10 percent with such strict purchasing procedures, just as you might save a small part of the commission by not using an ad agency, but these economics can cost you 50, 100, or 200 percent or more where it really counts: in response rates.

Of course, get competitive bids; but put service, cooperation, and creative contribution into the mix when you make your final decision.

Your suppliers are not servants, and they are not the enemy. They can and should be part of your team, involved in the creative process at as early a stage as possible. The contributions they can make are enormous.

For instance, a color separator can suggest a fine white line between two illustrations so as to avoid expensive premium services, or can show you how to prepare a scaled assembly of illustration elements. A color separator who is willing to work with you can save you much more than the difference between suppliers.

A printer can suggest a slight change in size that will make better use of paper sizes, or can help you develop a format that will do a better job of presenting your particular message at a better price.

A lettershop may offer ideas that can save you both time and money, such as widening an address window or changing a fold so as to facilitate inserting.

Too many marketers simply prepare their specifications and send them out for bids, without making suppliers part of the process. Three different printers, for example, may vary 5 to 10 percent in price; but one of them may show you how to combine two elements in the package and save 25 percent of the total cost. Isn't *that* the real economy?

The way to build a relationship with your suppliers is to make them part of the team and to let them know that they have work from you as long as they keep their prices in line. You want your account to be important to them, and it won't be important to them if they have to lowball their bids to get each and every job. My suggestion is to take bids on every job from new suppliers but to change suppliers only when you can save at least 10 percent. In that case, *change suppliers*; don't rotate them or play one against the other. When you find good suppliers, be good to them as long as they're good to you.

17

FULFILLMENT

The term *fulfillment* derives, as with most modern direct marketing, from this field's roots in mail order. Originally it referred to "fulfilling the order": opening the mail, typing a label, keeping track of the orders and deposits, and mailing the merchandise.

Direct marketing has, of course, evolved into much more than simple mail order. The "mail" response might be a phone call or a coupon delivered at a retail store. The "label" is more likely to be the input onto a computer record of not just a name, address, and key number but answers to a complex database questionnaire. The "merchandise" is more likely to be a membership, a donation, a subscription, further information about a product or service, or the activation of a sophisticated interactive service.

The common denominator is not what is being sold, but the advertiser's response to the consumer's response: the process of fulfilling the promise or offer made in the advertising.

MAIL ORDER

The mailing piece is attractive and inviting. You open the envelope and find yourself involved in an offer of a product that will make your job easier or your life more satisfying. Eagerly, you mail in the coupon. Like most customers, you then impatiently wait...and wait...and wait.

Finally, weeks later, a battered-looking carton arrives. Your name is misspelled. You break your fingernail opening the carton. You rustle through a mass of yellowed pages from an old newspaper, and there it is—broken!

Maybe it's not even what you ordered. The instructions may be in pidgin English. Sometimes the item doesn't come at all, but a polite postcard arrives six weeks later to tell you that it has been out of stock, or not available in your size, all along.

Whether you keep this item or not, or whether your return or refund is handled efficiently or not, you've already lost your enthusiasm for the product, for the company, and probably for buying by mail at all.

Avoiding this all too common scenario is what mail-order fulfillment is all about. Fulfillment should be concerned, but too frequently isn't, with fulfilling not only the order but also the customer's expectations. This subject is, technically, a matter of operations rather than marketing, but it can dramatically influence return rates, collections, reorder rates, and the entire future of direct marketing.

Good fulfillment practices, including prompt shipment, can significantly affect conversion and acceptance rates. Fulfillment expenses, including order processing, shipping, and service functions, are always a material expense, whether handled in house or by an outside supplier. Fulfillment problems can get your company in trouble with the Better Business Bureau, the DMA Ethical Standards Committee, the Postal Service inspector, the press, and the law. More important, it is unfair both to your customer, who trusted you, and to your fellow direct marketers, whose reputation will be tarnished along with yours.

DATABASE AND LEAD GENERATION

Most of the advice in this chapter deals with mail order, the most complex form of fulfillment. But the principles—particularly those involving speed and service—apply to any type of direct marketing effort. Whether you are developing leads for retailers, a sales force, a consumer or business proposition, or just building a database, you still have to perform many of the same functions.

Leads must be coded and transmitted promptly and accurately. They must be assigned to the correct geographic or specialty salesperson and transmitted by mail or by wire transmission in a usable form. In addition, there must be provision for information feedback: Was the party sold? Is a follow-up necessary? Should the party be sent information about a different product? If the original product was not sold, why not?

An information tracking system should be set up that analyzes the leads from every perspective: conversion by source, type of prospect, geographic region, type of industry if a business lead, advertising source, and the outlet or salesperson.

Usually there is a direct mail or telephone follow-up, in addition to simple transmission of the lead. List maintenance comes into play here, and so do economic decisions concerning how many letters to send, how long to keep sending letters, and whether letters should supplement or replace the field sales effort.

SUBSCRIPTION AND CONTINUITY PLANS

Other forms of fulfillment involve subscriptions—the method used by most magazine publishers—and continuity or club plans—used by book clubs, record clubs, and other businesses selling on a continuing basis.

These methods are even more complex, as they involve the continuing shipment of merchandise or the provision of services to a direct marketing customer.

Besides promptly shipping a single mail-order package, the fulfillment organization has the added responsibility of administering a two-way contract, to be sure that both the company and the customer honor their obligations to one another.

Subscription expiration dates, club commitments, and continuity cancellation privileges must be honored to the spirit and letter of the agreement entered into during the original transaction. Sometimes entire correspondence series must be created to persuade customers to honor their commitments: to pay for the last shipment, buy the required additional item, or renew the agreement.

Lead generation, clubs, subscription plans, and continuity plans could each occupy an entire chapter, and they do in my *The Direct Marketing Handbook* (McGraw-Hill, 1992). I recommend that those readers concerned about these specific approaches read the appropriate chapters in that book. The general principles described here—particularly those involving the need for accuracy, speed, and service—apply to any form of fulfillment.

FULFILLMENT PROCESSES

Each fulfillment process involves a complicated decision-making process. There are many tradeoffs. One is the standard of customer service you set as your goal.

Direct marketers aim for a high level of personalization, promptness, and performance—the three Ps of fulfillment. At each phase these must be weighed against the realities of time and cost, as expressed in added personnel, inventory risk, computer capability, and the expense of communicating with your customer by mail and telephone. Let's look at each step individually (see Fig. 17-1).

Opening Mail

Most firms count or number the mail first, to establish a control against loss. If there's cash involved, a "caging" process takes place, in which remittances are removed and the amount noted. The money is handled under supervision within a security area and deposited each day. Even outside fulfillment suppliers deposit payments in their customers' banks on a daily basis.

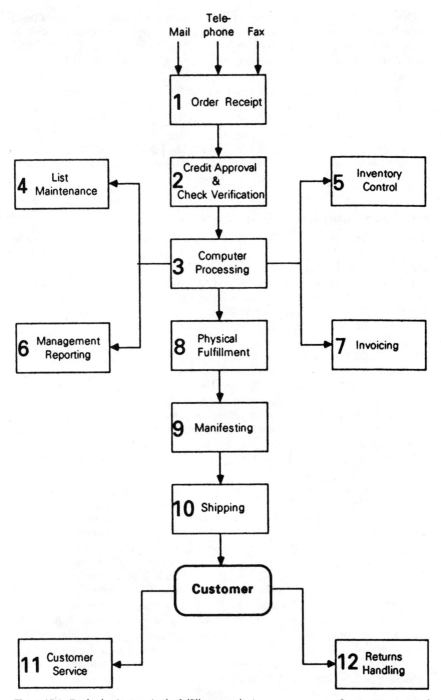

Figure 17-1. Twelve basic steps in the fulfillment cycle. [COURTESY OF FENVESSEY & ASSOCIATES, NEW YORK.]

Often the mail is sorted into types: payments, orders, general correspondence, returns. Advertising responses are sorted or counted, so that daily counts by key numbers can be supplied to marketing personnel. If the volume is large, the sorting and counting process can be helped by using different sizes or colors of reply envelopes, bold tag marks on envelope edges, windows with code number show-throughs, or optically scannable imprints on the envelope faces.

Large fulfillment operations also use very ingenious machinery that slits open envelopes and exposes the contents for easy removal. Other machinery can imprint checks with source and amount, both (1) generating deposits that can be quickly processed by the bank and (2) efficiently recording and controlling cash intake.

Handling Telephone Responses

For most types of propositions, the ring of the telephone is becoming as important as picking up the mail. The growth of telephone usage brings with it both problems and opportunities.

Toll-free WATS lines are the usual technique for providing such service, but the costs are high and getting higher. Marketers must provide not only for enough lines to handle the normal flow of inbound phone calls, but also for skilled and trained operators on all shifts.

To take full advantage of this medium, the phones should be answered day and night, seven days a week, whenever people are likely to be reading your message in their mail or in publications.

If your message is offered on television, however, usually it is uneconomical to have your own company handle the inbound calls. The intensive peak demand for inbound lines would result in expensive idle capacity most other times. Outside phone services are geared to handle peak usage at advantageous rates.

Most companies, especially those using direct-response television with its intense calling patterns, find it preferable to use a company that specializes in handling telephone responses. Matrixx telephone services, in Ogden, Utah, has handled most of my recent telemarketing needs for major clients. But, there are, of course, many other companies out there. Neither their rates nor the quality of their service is necessarily equal, so competitive bidding and reference checks are strongly recommended. At the very least, make some calls as if you were responding to current propositions they are handling, and see for yourself how they are handled.

There are companies with sufficient telephone volume to maintain their own 24-hour telephone services, customized to their own needs. With today's technology, a catalog company can identify a caller automatically and have their name and history on a screen before they've even answered the phone. "Hello, Mr. Jones, how can we at XYZ help you today?" is now entirely possible, as well as instant confirmation that an item is in stock and ready to ship.

One recent innovation is "on-line transfer," used in both outgoing and inbound telemarketing. This enables a caller to be connected, instantly, to a customer service representative who can handle more complex questions, or to a local dealer, insurance agent, stockbroker, or home improvement salesperson who can make an appointment or close the sale.

Whether your company handles its own phones or uses a service, the telephone contact is an opportunity to make a positive impression for your company by the way the call is handled. A courteous, efficient operator can do a lot to inspire trust. While on the phone, the operator can offer special trade-up offers or sell related items. Alternate colors or sizes or replacement items can be recommended. With credit card orders, the entire transaction can be confirmed and entered on the spot.

Data Entry

Fulfillment is a lot more complicated than newcomers imagine. The order or inquiry must be edited—examined for completeness and clarity. It may have to be coded in some way. Then it is put into a form where it can be compared with lists of former customers, lists of bad credit risks, lists for verifying zip codes, and other data. Codes are counted, and reports are compiled and perhaps even analyzed, depending on the sophistication of the system. The customer file then is used to send out acknowledgments and to generate shipping documents, invoices, statements, and offers of other items. Payments are recorded, and so are returns. All along the way, reports are generated that tell management whether the customer, the promotion, the product, and the business itself are sound.

Order-processing systems also guard against mail-order fraud, particularly with larger checks and credit card purchases of valuable merchandise. Many companies have manual or data transmission systems enabling them to call banks to verify balances on checks over $50 and to obtain credit authorization on credit card purchases over the same amount.

However, not every company faces the same problems, nor does every company start out on a scale requiring large-scale computer applications or sophisticated outside services. As recently as the first edition of this book (1982), many companies still were using label and ledger card systems. Today, however, minicomputers and software packages are available for various types of direct marketing applications. Consulting firms such as David Shepard Associates (New York) or computer services such as Blumenfield Marketing (Stamford) can often help a company to set up all the procedures it needs, on relatively simple data processing equipment with customized software. There is no need for any company today, of any size, to use manual procedures.

Many companies prefer to use an outside computer firm to handle order processing and list maintenance during the startup period, and then bring the functions in-house on minicomputers as soon as their systems have been debugged and their real needs fully identified.

Maintaining Lists

The heart of any direct marketing program is the database, or mailing list. Everything that comes in or goes out is part of some sort of list, and as I have already pointed out, a mailing list is likely to be a company's greatest single asset.

A customer list is more complicated only in that it carries more data: source codes, shipments, payments, returns, items ordered, and dates of transactions. Even the simplest system should be capable of quickly determining whether you want to make new offers to the customer (depending on credit), what the customer has bought, and when it was bought. Recency, frequency, and unit-sale data will be vital in eventual segmentation.

If you plan to rent the list out, you will need to be able to tag test rentals, so that the same names are not used for every test mailing and you can omit the tested names when a customer rents the list again. You may want to retain data that is not necessary for your own operation but that makes the list more rentable to others. For instance, renters definitely will expect you to know how old the name is (when it was put on your list), whether it is active or not, and how recently it has been active. They also can make use of source information. Direct mail sold names are generally more responsive to direct mail offers. Catalog mailers prefer "catalog buyers." Mailers may want to select one group or the other on the basis of which names came in on a sweepstakes offer and which did not.

In any event, the customer list should be maintained using DMA's standard formats and abbreviations, from the very beginning, even if only by sending a carbon copy of a typed shipping label to a computer service.

List rentals can be a very profitable source of income. Direct marketers should plan their systems to handle rentals in a manner that will render the type of fast, reliable, accurate service they want when they rent lists from others.

Shipping Orders

Assuming that you have hand-addressed, duplicated, or computer-generated the shipping labels, the most important action remains: shipping the customers what they ordered.

Shipping is a separate function from order entry and processing. The label may be created at one building and the merchandise shipped from warehouses close to the customer, or "drop-shipped" directly by a supplier. If outside suppliers are used, separate firms may be used for fulfillment and shipping.

In a warehouse, there are several major functions. One is receiving: keeping track of shipments that are coming in, spot-checking merchandise quality, verifying quantities, and getting the incoming merchandise to the right section of the warehouse.

Inventory control keeps track not only of everything that comes in but also of everything that is *supposed* to come in. Late orders have to be followed up, and the appropriate party notified when quantities appear to be low. Inventory systems, to be effective, cannot confine themselves to tracking the inventory as it is shipped, but must include a sophisticated forecasting function based on the expectation of new promotions. Reorders must be placed while there is still time to get additional merchandise. Customers must be promptly notified that the item ordered is not available, so that they still will be inclined to order something else.

Inventory and forecasting control is one of the most critical functions in the fulfillment process, and often makes the difference between profitability and loss for a mail-order company. This function concerns not only the quantity of merchandise received and shipped, but also its quality. Incoming merchandise and drop-shipped merchandise must be inspected, tested, or measured (as in apparel and other sized products) and reviewed for conformance to the original order. What goes out of your shipping department is *your* reputation, not your vendor's.

Once in the warehouse, the merchandise must be clearly marked and assigned locations so that it can be found again. I have seen desperate warehouse managers frantically tearing open cartons because a shipment couldn't be found. Marking cartons clearly and storing them so that the markings are visible can save your sanity.

Often the main bulk of merchandise—books, printed material, or whatever—is in cartons or on skids in one area of the shipping facility; a modest quantity is on shelves in a compact area closer to the shipping area. It would take too much time for order pickers to go through the entire warehouse to find a single item. Instead, a pick rack keeps some of each handy so as to minimize walking, searching, and time-wasting. Some larger firms have more complex systems with pick areas for different lines of merchandise, multiple documents, and high-speed belts or conveyor systems. The objective is the same: minimize walking so as to increase orders picked per hour.

Once the order has been assembled, it goes to a packer. The packer checks the item picked against the shipping document and, if correct, places it in a bag or carton. For most companies, pickers and packers are the heart of the shipping process.

The labels are affixed; the cartons are sealed. Then they are weighed, and postage or an air express sticker is affixed. Some larger warehouses have postal facilities right in the warehouse, to receive and sort the packages.

While most fulfillment operations use parcel post and UPS, there are a number of shipping variations that can result in substantial savings, cost reductions, or both. The late Stan Fenvessey and his associates recommended third-class bulk mail, first-class mail (for light packages where speed is a consideration), and other methods that may fit a company's special needs. UPS, for instance, sometimes is used to deliver packages in bulk to remote UPS distribution centers, which in turn make the local deliveries. Air express services also are being used more frequently by direct marketers, often at no extra charge to the customer.

The invisible part of a warehouse operation is administration: the managers, personnel people, and security guards who keep the whole thing together behind the scenes. Unless you've been involved in warehouse management, you can't imagine the variety and complexity of problems that are handled by administrators.

One important administrative area is security: guarding against unauthorized use of mailing lists, protecting goods from damage or vandalism, preventing loss through inventory pilferage or larger-scale fraud, detecting computer scams that would divert payments from customers or to suppliers, and protecting vital records. I know of one club that went out of business largely because of the accidental erasure of its commitment data during a tape-to-tape transfer. Good security procedures could have saved 500 jobs.

Another important area for administration concern is quality assurance: making sure that the fulfillment task is being done according to the procedures that have been laid out. This usually involves testing one's own service as well as the competitor's, sampling customer opinion (at least through questionnaires inserted in packages), monitoring return and cancellation rates, and conducting in-house audits and quality checks.

Much of this discussion does not apply to items such as single books, card sets, or magazines. These can be mass-packaged on automated equipment with automatically affixed labels.

Inquiries and Leads

While most fulfillment processes were developed to handle mail orders, it is just as important to assure speed and service for inquiries, leads, and questionnaires.

Certainly, sales leads require the fastest possible processing. Most companies fax or modem such contacts the same day they are received, directly to the sales office or dealer most qualified to handle them. In some cases, outgoing phone calls are made within hours, to try to set an appointment or to qualify the prospect. Several companies with field sales forces have been very successful in having their phone department make appointments for the sales representatives, using computers to keep track of individual schedules and the layout of sales territories.

It is just as important to respond promptly to booklet requests or other database-building requests. The interest or excitement generated by the direct-response effort in mail or other media fades quickly.

Recently I filled out a "bingo card" in a travel magazine for information about a dozen vacation destinations I was interested in. Three or four responded within a week, and we selected one of those for a vacation trip a month later. More than half of the booklets arrived at our home while we were away or after we had returned—a waste of the entire promotion. If you are going to offer information, send it promptly or don't bother making the offer in the first place.

Customer Service

Theoretically, customer service should be an unnecessary function. If everything went right all the time, there would be no need to handle complaints, inquiries, replacements, and special problems. The cost of maintaining a customer service department is one of the incentives to get it right in the first place: to hire the right people, that is, people who will prevent fires rather than wait until they occur and then try to put them out.

Correspondents are, basically, the human beings who read customer mail; make note of problems for management attention; and direct the computers or other systems to make an adjustment, accept a return, correct an address, or reship a damaged item. Oh, yes, they also do correspondence.

Once upon a time that meant they wrote personal letters to customers. This still happens, but very rarely, in the case of complex adjustments or explanations, or in companies where a highly personal approach is part of the image to be maintained. More often the correspondence is a form letter, a preprinted postcard, or at best, standard paragraphs on a word-processing system.

In a well-run business, customer mail—all of it—is answered within two days of its receipt. Any slower schedule will result in even more correspondence of an irritated nature, cancellations, returns, and a bad reputation. The best way to control speed of response is to mark each letter with the date received.

More and more, customer inquiries come in by telephone. Customers expect the person answering the phone to have instant access to their account record, and instant authority to make a required adjustment.

At Capitol Record Club I used to make it a point to accept one or two calls a day from callers who demanded to talk to the president. After they got over the shock of learning that they really had gotten through, I was able to learn a great deal about what was important to our customers and about the enormous anger and distrust that an incorrect shipment or unanswered letter can cause. I recommend that any executive concerned with customer service spend some time dealing directly with customers in this way, in order to find out what kind of feelings lie behind the cold statistics in customer-complaint reports.

FULFILLMENT REPORTS

In other chapters I have discussed the role of reports, results, and statistics in evaluating promotions. The reports generated within the fulfillment process evaluate everything else: the quality of the customers generated by promotions; the value of the customer base as a whole; the acceptance of the company's product; reactions to its service; forecasts to indicate expense levels that will have a significant effect on profitability; and the intrinsic health of the entire business.

Any business, large or small, simple or complex, should record all needed data in some type of regular reporting or review system. The data should be examined by the highest levels of management, by all relevant operating departments, and by consultants, ad agencies, or other suppliers in a position to influence the operations. Not all these kinds of data will be applicable to all businesses, of course, but they are included here as a checklist for your own operation.

Response Records

The simplest and most obvious record is the number of responses received. While this appears to be simple and superficial, it is more complex and critical than newcomers realize.

It is necessary to know exactly how many mail and phone order responses came in each day, so that the trend can be graphed and accurate forecasts prepared.

It is important to know what *kind* of responses. In mail order, the unit sale and merchandise mix are critical. For leads and inquiry offers, even if no other questions are asked, the mix of responses will be critical. For business responses, what size and kind of companies are replying? Are we reaching the people who really make the decisions? For consumer promotions, where are they coming from? Analysis will tell us that our better customers may come from certain-size cities, or particular regions.

For example, the success of our television commercials for Mutual of Omaha are, at a glance, first measurable by the number of calls received. But some calls come from states where a particular policy is not available. And even those who buy a policy are not all the same, according to the client's actuaries. Depending on age and area, they are more or less likely to have a life expectancy that will turn out to be profitable. And all of this varies by the kind of television spot aired, the stations it runs on, and the dayparts where it is finally seen. Decisions to pull unprofitable stations and add new tests are made every day, as soon as data is available. An extra few days on a weak station or the wrong daypart can be very costly, so this data is compiled and analyzed on an urgent basis, with custom software to expedite the compilations and analytical work.

Other Reports

Inventory Data. What's on order, what's needed, what's overstocked, and how much it all represents as cost of goods. Some companies obtain this data monthly, some weekly, some on a real-time basis with instant updating on a computer terminal.

Returned or Refused Merchandise. A cost factor, an inventory factor, and most important, an indication of promotional overselling or product deficiency. Alternatively, if the returns are for incorrect shipments or poor arrival condition, you know you have to review your picking and packing operation.

Work in Process.   Orders awaiting entry. Correspondence awaiting answers. Shipments stacked up in the warehouse. Promotional mailings held up. Reports on these matters will measure the efficiency of operating departments, and the likelihood of customer dissatisfaction.

Customer Service Reports.   Tabulations of complaints, inquiries, unfilled orders, and damage claims, to help point out problem areas for future correction.

Credit and Billing Information.   If you're selling on credit, you have to track the percentage of customers turned down. You have to know how many are paying and how many are not, what credit cards are being used, and how many customers are being turned over to collection departments.

Quality Control.   Spot checks should be made of all operations and departments to determine how well work is being done, in addition to other reports that indicate how fast it's being done. Computer programs should be checked. Work in process should be sampled and reviewed. Dummy orders should be put through the system and compared with the service being offered by the competition, which should be similarly monitored.

Reports should be compiled on everything for the information of department heads and management. Error rates should be recorded, as usually they are more significant when expressed as a trend than in themselves. An increase in error rate is a cause for concern in any function.

Productivity and Employee Reports.   Since fulfillment operations often are personnel-intensive, cost controls depend on the proper utilization of employees. Work loads must be forecast by department, and employees must be reassigned or staff levels revised to meet changing demand requirements.

In addition, the output of employee work groups or individual employees has to be monitored in order to identify exceptional producers or those who may need additional training.

Large mail-order companies such as Sears, Montgomery Ward, and Hanover House were pioneers in establishing productivity standards for office and warehouse tasks. In some such companies, most of the employees are on some sort of incentive plan—one of the major reasons for their fast service and the low costs the company incurs in handling orders.

Continuity Reports.   Organizations selling on a continuity, club, or subscription basis need many additional reports, including acceptance rates by cycle, renewal rates, commitment status, attrition rates, and sales projections.

This list does not include the financial and budget reports that would ordinarily be produced by the accounting department, or the reports prepared by the analysts in the marketing group. However, all reporting will depend on these fulfillment reports as input data for reliable financial projections.

Report Design Considerations

In setting up a direct marketing company's reporting system, there is one standard that is paramount: *usability*. Reports must be in a form that genuinely helps those who must use it, and that quickly indicates the significant trends, events, and exceptions that require management action.

The definition of *usability* depends on the level of management. Operating foremen and department heads may need every detail that pertains to their department. Interfacing departments and senior management may need only highlights.

Most sophisticated reporting systems include comparisons with previous months, previous years, annual budgets, and variances for each—for every single expense line. Other reports turn everything into trend lines, or relate each action to a plan or a profitability standard.

Every department circulating a report should have the responsibility for preparing a one-page summary, in simple language, of changes, exceptions, variances—the information that should be called to the attention of management.

FULFILLMENT PHILOSOPHY

Fulfillment is an operations process with a profound effect on marketing results, and an impact on profitability. The standards of fulfillment practice within a given organization are subject to a series of strategic decisions that, in total, derive from a company's philosophy.

This philosophy must be consciously and deliberately chosen by top management, not left to the sometimes myopic preferences of line managers. Let's look at some possible extremes, as a framework within which commonsense midpoints can be defined.

"Stop the Deadbeat"

Not a year goes by when I don't find that a zealous credit manager has guided ever-obliging programmers and customer service personnel on a course of "throwing out the baby with the bath water."

If credit is the priority, the philosophy begins with the offer. No credit at all is permitted. Merchandise is shipped only after checks have been received, deposited, and cleared. The weeks this adds to shipping time materially increase returned merchandise. More important, orders and reorders are materially decreased from a credit proposition.

Under this policy, a customer's claim that an item arrived broken may become the subject of lengthy correspondence, or a false claim that a billed item never arrived will be looked up and invalidated, and a collection process begun.

"The Customer Is Always Right"

This is preferable in terms of short-term expense reduction and long-term corporate reputation. In this philosophy, account look-ups are minimized, returns are accepted without checking shipping dates, and credits are issued on the customer's word.

The problem is that there are always some bad apples in the customer barrel who will take advantage of this policy. However, depending on the relative costs of products and fulfillment practices, it may actually be less costly to overlook the abuses and concentrate on pleasing the 99 percent who are the bread-and-butter customers.

"Cost Efficiency Über Alles"

Let the engineers and cost accountants reign supreme and you'll have a different emphasis: cutting costs ahead of all else.

Maximum efficiency in managing operating costs is important, of course, but it should not be attained at the expense of customer service. Daily batches are more efficient than continuous processing, and weekly batches more efficient than daily ones. This reasoning can lead to filling orders once a month.

Personal letters and phone calls are costly, both outgoing and incoming. One company, after finding that customers objected to having collect complaint calls refused, solved the problem by having their phone number unlisted. Very efficient! But is it smart?

Manpower planning finds peaks and valleys a nuisance. It's a lot easier to let a backlog of orders, payments, returns, and entries stack up so that personnel are fully utilized. One company built a wall to hide unprocessed returned merchandise from visiting management, rather than hire the people to process the returns. No, this is not a joke. I've seen the wall!

"A Rolling Stone Gathers No Loss"

"Keep it moving. Get it out. The customers are waiting." This should be the cry of every supervisor and department head.

Fast order turnaround and shipping materially increases customer satisfaction and sales levels. Slow handling leads to correspondence, refusals, and returns. Slow handling of correspondence leads to more correspondence, with higher and higher levels of anger and annoyance.

The industry standard is to deliver merchandise to the customer within two weeks of their mailing the order, and in even less time if the order is telephoned. "Allow six to eight weeks for delivery" is a phrase that may legally permit inefficiency and poor planning, but that doesn't justify it from the customer's point of view. One industry joke tells of the customer who goes down to the corner to mail an order and then, upon returning home, looks in the mailbox to see if the package has arrived yet. The joke may not be funny, but the expectation is a real one in the mind of the consumer; the closer we can all come to realizing this fantasy, the stronger our entire industry will be.

Every marketer should read through aggravated complaints and letters to government regulators. Such letters almost always begin with a phrase like "I've written three times and no one answered." Often there has been some kind of form response—but one so vague, so impersonal, so noncommittal that the customer did not even realize it was a reply.

"If I'm Your 'Dear Friend,' Why Don't You Know My Name?"

Nothing can so quickly destroy the illusion of a personal communication or a relationship-building program with customers as spelling the recipient's name incorrectly. The same applies to company names.

We know that the first thing people look at when they look at an envelope is their own name. And we also know that there is genuine annoyance if it isn't right, or if a Mr. becomes a Mrs., or if an executive's incorrect title is listed. People's names are icons representing themselves. They deserve to be treated with respect. Yet errors are rampant in most direct mailings.

One problem is the tendency to have large-scale data-input projects assigned to offshore countries where labor rates are lower. Though the operators may be efficient, they cannot be expected to spot names that seem uncommon, or to interpret the notoriously bad handwriting of most Americans. Where possible, they should be matched to other lists, such as compiled phone lists, before adding them to the file. Where there are contradictions, a decision should be made as to which source is most likely to be accurate. They also should be scanned by people with reasonable familiarity with common names, and the odd ones compared with the source document. When each prospect has a high value, these names should even be confirmed by telephone.

The simplest solution is to get the name right in the first place. Coupons should be large enough so that a name can be printed clearly. Some companies even insist on providing separate blocks, to encourage care in doing so. If the name isn't legible, the easiest way to check it is with a phone call or postcard inquiry when it first comes in.

Telephone responses should be keyboarded directly, which eliminates visual errors but adds phonetic ones. It is thus up to the operator to listen carefully and confirm spellings, particularly unusual ones. Yet most phone staffs are pressured to finish each call quickly, with no bonus for accuracy. Perhaps this emphasis should be reversed.

THE BIG PICTURE

If our service is not what we'd like, it may be because we have not set standards, defined policies, and established correct criteria. Systems designers and programmers, like copywriters, can be infinitely creative in meeting objectives and solving problems, but someone has to tell them what is wanted.

Computers originally were introduced as a way to improve customer service. Today, they are more often the excuse given for slow, inaccurate service. Don't blame computers; they do only what we tell them to do.

The place to begin good customer service is in the original advertisement or mailing piece. Don't make promises you can't keep, or guarantees you can't fill. Make the coupon clear and easy to fill out, with plenty of space so that your customer can print clearly.

Screen out the deadbeats before they get on your books. Screening by maintaining deadbeat lists or using outside services is cheaper than collection efforts. Offers that require some payment will knock out the professional coupon-clipper, and quality media and lists usually will produce quality business.

Go after the right customers in the first place, and treat them right in return. Good service is good business.

BACK-END
PROMOTIONS

The many direct marketing efforts discussed in previous chapters are sometimes referred to as *front-end promotions*. The equally vital techniques for making these customers, once acquired, profitable buyers of our products and users of our services are called *back-end promotions*.

In direct marketing, back-end promotions are particularly vital. Each new customer usually represents a sizable investment in advertising cost. Customers don't have to walk out of the store to abrogate this investment. They don't even have to make a negative decision. The effect is the same if they simply do nothing. Our hard-won customers—even those with the best of intentions—start to fall by the wayside from the very first contact.

Perhaps they simply inquire but don't buy. That's understandable. But what about the customer who orders and decides not to keep our product? Or the one who, worse yet, keeps it and doesn't pay for it? What about the retail customer who tries our product or service once, but never again?

HARNESSING INERTIA

One principle that helps us understand the dynamics of customer behavior at the back end is *inertia*. *Merriam-Webster's Collegiate® Dictionary*, Tenth Edition, defines *inertia* as "a property of matter by which it remains at rest or in uniform motion in the same straight line unless acted upon by some external force." Inertia is a human characteristic as well, and it can work for you or work against you.

Inertia is your ally if your proposition is a "club" with negative option, or a series of publications or products sold on a "ship-till-forbid" basis. It is your ally in the travel field if your customers have your company's reservation number in their pockets or by their phone, or in banking if they have authorized any type of automatic investment, sale, or savings—particularly with payments charged to an existing checking or charge account. It works for you in the packaged-goods field if your brand is accepted, valued, the first to reach for under normal circumstances. It works in the retail or catalog field if yours is the first place customers go to for certain items.

However, inertia is a formidable obstacle to be overcome for most marketers. Imagine this scenario. A customer returns from a hard day's work, greets the family, kicks off shoes, and collapses into a favorite chair to look at the day's mail. There are magazines to read, a letter from an old friend, a bill that demands attention, and an assortment of mail from both local and national advertisers. One of them is yours.

Your letter asks buyers to buy something that they have somehow managed very well without for all their lives thus far, to decide which of several models or subscription terms is right, to calculate not only the price but shipping costs and sales tax, to remember sizes, to find a charge card or write out a check—all right at that moment. Lotsa luck!

Some might say, "If people want my product, they'll go to the trouble to write a letter or deal with a complicated order form." In theory that's correct, but inertia gets in the way. No matter how good your deal, you will lose business because some people will put it off until later, and then just never get around to it. In most cases, "later" means "never."

OVERCOMING PROCRASTINATION

All this brings us to another important principle that should be kept in mind when planning back-end promotions: *procrastination*. The need for immediacy or urgency, more fully discussed in Chapter 12, Creative Tactics, applies just as much to the back end—but with greater opportunities for effective application. Expiration dates, limited supply, impending price increases, and special introductory offers all have greater credibility with a previous customer than with a front-end prospect.

EFFECT ON ALLOWABLE MARGIN

Chapter 19, Mail-Order Math, explains the concept of allowable margin: the portion of the selling price available for a combination of advertising (new-customer acquisition cost) and for contribution to advertising and overhead. Chapter 23, Database Marketing, and my separate book of the same name (McGraw-Hill, 1993) use similar approaches to determine the lifetime value of a prospect name added to a marketing database. The importance of back-end improvement becomes obvious after one has done some final projections this way.

Let's postulate a product with a $100 sales cost and a $40 allowable margin. In this example, the back-end figures include existing conversion, collection, return, and unit-sale experience. Imagine that we can devise an offer to sell some type of accessory costing $30, with a $15 margin and a $5 back-end cost per order, to one-half of our customers. This might be, for instance, a "bounce-back" promotion—an insert sent with the product shipment or other acknowledgments of the order. In this case, the supplementary contribution is $10 per order on one-half the orders, or a $5 overall addition to the new order margin (the total contribution, divided by the total number of customers). If our new-member advertising cost was $25 before, leaving us a $15 contribution per new customer, the effect of the back-end improvement—an additional $5 margin—goes directly to the promotion's bottom line and gives us a $20, rather than a $15, contribution per new customer. This one-third increase in profitability is the result of the back-end promotion.

Another way to look at this is to calculate what improvement in cost per order you would have needed to get the same result. In our example, the new-member advertising cost would have had to be improved by 20 percent—from $25 to $20—in order to get the same result. For instance, a 4 percent direct mail response rate would have had to become 5 percent.

One reason this is so important in understanding direct marketing is that there are business propositions that appear to be patently unprofitable, unless you understand the dynamics of the back end. There are magazines that lose money or, at best, break even on the first year's subscriptions, making their entire profit on advertising or renewals. There is at least one company selling incredibly low-priced maps or books, whose real aim is to amass sizable lists for promoting their other products and for renting to other direct mail users.

The balance of this chapter will be devoted to describing a score of possible back-end promotions. Almost all of them are adaptable, at least in theory, to virtually every type of product or service.

RESELLING EFFORTS

Every field has some type of reselling effort. The retail clerk tells the customer, "That looks wonderful on you!" The packaged-goods company prints a resell message on the box or label. The restaurant reprints a good review in the menu—a way of saying, "You've made a good choice in coming here." Direct marketing is no different.

In its simplest form, the resell effort can simply be a restatement of the basic appeals that motivated the customer to purchase from the original advertisement, commercial, or mailing piece. The less considered the purchase, the greater the need to resell at the point of delivery.

For example, one company advertised a revolutionary way to rid one's backyard of mosquitos and other insects without electrical grids and the noisy sound of bugs being zapped all night long. This was certainly an appealing-sounding item. However, the item delivered was basically an electric fan that sucked in slow-flying insects and dropped them in a tray of water to drown. Whereas the original appeal had presented the idea of relaxing in your hammock without annoying insects, the focus now was on the instructions, which indicated a need to periodically empty the water tray filled with assorted bug carcasses. Ugh! Of course, return rates were high.

A resell insert can change the focus back to the ultimate benefit to the customer. It should restate guarantees, and dramatize the manufacturer's offer to try the product for a reasonable amount of time before deciding. It might use a kind of peer pressure to tell, perhaps in letter form, how many people have ordered and reordered the item. A few testimonials certainly help to delay the decision to return a purchase.

If an item requires complicated assembly or operating instructions, care should be taken—even at the expense of rewriting the instructions completely—to make the use of the item as easy as possible.

If an item was sold as a prestige-giving asset, perhaps with some type of club membership or air of exclusivity, this should be carefully restated and consistently presented.

No matter what imagery was involved in motivating the original purchase, it should be carried through consistently in every aspect of this first impression: the shipping package, the wrapping, the bills or shipping documents. It is amazing how often a well-presented product advertised in a sophisticated magazine is fulfilled in a battered manila shipping envelope with tacky, uncoordinated inserts.

If you must generate additional income by accepting package insert enclosures from other companies, then at least be fussy and accept only those whose offers and appearances enhance your own product. Bargain offers of pantyhose, no matter how meritorious in their own right, simply have no place in the initial shipment of a Zubin Mehta recording to a new member of the classical division of a mail-order music service.

Resell involves not only the communications included with the product, but the entire first impression.

TRADE-UP PROMOTION

"Here's the shirt you asked for, sir," says the clerk in the haberdashery store. "Let me show you a beautiful tie that will go perfectly with it."

"As long as you're buying such a fine car," the automobile saleswoman says, "I'm sure you'll want the deluxe radio with stereo and CD player."

Trade-ups have long been accepted in retailing, but they have still to gain general acceptance in the direct marketing field. Yet they represent one of the easiest profit potentials for most ongoing propositions.

The front-end application is simple. "Check this box and we'll send you the deluxe edition for only $5 more." The deluxe edition might mean only a better binding, an extra section, or stamped initials.

The back-end application isn't so simple. It often means devising accessories, companion pieces, or refills of some kind. Encyclopedias offer yearbook subscriptions. Products offer large economy sizes. Services offer an extra premium for a longer term.

Perhaps one of the most innovative examples of a trade-up offer is the way sophisticated magazine advertisers are using direct-response television combined with inbound telephone. The two-minute announcement offers an introductory subscription at half the newsstand price: "One year for only $12." The customer calls an 800 number and the telephone operator takes the necessary information: name and address. Then comes the trade-up offer: "Instead of the one-year offer, ma'am, I can enter your subscription for two years for $20—a savings of 58 percent."

For $5 collectible-coin advertisers, I suggested offering a silver version for $50. More than 10 percent accepted the trade-up, the equivalent of ten unit sales of the original coin, doubling the total dollar volume. This one idea made several propositions successful where they otherwise might not have been.

In magazine circulation promotion, this technique sometimes is called *renewal at birth*. The trade-up effort can range from an elaborate mailer or bill insert to a simple line on the invoice: "Check here for greater savings...."

There are trade-up applications for virtually every product or service, and because they usually enjoy a "free ride" with an invoice or shipment, they are as close as one ever gets in this business to "a sure thing."

COLLECTION LETTERS

When you are selling on credit, sometimes the sale is the easiest part of the marketing problem. Collection efforts, like any kind of direct mail, can vary greatly in effectiveness. Three key factors are *convention, progression,* and *immediacy.*

Convention

The mainstay of any collection effort is, of course, the invoice. It should look like an invoice and be worded like an invoice—not like a colorful promotion piece. An effective mail-order bill often is a computer-printed invoice, complete with account numbers, computer codes, the exact amount, and if possible, a due date.

An initial invoice can include some gentle references to memberships in national credit bureaus, or a reminder that promptness counts when building a credit reputation. In my opinion it should always include an addressed reply envelope, though not necessarily one with postage paid by the addressee.

Convention is the governing force here, as in any kind of direct mail layout. People expect a bill to look a certain way, and if it meets their expectations, it will be treated like their other bills.

Graphically and typographically, even a bill and a payment envelope should maintain the imagery selected for the initial promotion. Even an invoice can look elegant, newsy, personal, or businesslike.

Progression

Subsequent bills traditionally take on added urgency. A gentle "Please pay" in handwriting, or a "Past due" in a formidable rubber-stamped impression will always have a place in any series of collection letters. A friendly note with a message like "Have you overlooked our invoice?" or "Is there anything wrong?" is always appropriate.

Flattery can get you somewhere in collection letters: "This may be a small amount to you, but it means a lot to us" is an effective theme.

Later in a progression of collection letters, the threatening approach has become routine, meaning overused. "Before I turn this account over to our collection manager..." is followed by a change in stationery, signature, and tone: "Please be advised that...."

I prefer a more sincere approach, with handwritten letters, perfumed notes, or a touch of humor. Most severe collection approaches are no longer legal or, more to the point, effective. A really heavy threat usually won't bring in enough money at that late stage to be worth the bad will created. Let the outside collection agencies or lawyers do the threatening. When all else has failed, you may as well turn the account over to collection specialists and let them do their thing in their way—which is much more powerful than the roughest letter you would want to send out.

Immediacy

The urgency principle applies in collection letters as in any other kind of promotion. Letters can have the deadline theme, as in "Last chance to renew without interrupting your subscription," "Last chance to reinstate your subscription," or "Last chance to pay and maintain your present excellent credit rating with us."

Billing letters are designed to collect money as their primary purpose, but there is another objective as well. That objective is to collect the money without endangering the basic customer relationship.

Notations such as "If you have already paid this invoice, please disregard this request" may reduce the level of correspondence somewhat, but customers still get very annoyed if they receive bills for accounts that already have been paid. Many companies wait a full month after the first bill to give customers a chance to make payments before getting the next bill. In this way the prompt payers—the largest and most valuable group of customers—are spared the annoyance of getting the second bill at all.

CONVERSION EFFORTS

How do you turn an inquiry into a sale? A trial subscription into a full-term one? An unused credit card or charge account into an active customer? A catalog request into a catalog sale? A simple kit buyer into a steady customer? An occasional customer into an active member of your marketing database? The answer: every way you can.

Conversion is the payoff effort to every type of two-step promotion. Traditionally, the first response, sometimes called the *acknowledgment package,* is an all-out effort to make every point you have to, in every way—to make the sale now or never. This is where the blue-chip brochures, broadsides, samples, letters, and testimonial flyers come in—and usually pay off. This is the first impression, the opening curtain, the grand climax, and the finale all rolled into one.

Your prospects asked for this package, in one way or another. They have identified themselves as prospects. They are almost sure to open the package and at least look through it. You have their names, addresses, and perhaps other information that makes it possible to highly personalize your communication. With a high order ratio expected, you can afford to do it right. This is no time to hold back.

Assuming that you have pulled out all the stops, your marketing problem here is not just to overcome buyer concerns but to deal with your real obstacle: procrastination.

The recipients who don't want your product or service, perhaps because of cost, aren't going to be persuaded to buy something they don't really want—no matter what you do. The presold prospect who has just been waiting for the specifications and an order form will buy it if you send a bundle of mimeographed pages. The real target is the person in the middle—the one who needs your product but can live without it, who would like to have it someday but has more pressing needs, who definitely wants to buy it but puts aside the order form to fill it out and mail it "someday."

For this prospect, you need "the works": facts, proof, guarantees. What is even more important, you have to overcome inertia. The key to making the conversion effort work is to provide effective motivations for acting now rather than later. Some examples:

- A packaged-goods advertiser offers a unique gift for purchasing several packages of their product—enough for the customer to get used to the flavor and buy it out of habit.

- A shoe company offers a free wallet with the first order from its catalog sent to a customer who buys a low-priced item advertised in a Sunday newspaper supplement.

- When filling a customer's initial order, a photo processor includes a coupon good for a 50-cent credit or a free enlargement.

- A car rental company offers a free roadmap book the first time their newly issued credit card actually is used.

- Political and philanthropic fund-raisers provide a moral incentive to act now, in the form of an immediate need: funds for a major television campaign; to finance a special effort in a key state; to get a tractor to a needy village in time for harvest; to feed a particular hungry child whose name, background, and photograph are enclosed.

- In one of the highest-unit sales efforts around, a precut home fabricator offers preseason specials—for each season.

That last example offers price discounts, offers of free insulation, and bonus garages—all for acting now, this season, rather than the next.

If the acknowledgment package is too heavy to go by first-class mail, a fast, simple letter is usually in order, thanking the customer and promising the requested information. This is sometimes called a *keep-warm letter.*

However, even with every possible device in the initial acknowledgment package, only 40 to 60 percent of the potential business will be derived from the order form it contains. The initial package should be just the beginning of a series of communications designed to remind and resell the customer. The main purpose of these mailings is to restress urgency and to make an order form available at the time when, because of personal finances, biorhythm, astrology, or change of mood, the prospect finally is ready to take the plunge and follow through on the interest expressed when the inquiry or trial originated.

Follow-ups can take many forms, but all should be aimed at combating inertia. They can include carbons of the original letter, reminders of special-offer deadline dates, and announcements of new special offers with new deadlines. To make each mailing look different, they usually should stress different points. One may have a testimonial emphasis, another may dramatize the guarantee, and still another may be a sincere letter from a company officer.

How many efforts should a conversion series include? As many as you need to do the job. As long as the allowable margin continues to exceed the order cost, try another mailing. You can always cut back if the last one doesn't pay. Usually my clients end up with between six and eight mailings in this type of series. Some companies, with large lists and sophisticated analysis methods, have refined follow-ups to the point of varying the eventual number of follow-ups according to the source. High-quality leads will justify more efforts than those from less desirable sources.

When I was marketing director of LaSalle Extension University, the number of mailings in my conversion series varied according to the course being sold, but always included half-a-dozen efforts. Our best approach was to gradually make it easier to enroll, with lower initial payments or shorter commitments with each effort, never lowering the overall tuition.

Table 18-1 shows a typical mailing series—a composite of several successful ones. It's a good starting point for your own experimentation with conversion techniques.

TABLE 18.1

	Effort	Theme	Offer
1.	On receipt: first class mail	Thanks: information on way	None (This is a keep-warm letter.)
2.	On receipt: bulk mail	Basic acknowledgment	Premium for fast action by date
3.	Two weeks	Carbon copy	Premium reminder
4.	Four weeks	Testimonial	Premium expiration
5.	Eight weeks	Letter from president	Premium extension
6.	Twelve weeks	Guarantee	Easy payment or low down payment
7.	Sixteen weeks	New premium announced	New premium
8.	Twenty weeks	Benefit theme	New premium reminder
9.	Twenty-four weeks	Questionnaire (Include referral request.)	Premium expiration
10.	Thirty weeks	Last chance	Prices not guaranteed later

If the value of the order is high enough, this series may be supplemented by telephone calls following up the letters at key points and making the same offers. The calls—starting with introductions such as "Did you get our letter?" and service offers such as "Do you have any questions?—can be effective if they are done well. However, care should be taken so that resentment about the telephone intrusion doesn't hurt overall response. Phone selling will show a quick lift in directly attributable sales, but it could depress the overall return depending on the script, the skill of the caller, and the sensitivity level of the typical customer.

What happens after letter No. 10? Do you write the name off and dispatch it to direct marketing limbo? No, just move it into a general file of previous inquiries to be solicited all over again, once or twice a year. House lists including such names as former customers, inactive members, and subscription expires always, without exception, become the most effective and profitable mailing list for subsequent promotions. Each name goes full-circle and becomes ready for the whole gamut of front-end approaches.

RENEWAL SERIES

Whether you have a home repair service, a term insurance policy, a membership of some sort, or a periodical subscription, renewals are the key to profitability.

In magazine subscriptions, one of the most demanding of all direct marketing fields, the first attempt to convert a trial offer to a full-rate subscription is called a *conversion* because the introductory offer is customarily at a lower price than the ongoing renewal rate. Perhaps 50 percent of initial subscribers "convert," and 80 percent of those who have already converted "renew."

The same type of ratio applies to any renewal effort. Because the expected response rate is so high, it is once again economically feasible to devote a major effort to this process. As in conversion or collection efforts, it is not uncommon to use a six- or eight-letter series over a period of months.

However, unlike conversion efforts, the major efforts in renewals are usually not at the beginning of the series but toward the end. Inertia is already on your side, and the writer should presume an intent to renew rather than dramatize the need to make a decision. A major sales effort presumes nonrenewal. A simple invoice or reminder presumes that no change in the inertia-driven status is expected.

The most effective opening renewal notice is, therefore, the simplest. Most publishers today use a "turnaround document," a simple notice and card designed to be mailed back to the publisher. To be consistent with the convention theory discussed in Chapter 14, I prefer that such cards be as official-looking as possible.

One technique is to ask the customer how many years of renewal or how many refills they want, or whether they want the plain or deluxe edition this year, rather than asking for a yes-or-no decision. This technique is based on one of the earliest examples of sales psychology: Coca-Cola's advice to restaurants to ask whether a customer wants "a large or small Coke" rather than "Do you want something to drink?" It is now accepted practice to invite a current member or subscriber to choose the "large or small" renewal without featuring the negative alternative. After all, the negative choice can be expressed by not responding at all.

Many companies combine renewal and billing efforts by asking for renewal only with payment, at least in the first few mailings. Later in the series, they offer the "Bill-me-later" alternative. This is one of those details that differs from one company to the next and should be tested, analyzed, and modeled financially.

A typical series begins about four months before the expiration of the series, unless the subscription was so short that only a few months have gone by since the first issue was received. After the first renewal effort, skip a cycle—that is, wait two months instead of one—before sending out the next effort. So many renewals are received on the first effort that you want time to get the responses before sending out the next mailing, which will then be a substantially reduced quantity. Perhaps 25 percent of the total response will come in from that first mailing, and avoiding a second bill will save the cost of answering a great many letters from people telling you that they have already paid or renewed.

The subsequent renewal efforts can then get a bit more urgent, with specific references to forthcoming expiration dates, missed issues, or possible reinstatement. Toward the end of the series, it is sometimes advisable to resell the benefits of the product all over again, to use sincere appeals, to devise questionnaires, or otherwise to dramatize the basic selling themes of the proposition.

As with conversion efforts, the length of the series may vary according to source. The economic analysis determining whether more letters are justified will show different results when different groups of members or subscribers are reviewed.

Some interesting experiments have been conducted with early-response incentives. The classic renewal series might offer a full-price renewal at the beginning of the mailing series and switch to a special introductory offer when the name gets placed in the expired file. Some companies have tried the reverse. A special incentive is offered for early renewal, justified by "saving us the trouble and expense of sending more notices." The approach is a very interesting one, though few publishers have used it. I suspect that the cost of sending the incentive to all subscribers (even those most eager to renew) might not be justified by the added renewals. Also, the added renewals at the beginning of the series may simply be accelerated responses that are offset by lower response later on.

For example, a premium or discount may cost $1 and result in a 10 percent increase in response. The effective premium cost of the increased response is $11, because the same premium has to be given to the original ten customers who would have responded anyway, as well as to the one additional customer.

It is a shame that renewal efforts, like billing and conversion efforts, are so often considered routine. Some companies use professional creative sources for their front-end material but feel that this type of letter is so simple they can handle it themselves. Yet the truth is that such back-end efforts demand the same care and expertise as any other part of the promotional effort, because the net effect on profitability is usually greater than the result of a slightly increased front-end response.

One additional approach to renewals is to build the renewal process into the proposition. There are three ways that this is being done that might apply, in principle, to other businesses as well.

One is the book club bonus-books system, in which the membership continues after satisfaction of the initial commitment. An offer such as "One book free for every two you buy" is sometimes dramatized with bonus coupons.

The second is the automatic shipment authorization, in which the publisher of an annual—say an encyclopedia yearbook—has built into the original agreement an authorization to ship and bill the product each year. Usually the customer is granted the option of returning the book without further obligation or shipments.

The third is the automatic renewal technique, where the original offer guarantees "the lowest rate available" for future renewals, and builds in the order for renewal. The only problem then is billing. One major advertiser has used such an offer without a material decrease in initial response. This advertiser later found that the automatic renewals held up, but that excess correspondence made the offer not worthwhile.

The same general principles apply to non-mail-order applications, such as packaged-goods database programs. For example, new triers of a product for infants were given a catalog of deeply discounted merchandise premiums that could be obtained only with proofs of purchase. A liquor offer sent to users of competing brands included not only an incentive for trial but also gifts that could be earned for subsequent purchases. Various cigarette companies, and even a manufacturer of motor oil, have published catalogs of merchandise that could be earned the same way. And what else are all the frequent-flyer, guest, and buyer programs but incentives to renew the commitment to a brand?

REACTIVATION TECHNIQUES

An attempt to keep a former relationship active or to reinstate it is a form of renewal, but it is actually closer to the front-end promotion in theory and practice. Every front-end creative and offer approach can be used in attempts to reinstate former relationships, with the single addition of reminding the customer of the previous contact.

One client, Avis Rent-a-Car, had millions of "Wizard Reservation Numbers," but found that a large percentage were completely inactive. The gamut of programs developed ranged from free gifts with the next rental to simply reissuing the stickers bearing the numbers. (The numbers originally were sent on labels, with instructions to affix them to a credit card, and the labels were discarded when the cards expired.)

Another interesting example was the RCA Music Service mailing, which referred, in giant ink-jet type showing through an envelope window, to the previous date and type of music: "To Mrs. Jones—our 1993 classical music member." This type of "We've missed you" mailing is used by many large mailers. Reactivation efforts are so profitable that this technique belongs in any direct marketing program.

Discover, the credit card issued by Sears, had millions of cards issued but relatively few in use. They had to be reactivated with a large-scale contest promotion: the more you use it, the more chances you have to win. American Express, which constantly analyzes usage patterns for credit reasons, uses the same information to identify cardholders to contact with letters and even phone calls. Land's End sends a particularly involving letter: "Have we failed you in any way?"

REFERRAL PROMOTIONS

Prospect lists are valuable assets to any company, and database building is an important activity to be considered. List-building activities come in many forms, but the most common are member-get-member (MGM) and get-a-friend (GAF) offers.

In the simplest form, you ask customers for a list of friends who might like to receive a catalog, learn about your service, or receive news about your activities. Such a request can be minimal—a P.S. on a letter or brochure in direct mail, or a message in or on a grocery package, or a simple display in a retail store.

One common theory is the "birds-of-a-feather" idea. Good customers tend to send in names of other potentially good customers. Bad customers tend to send in names of other potentially slow payers. Therefore, requests for names often are included only in package inserts, mailings to converted buyers, or early-stage invoices—never in dunning letters or initial conversion packages.

More ambitious programs actually recruit present customers as salespeople to some extent. Record clubs often enclose a brochure that a club member can give to a friend. Such brochures contain the basic offer and an order form or membership application. The only difference is that there is a space for the recommending member's name and address. The sponsoring member usually is offered a free gift or credit for recommending the new member.

Because the brochure has to contain the entire sales story and an application or order form, it is usually a multiple-page pamphlet. The same brochure may have a detachable flap containing the offer to the sponsoring member.

Some political candidates use mailings to their core supporters, asking them to each get five or ten new contributors by distributing the enclosed envelopes and pamphlets. This is a notably successful technique if there is genuine enthusiasm for the particular candidate. The same idea often is effective for religious fund-raisers.

Incentives to sponsoring members may include just about anything. I've seen bonus books or records, gifts matching those given to the new member, simple premiums, contest entries, and silver dollars. The gift can be as much as you are willing to pay for a new customer or member, less the allocated costs of the brochure.

CROSS SELLING

- You are an insurance agent with a list of people who have bought life insurance. How do you sell them accident insurance, property insurance, and retirement plans?

- You are a bank with a large number of checking account customers. How do you sell them savings accounts, Christmas clubs, traveler's checks, and home mortgages?

- You run a neighborhood gas station and have taken the trouble to get the addresses of customers who come to you for gas. How can you sell them auto repairs, tires, and oil changes?

- You are a toiletries manufacturer who has built a list of buyers of your perfume brand. How can you get them to try your line of cosmetics?

These are just a few of the many types of cross-selling opportunities. They exist in virtually every field. If you have a basic list of customers who are satisfied with their previous dealings with you, but you don't have a second product to promote, often it is worthwhile to develop a new product, or act as a retailer for someone else's product, in order to take advantage of the tremendous opportunity that cross selling offers.

The basic principle to utilize with cross-selling promotions is, once again, inertia. The present relationship is a bond to build upon, which is a far easier process than establishing a new relationship.

The application of this principle demands that you start with the present customer relationship, not only by reminding the mail recipient about it but by making the new offer appear to be a continuation in every way: in name, copy style, graphics, and offer structure.

One of the best cross-selling case histories I know was created for a large New York banking institution. As automobile and other loans were paid off, the bank sent out highly personalized mailings inviting customers to continue to make the same monthly payments as before, but as deposits to their own savings accounts rather than loan payments. The mailing piece included a computer-printed letter, a computer-filled account form, and a series of coupons bearing the customer's name and account number and the amount of the previous monthly payments. This mailing, tailoring the savings-account product to the present relationship by utilizing the familiar payment-coupon format, is an excellent application of both the inertia concept and the principle of convention.

Another example, also in the financial field, is the growing tendency of investment brokers, including such prestigious firms as Merrill Lynch and Dreyfus, to dramatize the liquidity of their investment vehicles by issuing checkbooks for instant access to funds. Merrill Lynch has since gone a step further by issuing Visa cards offering not credit but instant access to the holder's entire net worth deposited with Merrill Lynch. This concept has since been made available by Dean Witter and other major stockbrokers.

A simpler example of cross selling is one used by Time-Life Books. This enormous, highly sophisticated organization produces "libraries" of books on various subjects—animals, boating, history, cooking, and so forth—all sold by ship-till-forbid subscription. Once a relationship has been established with a subscriber to any one of these libraries, that subscriber is cross-sold other libraries, single books, videos, magazine subscriptions, or other products of the Time Warner family.

In the simpler efforts, statement stuffers describing one library are inserted with shipments and invoices for others. A unique technique of Time-Life is to make a cross-sell offer on a perforated extension of the billing invoice. The necessity for handling the extension when paying the bill assures its being noticed and relates it directly to the customer's present point of contact with Time-Life Books.

Cross selling presumes, of course, that your product and service have been well received. I know of one converse example: a photo-finishing concern that changes its name periodically so as to attract customers who would not do business with it again under its original name.

This type of offer not only introduces customers to other products, but can help to attract new customers as well. Mailings and on-pack messages offering a sample of another product or a savings coupon actually add value to the first offer.

REORDER SOLICITATIONS

Giant mail-order corporations devote the bulk of their marketing activity to sending catalogs and mailing pieces to their vast, scientifically segmented mailing lists. Merchandising departments are constantly looking for new items and analyzing previously used ones. Mailing lists are segmented by type of purchase, unit sale, type of product, and original source, to enable them to vary the frequency and scale of the promotions sent to each group of customers. Price-oriented buyers sometimes are sent only sale catalogs. Buyers of certain types of merchandise are offered specific specialty catalogs.

The number and scale of catalogs has evolved over years of testing and ranges from simple flyers to full-color volumes, localized for various regions and seasonalized for spring, summer, winter, and pre-Christmas.

On another scale, many smaller companies have a fall catalog as their most important and profitable effort. Unless they have segmented active buyers who merit year-round promotions, or they have seasonal merchandise, they can barely sustain one more catalog in the spring season. When a second catalog isn't profitable, it can often be revitalized by drastically changing the format, adding a sale theme, or restricting the size of the mailing compared to the pre-Christmas effort.

Of course every "free-ride" opportunity should always be taken advantage of. Statement stuffers—four- to eight-page flyers enclosed with bills—often are extremely profitable, as are bounce-back solicitations enclosed with merchandise shipments. Some types of companies (photo finishers, for example) have built their entire back-end business on bounce-backs enclosed with processed film. Often their promotions include some type of extra incentive: coupons good with the next film-processing order sent in by a certain date, credit certificates representing unprocessed prints, opportunities to conveniently enter a contest or sweepstakes, and most often, frequency bonus certificates.

These certificates can be used in virtually any kind of business. They involve enclosing some type of value voucher with each shipment, or some type of card that has to be punched or validated in some way. When five certificates are saved, or the card has been completely punched, they may be redeemed for another item free.

Back-end promotions require a strong commitment to positive thinking. If you are sending out your first catalog, don't get discouraged if the results seem disappointing. That's only a starting point. Take the result figures apart, piece by piece. Some lists or list segments probably were profitable even if the overall mailing wasn't. Some items in the catalog or some pages probably did well even if the total result was in the red. Find your strong points and build on them, even if they steer you into an entirely different product line or market than you had originally intended. A little objectivity can go a long way in direct marketing.

LEAD SELLING SYSTEMS

All the principles discussed above also apply to using leads. Converting inquiries by direct mail is a two-step proposition. In such a case, the lead selling effort is basically the conversion system outlined previously.

More often, leads are used because the second step is not only by mail but through some type of personal selling. Once a lead has been obtained, it is turned over to a telephone or field selling organization for further contact. This contact, in turn, can go directly for the sale, try to establish an appointment in the home or office, or invite the prospect into a sales office.

The simplest type of lead selling system is one used by Dictaphone for their dictating equipment. The lead, once obtained, is simply transcribed onto a multiple-part document and turned over to a local independent dealer. The dealers are expected to report on the disposition of the prospect (sold; no interest; bought other), but no added preselling support is given to the dealer at all. This can be effective only in those rare situations (so rare I don't know of one) where management believes that all members of their sales organization—in all parts of the country, new salespeople and old—are consistently effective at following through on leads and turning them into sales.

An effective lead selling system, in my experience, should sell the prospect as well as the salesperson or dealer. I recommend that a conversion-type series of letters be sent to the prospect independently of contacts by the sale force or dealer.

These mail efforts can be designed to persuade the prospect to visit the dealership or to call the salesperson for an appointment, or simply to keep interest in the product or service alive until the salesperson gets there.

International Gold Corporation had been giving dealer names to phone inquirers without any follow-up at all when I was invited to design a new Krugerrand marketing system. The one I put in provided for capturing the names and addresses of callers and forwarding the name to not one but three dealers, who then had to compete to make the sale. A five-letter follow-up series was sent to the prospect, not only selling the inquirer on the basic proposition but asking for the order on behalf of any of the three recommended dealers. All any dealer had to do was give a telephone price quote and arrange for delivery once the check had been received. In this case, our confidence level in the dealer organization was relatively low, necessitating a particularly high degree of preselling.

Even sophisticated sales organizations have conflicting priorities, varying confidence levels, and conflicting motivations. Salespeople have to be sold on following up leads. A very dramatic example of this occurred when two different offices of a major business equipment company followed up the same type of leads. One office was enthusiastic about leads and followed up every one by a telephone sales call; the other was skeptical and put in a minimal effort. The conversion rate in the enthusiastic office was 300 percent greater than in the other.

Salespeople and dealers are human beings, and like other human beings they don't want to be rejected any more than they have to be. This simple psychological fact results in what we call *prescreening*. This is what happens when a salesperson sorts through leads and decides, "This company isn't large enough," "This title isn't that of a decision maker," or even "This handwriting indicates someone I'd rather not have to do business with."

When I was vice president, marketing, of LaSalle Extension University, in the years before government regulations crippled the correspondence school business, I had inherited a system in which inquirers were mailed a school catalog and everything else was left to the salespeople, who eventually converted about 15 percent of the leads sent to them. In the meantime, in rural areas where we had no sales representative, a mail-order conversion sequence was signing up 10 percent of those leads completely by mail, without having to pay a substantial sales commission.

Our new system gave the lead to salespeople for only 60 days. They had this initial period to make their sales on a protected basis. After that, we cut in the mail-order sequence, with monthly letters, brochures, and a variety of premiums and trial offers, just as we had done in the rural areas. The result was amazing. We picked up an additional 5 percent conversion in mail-order sales even after the sales force had supposedly "worked" the leads. Amazingly, the average salesperson's conversion ratio, at the same time, increased from 15 to 20 percent. Counting the mail-order conversions, we were now getting 25 percent conversion instead of 15 percent. You can imagine the phenomenal effect this had on the bottom line. It seems salespeople increased their efforts for two reasons: one, they could no longer procrastinate because they would eventually lose their protected exclusivity, and two, they didn't want to be embarrassed by the mail-order department's turning up new enrollees from leads they supposedly had worked.

Did salespeople resist this new system? Sure. But only until they found that, despite their worst expectations, they were making more money. Also, we were able to sell them on the idea by demonstrating that the higher total conversion would make it possible for us to significantly expand the lead-procurement budget and provide each salesperson with a greater flow of leads than before—which we did. This simple change in the back-end follow-up system helped LaSalle to grow threefold in only two years.

An ideal lead system should be flexible. Too few leads discourage a dealer or salesperson. Too many result in the leads being "burnt off"— not given the full attention they would deserve if the salesperson had more time for each lead. New computer systems make it possible to issue leads to a sales territory automatically, to adjust lead flow according to past conversion experience for individual dealers or salespeople, and to adjust territories by spilling over surplus leads to salespeople in adjoining territories. Ideally there also should be an early warning system for the sales and marketing managers if any territory is getting too few leads. With timely information, territories can be revised, salespeople can be transferred, and supplementary lead-generation systems can be activated so as to provide leads in a dry area.

SPECIAL SITUATIONS

There is no way to anticipate every situation that may arise in the course of running a direct marketing business, but here are four unusual ones that may be of help to some readers of this book: cancellations, handling credit turndowns, out-of-stock situations, and dry-run testing.

Cancellations

Many subscription, continuity, and club relationships most typically end in a cancellation of some sort. Rather than the company dropping the customer as unproductive or because of slow payment, the customer writes "Cancel" on an invoice or returns an automatic shipment.

In the past, the cancellation was entered, the record dropped from the active file, and that was that. Since the previous edition of this book I have suggested to several clients that they make one last effort to reactivate, usually by telephone. A well-trained phone operator asks if there was a problem, expresses concern, and asks for another chance. Often the cancellation was a correctable annoyance, such as too frequent mailings of a product "of the month," or objection to too many scent strips and blow-in cards in a magazine. This simple step not only pays out in restored business, but also provides information that can be used to reduce annoyances and irritations that generate cancellation requests in the first place.

Credit Turndowns

Inevitably a certain number of new orders other than prepaid orders have to be turned down because of credit risk. This may be because the customer appears on a bad credit index or because of probability, as indicated by zip-code experience or other factors. Some companies just ignore the order; others send brutally frank letters. My own recommendation is to try to save the situation by tactfully switching the credit request to a cash order.

When turning down a credit order, first of all attribute the turndown to lack of credit information rather than to bad credit information or zip-code probabilities, either of which is bound to create ill will and useless correspondence. Then, instead of a cold turndown, offer a special cash deal. One record club, declining to send the advertised "6 records for $1" offered a no-strings-attached plan that let the customer select one free record for every one purchased, on a cash-with-order basis.

Out of Stock

A common situation with catalog houses and other mail-order vendors of products is the out-of-stock situation. FTC requirements now specifically spell out standards and procedures for notifying customers if an item can't be shipped within 30 days, and giving them an opportunity to cancel the order. These procedures should be followed to the letter not only because it is the law but because it is good business.

Even 30 days is too long to keep customers waiting when they have ordered something they want for themselves or as a gift. Don't substitute an item or send a different size or color, without explicit authorization from the customer, and don't keep customers on the string waiting for suppliers to replenish inventory. A prompt, no-nonsense letter explaining the situation is in order, along with a reply card giving the customer the option of waiting, canceling, or selecting an alternative. Where possible, a substitute should be specifically recommended. If the unit sale is large enough, a phone call may be in order, preferably followed up by a written notice and response card.

Dry-Run Testing

Dry-run testing is another problem for advertisers. Current regulations make it impossible to solicit payment for a product that is not yet ready to ship. Yet there are times when we want to test various factors before the product is complete: sizes, packaging, premiums, and prices.

A Knapp Publishing dry-run test for a *Bon Appetit* "Wine Journal" was able to determine whether or not to offer a leather-bound trade-up edition, whether to offer a premium, and which of several price levels would be most effective.

Such offers should be clearly labeled as preview or prepublication offers, and no prepayments should be accepted. If credit card charges are solicited, it should be made very clear—and scrupulously arranged for—that no credit charges will be processed until the item is ready to ship. Also, though this is not necessarily a legal requirement but certainly an ethical one, these test orders should be fulfilled, when finally ready to ship, at the lower of the new price or the price originally offered.

As you can see by the wide variety of techniques presented here, there is as much room for creativity and strategic planning in back-end promoting as in the more glamorous and highly visible front-end promotions. This type of program is not merely an adjunct to a good marketing program; it is an integral and vital part.

19

MAIL-ORDER MATH

In earlier chapters I have described direct marketing as both art and science, but it is first and foremost a business. As in any business, the fundamental objective is profit.

In direct marketing, each individual promotion can be evaluated in terms of profit or loss. Each mailing list, advertisement, or TV schedule can be examined as if it were a subsidiary business, and decisions can be made to expand that business or close it down.

While television and database marketing have their own applications, the underlying principles of direct marketing economics should be understood by anyone planning or executing any kind of direct marketing program.

To a certain extent, mathematics is the instrument of reality. It cannot be faked. If you spend too much money on a slick mailing piece, it will show up on the bottom line and may well make the difference between profit and loss. If you modify a headline or offer and improve response rates by 10 percent, a proposition that has previously produced a 10 percent profit can more than double its profitability.

Direct-response broadcast and infomercials produce less predictable responses, and success often depends on the ability to respond quickly to result information. In database marketing, name value must be determined first, before building or acquiring a list, depending on the calculation of lifetime value of a current or new customer. And with all the glamour of and excitement about new interactive methods, their final success will depend on the question so many of them are still avoiding:

the relationship between costs and sales. This will be discussed in coming chapters on these subjects, and will continue to evolve as the methods evolve. But for these applications, and others not yet conceived, a basic understanding of mail-order math is still the basic foundation.

THE BASICS

Cost per Response

CPR can refer to cost per lead, cost per member, cost per subscriber, or any variation that is relevant for a particular business, but the formula is always the same. Simply divide the cost of the ad or mailing piece by the number of responses:

Promotion cost ÷ number of responses = cost per response

There are some refinements that should be remembered. If you are doing a direct mail test campaign in small quantities, be sure to base your evaluation on what the campaign would have cost in quantity, rather than on the higher cost of the small test campaign.

Also, if you are testing in a relatively less efficient season, estimate what response you would expect in the better season when you would run the full campaign.

Allowable Margin

Allowable margin (AM) is what is left after you have paid for the product, shipped it, and written off any credit losses. In its simplest form, it is the amount of money available for profit and overhead after you have deducted every expense except advertising.

For example, let's say a widget costs 50 cents to make, 25 cents to package, and 25 cents to ship. The $1 total is subtracted from the selling price. If the selling price is $2, the AM is $1.

If, in addition, 10 percent of those ordering the product fail to pay for it, then that 10 percent is deducted, making the allowable margin only 90 cents.

Many advertisers add a charge per unit for administration or overhead before figuring the margin. In such a case, the AM is profit before advertising cost.

Profit per Response

Deducting the cost per response from the allowable margin gives the profit per response (PPR). If the figure is positive, you have a successful mailing; if negative, an unsuccessful one. The allowable margin concept, not used in ordinary accounting practices but a traditional approach in direct marketing, provides a simple rule of thumb for planning and evaluating promotions.

Return on Sales

This is the simplest and most common measure of profitability: the percentage of total sales that can be called profit. Return on sales is simply the profit on a business or promotional effort, divided by the sales.

Return on Investment

Increasingly, the standard of measurement is return on investment, or ROI. Sophisticated companies with diverse product lines and distribution methods rely on this standard to determine where to allocate their resources. Investors and bankers, deciding which companies to buy stock in or lend money to, also look at ROI. Catalog specialist Jules Silbert defines it as the net profit earned in a year divided by the average amount invested in the business during that year. In direct marketing, this investment consists of the average inventory, the accounts receivable, the plant and equipment, and the average amount of cash needed to cover payroll and other current expenses.

THE RETURN ON INVESTMENT MODEL

To simplify an understanding of return on investment analysis in the direct marketing business, Brian Hopkins uses two models: one for simple mail-order sales, and another for two-step or lead-generating businesses. Hopkins, as managing director of DMS Associates in Durban, South Africa, works with a wide variety of business and consumer organizations that now use this model.

Figures 19-1 and 19-2 are shown with examples filled in for specific applications. Basically, measuring the ROI calls for an analysis of the interplay of expenditure, market size, potential response, and potential contribution or profit. A variance in any of these four factors will have an impact on the return on investment.

In these models, advertising expenditure is referred to as PROMO COST, which in turn is made up of a cost-per-thousand rate, TOTAL CPM. In print or broadcast, this figure may be the media cost. In direct mail, it is the product of the mailing components, postage (POST CPM), printing and lettershop (MATERIALS CPM), and list rental costs (LIST MEDIUM CPM). The circulation, audience, or mailing quantity is shown as DISTRIBUTION QTY in this model, and is multiplied by the response rate (% RESPONSE).

GROSS MARGIN is the potential contribution, calculated from the value of each AVERAGE SALE. The percentage cost of sale or cost of goods sold (% COGS) is subtracted from total sales to arrive at the gross margin. The % COGS figure represents either the total of manufacturing or distribution costs and overhead, or a marginal cost factor.

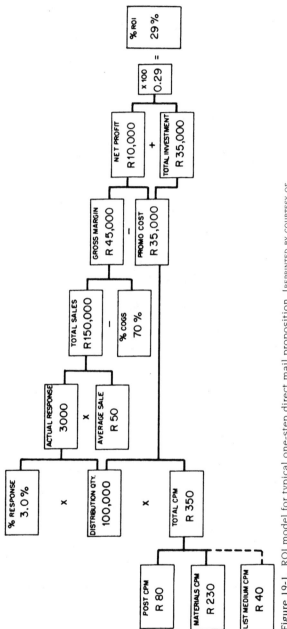

Figure 19-1. ROI model for typical one-step direct mail proposition. [REPRINTED BY COURTESY OF BRIAN HOPKINS]

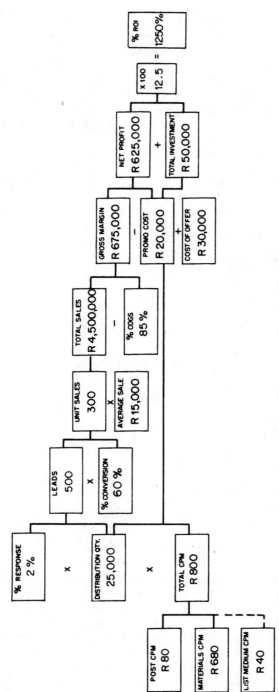

Figure 19-2. ROI model for typical two-step proposition, adding leads, conversions, and space for cost of offer. [REPRINTED BY COURTESY OF BRIAN HOPKINS]

To determine return on investment (ROI), subtract the total promotional cost from the gross margin to arrive at the NET PROFIT. Then divide this figure by promotional cost or total investment to arrive at a ROI factor. Simply multiplying by 100 then provides the % ROI figure.

Figure 19-1 shows the chart figured for a typical direct mail campaign. Note that "R" refers to South African Rands; the reader need only substitute dollars or another currency. The principles are the same.

Figure 19-2 is a modification providing for two-step marketing. Two blocks have been added: LEADS and % CONVERSION to determine the number of sales (UNIT SALES).

Another block appears in this example, COST OF OFFER, which is applicable to either one- or two-step marketing. This factor provides the cost of the incentive to respond: a booklet, premium, loss leader, initial introductory shipment, or whatever.

This model is a handy way to quickly test the interrelationships between different costs, response rates, media costs, and other factors. It often shows, for instance, that the higher response rates of direct mail do not justify its expense compared to media such as magazine and broadcast advertising.

MORE ECONOMIC CONSIDERATIONS

Here are some more factors that everyone in this business should be familiar with.

Conversion Rates

If you are offering a free booklet and then converting the lead into a sale, you will be concerned with conversion rates. The same term applies to a credit order, a trial subscription, or a membership. These transactions are not considered sales until they actually have been paid for.

If you have 1000 inquiries and 200 of them become buyers, you have a conversion rate of 20 percent. As an algebraic equation, this would be expressed

$$\frac{\text{Buyers}}{\text{Inquiries}} = \frac{\text{conversion rate (X)}}{100}$$

This kind of simple equation is resolved by cross-multiplying 100 times buyers equals X, the unknown conversion rate, times inquiries. You then divide both sides by the number of inquiries in order to isolate the unknown X factor. But it is not necessary to use this equation.

On a calculator, simply enter the smaller number of buyers and divide by the larger number of inquiries, then move the percentage point two places to the right. If your calculator has a percent key, press that rather than the equals key, and the two places will automatically be moved over for you.

Renewal Rates

Renewal rates are determined in the same manner as conversion rates. The term generally is used in analyzing the profitability of a subscription or service sold on an annual basis. Typically between 40 and 60 percent of first-year subscribers renew for the second year. Of these subscribers, perhaps 80 to 90 percent will renew in subsequent years. In the circulation field, these subscribers then are called *renewed renewals,* or RRs.

Attrition Rates

If you are selling a proposition on a continuity basis, or in a club that requires a purchase every month or cycle, you will have to deal with attrition. This is the number or percentage of "starters" (initial customers or subscribers) who drop out at the end of each cycle by canceling, failing to meet a purchase commitment, or not paying. Typically 50 percent or so will not "convert" by making the first purchase, dropping off by 5 or 10 percent in subsequent cycles—that is, as a percentage of those who survived the previous attrition.

Units per Response

In calculating profitability, take into account the number of units per sale. This can vary substantially, and can make the difference between success and failure. Usually a single-unit offer that has a gift appeal will produce anywhere from 20 to 50 percent more units than orders—a factor to be considered when projecting or analyzing profitability.

Average Take

In a catalog or club, you know that not everyone will buy from every mailing. If you expect 20 percent of your customers to make a purchase, the average take is 0.2. If half, then it is 0.5. One major club, with a tight definition of "active member" and strong incentives for multiple purchases, enjoyed an exceptional 1.2 "take" per cycle.

Name Value

All financial projections should provide an allowance for the value of a name—either for future sales as part of a company's house list, or as a contributor to list-rental income. This factor is an estimate of the net value as a name only. You cannot include the entire income, because future promotions will require both product and promotion investments.

Such house lists are worth at least twice what an outside rented list would be worth, and can be presumed to be rented internally at twice what you would pay to rent an outside list. The balance of the name value is an estimate of the number of times you or your list broker believe such a name would "turn" times the net income, after brokerage and computer costs.

Time Value

Some advertisers plan to break even the first year, then make their profits on subsequent years' reorders or renewals. Continuity plans and clubs make large up-front investments with the intention of pulling ahead months later as additional purchases are made.

The value of the money tied up in advertising and premium investments should always be taken into account in long-range planning. Whether you borrow money from a bank or you simply don't have your own funds available to invest, the current interest value of money is a factor to be considered. If interest rates are at 10 percent, then $1 invested now has to return $1.10 a year later just to break even. All long-term planning should be weighted for this time-value factor. Tables are available that show the value of a dollar in the future as compared with the present, at various rates. Similar tables show when it might be more profitable to take 90 cents now rather than $1 later—the reverse consideration. Your banker or accountant can supply such data easily.

CATALOG SPACE ANALYSIS

If you are mailing out a catalog or any type of multiple-item proposition, you will want to analyze not only the total proposition but also the profitability of each individual item in the catalog. This involves treating each page or fractional page unit as if it were an advertising promotion of its own.

Divide the cost of the entire catalog by the number of pages. For instance, if the catalog costs $90,000 and has 48 pages, of which 3 pages are used for covers and ordering information, then each page is worth $90,000 divided by 45, or $2000. Similarly, half a page is worth $1000, a quarter-page $500, and a tenth of a page $250.

In calculating the profitability of each item, the cost of the space has to be added to the cost of goods and to shipping and overhead costs.

If an item is very profitable, you will want not only to repeat it in future catalogs but also to enlarge the space used to feature it. If an item is unprofitable, you can either drop it or reduce the size of the space allocated to it.

What products will be successful will vary widely, depending on the positioning of the catalog merchandiser and the lists used. The results per item are examined individually and by category, to guide future selections and spacing. It is important to look for patterns—product type, price range, style, uniqueness, or markup percentage—so as to find the unique key to each catalog's profit potential.

Often it pays to do a separate calculation of this type for major list categories. It could be desirable to produce segmented catalogs with different merchandise for different list categories.

ANALYSIS MODES

The simplest report is a list of media in inverse order of cost per response, or a list of copy tests with "percent lift" indicated next to each.

The simplest profitability study involves taking the difference between allowable margin per unit and cost per response per unit, multiplying it by the total number of orders received, and indicating the total profit or loss.

Unfortunately, the simplest reports usually are not enough. Tables 19-1 to 19-4 show some examples of other reports prepared by Pierre A. Passavant (copyright DMA) and provided by the Direct Marketing Association.

The sample in Table 19-1 relates rollout costs to test costs, which is simply a matter of restating the cost per order as if the package were mailed at a quantity price.

Table 19-2 would apply equally well to any medium. In this analysis, line 3 represents a cost per inquiry, calculated from a magazine's cost per thousand circulation and a response rate. For magazines, it would be simpler to divide the space cost by the number of responses and get the same figure, without having to refer to circulation or response percentage. This example would be more applicable to direct mail; a cost-per-thousand figure would appear on line 1 and a response rate on line 2.

Line 4 takes into account the cost of the mailings designed to convert the inquiry into a sale, multiplying it by the number of mailings in line 5. This case indicates only four packages at an average cost of $400 per

TABLE 19-1
TEST VERSUS ROLLOUT COSTS

Test package	Quantity	CPM	Response	CPO
Cost	10,000	$600	4.2%	$14.29
Rollout cost	100,000	$270	4.2	6.43

TABLE 19-2
CONVERSION RATE IMPACT (TWO-STEP EXAMPLE)

1. Magazine CPM	$18.00
2. Response to ad	0.3%
3. Cost per inquiry	$ 6.00
4. Cost per conversion effort	0.40
5. Four conversion efforts	1.60
6. Total cost of inquiry and conversion	7.60
7. Cost per order:	
10% conversion	76.00
15% conversion	50.67
18% conversion	42.00

thousand. Telephone conversion costs might also be added at this point, along with the costs of a computer firm to handle the incoming mail.

Line 6 combines the cost of acquiring the lead (line 3) and converting it (line 5) to produce combined cost of inquiry and conversion series.

Line 7, then, is merely a projection of what the eventual cost per order would be at various conversion rates. You can see how dramatically changes in the conversion rate affect the CPO. Increased conversion effort costs are usually insignificant compared with the profitability of increasing the percentage rate, which is why six- and eight-part conversion series, with added telephone efforts, have become commonplace in this type of promotion.

Table 19-3 includes every factor applying to the profitability of a direct mail promotion, presuming a simple cash offer with 40 percent of the customers electing to pay by credit card and the others by check. It also indicates a 5 percent customer correspondence factor, 10 percent returns, and 3 percent bad debt.

Note that this analysis shows the profit and loss (P&L) in terms of total dollars rather than unit costs. While CPR and AM figures are handy for planning, P&Ls should always be in terms of real dollars. Table 19-4 then breaks down, in greater detail, the fulfillment costs included in line 7 of Table 19-3.

Table 19-5 shows the relationship between various profit objectives and the response rate needed. In this example the contribution per sale and the package cost are the same as in the preceding example. Note that only a 16 percent increase in response rate—from 2.4 to 2.8—is needed to produce a 100 percent increase in profit.

Back-End and Front-End Analysis

Common terms in the direct marketing business are *front end* and *back end*. Front end measures the initial cost of attracting the inquiry or first order, whereas back end evaluates how well those inquiries convert to a buyer status. The sum of the front end (inquiry cost) and back end (conversion cost) is the total cost of acquiring a new customer.

While great emphasis usually is put on obtaining the lowest possible cost per front-end response, ultimate success in attracting new customers depends just as much on back-end factors: what "quality" of customers were attracted; how effectively they were converted to initial and subsequent purchases; whether they paid; and how long they stayed active as customers, members, contributors, subscribers, or whatever.

A direct marketer can "hype" an offer with a sweepstakes or an exceptional premium, only to find that the incremental customers pull down the overall allowable margin and thus lower profit rather than raising it. More often, an added response rate up-front more than compensates for back-end deterioration. Either way, it is essential that back-end performances be monitored and that basic offer changes be postponed if possible until performance data is available.

TABLE 19-3
SIMPLIFIED PROFIT AND LOSS WORKSHEET FOR DIRECT MAIL PROMOTION

100,000 Packages Costing $280 per Thousand, 3.2% Response or 3200 Orders

	Unit value, dollars	No. of units	Total dollars
1. Selling price	$32.95	3200	$105,440
2. Plus shipping and handling	1.95	3200	6,240
3. Gross order value	34.90	3200	111,680
4. Minus returns (10%)	34.90	320	11,168
5. Net sales	34.90	2880	100,512
6. Cost of goods (delivered)	7.31	2944	21,521
7. Order processing, shipping, returns costs, customer service, and credit fees	4.53	3200	14,494
8. Premium (keeper)	1.20	3200	3,840
9. Promotion (CPO)	8.74	3200	27,968
10. Bad debt (3%)	34.90	86	3,001
11. Overhead (15%)	5.24	2880	15,091
12. Total expenses			85,915
13. Profit	5.07	2880	14,597
14. Profit % to net sales			14.5%

Explanatory Notes

Line Explanation

1. The price of the item is $32.95. In this example there are no deluxe options or accessories that might increase the price. If there were a separate deferred payment price (higher than the cash price), this line would show the weighted value of cash and installment orders.
4. 10% of gross orders received and shipped are returned by the buyer.
5. Net sales are orders left *after* returns but *before* bad debt.
6. The cost of goods delivered to the shipping point is $7.31. Each sale incurs this cost. In addition, it is assumed that 20 percent of returns cannot be refurbished and therefore become an additional product cost related to each sale.
7. This line includes mail opening, sorting of orders, credit approval look-up, transfer of checks and charges to bank, capturing customer identification and order history, and making shipping label. It also assumes an average charge card fee of 3.8 percent—lower for bank cards, higher for travel and entertainment cards such as American Express. The fee applies to 40 percent of the orders that are charged. Customer service includes complaints, inquiries, and special requests by customers; affects 5 percent of orders. Collection effort covers cost of following up on slow payers. See detail in Table 19-4.
8. The customer keeps the premium—even if the merchandise is returned.
9. The promotion cost assumed 100,000 packages at $280 per thousand, and a response of 32 orders per thousand, or 3.2 percent.
10. Some checks bounce, and some credit orders are erroneously approved by the company. This amounts to 3 percent of net orders after returns.
11. All other expenses (management, plant, equipment, insurance, utilities, etc.) not accounted for in items 6 to 10. The percentage comes from last year's history or this year's plan.

NOTE: Additional costs that could affect this profit, but which were not allowed for above, are cost of borrowed funds, retail credit checks, installment billing, and markdowns or merchandise disposal.

TABLE 19-4
DETAILS FOR ORDER PROCESSING, SHIPPING, RETURNS, COSTS,
CUSTOMER SERVICE, CREDIT FEES, COLLECTION

	Unit cost, dollars	No. of units	Total dollars
Business reply postage	$ .21	3200	$ 672
Order processing and customer setup	1.00	3200	3,200
Credit card fee @ 3.8% on 40%	1.33	1280	1,702
Customer service on 5%	8.50	160	1,360
Collection effort on 7.5%	2.00	215	430
Shipping and handling	1.95	3200	6,240
Returns postage on 10%	1.70	320	544
Returns handling on 10%	.60	320	192
Returns refurbishing on 80%	.60	256	154
Shown on line 7 of worksheet	4.53	3200	14,494

TABLE 19-5
RELATIONSHIP BETWEEN CONTRIBUTION TO PROMOTION AND
PROFIT AND RESPONSE RATES

$14.77 Contribution per Sale at $280 per Thousand Packages

Campaign objective	Profit per $34.90 net sale	Amount available for promotion ($14.77–$ Profit)		Promotion response needed ($280 ÷ $ Prom. per order)[†]	
		Per sale	Per order (10% returns)	OPM	Percent
Break-even point	$0	$14.77	$13.30	$21.05	2.1
5% profit*	1.75	13.02	11.72	23.89	2.4
10% profit*	3.49	11.28	10.15	27.59	2.8
14.5% profit*	5.06	9.71	8.74	32.03	3.2

*Percent to net sales †CPM/CPO = OPM

SEGMENTATION ANALYSIS

In the most elementary form of segmentation analysis, direct marketers
evaluate individual lists, publications, or stations, not entire campaigns.
In any campaign, some media perform better than others. It is axiomatic
that in future seasons we direct marketers will expand our usage of those
that did well, seek others like them, and drop those that did poorly. The
criterion is profitability, and using CPR and AM, we can quickly tell
which are likely to perform satisfactorily in the future.

Simply list all the media sources in inverse order of cost per
response—those with the lowest CPR first. For those on top of the list,

look for additional media with similar audience characteristics. For the ones on the bottom, drop them or find a new proposition to appeal to them. For those in the middle, proceed cautiously with test extensions. Over many years of direct marketing's history, this simple process was the key to planning future media campaigns. Then came segmentation, in progressively more complex forms.

Internal Segmentation.   This is the analysis of a medium by its built-in categories. The results of an ad in a magazine or in *The Wall Street Journal* can be related to the publication's geographic editions. Perhaps a national ad is marginal, but if only the best three-fourths of the circulation are used, it may turn out to be very profitable. Some larger advertisers use different propositions in different geographic editions of Sunday supplements so as to place the most profitable ones in each area, while still enjoying the economies of a national buy.

A run-of-station buy on a television station may also be marginal, but a breakdown of the results by different dayparts might show that it would be very profitable if you bought weekend only, nighttime only, or whatever the proposition called for.

Direct mail is especially sensitive to internal segmentation. With both house lists and rented lists, it is possible to break down results into a wide variety of segments: recency of purchase, size of purchase, type of purchase, original source, and demographic data. Credit card and insurance companies usually have age, income, marital status, and similar data available as well.

Any available characteristic can be analyzed in terms of relative responsiveness. Either assign key numbers in advance to predetermined segments, or arrange to analyze repondents in comparison with the characteristics of those mailed to.

There is room for imagination in defining segments. One client suggested converting birth dates into astrological signs and looking for patterns according to the supposed characteristics of different signs. Another suggested an age, or age-of-children, breakdown, on the theory that people at different points in the life-cycle will have different purchasing proclivities.

External Segmentation.   This refers to the analysis of characteristics that are not intrinsic attributes of the media. Generally applicable to direct mail, this form of breakdown has become a valuable tool for more sophisticated direct marketers.

There are many degrees of external segmentation. The simplest is the identification of areas of the country that produce either less than acceptable response rates or, in another dimension, acceptable member quality. In its purest sense, this would involve tracking the number of pieces mailed to a particular zip code and determining whether the response from the individual zip code was ultimately profitable. Unfortunately, such samples tend to be much too small to analyze in this pure sense.

At one time, such analyses were done by state. When zip codes came in, some companies started to analyze profitability and quality by sectional center. Both of these are very gross parameters. The most scientific application of this approach is cluster analysis, as popularized by Claritas and now available from several companies. Their refinements group zip codes together according to the latest available census data, as updated by commercial projections of population trends. In this way zip-code responses, mailing quantities, and eventual pay-up rates are assembled into patterns according to any and every type of data available in the latest U.S. Census.

Not only the obvious parameters, such as age, income, education, and home ownership, can be included, but also less obvious ones. *Field & Stream,* for instance, was found by Claritas to be most effective when they sent their mailings to zip codes with a high incidence of freezer ownership!

Knowing the characteristics provides a tool for the refinement of list purchasing beyond gross list selection. Desirable areas can be selected, or undesirable ones purged when the initial list buy is made. In print media, tougher credit standards can be applied to zip-code clusters that are likely to produce poor-quality business.

The added cost of a select or a suppress factor when buying lists is very small compared to the savings involved.

Zip-code analysis is not the only method of external segmentation. It is possible to match lists according to individual-name telephone book data, such as length of residence, single- or multiple-family occupancy, and ethnic last-name indications.

Financial institutions have been able to use what may be the ultimate form of external segmentation to predetermine the names to which they will mail offers of preapproved lines of credit. Names of prospective customers are sent to major credit bureaus such as TRW to precheck acceptability of credit, based on information in the organization's files. While many good prospects are screened out because of lack of available credit data, those who do match are already qualified. Credit cards, preapproved "instant-loan" plans, and other financing instruments are often sold this way. While the front-end results from such lists may be smaller than if larger and more responsive segments are used, the back-end quality makes this process worth its very high cost.

Decile Analysis

An extension of segmentation analysis, *decile analysis* is the practice of statistically analyzing the responsiveness of each segment of a mailing program, dividing the results into 10 segments, each representing 10 percent of the total, and then listing them in descending order of profitability. The top-performing segment, 10 percent of the total, might bring in 20 percent of the sales or profits. The two top deciles combined, or 20 percent of the total, might yield 35 percent of the total profits, etc.

This type of analysis generally lists each segment individually and then on a cumulative basis. Fixed costs such as overhead and mechanical production are not allocated but assigned as a lump sum at the beginning. Thus you can readily determine the optimal mailing quantity.

If you mail too small a percentage of the total, the fixed costs will not be offset. If you mail too large a percentage, you will be reaching down into the less profitable segments of the total.

The risk/return ratio also is obvious in such an analysis, as there is a point at which the next 10 percent of advertising investment would yield a much smaller percentage in profit increase, a factor to be considered in terms of overall objectives.

Decile analysis properly refers to a report breaking the total into 10 parts, but the practice and the name have been applied to breakdowns of 20, 50, or more segments as well.

Dimensional Analysis

In a hypothetical analysis of 10 lists, list categories, or lists arranged by profitability (see the previous discussion of decile analysis), it is presumed that some will do much better than others. Though the overall result may be good or bad, within that result some lists are exceptionally good and others very poor. Another possibility is that all may be good or bad, but with relative degrees of performance.

The usual practice has been to draw a line somewhere and decide which lists or groups are worth mailing to in the future and which are not. However, if each list, or each mailing as a whole, is further broken down by zip-code clusters or some other external factor, it is highly probable that the line drawn to designate which lists are to be mailed in the future and which omitted will be diagonal rather than horizontal.

Imagine that a cluster analysis or a state grouping indicates that some parts of the country or demographic groups do 25 percent better than the average and others 25 percent worse, and that these groups are shown across the top of a report. Down the side you have the lists themselves, the SIC codes for a business list, or the decile groupings or list categories. If these percentages are applied to the lists, either individually or collectively, depending on what kind of valid data are available, this additional result factor will be overlaid on top of the list results. This type of grid analysis usually can be made by combining list results with a zip-code analysis.

The chances are that even the best lists will have some areas that would be better omitted, and that even the worst lists will have some segments or parts of the country that are mailable. Many lists that would have been marginal producers can now be certain of producing a satisfactory profit.

It is theoretically possible to refine mailing-list results on a three-dimensional base, using a computer to compare and weight results for additional factors—say, the lists themselves, zip-code clusters based on demographics, and regional criteria based on other geographic factors such as size of market, area of the country, or weather (for a gardening or recreational product). House lists can be similarly refined based on recency, frequency, and unit sale—the three most important characteristics of customer lists.

Regression Analysis

Interest data from Polk, category and brand usage from Donnelly, individual purchase history from your own transactions. These can all be added to a list and then subjected to detailed analysis. This is the key to what is now called *modeling* and uses a mathematical probability process called *regression analysis.*

The details of regression analysis, and its variations, are more appropriate for a book on mathematics. Mathematicians and database consultants specialize in providing these services, directly to agencies and advertisers or as subcontractors of list compilers.

Generally they will provide such an analysis on a fixed or hourly fee basis, or as part of a continuing relationship with an agency or list supplier. Remember that they only analyze the data provided to them. The fees they quote will depend on the complexity of the analysis, and on the number of factors to be considered. If their client does not already have the data to be analyzed, they will arrange the necessary overlays through list compilers, but this will entail additional costs. It is thus not unusual for such an analysis, when done properly, to cost in excess of $25,000. For most marketers, though, the information developed will be worth any price.

ACCOUNTING PRACTICES

Direct marketing is like any other business, in that the rules of conventional accounting hold true despite the uniqueness of direct marketing. The following are some considerations that the direct marketer will want to learn more about from an accountant or tax adviser.

Inventory Valuation.   What you put in stock ties up capital, and often is subject to taxation. Drop-ship or installment shipping arrangements may be desirable.

Year-End Tax Treatment.   If advertising is expensed rather than capitalized, it may be possible to reduce current-year taxes by sending out mailings at the end of one year—an expense—and taking the resulting sales in the next year. This would defer taxes and make available more capital for mailing.

Capitalized Advertising. If showing earnings is your objective, as with a publicly held company, it appears reasonable to capitalize advertising costs, making them a current-year asset in the year they are paid for, and then write off the expense during the years when the income is produced. This would be most applicable to programs with long-term customer relationships.

Member Value. Direct marketing expenditures—both advertising costs and premiums to attract customers—should be treated as an investment in future sales. If money is put into building a new retail outlet, the expense is capitalized and spread over many years. Yet the money spent on bringing customers into a mail-order "store" often is treated as an expense for accounting purposes, leading otherwise sophisticated companies to bunch up their advertising at the beginning of a fiscal year so as to get back their yield in the same yearly accounting period. This attempt to satisfy artificial accounting criteria leads to poor investment decisions. Recognition of "member value" or "customer value" as an accounting practice—particularly in club and continuity programs—would offset advertising expense and give the reader of an annual report a more accurate picture of a company's fiscal situation.

Reserves. Holding reserves is another accepted practice, to allow for inventory write-off, returns, or bad credit, thus reducing current-year tax obligations.

Hidden Assets. One of the great frustrations of direct marketing executives is the extent to which major corporations fail to recognize the real strengths of a direct marketing business.

For instance, a direct marketing firm's greatest asset is its mailing list, which should be computed at a value based on the capitalized value of its list-rental income and internal solicitation potential. If a direct marketing company is sold, its list is the asset most in demand. Yet most companies fail to give it any value in computing assets or profits.

Similarly, control of key media positions, such as options on back covers or insert card positions, is a substantial hidden asset. So are fulfillment software that works smoothly, result data that guide a company in its marketing decisions, and trained, loyal personnel. Direct marketers accommodate figures to accounting methods; perhaps someday accountants will find a way to appropriately value the industry's greatest assets.

Other mathematical subjects are covered in the discussions of various media and testing. The reader is urged to read the chapters described next, which include other examples of mail-order math and economics.

Chapter 2 includes examples of offer testing and pricing comparisons. Chapter 6 reviews print media buying practices and the quality factor. Chapter 7 discusses the math of broadcast support advertising for preprints and direct mail, as well as the role of the penetration factor. Chapter 10, Testing, includes a discussion of statistical validity, which must always be considered when planning future campaigns. This pertains to the margin of error that should be considered when drawing conclusions from one season's efforts in anticipation of the next season's. Chapter 18 includes an example of the effect on profitability of back-end promotions.

This chapter was not meant to be a course on algebra, statistics, accounting, economics, or business math, for excellent books are available on all those subjects. To acquire more advanced knowledge of the math and finance of the direct marketing field, I suggest that readers enroll in the DMA's course on math and finance, offered in major cities throughout the country. For information, write the DMA Education Department in New York City.

DIRECT-RESPONSE
TELEVISION

It is convenient to think of broadcast as just another advertising medium for direct-response broadcast. In many ways, it is just that. But it is unique enough to merit special attention.

The fact is, many propositions work on television that are unsuccessful in direct mail and other media (and vice versa). Television can demonstrate, convince, and rouse enthusiasm as no other medium can.

As with other mediums, it is segmentable: by market, by station, by day of the week, by time of day, by type of programming. It also is testable—but with more of a trial-and-error approach. While there now are several good analytic approaches to media selection, the key to success is still to get results within hours of a placement, and to revise the schedule as you go.

While few general advertisers have taken advantage of the unique strengths of direct-response television, they have for some reason flocked to infomercials, which are merely a longer-form version. (I have devoted a separate, entirely new chapter to infomercials, and will include in that chapter other comments about how to use broadcast in database building.)

This chapter assumes that strategy, tactics, and copy platforms have been prepared just as they might be for print media or direct mail, but of course recognizing the opportunities and limitations of broadcast. It concentrates on the differences, and details the creative and production steps needed to convert a script into an on-the-air communication.

DIRECT-RESPONSE CRITERIA

The purpose of a direct-response commercial is to generate an immediate order or inquiry. Unlike general broadcast advertising, which only aims to impart awareness or a positive attitude, it must not only stop the reader and leave a positive impression but also convey enough sales argument and ordering information to generate a letter or phone call from the viewer.

In the early days of direct-response broadcast, little consideration was given to the attitudes being created toward the product, the company, and direct marketing generally. Consequently, broadcast direct marketing developed an image of loud, tacky, amateurish, and sometimes dishonest commercials for poor-quality records and fragile kitchen appliances.

Today the immediate objective of getting an answer must be tempered with the longer-range goal of building credibility for the industry and the sponsor. This will pay off in the short range too, as each airing of a commercial is building awareness and attitudes that may lead to improved response at the next airing.

TWO FUNDAMENTAL APPROACHES

There are two distinct philosophies about television direct-response strategies. The traditionalists, sometimes called "the Chicago school," believe that only 120-second spots work, that television produces poor-quality buyers for low-price products, and that production quality is less important than the availability of cheap time.

The so-called New York school, heavily influenced by the experience of the general advertising agencies with which they or their agencies often are affiliated, take a completely different tack. Their premise is that 60-second spots will often work better than 120s (particularly in terms of quality), that production values are extremely important, and that dayparts and adjacencies should be valued in terms of the characteristics of the audiences they deliver, not just the number of sets turned in. "Dayparts" refers to time segments such as Early Morning (6–9 a.m.), Daytime (9 a.m.–4 p.m.), Early Fringe (4 p.m.–7 p.m.), Access (7 p.m.–8 p.m.), Prime Time (8 p.m.–11 p.m.), and Late Night (11 p.m.–conclusion). "Adjacencies" refers to specific programs that the commercial appears before, during, or after.

The dilemma for the student of direct marketing is not to choose one of these two approaches but to recognize that both are valid—but for different types of products and audiences. The choice is not which philosophy to adopt, but which will work for a given situation. Let's look at some of the elements involved.

Length

We used to think that long, involved propositions or difficult-to-explain products or services always needed 120s. Now, after three years of testing the two lengths against one another, I find that the 60-second spot has a better chance of success with most products than the 120, provided it is professionally produced. The reason for this is simple: There is a scarcity of good direct-response time available at preemptible rates. Such time is priced at one-fourth to one-third the price paid by general advertisers, but is subject to being "bumped" (preempted) if a full-rate advertiser wants the time slot. Also, the station manager, who makes the final decision on what to run, is human—with his or her own sense of pride, taste, and self-image. In better time spots, when friends, relatives, and clients are watching, most managers would rather have spots that "pass" as general advertising rather than the old-fashioned scream-'em-into-submission direct-response clichés. These higher-quality spots often work better in the 60 length, and have the additional advantage that more 60-second time slots than 120s are available.

Production Value

The old direct-response cliché is an announcer sitting at a desk in front of a fake bookcase, next to an American flag or a potted palm, holding up a booklet about cancer insurance, desert land, or an effort to save whales, dolphins, or children. A more recent cliché is the smiling announcer, waiting for your phone call and the opportunity to send you a free calculator, telephone, radio, or vibrator—depending on the type of magazine or book club you are being asked to subscribe to.

The New York school of direct response (which is not necessarily practiced only in New York, just as the Chicago school's approach has been known to show up on Madison or Park Avenue) has a different approach. Its practitioners add story value, entertaining or interesting characters, and emotional intensity or excitement. They use mood lighting, musical backgrounds, and even song to make direct-response spots comparable to the best spots people see on their television sets at any time of day or night. The theory is that viewers are less likely to turn their TV sets off when they see these more interesting spots, more likely to believe the messages, more prone to trust the advertisers, and—not to be overlooked—more likely to make positive long-range associations with the products and the companies. The awareness by-product effect, discussed in Chapter 7, is a free bonus of this type of advertising.

Another key factor in favor of high-quality commercials is the station manager, who simply would rather have this type of spot on the station than the older type.

The old-school motto, which justifies buying time slots on late, late movies and afternoon game shows, claims, "The program must be less

interesting than the commercial." The new school, justifying higher production costs to achieve first-quality production values, says, "The commercial must be more interesting than the program." The statements may
sound similar, but the difference in emphasis underlines two fundamen-
tally different approaches.

Product Application

Since there are two approaches, which one should you use for your
company? The old school was established to sell records, knives, and
pots and pans—and it does a fine job for such mass-market, low-priced
products. In fact, direct-response methods were applied successfully to
opening up retail distribution in discount stores, drug chains, and auto
supply stores. If your product would ordinarily be found in such a mass-
market environment, this approach is fine, in my opinion, unless you are
concerned about the long-range image of your brand name.

Prominent advocates of the Chicago school declared emphatically that
only their method worked. At the same time they said that television is
not suited for intellectual or upscale products, for financial services, or
for narrow geographic or demographic appeals. They said television
advertising wouldn't work at all for such products, that it would bring in
only poor-quality business that would not pay off in the long run.

The New York school has proved otherwise, in all of the above categories. Head-to-head tests of commercial spots using emotional appeals,
user imagery, and musical themes outperformed the old approaches
hands-down. In test after test, 60s beat 120s, in most cases. And audience
selection media methods beat the pure bargain-hunting "haggle
method"—in some cases documenting a net back-end effect as good as
that produced by the company's best direct mail lists.

The best possible conclusion today is that poor-quality television spots
are fine if you can settle for poor-quality viewers. In retrospect, it seems
obvious that working people who watch movies or reruns will order better products and pay their bills faster than will insomniacs or game-show
viewers. It seems obvious that intelligent television advertising will
attract intelligent television viewers, and that such viewers are more likely to be interested in upscale magazines, investment products, books,
real estate, or luxury items for their homes.

CREATIVE CONSIDERATIONS

Once the basic philosophy has been established, the creative effort must
begin. In television as in any other medium, the basic creative strategy,
preferably in the form of a creative work plan, must be established. But
the creative skills required are more demanding than those needed for
one-dimensional, silent media. These skills must include an understanding of the unique requirements and capabilities of the medium itself.

Length Requires Pacing

The 60- or 120-second length of typical TV commercials makes pacing an essential creative requirement. The message should begin with an attention-getter: a diver jumping off a cliff, a display of fireworks, a tiger's roar, an airplane taking off, or any high-energy situation involving interesting characters. Preferably, your attention-getter should be relevant to the prospective customer and the theme of the message to follow.

The first objective is to stop the prospect from getting up and going for a snack or visiting the washroom. In the AIDA formula, attention is the first requirement, then interest, followed by desire and action.

The pacing of a commercial requires a pulsing of high and low involvement points. You can't keep the viewers in a continuous state of excitement. You have to bring up their interest, pay it off, bring it back again, and pay it off again—usually five or six times in one announcement.

Credibility Requires Sincerity

Because we are usually asking someone to order a product they have never seen, from an advertiser they have never done business with before, credibility is an absolute requirement.

There are many ways to build credibility. The obvious ones are to state why a product is a good value, well built, and backed by a reputable company. But remember, television, like any other form of communication, is nonverbal. No matter what you say, the tone or mood of the message will do more to establish or destroy credibility than any of the words in the script.

If an announcer is used, he or she must look reliable and sound sincere. This is no place for a flashy sports jacket or the bravado of most used-car commercials. (I don't believe used-car commercials are the right place for such devices either, but that's another story.) The setting, the music, the rates at which scenes change and the camera moves—all must contribute to credibility.

Action Requires Immediacy

Credibility might ordinarily lead you to a relaxed, soothing pacing of the commercial. The challenge is that we also are trying to elicit an immediate action, and that requires a sense of urgency. The announcer must deliver the message in a manner that sounds both sincere and slightly breathless, as if the offer being made is a once-in-a-lifetime opportunity. The skill required to accomplish this is the reason why some announcers demand premium rates while others find it hard to get work at all.

Casting

The choice of actresses and actors is crucial to the finished product, just as it is to a finished movie or television show. Characters in a dramatiza-

Figure 20-1. "Gardening" spot for Mutual of Omaha begins with a "life-and-death" discussion, but in a calm, nonthreatening setting, before turning to the price/benefits message. [COPYRIGHT BOZELL WORLDWIDE]

Figure 20-2. This "Faces of Crime" commercial for ADT Security Systems was designed to dramatize the consequences of not having alarm systems. [COPYRIGHT POPPE TYSON]

tion or demonstration must be believable, likable, and convincing to the audience. They must, in addition, reflect the aspirational goals of the audience, so that the audience can identify with them.

That is, if the commercial shows a magazine being handled by a reader, the actor or actress chosen to play the part should not represent precisely where the prospective viewers are, but where they hope to be; that is, the character portrayed should match the aspirational goals of the audience. Age, sex, and occupation need not be taken literally, but disposition, personality, confidence, and pride must be. Audiences identify with feelings more than with physiques.

Basic acting talent is essential. A model with a pretty face, for example, won't do on television today unless she can also act—play a convincing role. And you can't judge acting ability from head shots or composites. That's why it's worth the investment to use an agency casting department or an independent casting service that will direct actresses and actors in tryouts, let them read lines, and record them on tape. You can then, at your leisure, review the tapes, and see how each person comes across not in the flesh but where it counts for you: on the video screen.

Cost Relationships

How much should a TV commercial cost? It is possible to spend any-where from $10,000 to $100,000 on a television spot. Usually, $50,000 will do the job very nicely. It is also more economical to produce several spots at the same time.

The cost should be related to the size of the schedule and the type of programming. To compete for attention with an old movie requires much less talent and gimmickry than going up against prime-time program-ming and major packaged-goods advertisers, as the general agencies must do with "indirect" commercials.

A typical first-time television test might involve $25,000 in time and $20,000 to $25,000 in ad agency creative fees. To add much more than $50,000 for the production of the commercial would be to unnecessarily increase the downside risk.

If the commercial is a new one for a product line that has already been proved effective in direct-response broadcast, and there is a likelihood that a million dollars or more will be spent on the schedule, then the opposite is true, and no expense should be spared to make the commer-cial as effective as possible. If another $25,000 will increase response even 10 percent, it will pay off on even a $250,000 campaign.

To keep costs under control, the script writer should be aware of basic economics. It's expensive to have large casts with speaking parts, or hordes of extras. Distant locations or complicated sets add to the cost. Night shooting can more than double a commercial's budget. Most important, stay away from the big-name production houses who look down their noses at direct-response television and its cost realities. There are plenty of very fine production houses in New York and elsewhere that can give you what you want at reasonable cost.

Asking for the Order

If you are going to ask someone to remember an address or a telephone number, then give them every possible assistance.

Twenty or thirty seconds should be devoted to the actual presentation of the address or phone number, broken up by a premium sell or a basic offer resell.

Advance warnings help, particularly on radio where there is no visual reinforcement of the number. "Get your pencil ready" may be a cliché, but it's one that works.

It's a good idea to plan a commercial so that these ask-for-the-order seg-ments are self-contained. You may want to test a new price later, change the phone service, or work out per-inquiry deals with stations that want to insert their own local telephone service rather than your 800 number.

It's possible to edit the commercial so that the closing and any super-impositions of price or phone number can be changed later without hav-ing to reshoot the entire commercial.

Offer Modification

Often you cannot use the same offer in broadcast that was developed for print or direct mail. However, the reverse is true: A proven television offer can often be adapted for other media.

As discussed in earlier chapters, an entirely different strategy often must be developed to make the broadcast medium successful—perhaps even pulling for inquiries rather than orders, or changing the basic proposition completely.

Multiple add-ons are effective. "If you act now, we'll also send you this...and this....And if you call right now, even *this!*" Sets of knives, dishes, towels, tools all look impressive when the camera pans the merchandise or as additional elements are added.

Simplified responses are necessary. If you ordinarily give prospects a choice, you may want to offer only one version on television. You can always tell them about an alternate when they call in the order.

SUPPORT BROADCAST

Today, support broadcast is used only by advertisers who are supporting saturation mailings or large-scale print-media campaigns. The economics simply do not work out for others.

Two current examples of large-scale uses of support broadcast are Publishers' Clearing House and Columbia House. For most other advertisers, however, a response lift can be achieved simply by coordinating direct-response television efforts with direct mail drops or other advertising. While the broadcast spots are justified by the responses they produce, there is a measurable increase in response from other media appearing at the same time.

Length

Support commercials are not expected to make the sale at all, and need little time to ask for the desired action, which is to look for an ad or letter. Consequently they need much less time than direct-response commercials, and can be handled well in 30- and even 10-second formats. For some complex propositions, 60s may be used as well. The 10s, however, usually are used only in combination with the 30s, as an added reminder of a message that is being presented in the longer format. They don't provide enough time to do very much on their own.

Variety

When there is a high frequency of support commercials, usually it is advisable to present a few different versions in order to avoid fatigue. Generally these commercials are on the same theme but use a different example or setting. Publishers' Clearing House, for instance, used a series of interviews with prize winners for their direct mail support campaign. The subject matter in each interview was different because of the interviewee, but the theme—demonstrating that people really do win contests—was the same.

Television in support of a catalog mailing, for example, could present a different item in each commercial, but the main theme would be the value of the forthcoming catalog.

Cost Standards

It would seem that a support commercial should be much less expensive to produce. After all, if 120 seconds costs $60,000, shouldn't 30 seconds cost one-fourth as much? Logically, yes, but in reality, no.

It's possible for support commercials to cost even more than longer response commercials. The main reason is the difference in quality required. Support commercials are placed against the best programming in the dayparts they are up against. The adjoining commercials for packaged-goods products will be first-class, highly creative, well-executed commercials. You aren't up against the local furniture dealer or other direct marketers, so you've got to be good. Being good costs money.

Credibility versus Immediacy

Because you are not asking for an order or response in support commercials, credibility is less of an issue than with direct-response commercials, but immediacy is more of an issue.

In most cases, the medium that is being supported is a direct mail piece that is timed to arrive within one or two days of the commercial. It can also be a newspaper preprint or a *TV Guide* advertisement that is appearing the same weekend as the commercials are running. Prospects have to get that publication or look for that mailing piece, and act on it. There is no way for them to write down a phone number and call when they get around to it.

As a result, direct-response commercials can go all the way, to put stress on immediacy. This is the place for the breathless enthusiasm, the proclamation of "big news," the thrill of presenting a wonderful offer.

Support "Offers"

In the simplest sense, the immediate "offer" is simply "Look in your mailbox" or "Look in this Sunday's paper." However, the need to make a sufficient impression to get the message across is as important here as is giving the phone number on a response commercial.

If you are supporting a mailing, marketers agree that it is essential that you actually show the mailing piece. If it is a preprint or other ad, you must show the ad and name the newspaper. "Look in your Sunday newspaper" isn't enough, particularly as there may be several newspapers in any one station's viewing area.

The newspaper should be identified by name in a super (see Video Techniques, later in this chapter) or closing panel. One economy is to have your announcer say "in your Sunday paper" but have the super show the specific newspaper's name. You can change visuals at will, but changing the words the announcer says will require all kinds of extra costs.

The basic principle here is that there must be a visual association between the media. An excellent example is Ed McMahon appearing on both the envelope and on the television commercial.

The Transfer Device

One important innovation in support advertising is the *transfer device*. Attributed to Lester Wunderman, this device offers a premium "just because you are watching this message," as a reward for placing a secret mark on the card in the ad or mailing.

In one move, this ingenious device provides play appeal, immediacy, involvement, and a way of directing attention not only to the advertisement but right to the order form.

Transfer devices have become a mainstay of support commercials. Doubleday offers maps. Time-Life offers posters; their Home Repair Library commercials offer a handyman's apron; their magazines offer an extra issue or a free book. Record clubs offer an extra record. The premium possibilities are endless.

To increase involvement, extra play appeal is added by directing people to turn an S on the card into a dollar sign, or to circle the correct plane or animal, or to write a number in a box. As a plus, the transfer device can be used to measure the relative effectiveness of different commercials. One ad asks people to circle the panda, and the other asks them to circle the polar bear.

Transfer results cannot be "read" in the classic sense. The commercial has to be evaluated on the combined effect of the media being supported and the support costs, independently of the number of people who use the transfer device.

WRITING A TELEVISION COMMERCIAL

All of the steps and disciplines outlined in Chapter 13, The Art of Copywriting, go into the writing of a television script, but the dimension changes radically. If we liken an advertisement to a drawing, then a direct mail piece is like a sculpture and a commercial is like a motion picture.

You have infinitely more than words to create with. The 90 percent of communications that words on a printed page fail to convey all come into play on television. You have a setting, for mood. There's a narrator whose personality and sincerity can come across or not, and there are characters who portray self-image. You have realism, motion, and emotion—the ability to bring words to life. In addition you have sound effects, music, lights, and special effects to add allure, excitement, and entertainment value.

However, all this is no substitute for the sound thinking that has to go into any kind of direct marketing selling in any medium.

Timing the Script

First, take the time you are allotted—whether 30 seconds for a support commercial or 60 or 120 seconds for a response commercial—and set up a matrix on a blackboard or a sheet of paper.

Draw a line representing the length of the commercial and divide it into segments as if it were a ruler, using seconds, not inches, as your unit of measurement. Then break out the main components of your commercial—the "must" ingredients—and see how long each of them will run. For instance,

Opening	10	Here's a different combination:	
Subject sell	20	Opening	10
Product sell	20	Problem	20
Offer sell	20	Solution	10
Guarantee	10	Testimonial 1	10
Restatement	10	Testimonial 2	10
Phone	5	Testimonial 3	10
Premium sell	10	Product sell	20
Phone	5	Phone	10
Immediacy copy	5	Premium	10
Final phone	5	Phone	10

These are not formulas, just examples of how to approach this problem. The contents might consist of examples, demonstrations, case histories, applications, exhibits—any of the most graphic materials available to make the point.

Arrange the blackboard or paper in time segments, such as a frame for every 3 seconds. If you use this measure, draw 20 or 40 lines across the page—one for each 3 seconds.

Then draw a line down the page, dividing it into two horizontal sections. Label the left-hand column "Video" and the right-hand column "Audio," and start writing your storyboard.

Under "Video," describe what pictures will be on the screen. Examples are an announcer, a product shot, a close-up of a product detail, some footage of the product in use, a picture of the factory where it's being tested, or a home or office where it's being used. Include any words you want to show on the screen.

Under "Audio," write your text: the words the announcer will be saying on camera or off, the statements of others, sound effects, musical effects that you know you want. The video and audio should work together and reinforce each other.

Once the first draft is done, read it out loud, with a stopwatch. You'll probably discover that it's way too long. This is where the 10 percent inspiration gives way to the 90 percent perspiration: the careful, calculated selection of what can fit and what can't.

Every visual image requires a few seconds to be comprehended, unless it's part of a flurry of images designed to create an impression rather than be seen individually. Every phrase can be measured in seconds, every word in fractions of seconds. Rigorous selection of what goes and what stays is critical. The writer must play Solomon, and decide which copy point can stay, which must go, and which favorite slogan or play on words has to be sacrificed to nuts-and-bolts copy.

The temptation will be to cut down on those terribly uncreative phone numbers at the end, or to plan for an announcer who can talk faster— whichisfineifyoudon'tcareifanyoneunderstandsanything. In broadcast, the essence of creativity is in the choices you make.

Video Techniques

Once the basic script has been worked out, you can indicate some of the wide choice of effects that are available. Usually the writer thinks at first in terms of home movies, with announcers and scenes following each other. However, the skills and facilities of the production company can give you any effect you have ever seen in a television show or motion picture, including all the effects listed below.

Close-ups.   You can indicate exactly how close you want to get to a person or product. You can show a room full of people, close in on one of them, and then focus on something the person is holding.

In the jargon of the production industry, the group would be a long shot or a medium shot, the single person would be a medium close-up (MCU), a shot of the person's face would be a close-up, and the focus on something in a hand would be an extreme close-up (ECU).

Panning.   Panning is moving the camera sideways, to follow action or simulate it.

Zooms.   If you know what a zoom lens is, the term *zoom* speaks for itself. You can bring the scene closer (zoom in) or move back from it (zoom out). This technique lets you set a scene and focus on one person or object. In reverse, you can start with a close-up that arouses curiosity and pull back to show what it is.

Freezes.   Stop the motion with a *freeze* when you want to call attention to something. A freeze is a good way to relate an exciting scene to its photograph in a book.

Dissolves. One scene fades out, the other in—a much smoother way of changing scenes than the abrupt "cut."

Superimpositions. More commonly called a *super,* a superimposition is the placing of one image on top of another—usually a written message appearing at the same time as photography. Often it's a phrase under or across an image.

Split Screens. You can show two images at once on a split screen, or four on a quartered screen. The images are combined in the editing stage and can be used to add a feeling of motion to an otherwise static still shot.

Other Special Effects. I don't think there is anything you can think of that can't be simulated by the technician in a good production house. You can make images larger or smaller, add type, change backgrounds; you can speed scenes up or slow them down. You can paste scenes together to make new ones, change night into day, and mountains into oceans. If you've seen it on your home television set, there's someone who can do it.

Now that we've covered what you can do, let me add a word of caution, particularly to those producing their first commercial: Just because you *can* do anything doesn't mean you *should.* Too many good scripts are ruined because they get "gimmicked up" with flashy technique that distracts from the main theme.

Audio Techniques

There are three audio techniques that should be used together, in the proper balance: *voice, music,* and *sound effects.*

Voice. The announcer's voice, or on-screen dialogue, will be the primary delivery vehicle for your message. How a message is delivered is as important as what is said. The tone can convey enthusiasm or boredom, sincerity or duplicity. The manner of delivery cannot be specified in the script, except by means of occasional instructions such as "with enthusiasm." Voice is an essential consideration in casting, direction, and editing.

Music. Music offers almost as wide a range of communication as voice, except that it reaches the emotions rather than logic. No one will ever remember your musical backgrounds, behind the voice or as fill-in between spoken passages. They will remember that the commercial was soothing, thrilling, gentle, or powerful. All of these ideas—setting the tone for your message and conveying aural images to your product—depend on the music selected.

Most direct marketing budgets will not be able to afford original scored music, but there is an enormous range of stock music available, particularly in New York and Hollywood, to meet virtually any need. A skilled director can select from available music tapes to give your commercial any feeling you want.

Sound Effects. Since the earliest days of radio, sound effects have been used to convey images: the creaky door for suspense shows; horses galloping and livestock sounds for westerns; bullets ricocheting and sirens in the distance for detective shows—plus bells, explosions, traffic sounds, and in fact anything you can think of.

Sound effects can very inexpensively suggest an off-camera happening. Do you want an announcer to bring a kitchen gadget to a home by helicopter? Do it this way: "*Whirring noise.* BOY: Look, ma, it's a helicopter! *Pilot makes entrance.*"

Want Santa Claus to make an entrance? You can get bells, reindeer hoofs, and the sound of Santa sliding down the chimney.

All of these sounds are available on tape, and it's very simple to arrange to hear the ones you want and to get permission to use them for reasonable fees.

For one commercial we used old newsreels, but the sound tape had a news commentary and so was unusable. We were able to use stock sound effects to put the original's sounds back in.

PRODUCING A COMMERCIAL

In print advertising or direct mail, it is customary to treat production as if it were simply an execution process: setting the type that has been indicated, ordering the illustrations specified, and assembling the pieces into mechanical paste-ups for later printing.

In television, the creative process is only half done with the completion of the storyboard. Television production is a highly subjective process requiring artistic talent, skill, and experience to translate the storyboard into the message that will appear on the air. A professional producer is essential, regardless of the budget, the length, the medium, or any other variables.

Choosing a Director

A full-service advertising agency will have worked with production companies or free-lance directors, and can help recommend one based on their past experiences. Because of the volume of production work they handle, they will usually have some "clout" to assure the best prices and other arrangements.

If you are trying to produce television on your own, there are several ways to go.

The local television station usually will know some independent producers and directors, and the station itself may even do television production. A TV station's prices usually are unbeatable, but the productions usually are very poor. The problem is that stations are geared to simple news shows or local interview-type programs and don't have the exacting standards of commercial production houses.

Production firms are set up in business to work for companies requiring professional production of documentaries, training films, commercials, and other expressions of the cinematic arts. There are very large production firms and very small ones.

The larger firms may have commission representatives who do a wonderful selling job, and they may have one or two chief executives who have a fine reputation, but the only people who count are the producer and director they plan to assign to your project. Many of these companies may consider a direct marketing commercial a crass, unartistic venture, or they may resent having to work with budgets that don't permit taking the entire crew to Rome for a 3-second segment. The result is that your particular project may be delegated to a very junior manager who is learning the craft on your job.

A smaller firm usually is run by the principals who serve as both director and sales representative. You'll be working with the top people, but their crew may be assembled for each job. They may have technicians who have never worked together before, somewhat like the "pickup musicians" who make up the bands that play at weddings.

However, there is no reason why even a free-lancer can't rent the same facilities and assemble the same quality crew as a larger production firm.

My choice is usually a small, independent production company. The criterion should not be size, however, but the producer's attitude and the director's experience and involvement in low-budget television production.

Screening the Reel. Usually a production company seeking your business has one presentation and one only: a reel of work they've done for others. When you call a director you find in a telephone book or through referral, you'll be invited to a "screening."

Knowing how to watch such a screening is a skill in itself. It is a classic caveat emptor situation. First of all, take notes as you watch the work. You may be particularly impressed by some of the projects because of "big-name" clients or big-dollar budgets. Such projects are included to impress you. After the screening, refer to your notes and ask the production company representative:

- Did you make this film at this company, or when you worked for someone else?
- Who was the producer? The director? Are they still with you? Are they available for my projects?
- What was the budget? Is it comparable to the one I have in mind?

Then ask yourself these questions:

- What did I like about the reel? The acting? The special effects? The music? The humor or story line?
- Are the things I liked relevant to my project?
- Did the commercial come across as a well-integrated, continuous, consistent message, or were there good parts and bad?
- Do the producer and director seem enthusiastic about my project, or are they acting like they're doing me a big favor?

Once you've seen enough reels, you'll develop clear-cut standards of your own for comparing reels. Choose two or three companies you like best, discuss the specifications generally, and then ask for an estimate on your job.

Getting an Estimate

Always, without fail, get more than one company to give an estimate for your project, and always put your specifications in writing and make them identical for all bidders.

Begin by reviewing the storyboard, which should be self-explanatory but usually isn't. If you're showing a kitchen set, will you provide it for the filming or videotaping? Can the studio find a kitchen that generally fits your story? Or do you have such specific requirements that a set will have to be built to accommodate your needs? Obviously, the costs will be entirely different in these two cases.

Will you shoot on film or videotape? With union or nonunion talent? These factors also will make a big difference. The bid should ask the production company to specify exactly what crew will be used and whether the actresses and actors are figured on the basis of scale or above-scale fees.

Many of the questions about specifications for your particular commercial will arise in discussions with directors who are estimating for you. Directors can be very helpful in suggesting ways to cut costs or add creative strength to the finished product. Willingness and ability to make such suggestions should definitely be a factor in your final decision, even if the most helpful director's bid is a bit higher. Low cost certainly should not be the only criterion. In television production especially, you get what you pay for.

The proposal also should indicate, and make a commitment to, the shooting schedule and the completion date. Problems should be anticipated, such as what happens if bad weather spoils an outdoor shot, or who's responsible if an actor turns up drunk and can't work, yet the rest of the crew still has to be paid. That's what "contingency allowances" are for.

There are two ways to get such bids: *cost plus,* and *completion bid.* Cost plus means that the director gets a flat fee or a percentage of costs of what actual charges come to. This gives you a great deal of flexibility if you want to "play Hollywood" and get several takes on each scene, but it also means that you are signing a blank check because you have no way of knowing what the finished cost will be.

The most responsible bid is the completion bid, in which the director quotes a price on the finished product regardless of problems. Reshoots, editing problems, and uncooperative talent are the director's problem, and are paid for by the production company at no extra expense to you. Under this arrangement, directors may skimp when it comes to reshooting a scene, but they probably won't, because they too want to produce something they can be proud of.

Film versus Videotape

Almost every producer and director will have a strong feeling about the choice between film and videotape, and there are pros and cons to each. You should be familiar with both media even if you decide to leave the choice to the producer or director.

Advertisers with large budgets generally use film to do this shooting. Most directors are comfortable with this mode, and so are their camera operators and other technicians.

The equipment is more readily available, less bulky, and more portable. You don't need to rent expensive mobile control units if you're shooting indoors.

Videotape is more generally used by direct marketers. The advantage is that it is instantaneous. "Takes" can be played back while everyone is still on the set, and problems can be spotted and scenes reshot without having to call back the talent and crews. Special effects—"chroma-key" combinations of scenes, superimposition of text over photography—are much simpler to arrange.

The problem is the cost of the equipment needed to edit videotape. Editing facilities must be rented, complete with technical support, by the day or hour. Editing has to be done within a tight frame, and creative people, clients, and others concerned about the finished product have to stay at the studio until the editing has been completed, so that it can be done in one continuous process.

If very fine quality is required, as in food or cosmetic commercials, the slight extra cost you would incur by using 35- rather than 16-mm film or videotape may be insignificant. Film may also be advantageous when outdoor or location shooting is required.

Radio Production

Everything I've said about television applies to radio, except the obviously visual aspects. Sound studios and radio producers work the same way and should be interviewed and asked for estimates in the same way. They will always use tape, of course.

The key difference is in the creative aspects, where sound effects become more important and the creative challenge is more difficult.

Some radio commercials are done live, but this is very risky. If you listen to monitored tapes from live announcers in several cities, you'll be amazed at the differences in the style and the quality of the delivery. The only time when it's to your advantage to have live announcements is on a personality show, where a well-known announcer will deliver your script in a style that implies a personal endorsement of the product. For such shows, provide fact sheets and product samples to encourage improvisation.

The Shooting or Editing Session

Once the director has taken over, the advertiser's main concern is to respond to the queries, copy revision requests, and schedules set by the director. This is no time for second-guessing. The director is in charge—at preproduction meetings and casting sessions, on the set, and in the editing room.

That doesn't mean you have to abdicate responsibility. It does mean that you should respect the authority-responsibility structure and work exclusively through the director.

It is sheer disaster to have agency or client personnel on a set making suggestions directly to lighting people or camera operators, and it is worse yet to allow them to offer friendly advice to an actor who may be fighting off stage fright.

Be there, at every session. Watch, listen, scan the takes if they're on tape. Listen to the sound playbacks in either medium, but keep quiet. Pass your comments along at appropriate times, preferably in note form, to the director.

If there's a serious problem, ask to speak to the director privately. Never embarrass producers or directors in front of their staff and associates, or they will have to resist your suggestion in order to save face. This is the time for protocol, courtesy, and strict observance of the channels of communication.

Try to confine your comments to your interests: your concern for getting the message across in accord with the general marketing strategy. Try to resist the temptation to play movie mogul. Sure, shooting a commercial is a new experience for many advertisers. It should be a fun experience as well, but let's remember that, in direct marketing, the fun that counts is counting coupons.

21

INFOMERCIALS

Over the years I have seen one fad after another capture headlines in the world of marketing. And usually it is those least familiar with the basics of the underlying discipline who most quickly embrace it as the second coming of marketdom. Over the last several years, one of these has been the infomercial.

Is it a magical tool guaranteeing instant riches to all who try it? Certainly not. As with other forms of direct marketing, there are far more failures than successes. Not surprisingly, it is not the producers of the failures who tout their services at conferences or in press releases—at least not the honest ones. Is it all hype, then, a sucker game to be ignored? That is not true either. Infomercials are a tool that has its place among the many alternatives available to marketers, and when used correctly it can produce very impressive results.

WHAT IS AN INFOMERCIAL, ANYWAY?

First, just what are we talking about? It depends on who's doing the talking. Infomercials came into widespread use in the late 1980s, after the FCC deregulated limits on the amount of commercial time in programs. This was combined with the growth of cable, which in its early days eagerly welcomed any format that would contribute to revenue.

To direct marketers, infomercials are simply "long-form" direct-response broadcast commercials, usually a half-hour long. As with so-called "short-form" commercials—60- and 120-second spots—they require an investment in production costs and a purchase of media at economical rates. Leading infomercial sponsors believe the format has more in common with traditional long-copy direct mail than with short-form direct-response television.

The success or failure of a given infomercial usually is most dependent on (1) the proposition, meaning what is being sold or given away and at what price; (2) the media, meaning whether it is appearing on a station and at a time of day that will affordably reach the right market; and (3) sufficient interest values to attract or hold attention while still effectively presenting the sales message.

While general advertisers were late in discovering the effectiveness of this format, mail-order advertisers dominated the field. *The Jordan Whitney Infomercial Monitor,* a newsletter published in Tustin, California, reported the following top ten as early as 1992:

Victoria Jackson

SealOMatic

LaLanne Stepper

Prevention Magazine's Doctor's Book

Easy (Paint) Stripper Plus

Ray Stevens (Music) Video

Color Match

Ginsu Knives

Easy Step exerciser

Psychic Friends

The key is finding, or having, the right product. Many infomercial companies have built their reputation not on the quality of their communication or media buying, but on their ability (or luck) in finding a product that has "the right stuff." Often they take over the idea, arranging for manufacturing, paying for the advertising, and paying the originator a royalty. Here are some of the attributes such promoters look for:

- Five-to-one mark-up
- Blue-collar, mass-market appeal
- Easily demonstrated
- Unavailable in retail stores
- Available testimonials
- Price of $49.95 or less
- Promises a better life in some way
- . An impulse, not a considered, purchase
- Possibility of "back-end" repeat sales

To general advertisers, it is often their first introduction to the enormous sales potential of direct marketing. I am amazed that companies that have never sold their product directly to the consumer in safer and surer mediums such as direct mail or short-form broadcast will invest substantial budgets in the fad of the month, in this case infomercials. I know of one very large advertiser who refuses to put a phone number in its short-form TV ads even though all its print ads ask for responses. Yet they jumped into infomercials with both feet, as if somehow this was not television but something else.

To some, such as Braun or Singer or Estee Lauder, it is their first venture in any form of direct response. In these cases it is really direct marketing itself, not one particular media format, that has been responsible for their new source of riches. Here are just a few of the well-known advertisers who were among the early users of infomercials:

Volvo	Corning
Playboy	Toastmaster
Fidelity Fund	Microsoft
Infiniti	Time-Life
Braun	Black & Decker
Avon	GTE
Volkswagen	Kodak
Club Med	Coca-Cola
Apple Computers	American Airlines
Panasonic	Hyatt Resorts
Revlon	Singer

Other advertisers see infomercials purely as another communications vehicle—a view I endorse. In this case it is not their initiation into the world of mail order or even of database building; it is an opportunity to present their sales message in a more complete, more dramatic way than is possible in other media. Like a multipage brochure, there is space to explain, demonstrate, prove, and cover all the bases. Like any shorter form of direct-response commercial, it can use color, movement, and emotion, all dressed up in information or entertainment.

MEDIA CONSIDERATIONS

Infomercials, as most frequently used today, are most often compared to direct-response television, and are typically managed by the direct-response buyers within a media organization.

There are both similarities and differences. The similarity is that, for now, infomercials are constantly evaluated in terms of the orders, leads, or other responses they produce.

As with all direct marketing offers, this enables each placement to be evaluated on the basis of cost per response. And this, in turn, permits the media planner to test markets, stations, and dayparts, read the results, cancel some and repeat others. Usually a message must appear three times in the same station and daypart before a conclusion can be reached as to whether a station can be repeated over the long run. However, the winners and losers often show up very quickly. Usually as little as $25,000 to $50,000 invested in media is enough to determine if a product can be successful.

One source estimates that there are 500,000 hours per year available for long-form direct response on broadcast stations alone, not counting cable. A highly successful product could be placed on 200 broadcast stations and 10 major cable networks, with as many as 600 airings in one week. The media cost of such a schedule could run to $500,000 a week, but it would be bringing in between two and four times that amount in immediate income. And most amazing of all, a successful infomercial can run for *years*. No wonder some infomercial producers have made $10, $20, even $50 million dollars in profits from a single production!

As with direct-response television, rate cards are meaningless. The buyer must negotiate the cost and placement of each individual insertion. While a rate may be for an entire daypart, such as "overnight," there are dramatic differences in audience levels as each half-hour passes. I have seen 100 percent differences in response rates for the same spot scheduled only an hour earlier. Often a station will require a rotation package, i.e., 3 a.m. placements along with desirable midnight ones.

Compounding the scheduling problem is the fact that the most proven stations and times often are the most expensive. In order to run a schedule on the better stations, a substantial investment often must be made. Therefore infomercial planners generally have developed, through experience, smaller stations where results are projectable.

Some large mail-order users of this format have lowered their rates substantially by contracting for large packages over a long-term period. One of the pioneers in the field, Synchronal, went to cable stations such as BET and contracted with them to keep the station open past their regular programming time on a flat-fee basis. With the increase in channels, this opportunity will be available to others on many of the new channels.

Of course, such arrangements will be much more feasible for agencies or advertisers with enough different clients or products to make long-range commitments. If one product flops, they always have another to put in the time slot. Major agencies who place multimillions in conventional time-buying often also have an advantage. At Bozell we often have been able to clear a good placement for a direct advertiser by using the relationships and clout developed by BJK&E Media's regional buying offices.

One advantage of infomercials is that they are sold on a firm basis, rather than a preemptible basis as with direct-response spots. This enables them to be planned and promoted. One disadvantage, at least for smaller entrepreneurial firms, is that stations generally demand payment in advance.

CABLE				
DISCOVERY		MON	5:00–5:30 AM	$ 3,000
CNBC		SAT	3:00–3:30 AM	4,000
VH-1		FRI	4:00–4:30 AM	3,200
LIFETIME		SAT	12:00–12:30 AM	18,000
CNBC		SAT	5:00–5:30 AM	28,000
NICK-AT-NITE		SUN	12:00–12:30 PM	27,000
CBN		SAT	12:00–12:30 AM	22,000
BROADCAST				
WFTY	WASHINGTON, D.C.	SUN	9:30–10:00 AM	$ 1,500
KIFI	IDAHO FALLS, ID	SAT	5:30–6:00 AM	1,000
KSTW	SEATTLE, WA	THU	1:30–2:00 AM	2,700
WSBK	BOSTON, MA	SAT	1:00–1:30 AM	3,000
WDIV	DETROIT, MI	SUN	1:00–1:30 AM	5,500
KTHI	FARGO, ND	SAT	12:00–12:30 AM	900
WKBT	LACROSSE, WI	SUN	4:30–5:00 AM	1,100
WPHL	PHILADELPHIA, PA	SAT	10:30–11:00 AM	7,600
KFVE	HONOLULU, HI	SUN	7:30–8:00 AM	750
KGO	SAN FRANCISCO, CA	SUN	12:30–1:00 AM	4,000
KWHY	LOS ANGELES, CA	SUN	8:00–8:30 AM	2,600
WEVU	FT MEYERS, FL	SAT	12:30–1:00 AM	950
KTVN	RENO, NV	SAT	3:30–4:00 AM	1,300
WJYS	CHICAGO, IL	THU	11:00–11:30 AM	950

Figure 21-1. **Typical infomercial rates.** [These rates have been supplied by Hawthorne Communications, Fairfield, Iowa, a major full-service infomercial production organization. As all rates are negotiated, these rates may not apply for a different advertiser in a different season.]

Media rates vary from season to season, and probably will escalate each year as more and more advertisers use this format. The average cost of a half-hour is about $1500 for the most effective dayparts. These are late-night, Friday through Sunday, and daytime Saturday and Sunday. Figure 21-1 shows some typical rates, as of this writing, for a variety of markets, stations, and dayparts. All are for a half-hour.

CREATIVE ALTERNATIVES

Just as some early direct-response commercials looked as if they were shot on a home camera in someone's garage, some early infomercials looked equally primitive. It only makes sense, when there is no certainty that a format will be successful, to limit the production investment.

Within these budget limitations, the early infomercial producers developed formats that looked as good as, if not better than, some of the talk shows and other formats produced for conventional programming. Most had one or more of the following components:

- Inventor or author as guest
- Interviewer, lecturer or emcee
- Studio audience
- Celebrity or other authority
- High energy, fast pacing
- Enthusiasm, excitement, sincerity
- Interesting demonstration
- People who have succeeded with the product's aim
- Details and demonstration of the product or service
- News announcer
- Traveling demonstrator
- Documentary
- Multiproduct home shopping mart
- Anticipation of all possible objections
- Promise of significant benefit: success, good looks, popularity, material comforts
- An immediacy incentive: a gift sent only if the call is received before the program goes off the air

While many of the formats were similar, they varied greatly in production values. Some had large audiences. Some were shot in exotic locations, such as a Hawaii beachfront home. Others had celebrity participants who added real value to the show.

Probably some of the best-done infomercials, and the most successful, were for the Victoria Jackson cosmetic line, which included Cher as an enthusiastic endorser. A very creative execution was Richard Simmons for his Deal-a-Meal diet program, traveling around the country "surprising" customers who had used his program successfully. And who can forget Susan Powter, the former fat lady with the close-cropped haircut, screaming "Stop the insanity!"?

Note that all these direct-response infomercials (see Figs. 21-2 and 21-3) not only sold direct to the consumer but built brands and personalities that can add value to magazine covers and retail products alike.

Susan Powter, for example, is now so well known as a result of her infomercial appearance that she has been featured on the covers of national magazines and has a book on the best-seller charts. In general, infomercials are one of the best examples of the idea that new products can best be introduced through direct marketing, where the advertising-to-sales ratio is ten times that of a retail-distributed product.

Figure 21-2. Hawthorne's Braun demonstrations sold this kitchen appliance by mail order, while simultaneously lifting retail sales of all Braun products.

Figure 21-3. USA Direct made Susan Powter a household name with the now-classic "Stop the insanity!" infomercials, which dramatized the fat content of everyday foods.

The Length Factor

One common denominator of all infomercials, past and present, is that they have to make good use of the longer programming time. Just as direct mail can work so much harder than a print ad, so an infomercial must work harder than a one- or two-minute spot. The infomercial is best used, therefore, precisely when it is essential to cover much more ground in order to make the sale.

The unique role of the infomercial lies, to a large extent, in its ability to tell the whole story the way direct mail does, when there are not enough specifically targeted mailing lists. It therefore combines two concepts discussed in earlier chapters: *high-penetration selling,* and a *skimming media opportunity.*

The Channel-Surfer Factor

A very important creative consideration for most mass-market infomercials is the recognition that most viewers have not tuned in to watch your show, but have stumbled across it while zapping a remote controller looking for something to watch.

This means that, as far as many viewers are concerned, there is neither beginning nor end to the presentation. And there is no assurance that even those who develop an interest in the proposition offered will stay to the end.

Therefore all the AIDA elements must be present in each five- or six-minute segment. There has to be something unusual—the setting, the personalities, the tone of the dialogue—to get Attention. You need enough of a product story value to develop an Interest, then enough of a benefit message to create Desire. And last but not least, the Action element: call this number now, and here's what we'll do for you.

Production Values

In theory, the offer and the product story are more important than the form in which the the message is delivered. This is true, to the extent that the most elaborate presentation can't sell something that people don't want. But for a successful product, a quality commercial can sell much more than a cheap one.

There are two reasons for this. One is that production values which resemble those of general advertising are reassuring to the viewer. They suggest that the sponsor is a big, established, reputable company, and that therefore he or she can believe the promises made and implied.

The other is that, as with direct response, station managers often are more willing to give better placements to programming that reflects well on their station, meaning infomercials that look more like "real" programming rather than obvious sales harangues.

TESTING AND REVISION

Although infomercial production can represent an investment averaging $250,000 for a half-hour (about the same as some 30- or 60-second general commercials), it is never considered finished. If the test is marginal, and even if it is successful, it usually requires some form of re-edit or revision.

Some of this is generated by reports from the telephone operators, possibly indicating that there is some confusion about the offer. Often, focus panels reveal a problem or opportunity—especially when the participants are callers who did not order. Such research is much more meaningful after the first results are in, as the respondents can be profiled and analyzed so that focus groups represent typical customers.

The usual process is to

1. Expose consumer groups to the product and general message prior to final scripting and production

2. Produce an inexpensive commercial for on-air testing

3. Research the respondents and revise as required
4. Roll it out as fast as good media buys become available

A word of advice, from my own experience: Be sure to test the reaction to the spokesperson or host as well as to the product. A skin-care product created by a woman with a Hispanic accent, and a fitness product endorsed by a champion African-American athlete, failed to realize adequate responses from general audiences. While there were many respondents with similar ethnic backgrounds, somehow these spokesperson choices triggered the "not-for-me" reaction in other prospects.

Another source warns against having psychologists endorse anything, because his research has shown that the blue-collar audience attracted to typical mail-order infomercials believes this profession is a sham, and relevant only to sick people. As infomercials are still relatively new, each producer relies on specific experiences such as this one involving psychologists. Such lessons may or may not be universal (or even relevant to other clients).

PRODUCTION CONSIDERATIONS

What's involved in producing an infomercial? And how much should it cost? The answer to both questions is "It depends."

At one extreme, you can start with a copy platform and travel around interviewing people trying your product at interesting locations, the way Joe Sugarman did for his BluBlocker sunglasses. It would have been impossible to script such interesting characters and enthusiastic endorsements. One participant even wrote a rap song about his glasses. It was all assembled with great creative skill in the edit room, to become one of the most creative infomercials I've seen.

I don't know what this particular commercial cost, but I've done infomercials with top-grade talent for less than $100,000, and I suspect this one was also.

On the other hand, you can hire a production company to plan the entire production—concept, script, sets, casting—and easily spend between $250,000 and $500,000. Sometimes it's worth it, especially if it's a continuation of a successful campaign or there are secondary uses, as described later in this chapter. Figure 21-4 shows two budgets for two different infomercial projects.

The trick is to get real value for whatever amount is spent. The infomercial specialists responsible for past successes are not the only choice, though they may be the safest ones. New users of this format will have to break the mold and come up with fresh, creative approaches as this format becomes not just popular but over-used.

I have seen very fine work produced by companies whose past credentials were in documentaries, news productions, industrial films, and

	High	Low
Concept and treatment (3)	$ 10,000	$ 5,000
Scripting (3 drafts)	30,000	10,000
Preproduction	20,000	5,000
Production	300,000	45,000
Talent fees	150,000+	10,000
Music	10,000	2,000
Computer graphics animation	25,000	5,000
Postproduction	50,000	15,000
Tape duplication (test)	5,000	2,000
TOTALS	$600,000	$99,000

Figure 21-4. **Infomercial production budgets.** Note these are not for the same client or product. [These figures have been supplied courtesy of Hawthorne Communications, Fairfield, Iowa.]

of course, advertising commercials. All that is needed is a general knowledge of direct marketing basics if a response is needed, and a creative plan that assures that correct imagery objectives are established and delivered. Companies with integrated full-service advertising agencies on retainer should certainly leave the direction and supervision of this medium to them, just as they would any other medium.

It makes no more sense to hire hard-sell mail-order producers to write and produce a general advertiser's infomercial than it would to hire the team who sold Ginsu knives to sell cars and colas. Yet otherwise brilliant general advertising executives, unable to differentiate between infomercials and the equally successful direct-response media, have raced to affiliate with any self-proclaimed expert in this field. This is particularly dangerous as some operators seem to have exaggerated their past involvement in this field. Reference checks are always in order.

TELEMARKETING CONSIDERATIONS

Another thing infomercials have in common with short-form direct-response television is the response device. Typically viewers are asked, repeatedly, to call a toll-free 800 number. Thousands of calls can come in during and soon after each airing, so it requires a very large telemarketing operation to handle the calls.

Cincinnati Bell is the leader in this field, operating both the Matrixx facility in Ogden and the Wats Marketing operation in Omaha. Their computerized phone stations can handle the volume peaks of short- and long-form direct-response television, including entry of orders and information requests directly into a computer terminal, credit card verification, upsell scripts, and dealer locators. There are also many smaller companies in this field who may be better able to provide advice and service to the new entrant. Some very large telemarketers maintain their own facility, but this is costly unless there is a predictable order flow on a year-round basis. Usually this is convenient only for a marketer who has many different products that suit this technique.

Some advertisers also have used 900 numbers, where the payment is made by billing the customer's telephone account. However, this appears to be used generally for smaller-unit sales, or propositions that might appeal to younger people or others who do not have credit cards.

There are also substantial facilities for automated answering, where the customer is asked to press phone buttons indicating choices. The message then asks for the customer's name and address. It is also possible to capture the caller's home phone automatically, which then can be translated into an address with a simultaneous or subsequent look-up. In this case all that is requested is the name of the individual for keyboarded entry.

RADIO INFOMERCIALS

The same techniques developed for television infomercials also are being developed at this time for radio. The same kind of economics applies, and virtually all of the same advantages except the ability to demonstrate visually.

One company developed a format, called FutureNow, that is being tested on twenty radio stations, offering a varying range of products that don't require visual demonstration. These include video equipment, self-help tapes, and even surge suppressors for computers. These are products that lend themselves to explanation rather than demonstration, and may well be successful.

While no results are available at this time, the idea does seem logical and I would not be surprised if, by the time this book is in the bookstores, there are many more examples of radio infomercials.

APPLICATIONS TO GENERAL ADVERTISERS

If the great advantage of infomercials is their length, then they certainly have a place in marketing any product or service that requires detail and demonstration.

This has already taken place in specialized cable categories, where financial institutions have placed messages on financial stations, and in the medical field, where pharmaceutical companies explained complex medical data on the Lifetime network when it devoted Sundays to such material. With the rapid expansion of channel availability, there will be many more such opportunities, in many fields. In fact, during the initial stages of some coming specialty channels on topics such as equestrian sports and sailing, there will be a dearth of station-sponsored programming. Infomercials, particularly in well-done series, will be needed and appreciated, which should result in favorable rates.

Already there are infomercial applications in development, many of them independent of any mail-order or database-building objective. Automobile manufacturers can introduce a new model and present not just specifications and choices but all the experience of a test drive. Financial and investment firms can educate viewers to the fine points of sophisticated annuity and investment alternatives. Travel and resort advertisers can portray amenities and events fully and realistically. Political candidates and advocates of issues can present their issues, hopefully in a more interesting manner than a candidate with a stack of charts. The list is endless.

The problem is that the expense of the long-form commercial in effect wagers a large investment against a relatively unpredictable market segment. To make the format more cost-effective, some audience-building efforts can be very productive.

Building Audience

Stations promote their programs with listings in television guides, and free promotional spots elsewhere on other programs. Advertisers don't have these options, but they do have the other tools of direct marketing.

Advertisements and TV spots can direct viewers to the scheduled infomercial, provided it is in a format that promises some sort of benefit for watching. For this it needs a title suggesting a value to the consumer.

When a company has built a prospect database, it can be very effective to mail an announcement inviting interested prospects in the station's area to view this as a special event.

The Videotape Option

The same expense that can produce an infomercial can do double duty in the form of a videotape, either in addition to or instead of on the air.

Mailed videotapes can reach exactly the right audience—either of selected outside prospects or of names on a database. Depending on length and quantity, specialists such as Duplication Factory (Chaska, MN) can produce and mail tapes for as little as $2 including packaging, postage, and a reply form. The key is the same as any in direct mail effort: the extent to which mailing lists offer greater selectivity and penetration of a target audience than mass media.

For one client we mailed over 300,000 videotapes presenting a sophisticated investment alternative, with very impressive results in new and enlarged accounts. In such a case where affluent investors were the objective, a mass medium like television would not have provided either the coverage or the cost efficiency.

One variation I have recommended is a combination one. In this case, prospects for a new computer terminal would be invited to watch an infomercial, billed as a special national event. The same mailing would include both a reminder card with local channel numbers and an order form for a free videotape "in case you miss it."

HISTORICAL NOTE

If we pull back to take a broader view of the emergence of infomercials, we perceive a certain irony. Historically, in the earliest days of television, most advertising was what we now call infomercials.

Agencies created programming to build the image of their clients, with names like *The Colgate Comedy Hour* and *The Hallmark Hall of Fame.* Charities bought hours for telethons. Even today, programs such as *The Chrysler Showcase* provide effective vehicles for national brands.

Ross Perot is given credit for using infomercials in his bid for the presidency, as if it were a stroke of marketing genius. Yet I remember, when I was still too young to vote, Eisenhower and other candidates routinely buying an hour or a half-hour of broadcast time to air rallies, fireside chats, or election eve wrap-ups. (Not amazingly, voters responded to lengthy discussions of issues and philosophies that could never be expressed in today's sound bytes and thirty-second "smear n' slogan" spots.)

And even mail-order advertisers began by buying segments of time for "Great Moments of Music" or demonstrations of the Vitamix blender. For cost efficiencies, 30 minutes became 15, and then 5, and finally the 2-minute commercial became the standard for direct-response television. I was in the vanguard of those advocating 60-second spots, which at the time was highly controversial and the subject of heated debate.

Today the 60- and 120-second spots are accepted as conventional tools that have a high probability of success. Are there failures? Yes. Too many. And are there examples of entrepreneurs becoming instant millionaires by means of these short-form direct-response commercials? Yes, many. Topsy Tail and Nordic Trak were successful short-form commercials long before they experimented with the long form. And are many general advertisers using this format to build mighty databases or supply leads to legions of sales representatives? Yes. Today, the short-form direct-response commercial is no longer news. Instead, the fad of the day is, without doubt, the infomercial.

Within a few years infomercials too will be just another medium, and the headlines will, properly, deal with the successes that spring from its innovative use, not the fact that it exists at all.

Already the pressures are to return full-circle to a recognition that infomercials are simply the purchase of time to be controlled by a sponsor. And while there are consumers who have nothing better to do than watch home-shopping stations or half-hour testimonials for a steam iron, the larger mass of both general and direct marketing consumers want something of value on their home television: information, entertainment, amusement, education.

With the proliferation of infomercials, those that are clearing time on the better stations and attracting the better audiences are those that have the same standards as nondirect advertising.

First of all they are well written, and rely on facts and demonstration rather than faked oohs and aahs by a host or the rabid enthusiasm of a computer tutor or self-styled fitness fanatic.

Secondly, they are well directed and well cast. Celebrities may add interest and credibility if they are relevant, but more important is the ability to deliver an effective message that is welcomed by those market segments whose intelligence and taste levels go beyond lusting for bargain-priced gold chains.

Third, and most important, is a format and concept that is appropriate both to the audience and the product. More and more we see news formats, interview show formats, game show formats—all attempts to make the half-hour of advertising seem no different than a station-provided show.

The circle is being completed once again. The Great Moments of Music format is back, with music or videotapes providing entertainment values for programs designed to sell them, as is softer-sell exercise advice as a prelude to an intelligent pitch for fitness equipment.

In a meeting I had with one major direct-response advertiser seeking greater exposure for their many spots—both short- and long-format, as appropriate for each product—we discussed starting their own channel, or buying blocks of time where they could run their shorter spots so as to attract special audiences. The conversation then evolved in the very direction I think this whole industry will eventually go:

1. Do we have enough of our own material to fill up the time?

2. If not, what can we get—reruns, old movies?

3. Why not develop our own programming, uniquely designed to attract the audiences we want?

If this logic sounds like the steps that led Procter & Gamble to develop the soap opera genre, or Hasbro to facilitate children's shows about G.I. Joe or My Little Pony, maybe that isn't accidental. It's logic like this that will bring infomercials closer to general programming, just as direct-response advertising in all media, including direct mail, is moving closer to general advertising.

This viewpoint was best expressed by Tim Hawthorne, whom authors Stan Rapp and Tom Collins call the "King of the Infomercial":

> For 10 years, infomercials have been a rudimentary precursor to the
> electronic marketplace in tomorrow's information superhighway.
> Although the infomercial's roots are in direct response, the industry
> will soon become dominated by general advertisers using this
> format to build databases as well as image and awareness. After a
> decade of ignoring this powerful marketing tool, marketing directors
> everywhere are now recognizing the truth of the infomercial's
> underlying premise: the more you tell, the more you sell.

INTERACTIVE
MARKETING

Nothing has captured the imagination of marketers, media, and the communications world as much as Interactive. Vice-President Gore has made the inevitability of the "Information Superhighway" a major crusade rivaled only by his interest in environmental cataclysm. Not millions but billions of dollars have been put at risk by investors who see this development as the herald of the twenty-first century. Telephone companies, cable companies, and movie studios engage in mergers and legal battles for the high ground in the inevitable shakeout war. Press releases, each heralding the newest "ultimate" system, flood the desks of editors and executives.

But what *is* interactive marketing, really? Like the story of the blind men and the elephant, the observers are biased by their own individual perspectives. Some are fascinated with the technology. Some see it as a revolution in home entertainment, or information. Some see it as an advertising medium. Some see it as an investment opportunity.

Actually, Interactive began almost two decades ago, with Warner's QUBE cable system in Columbus, Ohio. Used mostly for research, it included five selector buttons that could transmit an upstream signal. Later, Cox brought out a 12-button system in San Diego, but both soon were abandoned.

In the eighties a rash of entrepreneurs again introduced a variety of services based on interactive technology. Of these, pay-per-view—particularly in hotels—found a niche, and eventually became widely available. Despite many obstacles imposed by the home-video industry, it has reached $625 million a year in the United States and is still growing. In the meantime, Videotex—limited by its silent, screen-by-screen selections—failed, with over a billion dollars in losses.

It was not until Great Britain deregulated telecommunications that U.S. telephone companies entered the interactive market here in a big way, pushing cable companies to accelerate their own efforts. In England, with free competition, cable companies emerged from the competitive fray with a 25 percent share of the voice-to-voice business. As a result, U.S. phone companies consider entry into interactive to be a defensive move against the cable and out-of-region telephone companies. As a result, investments are pouring into this arena. Next Century Media estimates that current plans will result in at least 20 million homes being interactive-ready.

Unlike some writers on this subject, I admit my own bias, which is to look at these developments from a marketing viewpoint—both as a challenge and an opportunity. As this chapter is written within the framework of a book on direct marketing, this should come as no surprise.

INTERACTIVITY REDISCOVERED?

Once again we see the same people who scoffed at putting coupons in their ads or phone numbers in their commercials, as direct marketers have always done, expressing amazement at the fact that consumers like to have the ability to respond. Executives from a wide variety of industries are leading the way in seeking applications of the interactive aspects of new technology, or the ability to deliver entertainment or commercials precisely to those most interested.

The truth is that we have had interactive advertising as long as we have had advertising. I cannot rummage through the yellowing pages of old *Collier's* or other mass magazines without finding coupons that offered information, which became leads for salespeople, and long-copy mail-order advertisements "asking for the order." And what is telephone marketing but a personal and interactive selling method, lacking, for now, only the visual transmission of advertising messages.

Isn't the mail-order business already designed to "bring the store to the customer"? In many ways, the new forms for facilitating interactivity will achieve their greatest successes only for those enlightened companies who recognize that they are not so much opening a new channel of distribution as entering a proven one. Yes, the potential is enormous. But that potential exists *now,* with no need to wait for the new technologies to be perfected. Interactive will similarly encourage even more companies who presently rely on indirect marketing to try database marketing—adapting the lessons of mail order to the support of retail sales.

A basic tenet of direct marketing has always been "Response-ability," meaning making it easy for the prospect to respond. We filled in customer names and addresses on order forms, tipped on reply cards, provided toll-free phone numbers. Therefore it is only logical that new forms of interactivity, making it easy and convenient for the customer to respond, should merit our attention.

But what is too often forgotten is that ease of response is only one aspect of generating a lead or involvement. We must still attract attention, generate interest, involve the prospects, motivate them, overcome objections, and give them a reason for acting *now*. That is exactly what direct marketers understand better than anyone in the world of marketing, and why any interactive concept or process that disregards this body of experience will be among the first to vanish from the scene.

INTERACTIVE'S BASIC COMPONENTS

Each new combination of delivery systems and interactivity is heralded with major fanfare and imaginative new names. As of this moment, there are no less than 118 "test beds" dealing with one form or another of the information highway. The activity is so frantic that Bozell and other major agencies maintain full-time executives just to keep track of the options, with high-level task forces seeking ways to use them for clients.

But when you sort it all out, there are only a certain number of components, which are much clearer if they are considered separately. These are

1. The communications channel
2. The communications terminal
3. The incentive for consumers to participate
4. The incentive for advertisers to participate
5. The resources behind the system

The Communications Channel

Basically, this is the "highway" that connects a source of communications or advertising to the consumer or business customer, called *downstream*, and possibly back again, called *upstream*. It is financed by user fees, such as a phone or cable bill, by advertisers, or by companies who hope to profit by the sale of hardware or entertainment.

Cable. Wire connections with a copper center strand and a foil outer layer—the primary system available to a majority of homes in the U.S. Of these, a large percentage also subscribe to premium channels such as HBO. Most systems can accommodate about 70 channels, each with sound, motion, and color. Original systems were "one-way" and not "addressable," meaning that there could be no customized transmission of signals.

Phone Lines. The original "paired-wire" connections available to almost every home in the United States. These have had limited carrying capacity—sound, or simple graphic messages—but are completely addressable either way. However, the new compression technologies now make it possible to use these lines for video, except in areas far from a switching center.

Fiber Optics. In essence, fiberglass connections sending light pulses rather than electronic signals. Being installed for most new long-distance telephone lines, and many local phone companies and cable operators. Capable of two-way transmission of voice, picture, color, and motion.

Satellite Transmission. USSB and Direct TV are offering "cableless cable" with up to 150 channels. Modern technology permits both address-ability (via telephone modem) and two-way transmission of sound and picture with exceptional high fidelity. Early versions required a roof or back-yard dish as large as a small car; these work with an 18-inch RCA dish, easily installed indoors or out.

Addressability. The ability to direct a signal, whether entertainment or advertising, to a specific household. It is this feature that permits pay-per-view broadcasts of films or sports events.

Upstreaming, or Return Signal Capability. Addressable features such as pay-per-view can currently be accessed with a phone call to a live operator or automated system. And interactive direct-response advertising is alive and well, thank you, using the same response mechanism. The difference here is one of added convenience in the form of one or more buttons on a remote-control unit, dispatching a signal directly to the transmission source without dialing a number. This feature, like its telephonic predecessor, has been used for research or poll-taking, and it is easily adaptable to requests for information, samples, or mail orders.

Digital Compression. A method of translating signals into a more com-pressed digital form that increases capacity—the number of signals that can be carried simultaneously.

Conventional Delivery. The mails, as well as UPS, Federal Express, etc., should not be overlooked. Many of the same objectives can be accom-plished, at least for now, by sending prospects videotapes or computer disks. These are more than addressable, for combined with advertising in mass or specialized media they can be requested, possibly with variations. They can be customized with different versions for different prospects, as a product of database marketing programs (discussed in the next chapter and in my separate book on this subject), and they can even be attached in one way or the other to the pages of a specialized magazine, as a sort of super-ad. These more conventional delivery systems may effectively be used to pretest the more exotic channels and terminals. If a marketer can't make enough sales with a videotape that a customer asks for, they won't with a high-tech version of the same selling proposition.

Fiber optics are the cement of the new information highway—literally the connector that makes most of "tomorrow's" communications conveniences possible. Today miles of fiber optics are being installed by both phone and cable companies. Many of the cable/phone company alliances are designed to share existing fiber-optic installations, or the expense of installing new ones.

The Communications Terminal

This is the hardware that turns the electronic or light signal into sound and sight, or back again—in its simplest form, the phone and a television set. Complex modem-connected computers already are in millions of homes. And soon there will be many new combinations that do it all.

Television Set.   The standard of visual reception, getting larger and flatter, and with more options. Projection systems will let you cover a wall. New head-mounted devices will give you three-dimensional images of "virtual reality." "Picture-in-picture" features will let you see more than one channel at a time. And with multiple channels —as many as 500, by some estimates—choice will be greater than ever. One improvement will be variable starting times: movies that start again every half-hour or so on different channels. If the movie you want has already begun, wait a bit and watch it from the beginning on a different channel. But all in all it's a dumb terminal, able in its present form only to view whatever is selected from whatever is being broadcast or "addressably narrowcast" at the time.

Telephone Instrument.   The familiar voice-communication tool in a growing number of unfamiliar formats: redesigned instruments, variable sound levels, caller identification, and now voice dialing. In the new world of interactivity, picture-phones—first introduced at the 1939 World's Fair—may finally become a consumer reality.

Mobile and Cellular Phones.   Once the symbol of affluence or intrigue, now a common business tool used by traveling executives in enlightened corporations as well as by homemakers out doing neighborhood chores. The phones themselves are getting smaller and lighter, and even the Dick Tracy fantasy of a wrist-phone is now practical and inevitable.

Computer/Modem.   Computers of every type can be at the other end of any wired, cabled, or transmitted signal. Within the "pure" world of computers, all kinds of services are available: electronic mail, grocery shopping, travel schedules, theater tickets. The options are limited only by what a subscriber or advertiser is willing to pay for. One interesting application is the computer bulletin board—an "anything goes" version of the classifieds, including the most personal of personals. While computers have the ability to, well, compute, and can be as addressable as any phone, they have for the most part been limited in their graphic capability. Most visuals have been still "screens" lacking photographic clarity or motion, except within subscreen "mortices" or "windows."

Special-Purpose Terminal. Somewhere between the computer and the terminal are special-purpose terminals for office, home, or portable use. At one extreme, news organizations such as Reuters and Knight-Ridder and others already install TV-size terminals as the modern equivalent of a stock ticker, customized to display up-to-the minute data on stocks, bonds, currencies or any other financial instrument, complete with preset alerts or a memory bank of trend data. On the other, pocket-size beepers can deliver news services, weather, stock prices, or simple messages.

And don't forget the PDAs—personal digital assistants, such as the Apple Newton and MadCap software. These are designed to be a secretary in your pocket, keeping track of appointments, accessing files, calling up reference sources, placing your phone calls. And for those idle moments, they can become your newspaper, with up-to-the minute news of all kinds, or you can play your favorite game or study a language or other subject. Only 50,000 had been sold as of 1993, but the computer industry is gearing up for another three million over the next five years.

Printer. As with any computer printer, it provides the instant hard-copy transmission that some say will one day replace the mailed letter completely. Interactive system promoters see printers as vehicles for printed information, store coupons, and financial records, among other uses. Next Century Media believes that in-home couponing "is the biggest revenue growth potential that TV stations have had in 40 years."

Electronic Game System. Game systems such as those by Sega and Nintendo are truly interactive, with their control rods, target guns, 3D glasses, and scoring systems. Players can play tennis, sail, golf, play football, or drive a racing car—all on realistic playing fields. While they have always been capable of display on a television or computer screen, the difference is that now the games themselves can be transmitted on a pay-per-game or other basis for downloading. Game software can be delivered on phone or cable, and perhaps also by satellite or local transmission as well. Already AT&T sells a special modem that lets Sega Genesis owners play games over phone lines while talking. And a cable Sega channel is in the works to transmit game software on command.

CD-ROM. Not a transmission method, but a computer storage system capable of storing over 2000 pages of text. Over 5 million are in use as of 1994. They make possible the storage of almost limitless video games, encyclopedias, or entire libraries—which can be purchased by mail order or at software stores. On a simpler basis, the common VCR (videocassette recorder) can be used the same way but with less capacity.

Camera. Some prototype systems already are equipped with built-in cameras for interactive visual images, meaning that telephonic conversations between two similarly equipped locations can include both sound and moving picture.

Scanner/Keyboard. As with any computer, these are convenient ways to transmit pictorial or keyboarded information: test answers to a teacher, order forms to a direct marketer, written instructions to a stockbroker, etc. Some devices receive and transmit handwritten notes as well.

Kiosks. Any free-standing unit in airports, shopping centers, street corners, or even—combined with ATMs (themselves a form of kiosk)—in banks and large retail stores.

Mailbox. Not to be forgotten in the rush to new technology is the fact that information or merchandise requested through any channel and on any terminal can also be delivered the old-fashioned way—in printed or videotape form—through the mails or by express shippers.

Omnisets. This is just my name for "any or all of the above." Many of the technology advances have consisted of combining features of these terminals and adapting them to the various strengths and shortcomings of the channels. The ultimate goals are the addressability of the phone system, the visual clarity of digital television, the creativity of the game systems, the portability of a cellular beeper, and the user-friendliness of a Macintosh computer. Is this too much to ask? Not at all. There are no theoretical obstacles, only financial ones.

The Incentive for Consumers to Participate

People buy ad-filled newspapers for news. Magazines for entertainment. They sit through commercials as the "price" to pay to see a favorite show, sports event, or movie. Or they pay a fee for the channel. Or for the terminal. But all the technology in the world can't force someone to pay for programming or watch a commercial unless they want to.

Motion Pictures. The power of Hollywood to amuse, arouse, and entertain remains unchallenged as the surest way to build an audience, dependent only on how new, good, and convenient the movie is. It is movies that built the home videotape rental business. It is movies that drive cable subscribers to pay more for premium channels. And it is movies that mostly motivate pay-per-view. What better evidence of the power of the motion picture could anyone need, than the frantic bidding that took place between the QVC shopping network and Viacom for the control of Paramount Studios?

Sports. While no sports event has universal appeal—except perhaps the Olympics—each has its cadre of loyal followers who will always find the time and the money to see their favorite competition. Pro or college football. Golf or tennis. Baseball and basketball. Auto and horse racing. And if more soccer, sailing races, chess games, or rodeos were broadcast, they too would attract and hold audiences willing to pay for the privilege, and advertisers willing to pay to reach them. With the availability of more channels, such narrow interests finally can be reached effectively.

Broadcast Network Programs. With all the media fuss over cable, it's easy to forget that on an average evening a majority of the audience is tuned into prime-time programs, developed and paid for by networks as an investment that will attract audiences for advertisers. This is, and probably always will be, a formidable competitor against new forms of communications, no matter how interactive they may be.

Cable Network Programs. Although cable networks built their appeal on first offers of recent movies, they now compete in the broadcast network's own arena by producing their own exclusive movies for television, as well as other programming, including national and international news.

News and Programs. It would be a mistake to underestimate the pulling power of news broadcasts: national and international developments, business news, special-interest news and features. This particularly applies to local events, familiar faces, political issues that affect home and workplace. "News on Demand," or customized news, is sure to be part of all of the new systems.

Special Interests. Business news. Investment news. Religion. Weather. Opera. Crafts. All these interests can be catered to with special programming and relevant advertising that people with these interests will want to watch. I came home from a meeting tonight and found my wife watching The Food Channel—a full day of watching chefs cook and diners eat, sort of a *Gourmet* magazine of the air. And why not? If magazines are gravitating to special interests, why shouldn't television?

Education. Many forecasters, including this writer, believe that one of the great opportunities of the interactive era will be the growing availability of educational courses of all kinds, complete with tests, credits, diplomas, and maybe even two-way dialogues. Today's college student population is growing older, with people of all ages returning to complete their education or take advanced courses. When the convenience of home education is generally available, offered at competitive fees by leading colleges, even more will opt to learn languages, develop skills, study in areas of cultural interest, and learn to repair, remodel, or even build their homes. Many consumers may not want to pay for new channels and terminals for entertainment they can get on advertiser-sponsored television, but I think they will be delighted to do so to acquire new skills and knowledge at Information Highway U.

Business Data. While most of the news involves consumer applications, business and professional users are the most price-elastic prospects for information and communications, and always will be. Many of the new channels and methods will find their most valuable application in sales kits, travelers' briefcases, ambulances, and repair service trucks. Even now, people in my agency are developing a Next system that will give us access to enormous databases of media information or result records, even through a laptop while traveling or in a client's conference room. With both wired and wireless applications being perfected, any type of instruction, reference, supervision, or consultation can be made available for any type of business use, anytime, anywhere.

Games. Not just for the younger set, electronic games will become genuinely interactive and convenient. Computer networks already enable strangers to challenge each other to a simulated soccer match or bridge game. Or imagine a game arcade of the air: Press the button, and for a nominal charge you play the latest version of Pac Man or Super Mario. While perhaps not generally applicable as an advertising medium, teenagers will pay to play the latest electronic games or simulate flying a jet fighter. These games will probably be downloaded into a memory unit of some kind on what will undoubtedly be called "pay-per-play" or the "home video arcade." Such games can even be competitive with other players in the same home or in other homes. And scores can be signaled back to a station for instant national or local recognition of the winners.

Shopping. Some interactive developers believe that the driving force behind interactive technology will be home shopping. Certainly the success of the Home Shopping Network and QVC would indicate that there is a large number of people who are willing to purchase goods and services they see on such continuous shopping shows, and that such shows can sell millions of dollars in goods this way. While the early shopping shows were somewhat primitive in their entertainment value, they are evolving into an entertainment medium in their own right, with celebrities and talented actors raising the production standards. Such shows have been successful with the interactivity limited to the household telephone. It remains to be seen whether the ability to order by pressing a button, or being able to see a garment or a car in your choice of color, will provide an increase in sales worth the increase in costs to advertisers.

Infomercials. To the extent that infomercials combine both reason to watch and incentive to buy, they are ideal for interactive applications. On an interactive delivery system, they can be expanded to provide answers to objections or emphasize areas of special interest. For example, a program featuring a weight-control program can provide specifics to viewers who punch in their present height and weight. Or a wallpaper pattern can be projected onto a preprogrammed view of a room. And the order can be placed with a push of a button, the purchase charged to a preregistered credit card or the cable or phone bill. Some advertisers have discussed sponsoring new channels just to run infomercials, or to be able to offer infomercials on demand.

Bribes.   This may be an ugly word, but it sums up one approach that is an integral part of some of the major interactive tests. "How can you get viewers to participate in some interactive selling messages?" system sponsors ask. "Pay them, by letting them watch movies they would otherwise have to pay for." It sounds logical, but I have serious reservations about the value of a prospect whose attention has been purchased. These schemes have even included requiring a viewer to press a signal button several times during a purchased message to be certain they haven't left to go get a snack!

The Incentive for Advertisers to Participate

Market Coverage.   As I will discuss more fully later in this chapter, there may well be two separate market groups in the future: those easily reached by traditional media, and those that will best be reached through new technology such as interactive terminals. If advertisers want to reach all prospective customers, they will have to use all media that reaches them. To top it off, the interactive prospect may well be the segment that is more affluent, better educated, has a higher income, and—by definition—is more willing to try new products and services. This new segment will represent a market that cannot be overlooked.

Media Targeting.   If, as everyone expects, hundreds of channels will make possible dozens of special-interest channels and programs, many advertisers will be able to direct their messages very precisely to niche markets previously unreachable on television. Just as *This Old House* made it possible for lumber manufacturers to use television effectively, so too segmentation will bring in hundreds, perhaps thousands, of advertisers who previously had never used this medium. Some schemes claim to be able to combine database information and deliver different messages to different homes depending on product usage, demographics, and lifestyles. Certainly it is technically possible. The major difficulty, as always, is financial feasibility.

Involving Messages.   More than anything else, interactivity will involve viewers: with choices, with personalization, with curiosity. It will also be a source of advice—the best form of selling—as the viewer can "ask" for messages about the subjects that most concern them. Of course this will be most applicable for products that are "considered purchases," such as an automobile or a major vacation. A Bell Atlantic demonstration I saw for travel advertisers enabled users to indicate their hobbies, interests, price ranges, etc., and then provided details on those resorts that met each viewer's needs.

Prospect Data.   With the growing recognition of the value of database marketing, information about individual consumers—their interests, their purchasing behavior—is becoming more important. Promotions that respond to such individual behavioral differences are always more effective than those that are simply based on generalized demographics. Today, telephone companies can plan their offers based on usage patterns known only to them: where you call, when you call, what options you have already accepted. Banks are able to do the same, with knowledge of your bank balance and the details of your financial situation.

With interactive data, cable companies will be able to track what kinds of programming you watch regularly, what specific actors you seem to like or dislike, which commercials you watched and which you turned off, and what movies or sports events you liked so much that you were willing to pay for them. If you interact with a commercial game type of message, your choices and preferences can all be recorded and used in future marketing plans.

Imagine how detailed individual communications can be if you have revealed your favorite color, your dream holiday destination, your clothing size, and what kinds of products you have asked to get more information about.

Mail-Order Sales.   To the extent that marketers accept the idea stated earlier in this book that "to serve all consumer segments you must use all distribution channels," interactive marketing will dramatically increase their opportunities to sell direct to the public.

An interesting new application combines retail and mail order. Both Pizza Hut and McDonald's are testing Interactive for home delivery. The customer can see a commercial, ask to see a detailed menu, and then with the press of a button place an order for home delivery. The only thing Interactive hasn't figured out yet is how to pop the pizza out of the TV set—but give them time!

Classic mail-order companies will need no convincing; their decision will be based, as always, on cost per order. As with direct-response television, mail-order companies will be standing by to take advantage of unsold participations at remnant rates or on a per-inquiry basis. The difference is that whereas today's direct-response television features one item at a time, the new interactive methods will enable manufacturers and retailers to offer whole catalogs (or "shopping malls of the air") of merchandise.

Let's say someone watching a craft show becomes interested in a power sander used on the show. A press of a button can provide specifications and advice on the sponsor's entire range of sanders and ask for the order on the spot, while interest is still high. Then other questions can inquire of the prospect about other tool needs, and respond accordingly. The potential is there for the kind of interaction that consumers once expected to get from helpful, knowledgeable salespersons.

The Resources Behind the System

Both private investors and public companies have poured millions into the race to become dominant forces in the new age of interactivity. Even the Federal budget, supposedly concerned with reducing the deficit, found $100 million to invest in developing the "Information Superhighway."

As part of this change, both cable companies and broadcast networks are unwittingly stimulating the growth of paid, commercial-free programming. They are adding so many of their own promotional announcements to paid commercials that for many programs the viewer must sit through more than 13 minutes of sell for every 47 minutes of entertainment. If watching commercials is "the price the viewer pays for free TV," the price is getting too high.

The most ambitious experiments are being launched by companies who already have something to bring to the party. Phone companies have their switching experience, home shopping companies the systems and products to sell, cable companies their connections, movie studios their treasuries of movies and the capability to create new material. Some are cautious. Some, like Bell Atlantic and Pacific Telephone are jumping in with massive roll-outs. Time Warner—with several operating companies, its ownership of Warner Brothers studios and HBO Network, advertising/sales experience from its magazine division, and direct marketing from its Time-Life Books operation—is one of the few that is self-contained. AT&T and Viacom also are conducting interactive tests. Others are forming alliances and raising money so that they won't be left out.

Will it be worth it? Bob Smith, executive director of Interactive Services Assn., says, "Interactive advertising is inevitable. It's not whether it will catch on, but rather, how big and how soon." Allen Rosenshine, president of BBDO, says, "I wish I had...a percentage of the money going in the toilet in the name of building the Information Superhighway. It's going to make the financial fiascos of the eighties look like small change."

I tend to go along with Bill Harvey, whose Next Century Media is one of the most respected consultants in the field. He believes that Interactive Marketing represents an important opportunity for marketers, but that it must be used creatively; simply putting old commercials and marketing methods into new formats will not be enough. But when used correctly, it can be a powerful tool for marketers to build share at retail or to profitably exploit the direct marketing channel. However, he agrees that there is no chance that conventional media will disappear from the scene—at least not in this generation. In the meantime, the race is on.

As developments are taking place very quickly and this book is intended for use over several years, I have refrained from including a list of current entrants, preferring instead to abstract their common elements. Here, then, are some of the most visible types of contenders.

Cable Companies. With two-thirds of America's homes already wired with cables, this industry has the most to gain, short-term, by adding new sources of revenue such as interactive communication in its various forms. However, the more advanced levels will require the replacement of most of those cables with fiber-optic ones. Both local operators and networks have had valuable experience in the marketing of new technologies, as cable itself was new only a few years ago. Accessing movies and shows is routine for them.

Phone Companies. Who knows more about two-way communication and "addressable" switching than the phone companies? And what interactive function is as indispensable as communicating with friends, family, and business associates? However, conventional wire channels so far can't carry moving pictures, because it takes too long to compress the signal to fit the narrow lines. To accommodate movie-type entertainment, or picture quality suitable for most catalog or advertising use, they too will have to install fiber optics. In many parts of the country they are doing just that. Although Bell Atlantic and others are using phone lines for early video delivery, this is an evolving strategy that will eventually lead to fiber-optic and coaxial cable installations.

Entertainment Companies. The medium may be the news, but it is not the message, according to the producers of shows, movies, games, and other forms of entertainment. While few of the channel-driven enterprises are paying much attention to what is going to go through those channels, it is likely that, as with conventional broadcast, whoever controls the programming will control the medium.

Already MTV is planning MTV Express, where viewers can order a video or CD of music they see on the channel. And the international music and book giant Bertelsmann is working with major cable operator TCI (Telecommunications, Inc.) on a similar venture. BMG now owns and operates the former RCA Music Service, as well as what used to be called Doubleday Book Clubs, while TMI, which has made over 500 acquisitions, now has about 20 percent of all cable subscribers. Others starting music shopping channels include Warner, Sony, Polygram, and EMI, which owns the HMV music chain and Capitol Records.

Publishers. I personally believe that the key to the future of the new technologies will be in the hands of publishers. The news, features, advice, and reference works they generate may well be more useful and more timely in interactive formats than in printed pages. Many already are offering such services, but mostly to business audiences.

In California, the powerful Times Mirror publishing group announced a joint venture with Pacific Telesis to produce an interactive shopping service designed to meet routine shopping needs. Initially the service will deal with such mundane items as used cars, restaurant listings, and hotel rates. At the same time, Cox Newspapers is combining with Bell

South to offer a combination of the classified pages and the yellow pages to help consumers find anything from apartments for rent to the nearest all-night drug store.

The potential is enormous, for news as well as shopping. Any channel-surfer will appreciate the idea of news stories that can be skipped or extended, depending on the viewer's interests, or sports events where facts, figures, and replays can be called up on command.

Broadcast Companies.   Anyone who thinks that major networks will just stand by and watch their ratings be diluted into unsalable fractions on hundreds of separate channels should think again. Some of these same networks started in radio; they were not the first television broadcasters, but they ended up being the dominant ones. And despite all the attractions of cable, their free, advertiser-supported movies and shows and events still attract the largest audience by far. I would guess that they are sitting back and waiting for the dust to settle. When they do make their move, it will be a strong one.

THE INTERACTIVE LADDER

In the previous section, we have looked at the elements of interactive communication. These must be understood before anyone can attempt to use interactive methods to sell other products or services. Bill Harvey of Next Century Media puts the pieces together in terms of degrees of inter-activity. These "levels" (copyrighted by his newsletter, *The Marketing Pulse,* Woodstock, NY 12498, and reprinted by permission) are the best way to follow the many test opportunities being offered to marketers.

> *Level 1—Analog + Upstream Buttons.*   Viewers have about the same TV choices they have today, except that they can play along with quiz shows, second-guess during sports events, order products, and get information using one or more buttons on their remote.
> Of course, "ordering products" includes pay-per-view events and movies.
>
> *Level 2—Near Video On Demand—NVOD.*   There are some hit movies and other programs starting at staggered times, so that the viewer can, with only a short wait, watch PPV programming at his/her convenience. Some of this programming might merely be broadcast/cable network/syndicated shows the viewer has missed but is now willing to pay to see.
>
> *Level 3—Some True Video On Demand—TVOD.*   Programs that the viewer can literally call up at any time. This may be a home application of the services now in many hotels, where a limited number of guests can choose from a list of shows.
>
> *Level 4—TVOD.*   At this level, *all* of the programs are available, with no wait whatsoever. This level is distinguished from the prior level

by the enormous difference in the capital investment cost of doing *some* versus *all* TVOD.

Level 5—TVOD With Substantial Branching. In this case, not only is it all TVOD, but there are lots of programs available that are interactive, to the point of changing the on-screen action by means of individual viewer response. Essentially, ACTV (Advanced Cable Television) is a Level 1 network operating today, which allows branching among four options. However, the production cost of truly realizing the potential of branching, via so-called "movie-like games," is so high that ACTV at current penetration levels can only dabble in the kind of rich branching that we use as the litmus test of Level 5.

Level 6—TVOD/Branching + Camera. In this level, there is also a TV camera or camcorder hooked to the system, so that the viewer's face can appear in a TV show seen in many homes, videoconference, or work at home with others who are not there.

Level 7—Viewer As Creator. Here the viewer has at his/her command editing and/or animation tools, permitting creative participation in television programming above and beyond the talking-head limitations of Level 6.

THE TECHY MARKET

When levels 5, 6, and 7 are available to the consumer, it is doubtful whether the average homemaker will rush to subscribe, or the average advertiser will have the economic motivation to sponsor them. But that's the *average* consumer.

There will always be a segment of the market that will rush to take part in whatever the latest technological innovation is. These are the "techys," people fascinated by technology for its own sake, far beyond the "new triers" who were the first to own microwaves and CDs. They are the amateur photographers who put aside excellent 35-mm cameras because a new model has "matrix metering" or "memory chips." They are the people who bought a new BMW because of its trip computer, or other cars because they have GPS map-locators. They run up hundreds of dollars in phone bills communicating with strangers on the computer Internet. And they trade up perfectly good computers and software because of new features.

This group has the time, the money, and the compulsion to get the latest and most advanced technology, whether they need it or not. And they will be in the forefront of those clamoring for the highest levels of interactive technology—whether they need it or not!

The trap is to presume that crowds at trade shows, and the initial subscribers for such innovations, are necessarily typical. In fact, it's just the other way around. For example Macintosh's success was based on being user-friendly. Anyone could handle basic job processes without any prior training or complex manuals. But the techys in the marketplace and in the company couldn't leave well-enough alone. To impress their peers, they designed more complex programs that needed more advanced system software that in turn needed larger-capacity machines. The price went up, the ease of use went down, and Macintosh boxed itself into the highly competitive technology niche when once they could have aimed to be in every home.

Interactive technology faces the same challenge. To be accepted in the mass market, it must be user-friendly. To be user-friendly, people of any age, techy or not, must be capable of using it. I just gave my senior-age parents cable TV, and even the remote control was too complicated, with two-dozen closely spaced black buttons. I had to program it for them, and highlight the two buttons they most needed.

Most important, the technology must be a means, not an end. The end product in marketing and all types of communication must always be some user benefit: entertainment, information, convenience, choice, savings. People must want to use the system to access the messages, not just as a symbol of their technical prowess.

This is why I believe it is a mistake for advertisers to start with an interactive test of a new communications system if they have failed to develop products and propositions that work on the existing systems. If it won't sell in a mailpiece or a direct-response short- or long-form spot, then it won't sell in interactive.

THE HAVES AND HAVE-NOTS

Judy Black, chairman of the AAAA committee on technology and an associate of mine at Bozell, predicts that in the short run the country will resemble a patchwork quilt. Financial constraints will limit the roll-out of the new technologies that allow for interactivity. Cable companies that have upgraded their system over the past few years without a high level of interactive capability will not upgrade again for some time. Thus, one community may have an advanced interactive television system available, while an adjacent community will have fewer options.

Eventually we will have "the connected" and "the unconnected." Once the different systems shake out and there are only a few dominant systems, there will be people who have them and others who do not. And they will be two entirely separate markets.

The "connected" households will be those who are comfortable with the new style in communications, who may prefer to read their newspaper and consult reference books on the same instrument they use to talk with friends, order groceries, shop for clothes, write letters, and watch movies. The instruments may be in the home, the office, or worn on a belt.

Those who can afford to and who are comfortable with these new systems will use them routinely, updating their services and terminals as new features attract them. Those who prefer to use phones, catalogs, magazines, pen and paper, free TV, and trips to the video rental store will continue to do so. And marketers will have to find ways to reach both groups.

INTERACTIVE AS PRODUCT

How will Interactive impact direct marketers? One way is that the interactive media will have to be sold, and direct marketing will undoubtedly prove to be the most effective way to do so.

The more complex the sale, the more it requires multiple contacts, and therefore databases. And so all advertising for interactive services will have to involve direct marketing expertise. Only direct marketers have the lists and the experience in mass media that will make such introductory campaigns cost-effective. Only direct marketers have the know-how to turn interest into action.

INTERACTIVE AS MEDIA

Both media managers and creative directors have become fascinated with the power of interactive marketing to present messages in dramatic, involving ways never before possible. Every agency media department is following with great interest the various combinations of resources and opportunities to participate in the new "test beds"—currently over 100 of them.

Some large companies—including all of the major automobile companies, investment institutions, and even the U.S. post office—have invested hundreds of thousands of dollars to explore some of these systems in their early test stages. For all of them, there is a single question: Will these new communications channels enable us to reach our prospects effectively and economically?

As of the date this manuscript was completed, in early 1994, the answers are unknown. Some early tests already have been abandoned. Some show encouraging initial response, but there is a question as to whether it can be sustained after the novelty has worn off. Some of the largest tests—including Time Warner's in Orlando, and PacTel's in Southern California—are just being launched.

Of particular interest to direct marketers is the ability to measure involvement in exactly the same way that we measure the success of a direct-response effort. There is no way these systems can pay out simply on the basis of the number of homes reached. They have to be justified on the basis of reaching people who, by requesting additional information screens or requesting a booklet or sample, have revealed themselves, individually, to be active prospects. The standard of measurement will therefore not be "target audience reached" in terms of demographics, but "individual prospects reached" as evidenced by interactive responses of some sort.

Let's stop for a second and look at some basic media math. Say direct mail costs $1 apiece and produces a 10 percent response, thus costing

$10 per response. If mass broadcast reaches homes at 1 cent each, then a $10 cost per response is the result of motivating 1 out of 1000 people—not a difficult goal on direct-response television. Interactive communications may cost as much as direct mail, but with a similar combination of selectivity and effectiveness the cost per response could turn out to be competitive.

Some comparisons can be made to Prodigy, which has been operating an interactive computer network for several years. While subscribers use Prodigy to pay bills, check the news, book airplane flights, or review electronic bulletin boards, messages appear inviting them to visit the offerings of their advertisers. Interestingly, these messages are targeted depending on age, sex, and viewer on-screen activity. They charge advertisers $27,000 a month for a sequential five-screen advertising message that is voluntarily looked at by about 20,000 people a month. Of these, about 5000 request more information, which comes to a reasonable $5.40 per inquiry.

If, as direct marketers already do, we look at media expenditures in terms of people motivated to act rather than simply people exposed to our messages, Interactive can be cost-effective. But prospects must be selected effectively, using criteria beyond demographics.

As a result, all the media mavens who once looked down their noses at direct marketers are now "picking our brains." Direct marketing experience on a resumé is now a plus not just for direct marketers but for any executive. And all of the devices we have developed to test media and copy, to facilitate response and to incentivize action, are meaningful to all marketers and not just those whose primary business is selling by mail order.

INTERACTIVE AS MARKETING TOOL

The opportunities here for direct marketers are obvious. Interactive can allow us to be more selective, to place offers in a wider variety of hospitable editorial environments, to offer our goods and services when the customer is in the mood to shop at home and to order on the spot.

The resulting expansion of channel capacity will give us more opportunities for long-form direct response, more remnant time, more per-inquiry deals. And the interactive techniques themselves will enable us to use new methods to give prospects just the information they need to make a decision, without trying their patience.

If I can sell a blender by mail, why not a refrigerator? For that matter, why just take leads for an automobile, when you can sell the car itself? Imagine this message on your screen: "If you wish to buy the make and model you have just selected, press button Z and your local dealer will arrange to bring one to your home. If you complete a lease or purchase within 5 days, you will receive 100 pay movies free, courtesy of the dealer."

As fascinating as the many new opportunities sound, let's remind ourselves that a direct marketer's focus must always be on the bottom line. We are being offered a wonderful array of new tools, but as of this moment no one has told us what the cost will be.

I can't help but think of the direct mail printers who are always coming to us with new kinds of embossing, pop-ups, and voice messages. Yes, they do attract more attention than an ordinary mailpiece. But no, seldom do most of them bring in enough additional orders to pay for their added cost. Nonetheless, a few, such as scent strips, closed-face personalization, and the use of quality photography that generates emotional response, have turned out to be very good investments that more than made up for all the others.

The many variations of interactive will shake out in much the same way. Some will be marketable; some will not. Some will be profitable; some not. With all the research and testing methods available, we still cannot predict with certainty which interactive methods will be among the survivors.

DATABASE MARKETING

Database marketing is where it all came together. The dollar-wise common sense of mail order. The psychological creativity of general advertising. The mathematical sciences of mailing lists and of all the direct-response media.

It hasn't made headlines like the relative handful of genuine infomercial successes. It doesn't have the Hollywood glamour and space-age technological fascination of interactive marketing. But it's here. It's growing. And it works—so well and so often than many of its most frequent practitioners go to great lengths to keep their successes secret.

WHAT IT IS

The word *database* has come to mean any collection of information, including marketing results or sales data. Let's look at the two parts of the word separately.

Data. As we refer to it here, *data* means the names and addresses of individual customers and prospects, along with enough information to select those most likely to respond to a given promotional idea.

Notice that I am saying *individual*. For direct marketers, there is nothing new in finding *groups* with a high probability of responding. By picking the right list and selecting geographic areas, let's say a mailing produces 5 percent response. But if the 20-80 rule is true, and we could mail only to the one of five individuals who account for the 80 percent, we should be able to get four times the response rate, or a 20 percent response!

Does this seem unlikely? Too optimistic? An exaggeration? Not to those who are actually involved with database marketing rather than just talking about it. That's why my most recent book, *Database Marketing* (McGraw-Hill, 1993), includes statistical variation tables to 30 percent. And because of later results, the next will go even higher.

With this kind of arithmetic, the whole game changes. Suddenly it is clear and obvious that direct mail can be more cost-effective than mass advertising to the extent that a company has built an effective database. And that's *before* adding in the lift of greater segmentation, involvement, personalization, and the space to include samples, provide proof, and tell the whole story.

What kind of data? To begin with, the knowledge that a customer really is a customer, and not just a trier. That a prospect really is a prospect—someone who already uses the category of product, who has asked for information, or who has a clear need for what we have to sell.

Add to that the name in proper format, with separate salutations, first names and last names. With addresses, cities, zip codes in DMA-recommended abbreviations and standards. With annotations for date and source and any segmentation data. Then be prepared to add enhancement or sales generated.

If all this sounds like ABCs to any mail-order company, that is exactly the point. Database marketing is an application for nonretail products of all the methods and experience of the direct marketing field.

Base. The other part of the word is *base*. More than anything else, this suggests a starting point, a place to begin. It does not mean a collecting point for academic information to go into research reports. Nor does it suggest a repository of names and addresses as part of some corporate archive. Yet these cases seems to persist as often as those that are used as they should be.

A database is a *tool*. It should be designed actively to achieve goals—distribution goals, share goals, sales goals, profit goals. Names should be collected and transcribed into electronic formats only if they will produce a profit. Information should be added to these lists only if the added effectiveness can be cost-justified. That is, information should be actionable! That's why I'm cautious about database projects managed by computer specialists or research departments. A database is a marketing tool, and should be designed to achieve marketing goals.

WHAT TO DO WITH IT

Database marketing is the "missing link" between mass advertising and sales. Today, when advertisers are increasingly demanding accountability in advertising as in every other expenditure, database makes the connection between money expended and sales.

Sometimes called *integrated marketing* or *relationship marketing* or even *maxi-marketing,* the principle seems simple. Make every marketing communication work twice as hard—building brand identity at the same time as it asks for an order or at least an expression of interest. In other words, build brand equity and a marketing database at the same time.

To the extent that customers or prospects are identified, marketing funds should be addressed directly to them, usually by mail. Mass advertising should be directed at everyone else, with a secondary objective of getting new names or information for the database.

Mass advertising, whether in broadcast or publications or even in some badly designed mail and door-to-door media, usually has the time or space to get across only a single message or image. It therefore must be addressed to the lowest common denominator of prospect. And it must rely on package design, store display, or retail sales clerks to close the sale. With the growth of megamarkets and the decline of both service and salesmanship, the relationship between building "intent to buy" and "share of market" has become increasingly distant.

SIX BASIC ELEMENTS

Database marketing is the solution, when it's done right. There are six basic elements to be considered in order to develop and use a database:

1. Building it
2. Enhancing it
3. Using it for conquest
4. Using it for trial and cross-sell
5. Using it for loyalty and frequency promotions
6. Using it for advocacy

Let's look at these six elements.

Building a Database

Where do you start? There are four basic methods.

1. *Existing names,* usually from promotions, contests, inquiries. This is the easiest place to begin, but not necessarily the best. Such names may indicate more interest in the contest or promotion than in your product or service.

   Customer names usually are much more useful, particularly for service companies such as banks insurance companies, investment brokers, cable companies, telephone companies. In these cases there is often an application with useful information or a record of purchases.

2. *Compiled and survey names* are purchased through list brokers from companies who have built their business and reputations on their ability to supply lists that will do the job.

   The most useful are what I call survey names. Half of all households have filled out a questionnaire that they received in the mail or in a newspaper, asking about purchase intent, category usage, and brand preference.

   Other lists provide stated interests, product purchases, personality indicators, individual or neighborhood characteristics. Often these are just as valuable.

3. *Custom-built lists* are always in order, even if substantial other lists exist. There is always a need to add fresh names and reach out to new prospects. This is especially economical if this effort is a by-product of other promotional investments—inviting offers on packages, shelf-talkers, and as a secondary objective in mass advertising.

   Often it is necessary to compromise, as there may not be enough names of qualified self-identified prospects. The procedure then is to try all of the various sources, including those that may not have all of the desired information or may be more conjectural or may offer a degree of probability rather than certainty. This is very similar to all direct marketing list-testing. The chapter on that subject (Chapter 5) should be read as carefully by database practitioners as by circulation and catalog companies.

4. *Name-generation offers.* Once you have established the value of a new or purchased name, based on the possible applications of database marketing over time, you can test and rank all of the different ways of doing so. Usually it will pay for you to develop promotions in which the primary or secondary objective is to get names.

   Whether you use the cost of buying a name from an outside compiler or an estimate of the long-term profit potential, you can establish an "allowable cost" for a new name. Often it is less expensive to develop your own list than to buy an outside one.

Planning Tips.   Our approach has been to conduct a typical direct marketing grid test, simultaneously testing different offers, different creative treatments, and a wide variety of media options. Typically they include solo mail, co-op mail, small-space advertisements, full-page insert cards in specialty magazines, radio and television. The end result, once all the split runs and rate adjustments have been taken into account, is a ranking in terms of cost per incremental name. Notice the word *incremental*. Often the client has names that have been developed from a logical source. New promotions to that source may generate responses, but from people or companies who had already responded.

Another consideration is that different sources will turn out to vary in their responsiveness to future offers. For instance, a self-identified prospect who asks for information from an advertisement will obviously be better than someone who is included on the basis of calculated probability. Someone who sends a token amount to buy a "Guide to Buying the Right Vacuum Cleaner," for example, will be of better quality than someone who simply calls in for the same booklet free.

Don't overlook your company's "free" media: bill inserts, package enclosures, "on-pack" offers, etc. The most economical name sources are always the free rides derived from approaching all advertising and sales promotion on an integrated basis. Other than the cost of a booklet or premium, it costs nothing to add a free offer coupon in a free-standing insert that would have run anyway as a sales promotion expenditure, as we do for Jolly Time Popcorn. Or to add a coupon or phone number to advertisements primarily designed to announce a new product or build brand image, as we do for Chrysler. Or to offer a free sample at the end of a television spot, as P&G does for Attends.

List Enhancement

Most companies find that they do have names to start with, perhaps from an old promotion or, in the case of a service organization, present and former customers. Sometimes these names are properly collected in electronic form, more often they are original documents stored in a warehouse somewhere.

Editing. Either way, the first step is to edit the list and get it in proper order. Every direct marketing computer service firm is geared up to handle this type of project. If the list has to be entered, they may use optical scanning with new character recognition software. Or they may subcontract to one of the very capable data entry firms in Ireland, Jamaica, India, and elsewhere, to keyboard-enter the information in the traditional way.

For many reasons, lists should be maintained in DMA-approved formats, with separate fields for first name and last name, proper zip codes, and standardized abbreviations. Even if the name and address are accurate, a nonstandard list cannot effectively be matched with other lists. Standard formats are needed in order to eliminate duplicates though what is called a *merge-purge process.* They are needed to efficiently add enhancement data from outside lists. And they are essential if the list is going to be exchanged with others or placed on the list-rental market.

Internal Data. To the extent that other usable information is available, it should also be preserved in the basic list. At the least this would include the date when the name was acquired, and the source of the name. To the extent that the information is relevant and the quantity of names with it is significant, it would be valuable to have any information about what kind of purchase or service was provided, or what type of inquiry, or the price and type of any transaction. Ultimately the use of the lists will be influenced by the mail-order standard of recency-frequency-price (of transaction), regardless of the intended use.

External Data.　Any list can be enriched by adding information available from commercially available sources. There is an incredible wealth of such information, but I suggest that you resist the temptation to load the list with data that may be interesting but will not make money for your business. Remember, you are building a marketing tool, not a research report.

If your list is somewhat dated, your computer service can match it with NCOA (National Change of Address) lists provided by the post office, or telephone and resident lists compiled from telephone directories. These will give forwarding addresses for a substantial portion of the moved names, and let you remove those names whose current addresses cannot be confirmed.

Demographic data can be added—about half from available individual information, and the remainder from neighborhood characteristics. Or you can just use the neighborhood lists, which for most uses is more than adequate. These suppliers can add any information that has ever been asked on a warranty card, survey program, or census questionnaire. This includes age, occupation category, estimated income, home value, education, and many other factors. Finer geographic delineations often are available, down to individual carrier routes.

Present product use and intent-to-buy information can be added from many sources. Survey sponsors have on file so much data that it is best to presume something is available and try to find it than the opposite. I have found prescription usage, personal health ailments, oil-change preferences, cereal preferences, and car-buying intentions. When you see such a survey in an FSI or in a Tucker or Carol Wright coop mailing, study it carefully and you'll be amazed at the diversity. Of course, some items are blocked from some suppliers because the data was sponsored by another advertiser on an exclusive basis. But then you can probably find it from a different supplier, or you can sponsor questions yourself for a fee and control your own new information sources.

Most response lists are too small to be used for enhancement by themselves, but there are some notable exceptions in some special categories. Some huge multimillion-name lists such as Fingerhut, or Warshawsky auto accessories, or Boardroom publications, are large enough to make it pay to combine their data with yours. Such overlays can provide specifics that can make the difference between success and failure in a database application.

Other suppliers have combined data from many lists, so that those names on your list who have responded to any direct-response offer within the last year or other time period can be coded as such. These will respond to your own company's offer at a much higher rate than those who have not. Often, recent car buyers or type of car owned, recent appliance purchasers, recent movers, music and book preferences from club lists—all of these may be valuable if that information is significant to the purchasing profile.

Which data is worth adding? That is what regression analysis (see Chapter 19) is all about, a mathematical process to determine the degree of matches between known buyers and available enhancement data. This is an important process, and one that should be conducted by any major mailer in the early stages of marketing development. However, it is too complex to explain within this chapter. My book *Database Marketing: The Ultimate Selling Tool* (McGraw-Hill, 1993) has an entire chapter devoted to this single subject, just as it has for the other broad areas discussed briefly here.

Conquest/Trial/Cross-Sell

The most exciting application of database marketing is the ability to concentrate promotional efforts against exactly the right target markets. In a decade when mass advertising is under pressure to justify itself, direct or database advertising has no problem at all in doing so. In fact, it is the need to develop names for database marketing that provides the missing link between general advertising and direct marketing, making both more cost-effective.

In general, it involves sending highly persuasive communications, coupled with incentives for trial, to businesses or consumers more likely to be interested than those reachable in mass media.

As with all direct marketing efforts, it is not a panacea. The cleverest ideas must still take a backseat to the simplest spreadsheet forecast. To be effective, a database marketing offer must include the following elements:

- Clearly defined prospects or self-defined inquirers
- Product or service stories that are benefited by space for demonstration or the ability to provide samples
- A narrow category, a major purchase, or nondominant share—otherwise mass communications may be more effective
- Product or service advantages that would be obvious to a trier and so lead to additional sales
- A substantial "lifetime value" of a product user—in either long-term value of smaller purchases (e.g., shampoo) or high-profit individual sales (e.g., an automobile)
- A creative approach that is genuinely interesting and that uses the mail format effectively, not just "an ad in an envelope"

Conquest advertising can be addressed to users of the same category but different brands, or simply to people who are likely to respond to the offer. Sometimes the offer, for instance a premium, is selected to fit a specific market segment.

Often a conquest offer can be combined with the name-generation advertising described earlier, or it can be used to promote more than one type of product. Some of the most successful promotions my agency has worked on are cross-brand promotions, sending multiple communications to people with certain age or lifestyle similarities.

I am amazed at the number of major corporations—including one of the big-three cereal makers—who use databases to send out single or multiple coupons, as if the prospect can simply be bribed into trying the brand. They overlook the demonstrated research that shows that the easy triers who will respond to such an offer will just as easily switch back when someone else's coupon comes into their possession. As P&G has stated publicly when they announced their value-pricing policy, using coupons indiscriminately simply trains the customer to buy with any coupons.

It is also quite accepted that most such coupons are redeemed by people who have already tried the product, and that perhaps only 1 of 10 represents new trial. That's why conquest marketing is most effective when you can identify new prospects, eliminating present customers. Research that shows that the extra creative effort isn't worthwhile is faulty—a product of the core-market fallacy discussed earlier in this book. The present users polled don't need the extra selling, but they are not the payoff of the promotion. It is the new customers whom we want to try the product or service because of its merits, rather than just because of a bribe, that do appreciate and respond to a well-done creative execution.

Frequency and Loyalty

Here again, the relationship between mail-order and database marketing is indisputable. In mail order, it is common to design programs that may do no more than break even on the initial customer acquisition. The profit is in the "back end"—magazine renewals, donation upgrades, sales from subsequent catalogs, the fulfillment of a continuity obligation, etc. The "front end" is a business-building investment; the "back end" is where the profits must come from, and striking a balance between these two programs is the key decision management must make each and every year.

I have seen several financial studies in which companies not only received the proverbial 80 percent of their sales from the top 20 percent of all customers, most of whom are repeat buyers, but this group produced 100 percent of the company's profits. (Jerry Pickholtz, O & M Direct's president, confirmed this relationship, but reports that the actual figures are not 20–80 but 30–75—that is, 30 percent of the customers produce 75 percent of the sales.) I recommend reading the Clancy/Shulman work *The Marketing Revolution* for a more detailed and more colorful discussion of this observation.

I share these authors' amazement that general advertisers have given so little attention in the past to retaining customers as opposed to winning new ones. The right approach, which many companies are beginning to adopt, begins with budgeting marketing funds. It is as simple as making the "first cut" an allocation for "identified customers" and "identified prospects" based on the percentage they represent of customers, or of sales volume, or of profit margins. The second step, then, is to take what's left and invest it in advertising that builds brand equity and/or at the same time identifies new customers and prospects. Some companies separate these last two functions as well, with different budgets assigned to each priority.

Database programs, and in my opinion all marketing, should be looked at in the same way. Mass advertising should appropriately be bringing in new triers and first-time customers, with a secondary objective of identifying high-potential prospects and current customers. There are countless ways to motivate new trial, especially if you're willing to invest a large part of the initial sale's income in doing so.

There is a different standard, however, for present customers. The object here is not volume but profits, and therefore the investment to induce incremental sales must be limited. Remember, these are the people who are likely to buy your product anyway, and the promotion investment must be appropriate to the profit goals from this segment. The object here is to either

1. Increase frequency of usage or purchase
2. Upgrade to a more profitable variation of the product or service
3. Extend product loyalty to related products
4. Defend market share against competitive conquest efforts

Obviously, sampling and extensive argument should not be needed for present customers. However, it is often beneficial to give customers information to support their original decision, and to reassure them that they did the right thing. Mostly, however, present customers are successfully motivated in one of two ways: *relationship* and *reward.*

Relationship.   The object here is to build a bond between the company and the customer.

Often, publications are used. Sometimes these share information and give advice, to show the customer that he or she is important to the company. Sometimes they are entertaining, with stories, games, and other involvements. Or they can provide news about a related interest, reinforcing the product's association with its imagery. An example of this would be news of off-road adventures sent to Jeep customers, a guide to new hairstyles for Vidal Sassoon shampoo users, a magazine with advice for parents to users of Pampers.

Publications may be in any format. DBM/Scan, the principal database archive service, has reported such efforts in the form of newsletters, newspapers, magazines, booklets, and even bound books. And increasingly, similar promotions have been offered in videotape or computer software form.

Some companies send gifts. Small businesses have been sending gift calendars, pencils, and notebooks for years. An oil company uses baseball caps with their logo. A laundry product sends its identified customers a convenient dispenser unit. These often have a secondary objective of keeping the advertiser's brand or phone number visible. In these cases it's not the value of the gift that's important, but the idea of it.

And don't overlook common courtesies. A thank-you letter. A Christmas card. A letter celebrating the anniversary of a business relationship. Advance news of a product or service or sale before it is offered to the general public. While some of these may come with reminders to rebuy, or plugs for related products, the main objective is to build the relationship and make customers feel they are "family."

Reward.   "This free gift if you send three proofs of purchase!" "Save ten proofs, and get this accessory at half price!" "A discount coupon if you buy a carton of our cigarettes instead of a pack!" "Try all three flavors or scents and get a rebate!" All of these are approaches to combining incentives to buy more with reward for being a present customer.

Often this takes the form of a whole catalog of products—free, or at a discount price for proof of various levels of purchase. Such gifts can be self-liquidating; that is, priced at a level that represents a significant savings to the customer but is really at or near the advertiser's actual cost. Or they can be free. Certainly the earliest promotion of this type I ever saw was my mother's hosiery card, which was punched each time she bought nylons, and which was good for a free pair when all 12 spaces had been punched.

My preference is a two-level pricing program. The lowest price requires substantial quantity of usage, and represents the actual cost or even a subsidized cost. In this case the customer might get interesting items at half-price. But each item also has what has been called a "Speed Plan," where fewer proofs of purchase are required but the discount is only a third or so. Promotions of this type, for Betty Crocker and Kool-Aid and many others, often involve millions of customers and enormous volumes of merchandise.

Some sales promotion specialists put together programs such as this for manufacturers—on either a single-product or a catalog basis—and will even supply the promotion materials, as long as they can handle the sales and take a small profit margin. I have put together deals like this myself. While it is more costly than setting up your own program, some companies prefer to have a turnkey arrangement where they don't have to concern themselves with the details of merchandise selection, inventory levels, fulfillment practices, and customer service.

Certainly the frequent-flyer or buyer programs have to be considered in this category. I have reservations about giving away the same product you are trying to sell, but in most of these cases the plane seats or hotel rooms would be empty anyway, and so have little incremental cost. Also, the flights taken often are vacation trips that do not displace business trips anyway. But effective they certainly are. I must confess to personally having taken some strange routings in order to reach the mileage goal needed to maintain my "Gold Card" status with American's Advantage Club!

That's why most plans offer merchandise that is related but not the same as what is being sold. The Barbie pink-stamp plan earned points with purchases of doll clothes, cars, and other accessories, but could be redeemed only for items such as Barbie-branded clothes, book bags, and portable radios intended for use by the girl herself. AT&T's Opportunity Calling, and Citibank's Citidollars, offered neither phone nor banking services, but merchandise at discounted prices.

There are other variations as well. A program I did for Beneficial Finance offered a contest entry every time the card was used. Banks offer personal banking conveniences (no lines) and reduced rates if you consolidate all your accounts in one place so as to keep a minimum balance. Even supermarkets offer price-off specials to those who join their club plans and use them consistently.

Advocacy

The most neglected lesson from the world of direct marketing is the use of *advocacy programs,* sometimes called *member-get-member* or *get-a-friend programs.* This subject is discussed at great length elsewhere in this book (Chapter 4), so I will not duplicate it all here, but I can assure you that they are worthwhile.

Offers to be passed along to friends, or requests for friends' names, have been very successful in database offers, mostly as a way of getting additional names. Some major programs have generated an additional 20 to 40 percent in added responses.

Usually your new customers are your most enthusiastic word-of-mouth generators, especially during the "honeymoon" period soon after the initial purchase. A program I once recommended for Nissan included a coupon book that new customers would keep in their glove compartment. If a friend admired their new car, the owner could pass out a coupon that introduced the friend to a dealer and entitled both the friend and the owner to extra accessories if another sale resulted.

My usual approach is to offer a gift to both the referrer and the referee if a sale results. Or the customer can send a free sample of a product, or a promotional booklet or publication, to the friend. For instance, every issue of *The Jolly Times,* a family-fun newspaper we do for Jolly Time popcorn, invites the reader to send us the name of a friend who would like a copy. The copies sent then suggest that to continue the subscription they will have to send in a proof of purchase.

AN EXAMPLE OF AN INTEGRATED DATABASE PROGRAM

While working on this chapter, one of my Asian associates called to discuss a database program for an airline based in a European country. We had to work out a strategy right there, over the phone, and while it may not be as creative as it could have been if we had had more time, it's a good example of how the pieces fit together. Here's what we recommended:

- *List-building.* Several thousand identified nationals who had flown with the airline before—customer lists. Members of a business group dealing with the European country. Senior executives of major international corporations. Plus, to identify those planning business trips, a small-space advertising program in business publications offering a booklet on "How to Do Business in Europe."

- *List enhancement.* Two projects. One, a questionnaire with an offer of several thousand mileage points just for filling it out. The other, a win-a-trip-to-Europe contest asking contestants which country they would like to visit and at what time of the year, if they win.

- *Loyalty/frequency.* A typical frequent-flyer campaign, but one recognizing that most visitors from this country flew only on business trips and that free trips would reward their companies but not themselves. The plan we worked out emphasized other personal rewards, especially trips for companions and pleasure-trip extensions to other cities in Europe.

- *Conquest/trial.* Mostly aimed at more flexible vacation travelers, this included a program of special offers during seasons of high vacancies—upgrades, or hotel and recreation perks. These would apply only for trips taken during specific seasons or leaving on specific days. These offers would be sent to prospects based on the information provided in the list-enhancement questionnaires.

In many ways, database marketing—selling to individuals rather than groups—is the most sophisticated form of direct marketing.

Its uses are just beginning. But its roots are as wide as the many applications of direct marketing in use today and as deep as the earliest ads, catalogs, and mailings that unashamedly offered goods by mail order.

EPILOGUE

In the first two editions of *Direct Marketing,* I included a chapter on "The Future" at the end of each. I have not done so in this edition because the future is here.

If the chapters on infomercials, interactive marketing, and database marketing don't suggest the future of direct marketing, what does? Yet each of these disciplines is still evolving.

The thing to remember is that no matter where the business goes, its roots are still in the experience and history of the mail-order business. To explore the future of direct marketing without understanding its past is to court disaster. We who have seen this business grow and evolve have already made most of the mistakes that anyone new will face, and have learned not to argue with results. I believe the saying goes, "Those who are ignorant of the past are condemned to repeat it."

What I do see is a change that I have wished for during my whole career. Direct marketing is now accepted as a serious marketing tool in every size and kind of business. Sophisticated marketing executives who used to demand "company learning," and who stuck to what they knew from their basic advertising classes, now respect the fact that direct marketing is different, that it is professional, and that the lessons of one advertiser apply to all. Today and tomorrow, we in direct marketing are experiencing what we have earned and most desired since the first order form was sent in the mail or placed in a magazine: RESPECT!

INDEX

Note: The *f.* after a page number refers to a figure; the *t.* to a table.

ABOUT THE AUTHOR

Edward Nash is one of the most famous personalities in the world of direct marketing. For over 30 years he has "done it all" for corporations large and small, from lifting response rates for traditional mail-order companies such as Time-Life, Doubleday, and Mutual of Omaha to developing unique new applications for clients such as Procter & Gamble, Merrill Lynch, and Mattel Toys. (The latter won him the Henry Hoke Award, the industry's highest recognition.)

His career has spanned the modern development of direct marketing from its roots in mail order to today's most sophisticated psychological, mathematical, and technological innovations. He started as a copywriter with Schwab & Beatty, and still writes ads, mailings, and TV spots for clients. He went on to serve as marketing vice president for LaSalle Extension University, president of Capitol Record Club, executive vice president of Rapp & Collins, and president/CEO of BBDO Direct, which he founded and ran for five years. Currently he is executive vice president of Bozell, Jacobs, Kenyon & Eckhardt, responsible for developing direct marketing in all of the company's offices around the world.

Ed Nash has been called the "master strategist" of direct marketing, in recognition of his work as chairman of the DMA Marketing Council and its Awards Committee. He has been chairperson of New York's Direct Marketing Days and a frequent keynote speaker at DMA Annual Conferences and the Montreux International Symposia as well as similar events in virtually every city in the United States and in two dozen countries. He is on the Editorial Advisory Board of *Direct* magazine and the *Journal of Direct Marketing*. He is also the editor in chief of *The Direct Marketing Handbook* and author of *Database Marketing*, both published by McGraw-Hill.

The Edward Nash Institute for Direct Marketing offers weekend workshops and corporate training programs in basic and specialized direct marketing subjects. These are conducted by Mr. Nash or other prominent authorities in various cities in the United States as well as in other countries. Information may be obtained by writing to the Institute's director, Diana Bright, at 190 East 72nd Street, New York, NY 10021.